FIRST
WITH THE
NEWS

FIRST
WITH THE
NEWS

The History of W.H. Smith
1792-1972

CHARLES WILSON

JONATHAN CAPE
THIRTY-TWO BEDFORD SQUARE LONDON

First published 1985
Copyright © 1985 by W. H. Smith & Son Limited
Jonathan Cape Ltd, 32 Bedford Square, London WC1B 3EL

British Library Cataloguing in Publication Data

Wilson, Charles, *1914*–
First with the news: the history of W. H. Smith
1792–1972
1. W. H. Smith & Son——History
I. Title
381′.456762823′0941   Z325.S66
ISBN 0-224-02156-7

Typeset by Gloucester Typesetting Services
Printed in Great Britain by
Butler & Tanner Ltd, Frome and London

Contents

Illustrations

The author and publishers are grateful to the following for permission to reproduce illustrations: Guildhall Library, nos 2 and 3; Illustrated London News Picture Library, no. 11; Alan Wofsy Fine Arts, no. 34. All other photographic material comes from the archives of W. H. Smith & Son Ltd.

TABLES

Preface

I WISH TO acknowledge the help given me in the preparation of this book by the Directors and members of W. H. Smith & Son Ltd, who have spared time to advise me on the various aspects and problems of the business. I would particularly like to mention the Chairman, Mr Simon Hornby, Mr Julian Smith, Mr Brian Jamieson, Mr Peter Bagnall and, from among former or advisory Directors, Mr Michael Hornby, Sir Charles Troughton and Mr Geoffrey Chandler (of Cazenoves) who have given me the benefit of their unequalled knowledge of the business and its history.

Personal contacts such as these have been particularly important because the documentation of the W. H. Smith history is, at best, fragmentary. Much of the business of the partnership from the beginning to 1929 was transacted between the partners and staff verbally. By far the greater part of such business correspondence as may have formed part of the firm's records at one time or another has either been destroyed or has disappeared in the course of removals, wars, paper drives and all those vicissitudes which afflict historic institutions to a greater or a lesser degree.

Fortunately, some of the episodes and developments in the history can be constructed from other sources, notably the records of the railway companies and the newspapers. These were the two leading institutions with whom Smith's conducted its most important commercial relationships for over a century. In this connection I wish to express my deep appreciation to Dr Christine Shaw whose assistance in locating and investigating the records relevant to this study has been as indispensable as it has been meticulous. Without it, it would have been impossible to write this book. Similarly, the archivist of Messrs W. H. Smith, Mr

T. W. Baker-Jones, has put at my disposal his meticulous knowledge of the sources of the business and has afforded advice and criticism for which the outside intruder into this complex and arcane citadel must be suitably grateful.

For much friendly administrative help I am indebted to Mr Lawrence Hammond and members of the staff of the Public Relations Department of the Company. To Miss Sally Williamson especially I owe a great debt for her patient decoding of my so-called handwriting as well as for a score of other problems solved. Likewise to Mrs Barbara Gildert I am grateful for help in the arrangement of interviews and other contacts within the business.

Acknowledgment of a different kind is due to the late David Keir. Mr Keir left at his death an (incomplete) history of the firm in typescript which provided a very useful introduction to the subject. It contains no indication of the sources he used and cannot therefore be used as a basis for more detailed research. I have, however, followed Mr Keir in using a famous advertisement in the title of this history.

The *imponderabilia* of public taste, opinion, 'censorship', legal conflicts over alleged libel, defamation, obscenity, etc., which arose as a consequence of the sale or lending of 'literature', form the matter of Chapters XVI and XVIII (Part II). Their location at the centre of the book is deliberate. The problems they discuss affected the firm throughout at least three-quarters of the period covered by this book. Piecemeal references scattered through its pages, or relegation to a final Appendix could not have done justice to their true importance in social history.

The last section dealing with the period 1949–72 represents a different form of historical treatment from the earlier part of the history. The decision to include it was reached only after long discussion. For a variety of reasons, similar to those which have prescribed a postponement in the release of public records, it was agreed that this period of almost contemporary history should be covered, but in outline form only.

The principle that half a loaf is better than no bread can never be historically satisfactory, but in this case was unavoidable. I can only hope that the outline provided will give the reader some impression of how the whole period, when W. H. Smith & Son, limited or not, was goverened by Smiths of five generations, culminated in a great modern public company. Some later hand will no doubt be able to fill out the contours sketched here.

Cambridge 1985   C.W.

W. H. SMITH

THE FAMILY TREE AND PARTNERSHIP

PARTNERS 1792–1949 (Strictly, Directors from 1929)

Note: Z. Coates omitted (1800–12?)
H. & W. Smith dissolved 1828 (1816–28)
Style W. H. Smith & Son from 1846
W. H. Smith Snr retired 1857

H. W. Smith = A. Eastaugh
1738–92   1756–1816

H.E. Smith
1787–1846

W. H. Smith = M. A. Cooper
1792–1865   1792–1851
(W.H.S. 1)

F. D. Danvers = C. M. Rawlinson
1795–1867   1808–91

W. H. Smith = E. Leach née Danvers
1825–91   1828–1913
(W.H.S. II)   1st Vct

Rebecca = S. B. Power
1834–1902   1823–92

A. D. Power
1875–1959
WHS 1911–
Ptn 11/51
(Arnold)

Emily = W. A. D. Acland 2nd Bt

Helen = H. S. Seymour

B/tric = A. D. Acland
1858–1937
WHS 1885–
Ptn 90/1924
(Alfred)

W.F.D.S. = Lady E. Gore
1868–1928
2nd Vct
WHS 1890–
Hd 91/1928
(Freddy)

W.H.S. = Lady P. Herbert
1893–48
3rd Vct
WHS 1925–
Hd 28/48
(Billy)

D. J. Smith = Lady H. Pleydell-Bouverie
1907–76
WHS 1930–
Ptn 35/72
(David)
(Chmn 48/72)

J. F. A. Smith
1906–80
WHS 1928–
Ptn 33/46
(Jimmy)
(Hdgs 49/74)

W.H.S. = M. di Adelfia
1930–
4th Vct
WHS 1952–5
(Hdgs 1956–)
(Harry)

P. H. Smith = S. A. Bennett
1939–

E. J. Smith
1934–

J. D. Smith
1932–
WHS 1950–
Ptn 1965–
(Julian)

(Joanna)   (Peter)

W. H. D. Acland
1888–1970
WHS 1909–
Ptn 14/40
(Robin)
(Sir Wm 1924)

E. W. Seymour
1897–1979
WHS 1921–
Ptn 24/44
(Eddie)
(Co. Secretary)

A. W. Acland
1897–
WHS 1920–
Ptn 24/63
(Arthur)
(Hdgs –1968)

D. A. Acland
1929–
WHS 1951–
Ptn 58/78
(David)

W. Lethbridge
1824–1901
WHS 1862–
Ptn 76/1912

C. Awdry
1847–1912
WHS 1870–
Ptn 76/1912

C. S. Awdry
1877–1918
WHS 1901–
Ptn 04/18

C. H. St J. Hornby
1867–1946
WHS 1893–
Ptn 94/1946

M. C. St J. Hornby
1899–
WHS 1921–
Ptn 24/65

S. M. Hornby
1934–
WHS 1958–
Ptn 1965–

C. H. W. Troughton
1916–
WHS 1946–
Ptn 48/77

PART I

1792-1949

I

A Tale of Two Cities

HISTORIANS (AND PROPHETS) have looked at the Industrial Revolution in many different ways. To some it has seemed a predetermined march of society to the scaffold, passing from the stage of early merchant capitalism, through industrial and finance capitalism, to economic imperialism, to ultimate collapse. For others, less pessimistic, it is a progress from simple to more complex forms of industrial capitalism. For the optimists, it is a long preparation from ages which had steered a course of two steps forward – two steps back – to a state in which continuous investment brings continuous expansion of personal and social wealth. Somewhere between lies the notion that it comprises a series of movements which carry society forward (or sideways) from the achievement of basic, essential economic techniques – the cheaper, near-mass production of iron, cotton stockings and such like essentials – to the production of less essential, ultimately luxury, commodities.

At this latter stage the British economy became more variegated, society more 'miscellaneous'; as Sir Robert Giffen said from the Presidential rostrum to the British Association at Manchester in 1887, the production of 'staple articles' was increasing less fast, but 'the larger numbers engaged in . . . miscellaneous industries, and in what may be called incorporeal functions, that is as teachers, artists and the like, prevents the increase of staple products continuing at the former rate.'[1] That master of Victorian studies, G. M. Young, seemed to be saying something very similar when he wrote of the late Victorian economy how '. . . the lead of the great industries was shortening: and, in compensation, capital, labour, and intelligence were flowing away to light industry, distribution, and salesmanship'.[2] The Armstrongs, Whitworths and Brasseys were giving way to, or being joined by, the Levers, Harmsworths, Boots, Harrods and the like.³

Among the geniuses of distribution was also W. H. Smith, fifth head of a business known wherever newspapers, books, journals or magazines were bought, sold, lent, or borrowed in late-Victorian Britain; later in life famous as a pioneer in social and educational reform, in Parliament First Lord of the Admiralty, Secretary for War, Secretary for Ireland, Leader of the House of Commons, *Punch*'s 'Old Morality', and guyed by W. S. Gilbert (in spite of later denials) as Sir Joseph Porter in *H.M.S. Pinafore*. No entrepreneur of the late-Victorian age more vividly fills the role in social development jointly described by Giffen and G. M. Young than 'Old Morality', standing as he did between the world of new technology and the world of Victorian culture.

Historical generalisations can always be faulted or modified. The socio-economic trend discussed by Giffen and G. M. Young was certainly increasingly characteristic of late-Victorian England. The W. H. Smith business was much older: 'Old Morality' was the third generation of the Smith family to be a newsagent and bookseller – and certainly the greatest: but the founder of what came to be a nation-wide system of buying, selling, distributing and lending newspapers, books, journals, etc., a century earlier, was 'Old Morality's' grandfather, Henry Walton Smith (1738–92); its first architect was Henry Walton's second son, William Henry (often called W. H. Smith I) (1792–1865): its second ('Old Morality') was William Henry Smith II, his son (1825–91). Others worthily carried on the tradition thus established: William Frederick Danvers Smith, Second Viscount Hambleden, was head of the firm 1891–1928; W. H. Smith II's widow was ennobled by the Queen in 1891; William Henry Smith, Third Viscount, was head of the firm from 1928 to 1948 and was succeeded by his brother, David Smith, from 1948 to 1972. Other members of the family were partners, directors or managers.

It was, conspicuously and proudly, a family business and so, up to a point, it remained, even after its transition to a public company in 1949. Writing as 'your affec. cousin' in July 1910, to Arnold Power, W. F. D. ('Freddy') Smith (Second Viscount) explained: 'Circumstances make it advisable for me to get another man of business experience & capacity as Partner . . . The fact that you are a member of the family would make you welcome amongst the Staff as they always look upon it as a family business.'⁴ That it could remain so was, however, not least due to the shrewd choice of non-family partners and managers whose contribution to the business is described later in this book.

In his late forties, W. H. Smith I applied for a grant-of-arms (in 1842); he described himself as 'youngest son of Henry Walton Smith, late of Hinton St George in the County of Somerset, Gentleman deceased.'[5] Whether or not his description of his father was correct has never been confirmed or denied. That Henry Walton was born in 1738 seems certain: that he came of a good family also. These facts William Henry apparently had from his mother — as we shall see, a reliable source. Nothing more is known of Henry Walton with certainty until the 1780s. By then he had become a kind of personal assistant to a person of some contemporary minor importance and a more substantial significance to later generations. This was Charles Rogers, a high official in the London Custom House who typified that mixture of erudition, culture and *bonhomie* to be found in the Civil Service before the days of competitive entry and which occasionally survived it afterwards. Whether he was competent at his job is now a matter of small consequence. What has become more important with the passage of time was his eye for the visual arts and his literary sense, which, over a socially crowded lifetime, ensured the steady accumulation of books, drawings, paintings, bronzes and manuscripts which he left to his friend and colleague of the Custom House and husband of his sister Charlotte, William Cotton. (Some of it now forms the Cottonian Library in the Plymouth Museum.)

Rogers's City house at 3 Laurence Pountney Lane and his country retreat at Richmond were the meeting places of his friends: among them Horace Walpole, Romney, Angelica Kauffmann and Sir Joshua Reynolds. Rogers was extraordinarily versatile: besides becoming a notable collector, he was a Fellow of the Royal Society, Fellow of the Society of Antiquaries, translator of Dante (in his 71st year) and author of a number of papers on antiquarian problems: anyone interested in ancient masks or the antiquity of the horseshoe must still read Charles Rogers. His portrait by Reynolds, his collection of bronzes and his magnificent collection of engravings at Plymouth still commemorate his passion for the arts.

Like most of the old, large cities, London suffered a high death rate. Its rapid expansion in the seventeenth century had depended on a continuous flow of immigrants from the country, where death rates were lower and the natural increase of population greater. There was therefore nothing surprising in Henry Walton's seeking social preferment in London rather than in rural Somerset. He was not only literate but apparently tolerably well educated. He must have arrived about the time the gates of the City of London proper were being dismantled, chopped up by the contractors and sold off profitably to the souvenir hunters. The event was a symbol of the persisting old duality of London. The old City was ceasing to be residential. For half a century its population had been dropping. Many merchants still lived, as they had done for centuries, 'over the shop', but their numbers were dwindling. More were converting their dwellings into offices and counting houses and living 'outside the walls', in the 'Liberties' between the walls and the 'Bars' (or gatehouses) beyond; the really rich might live even farther west in the other London – Westminster, the real capital of England – or in the new fashionable squares north and south of Piccadilly – St James's, Grosvenor Square, Hanover Square, Bond Street or Clarges Street.

Here, since the late seventeenth century, the real development of London had been continued by a profitable alliance between the great landed nobility (such as the Earl of St Albans and the Duke of Westminster) and a group of speculative building developers – Sir Thomas Bond, Thomas Clarges, Gregory King, and Nicolas Barbon (son of 'Barebones'). These 'two Londons' were linked by the Strand, where the once great noble palaces had mostly crumbled away, by Whitehall, and the Charing Cross Road. Westward beyond, and along the green and tranquil banks of the Thames, sprang up the new *palazzi* of the great merchants and bankers, at Fulham, Putney, Kew and Richmond; at Richmond Charles Rogers was in affluent company.

Henry Walton certainly knew Richmond too. There were no doubt long weekends and summer holidays when his employer took him there. The West End he would also know from errands to deliver letters, invitations, and acceptances to Sir Joshua Reynolds at the Royal Academy or Leicester Fields (now Square), to George Romney in Great Newport Street, to Horace Walpole at Arlington Street, or Bartolozzi in Golden Square. Yet his principal home in London was in the heart of the City, with his employer at Laurence Pountney Lane. From there a few steps took him to Cannon Street. He had only to walk straight on and he was in Fleet Street, and, half a mile farther on, in the Strand. In the Strand stood the newly built Somerset House which he had a number of reasons to visit. As a lair of government revenue offices of various kinds it would be familiar to him as the servant of Charles Rogers the Customs officer: as the servant of Charles Rogers, FRS and antiquarian, it would be familiar to him (after 1780 at least) as the home of the Royal Society's museum. But as he walked along Fleet Street he could hardly be ignorant that the area was fast becoming the centre of a growing printing and newspaper industry. A major reason for this was the newspaper stamp duty which from the early years of the eighteenth century had made it necessary for the paper for printing newspapers to be taken to the Government Stamp printing office to have the duty stamp impressed on it. Up to 1837 the only stamp office in the Kingdom was in London (first in Lincoln's Inn, later in Somerset House). 'It was for reasons of proximity to Somerset House that many of the printing houses were set up near at hand – mainly in or around Fleet Street.'⁶

As assistant and protégé of Charles Rogers, Henry Walton would have been concerned with Fleet Street and printing. Rogers the Customs officer was responsible for a great deal of printing of official documents. (John Walter I, founder of *The Times*, did a large amount of printing for the Custom House: Rogers the antiquarian was fascinated by the possibilities of printed engravings of the great masters.) On both counts, Henry Walton's visits to Fleet Street must have familiarised him with the printers and publishers who flourished along and around the route from St Paul's to Charing Cross.

By 1782 the time was not far off when Henry Walton's knowledge of both the cities of London was to prove his salvation. Charles Rogers was then in his seventy-first year; he was feeling his age. Soon after Christmas he was knocked down in Fleet Street by a butcher's boy in a hurry. The accident set off a decline which lasted through the whole of 1783. He spent the year, an almost total invalid, at his Richmond house. Henry Walton stayed with him. He too was far from well, suffering from a kind of nervous debility made worse, no doubt, by the boredom and loneliness of nursing his employer at Richmond, away from his friends in Laurence Pountney Lane. First in his thoughts was a girl at 95 Watling Street, a domestic servant to a coal merchant's widow, Mrs Brown. Anna Eastaugh was another immigrant to London – but from Suffolk (her name often shortened in Suffolk fashion to 'Easter') and she was twenty years younger than Henry Walton, now in his middle forties. Neither the poor girl's social status nor her age endeared her to Henry Walton's family and there seems to have been a family break over the apparent mésalliance. But Henry Walton, though in some ways difficult, timid and something of a hypochondriac, had his family share of other qualities. He was dutiful and tenacious: once his mind was made up nothing could shake him. In his lovesick letters from Richmond to 95 Watling Street, she is his 'dearest Anna', his 'dearest Nanny' or 'my Nanny'.⁷ Will she send him something to read to pass the time? Another volume of *Pamela*, for example?

Pamela, or Virtue Rewarded was now some forty years old. It was Samuel Richardson's first novel and had enjoyed a stupendous popular success. Pope had lavished his praises on it: at Slough (the scene of the heroine's triumph over attempted seduction) the villagers had rung the bells for joy. In France it had won praise from Diderot, Rousseau and Voltaire. In Germany, Lessing and many others imitated him. Coleridge believed him to have influenced Schiller. Were these Richardsonian triumphs what attracted Henry Walton? Or was it, more simply, that *Pamela* was written (in the author's own words) 'to instruct handsome girls who were obliged to go out on service . . . how to avoid the snares that might be laid against their virtue'? (The problem was one that seems to have been a constant preoccupation of Richardson.) There was no need for him to worry: Anna was a faithful and stout-hearted girl.

But there were other causes of distress. At Christmas, 1783, the strain of Henry Walton's nursing duties had brought him very low. He wrote at 3 o'clock in the morning to Anna:

> Mr. Rogers is in a state that would alarm a stronger mind than mine. I have been up with him ever since we have been here, and I believe his stay in this variegated life is of very short duration. The melancholy situation in which he lies makes nature shudder, and at the same time tells me the miserable state of man . . . [8]

The style shows that Henry Walton was not only literate: it suggests the conscious literary contrivance of his day, Augustan, a little artificial but witness to the atmosphere of cultivated poetic sentiment and everyday philosophy in which he had lived at Laurence Pountney Lane. Rogers's Christmas present – a quarter guinea,[9] passing generous by contemporary values – had not been enough to dispel his faintly conscious self-pity that follows:

> I cannot say I am well; if I did it would be flatt'ring myself too much, therefore if anything should happen it will only rid you of a troublesome fellow and make you once more easy; and then perhaps you may form connexions with one who will better deserve your esteem . . . [10]

Richardson himself could not have done better.

To complete the dramatic *ensemble*, Charles Rogers died a day or two later, on 2 January 1784. The faithful Henry was at his bedside. Rogers was buried in the St Laurence Pountney cemetery. The estate was settled. The art collection, manuscripts and all his other possessions passed to William Cotton and his wife Charlotte, Rogers's sister, whom Henry Walton had come to know well. Henry Walton expected nothing from the estate. He was not disappointed. (It may well be that his employer had provided for him earlier.) For some months, until October 1784, we know nothing of his movements. Probably they were spent in clearing up the house at No. 3. But by 27 October Henry Walton was ready to marry. Evidently he had moved northwards by then to Spitalfields. On that day, the marriage took place at Christchurch in the midst of the now large and well established colony of French Huguenot silk weavers who had settled there since Louis XIV had expelled them from France nearly a century earlier.[11] The two immigrants from rural England (now described as 'of this Parish') chose as their witnesses of the marriage two second-generation descendants of those original French immigrants, John Rondeau and Abraham Duprée. That Anna signed with a cross has no significance (as late as 1859 Lord Campbell declared he had seen many documents bearing such a mark as the signature of persons who could write perfectly well).

For three years after the marriage the only evidence that exists of Mr and Mrs Henry Walton Smith suggests they were not only literate but numerate. From 1783 to 1787 Henry Walton received a small income from the Bank of England on his 3 per cent Consols. He was also active as a small buyer and seller of stock. He was buying from 1783 to 1786 and selling in 1786 and 1787, possibly to buy the small news business described later.[12] The address of the principal was still registered as Laurence Pountney Lane. Was it a gift from Rogers? We cannot know: if it was, it was not part of his testamentary estate. That all went to the Cottons. In 1787 the account was closed, almost certainly coinciding with the Smiths' removal from the old City to the new; to Mayfair. How they made a living between 1784 and 1792 is less clear than that they managed not only to remove and survive but to raise and maintain a family. The family attended St George's, Hanover Square. Their first son, Henry Edward, was baptised there in July, 1787. The second child, Mary Ann, similarly in March, 1789.[13] The youngest, William Henry (later referred to as W. H. Smith I) in August 1792[14] – only a fortnight or so before the untimely death of his father, Henry Walton, on 23 August, at the age – early even for those days – of 54: not, however, before he had established a small 'newswalk' business (i.e. paper round) which his widow managed, singlehanded, until 1800 and thereafter in partnership, until her death, at the age of 60, in 1816.[15]

In a note probably written in the early 1850s, William Henry later recorded the facts of his father's death; punctuation was not his strongest point:

Memoir: On the 7th of July 1792 I was born my parents carried on a small Newspaper trade at No. 4. Little Grosvenor Street Berkeley

Square on the 21st of August in the same year my Father was wet
through in a sudden Storm of rain and instead of changing his clothes
he had his feet rubbed with Brandy this caused the cold to take effect on
his bowels caused an inflammation thereof which caused his death in
3 days thus when only 39 days old I became an Orphan and my Mother
a Widow thus left with 2 other children a Brother and Sister . . . [16]

An advertisement in *The Times* (1792) gives an impression of the kind
of establishment the newswalk was and the very modest prospect it offered
the purchaser:

An old-established NEWS WALK to be disposed of that brings in £1. 12s.
per week clear profit; situated in the best part of London, and capable,
with care and assiduity, of great improvement: such an opportunity
seldom offers for an industrious person. Enquire tomorrow at No. 14,
Portugal Street, Lincoln's-Inn-Fields.[17]

(Thirty-two shillings a week was approximately the wage of a skilled
workman.)

The record of the little business was to be patchy. The age of the French
wars was not an easy one. News was in demand, certainly; the business,
at No. 4, Little Grosvenor Street (no longer on the map: it is now a blank
and featureless street of tall office buildings re-named Broadbent Street)
was well placed for the carriage trade. But even in this fashionable area,
sixpence for a newspaper was a high price for any but the devotees of
politics or trade. Wartime difficulties were harassing, inflation rampant.
The expense of a growing family pressed hard on a widow. But whatever
she may have lacked in social credentials she certainly added thrift, shrewdness and reliability to the family stock of heritable propensities. Even in the
year of her husband's death, the business was under way. The West End
was attracting the wealthy and the major flow was of wealth and affluence.
In Mayfair houses were scarce.

The stuff of the newswalk must have been the eight regular morning
dailies then on sale in London. The oldest was the *Daily Advertiser* founded
over half a century earlier. As its name explained its object was largely to
advertise – theatres, concerts, patent medicines, razors, books, schools and
jobs. Its readership was wide, both inside and outside London and included
'the lower orders'.The *Morning Chronicle* (1769) and the *Morning Post*
(1772) were more recent, more seriously dedicated to news and appealing
more to persons of rank. The newspaper which in 1788 became *The Times*

had been founded three years earlier under the name *Daily Universal Register* by John Walter, an adventurer and entrepreneur anxious to outpace his competitors as proprietor of a paper that was a news medium as well as an advertising sheet. Under his vigorous, even ruthless direction, *The Times* achieved his object: its circulation, claimed to be 2,000 daily (an exaggeration but not a wild exaggeration), by 1794 was higher than that of his rivals. Besides the dailies and advertisers there were the nine evening papers and the newly founded *Observer* (1791).

In a world where the newspaper was still thought of as a 'party' organ, government or opposition, and subsidised or victimised accordingly, the growth of advertising was a crucial development. It was industry and trade and the supplies and demands of the new commercial world that needed, and helped to create, the world of advertising. And advertising gradually made possible an existence for the press independent of political strings. This was to be the major claim to survival and reputation of *The Times* under John Walter's son, his staff and successors. Yet for the present it was not yet a national paper: much less its rivals. The Smith news round was typical of the methods by which the London papers were distributed: in London, in relatively small areas of 3 or 4 square miles: not more.

The times offered opportunities and problems: both in abundance. The French Revolution, the wars in Europe that followed and the end of the Empire in North America plunged Europe into prolonged crisis. Gradually England became the centre of the struggle for power. At home, politics came to the boil. What for some was a triumph of libertarian idealism over the mouldering corpse of privilege, tyranny and corruption seemed to others a new, and far worse, threat of permanent and brutal despotism. The reign of terror in France and the guillotining of Louis XVI and Marie-Antoinette put successive English governments into a fright over threatened sedition, espionage and revolution. The assassination of Gustavus III in Sweden confirmed their fears. Parliament came to vigorous life and it was plain that full publicity for its debates, long shrouded in veils of constitutional privilege, could not be withheld for ever. All this was a prelude to a quarter of a century of war, political upheaval – and news in abundance. So were the riots against machinery in the midlands and north, the strikes of sailors in the east coast ports for more pay, and outbreaks of criminal violence by thugs in the large towns. The problems were those common in wartime – shortages of everything, but of paper especially, alarming monetary inflation, unemployment in some industries, labour shortage and rising wages and costs in other. *The Times*, originally sold at 2½d. cost 6d. by 1797. The press was heavily encumbered by the increase in stamp duties on newspapers, by taxes on paper and on advertising. All this combined with the slowness of hand printing – a maximum of 250 copies an hour – to restrict positively both the production and the distribution and sale of newspapers.

In the circumstances, it was a tribute to the 'care and assiduity' which Anna Smith brought to her new business that she was able to show a good balance on her account at the Bank of England. In August 1793 she bought stock worth £75, in September 1795 another £70 worth and in 1796 double that value again: for if family tradition handed on by her son was true, she received neither help nor notice from Henry Walton's family in Somerset.[18] Either she had been left better off by him than we know or, more probably, she managed her affairs at Little Grosvenor Street profitably and efficiently enough to make some prudent saving possible for her family: to consider also some way of lightening her own burden – she was now approaching her middle forties. The answer was to take a partner.

In the autumn of 1800, on 7 October 'in the Fortieth year of the Reign of our Sovereign Lord George the Third etc. . . .' Mrs Anna Smith of Little Grosvenor Street, Widow contracted with Zaccheus Coates of the same place, 'Newsman', to become her co-partner. (The description suggests he may have been already in her employment.) Coates was, plainly, to be a manager ('from time to time . . . use his utmost endeavour skill and dilligence to manage and improve the said News Walk'). The articles were precisely drawn. They were to last for up to seven years. During that time, although the initial capital was provided by Anna Smith, they were to be 'equal Partners', each accounting to the other for any cash received, dividing profits and losses equally, bearing an equal share of all 'Debts . . . Duties and Expenses and Wages of Servants used and employed in the management and carrying on of the said business.' Neither was to carry on any other business or sell off any property of their jointly-managed assets. 'Proper Books of Account' were to be kept and each 1 January was to see 'true, plain and perfect account in writing of the whole Partnership in Cash Goods and other Effects . . . and that the Balance . . . be settled and struck . . .' There was provision also for dissolving the partnership. In that case Coates undertook to instruct his successor for one month in the art of running the business, and to refrain from harming the business by competing for custom in newspapers or other publications.

The occasion was important enough to warrant a thorough act of law. Thomas Dangerfield 'of Berkley Square in the Parish of Saint George Hanover Square . . . Bookseller' and 'William Latty of Bell Yard in the Liberty of Rolls in the Parish of Saint Dunstans in the West . . . Bookseller' were empowered to inspect the books. Dangerfield stood guarantor for Anna Smith in the sum of £100. James Smith 'Publican Davies Street Berkley Square' bound himself for Coates (was he a regular buyer of papers for collective reading to his customers?). The articles bear witness not only to the need of the expanding business for a partner but to its ability to sustain the costs of legally establishing and maintaining a partnership in Mayfair. The mention of Bell Yard echoes either Henry Walton's City connections of a decade earlier, or the continuing dependence of Little Grosvenor Street on Fleet Street or the Strand for its supplies of newspapers and other publications.[19]

Again William Henry recorded the brief history of the co-partnership, its dissolution and his own return to Little Grosvenor Street:

> ... during the next 20 Years my mothers income did not reach quite one hundred pounds per annum with such limited means of course only a plain education could be obtained When about 14 Years of Age I was bound as Apprentice to Mr W. H. Wilson of 1 Vigo St. St. James (Silversmith) the *same house* is still standing in Regent St. now occupied as a Man's Mercer or more properly as a shop for Scotch made fabrics from imperitive circumstance it became needful to dissolve the co-partnership between my Mother and Z. Coates on the 6th of December 1812 Mr Wilson very handsomely allowing me to quit 6 months previous to the expiration of my apprenticeship.[20]

Thus, mysteriously but finally, Zaccheus disappears from the story. The eldest son, Henry Edward, was still there but he was a frail prop for Anna to lean on. William Henry was made of sterner stuff: it was badly needed at No. 4: 'Duty [he wrote many years later] called me to its management. It was in a very sickly state.'[21] Whether inadequate attention by Coates, or the government's decision to increase the stamp duty on newspapers by one penny to help to meet the rising costs of the long war with France, were the basic cause of this 'sickly state' is not clear: probably both contributed. William Henry put down his recollections of 1812, with its rising costs and the stagnation of trade in Mayfair, in later life.

> Newspapers in my Boyhood sold for 6d each. When I returned home after my apprenticeship to Mr. Wilson the Silversmith, they sold for 7d each, the duty having been increased. The Circulation of papers had not in my opinion increased. The amount of composition in a daily paper of the present time must be fully 20 fold more than it then was.[22]

In rather jumbled recollections that telescoped the events of some fifteen or twenty years, W. H. Smith I put together the momentous history of newspaper technology of the first quarter of the century: his spelling was as uncertain as his memory of newspaper statistics.

The Daily Newspapers where in my boyhood about one-forth of the one sheet of the present Newspapers The Type widely set. Advertisements few, say about 3 or 4 for Shipping, 8 sales by Auction and about 20 Adts for other things – reporters where not allowed to take notes in the Houses of Parliament. The late Mr. Perry of The *Morning Chronicle* [James Perry, 1756–1821] had a retentive memory and caused a sort of summary of the debate in that paper to appear each day, during the season its common hour of publication was between 9 and 12 o'Clock. He was a Whig in politics. It was the highest in Nos. say 3,000. The *Post* and *Courier* where then called Tory papers. The *Courier* I think averaged about 3,400 except when news of any Battle arrived, then the Public where arround the offices in crowds.[23] (See pages 53–4.)

To these rather rambling memories he added one other: it confirms other evidence of newspaper production and technology. 'The printing was very slow, all by hand. What they called a full form about 250 per hour, a half page of the size mentioned 500 per hour.'[24]

This was the essence of the problem at Little Grosvenor Street: not, basically, taxation – a progressive industry might have absorbed that – but a static technology and production. This, not the market for papers, or illiteracy, or poverty of consumers, was the problem: there was an absolute shortage of newspapers in face of potential and actual demand. Yet, even as William Henry was called back from his apprenticeship, change was in the air. It came in the persons of two inventors of German origin, Koenig and Bauer, with a new steam printing press: thereafter with two printers who successfully developed their press into applied form, Cowper and Applegath. All this occupied the years between 1803 and 1827. The results in production were spectacular (see Table I.1).

The new methods offered Smith's at Little Grosvenor Street one avenue of escape from their dilemma: more newspaper copies to sell: more turnover. They were also helped by new technology in other directions: gas lamps lit the streets from 1810 for newer, faster and less cumbrous carriages – first the lighter hackney-chariot, then the even handier cabriolet. Prices, in Mayfair, were less of a problem. Thus encouraged by more managerial help and more plentiful supplies, and in 1815, by the end of the war with

France, Anna Smith saw her way clear for another step forward. Near by, in Park Street, Grosvenor Square, was a rival newswalk: that of William and Mary Massey, booksellers, newsagents and stationers. In 1815, by an

TABLE I.I IMPROVEMENT IN PRINTING TECHNOLOGY, 1803–27

	Hourly output
Hand press	250 sheets
Koenig	1100–1800 sheets
Cowper	2400 on both sides
Applegath	4000 on both sides

agreement witnessed by her old friend and bookseller, Thomas Danger-field, Anna Smith acquired her nearest rivals, together with an undertaking that they would not henceforth set up newsagency premises within one and a half miles of Park Street.[25]

Thus, on an expansive note, the Smith business entered the new era of peace: but Anna herself was failing. Anna Eastaugh came from Suffolk; a woman of character with the phlegmatic temperament of the rural East Anglian. But even she was soured by the neglect she had suffered from members of her family after she left home: even more soured when they blamed her on her widowhood for not writing to them. She was provoked into a letter to her sister and brother-in-law at Wangford; detailed, dignified but edged with an understandable bitterness.

> . . . As to not taking notice of any of my relations in the country before I answer that question let me ask you . . . have any of them taken any notice of me or my sister . . . When my Mother died, I wished as well as my sister to have some small article belonging to her such as a bible . . . the letter . . . was not even answered by any one . . . I will ask yourself would you write to those persons that would not even answer your letters. I should wish to live in friendship with all mankind and in particular with my own family as we cannot tell what time we shall quit this world. My best love and respects . . .[26]

Early in 1816 she made her Will. Three months later she was dead. Her Will was proved on 9 April 1816. She left £10 and her clothes to her sister, Sarah: £20 each to her executors (one being Thomas Dangerfield).

The rest of her worldly goods, her business and its goodwill at Little
Grosvenor Street, were divided equally between her two sons, Henry
Edward and William Henry; they were entreated to 'carry on the same
Business in Copartnership together to and for their mutual benefit and
advantage and that the profits thereof may be divided amongst them in
equal shares and proportions share and share alike . . .'[27] Six months later,
Henry Edward and William Henry, each described as 'Newsman',
received £500 each from the account at the Bank of England marked
'Anna Smith'.[28]

The partnership thus created was known as H. & W. Smith. Looking
back on his return to Little Grosvenor Street William Henry indicates
very clearly that the new partnership was cradled in melancholy circumstances which left their mark on his character. In his later years he wrote:

> I often regret that I cannot enter into society with that enjoyment which
> others evidently feel which I think must arise from the way in which
> my youthful days were passed, ground down by many years of great
> oppression and also seeing year after year the great sufferings of those
> I then loved and whose memory I still love and trust I shall while life
> and reason are continued to me – do not think that writing thus that
> my spirits are low, this subject always brings the feeling of gratefulness
> for the many blessings the Almighty has conferred upon me.[29]

What he had in mind is not wholly clear. That these last years of his
mother's life were difficult financially? That she had some lingering and
distressing last illness? That he was concerned about his brother Henry –
a lethargic personality without practical capacity or ambition, whose
inactivity was a constant problem and anxiety? Even allowing for William
Henry's propensity – inherited perhaps – to dramatise his situation, his
youth had without doubt been difficult. But he was justified in exonerating
himself from the charge of self-pity. On the contrary, his problems were
always a challenge to action, not an excuse for inertia. After his mother's
death, he threw himself into the rescue of her work with all that highly
strung, nervous energy and determination which was to be the major
distinguishing mark of his character.

In 1818, the brothers leased No. 41 Duke Street, Grosvenor Square:[30]
here there was not only more room to expand the business but also a
family house. William Henry could live 'over the shop' with his family –
for in 1817 he had married at St George's, Hanover Square, his parish
church, Miss Mary Ann Cooper.[31] She came of a strict Wesleyan family,

a circumstance which was to be of some personal and family consequence later on (see page 80).

The description of the new partnership was duly raised on to a more ambitious plane: H. & W. Smith were no more merely a 'newswalk' but 'Newspaper agents, Booksellers and Binders'.[32]

But while Henry Edward seems to have stayed behind for a year or two at Duke Street – it became his standard role to form the rearguard of the business – William Henry pressed on back towards his parents' original home and the City. The new address from the autumn of 1820 was 192 Strand, formerly occupied by W. I. Clement, the publisher of the *Observer*.[33] He has been described as 'a syndicate' and one who 'excited the suspicions which were attached to the Northcliffe press'.[34] Up to this time he was also 'one of the most extensive newsvenders in London'[35] and appears to have sold his newsvending business to the Smiths in preparation for purchasing the *Morning Chronicle* from James Perry. The impact of this step on the Smith business can be seen in two surviving bank accounts of 1826 and 1831 which show turnover increasing roughly fourfold in five years from £13,147 to £51,052. In both years the eleven largest suppliers were paid over 70 per cent of the total, comprising wholesale stationers as well as newspaper publishers in 1826 and a sum of nearly £7,000 to Clement in 1831.[36]

In December 1821 the brothers opened a 'New Reading Room' at 192 Strand. Here for a subscription for a month, or months, or a year, subscribers might read newspapers, 'the most approved Reviews, Magazines etc. ... from Nine o'Clock in the Morning till Nine in the Evening; Sundays excepted'.[37] William Henry moved in himself, with his wife and growing family, to the same address, once again living, in the traditional style, 'over the shop'. Part of the functions of the business was left at Duke Street with Henry Edward, who (tradition says) continued to be responsible for addressing the newspaper wrappers; his indolence and unpunctuality was a constant source of contention to his younger brother. At times, William Henry's nervous irritation would drive him out into the Strand where, in his short-sleeves, watch in hand, he could pace up and down awaiting the approach of his brother's consignment of wrappers. (A few more years and Henry Edward would be gently, and doubtless neither ungenerously nor unwillingly, eased out of the partnership – this in August 1828).[38]

The removal of the Smith business to the Strand was one of the most crucial decisions in its history. The ties with Fleet Street and Printing House Square had never been broken, for this had become the major centre of the printing, publishing and press industry and trades. This in turn was closely connected with the proximity of the government stamp duty and revenue and other offices, and especially, after 1775, of Somerset House, only a stone's throw from the new headquarters at 192 Strand. Not far away again, opposite the great coaching inn, the *Bull and Mouth*, the new General Post Office was a-building: it was designed by Robert Smirke, the pompous (John Summerson appropriately coins the word 'prolix' for him)[39] architect of a number of buildings in the same Greek Ionic manner — the Covent Garden Opera, the new Custom House and the later stages of Somerset House were all among his creations. Both Somerset House and the Post Office were crucial to William Henry's decision to move to the Fleet Street end of the Strand. For it was at Somerset House that the newspapers were stamped; in Fleet Street or nearby that they were printed; from the General Post Office that the mail carts delivered to the mail and stage coach starting points, both for London's centre and West End and — increasingly important — for the country at large: the *Bull and Mouth* was the nearest and largest. And, after the West End, it was the country at large on which William Henry had his eye.

Communications and Culture

THE SUCCESSFUL DEVELOPMENT of the W. H. Smith business resulted from the skill and decision with which its successive owners and directors seized opportunities for expanding their trade offered by the changing economy and society in which they lived and operated. In the later eighteenth and early nineteenth centuries two major economic trends combined to create new opportunities for enterprise. One was the resumption, after a long pause, of the expansion of London: the other was the movement known now for over a hundred years as the industrial revolution. Both need to be briefly described if the growth and development of the Smith business is to be understood.

London, where the Smith business began, had been the biggest town in Roman Britain and the capital of England since 1066. The road system of the entire country fanned out radially from London and ensured that it effectively dominated the country as a whole. Its growth in the seventeenth century (not least by immigration) had been specially rapid, continuous and impressive. Neither civil war, plague nor fire had done more than halt it for short periods. By 1700 London's population was a tenth or thereabouts of the whole national population. Then followed a pause, in some senses a decline, for half a century or more. Its causes must be sought perhaps in a general demographic pause; more specifically in the high mortality which was to mark out London as a particularly unhealthy place as late as the 1780s; in the congestion of its approaches and internal road system and of the Thames's waterway and bridges; in the inadequacy of its port, wharves and quays. With the opening up of a system of improved roads and the increased number of better designed vehicles which used them, inside and outside London after the mid-century (described later in this chapter), and the rising birth-rate outside London, demographic growth was at last resumed: not, it must be added, in the old City, where the decline begun after 1700 was to continue steadily down to the twentieth century as the area 'within and without' the ancient walls ceased to be residential and became a place of counting houses, offices, banks and the like. Westminster, even the 'Liberties', inner and outer suburbs resumed their growth; slowly until the nineteenth century, rapidly thereafter, until the half million of 1700 was over six-and-a-half million by the Census of 1901. Cobbett's 'great wen' was again a major national problem, more complex and insoluble than ever.

To some extent, the second development – 'industrial revolution', to which must be added the scarcely less important phenomenon of 'agricultural revolution' – contributed to this new metropolitan growth: to some extent it mitigated or at least modified it. The apparent paradox is explained by the ambiguous and misleading sense of the term 'industrial revolution'. In the long run, industrialisation certainly revolutionised the character of the English economy and society: but it did not do it suddenly. The word 'revolution', borrowed from older political terminology, is too indiscriminate and sharp a description of the process of socio-economic change in town and country, which was slow, regional, partial. This was as true of the consequences of turnips and enclosures as of steam engines and spinning jennies.

For England as a whole there was no sudden transformation. Trade, industry, exports and imports had all been growing steadily for a century by 1760. By 1830 (or even later) England was still far from fully industrialised. The output of coal, long growing, grew ever faster in the coalfields of the midlands, Yorkshire, Lancashire, Durham and Northumberland: yet its organisation, and the miners themselves, still bore the marks of feudalism. New technology, mechanical and metallurgical, was transforming the textile industries and creating a modern factory industry for cotton in Lancashire and a few other areas, while midland England was rapidly becoming a vast network of metal industries. A few, like the famous establishment of Boulton & Watt, were relatively large. Most were small. This is to emphasise how gradually, almost reluctantly, England left behind the age of agriculture and handicraft industry. Even by the time of the Great Exhibition in 1851, only a small fraction of the adult population of England had ever seen the inside of a factory or been down a coal mine – perhaps half to three-quarters of a million out of a total of 16 millions. Otherwise the English people were still countrymen sustained by those changes in rural economy often called 'the agricultural revolution' – farmers or farm servants, domestic servants, craftsmen and small masters, builders, black-smiths, millers, sawyers, carpenters, wheelwrights, printers, tailors, tinkers, milliners, dressmakers, sailors, fishermen ... Long after the arrival of railways, from the 1830s onwards, far more people were employed about stables, coach houses, inns and posting houses dealing with horses, coaches and carts than were employed about the new railways.

By the second half of the nineteenth century, by the 1880s certainly, the tide would flow strongly in favour of industries gathered into factories, heavily invested in machinery, consciously divided into employer-capitalists and workers organised in trade unions. The social structure would change accordingly as the world of small masters and craftsmen crumbled, but the changes were slow to come. Politics changed equally slowly. The transition from cottage to factory industry brought, in time, greater wealth, but it brought agonising problems for those displaced by machinery, like the handloom weavers. Town and country both witnessed the violence of desperate men, Luddites and rick burners. In politics there was a rapid growth of Radicals and Radicalism: but the reformers still aimed at politi-cal, not economic targets. Salvation from the troubles of the times was sought not through any socialist reform of industry or the economy but through the reform of Parliament. For most of the nineteenth century, the target of most reformers was still in the spirit of the European reform move-ments of the previous century: the abolition of hereditary and traditional privilege, and of parliamentary and government corruption through the reform and steady broadening of the franchise.

In the early part of the nineteenth century, then, the growth and develop-ment of provincial England (rural as well as urban) was the dominant economic and social feature of the times. London lost to the provinces a number of industries which had previously marked its suburban economy – ribbons to Coventry, hosiery to Leicester, cutlery to Sheffield; Thames shipbuilding gave way to the Clyde, the porcelain of Chelsea and Bow was edged out by the Potteries: all this in addition to the textiles and chemicals of the north west, the woollens of Yorkshire, the coal of the midlands and the north. The western ports benefited most by the important export trades generated by all this industrial growth outside the metropolitan area. Thus the economic unbalance of centuries between the wealth and power of the metropolis and the relative poverty of the provinces was steadily brought into equilibrium. London remained the greatest port, trading and financial centre, the hub of politics, fashion – and news. Provincial England became the location of more and more industries, old and new, and an agriculture uniquely advanced.

Yet to achieve the desired equilibrium, another form of economic innovation and improvement was essential: transport. For transport and economic development are interdependent. Roads, canals, railways handled traffic and by doing so created more traffic: more traffic created the need for more investment in transport and the means of transport. For the carriage of heavy, bulk cargoes, canals were the cheapest and most convenient form of transport, until they were overtaken and put out of business by the railways. But coal, grain, iron, pots and pans were not the whole story of industrial growth. There were other, lighter packages, and for these freight costs were less important than speed of delivery – newspapers among them. And because London remained the centre of politics, and the largest centre of consumption and therefore of the growing business of advertisement and news, the provinces needed the swiftest possible means of access to the London press – news of Parliament and government, of markets for commodities and money, of investment opportunities and problems. People also needed to be carried to and from the metropolis in increasing numbers. Thus the services of the engineers, often the same who were designing and building the canals, were called in to provide improved roads and bridges. Among them was Thomas Telford; but the best known name was that of John Loudon McAdam. Both were Scots.

The improvements of inland and coastal navigation and the building of roads had been in progress since the Restoration. But the recruitment of the capital and labour, and, no less important, the marshalling of political support to overcome local patriotism and the private interests that stood in the way of its success only bit hard by the second half of the eighteenth century. There is no reason to disbelieve the letters and diaries of travellers and writers who left excoriating accounts of the generally bad state of the roads in the seventeenth century and even long into the eighteenth. Coach services certainly were available and advertised in the seventeenth and early eighteenth centuries: how regular or reliable they were is doubtful. It seems improbable that either regularity or reliability could be expected so long as no system of financial support or consistent construction policy for roads extended much beyond each parish boundary. In any case, the early road improvements seem to have been confined largely to the Home Counties and a few areas bordering on them. It seems fair to infer that reliable road travel had to await the coming of the Turnpike Trusts and particularly the General Turnpike Act (1773) which reduced the considerable expense of procuring a separate Act for each new stretch of road. But the road mileage under Turnpike Trusts represented only a small proportion of the total road mileage and even this was far from perfect. Yet travellers were thankful for small mercies. 'I have been thinking, as I rode alone in a post-chaise from Hereford hither [to Breconshire]' wrote a lady traveller 'that, if ever I subscribe money towards the erection of a statue, it shall be to that of McAdam. Nothing can better prove the utility of his plan than this road, which is composed of alternate patches of new and old; on the former of which one runs as on a bowling green, while the other grinds one's bones.'[1]

Another lady traveller was less enthusiastic. McAdam's methods of road building did well by carriages and draught horses: for human beings, in dry weather, they threw up intolerable clouds of dust, suffocating the travellers, ruining all decent clothing, covering roadside cottages and destroying all cleanliness. 'If Mr. McAdam could lay the dust as *well* as the roads, he would be a clever fellow.'[2]

The most famous of all the published works dedicated to the description of a British road system was *Paterson's Roads*. When Edward Mogg issued its eighteenth edition in 1826–8, the system was at its apogee. Mogg follows the original author in dividing the roads into three types. Direct roads: mail coach roads: cross roads. It was the second category which formed the backbone of what today are (or were, before motorway construction) the main trunk roads of Britain. Apart from a minor complex of coach and direct roads in the midlands, converging on Birmingham, the heart of the entire system was London. Only in the outlying counties do the recorded roads do anything but point the way to the metropolis: even in Wales, Cornwall, East Anglia and the north, the main purpose of cross roads seemed to be to get passengers on to the London roads. Out of the 618 pages of Paterson which help the readers to follow the road, enjoy the history or topography of towns and villages and follow the vicissitudes of the owners and builders of the family seats which embellished the landscape and relieved the tedium of the journey, 353 pages concern themselves with roads which began or terminated in London. A foreign professor who was visiting England in the late eighteenth century found that the only way to get from Cambridge to Oxford was to travel via London. It was still arguably the best way in the twentieth.

Thanks to the combined talents and enterprise of road engineers, turnpike investors and coach-proprietors and designers, a nation-wide network of road transport emerged which employed at its peak over 30,000 men and 150,000 horses. At Hounslow alone, the first staging post to the west of London for the Bath and Exeter traffic, more than two and a half thousand horses were stabled. The post-horse proprietors operated a private hire system of horses and post-chaises – private but less comfortable than the public stage coaches. Even these ran the peril of overturning until patient experiments with safety coaches reduced the risk. The safety coach distributed the weight over a broader wheel base and the centre of balance was placed lower. But the fastest way to go on a long journey between 1784 and 1825 was certainly by the mail coach. It had its own roads. It was exempt from tolls. It took precedence over all other coaches in cases of obstruction. It was punctual and in the earlier period more exclusive. Gentry, merchants, professional men, army and navy officers were prepared to pay for speed, reliability and the security provided by the statutory armed guard.

To Pitt goes the honour for backing the proposal by John Palmer, an enterprising theatre proprietor of Bath, for the reform of the older system of slow, unarmed coaches in 1784. Overruling Post Office objections, Pitt gave Palmer the chance to try out his proposals – at his own expense. Thus, in triumph, the first post mail coach left on the run between London, Bristol and Bath in August 1784, inaugurating the system which maintained its supremacy for forty years. During this period the mail coach gradually put out of business the older, smaller proprietors whose coaches had been serving the provincial routes to London increasingly since the seventeenth century. Much of this pioneering coach business (like Palmer's) sprang from provincial enterprise: it was especially the men of the midlands and the north who were apparently 'more anxious to link themselves with London than London . . . was to be linked with them.'[3]

Steadily the coaching network had grown: from Warwick, Birmingham, Manchester, Newcastle, Cambridge, Carlisle, Glasgow, Liverpool, Leeds and other provincial centres, the links of relatively regular services, slow, uncomfortable, vulnerable to highwaymen, floods and accidents, were forged. But the competition of Palmer's reformed mail coaches was too strong. In the ensuing struggle many of the small proprietors went under. Except for the services on the 'cross' roads, they were squeezed out by the three or four large operators who operated in each town of any size. The result: a new type of competition developed from those stage coach proprietors, more often than not Londoners, who had the enterprise and capital to build and operate improved coaches which could travel as fast and reliably as the mails. These were provided with horses and coachmen capable of making the 10 to 11 miles an hour in reasonable comfort which was the standard set by Palmer.

Two distinct types of coaching emerged in the course of time: the horsing of mails, and the stages. After Palmer's finances were exhausted he retired on a government pension. The mail business thereafter was subsidised by government and put out to contract by the Postmaster-General to the big stage coach operators. They hired their vehicles from the London coach builder, Vidler, of Millbank: and Vidler's hire charges were such that horsing mails was in itself never very profitable. But each mail contract carried with it the right to style the booking office a 'Royal Mail Coach Office' and this was in itself a prestigious title which brought other coaching custom with it – even though for passengers it meant travelling by night.

The nerve centre for the mail system was the General Post Office, originally in Lombard Street: after 1829 the new GPO at St Martin's-le-Grand. The mail coaches for the north, east and south would load up their passengers at inns in different parts of London, moving off to the GPO about 7.30 p.m. Coaches for the west of England gathered in Piccadilly or Oxford Street: their mail bags were delivered to them by carts from St Martin's-le-Grand. By 8 p.m. the mail coaches were all on their way.

Among the great mail contractors were the four biggest London stage coach proprietors, William Chaplin, Edward Sherman, Benjamin Worthy Horne and Robert Nelson. All operated from famous inns in the City. Chaplin's principal headquarters was the *Swan with Two Necks* in Lad Lane off Gresham Street, previously used by Palmer's first mail coach from Bath in 1784. Chaplin worked on a very large scale. At his peak he had 1,800 horses and some 2,000 coachmen, guards, ostlers and others, serving 68 different coach routes. Fourteen out of a total of 27 mails leaving London every night were horsed by Chaplin. But unlike some of his competitors Chaplin fell behind by too great a reliance on his mail contracts: by the 1820s and 1830s travellers were coming to appreciate the pleasure of travelling by the fast *day* coaches: night travel was boring. Edward Sherman, Chaplin's rival, was established at the *Bull and Mouth*, St Martin's-le-Grand. This was, providentially, immediately opposite the new GPO and had been the headquarters of Willans, one of the earliest mail contractors. But Sherman had a special claim to originality: he inaugurated the fastest and most efficient *day* coach service. His Shrewsbury *Wonder* of 1825 beat the previous day coach record by making Shrewsbury in 15 hours: until then, Birmingham had been the farthest limit. His underground stables at the *Bull and Mouth* held 700 horses. Robert Nelson, working from the *Bell Savage* on Ludgate Hill with some 400 horses, was the son of Mrs Nelson of Aldgate, a monopolist of eastern coach traffic. Her son operated to the north and west as well. So did the energetic and aggressive Horne (of the *Golden Cross*, Charing Cross) whose competitive spirit drove not only his rivals but, in the end, the exhausted Horne himself into the ground.

In the last years before the spread of the new railway system, the coach proprietors were coping with a seemingly boundless market for travel. More and more travellers were demanding services between Liverpool, Birmingham, Manchester and the metropolis. Unless they booked well in advance, they stood little chance of finding a seat either on the night mails or the fast day coaches in and out of the growing industrial towns. The rivalry between the operators for business became hectic. On May Day, 1830, Horne's *Independent Tally-Ho* beat Mr Mountain's *Tally-Ho* (*Saracen's Head*, Snow Hill) and all previous coaching records by covering the 109 miles to Birmingham in 7½ hours, an average speed of 14½ miles an hour. On the much longer Manchester run (186 miles), Sherman's *Telegraph* in 1833 left the *Bull and Mouth* at 5 a.m. and reached its destination by 11 p.m.: the 18-hour run included two 20-minute halts for meals and 18 stops to change horses.

The pace was, literally, too hot to last. The new railways offered a way out. One by one, the stage coach operators, tough though they were, moved out of coaches into rails. When the line to Birmingham opened, in 1838, Chaplin took his crack coach, *Greyhound*, off the road, and persuaded Horne to join him in a contract with the new line as a carrier of goods and parcels. He was also one of the first investors in the new London–Southampton line. Sherman lasted a little longer, doggedly cutting fares in an effort to hang on: the cost – £7,000 in losses – was too high. Between 1838 and 1847 the horse-mails steadily dwindled. At both ends of the Kingdom – Edinburgh and Dover – the mail stopped running. By 1842, the *Bull and Mouth*, historic centre of so much coach traffic, had only 3 of its original 73 coaches still in service. Only a few slow coaches, short stages and services to remoter parts of the country survived. Here and there, the occasional inn, out of imagination or oversight, still exhibits an ancient bill recording a coach service of the 1870s or 1880s flying between London and the north and east (as one at Buntingford still advertises a service via that sleepy Hertfordshire town between London and Cambridge). The carrier's cart, with its picturesque cargo of farmers' wives, their butter, chickens and vegetables, was the last survivor in the 1920s and even 1930s in remote Lincolnshire. But in general what has sometimes been called 'the long sleep' had begun by 1850; the old inns quickly became dilapidated, shabby, deserted; the roads, cross roads especially, overgrown with grass and weed. They would not revive until the coming of the bicycle, the internal combustion engine and the temperance enthusiasts who founded the Trust House movement at the turn of the century.

It remains to note two points. The first is the important distinction between the two systems of coach service between London and the provinces:

the night mail services, subsidised by the government to carry mail at standard rates, but gradually and by a complicated and eccentric progression (see page 40) coming to carry newspapers as a free service; and the fast day coaches which also came to carry newspapers, at a price, for those distributors who believed the extra cost was worth the expanded markets it opened up to their enterprise. This distinction was to be vital to the growth of W. H. Smith's (see pages 44-5).

Secondly, we must sketch briefly the connection between the coach system as described above and what is popularly called 'culture'. If we use the word 'culture' we use it simply, and without overtones of superior morality, to mean the way people pass the time when they are not working, and the influence this has on their mental activities both at work and in leisure; a literate factory worker is not necessarily better than an illiterate peasant: he may be less intelligent, more gullible, less generous, more greedy: but he is different. The society composed of more literate and (supposedly) more rational persons will also be different. If, as such writers as Karl Marx, Thomas Carlyle, Lenin and E. H. Carr inform us, history is in large part a matter of numbers, we should be duly impressed by the importance of mail and stage coaches. More than Caxton or Gutenberg before them, or free popular education after them, they spread the habit of reading by spreading material to read. Let us look at the beginnings of this process in which W. H. Smith I and II played such an important role.

The technological and industrial 'revolution' emphasised a division of functions between London and the provinces which was to last until the twentieth century. The provinces and outlying Britain – Lancashire, Yorkshire, the midlands, the north-east, Wales and southern Scotland – became the major centres of industrial production. Thus the time-honoured abuse of London as a monopolist of trade, industry and power was to some extent muted. But neither the sacrifice of industrial supremacy, nor the rivalry of provincial ports in overseas trade, nor the reform of the Parliamentary system from 1832 onwards did much to shake the role of the metropolis as the centre of political power, national administration, high fashion, amusement and opinion. The monarchy might divide its time between its London, Scottish, Welsh and provincial seats. Neither Parliament nor Whitehall contemplated similar concessions to devolution until well into the twentieth century. So, while London grew steadily less unhealthy, and more capable of a measure of self-sustaining growth, immigrants continued to head for the capital from Scotland, Wales (both

traditional sources of supply) and from the provinces, where the birth rate
had long exceeded the death rate. By the early nineteenth century Britain
was breeding enough people to supply both the needs of the industrialising
provinces and the renewed expansion of London. The process was made
easier by the growth of cheaper and more regular forms of transport.

Not everybody was as pleased with Mr McAdam as were lady travellers
(especially pregnant mothers), progressives and (generally) Londoners.
Reformers and preservers of rural Britain were critical, Cobbett and
Arthur Young among them. Young wrote:

> ... the power of expeditious travelling depopulates the kingdom.
> Young men and women in the country villages fix their eyes on London
> as the last stage of their hope. They enter into service in the country for
> little else but to raise money enough to go to London, which was no
> such easy matter when a stage-coach was four or five days in creeping a
> hundred miles. The fare and the expenses ran high. *But now!* a country
> fellow, one hundred miles from London, jumps on a coach box in the
> morning and for eight or ten shillings gets to town by night ... the
> numbers *who have seen London* are increased tenfold ...[4]

An observant if irascible traveller wrote of the turnpike roads 'which
have imported London manners, and depopulated the country. – I meet
milkmaids on the road, with the dress and looks of strand misses; and must
think that every line of Goldsmith's *Deserted Village* contains melancholy
truths.'[5] The unification of Britain was not without its pains and penalties.

The new transport industry brought travel within the reach of many
people for whom it had been hitherto impossible or at best extremely
difficult. London was the magnet: a high proportion of those who were
not drawn to it permanently visited it, not least, because they already had
relatives there. For a variety of reasons, therefore, London's news was
everybody's news: there were high politics, war, diplomacy, the Court
circular and fashionable scandal for the great; trade, finance and advertisements for the middling; positions as footmen or ladies' maids for the
humble; jobs as bank clerks and mechanics for the Scots and as ushers for
the Welsh. The provinces had very few daily papers. Their weeklies were
steady, reliable, respectable and accurate: but, truth to tell, dull reading.
It was the wars in Europe, the rows in Parliament, the scandals at Court,
the crises in Threadneedle Street, the swindles and the bankruptcies,
divorces, rapes, suicides and murders which made the London papers
worth buying. As Arthur Young's stream of hopeful, rustic immigrants,

male and female, flowed into London, the coaches which carried them in carried out a growing supply of London newspapers, journals, and books, mainly novels. This growing market in literature was another function of industrialisation which multiplied and magnified the impact of London on rural and provincial Britain.

The inns of Britain, to which the turnpike traffic had brought a Golden Age, had been among the first to enjoy news and literature from London. The Hon. John Byng was no friend of the turnpikes which he travelled so frequently: but his diaries contain copious references to the relief from the tedium of travel (there were not many) to be derived from reading the London newspapers supplied by the inn-keepers. At Bagshot he wrote letters or relaxed 'by old news-paper reading'. On arriving at Caernarvon the 'abundance of letters, and newspapers, prevented any wish of rambling'. At Hereford he 'read the London news-papers'. At Leicester in 1789 he read 'at the coffee house the latest London papers'. At Bedford in September 1790 he rose in the morning 'after reading newspapers (for I cannot move till I have read about the Spanish War) . . .'[6]

Such references may be found in the diaries of travellers: they multiply as the communications system itself spread and improved. And they include increasing comment on books as well as papers. That sharp correspondent Maria Edgeworth observed that both news and fiction provided topics of conversation as they circulated round the country. 'Do you recollect our seeing in the newspaper an account of a man who poisoned several race-horses by putting arsenic in the water-troughs? Also an account of a horrid woman who made her servant boy murder her husband; and ordered him to go back and *finish him* as composedly as if she had told him to kill a pig?'[7] The transmission of newspapers was growing at a rate which compelled the Post Office to provide special waggons for their carriage. The growth of this traffic was connected with two developments: the spread of literacy and the coming of the free post.

It has been suggested in recent years that the result was the development of a press which corresponded to liberal ideas (past and present) of the early Victorian age – virtuous newspapers read by either uncorrupted working men or an educated and pious middle class: and an underground press of pornography, scandal and violence read only clandestinely or by readers who failed to qualify as full citizens. This Golden Age is supposed to have collapsed only in face of the combined onslaught of capitalism, technology and the greed for profit: Northcliffe represents the climacteric and the perversion of the objectives of W. E. Forster, the north country Liberal M.P. (and friend of W. H. Smith II) whose Education Act used popularly to be supposed to have converted an illiterate England into a world of readers just in time to be seduced by a debased press. If common sense and a reasonably realistic view of human nature were not enough to reject such a comical distortion of history, now almost an orthodoxy among progressives, the evidence will do the rest. The 'Last Dying Speech or Confession' of William Corder, the murderer of Maria Marten in the Red Barn, sold over a million copies. Maria Edgeworth wrote, on 29 December, 1821, with more excitement than syntax: 'Thanks to the printing press – the mail coach and the steam packet gifts beyond the gifts of fairies we can all see and hear what each other are doing and do and read the same things nearly at the same time.'[8]

She was no prig. Like the majority of readers of all classes, in her own age, before or later, she read out of curiosity and for amusement. The willingness to satisfy these natural desires has been found among publishers, authors, journalists at all times. Maria would have been bitterly disappointed if the fairies had not numbered among their gifts a good sprinkling of ripely human, and inhuman, episodes. So would the growing thousands of new readers in her day and later. Fiction, good and bad, was similarly distributed. G. O. Trevelyan recalled apropos a letter of 1820 how his uncle 'would walk miles out of Cambridge in order to meet the coach which brought the last new Waverley novel.'[9]

In the buying of fiction generally, most people found themselves victims of the high prices which ruled all forms of literary output. There were, nevertheless, examples of publishers who exploited particular areas of the market – almost exclusively crudely sensational – and thus successfully combined low prices with very high sales. One was James Catnach, publisher of William Corder's speech and confession and similar crime literature. His imitators specialised in 'Gothic' novels of horror; salacious tales like *The French Novelist, Legends of Terror and Tales of the Wonderful and the Wild, Varney and the Vampire, or The Feast of Blood* vied for readers with *Fatherless Fanny, or The Mysterious Orphan, The Death Ship, or The Pirate's Bride and the Maniac of the Deep*. These 'pariah publishers' of early Victorian England may have taught modern American publishing a few tricks of presentation or the lowest wiles of salesmanship: there are many similarities between them. Yet, as one historian of literacy has remarked, they and their schemes 'deserve much credit for spreading the reading habit among the semiliterate.'[10] It is at least a refreshing admission from among the historians of culture (usually so critical of capitalist contribution to social progress) that the worse could occasionally lead to the better.

It is now in fact evident, and generally accepted, that long before Forster's

Act could affect the rates of literacy in England, a high proportion of men (slightly fewer women) had somehow learned to read: fireside Bible reading, Sunday School, Dame School, Charity School, smutty novels and magazines: wholesome and virtuous, unwholesome and sinful, solemn and frivolous – every little helped. At least one provincial newspaper was launched in the belief (of the founder) that the area (East Riding of Yorkshire) was one of 'almost universal reading and writing'. The particular area may have been rather stronger than average for literacy but, all in all, it seems probable that by the first half of the nineteenth century some three fifths or more of the people could read and write. Of course there were wide differences between this region and that. But by the 1890s no area fell (officially at least) below 90 per cent. Forster's Act was important but its role was to complete, not initiate, the processes by which England became almost entirely 'literate', at least in a technical sense – 'literate' is not the same as 'educated'.

Before the 1870s there were few newspapers, except *The Times*, which could have claimed to be 'national': and the sale of London papers – even of *The Times* – and of local papers was far, far smaller than the number of potential readers might have led one to suppose. If so large a proportion of the people was able to read, why did they not buy a newspaper? The answer was: first, most of them could not afford the high price (see page 60); second, there existed a traditional system of 'collective' purchase and exchange of newspapers. This had become tolerable by long-established custom. Papers passed continuously and no doubt increasingly grubbily, through the post, especially as the post gradually became free, to some and then to all; buyers passed them to relations, neighbours exchanged with neighbours. Members of reading rooms and clubs read them, or were read to, on payment of a subscription. Inns and public houses bought a newspaper for the use of customers, among whom it was not difficult to find one who was only too ready to read aloud to defray the costs of his own entertainment.

A vast mass of evidence, mostly local and casual, exists about these tabernacles of literary ritual and their devotees. Being by its nature unsystematic, any inferences drawn from it must be impressionistic. Yet some outlines are clear, as a brief survey will prove. An article in the *Monthly Magazine* for June 1821 (signed 'A Traveller') estimated that there were not less than 6,500 Reading Societies and Literary Institutions in the United Kingdom and 'owing to their convenience and proved utility, above 1,000 new ones have been formed within the last three years . . . hence above 30,000 families become by these means more or less literary, at an individual expense, varying from half a guinea to two guineas per annum.' Commercial circulating libraries, supplying 'novels and high-seasoned productions for sickly or perverted appetites' totalled some 1,500 'supplying . . . 100,000 individuals regularly; and another 100,000 occasionally' and (concluded the 'Traveller' surprisingly charitably) 'as far as they exhibit the passions and foibles of mankind, amend the heart, and extend the influence of sentiment and sensibility, they must be regarded as useful establishments.'

Quite separate were the Newspaper Societies, said to exist in every parish and hamlet, not less than 5,000 in all, 'serving with mental food at least 50,000 families'. In these societies, 'seven, eight or nine persons club their sixpence a week to take in and circulate from one to the other, a London, and one, two, or three provincial papers. In poor districts [the special mention shows that newspaper clubs were not limited to 'the poor'] twelve or fourteen club their weekly penny for one or two of their favourite provincial papers, which they wear out in passing from hand to hand.'[11] (All but a very few local provincial papers appeared once or occasionally twice weekly.)

How accurate the 'Traveller's' facts were is impossible to know: but generally they are in line with other available information about conditions in local regions and cities. This tends to support the view of a number of historians of Scotland and the north of England that (as Brougham, among others, always maintained) the whole of this area was better off for grammar schools and Sunday schools than the south: if existing endowments were properly used and distributed, the majority of children could be assured of facilities for at least rudimentary education. In Scotland, education was strongly believed in at all levels up to university, not to speak of scientific and technical training. In the north, the influence of old and new Dissent, itself closely connected with the aspirations and ambitions of the intelligent artisan and thoughtful shopkeeper, helped to spread literacy. Religious books and pamphlets were one of the most common forms of reading in town and country and John Wesley himself published and circulated quantities of cheap books and pamphlets. Hymn-singing has always been a favourite part of the Methodist chapel service: it demanded a knowledge of reading, if not of music. (In the 1920s the mentally-retarded organ blower at a Lincolnshire village chapel threatened a personal strike if he was not provided with a hymn book containing words *and music*.) Methodist local (lay) preachers were capable of composing extempore prayers and sermons, biblically derived, of astonishing power and eloquence – and length. Prayers lasted up to twenty, even thirty minutes; sermons up to an hour.

The generally high standard of written composition by mid-Victorian times owed less to school lessons than to regular practice in writing letters. The results were simple, effective and sometimes eloquent. An American writer is sceptical about the statement in the 1790s by James Lackington, the shoemaker turned bookseller, that poor country people widely read each other stories to shorten the winter nights: he thinks reading was more an urban than a rural occupation. But his scepticism seems to be based on little more than logic (thus: city clerks need to read; ploughboys do not) and even this is not beyond doubt.[12] The East and North Ridings of York-shire, where literacy was high, were not as urbanised or industrialised as the West Riding or Staffordshire, where literacy was low. Literacy in the country was also often highest among women: it was therefore passed down to the children more easily.

These continuing debates underline the uncertainty of knowledge about these grey areas of social history where mental and material matters and evidence are equally involved. One or two points are nevertheless clear: we return to the great increase in wealth and influence in the provinces, especially the north; to the resumption of the growth and influence also of London, more than ever the source of information, news, literature and communications and the major centre of printing. We need to recall, nevertheless, the important gap that still separated 'literacy' from the economic consequences that might have been expected to follow upon 'literacy'. The communal, collective arrangements for buying and reading newspapers and other literature were to survive long into the nineteenth century (and even beyond). This phenomenon, to which too little attention has been given, is apparent from the evidence of the largest and most opulent industrial cities of the midlands and north. Certainly individual purchasers of newspapers and books existed, for example in Birmingham: but there was also a demand for the creation of reading clubs of various kinds. Reading clubs *were* clubs, social as well as utilitarian.

On 10 February 1772, *Aris's Birmingham Gazette*, a paper combining news, notices and advertisements, announced the formation of a Book Society at Mr Swinney's, Printer and Bookseller, High Street. It was many years later, in 1808, that the *Gazette* carried news of proposals by Messrs Thomson and Wrightson, Booksellers, at the Stamp Office, New Street, to open in 'an elegant and spacious Apartment at their Residence' – a *News Room*. It was to be supplied with four London dailies, *Lloyd's List*, *Prices Current*, a Sunday paper, three provincial papers, three Birmingham papers, reviews and popular magazines. Its purpose: to afford opportunities for 'Merchants, Tradesmen and others' (not the poor) to meet and obtain

'Information without the Hurry and Inconvenience naturally attending upon a Public Room . . .' It is worth noting that when the room opened, the London dailies were evening papers (delivered presumably by the night mail): no London morning papers were available. By 1822, a number of newspapers had been added to the list. It now included at least one morning paper – the *Morning Chronicle* – one of the several smaller rivals of *The Times*. *The Times* remained an absentee.[13]

Birmingham had been somewhat isolated from the rest of England in the first half of the eighteenth century. Not even turnpikes had done much to mitigate a solitary situation in which Birmingham had been content – of necessity – to rely on its own newspapers and what they could crib from London sources. By 1800 this was changing: it was to change even more, and more quickly as the nineteenth century went along.

An air of liberality seems to have characterised Manchester's arrangements – a circulating library with nearly 400 subscribers, 5,000 to 6,000 volumes and membership transferable 'by sale or legacy', seems to have competed with several other similar institutions to which was added in 1803 a 'New Library and News-Room' on a grand scale and for a grand entrance subscription: 20 guineas was evidence of growing Mancunian opulence. The 'Coffee, or News-Room' was nearly the length of a cricket pitch: members (and their ladies) might not only read but drink coffee, tea or soup in its pleasing surroundings.[14]

By the 1830s, another 'Coffee and News-Room', but with a strongly progressive slant, made its appearance in Manchester. In 1833 John Doherty, the Irish Radical reformer and trade union pioneer, advertised the opening of his reading room, with 96 newspapers and publications weekly; the *Edinburgh Review* and the *Westminster Review* ensured the readers access to the élite intellects of London and Scotland. Pointedly, the Tory *Quarterly Review* was excluded. Doherty was at pains to enlarge with Hibernian eloquence on the total *respectability* of his establishment, affording as it did '. . . advantages never before offered to the Manchester Public, combining Economy, Health, Temperance, and Instruction, in having a wholesome and exhilarating beverage at a small expense, instead of the noxious and intoxicating stuff usually supplied at the Alehouse and Dram-shop, together with the privilege of perusing the most able and popular publications of the day, whether political, literary, or scientific, in a comfortable and genteel apartment, in the evening brilliantly lighted with gas.'[15]

But for confirmation of Brougham's faith in northern virtues, those at Newcastle-upon-Tyne surpassed, if anything, the cultural facilities of Manchester. By 1831, Newcastle enjoyed splendid coach services to north and south. These enabled its coffee-houses to be plentifully supplied with newspapers: Thomas Oliver, the local historian, writing in 1831, even remarks (rather stuffily) that only one coffee-house (the *Eldon* in Blackett Street) was truly a coffee-house; 'those others so called, being properly news rooms, and devoted to the use of their respective subscribers'. The *Exchange News-Room*, he observed, was 'well supplied with London and country papers, and several foreign Journals'. Taken along with his account of its 14 or more schools – infant, charity, grammar and others – and its literary institutions, Oliver's picture is one of a thriving and intellectually vigorous city.[16] It compares well with (for example) Reading. Here, in spite of good communications by road with London, the prevailing spirit seems to have been one of torpor, at least before the railway age. Schools were few, small and obscure. The postal service, even to London, was poor. A local critic wrote caustically in 1810: 'The book most read here is the *Bible*; next to that is *Moore's Almanac*'. The history of its social-literary institutions seems to confirm that Reading was not a centre of intellectual ferment. A small book club founded in 1802 quickly became 'convivial rather than intellectual'. By 1839 its subscription library was described as 'somewhat antique' and it was merged with an equally languid philo-sophical institution under the fashionable title of the *Athenaeum*. A Mecha-nics' Institution of 1826 enjoyed (if that is the right word) only a brief life. A successor founded in 1840 did little better: after three years it could only claim 15 'mechanic' members. Its finances were rescued – often the fate of such institutions – by the patronage of 'respectable tradesmen' who renamed it the 'Literary, Scientific, and Mechanics' Institution'. Earlier the only arrangement (and it was far from specific) made for disseminating news among the minority interested in such things was for sporadic meetings at which *The Times* was read aloud 'in a large room'.[17]

Reading, it seems, had neither the vigour of the industrial cities of the provinces nor the surviving thirst for cultivation which enlivened the – often remote – old cities and towns important in earlier centuries and now famous mainly for their cathedrals, abbeys, markets, an occasional *Athen-aeum* or Assembly Rooms, where the 'county' met the local worthies, the Bishop or Archdeacon could witness the annual Ball, or play whist or simply read and talk: such were Norwich, Stamford, Bury St Edmunds, Colchester, York, Lincoln, Chester, Exeter, etc. Among these Lincoln has been very fully recorded by recent studies marking its progress from Roman and post-Roman times down to the present.[18]

Geographically, Lincoln has been off the map of England since Roman times, accessible more from the sea than by land. The 'north' road proper led straight up to Edinburgh. The branch road to Lincoln and beyond merely led the unwary traveller straight into the mud flats of Humberside and *ultima Thule*. Why go to Lincoln? Only to see Lincoln. Its claim to be viewed rested on its superb cathedral, its castle . . . what else? Yet by 1786 it had a county newsroom, 'with twenty-one gentlemen of the county and thirty gentlemen of the town as members. Gentry and clergy were prominent, with some doctors . . . Here were newspapers and a book club, and glimpses . . . of whist and the periodical distribution of books.'[19]

By 1792 Lincoln had another book club: it met at the *White Hart Inn* (still there in the shade of the cathedral) for tea, whist, talk and the auction of books. By 1814 it had a library, with 270 'proprietors' – gentry, clergy, merchants, farmers and tradesmen – owning in all some 6,000 volumes. It was enlarged in 1822 by a decision to extend membership to mechanics, apprentices and inhabitants of surrounding villages at a nominal subscription. As to newspapers (there were two weeklies – the *Lincoln Chronicle* and *Lincoln Gazette*) their circulation was small. A local printer, Edward Drury, editor of the *Gazette*, told Tennyson in 1834 that 'only one in twenty people saw a newspaper, and that often only once a week.'[20]

Such local evidence is too fragile to form any solid basis for confident generalisations on a national scale. Yet, unsystematic as it is, it leaves the impression of a society varied, diverse, uneven – yet aspiring and full of promise. This was a society full of curiosity, bubbling with social, cultural and political potential. Here in the making was a market for news and literature. London had both the news and the literature: the task was to bridge the gaps in transport and communications. This was the self-appointed task of William Henry Smith I. The improvements in printing, the development of fast day coaches out of London, the demands of provincial readers of newspapers, individual and collective – all features of the 1820s – were for William Henry both challenge and opportunity.

III

London and Provincial: The First W. H. Smith

The Age of the Coach

SOMEWHERE BETWEEN the end of the 'French War' in 1815, and 1830, the business known from 1816 to 1828 as H. & W. Smith changed its direction. From being a small, London (mainly West End) newswalk, it became a vigorously growing enterprise increasingly concerned with the transmission and sale of London newspapers to the provinces – especially to the large cities, Manchester, Liverpool and Birmingham. This concern was not, however, exclusive. William Henry I's purchase of 192 Strand symbolised the change, but No. 192 was also a local newsroom; and there is enough evidence to show that the carriage trade originally established at Little Grosvenor Street continued. In the late 1820s, the Smiths were publishing, 'at four o'clock every Saturday afternoon, *Bell's Life in London and Sporting Chronicle*; combining, with the News of the Week, a Rich Repository of Fashion Wit and Humour, And the Interesting Incidents of Real Life'.[1] In this versatile journal, in 1828, they also begged to inform 'the Nobility, Gentry, and Public' that they had 'for *Sale* an extensive *Stock of Writing* and other *Papers*, of the most *superior* quality' at 192 Strand, 'second house from the Crown and Anchor Tavern.[2] In 1829 W. H. Smith were advertising in the *Morning Post* 'Splendid Annuals, Almanacks, Writing Paper, Scrap books, Pencils, Travelling Desks and Dressing Cases, Ink, Merchants' Journals and Ledgers. Etc.'[3]

This was evidently an upper-class trade to both London and the country: for example, *Bell's Life* was available by post, in any part of the country 'within one hundred miles of London' on the Sunday morning following Saturday's publication.

Some fragments of this country gentry trade have survived. In November 1822 Sir Thomas Staines of Margate asked to be sent 'by the Margate Corn Hoy which will Sail tomorrow from Chester Quay near the custom House', a large package of 'Good Post Paper'.[4] The *Standard* advertised all the usual stationers' materials, including pocket knives, scissors, playing cards, etc. available at Smith's.[5] Journals, reviews and gazettes were despatched all over the British Isles. In the west of England the Bishop of Worcester took the *Courier, Standard* and *John Bull*.[6] Lord Willoughby de Broke would have the *Albion* (evening paper) sent to Compton, instead of the *Morning Post*.[7] The Duke of Buckingham,[8] Lord Midleton[9] and Lord Dunsany[10] likewise made their pleasure known: from Scotland, the Marquis of Breadalbane his displeasure: 'Lord Breadalbane' (his secretary wrote) 'expects you will *always* send him the latest additions [*sic*] of the Evening Newspapers – his Lordship is surprised that you have not done this lately, therefore you will be so good as return him an answer stating the reason.'[11]

Evidence of individual buying of newspapers and journals covers places as widely spread as Selkirk, Stirling, Falkirk, Stratford-upon-Avon, Godalming, Buxton, Manchester, Bradford, Ludlow, Tadcaster and Dublin.[12] Many were probably evening newspapers, despatched by the mail coaches: others may already, by 1825 at least, have gone by fast day coaches. In all cases, this country trade probably sprang directly or indirectly from the original carriage trade of Little Grosvenor Street. For it was the common practice of the nobility and gentry, upon leaving their town house for their country seat, to order Smith's to send their London papers and journals on to them. The coming of the fast day coach services (see page 43) by the second half of the 1820s gave this burgeoning trade a major boost.

Another development of the years immediately after the Napoleonic wars may have added to the newsagents' interest in the country trade: the fall in circulation accompanying the peace. The *Westminster Review* in April 1829 wrote:

At the close of the late war the public, who appeared to have been satiated with news, and to imagine that a time of peace could never furnish sufficient incident to keep up the interest of a daily paper, evinced a pretty general indifference to news; and many persons with whom the purchase of a daily paper proceeded from mere excitement, discontinued their subscriptions, and contented themselves with reading the news once a week instead of once in evrey twenty-four hours, but this was only for a time; within the last four or five years there has been a good demand for daily papers . . .[13]

Whether the pause from 1815 to (say) 1825 was psychological (as the *Review* argued), or a result of the temporary dislocations in the economy resulting from the war, or simply of the increase in the stamp duty on newspapers in 1815, is impossible to say. But it was evidently felt more in London than in the country: all the more reason to attend as vigorously as possible to the country trade, as Smith's evidently did. By 1829, the pause was over. The *Westminster Review* calculated that through the growing number of coffee houses and communal reading centres, half a million new readers had been added to the London reading public: counting 30 readers to each paper, this meant one newspaper to every 400 people, 'an astonishing number . . . exceeded in no part of the globe, except the United States of America'.

Allowing for the progressive enthusiasm of the *Westminster Review* there was something in its argument that, for the moment, with swords sheathed, 'the schoolmaster is indeed abroad' in Fleet Street. Battles and sieges gave way to 'more useful and instructive matter': outwardly, at least, man seemed to have become 'more of a reasoning animal'. This in turn had re-stimulated the public interest in the press – certainly in London.[14] The provincial press (according to the *Westminster Review* in January 1830) was 'absolutely without original articles . . . mere . . . registers of the news and occurrences given in the London papers'.[15] Provincial papers might be cheaper, being less costly to establish, maintain and finance, but the initiative and prestige remained firmly with London. For the provision of genuine 'news' it remained cheaper to print and publish in London and send the London newspaper to the provinces than to send the news by post from London to Liverpool for the use of a daily paper printed there. The local papers remained late echoes of the London press.

This was the background against which William Henry I developed his famous 'coach trade' in London daily papers to the provinces. He vested his decision upon one simple observation: the correct timing of his means of transport. It has been a popular fallacy to suppose that he was unique in spotting this opportunity. This is not correct: others did too. What was unique was the vigour and determination with which he laboured thereafter, year in, year out, to provide reliable and punctual services. It was this which led him into a position of near-monopoly in the transmission of the best London dailies to the country.

In time, the name of the Smith business would be increasingly – for a long period predominantly – identified with the transmission of London newspapers and other literature to the provinces. Smith's did not however either initiate or monopolise this function in the 1820s or for some time after. Originally it lay with the Post Office and it is to the conditions of the postal services that we must first look to understand what William Henry and his successors altered.

Among those who had long enjoyed the privilege of sending newspapers freely through the post were members of the House of Lords and the House of Commons. By the 1760s about a quarter of all the newspapers sent through the General Post Office could be traced to this source. The Franking Act of 1764 (designed originally to prevent forgery) gave these classes of person the right to send written orders to the Post Office demanding the free delivery of their papers. By the 1770s members of the Opposition were making the most of their privilege, sending large orders on behalf of printers, dealers and booksellers as well as to themselves, their families, friends and constituents. Provided the sender's name was written on the outside of the packet, it passed through the post free.

By 1772, over 2,000 such notices from MPs were registered at the General Post Office (still in Lombard Street), roughly one third being for constituents and friends and two thirds on behalf of printers and booksellers. These were thus able to compete with the original managers of the newspaper post, the Post Office 'Clerks of the Road'. By 1790 the number of notices had more than trebled: it now represented free postage for over 65,000 newspapers a week passing from London to the country, or more than half the annual total flow of London newspapers countrywards.

All attempts by the GPO to restrict Members' orders ended in failure: so did the experimental imposition of a penny postage for newspapers in 1782. This had, nevertheless, one by-product: the special Newspaper Office of 1787. This had been set up because the increasing volume of newspapers hastily despatched by printers and dealers, clumsily folded and still wet from the press, was damaging and defacing the rest of the mail.

The foundation of this new office, which was to be a familiar place to William Henry and his staff, virtually coincided with the final merging of what had begun as a Parliamentary privilege into a general free-for-all newspaper post. In a characteristic eighteenth-century way, considerations of convenience had united with a good deal of political jobbery to produce a remarkable arrangement of tremendous value to all. Freedom had, literally, broadened down from precedent to precedent: private vices became public virtue. Universal acceptance of a free post for the press did a great deal to multiply the continued attempts of government to squash opposition newspapers by anti-sedition legislation, while financial favours went to the pro-government papers. But far from becoming more susceptible to government attempts at control, the press became bolder and more critical. By 1825, the law was finally made to correspond with reality: by Act of Parliament newspapers passed free by post. They continued to do so for nearly another half century. (After 1855 they were subject to a voluntary stamp duty.)

The free carriage of newspapers had come to represent an important – in London preponderant – part of Post Office business. Of dubious origin legally, it continued to furnish illicit attractions to the economically minded. From Scotland successive Parliamentary Select Committees were to hear from witnesses of the ingenious ways in which newspapers were used as a means of communication 'a great deal' by the canny inhabitants of north Britain. 'One lady told me she corresponded with a friend all last summer by writing [upon her newspapers] with milk, which, upon being rubbed by burnt cork, was visible.' Secret codes were not unknown: 'I knew a young man in Edinburgh who always sent the *Scotsman* newspaper to Glasgow, and by making marks under the letters in rotation, he was able to communicate with his friends in Glasgow'. The inhabitants of Cirencester used methods less subtle but equally effective: they sent a newspaper as a simple code meaning 'money received' or 'arrived safely' or 'all is well' or 'nicely thank you'.[16]

In 1798, the joint Secretary of the Post Office had been ordered to carry out part of a secret census of the press to assess how public opinion was influenced by opposition newspapers. Francis Freeling's report had some interesting comments on the papers travelling from London to the country. 'The Numbers . . . perpetually varies, many are sent for a few Days only and then discontinued; when Persons of Consideration visit the Capital, the Newspapers sent to the Country are of course proportionally fewer. In short nothing can be more fluctuating.' As to numbers received in the country, 'many of the Morning Papers are sent by Stage Coaches etc. to Places within 100 Miles of the Metropolis . . . Canterbury Oxford Cambridge Bath Salisbury Colchester . . .' But in general, he concluded 'that the Morning Papers are not much circulated in the Country. People at a Distance from the Capital prefer an Evening Paper which they suppose to contain all the Intelligence of those published in the Morning together with all the occurrences of the Day.'[17]

This was how it still stood in the early 1820s: an inner distribution area within a hundred miles or so of London where some morning papers (but

probably more evenings) circulated, surrounded by the whole outer part
of the British Isles depending on the evening papers, the greater part served
by the night mail coaches and a few morning stages.

In the early days at 192 Strand, William Henry seems to have used the
night mail coaches, as did most newsagents or printers. The mail coaches
left London at about 8 p.m. after being loaded with the newspapers from
the Newspaper Office in Lombard Street (or later St Martin's-le-Grand).
For some time the Clerks of the Road seem to have used their privileged
position at the Post Office to get the lion's share of the trade in London
evening papers to the country. Their advantage was to be able to receive
later editions than the private newsagents and newsvendors who had to
have their papers ready for despatch at the Newspaper Office by 6 p.m.
The Clerks of the Road could hold off until nearer 8 p.m. and thus supply
the country with later news than their private enterprise rivals. The *Westminster Review* in January 1829 strongly attacked the corrupt privileges of
the Clerks of the Road. The machinery of a public office ought not to be
used for private gain: 'It is to be feared that much irregular lucre makes its
way – through such crooked channels as these to the pockets of official
persons'.[18]

The *Westminster Review* was quite correct: the Clerks had made large
incomes out of their strategically located positions for over half a century.
But long before the wind of reform swept away their privileges in 1834,
they had felt the stiff breeze of private competition from the small army of
newsagents and newsvendors (estimated by 1829 at 2,000) who had taken
over the distribution of the increasing volume of newspapers in and from
London. They shrewdly perceived that the demand for evening papers in
the country was comparatively limited. The six London 'evenings' had
an aggregate circulation of slightly more than that of *The Times* alone. It
was the mornings – the *Morning Post*, the *Morning Chronicle* but, increasingly and above all *The Times* – that the political and commercial classes
wanted. And for political and commercial reasons they wanted the parliamentary news, the commodity prices and the daily movement of the
Government Funds as early as possible; for a service of prompt despatch
and distribution they were prepared to pay. How could it best be provided?

The Post Office mail coaches left London at 8 p.m. or soon after in the
evening and travelled by night. Any morning papers (printed in the morning) would be at least twelve hours old before they left the capital. Even
subscribers in the inner (Home Counties) ring round London were never
able to read their paper on the day of publication. In distant towns –
Manchester, Birmingham and beyond – they had to be content with

papers two days old. By the mid-1820s there was a remedy for this: the new, fast stage coach services by day could carry the morning papers from London to the provinces. A network comprising well over seven hundred coaches was available for such service, leaving their home base – one of the large coaching inns – at various times in the morning. This was William Henry's opportunity. He seized it and made the best of it, adding his own auxiliary London service of light, speedy carts as a link with the coaches. A fleet of these highly manoeuvrable flyers, driven by handpicked men, waited at the newspaper offices, collected the papers fresh from the press, drove them straight to 192 Strand, waited for them to be packed and addressed, then speeded to the inn from which their particular coach would leave for its country destination.

William Henry I's national plan of distribution was based on a careful study, not only of the main routes, but of the minor, local cross-routes which linked the London roads to the more remote towns and villages, whence papers were redistributed by the motley of grocers, barbers, publicans and the like who acted as newsagents and distributors locally, or held the parcels until they were collected by the servants from hall or office. The major services he used were, in the south, the Brighton coach, famous from 1824 for the excellence of its coaches and horses and the relative civility of its drivers, and the Dover, and Portsmouth coaches; to the west, the coaches for Salisbury, Bath, Bristol, and Exeter; to the north, those for Shrewsbury, Holyhead, Birmingham, Carlisle, Leeds, York, and New-castle: and over the Border for Glasgow, Edinburgh and Aberdeen. If the many other direct coach services to London are included, together with the local links to the trunk services with London, there were some 9,000 towns and villages in Britain to which Smith's could deliver papers and parcels by adroit use of the coach time tables. If, for example, the van chanced to miss the 6 a.m. coach for Bath from the *Angel* (Inn still), a quick run to Ludgate Hill would connect with the 6.30 a.m. Bath coach leaving from the *Bell Savage* (Belle Sauvage) on Ludgate Hill. If the driver failed to connect with the famous fast coach, the *Aurora*, from the *Bull and Mouth* (near the GPO) for Birmingham, he still had a choice of three other coaches from the same inn, another three from the *Swan with Two Necks* Inn in Lad Lane (the *Royal Mail*, the *Royal Birmingham* or the *Balloon Post Coach*), as well as others later in the day.

The legend that William Henry I was the sole inventor of the paid fast day coach service as the alternative to the free mail coach was hardly ever credible: nor does it bear careful scrutiny. In 1832 (4 July) *The Times* carried an advertisement by William Lewer, also of the Strand, wholesale newsvendor. 'By a special arrangement . . . with the proprietors of *The Times* newspaper', he was enabled to forward that newspaper punctually into the country 'by morning coaches' to Birmingham, Manchester, Liverpool and all the great northern towns, 'quite as early as any contemporary morning journal'. In case of 'important political excitement', *The Times* could be forwarded *by express*.[19]

Why did William Lewer (and no doubt a number of others) not survive to build similar businesses to the Smith's? The only answer seems to be that the total business available in this London-provincial distribution was still small, the rewards still exiguous, the necessary personal supervision exigent, demanding as it did long hours of scrupulously detailed management and punctuality. The world of the London newsvendors was not conspicuous for such qualities. On the contrary, it was medievally casual and muddled, ill-rewarded and ill-managed. Newsagents came and went. Only the fittest survived.

William Henry had the qualities to survive, though at great cost to his health. His indolent brother was the first, but not the last, to feel the edge of his irascible personality. The brothers' partnership ended in August 1828.[20] The sole partner was now free to concentrate his formidable powers on the Strand house. Here the legend of his daemonic energies is well-attested. By 4 a.m. he would descend from his living apartments into the offices below, driving on his staff with the parcelling and despatching of papers, joining himself when necessary in the lowliest jobs, packing and addressing labels alongside the employees, issuing the while a string of orders or giving the clerks instructions about the office correspondence. (There was a standing offer of an extra shilling's wages to any packer who could put a parcel together quicker than the head of the business. It was seldom claimed.) All this until dusk when he turned to the checking and balancing of accounts or ledgers and the close scrutiny of the 'coach book' with its list of orders for the following days.[21]

Fragments of witness to his meticulous direction of affairs, and to his readiness to advertise it to potential customers have survived. The *Newcastle Chronicle* of 5 June 1824 carried an advertisement headed 'Great saving!!!' with a list of London newspapers offered by Smith at terms which 'will, on Inspection, prove to be at a much lower Rate than if ordered through any other Medium.' Fourteen London dailies, 35 weeklies and other periodicals on the law, literature, farming, etc., were offered via Mr Horn, a Newcastle book and music seller, to the gentry and commercial élite of the area.[22]

The Parliamentary sessions were particularly demanding, more especially when a late sitting complicated the problems of early despatch and called for skilful improvisation. The brilliance of the service was not allowed to go unnoticed (by customers or by the proprietor of *The Times*). *The Times* of 5 March 1828 carried a notice, written and inserted by William Henry, of one such feat. '*The Times*, published on Saturday ... at half past eight o'clock in the morning, was forwarded by *special express*, to Birmingham, where it arrived in time for the inland mail, by which the subscribers to the above paper in Birmingham, Liverpool, Chester, Warrington, Manchester, Rochdale, Preston, Lancaster, etc., obtained their papers *14 hours before the arrival of the London mail*. The above express was sent by Messrs. H. & W. Smith, newspaper agents, 192 Strand, London, who have sent several expresses [coaches] since the Parliamentary sessions commenced.'[23]

Two years later (it is said) he brought off another coup, at the death of George IV. To get the news to Dublin he chartered a special boat and beat the Royal messengers by twenty-four hours.[24] Another advertisement was inserted by William Henry in *The Times* of 9 August 1839, when the debate in the House of Lords on Lord Brougham's resolutions with regard to the administration of justice in Ireland 'caused the morning newspapers of Wednesday to be published too late for the morning mails. W. H. Smith, newspaper agent, 192 Strand, sent expresses to Edinburgh, Glasgow, Dublin, Newcastle-upon-Tyne, Carlisle, Preston, Leeds & c. by which the morning newspapers of that day were delivered at the usual hour.'[25] This was presumably the time when the phrase 'First with the News' was coined to advertise William Henry's achievement. It was to become a tradition.[26]

Careful to the point of stinginess in his personal expenditure, William Henry never stinted his business outlay in what he rightly regarded as vital investment to bring in more business. He was always ready to extend special express services not only for the late papers but also for the 'slips' – stop press news items – printed by *The Times* to cover specially important late news. These were also carried by special vans and coaches for the benefit of local newspaper retailers, on the strict condition that 'slips' printed by one newspaper were not communicated to another. By such prompt and punctilious attentions William Henry slowly and painfully built up his business and reputation as a wholesaler with his country clients and with the growing London press.

One of the major problems commonly emphasised by observers of this kind of business was bad debts. William Henry had his share; but he tackled the problem with his usual resource. When Joseph Green, stationer, of New Bond Street, Bath, was declared bankrupt in July 1830, his largest creditor – for £819. 16s. 7d. – was William Henry; but while the settlement allowed the other creditors to be paid off, he was assigned Green's stock and goodwill so that he could carry on Green's business.[27] Thus the original London retail business had given rise to the country wholesale business: now this had thrown up an uncovenanted opening for a country retail business; and here perhaps was first a harbinger of the future not far distant when a vast congeries of retail businesses under the name of W. H. Smith would be identified in the popular mind with the world's first great railway system.

The Age of Rail

Between 1825 and 1843 the railway network of Britain assumed its essential shape. Its beginnings were in the north-east (the Stockton and Darlington) and the north-west (Liverpool and Manchester), its original promoters merchants, many of them Quakers; their original purpose, to carry coal in the east, cotton, sugar and foodstuffs in the west. Building went on through the 1830s: by 1843 the total mileage was over 2,000 miles. The network of the whole north was beginning to look like a quadrilateral of iron – Carlisle to Tynemouth, south to York, Hull and Leeds; across to Manchester and Liverpool, north to Lancaster. In Scotland, Edinburgh was linked to Glasgow and Ayr. Southwards, Lancashire and Yorkshire were linked to the midlands complex – Derby, Stafford, Birmingham, Leicester, Northampton. Then, southwards again, to Gloucester. Then, from London, a long web of rail had crept outwards to link the metropolis to the midlands, to Bath, Bristol, and Taunton; to Southampton and Portsmouth, to Brighton and to Folkestone. In the west, Wales, and in the east practically the whole of East Anglia, north of Colchester, through Suffolk, Cambridgeshire, Norfolk, the Fens, and the East Riding, remained untouched by the hand of the engineer; so, too, except for one or two short stretches of mining railway, did Devon and Cornwall.

By 1855, nearly four times as much rail had been built (8,280 miles): neither the suspicious attitude of many Londoners nor the eloquent opposition of Charles Dickens, champion of the stage coach, could finally thwart the victory of the engineer. The British method was to build in bits. Already in the 1840s, competition and unsound finance brought on the first attacks of amalgamation. *Bradshaw* for 1846 had 200 separate railways: by 1848 they were reduced to 22 large and a few small – but this more consolidated system had also grown. The major permanent rail lines were the London & North Western, Lancashire & Yorkshire, North Eastern and (later) the Great Eastern (1862). The Great Western had extended into Cornwall and South Wales. The Midland (which had begun as a link between the north east and south west) was in 1860 planning its own route between London, Derby and the north. The modern rail network of Britain was essentially complete.

It is difficult (*pace* the cautious approach of modern economic historians) to over-estimate the effects of railways. They created new business, reduced transport costs, standardised trade routes, made people more mobile and brought new recreations and opportunities to large masses of the population who had previously never had them. Among the latter was greater access to newspapers and other forms of literature.

The growth in the number and total circulation of newspapers was one of the numerous wonders of the age. England and Wales had 76 newspapers and periodicals in 1780: by 1821 there were 267 newspapers alone; by 1851 this number had more than doubled. Within this total the number of provincial papers had more than quadrupled – the beginnings of an important movement. The total sale of papers (excluding the 'illegal', unstamped) rose from 14 to 85 million between 1780 and 1851. To 1836 the increase just kept pace with the increase in the numbers of the reading public; after 1836 there was a new and genuine increase in the number of papers available *per capita*. This was partly due to changes in the system of taxation, so that tax bore less hardly on the press at large (see page 64). But it was also due to the growth of the railway network, which took over, in regard to volume, lower cost and higher speed, where the stage coach left off exhausted (see page 26).

Charles Knight, in a magnificent six volumes on *London* which commemorated the decade that was to culminate in the Great Exhibition of 1851, described in detail how the railway had replaced and bettered the day coach system. Morning papers sent by the Great Western had to be at Paddington by 6 a.m. and reached Bristol by 11 a.m. Those for the north of England via Birmingham left Euston at 6 a.m. also. But it was the Gosport and Isle of Wight service that specially caught his eye. Leaving Nine Elms (the L & SWR terminus before Waterloo) at 7 a.m. the train reached Gosport 3½ hours later. There it was met by a steamer which had the papers in the Isle of Wight by 11.30 a.m.

The inhabitants of that island are reading their *Times*, while the London publication of the paper has scarcely finished. An agent who supplies the early papers to Gosport and the Isle of Wight, informs us that his

Gosport customers are often supplied before his town customers. The publisher of *The Times* gives off the papers that are to be sent by railway first, and the agents who receive them are not allowed to supply their town customers with these first oozings of the press.[28]

The London agent who supplied the country ('though by no means so topping a character as the publisher') was a much bigger fish than the common or garden newsvendor (cum-stationer, greengrocer, barber). Men of this (wider) class generally took large supplies of paper direct from the newspaper offices. Ten or twelve of them sent their papers by railway-trains: 'One we know whose papers cost him [£] 1000 a-week.'[29] (Was this William Henry? In all probability yes. In the late days of coaching, the Smith 'coach book' contained addresses of customers to whom deliveries were to be made at Portsmouth, Petworth and in the Isle of Wight at Ventnor, Newport and Ryde. Seven were retail or individual buyers of *The Times.*) Certainly William Henry's purchases of morning dailies alone for export to the country may well have been costing him between £700 and £1,000 a week by 1843. At this stage he had risen to somewhere near the top of the London newsagents for the country trade, if not the very top itself. He was not 'a product' of the railway age: far from it. But he had eyed or seized the opportunities it offered, just as he had earlier explored the opportunities of the fast day coaches, until they were outclassed, outpaced and outfaced by the railway. For some years the battle between the two systems swayed backwards and forwards.

A specially severe winter in 1836 which began early, on Christmas Eve, underlined the advantages of the infant railway system. For several days heavy snowfalls blanketed the whole country. Communications by road in and out of London and all over Britain were in total confusion: coaches and mails were everywhere stuck deep in snowdrifts. 'Never before, within our recollection' said *The Times* on 28 December 'was the London mail stopped for a whole night at a few miles from London; and never before have we seen the intercourse between the Southern shires of England and the metropolis interrupted for two whole days'.[30] Yet a correspondent in an evening paper observed that rail travel had been little affected (unlike its present-day counterpart in snow time). *The Times* of 5 January followed up:

... we have learned from a gentleman recently come from that [northern] part of England, that the travelling [by rail] has never been impeded by the snow. The little which may lie on [the rail track] is brushed off by the engine itself . . . All the information which we have hitherto received tends to make us believe, that had railways been laid down in every direction, the late storm would scarcely have impeded the communication between the most distant parts of the kingdom more than an hour or two . . .[31]

None of the benefits offered by rail transport caused any immediate or wholesale desertion of the coach. By 1838, however, William Henry I was making enquiries about rates on the Grand Junction Railway (from Birmingham to Manchester and Liverpool). His object was to make an agreement that his newspaper parcels should be carried from Birmingham to Liverpool for not more than 1s. 3d. The Grand Junction directors did not favour this: but they were willing to arrange with the London and Birmingham Railway (they were soon to be joined together as the London and North Western Railway) to carry for a 3s. charge all the way from London to Liverpool, dividing the sum equally between the two companies. The pace quickened through the 1840s. New lines such as the London and South Western Railway (between London and Southampton) were taking increasing numbers of papers; but coaches were also still much used.

William Henry's brief and sometimes astringent letters to his son, William Henry II, a pupil at Tavistock Grammar School, provide glimpses of the progress of the business in those early years of rail. By 1841, for example, the delivery of papers to York was assured; trade at Leicester was going on 'as usual'; so also business with the 'Gt. Western folks'.[32] 'Willmer' (a wholesale customer) was 'into some trouble with the Railway Cos they charge his parcels by weight . . . business keeps up. *Times* 52.18 [quires].'[33] In York 'business is really quite brisk again . . . instead of dropping papers they are really getting up again'. In November 'the Birth of the Royal Prince' has caused a flurry of business . . . 'it made us very busy in getting parcels off in every way I could think off [*sic*] . . .'[34] One other prophetic touch enlivened a year of promise: the first railway station bookstall was opened on Fenchurch Street Station.

As 1842 opened, William Henry was optimistic. The purchase and sale of papers was steady . . . 'about 50 to 51 quires of *The Times* every day, 29 quires of the *Chronicle*, 15 of the *Herald*, 11 or so of the *Post* . . . all others in proportion . . .' One or two large debts from wholesalers were outstanding but 'the balance at Bankers 31 Dec was within 50£ of last year so that as far as property and business there is every cause for satisfaction.

There is a New News Room at Glasgow 14 papers per day which have
come to me through Rutherglen . . .'[35] As the year went on, business
increased. By February, with the re-opening of Parliament, sales were up:
The Times especially (to 78 quires) and the *Chronicle* to 46; the rest proportionately. *The Times* was 'cleverly got off by express Train.'[36] The opening
of Parliament always lifted the demand, but it was not the only cause. Less
august, more grisly events also acted as a spur. 'No doubt, you have
remarked the dreadful murder at Roehampton. The wretch has been taken
and is at this moment before the Magistrates at Bow Street . . . this will
cause a severe pressure this afternoon and being Monday it will be more
felt.'[37]

This was well in its way, but the effect on William Henry's health was
beginning to alarm his family. In the mid-1830s he had moved out of the
residential part of the Strand House to St John's Wood and later to Kilburn
House. If this was a move to detach himself from business cares it failed.
At 4 a.m., sometimes 3, he rode on horseback, in all weathers, to the
Strand, putting in appearances which his staff learned to await with some
apprehension; he was moody, depressed and plagued by involuntary and
uncontrollable nervous irascibility which shows through his letters. In
October 1841, to his ever-dutiful son:

> My Dear Son
>   I think you was rather unreasonable to expect a letter by return,
> there being enough to do on a Monday . . .[38]

To another letter time could not be spared for a reply . . . 'you may judge
that all about me have enough to do by the following [figures of papers
despatched] . . .'.[39] *The Times* was said to be 'troublesome' in not supplying
enough copies.[40]

The family's anxieties grew. William Henry II, now 16 years old, wrote
from Tavistock School:

> . . . I am sorry to hear that Father feels the 'push of the season'. I had
> hoped that some arrangement would be effected, by which the work
> would be rendered more easy to him, rather than otherwise . . . I had
> some misgivings when I left town [for school] lest he should take too
> much upon himself; but still so many assurances were given by him to
> me that such would not be the case, that I had almost succeeded in
> persuading myself that Father for the first time in his life would take a
> little care of himself on that score.[41]

For exactly thirty years William Henry I's entire physical, mental and emotional energies had been channelled into his business. It was too late to reverse a way of life that had become second nature to him. The wear and tear was not diminishing with material success and new opportunities for business expansion: very much the reverse. The exact symptoms of his malaise are not clear. They were mainly psychological but certainly included physical troubles, probably eczema and gout. (These were akin to the illnesses which preceded the premature death of William Henry II – a much more equable character – half a century later.) For another fifteen years, until he retired in 1857, William Henry I plodded doggedly on in the business, clear-headed as ever; and his physical strength, although diminishing, did not give out. But the urgent need for help was evident. Not even William Henry I could hide it from himself. His son was also painfully aware that before long he would be called on to share his father's responsibilities; a prospect which he was far from relishing. He saw his future quite differently. Hence, perhaps instinctively, his efforts to save his father's strength for the business. For his conscience was uneasy.

The Taxes on Knowledge

'No article of consumption, with the exception of salt, was so highly taxed as the Newspaper.'[42] When Charles Knight, the famous Victorian journalist and editor wrote this, the 'taxes on knowledge', so hated by Victorian progressives, had finally disappeared (between 1855 and 1861) after a struggle lasting nearly a century and a half. This fiscal network, created, modified and complicated by successive governments from 1712, forms an important part (but not the whole, as is sometimes represented) of the formative context of the British press in this period of growth: it has long been represented primarily as an era of growing press freedom, but more recently by Marxist, post-Marxist and semi-Marxist historians as one of a struggle for power between a capitalist government-cum-press and a 'working class' underground press. The point of central importance for Smith's was relatively simple: the output and sale of newspapers, journals and books grew, not at a steady rate but by a series of spurts. Within (and in spite of) a framework of government fiscal controls, laws of libel and sedition, and economic and material progress, there was more literature to sell and there were more customers to buy it. The opportunities for newspaper distribution were general: to keep a newsagency afloat and solvent, let alone profitable, called for a careful probe to find where the particular areas of profit lay.

A legend of the business was William Henry I's reply to a customer who suggested he might round his account to the nearest half-penny. 'Man! – man! – ' came the reply, 'this house was built up on farthings'. It was not more than the literal truth. The Mayfair period of the original newswalk was a retail trade built on farthings: the years from about 1825 to 1842 saw a change to wholesale trading in certain London papers from the metropolis to the country but the profits were still in farthings. Only as the railway age continued and the railway bookstalls sold both wholesale and retail, newspapers and books, and organised lending libraries, could it be said the age of farthings faded.

The first Stamp Act of 1712 taxed every copy of a 'news' publication at the rate of a penny for each full sheet. A tax of one shilling was laid on every advertisement. Neither this nor a more tightly drawn Stamp Act of 1725 killed the press but they did raise the cost and the price. The difficulty of defining, legally and precisely, what constituted a newspaper left loopholes for papers claiming to be pamphlets or miscellaneous commentary to pay reduced duty, or escape stamp and payment entirely. In the second half of the century, output and sales grew; so did the transmission (first via the Post Office) of London papers to the country. The million odd London papers thus exported from London quadrupled by 1790. In London, coffee house and tavern reading grew. The advertising duty paid, less than £1,000 in 1713, rose to £40,000 by 1781. Neither taxation nor prosecution proved able to suppress the vigorous if often disreputable expression of opinion by the press.

With the onset of the French Revolution, government apprehensions about the press were renewed and sharpened. Duties were again increased. 'Hiring out' newspapers was made illegal: but like most other attempts at repression, the law was honoured in the breach. In 1797 the newspaper tax was increased again to 3½d. a copy: the price of *The Times* rose to 6d. In 1815 (for the last time and after much debate) Vansittart, the Chancellor of the Exchequer, raised stamp duty to 4d., the advertisement tax to 3s. 6d. and the tax on pamphlets to 3s.

Whether these heavier duties were the sole cause or were supplemented by generally bad times economically, following the end of the French war in 1815, there was certainly a pause in newspaper expansion over the next twenty years. In these two decades the sale of stamped papers increased by some 30 per cent: after 1836, when the duty was reduced from 4d. to 1d., sales increased by 70 per cent in six years. But again times had changed: the economy was more buoyant.

True comparison and isolation of the effects of taxation by itself is exceedingly difficult. What was clear was that in so far as heavier taxes increased the problems of legitimate newspapers, they also increased the advantages of the unstamped press. A further Act of 1820, which broadened the definition of a newspaper, dealt a heavy blow to the Radical unstamped, especially Cobbett's *Weekly Political Register* which had sold widely and successfully as a reforming paper.

Broadly, the continued government controls and taxes, and the attempted extension of the libel and sedition laws were only very partially successful. The courts, judges and especially juries, showed remarkably good sense. Unlike the governments, they refused to be panicked into wholesale repression. But bad times and heavy taxation certainly had the effect of reducing the numbers of newspapers and publishers. At 7d. each a newspaper was a considerable luxury. It had to be organised as a business very efficiently and edited as a medium of news, independent opinion, essential information – commercial information especially – and entertainment with utmost intelligence (and courage) if it was to survive. The worst trials of the press were over by the 1830s: the stamp on pamphlets was repealed in 1823, the advertisement duty reduced by half. The year 1825 saw the paper excise duty lowered to 2d. Finally, in 1836 the newspaper duty was reduced from 4d. to 1d. Final repeal was not to come until 1855; and with the disappearance of the duties on paper in 1861, the shackles on 'knowledge' finally went.

This was the immediate context in which, paradoxically as it might seem, William Henry's business found its first springs of growth. His target was the capture of as large a share as possible of the export of London newspapers to the country. This meant, in the first half of the century, the 'quality' papers – *The Times, Morning Chronicle, Morning Post* and *Morning Herald* especially – for these were the papers which the gentry and the more affluent middle classes read for their political and business news: they were also, because of their price – 7d. a copy – those on which William Henry could make a profit. These were the papers favoured by the heavy duty and attendant regulations. *The Times* especially explored with conspicuous success the opportunities it saw in laws intended to defeat an independent press as a whole. It therefore won for itself – until the final repeal of the anti-press taxes in 1855 – a near-monopoly position among the quality papers. Accordingly it became, in the eyes of Cobden, Bright, Brougham, Whigs, Radicals – and its thwarted rivals – a major target for green-eyed criticism from the 1790s to 1855. Its only real rival, in circulation, had been the *Chronicle* under its great editor, James Perry, until his death in 1821 – Perry the 'incorrigible' and 'incorruptible' ultra-liberal as the French

Ambassador called him;[43] more practically (as William Henry remembered twenty years later) a Whig with a retentive memory (see page 14): but a great editor whose like the *Chronicle* was not to see again. The way was thus open for *The Times*. By 1841 it sold more than twice as many copies as the *Chronicle*, *Post*, and *Herald* put together; by 1850 four times as many. These statistics and proportions were reflected in William Henry's returns of London papers exported to the country by him in these years. They were its most scintillating years.

The victorious progress of *The Times* rested not directly upon the system of taxation (as its enemies alleged) but upon the twin pillars of brilliant and independent editing; and acute business management. Launched originally as the *Universal Daily Register* in 1785, it changed its name to *The Times* three years later. It was the creation of three members of the Walter family (John I, II and III). Gradually – and wisely – they surrendered the editorship to independent professionals. The first of these was the great Thomas Barnes, a large, benevolent, carelessly Bohemian figure, who 'seemed to regard all public men with equal indifference'.[44] His style was as trenchant as his courage was indomitable. From 1817 to 1841, first as a Whig and later as a Tory, Barnes fought to extricate *The Times* and public opinion itself from subservience to the political authority of ruling cliques, and to establish the dignity and integrity of journalism. He was quite frank about his tactics: John Bull's 'densely compacted intellect' needed to be shocked into wakefulness with the aid of ten-pounders 'before you can make it comprehend your meaning or care one farthing for your efforts'.[45]

Barnes fought one battle after another to establish the independence of his paper. After 'Peterloo' he called for open publicity and enquiry. He attacked the government's Sedition Acts. He supported the case of Queen Caroline: then, as the justifiable radicalism of the 1820s turned into what he regarded as the unjustified mob demagogy of the 1830s, he denounced the Irish Catholic politician Daniel O'Connell as 'unredeemed and unredeemable'.[46] He doggedly opposed Bulwer Lytton, Brougham (the Chancellor) and denounced the *Penny Magazine* (Brougham's chosen instrument against *The Times*). Consistently, he denied the charge of his enemies that the rise of *The Times* depended on the shield provided by the stamp duties which kept up the price to 7d. and excluded potential competitors from entry to the newspaper business. Barnes argued that the duties, wise or otherwise, necessary or not, gave *The Times* no advantage not accessible to its less successful rivals. Its success rested on the better services it gave the reader for the – admittedly – high price he had to pay. He was proved right. After the clumsily contrived Act of 1836 which reduced the stamp from 4d. to 1d., *The Times*'s circulation rose again: that of its rivals fell.

Barnes made his mistakes: and his courage naturally brought down on his head and those of his successors the political venom of his infuriated rivals. Combined with the genuine conviction of moderate social reformers that a changing society also deserved a cheaper press and newspapers more appropriate to its needs – tastes might be, and proved to be, a rather different question – the aggressive independence of *The Times* raised up a high tide of jealous criticism by 1850. The great flood of 1851 was the result: but it was not simply a consequence of *The Times*'s policy but of economic and social change without precedent.

Under Barnes, *The Times* became history, 'The Thunderer', the Fourth Estate, on the whole justifying to reasonable men, if not to fanatics or diehards, the validity of its claim to speak not to one but to all classes, over the heads of parties, cliques and governments. Yet none of this would have been possible but for a sound and realistic business policy. The efforts of Cobbett, a brilliant journalist, failed for want of such a policy: *a fortiori*, the scores of unstamped protagonists of reform. In the end, they succumbed through the boredom of the average reader and – vital to the economics of any newspaper – the absence of any income from advertising. Proprietors and editors combined to achieve a judicious combination of 'superior amusement'[47] and advertising income. The first was provided by vigorous and independent leading articles, piping hot news and contributions from Disraeli, Thackeray, Lamb, Macaulay, etc.: the second by owners of houses to let or sell, seekers after office or domestic staff, booksellers, milliners, wine merchants, auctioneers, theatres, tailors, patent medicine dealers, etc.: increasingly, by company meetings, ship passages and freighting, stock exchange news, sporting events and so forth. *The Times*'s advertising policy was directed towards its known markets and was correspondingly staid and conservative. (In its early days it had engaged in a struggle for circulation with the *Daily Advertiser*: in the end it had left the market among the humbler orders of society to the *Advertiser*.) Thus, upon advertisements and especially on its advertising supplement, *The Times* could construct its independence both of government and of sectional opinion.

A carefully observant foreign traveller remarked in the same decade on the contribution of newspapers in England to 'that general diffusion of a moderate degree of knowledge' which seemed to him 'the distinguishing characteristic of England' in the 1820s. The 'social machine' worked smoothly and efficiently; orders were despatched promptly and without fuss; civilisation proceeded 'at full gallop' . . . so that . . . 'all those fluctuations, that consume so much time and power in countries not so well organized, are wholly avoided.'[48] The insertion of advertisements, he continued:

> relative to business forms a considerable part of the profit of an English newspaper. This branch of revenue for *The Times* alone produces, I am told, more than thirty thousand pounds sterling a year. The advantage of the most extensive publicity is so fully appreciated by the merchant, the shopkeeper, the manufacturer, and every one who is desirous of selling the produce of his labour, or calling attention to a new undertaking, that no expense is spared to promote this object . . . a bookseller . . . in a single year expended £5,500 sterling in advertisements.[49]

Such was the business world in which John Walter moved; and William Henry Smith I was no less sensible of the selling power of *The Times* advertising (as the Baron de Stael-Holstein put it) 'from Dover to the extremity of Scotland'.[50]

The idea, often propagated in recent years, that newspapers ought to be independent of governments, readers, and advertisers, to live in piety in a social vacuum regardless of their cost (yet still representative of a liberal progressive consensus where changes of ethos are only in a presumed progressive direction) finds no support in the history of the press. The press secured its independence of government autocracy only through individual resource.

In the last days before the railway age, an observer remarked how the current regime of taxes, costs and prices affected the distribution of newspapers. When papers were printed (wrote the *Westminster Review* in January, 1829) the publishers supplied them to the 'newsmen' in 'quires' of 27 papers for ready money at 13 shillings a quire. The papers were thus disposed of for just under 6d. each from the printing office, which by this method had no risk of debts and was therefore satisfied with a smaller return; bad debts being the curse of the publishing trade. If the printers did receive orders for newspapers, they were passed on to the newsagents who supplied them at the regular price of 7d. each: 'the trouble and risk of getting in the accounts is shifted to them from the proprietors'.[51] (We are reminded of Mr Green of Bath, pages 45-6.)

The exact price to the newsmen was in fact 5⅞d. per sheet. From this the newspaper proprietor had to find all his expenses, and pay the stamp duty. From 1⅛d. the newsagent had to recoup himself for his outlay of capital and labour in distribution and against the risk of bad debts by other retailers and private customers: regard for the tradesman was not a particularly noticeable trait in the social demeanour of the nobility and gentry. This was, indeed, a house built on farthings.

From the 1820s to the days of the Great Exhibition, these trends continued. All round, the castles of the old mercantile state were tumbling before the new doctrines of *laissez-faire*. One after another, tariffs, subsidies, corn laws, indirect taxes were to fall beneath the axe of Huskisson, Peel, Gladstone. It was unlikely that the taxes on knowledge would survive. In the year after the opening of the Great Exhibition the sessions and records of the Select Committee of the House of Commons on Newspaper Stamps give us a series of portraits – and self-portraits – not only of the newspaper business but of the newspaper distribution trade. It includes a self-portrait of the business known, after 1846, as W. H. Smith and Son; the portrait was still drawn by the father, William Henry I.

The Press Unbound: The Wisdom of William Henry I

The 1851 Committee of the House of Commons on Newspaper Stamps, wrote the *Edinburgh Review* in October 1853 (when the Committee's Report was still under debate) 'was got up, and virtually managed throughout, by a society in London, called "The Association for Promoting the Repeal of all the Taxes on Knowledge" . . .' The *Review* was not (it added) 'in the least blaming [the Association] for doing with zeal what they think a good work.'[52] *The Times*, in July of the following year, added its own flavour to the debate: 'Mr. Cobden and his school wish to destroy the influence of the metropolitan press, because it interferes, as they think, with the provincial . . .'[53]

Both statements by the *Review* and *The Times* were substantially true, though not perhaps quite the whole truth. The Association for Promoting Repeal was certainly the motive power behind the Select Committee. It was itself an offshoot of the People's Charter Union which had persuaded Cobden to put the repeal of the newspaper stamp high in his 'budget' proposals of 1849. The Union's secretary, C. D. Collet, was among the majority of well-known favourable abolitionists called to give predictable evidence to the Select Committee. The proceedings of what one historian has recently called 'a markedly successful propaganda exercise'[54] were imbued with the reforming spirit of Chartism and their organisation was modelled on the Anti-Corn Law League. The spirit was represented by Collet (the letter too; he was a lawyer); the organisation by Milner Gibson, who had won his spurs in the Anti-Corn Law agitation. Among the Association's members were also John Bright, Joseph Hume, and William Hickson (an 'educationist' but gifted with a practical imagination and earthy common sense rare in that breed). Nobody doubted, however, who the real architect of the grand plan for repeal was: it was Cobden, who combined the passion and sentiment of the Chartist with the manipulative ideology of the classic economist. His speeches combined lamentations over the size of the non-reading public (was it two or three million? Whatever it was it was deplorably and unnecessarily large) with, in the early stages of his campaign, compliments both fulsome and sly to *The Times* — 'at 5d . . . as cheap as any paper in the world' (untrue) but 'too good and too large' for the poor peasant . . . 'he had not a table on which he could spread it out, and his feeble rushlight would not help him over its vast surface of print'[55] — and much in the same vein.

Mob oratory and false sentiment perhaps, but when Milner Gibson came to write the Select Committee's final Report, it was the apparent objectivity and fairness of Cobden's style and methods which persuaded men that if he was now converted to a less favourable view of *The Times* and its influence, there must be weighty reasons for his change of heart. Only total repeal could loosen the stranglehold of *The Times* and make way for cheap — but still good — papers 'suitable to the means and wants of the labouring classes'.[56] Thus what in fact was simply the automatic application of doctrine, was represented as the outcome of long and reasonable cogitation and the balancing of all the possible *pros* and *cons* by minds open and unprejudiced, concerned only, and piously, with the public welfare and especially the welfare of the poor and underprivileged.

The end, not only of the stamp duty, but of the advertisement and paper duties too, was compassed by a skilful and ruthless campaign by the abolitionists . . . 'a dazzling display of political virtuosity in which civil servants were secretly lobbied and converted, loyal party men were assigned to lobby their colleagues . . .'[57]

Particular care was given to the selection and interrogation of witnesses. One by one they paraded before the Committee, these 'representatives' of British opinion, carefully selected to ensure that the predictable outcome of the sessions would be a majority in favour of abolition: it was, but even Cobden's experienced management could not avoid what was, echoing the Duke of Wellington's words, 'the nearest run thing'. For, as before all tribunals where witnesses are allowed to speak *extempore*, some were confused by the complexity of the issues and said things they were not intended to: others were honest enough to admit that the issues *were* complex and that they were not able clearly to predict the outcome of abolition or non-abolition.

The witnesses divided naturally into a few main groups. There were the spokesmen of the press 'establishment': *The Times* and the Provincial Newspaper Society, both opposed to abolition. Against them, and favouring abolition, was a group of new pressmen – Michael Whitty (founder of two Liverpool papers); F. K. Hunt, of the ailing *Daily News*; John Cassell, proprietor of the *Working Man's Friend*; and – an ingenious stroke this – the American, Horace Greeley, of the radical *New York Tribune*. There were social reformers, fanatic and moderate; the Rev. Thomas Spencer (uncle of Herbert Spencer and editor of the *British Temperance Advocate*) typified the former; W. E. Hickson, an abolitionist and reformer but a man of good sense and wit, typified the latter. So did Thomas Hogg, secretary of the Mechanics Institutes of Lancashire and Cheshire. Three witnesses were drawn from the world of newspaper distribution: Samuel Bucknall, a Stroud (Gloucester) printer and publisher; Abel Heywood, a Manchester publisher and wholesale distributor of newspapers, journals and the like; and W. H. Smith I. Finally, there were public servants such as Rowland Hill of the Post Office; and finally Collet, the indispensable secretary of the Association for the Repeal of the Taxes on Knowledge.

The chairman of the Select Committee, Milner Gibson, and Cobden, who organised the questioning, along with three members of the Committee, were committed by doctrine to abolition. So were at least three of the witnesses, plus at least another nine whose opinions were not in doubt. Such was 'the model agitation', as it was rightly called at the time and since. Propagandist and artificial as much of the Committee's proceedings were – by no means an unusual circumstance – the evidence given threw, wittingly and unwittingly, a vivid light on the state of the press and on public opinion regarding the press, in the year of the Great Exhibition.

The press spokesmen, both abolitionist and otherwise, were, naturally, concerned in large measure with their own interests, but these did not necessarily exclude the public interest and the two were frequently, and not unnaturally, seen as coincidental. John Cassell, publisher of the *Working Man's Friend*, a teetotal paper, and various other journals, announced himself to be 'one of those individuals who have sprung from the working classes; I have associated with them, and I know their sympathies well . . . the people want cheap publications . . .'[58] So did Mr Cassell: but his business (and the desired improvement of the working class) was obstructed by the newspaper stamp, the élite press it was said to protect, and by the failure of the Post Office to compete with the ingenious combination of newsagent-cum-railway which contrived to get the London morning papers to the provinces on the day of publication. If the stamp was removed, 'I consider there would be a complete revolution in the newspaper press of this kingdom.' The effect would be: 'Decidedly to increase the circulation of local newspapers, and also to create a new class of newspapers, though [Cassell added hastily] at the same time the old newspapers would endeavour to meet the altered circumstances in which they would be placed'.[59] Omitting from his loquacious and extremely lengthy survey no aspect of the economics of the trade, and especially the hopes of future profit, the apostle of teetotalism and universal education through the press included a word of cheer for the Chancellor of the Exchequer. It was his fervent hope that the Post Office would pull itself together and compete with the newsagent–railway alliance for newspaper distribution. 'I have always supposed that the Chancellor of the Exchequer, keeping an eye to the revenue, would compete with private enterprise.'[60] At this, Sir Rowland Hill must have lifted an eyebrow.

The other aspiring press–publishers were, mercifully, less eloquent. Michael Whitty, of the *Liverpool Journal*, made the point that 'newspapers are the only things that people will ever read[61] . . . All the information they get is through that means and conversation, all of which originates in the newspapers'.[62] His motto: abolish the stamp and vote for a cheap press. F. K. Hunt of the *Daily News* agreed (he was right – the *Daily News* though temporarily in difficulties had a future before it as a cheap Liberal newspaper): everybody except *The Times* ('which I do not think is so much interested in removing the stamp, because it being now in the first position, any change could not improve but might injure it') would benefit by abolition – always provided good newspapers were protected against piracy and plagiarism.[63] He thought about one-third to one-quarter of papers published and printed went to the provinces.

From a relatively poor agricultural area, Henry Watkinson, proprietor of the *Spalding Free Press*, briefly agreed. He would sell six or more papers where now he sold one, if the stamp were abolished. Like several other witnesses he believed, quite simply, that if the price were reduced, the lowly-paid agricultural labourer would buy his own paper at 1d. or 1½d. instead of contributing ½d. as a group of six or so collective buyers of a newspaper shared between them for a price of 3d. or 4d.: 'Collective' reading was a rural as well as an urban pastime.[64]

It was left to the Yankee press tycoon, Horace Greeley, to plunge his North American harpoon into *The Times*. Its success, he declared, was due to the advertisement duty *and* the stamp duty, which worked together to limit newspaper circulation generally and to cause readers and advertisers to 'take *The Times*, because everything is advertised there; consequently they do take it . . .'[65]

Much of this was plausible and persuasive, especially for a liberal audience to whom *The Times* represented Toryism and high-handedness amounting to a monopoly. Mowbray Morris, *The Times* manager, had a good case; but success in business is never easy to defend, and patience and diplomacy were not Morris's *forte*. The abolition of the stamp, he agreed, would have little effect on well-established papers: it would shake the less secure by raising up against them 'rivals who would destroy them'.[66] There might be papers advocating 'opinions not quite so advantageous to society as are advocated now by the press'.[67] This stung Cobden the radical into action: did the manager of *The Times* think that the character of the press was improved by being in the hands of large capitalists 'because those large capitalists are themselves of a superior character; or is it because the public are confined to a higher priced article, and therefore the common people have not an opportunity of buying newspapers at all?'

Morris was stung into an equally choleric rejoinder: 'If . . . the Honourable Member infers that the common people do not read newspapers, I think he is mistaken; I think the common people do read the best newspapers now . . . *The Times*, for instance . . .'[68] Cobden: 'By what process have they arrived at the preference which they have now for *The Times*?' Morris: 'The other papers . . . are perhaps as good, only perhaps *The Times* has got the ear of the market; and . . . prestige attached to its name . . .'[69] Cobden: '. . . might you not leave it to the sagacity of people, to their own self-interest and love of truth, to find out what was sound?' Morris: 'I have very little opinion of the sagacity of uneducated people.'[70]

Tactically, Morris was not a good witness to his own cause: it was better than he allowed the world to think. Alexander Russell, editor of the *Scotsman* and member of the Provincial Newspaper Society, did more good by precise and judicious evidence. He saw the stamp duty not as 'a tax' but as 'a payment made [indirectly] to the Post Office for services' which could not be so cheaply provided in any other way.[71] If it were removed a 'postal rate' would be the inevitable alternative.[72] This would certainly favour the rise of purely local papers. The result might well be that information would become local and sectional . . . 'the promotion of local prejudices, and . . . the narrowing and embittering of political and all manner of discussions'.[73] I propose (said the *Scotsman*) 'that things should remain as they are.'[74]

From such technical and economic complexities, the Committee was doubtless glad to turn to the newsagents, human interest and light relief.

Not that there was anything light or frivolous about Samuel Bucknall of Stroud. He was, on the contrary, ostentatiously pious; though pliable. He did his best (he protested) to raise the moral standards of the readers whose literary needs he supplied; but seemingly in vain. However much he plied them with serious works (such as *Chambers's Journal* and *Miscellaneous Papers*,[75] or the *Family Herald*)[76] it was most regrettable to find 'that upon an important trial, or when anything very particular [i.e. morally peculiar] has taken place, the demand for newspapers is increased, and even persons who never purchase a well-written periodical will buy a newspaper'.[77] Worse even were the large numbers of demoralising novels he found himself selling – *Dick Turpin*, *Jack Sheppard*, the *Highwayman* or the *Black Pirate*; 'all those, the foulest filth of the printing press', cried Mr Bucknall, warming to his theme 'are read by those persons eagerly, and they encourage a love of adventure which may be natural, but . . . ought not to be encouraged beyond very restricted limits . . .' Such were examples of acts of heroism and daring but acts morally wrong and consequently (Mr Bucknall expired, exhausted by his own logic) their education was 'bad instead of good'.[78]

The Committee, disturbed or at least intrigued by the moral condition of Mr Bucknall's customers, pressed him further. Were *many* immoral publications sold at Stroud? Mr Bucknall regretted his inability to answer 'with any degree of accuracy', adding primly 'we endeavour ourselves, as booksellers, as much as possible to discountenance them . . .' This apparently meant he took no orders for them 'unless we are paid beforehand . . . if a person comes and orders a single number, we tell him that we will not sell it; that he must order half a dozen'. Thus was immorality vended, at Stroud, by the pound. Coyly, Mr Bucknall admitted there were 'channels' through which they were circulated: they were 'below my own observation . . .' though he knew 'one man . . . who gets his living almost entirely' thus.[79] Other men in other towns did the same; not Mr Bucknall. This was (in his view) a back-street business: in London and provincial towns, he concluded, with obvious pain at the memory 'you will see very often shops open on the Sunday morning . . . out of the general reach of observation; and unless you go there and positively watch the sale, it is impossible that you can have any idea of the amount of moral depravity of these things.' Worse still, there were shops like that, in 'pretty nearly' every country town.[80]

Less deprecatory, more robust and cheerful, were the views of another distributing bookseller, general publisher and newsagent, Mr Abel Heywood of Manchester. Mr Heywood, a natural entrepreneur but a former activist for abolition and (predictably) future Mayor of Manchester, was a cheerful and confident North Countryman in a very large way of business in 'cheap publications' and proud of it.[81] '. . . you have probably the largest experience of any one in the kingdom in the sale of those publications?' Mr Heywood (with modest satisfaction): 'I think so; the trade say so.'[82] More specifically, he supplied Manchester and the towns for 20 miles around with their needs for small and weekly publications which came down from London by rail. He was a wholesaler of such publications and they came in many shapes, sizes and colours – political, domestic, religious, and fiction, pure and otherwise.

Mr Heywood's personal opinion on this stream of publications that passed through his hands was similar to Mr Bucknall's. He strongly approved of those which were domestic, religious and socially improving. The *Family Herald*, with a weekly circulation of 200,000, he thoroughly endorsed:[83] 'it addresses itself to the fairer sex in a great measure, and to that perhaps may be attributed its very large circulation'.[84] Mr Heywood took it for his family, and 'read it with a great deal of pleasure, and it is read by every member of my family'.[85] Other improving or religious issues also won his sympathies; the Roman Catholic *Lamp*, for example; the *Christian Socialist*;[86] the *Friend of the People* (renamed from its earlier manifestation as the *Red Republican*);[87] there was *Eliza Cook's Journal*, Dickens's *Household Words*, and many other 'respectable' publications.[88]

Apart from these stood two debatable publishers and their publications: Lloyd and Reynolds. Lloyd, to be more widely known later, published many things, principally novels . . . 'rather of the extreme novel class, and deal more in bloody murders and all other crimes which it is possible for the imagination to invent' . . . among them the *Adventures of Tom King*, the *Black Monk*, the *Blighted Heart*, etc.[89] In a similar publishing class stood George Reynolds, whose *Miscellany* and *Mysteries of the Court of London* were already casting shadows over the hoped-for purity of the working-class reader. Lloyd and Reynolds were destined to puzzle the morals of devout socialists. Abel Heywood was more tolerant than they were, or Samuel Bucknall. 'I have read some portion of it [the *Mysteries of the Court of London*] he confessed a shade reluctantly, 'and it draws scenes of profligacy as strongly as it is possible for any writer to do, and the feelings are excited to a very high pitch by it; indeed some look upon it as an indecent publication; it is not in reality an indecent publication, because I do not believe that any words appear that are vulgar; but certainly the language is of a most exciting kind, and directed to excite the passions of its readers.'[90] The quality of writing was 'very good'; like the *Family Herald*, but by very different methods, the *Mysteries* appealed, apparently, to the fairer sex, and others.[91] 'A great many females buy the *Court of London*, and young men; a sort of spreeing young men; young men who go to taverns, and put cigars in their mouths in a flourishing way'.[92] Yes, Abel Heywood was a sound judge of the contemporary reader ... 'I believe that you could not educate people so that there could not be found 10,000, 15,000 or 20,000 of people in this country disposed to buy it'.[93] But what subjects were 'most attractive' to the lower classes in *newspapers*? 'Foreign news is as attractive as' anything else.[94] Was the penny newspaper stamp unpopular among working people? When the stamp was 4d., yes; now they could buy a paper at 3d. there was less feeling. Abel Heywood was for abolition: plainly he was not anxious to go to the stake for it ... but he was open to persuasion.

The other abolitionist witnesses were predictable – Collet, secretary of the Abolitionist Association, complained there was 'no press for the working classes' but his evidence was purely a matter of form.[95] Thomas Hogg's evidence was remarkable for its pathos rather than its originality. The Mechanics Institutes (he confessed) suffered from a 'want of interest on the part of the working classes', though the Institutes bore their name and were established by them, assisted by the wealthier classes.[96] The working classes were not generally a majority of his members: these were drawn from 'young men in offices, and others engaged in retail establishments, and the like'.[97] Short of papers, they had to beg from friends of the Institutes for second-hand copies of *The Times* and other papers. What did they mainly read in the papers? 'Chiefly, when Parliament is sitting ... the debates in the two Houses, and ... events going on on the Continent and in other parts of the world.'[98]

There remained the two social reformers. The Rev. Thomas Spencer was a convinced abolitionist largely because he was a convinced teetotaller. The stamp duty put a premium upon drunkenness. A drunkard in his parish had told him, with an ingenuity evidently lost on his passionate listener:

'I tell you, Sir, I never go to the public-house for beer, I go for the news; I have no other way of getting it; I cannot afford to pay five-pence, but unfortunately I go on drinking till I have spent a shilling, and I might as well have bought the paper in the first instance ...' and that [cried the Rev. Spencer] is the case with the working classes all over the kingdom. They go to the gin-shop, or the beer-shop, or the public-house ... and when they are in liquor, and have spent their money ... they are angry

... and are ready to entertain the most desperate feelings against any class, and ... government ... There is not the slightest danger to be apprehended from any working-man, a domesticated man and a sober man; there is an innate love of peace and quiet and order in every Englishman if he is not a drunken man.[99]

What would be the effect of abolition? ... 'a moral revolution ...'[100] A cheap press would diffuse moral principles through the country and the newspapers would become 'the great teachers of the people'.[101]

Compared with the Rev. Spencer's short cut to the New Jerusalem, William Hickson's evidence was sober, common-sense stuff. Abolition would bring out journals 'inferior to *The Times*' – but a good thing too.[102] Half the news in *The Times* was above the level of comprehension of the evening class of agricultural labourers in his village. They needed a paper that would report 'some trial at Maidstone assizes' or a stackyard fire.[103] There was another important function of the newspaper that could be more easily read, inferior though it might be; he had often observed that boys at the National Schools, apparently once taught to read, could forget completely. They had been taught to spell 'painfully', chapter by chapter of the New Testament, but 'nothing was afterwards put into their hands that had sufficient novelty to induce them to keep up the habit of reading ...'[104]

But (asked a Committee member) did Mr Hickson conceive that accounts of murders and rick-burnings were exactly the subjects best calculated to humanise the mind and affections and most conducive to the formation of moral habits? Hickson was unrepentant; yes, as a child he had been fascinated by the accounts of 'accidents and offences' in his father's newspapers.[105] He wouldn't read them now, but then ... 'it was the means of developing my intellectual powers, and I believe that a similar kind of reading would produce the same effect generally throughout the country.'[106] If he could read a paper about rick-burnings, he would know that the farmer was not really harmed, because the stacks were insured ... 'readers are not rioters; readers are not rick-burners'.[107] Hickson was that rare bird; a rational radical.

It remains to isolate from the evidence of Rowland Hill, whose penny post had been in operation over a decade, his conclusions bearing on the failure of the Post Office to prevent the carriage of newspapers from London to the provinces by private competitors. Hill was a supremely independent witness, as always. He frankly admitted that 'the Government always works more expensively than a private individual'; but he stuck to his point that the Post Office was primarily concerned with letters and the letter post.[108]

Mail times were fixed with this in mind, and the despatch of newspapers by early trains (not mail trains) was something which would demand special and very expensive arrangements. The final delivery of newspapers to customers, again, was by delivery boys; the delivery of letters could not be so entrusted. And so on.

Such was the background sketched by the witnesses: a mixture of self-interest and public concern, some genuine, some assumed. Plainly, news-papers, journals, miscellanies and the like were, then as now, a mixture of news, information and entertainment ranging from the intellectual to the near-pornographic. The press audience was still, in 1851, one of tinkers, tailors, candlestick makers; in so far as it was a 'working class' audience the workers were still mainly agricultural labourers or village craftsmen; self-employed or small workshop artisans. This was ceasing to be true in Lancashire but it was still true in London and most other parts of England. The 'popular press' and the fortunes of 'radical' newspaper proprietors like Edward Lloyd and George Reynolds were still in the future; but that future, rooted in the reading habits and tastes of the lower classes, was already clearly discernible. In short, the condition of the press was in pro-cess of being radically transformed. Preoccupation with the effects of the newspaper stamp, good or bad, was, in an important sense, misplaced; for it was not only the stamp, or *The Times*, that was the centre of change. This would presuppose, as it were, a pre-Copernican type of economic universe. By 1851 the whole economy was in a state of motion. Nothing in the proceedings of the Select Committee was more significant than the concluding remarks of that unhappy witness, Mowbray Morris of *The Times*:

> *Question:* 'Do not you consider that the tone of the newspapers . . . has very much improved of late years?'
> *Answer:* 'Yes; because the tone of society has very much improved.'[109]
> *Question:* 'May not this change in national manners, tastes, and feelings have had, rather than the stamp duty, a considerable influence in causing the improvement in the tone of newspapers?'
> *Answer:* 'That is my opinion; *I do not think that the stamp duty has anything to do with it* . . .'[110]

Against this background of material expansion and varied human demand we may now consider the evidence given by W. H. Smith I to the Select Committee. His first words characterised his style as a witness:

Question: 'You are a Distributor of Newspapers for the London Press, are you not?'
Answer: 'Yes, a Newspaper Agent.'[111]
Question: 'Do you carry on a considerable business?'
Answer: 'A very large one.'[112]

For several years his family and colleagues at the Strand had been anxious about his health, the strain of the business and his fits of nervous irritability and depression. However justifiable their anxieties may have been, his ailments did not show in William Henry's evidence. He was terse, accurate and clear. He did not fall into moralisings like Bucknall. He was not long-winded or pompous like Cassell. He did not turn truculent like Mowbray Morris. His was the evidence of a professional, conscious of his complete mastery of a complex business acquired over nearly forty years; confident also that this mastery of affairs was enough not only to maintain what – to an outsider – might seem a precarious business situation, but to extend and expand it in face of any competition he might have to face from private, or public, rivals for his trade, e.g. the Post Office. The only other witness comparable in technical mastery was Rowland Hill and his evidence as to the unshakeable hold Smith had acquired on the railway trade was the best compliment William Henry could have asked.

Of all the witnesses, he made the best use of figures. His first task was to outline quantitatively the character and extent of his business. The circulation of London daily papers, he began, 'scarcely exceeds 60,000'.[113] Of this he himself transmitted about one-seventh, or say 9,000, to the provinces. In London itself his circulation was mainly 'confined to those persons who may be coming to town for a season'.[114] What he transmitted to the provinces were principally morning dailies: there were fewer weeklies. He confirmed what several other witnesses had said: a very small proportion of morning papers was sent by post . . . 'the majority are sent by railway trains to large towns in the country'. He described his business routine:

We obtain the papers at an early hour, about five o'clock in the morning, from the [newspaper] offices by carts; they are then made up in parcels for the principal towns, and we dispatch them by the first trains, at six or half-past six; then a second dispatch is made by the Post Office to the country villages, chiefly in the neighbourhood of large towns, and to distant parts of Scotland which are not reached by the parcels, and the dispatch of the morning papers then ceases. In the evening the papers are made up chiefly in single copies for the distant parts of the country; but the second editions are forwarded also by parcels to the large towns, in order to save the expense of a halfpenny postage which is charged by the Post Office, and to ensure an earlier delivery.[115]

Was there, a questioner asked, any additional cost to the purchaser for the services he provided? 'Scarcely any'. The cost was paid by the country agent who was glad to attract to himself the whole business of the district. '. . . the cost averages a farthing a paper'.[116] A customer demanding long credit would have to pay something for it, of course.

Next, with some satisfaction, he enlarged on the process of 're-transmission' of stamped newspapers by the free post which supplemented his own initial distribution by rail. This was important because to some extent, though not entirely, it answered the criticisms of those who saw Britain dominated by a *Times* newspaper selling at a price beyond the pockets of the man-in-the-street. Had he found this 're-transmission' to be 'a very great convenience to the middle classes . . .'? Yes, he had. The system was practised 'to a most enormous extent, and it reduces the cost of the paper to those least able to pay for it, to a perfectly wonderful extent'. He had no doubt that 'every daily paper published in London is read by three or four distinct persons' . . . 'I was in the country, and a clergyman told me that *The Times* only cost him a penny. It was forwarded first and read at a news-room in Norwich; it was sent off from that room in the afternoon to some person residing in that city, and next morning forwarded by the Post Office to a village about eight or nine miles off, and then it travelled round the country . . .' Was this class of persons very numerous? 'I should think so; exceedingly numerous'.[117] Enough, he added, to ensure that if the stamp were removed, this would not in itself ensure that the numbers of persons reading the papers would necessarily increase correspondingly.

Cobden pressed him at this point. Would it not be possible to publish a 'good' newspaper for 1d.; like the *Family Herald*?[118] William Henry did not think so. It could be done if the paper cribbed its matter from better papers or lowered its tone; but in any case, the *Family Herald* was not a 'newspaper'; it was 'a number of scraps . . . respectably done . . . short articles . . .' but emphatically not to be confused with a newspaper.[119] It was not enough, if you wanted a good newspaper and a high circulation, simply to avoid 'improper matter' and preserve 'a high moral tone'.

But did he think 'the general taste' was for the 'low and immoral'? William Henry avoided the Cobdenite trap into which Morris fell. 'No, I do not; but I do not think it would be possible for a newspaper publisher, at a penny or 2d to publish at a profit without pandering to a very immoral taste'.[120]

Victorian morality? Not at all: what William Henry said was essentially what latter-day progressive critics are still writing about the great capitalist captains of the popular press from Lloyd and Reynolds to Northcliffe, Rothermere and Beaverbrook.

The other major question for the reformers was that the stamp duty was popularly regarded as a substitute for a postal rate for papers. Would it not be a general benefit, not least to the national revenues, if the stamp were removed and then a postage of 1d. for a single posting were instituted? No, it would not. The only result would be that private enterprise would immediately contrive means of delivering papers; 'we could derive a very profitable trade by conveying newspapers to any part of the United Kingdom for a halfpenny a copy'.[121] William Henry's mastery of the subject was too much for the Committee; after a few more desultory and feeble questions, the Post Office was abandoned, and the Committee turned with relief to hear William Henry describe his provincial trade.

William Henry had none of the businessman's common love of secrecy; he was shrewd, and honest enough to see that he had nothing to lose and something to gain by opening his books. They showed that in 1836 (before the stamp was reduced and prices were at their maximum) he had sold daily a total of 215 copies of *The Times* in Liverpool and Manchester. Of 'other papers' he had sold in those two cities 1,024; by 1846, in a decade of a reduced (1d.) stamp, he had sold 1,171 *Times* and 917 'others', plus 567 copies of the new, cheaper *Daily News*. By 1851, his daily sales in the same areas were 1,354 *Times* and 845 'others'. The overwhelming upsurge of *The Times* only reflected its national performance. Its annual sale of just over 3 million in 1837 had risen to just under 12 million by 1850. Except for the *Morning Advertiser* (which just about held its own) all its other great rivals – *Chronicle, Herald, Post* – had fallen back in disorder, especially the *Post* which had dropped by over 50 per cent between 1843 and 1850. Significant for the future of popular journalism was the sensational rise of the *News of the World*, harbinger of the popular 'Sunday'; and, in its own class and harvesting the gains of the new technology of photographic illustration, the *Illustrated London News*. As William Henry observed when speaking of the provincial newspapers, it might be that the abolition of the stamp would stimulate their production and sale, but he felt bound to observe the tendency of things was decidedly in favour of the London press; 'every change has been in favour of the London press'.[122]

The London newsagents (he told the Committee) had not been favourable to the reduction of the newspaper duty in 1836 because their profits had likewise been reduced, 'which [said William Henry] was a very reasonable objection . . .'[123] What would their (meaning 'including your') response be to abolition now? His reply was not the least striking observation among his evidence.

> . . . as a body, the London newspaper agents would be unfavourable to it now. As an individual, and considering only my own interests, I should strongly desire it; because, having a very large business already in those manufacturing towns, it would concentrate that business still more in my own hands, and I could afford to convey newspapers for very much less than the Post Office, let them do what they choose.[124]

With that, and mingling just a touch of asperity, and a touch of defiance to the abolitionists, he rested his case. His performance had added to his stature. He had shown the Committee and the men of public affairs that he knew how to mind his own business; while avoiding anything so crude as to suggest others might do well to go and do likewise, he had at least taken some of the wind out of the abolitionists' sails. True, he had not blocked abolition, neither, as he explained, was it in his personal interest to do so. But his evidence, replete as it was with chapter and verse, and taken along with warnings from Rowland Hill, helped to prevent any imposition of onerous new postage rates on newspapers to compensate for the discarded newspaper stamp. Here the abolitionists had to be content with a malevolent surcharge on weight; for if the clause had carried the sub-title 'the anti-*Times* clause', its aim could not have been more clear. Writing to his son on 16 March 1855 when the Bill appeared, William Henry remarked, '. . . The plan stated in the *Globe* I do not think will please Mr. Walter the Tax or Stamp graduating according to the size of the paper though quite just will not suit the *Times*'.[125] Yet, yoked together with *The Times* as his fortunes at this point might have seemed to be, he never showed the slightest subservience to 'The Thunderer', whether in the persons of Barnes or Delane as editors, or Mowbray Morris as manager, or John Walter as owner. His relations with *The Times*, as with the rest of the press world, were strictly on a basis of business; they did their job; he did his. So it was to remain into the twentieth century.

His evidence was not only a model of precision; because it was precise, and his mind uncluttered by false sentiment or social rhetoric, it also proved to be prophetic. When he said that he would profit by the removal of the stamp duty he was simply stating a fact – the conclusion of calculations which proved that such a move would tend to concentrate the business of distribution in fewer hands. When he said he would compete successfully with the Post Office, he was not boasting but, again, stating a fact – to him a simple fact; and he gently reproved the questioner who asked him if he believed he could 'so compete with the Post Office as to prevent them [i.e. readers] purchasing their papers, and having them sent through the post'? William Henry corrected him: 'We should not do it to prevent them purchasing their papers, but to get a profit out of the difference'.[126] When he said he did not think a paper could sell for 1d. without pandering to low tastes, he was not moralising; simply describing the gap between *The Times* as it was and the material he knew from *Mysteries of the Court of London*. This latter would form a necessary selling ingredient in really cheap newspapers. There would be time enough for the intellectuals of the future

TABLE III.I NEWSPAPER STAMP 1851 – W. H. SMITH SALES OF LONDON
NEWSPAPERS TO CERTAIN PROVINCIAL CITIES[127]

		The Times	Other papers	
31 August 1836	L*	127	481	
Stamp 4d., price of paper 7d.	M*	88	543	
30 July 1837	L	148	577	
Stamp 1d., price reduced to 5d.	M	117	606	
		The Times	Other dailies 5d.	Daily News 2½d.
1 July 1846	L	437	413	277
	M	734	504	290
26 Jan. 1847	L			163
	M			235
31 Jan. 1849	L			134 (3d.)
	M			180
3 June 1851	L	506	411	
	M	848	434	

* L=Liverpool, M=Manchester

TABLE III.2 NEWSPAPER STAMP COMMITTEE 1851 *(Appendix 4, Return of 1d news-*

	1837	1838	1839	1840	1841	1842
Atlas	105	140	136.5	125	90.541	125
Athenaeum	30.25	55.65	63.5	70	68.9	75
Bell's Life in London	851	1,040	1,180.5	1,173.5	1,029	1,014
Britannia	—	—	66.6	161	199.5	289
Court Journal	53.785	86.5	99	74	76	58.5
Evening Chronicle	220	236	226.5	219.5	204	194
Evening Mail (evening edn. of *The Times* 3x week)	318	275	360	380	445	475
Illustrated London News	—	—	—	—	—	932.95
Morning Advertiser	1,380	1,565.225	1,535	1,550	1,470	1,445
Morning Chronicle	1,940	2,750	2,028	2,075.5	2,079	1,918.5
Morning Herald	1,928	1,925	1,820	1,956	1,630	1,559.5
Morning Post	735	875	1,006	1,125	1,165.210	1,195.025
News of the World	—	—	—	—	—	—
Observer	299	275	118.5	216	182.5	210
Standard	1,330	1,075	1,030	1,040	1,025	1,000
Sunday Times	407	695	690	1,050	1,100	1,080
Sun	794	1,344	1,231	1,281	1,225	1,173
The Times	3,065	3,065	4,300	5,060	5,650	6,305
Weekly Despatch	2,606	2,691	2,750	2,275	2,975	3,275
Weekly Times	—	—	—	—	—	—

paper stamps issued to newspapers 1837–50: (Principal London Papers) (1,000's)[128]

1843	1844	1845	1846	1847	1848	1849	1850
107	87	84	72	83.25	85.5	90.668	98
78	93.25	103.5	117	117.5	125.5	127.5	144.158
992.5	948	1,520.5	1,250	1,311	1,236.5	1,176.5	1,285.5
261.5	258	257	252.331	216	203.3	182.35	163.875
40.4	42.1	40.7	41.5	37.697	26.007	18.559	17.543
150	144	134	93	39.6	—	—	—
500	550	525	530	550	600	675	650
2,110.353	2,532	2,618.8	2,367.067	2,267.601	2,964.658	3,600.169	3,467.007
1,534	1,415	1,440	1,480	1,500	1,538	1,528.22	1,549.843
1,784	1,628	1,554	1,356	1,233	1,150.304	937.5	912.547
1,516	1,608.07	2,018.025	1,725.5	1,510	1,335	1,147	1,139
1,900	1,002	1,200.5	1,450.5	990.1	964.5	905	828
101.205	674.018	1,251.150	1,878.5	1,981.853	2,478.955	2,806.767	2,926.269
141.5	154.5	149	177.5	212	281	360.5	324
920	867	846	780	659.5	652.5	539	492
915	880.5	945.5	932.5	785	757	735	675
1,098	868	1,098.5	1,104	909	893.312	873	834.5
6,250	6,900	8,100	8,950	9,205.230	11,025.500	11,300	11,900
2,865	2,600	2,457	2,421.5	2,203.5	2,112.790	2,250	1,950
—	—	—	—	805.580	1,077.033	1,808.190	2,037.703

to wring their hands over the betrayal of working class morality by *Lloyds Weekly*, *Reynolds News* and the *News of the World*.

For Morris had been right. The stamp duty had been credited with too much influence, for good and bad alike. In the long run, 1851 was to be less remembered as the year of the Select Committee on Newspaper Stamps than as the year of the Great Exhibition, the best outward proof of the upsurge of wealth and income which was to transform the British economy and British society: simultaneously to revolutionise, for good or ill, the British press and with these great transformations, the business of W. H. Smith.

IV

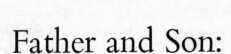

Father and Son:
A Crisis Resolved

WILLIAM HENRY SMITH the younger must have been among the first small boys to cherish the ambition of driving a railway train. He was born in 1825, the year when George Stephenson, inventor of the railway steam engine, engineer and manufacturer of steam engines and rails, opened his first steam railway between Stockton and Darlington. He was a child of the new age of steam power. He saw the steam railway evolve from its early partnership with the horse (carried in the 'dandy cart' on early railways to help on uphill stretches) and the steamboat emancipate itself from its partnership with sail. His life and business career were inextricably entwined with the improvement of the railway system as it spread ever more widely, replacing the coach and road system which William Henry the elder had energetically exploited for the distribution of newspapers.

The change from road to rail was progressing steadily as young William Henry was put through school. There was now enough money to ensure that William Henry I was able without difficulty to fulfil his ambition to give his son a better education than his own mother had been able to afford for him. William Henry II's early schooldays were shared with his four elder sisters and a governess. Then came a young tutor fresh from Trinity College, Cambridge, William (later the Rev. Dr) Beal who was to marry the eldest of the sisters, Mary Ann. Her husband was appointed Headmaster of the recently revived Grammar School at Tavistock. Thither, as a boarder, went William Henry on the eve of his fourteenth birthday. His career was so promising that he returned home for more coaching; in 1841, when he was sixteen, he went back to Tavistock as a private pupil of Beal's. Tavistock was ruled with a firm hand and Beal, though an 'excitable' character (as William Henry regarded him) helped to turn William

Henry II into a competent classical scholar who could construe his Virgil and Sallust, struggle through his Euclid and comment on the world about him with an observant eye and a shrewd pen.[1]

His later years at school and after were a time of crisis and decision. By the late 1830s, his father was already showing increasing signs of physical and nervous strain as the business grew larger and more complicated: and he was not a man who took easily to co-operating on equal terms with a partner. In his unpunctuated, telegraphic, nervous style he would write to his son at Tavistock; most often about the state of the business but often adverting to his other favourite topic: the perils of extravagance and the virtues of thrift and accuracy. Was it a tuck-shop bill that provoked a minor explosion on 7 June 1839? 'I inclose the half of a Five Pound Bank Note, pray do not leave a farthing unpaid I cannot bear Debt ...' (the other half, characteristically, was to follow by a later post for safety's sake).[2]

William Henry's letters to his father were long and dutiful. Unlike most schoolboys he enjoyed writing letters. (His first surviving letter, written when he was nine, was to his favourite sister Augusta ('Gussie') congratulating her on being eleven years old, enclosing a geranium and wishing her to be 'joyful on this always happy day and that you might prosperously go on'.[3] William Henry II always had a sense of occasion.) To his father, for whom he had a real affection which survived the temperamental fits that punctuated relations between them, he wrote precociously long and careful letters, mainly about public affairs and the family business. On 15 April 1839, he wrote from Tavistock:

> ... I see that a very important debate comes on tonight in the Commons, and I should think one very likely to influence the fate of the ministry. I should like to be with you tomorrow morning to see what help I could render, and I can assure you that often of a morning when up at 6 o'clock learning my lessons, I have thought of the Strand & you, & could imagine how busy you were at any particular moment when I was enjoying myself. I suppose that you have not yet had any occasion to use the Preston route, as I have not heard anything of it. The Newspapers I can assure you are very welcome reminding one of one's work at home ... Although away from you & the business my mind frequently reverts to you hoping that you are well in health and especially that you do not work so much as you did.[4]

Even more remarkable, for a 17-year-old boy, was another letter (23 April 1842) commenting in detail on the distribution of the London papers

(*The Times* especially) in the west of England and shrewdly detecting the weaknesses of his father's business rivals.

> . . . In Bridgwater I observed a placard, announcing to the world, that John Tiver, bookseller, received *The Times* daily at one (or two) o'clk. We left Bridgwater at 2 by one of the coaches that wait the 8 o'clk London train; this, I found carried a parcel of about a dozen papers from Westley's for a Mr. May of Taunton wh. had been enclosed in Tiver's parcel, and had come down by the 8 o'clk train. There are no other papers carried to either Bridgwater, Taunton or Exeter . . . so you see these are all the wonderful exertions of Mr. Westley wh. are advertised in *The Times*; indeed it must be at a most terrible expenditure of trouble that he can manage regularly to send not quite a quire of papers, and all folded too, by 8 o'clk from the terminus at Paddington. If he was but to make the least exertion he might very well get a good business in that part of the country . . .[5]

Father, his eye always sharp for business aptitude, did not fail to take careful note of his son's remarkable, rather precocious, intuitions of enterprise. It was, as he remarked in a letter at Christmas 1841, 'a great thing to keep so large a business together . . .';[6] and that business was his personal creation; its welfare and preservation his daily anxiety. Who would help him to look after it when he was no longer able to take the whole responsibility himself? Between 1839 and 1842 he became daily more convinced that his mantle must fall on his son, who showed such dutiful interest and aptitude for business. As he felt more and more unsure of his own health, each letter from Tavistock determined him more surely that William Henry the younger must take over. In January 1842 he was feeling acutely the 'push of the season' (as his wife described it):[7] but not enough to overlook a fault in his son's personal budget.

> . . . I only observe one item to complain off [*sic*] that is 1/9 Late Postage – it is not the amount but the habit or practice of being to the last minute that I dislike no tradesman ought to do so – as far as he his [*sic*] concerned he should always be before the time required not after it . . .[8]

For the young William Henry the apparent reference to his future was ominous. He was a highly intelligent boy of delicate perceptions and sensibilities and he had already created in his imagination a quite different future for himself. His only confidants were his sisters and his brother-in-law,

William Beal. William Henry was, in fact, going through a genuine crisis of the spirit. Brought up to an evangelical brand of Anglicanism nearer to John Wesley than to Newman or Pusey, he cherished a deep hope at this period to be ordained into the Anglican priesthood: he himself disliked the Oxford Movement. 'Don't be afraid', he wrote in 1845, 'that I am becoming a Puseyite, a Newmanite, or Roman Catholic . . . I am only confirmed in my dislike for Wesleyanism as now carried out by Preachers and people and in my decided preference for the Church . . .'9

Yet what, at a distance of a century and a half, seems a turn of only a degree or two, was enough to cause an explosion in an early Victorian family. In some ways moving, in others ludicrous, for William Henry the younger it meant several years of personal agony. His sister Mary Ann and her husband, though middle-of-the-road Anglicans (as was, formally at least, William Henry the elder himself) were terrified that his frame of mind would be interpreted by his father as disloyalty and ingratitude, besides being a kind of apostasy: for at heart the Smiths had remained Methodists, though outwardly conforming Anglicans. And when the suspicion slowly dawned on them that their son not only disliked Dissent but leaned towards the priesthood, their old anti-clericalism was roused, first to wrath, then to distress.

The first move was precipitated by a gradual worsening of the father's health. William Henry the younger had for some months been travelling the two hundred miles between Tavistock and the Strand in a desperate attempt to share his father's load. Now it was decided he would join the business – as yet in a junior capacity with an allowance of £200 a year. He was later to live at the newly acquired Smith residence at Kilburn and have a horse '. . . a very beautiful one indeed on which I am to ride backwards and forwards (to the Strand) . . .'10

Not for the first nor the last time, however, William Henry the elder, whose powers of recovery were as remarkable as they were disconcerting, plunged with renewed energy into the business, now with the object of driving his son as well as everybody else as hard as he drove himself. His son stood, determinedly as ever, to his private resolution to enter the Church. For three years the two faced each other without either budging from his unspoken position. The silent reserve which obscured relations between father and son like a fog, made things worse. The health and nerves of both suffered equally. It was the younger man who threatened to crack first. In an undated letter to his sister at Tavistock he described life with Father:

I never remember such a period of excessive excitement and hard work.

I have been in town, with Father, once at 3 oclock in the morning, and every other day ... before 5 ... and we have already had 9 Special Express Engines to Liverpool, Manchester and Birmingham and they will run every day this week. All this I have *mainly* to arrange and I can assure you it has worn me not a little. Constant excitement and anxiety during the days and short and disturbed sleep at nights, as the consequence, are gradually making me feel as low and nervous as I was a few months back ...[11]

Yet somehow he kept going, even managing to fit in 'an interview with the great George Hudson, the Railway King'. The occasion was a joint visit by a *Times* representative and young William Henry to remonstrate with Hudson about the unsatisfactory arrangements of newspaper trains to the north. William Henry was not impressed:

... I think he is a cunning clever man, but very deficient in every thing that is noble and commanding respect; very much of a bully in conversation – if he thinks he can succeed – if not, possessed of little courage, if any; at first he was disposed to treat me very slightingly and I felt angry, and in the course of conversation brought in the names of the conductors of *The Times* and *Chronicle* which had such a magical effect upon the honourable gentleman that both my companion and myself could hardly refrain from laughing in his face ...[12]

His verdict was prophetic. Hudson was to be the chief victim of the great financial debacle of 1847-9. He had too long financed himself (in the words of a subordinate) 'by cooking the accounts in order to make things pleasant'.

By 1845, no progress had been made towards resolving the family impasse. Both father and son were feeling increasing strain. The elder had a recurrence of the lameness which had on earlier occasions been an early symptom of danger. The son, also suffering from overwork and strain, was sent down to Dover and Ramsgate in the hope that the sea air would give him back physical and nervous strength. William Henry the elder, true to form, visited his son, principally to impress on him the effect of the overwork that fell on his own shoulders in his son's absence. He has still, wrote young William Henry, 'a great wish that I shd go on with the business but seems aware of my desires to do something else, and is afraid to press the subject lest the result might realise the Doctor's prediction.'[13]

It seemed a small straw to grasp at but in fact both men were within

sight of a solution of their problems. The younger man had earlier observed
– wisely as it was to prove – 'Evils must always reach a climax before they
are remedied and frequently the longer they are left, the more complete is
the remedy . . .'[14] Genuine as the younger man's spiritual crisis and sense
of religious vocation undoubtedly were, his father, also a man of acute
intuitions, seems to have sensed an element of adolescent emotionalism in
his son's state of mind which would probably pass with time and involvement in a steady rout ne of work. The older man tried to break the deadlock by hinting – at last – at the possibility that he himself might retire.
The son wrote to his sister that his father:

> . . . began to think that there was no absolute necessity for him to
> labour on, and after turning the matter over in his mind a great deal,
> and very frequently representing to me what an enormous fortune I
> shd have in a few years, if I could continue the business, he at last made
> up his mind to retire as soon as he could possibly get things in order.[15]

To his father's chagrin, William Henry II took his father's decision not
as the occasion for himself, but for some other suitable incumbent, to
replace William Henry I. His dislike of the prospect of a business career, of
his parents' Wesleyan friends, of family plans to encourage him towards
'a suitable marriage', remained intense. As late as November 1845, he
wrote (with evident distaste and in the context of the ethos of the same
Dissenting friends of his parents):

> The present panic as a result of the late feverish haste to get rich is
> beautifully developing this amiable quality which seems inherent in us
> all (i.e. selfishness). The cry is 'every man for himself' and *not* 'God for
> us all' but 'the Devil take the hindermost'.[16]

It took from the autumn of 1845 to the end of the summer in the following year for the crisis to resolve itself. Some undated notes in pencil show
William Henry bracing himself to put his final answer to his father. The
gist of them is that it had for many years been his wish to enter the Ministry,
but until Providence had created a favourable opportunity in the shape of
his father's recent change of mind (i.e. his decision to give up the business)
no occasion had presented itself. Now he asked to be allowed to enter the
Church. Of what happened at their meeting no more is certain than that
the request met with a flat refusal and probably provoked a predictable
explosion. On 6 August 1846 he wrote:

1 W.H. Smith I, 1792–1865, son of the founder, Henry Walton Smith
(portrait by unknown artist)

2 Above: the *Bull and Mouth* Inn was conveniently placed, opposite the Post Office in St Martin's Le Grand (after a drawing by Thomas Allom, 1829)

3 Below: The *Bull and Mouth* Inn (after a drawing by T.H. Shepherd, c.1830)

4 Newspapers being loaded on to a Royal Mail coach outside the *Swan with Two Necks* (interpreted by P. W. Dooner, 1948)

Hble & Rt Revd Lord Bishop of Worcester

To H. & W. SMITH,
Stationers and Account-Book Manufacturers,
AND AGENTS FOR ALL THE LONDON NEWSPAPERS.
NEWSPAPERS SENT BY THE EARLY MORNING COACHES.
192, STRAND.

H. and W. SMITH beg to solicit your attention to the following List of Prices for Writing Paper, of the very best quality:—

	QUIRE. s. d.	REAM. s. d.		QUIRE. s. d.	REAM. s. d.		QUIRE. s. d.	REAM. s. d.
Excellent copy	0 N	12 0	Bath post	0 7	10 6	Super large Bank post	1 2	20 0
Very best lined brief	1 6	29 6	Ditto	0 8	12 0	Best 8vo. note	0 6	9 0
Good laid post	0 8	12 0	Superfine Bath	0 9	13 6	Ditto ditto, gilt	0 7	11 0
Thick ditto	0 9	13 6	Ditto hot pressed	0 10	15 6	Superfine foolscap	1 0	19 0
Superfine ditto	0 10	15 6	Ditto ditto ditto thick	1 0	17 6	Thick ditto	1 2	21 0
Do. very best laid do	1 0	17 6	Very best thick Bath gilt } or black edge	1 1	20 0	Ditto	1 3	24 0
Bath post	0 4½	6 9				Very best ditto	1 4	26 0
Ditto	0 5	7 9	Bank post	0 10	15 0			

Superior satin and tinted post of various colours; best foolscap copy-books, 3s. 6d. per dozen; post copy books, 5s. 6d. per dozen; pinions and pens equally low in price; also drawing paper and Bristol boards; very best sealing-wax, 4s. 6d. per lb.; steel-nibbed pens, 1s. 4d. each; strong brown paper, 10d. and 1s. 6d. per quire; small hand, 4d. per quire, or 5s. 6d. per ream.

Also a large assortment of Travelling and Dressing Cases, manufactured from the best materials, and of superior workmanship. 12-inch Soufflet, 20s.——14-inch ditto, 22s.—5s. extra for Patent Lock.——Double-fold Writing Desk, 20s.——14-inch, 31s. 6d.——Pouch Dressing Case, with Instruments, 12s.——Large Box Pouch, 20s.——Ditto, with the very best Instruments, 42s.——Real Russia Dressing Case, with Brushes and Instruments, complete, 35s.

FOR READY MONEY.

1827   Courier   1 April to 25 Augt   4. 5.

J Bull   1 April to 31 March   1. 14.

Standard   25 Augt. to 31 March 1828   6. 6.

£ 12. 6

My Lord   Above we send your annual accts. We return our most grateful thanks for favours conferred & are

Your most

5 The Lord Bishop of Worcester billed for his newspapers by W.H. Smith I, 1829

The past twelvemonth has been one of great importance to me and as far as man may be permitted to judge, determining the particular course of life I shall lead, and the objects to which my best energies are to be devoted.

The decision on these most serious matters, was not perhaps in accordance with the hopes and desires I had long cherished.

Those who have a natural claim upon my respect and obedience so strongly opposed the schemes I entertained and in such a feeling as to render it impossible for me to carry them into effect . . .

But it is not so – at least apparently – for he whose power is absolute in the matter – under Providence itself – by the strong expression of his wishes and intentions obliged me to yield my own desires and views, and adopt his instead.

By this I do not mean that he acted otherwise than from the kindest motives, as he no doubt considered the course of life he contemplated for me the best and the most useful and that in fact for which I am designed . . .[17]

The long contest had ended in a victory for the elder man and an imposed peace. The son was bitter and disappointed, but, with a philosophic acceptance that was to become a marked feature of his character, he quickly mastered his feelings. Deeply hurt though he was, he commented only that: 'it is my duty to acknowledge an overruling and directing Providence in all the very minutest things, by being in whatsoever state I am, therewith content . . .'[18] Perhaps his father had not been so far wrong in his strategy of attrition, in his persistent intuition that, given time, the emotional crisis of youth would slowly pass, yielding to a revival in new forms of the still remembered boyish ambition to solve the related jig-saw puzzles of newspapers, trains and time-tables.

The next month, on 28 September 1846, the 'Articles of Partnership between William Henry Smith and his Son' were signed. The deed was in no sense vindictive: on the contrary it offered young William Henry, who had only just attained his majority, substantial advantages, with the obvious incentive of that great fortune dangled earlier before him by his father if all went well. But the father was a Victorian father true to the fictional image if ever a Victorian father was. For him, a genuine relationship between father and son, like the relationship between partner and partner, was a matter of strict observance of mutual duty, responsibility and authority. The existence of family affection (and in his shy, brusque way he was not lacking in it) was no excuse for blurring the nature of authority. The partnership deed therefore made no effort to disguise the nature of the older man's victory or the necessary acceptance by the son of the consequences of that victory. The phrase 'junior partner' is not used in the articles: they simply assumed that the new partner was, in every respect, subordinate to his father – for the seven years duration and subject to his strictly legal rights. The character of William Henry the elder stands out from every line of the parchment as sharp and taut as from the telling (but anonymous) contemporary portrait.

The articles recited, first, that William Henry the first had 'for many years last past carried on the trade or business of a News Agent and Whole-sale and Retail Stationer'. He had 'by great labour and attention and at considerable expence increased the said trade or business so that the same is now become very lucrative and beneficial to him And whereas the said William Henry Smith the younger hath for many years last past served his Father . . . with great fidelity as a clerk in the said business' he is to be admitted to 'a share of the said trade or business, for . . . seven years'. The rewards and conditions follow. The business will be carried on 'in the same manner in all respects . . .' At the end of the partnership the younger partner will have £2,000 but no interest on it. He will have £500 a year and necessary expenses but no detailed account of his father's estate, effects and profits. The bank account remained the sole account of the father. He alone could draw cheques and, likewise, he bore any losses incurred by the business. Credits were likewise strictly controlled by father. The son was to render to him when asked verbal or written explanations 'of all his dealings and transactions'. His share in the business was not transferable and any failure to perform his duties could result in deductions from the £2,000 and any other sums due to him. The partners – both – were to be 'true and just to each other' in all their dealings. Any disputes should be referred to arbitration by two 'indifferent persons' one appointed by each party. Only if this provision was neglected by one party could the other go to the Courts.[19]

Tough? Certainly, but given all the circumstances, fair and reasonable. The new partner seems to have looked at it in this light. More than a decade later, when the father finally made over the whole business to his son, he recalled that the value of his property on the eve of the partnership was £80,527. 8s. 6d. 'The next day my Son's name was put into the business to have from that date £500 per year, free from all charges for Board, Lodging, Horse, Brougham, Groom Etc. Etc. Etc.'[20] The note was per-haps designed to clear his conscience: he had been generous to his son and discharged a father's duty and authority. But had he perhaps been overgenerous? Had the rein been tight enough? Just in case he had relaxed too far, he continued his periodic bombardment of the Strand with helpful criticisms. One of 1 October 1859, survives:

> . . . I requested that *The Times* of Friday 15th should be sent here and also the *Saturday Review*. Friday *Times* not sent. Saturday *Times* sent by night mail arrived here Sunday Mg. *Saturday Review* not sent at all. *Illusd. News* sent 2 Weeks . . . though ordered to be stopped it is sent again this Week. I inclose the 5d for it do not it [*sic*] send again. I really hope my old business is not generally conducted in this neglectful and blundering way . . .[21]

His son had remarked, before he entered the partnership, that his father seemed resigned to the idea of a more peaceful life . . . 'on doing less . . . on playing the Gentleman Tradesman . . . to dine *here* [Kilburn House] regularly at 4 o'clock, excepting on Saturdays . . .'[22] But it was only fancy. William Henry I was not ready to change his way of life and never would be.

The arrangements of 1846 did not solve any of the fundamental problems. Co-existence between father and son was a traumatic trial for both: for William Henry I would not share authority and William Henry II was not allowed to exercise it. More than another decade of intermittent purgatorial misery followed. The major burden of a rapidly expanding business fell on William Henry II: in this he had less and less help and more and more nagging criticism from his father; decisions were taken only to be cancelled: the tension continued, and his loneliness was relieved by only one trusted friend and confidant, William Ford, partner in the firm's solicitors. Until his father finally retired completely from the business and allowed him to introduce a partner, Ford was William Henry II's only source of advice and encouragement.

In April 1855 he wrote to Ford from Torquay: his father and he had agreed that the prestige the Smith business had acquired made it opportune 'to sell the Good-Will if we can obtain purchasers for it on fair and reasonable terms'.[23] But consistency was no longer in his father's nature. A year later the son was still writing desperately to Ford from Dublin to ask him to:

> drop in upon my Father . . . Talk also if you can about me. This must really be the wind-up of my work in the business, or the fair beginning of the end. How is the whole affair to be wound up. To respect each other as we ought, we cannot get on together as Father and Son much longer. Somehow or other the connection must be brought to an end

even if the business is to be continued, and I honestly confess I do not like that, as it involves transactions with Newspapers and Railway Companies which it is difficult for an independent man to carry through without a sacrifice of feeling which I have no motive to make – unless the possession of money in excess of one's wants could be a motive.[24]

Late in the autumn of 1856, the situation was, if anything, worse. 'I am, personally, very low', he wrote to Ford on 25 November. 'My Father is more excited and anxious than ever, and I really cannot help differing from him. I do heartily wish that he was in thoroughly sound health so that I could safely put a few thousand miles between us for a month or two. It would do us both good.'[25] To crown the problems of increasing work and responsibility, and his father's obsession that his son was spending too much money on business innovations – railway contracts, stocks of books, advertising expenses – came a wounding quarrel picked by the proprietors of the Radical *Standard* with Smith's. William Henry II was still a Liberal, and the *Standard* was doing its best to wreck his relations with the South Eastern and London & South Western railways.[26]

Perhaps worst of all – for behind the calm face he put on to the public he was deeply emotional – William Henry II was still suffering a wound of passion suffered some years earlier. In the late 1840s, as part of his search to compensate for the lost vision of a life in Holy Orders, he had joined the managing committee of King's College Hospital, with which he was to be closely connected for the rest of his life. This brought him into contact with the family of Frederick Dawes Danvers, clerk to the Duchy of Lancaster and father of several attractive daughters. William Henry II conceived a hopeless passion for the eldest daughter, Emily. For Emily preferred his rival, Benjamin Auber Leach, a young man of sternly puritanical views who added insult to injury by attacking his rival for selling (on the new W. H. Smith bookstall at Waterloo Station) a copy of Byron's *Don Juan*. Mr Leach wrote (of course) 'as from a friend', but one whose aim was also 'to stop the stream of iniquity which seems to threaten us, in the shape of immorality flowing from the press . . .'[27] This was in October 1853. Fate did not leave poor Leach to suffer iniquity long. In under two years he was dead, leaving Emily a young widow, and pregnant.

For several years this shock only added to William Henry's uncertainties and anxieties. Where did his moral duty lie? Was it mortal sin or Christian succour to harbour ideas of winning, after all, his heart's desire? His recorded thoughts and prayers were witness to another bout of deep agony of spirit. On 7 and 8 June 1856, he wrote in his diary: 'The first day of an intended new life. Oh Lord help and save me. I thank God for enabling me to strive against known Sin this day. See 2 *Cor.* 6 ch. 17, 18 vs.'[28]

In the end, and after a decent interval, common sense won, cheerfulness broke in and in an ecstasy of happiness William Henry married the young widow. It was to be a happy marriage. Emily was an affectionate and understanding wife. If she had any critical or contrary opinions she kept them to herself: her job was to comfort and support him. And he needed all she could offer.

The marriage took place, with a sound Victorian disregard for superstition, on 13 April 1858 at St James's, Paddington. Everyone was happy: even Father. 'For a very long time', wrote the bridegroom, 'I have not been so free from care or anxiety . . .'[29] Father had enjoyed a 'wonderful preservation from serious attack . . . and he appears to feel almost as warmly about our marriage as I do. Have we not the promise of happiness?'[30] He had, though Father's natural discontents were not long assuaged. A month after the wedding William Henry was writing to Ford once more of his concern at his father's 'frequent change of purpose' and his embarrassment that he could not bring himself to confide in his wife about the apparent change in his father's feelings towards him.[31]

Even the shadow of Father grew less with his final decision to withdraw from the business in 1857. The deed of 1 July of that year recalled that the partnership of 1846 had expired in 1853 but had been continued informally as if nothing had happened. William Henry II had been undemanding. His drawings of cash had never reached £500 in any year and he had never claimed the £2,000 due to him. For some years (the deed went on) his father 'by reason of Illness' had not taken any active part in the management of the business and consequently – 'the whole burthen of conducting the said Concern . . .' had fallen on his son. Now the father wished to retire. He was to have an annuity of £4,000 for life and be quit of the liability (generously waived by his son) to pay either arrears of income or the capital sum of £2,000 due to William Henry II. So William Henry II, at the age of 32, became legal as well as actual head of W. H. Smith and Son.[32]

The year 1858 brought him Emily. Following years added strength in the shape of an assistant to help with the management of an expanding and exigent business. This was William Lethbridge, an old school friend from his Tavistock days and later a schoolmaster at Rossall, St Paul's and Highgate. They met again sometime in late 1857 or early 1858, after the dissolution of the family partnership. William Henry was now free (1862) to invite Lethbridge to join him in the business. He was to prove resourceful, a patient but firm negotiator, loyal but independent by nature, always preserving his function of colleague and, when necessary, critic and adviser. From 1864 when he became a full partner, for over a quarter of a century, Lethbridge played a major role in shaping the W. H. Smith business. Without him William Henry's career could never have taken the course it did.

The end of the partnership with Father, marriage, the arrival of a dependable business associate – all combined to give new vitality to William Henry's policies. The charges made by the *Standard* (that he was refusing to sell the paper on fair terms) were publicly rebutted and the authors strongly rebuked. The distractions and overwork that seemed to account for a lassitude or exhaustion that had lost railways contracts (the North British Railway for example) were no more. The advance of the business on all fronts – newspapers, books, libraries, publishing and advertising – went forward with new vigour. With one contract after another Smith's began their advance towards the steady conquest of the railway world of reading.

Business success is built on several foundation stones: a flair for commercial opportunity, the ability to manage people, attention to detail, broad vision, stamina. In some measure, old William Henry possessed all these: but undoubtedly the quality which he himself would have selected – and in his chosen walk of business life perhaps he was right – meticulous attention to punctuality and accuracy came first. It remained first until he died, at the age of seventy-three; a remarkable evidence of stamina after a life of apparently unbroken tension.

The long crisis recounted here is not merely a comment on Victorian life and beliefs: it is directly relevant to the history of the W. H. Smith business. The son inherited many of his father's qualities: the proportions in which they were mingled in his character were different. The difference was partly inherent but it was also owed, in part, to the critical years described above. In his own perceptive phrase, the 'evils' had been a long time gathering. He survived the long trial and in the process many of the transient weaknesses of adolescence were eliminated. He emerged stronger, more relaxed; his natural intelligence, good nature and wisdom asserted themselves. He had learnt enough to be capable of learning more and going further. But though he yielded to his sense of duty, the habit of looking beyond the confines of the Strand, the business, the attractions of wealth, success, family and social satisfactions – this habit never left him.

In 1865, a shade less than twenty years after he came into the business as a partner, he wrote to his favourite sister Gussie of his intention to stand for Parliament.[33] This was a natural consequence of the passionate interest in social and educational reform and public philanthropy which he had maintained throughout his years as head of the W. H. Smith business. They can probably be traced back to his schooldays at Tavistock and a half-holiday visit with the Rev. Dr Beal to the Tavistock workhouse – his first recorded demonstration of interest in social problems: he was then in his fourteenth year.

The spiritual crisis which he experienced from then onwards until 1846 was not simply a crisis typical of adolescent psychology. His aspirations to join the priesthood were abandoned after a long mental struggle between personal desires and a sense of filial piety: but he never forgot them. They were diverted and sublimated through other channels – especially social reform and political service. Thus while he was to remain the titular (and actual) head of an expanding personal and family business – an interest always meticulously declared – his service in Parliament and the Cabinet was to make it necessary to leave the daily management of W. H. Smith & Son to others.

The firm was to become in effect an early and in many ways unique example of a business that remained strictly private yet professionally managed. In a sense, its most famous head, and one of the most celebrated of great Victorian business men, was a reluctant entrepreneur. It was, however, characteristic of him that even when, from filial piety, he felt duty bound to yield to his father's will, he applied his natural habit of thoroughness to his business tasks as to all his other duties.

The story of William Henry II's public career has been told twice: in Sir Herbert Maxwell's biography published in 1893, very soon after his death in 1891: more recently by Viscount Chilston in his *W. H. Smith* (1965).[34] The latter work, a balanced picture of its subject and his political background, career and achievements makes it unnecessary for the historian of the W. H. Smith business to do more than explore and refer to its author's researches and conclusions: enough for the moment to say that though William Henry Smith was, after 1874, much more often absent than present in the business he still owned, his influence lived on in those to whom with complete confidence he entrusted the management of its affairs.

V

Building the Bookstall Empire,
1848-75

... you recognize that if the English are immensely distinct from other people, they are also, socially, ... extremely distinct from each other. You may see them all together, with the rich coloring of their differences, in the fine flare of one of Mr. W. H. Smith's bookstalls – a feature not to be omitted in any enumeration of the charms of Paddington and Euston. It is a focus of warmth and light in the vast smoky cavern; it gives the idea that literature is a thing of splendor, of a dazzling essence, of infinite gas-lit red and gold. A glamour hangs over the glittering booth, and a tantalizing air of clever new things.

Henry James, 'Essay on London'[1]

... Railway Travellers include ... every individual of rank, property, or influence in the three kingdoms ... the number of passengers ... in the year 1850, exceeded *Sixty Millions* ... these immense numbers – the possessors of the aggregate wealth of the country – are concentrated, day by day, at the Railway Stations; and the circumstances of every journey are such, that either on the departure or arrival, or in the course of transit, every passenger must of necessity become acquainted with the announcements which will present themselves to his notice.

... no other mode of Advertising presents so favourable a means of reaching that class which the Advertiser desires most to attract ...

W. H. Smith & Son, Printed letter, c. 1851[2]

Mid-Victorian Transformation

Economic and social history is short of exact dates that really matter. The years 1066, 1688, 1789, 1848, 1914 . . . are landmarks for political history: but economic and social history flows endlessly, and the experts still argue endlessly over where its major trends begin, where they end, even whether they exist. An exception to prove this rule might be 1851. The Great Exhibition seemed to symbolise, as nothing else did, the confluence of all the forces that were changing economy and society in England but previously only partially and disparately: steam power, transport, technology, railways, population growth, manufactures, the spirit of enterprise, political reform and improvement, the emergence of an economically unified state. The year 1851 was half way between the first great Reform Bill and the second. It started a quarter century of unprecedented railway construction and continuous economic progress.

For W. H. Smith's it was the year of the first of those stirrings which were to transform the world of newspapers and popular reading and ultimately to level up provincial England with the metropolis; to give the *Manchester Guardian* and *Birmingham Post* their chance against *The Times* and *Chronicle*: to create five times as many provincial papers by 1887 as there were half a century earlier.

As men of the world settled down in Parliament, their London clubs, town houses and country mansions to read what the pundits thought of Cobden's Committee against the newspaper stamp and the news of the latest railway building they could also read the news, if they were any longer interested, of the death of James McAdam, son of his great father who had inherited some of his ability and some of his jobs. By 1852 his income was much diminished; the McAdams and their roads were overshadowed (as McAdam's latest biographer has remarked) 'by an advancing railway locomotive'.[3]

It was not only geographically and politically, but economically and socially, that unification proceeded. In the 1850s the cogs, wheels and shafts of the economy all slid into place. Distance, the technical problems obstructing industrial growth, the social remains of feudalism itself faded away. 'I rejoice to see it' (cried Dr Arnold ecstatically of the railway train, 'and think that feudality is gone for ever.'[4] Such was the mood of the age, and William Henry II shared it to the full. Ingenious historians have recently argued that the contribution of railways to economic development in history has been exaggerated. Canals could have been a substitute? Perhaps: but certainly not for the needs of the Smith business.

However much he may have differed from his father about his future, William Henry had imbibed the basic truths and needs of the family business: speed, accuracy, reliability. The day-coach had bettered the mail-coach; the railway bettered the day-coach and the road. The first use of the railway by Smith's was therefore to improve their system of distributing the London papers to the provinces. But, as we shall see, the railway, railway passenger travel and railway stations offered other, and ultimately wider and more important, openings for enterprise.

The purpose which inventors and promoters had in mind for the locomotive engine was to carry goods, just as its predecessors, the horse-drawn railways, had carried coal and iron. It was to do the same job but at double the speed (of 9 or 10 miles an hour) achieved by a fast coach. By 1831 these hopes had been surpassed: the steam locomotive was running at 25 to 30 m.p.h.: by 1850, at 50 m.p.h. or more. For more than half a century after that the gain in average speeds was relatively small. Progress was first and foremost in the sheer growth of the track system – most rapid in the period of William Henry II's accession to the management of his firm's affairs (1846–74): the railway mileage to which he strove to gain access grew as shown in Table V.I.

TABLE V.I GROWTH OF RAILWAY TRACK

Year	Miles of track
1840	1,331
1850	6,635
1860	10,410
1870	15,310

Thereafter construction and improvement continued, but at a diminishing rate, until 1900 and after.

The other twist to railway development was that the fears of the early days that the new system would never be able to move passengers safely at its much higher speeds were proved false. Railway projectors after 1830 changed their minds; they thought mainly in terms of profits from passenger traffic rather than from freight. But in the industrial England of the north, freight was always important; and in 1852 the rapidity of industrial progress was reflected in railway economics when, for the first time, freight receipts were larger than passenger receipts on the railways of England and Wales.

Railways, for freight or passengers, opened up multiple opportunities for Smith's. Against the doubts and criticisms of his father – watchful as ever for rash expenditure – William Henry II vigorously probed the whole expanding transport system. Fast trains meant faster and more reliable deliveries of the London papers in the great provincial cities. As the railway network crept outwards in the 1850s and 1860s – beyond the midlands to the north and Scotland, westwards to Wales, south-west to Bristol, Taunton, Exeter, south to Dover and Brighton, rather more slowly into East Anglia – William Henry II kept pace with deliveries of papers and journals by his express carts to the growing London rail termini. The 1840s saw newspaper distribution revolutionised by rail.

Yet it was not only speed and punctuality that was improved by the technical superiority of rail to road: the whole character of Smith's business was transformed as the organisation and physical structure of the railway system was adapted to the demands of its passenger services. For these services, railways needed railway stations. Stations needed booking halls, waiting rooms, refreshment buffets. Passenger trains drew specially designed passenger carriages, designed to match contemporary economic facts and contemporary social expectations about the different levels of comfort different kinds of passenger could afford, or were entitled to.

Business men were the first to be catered for – in the first class. More slowly, railway companies recognised the existence of persons who might suitably be carried in second class and in 1844 Parliament ordered every company to run at least one third class train a day at a charge of a penny a mile. First-class passengers and, by 1850, those in the second class were provided with the luxury of closed carriages fitted with glass windows. The third-class passengers sat in the open air to face wind, rain and storm – worse still, the hazards and torments of smoke-filled tunnels. *Punch* of 1846 published its own *Rules for Railways*: 'No third-class carriage is to contain more than a foot deep of water in wet weather, but, to prevent accidents, corks and swimming belts should always be kept in open carriages.'⁵

Much of the rest of the history of Smith's, into the twentieth century, is concerned with the economic consequences of rail travel and travellers. The conditions of coach travel had made reading virtually impossible for travellers except while waiting at inns where newspapers and journals were occasionally provided. Now – for first- and second-class passengers (at least in daytime and later by night too) – reading was not only possible: it was almost indispensable to the business man and the educated traveller. For the one, time was money: hours of travel could be profitably spent bringing the traveller up to date with the latest news of markets, commodities, prices, the Funds etc. etc. For the other a newspaper, the *Illustrated London News*, *Punch*, the *Quarterly Review* or a novel, bought or borrowed, whiled away the tedium of a long journey. For the young, an improving book, even if it failed of its highest purpose, at least kept the victim quiet and gave Mama a rest from enquiries. So the demand for reading and its provision went ahead.

In addition, inside and outside the carriages, in waiting room and booking hall, and on station walls or on hoardings erected along the approaches to railway stations, advertisements multiplied like mushrooms: wide-eyed, fascinated, or unimpressed, travellers gazed at W. H. Smith's panels and posters which decade by decade celebrated the claims, merits or powers of Rowntree's Cocoa, Reckitt's Blue, Mazawattee Tea, Pears or Sunlight Soap, Bovril, cures for anaemia, coughs, constipation, indigestion, and other physical and nervous weaknesses, to say nothing of the miraculous healing powers available to visitors at Skegness or Buxton, and notices of meetings, concerts, games, theatres and other entertainments.

Starting with Euston and continuing with Paddington, St Pancras, Marylebone, King's Cross and Liverpool Street, the great London termini offered the largest concourses of passengers and the most profitable opportunities for the concentrated sale of papers and journals. To these William Henry swiftly added books and the display of advertisements. Increasingly, from the mid-century, the Smith business ceased to be simply the distribution of London papers to the provinces and began its long and steady diversification into a number of those services for the reader-traveller all over the British Isles with which its name was to be principally associated in the public mind until the period following the Second World War.

'A Railway There, A Tunnel Here, Mix me this Zone with That'[6]

In the 1830s and 1840s William Henry I looked on, a little sceptical, while the railway n⸱ ⸱⸱rk grew. After the early swallows (the Stockton & Darlington, Liverpool & Manchester, Bodmin & Wadebridge, Festiniog, etc.) there was a pause while the world waited. Would summer follow? Or not? Opinion swayed to and fro between the optimists and the pessimists. The first bathed their imaginations in a sunlit future unsullied by the evils of aristocratic privilege, landed feudalism and political tyranny: corruption would be banished and the fruits of prosperity would be enjoyed by all. The second were gloomy. They included that prudent Scot, J. R. McCulloch, the distinguished economist. McCulloch saw no future for railways: their prospects 'had been much exaggerated'. William Henry I inclined towards McCulloch.[7]

The first tonic for the optimists came from the London and Birmingham Railway, soon to link up with the Grand Junction and thereby with industrial Lancashire and Liverpool to become the solid centre of the British railway system under the title of the London and North Western. The LNW's abiding symbol was the Hardwick Gateway at Euston, a noble public monument, and later the Great Station Hall. It stood outside the apparently hopeless chaos and cut-throat railway competition that culminated in the 'railway mania' of 1846, and outside George Hudson's railway empire. Whatever Hudson's faults and failings as a great promoter of railway companies he was the one railway politician who had grasped the need for amalgamations. His greatest achievement was the other great main line, the Midland. The Midland was centred on Derby but later its romantic towers were to arise in noble neo-Gothic at St Pancras. For its vast hotel Sir Gilbert Scott retrieved (or so it was alleged) from a forgotten file a design for a new Foreign Office in Whitehall, rejected – happily for Whitehall – for that purpose. Also outside Hudson's empire and adjoining St Pancras was the Great Northern, begun in 1846; King's Cross, its London terminus, boasted, until 1888, what was claimed to be the largest wooden roof in the world, copied from that of the Czar's riding stables. By 1852 the major phase of main-line construction was complete: it only remained in the next years to amalgamate most of the lines north of Leeds and Selby into the North Eastern Railway, and the East Anglian lines into the Great Eastern.

All this was watched by William Henry II with keen interest. Even before he became his father's partner in 1846, his imagination was stirred by the possibilities offered by railways to the family firm, and by the varied characteristics of the different railways which either endeared them to the public or did the opposite. The Midland was famous for its sense of business enterprise. It was the first to see the economic importance of the humble third-class passenger. To the indignation of its rivals it pursued him with a zeal even exceeding that recommended by Gladstone, compelling them to follow suit. In doing so the Great Eastern too was not only to become 'the poor man's line' but to succeed in putting behind it the ridicule that *Punch* (and thousands of frustrated passengers) had heaped on it in earlier days for its unpunctuality and inefficiency.

By contrast the Great Western came to be thought of as the rich man's line – and 'high-class passengers' meant a corollary of high class stations with high class hotels and high class amenities. The broad-gauge line (claimed by Brunel and his disciples to provide greater comfort and safety) and the miracle of the Severn Tunnel for long maintained the same profile of technical originality and distinction.

The Great Northern, with long distances to go and fewer stops, went all out for speed, breaking record after record with its famous expresses to Doncaster, York and Edinburgh.

This was the core of the railway system which impressed young William Henry II as much as it raised doubts for his father. It expanded, reached its climacteric, stabilised, slowed down and eventually stagnated. The rail competition of the 1840s and 1850s was the sign of youthful vigour and optimism. The third quarter of the century witnessed a very different kind of competition: a game of desperation as costs went up and profits down. The late nineteenth and early twentieth centuries were to be a time of railway conferences, joint committees, collaboration and collusion. The opportunities that Smith's seized in the 1850s were to turn into very tricky conundrums by the 1890s. Only the continuing growth of London offered real openings: underground. The first experimental Metropolitan Line was to open in 1863, from Paddington to Farringdon. Uneasy partnership with the District Line brought the Inner Circle into being twenty-one years later. But their 'tunnels' were all shallow, only a little under the ground. By 1890, twenty years of research produced the first deep tunnel, the City and South London, and this was to be the parent of later 'tubes' still with us: the Piccadilly, Central and Bakerloo. Travel by Londoners grew four-fold between 1864 and 1884. By 1913 the underground railways carried a record total of 426 million passengers. All this was to be the vital backdrop to the growth and vicissitudes of W. H. Smith & Son.

The impact of the new transport system on Smith's business was twofold and it came in two stages. The first involved simply the substitution of a much more rapid and much more systematic mode of distribution of papers, periodicals and magazines from London to the main provincial cities, especially Birmingham, Manchester and Liverpool. As early as 1838 an application by Mr Smith (presumably William Henry I) to the London and Birmingham Railway for specially favourable rates for the carriage of newspapers to Birmingham, sent that company post-haste to find out from the Grand Junction what was *their* policy towards Smith's transport from Birmingham to Liverpool. Out of these consultations emerged a proposal 'to assimilate' newspaper parcel rates between the two companies, 'short parcels [to] be only charged 6d each by either Co. which would secure to us the W'hampton [Wolverhampton], Stafford, & New-castle Parcels, otherwise entirely lost to us.'[8] This was life-line traffic for Smith's. Negotiations went on intermittently for many years.

Meanwhile, at the London end, Smith's red carts, which speeded the papers from their printing houses or the Smith headquarters in the Strand to the rail head, were already a familiar sight at the new Euston terminus. Connecting Printing House Square or Fleet Street with the train was already a problem – a tribute to the strict punctuality which was already the sternest rule on the new railways. In January 1844 William Henry II (signing on behalf of his father) sent a sharpish complaint to the Euston traffic manager. '. . . I have to inform you that the Daily Morning Papers of Thursday last for all the Towns served by the Birmingham Railway were delayed *three* hours . . .' His cart, he explained, had been accidentally delayed on its way to catch the 6 a.m. train. An over-assiduous clerk in the Parcels Office refused to countenance the two minutes delay necessary for the papers to catch the train so that 'the Exchanges and principal News Rooms of Liverpool, Manchester, Birmingham, Nottingham, Derby, Sheffield, Leeds, Coventry and other Large Towns were wholly without their papers at the usual hour . . . in case of a failure of my parcels, not one individual but many thousands are sorely disappointed and injured.'

The injuries to thousands of newspaper readers did not impress the officials of the London and Birmingham: they were concerned with punctuality for their passengers and the *amour propre* of at least one of them was affronted. He endorsed William Henry I's letter of protest with comment as brusque as Smith's was peremptory: 'who is the writer of this letter?' he asked. When told, he wrote:

> Mr Smith, who is only a News Agent, ought not to run his Papers in the morning so close to time – the 6 o'clock Train generally has to be kept a few minutes for the morning Papers and Mr Smith's lot is usually the last. It is essential that we should be punctual with this Train, it being in connection both with the Yorkshire and Lancashire Trains, the former taking Passengers to Newcastle . . . the latter to beyond Lancaster . . . he [Mr Smith] deserves no great consideration from the Company and he should be charged the usual rate of *8 shillings* a mile for a Special Engine on requiring one when other Agents have been in time to save the Train.[9]

If William Henry II (whose complaint was probably the voice of Jacob and the hand of Esau) had pursued the quarrel he could have explained that his problem was *The Times*, which regularly and notoriously delayed publication in order to include the political news up to the last minute: a severe embarrassment to its distributors, especially Smith's. But William Henry II was not his father: honey caught more flies than vinegar in dealing with the railway companies as with the rest of mankind. On great Parliamentary occasions especially he needed a 'special' to ensure that all Britain outside the metropolis received the swiftest news of proceedings. Thus, to the superintendent of locomotives at Euston at 3 p.m., Thursday, 1 February 1844, went a polite but urgent request. 'Sir, I am anxious to obtain a Special Engine either to precede or to follow tomorrow's 6 a.m. train' (the lesson had been learnt) 'with all the Morning Newspapers containing the Debate on the Address.'[10] All charges would be met: all regulations observed. Might he have a reply by the bearer in order to complete all his arrangements? He had his reply and his engine.

As William Henry II tightened relations with the railways, especially with what soon became the LNW lines to the industrial midlands and north west, the British railways became more and more familiar territory to him: he became a correspondingly more familiar figure to them and their managers. It was the railway managers, a band of men dedicated to the needs and discipline of the railway service, often ex-army or navy officers, who welded together the original creations of the engineers – the Stephensons, Brunels etc. – into a relatively compact transport system. A certain corporate sense slowly replaced the bitter rivalries of the early days as amalgamations brought some sort of collective order out of the early furies of competition. Among them was the able if equivocal Captain Mark Huish (late Bengal Native Infantry), manager first of the Grand Junction, pioneer of the LNW amalgamation, manager at Euston, later general manager of the line and for years the leading exponent of roving rail diplomacy. Variously described as 'able', 'resourceful', 'mysterious', 'deplorable', and 'monopolistic ogre', he finally resigned over a row with the Warrington and Chester line in 1858: but during his reign over the LNWR he was a friend and neighbour (at Kilburn) of the Smiths and appears fairly regularly in the Smith history. His spectacular aspects have been much commented. Only comparatively recently have his serious contributions to the improved administration and financial arrangements of his railway company been adequately recognised.[11]

Was Huish behind the extraordinary and somewhat out-of-character enterprises of young William Henry II in 1847 and 1848? On the first of these (November 1847) William Henry II chartered an express train to take a large consignment of newspapers from London to Beattock in

Dumfriesshire, then the most northerly point to which the railway connections from the south had reached. The trip involved three separate lines: the London and North Western, the Lancashire and Carlisle, and the Caledonian. The express left Euston at 5.30 a.m., reached Manchester at 10 a.m., Liverpool at 10.30 a.m., Carlisle at 1.6 p.m., Beattock at 2.5 p.m. Engines were changed at Rugby, Warrington, Preston and Carlisle: there were stops for water at Tring, Wolverton, Tamworth, Stafford, Crewe, Wigan, Lancaster and Kendal. The manager of the L. and C. (Mr Worthington) drove the train over his company's part of the track. From Carlisle to Beattock the chief engineer to the Caledonian took charge. The remaining part of the journey to Glasgow had to be done by post-horse and at 8 p.m. the newspapers were handed in by William Henry at the Glasgow coach terminus.

On 19 February of the following year another remarkable operation was mounted. Once again the target was Glasgow: the event was a speech on 18 February by Lord John Russell's Chancellor of the Exchequer, Sir Charles Wood, which was to decide whether income tax would or would not be increased from 7d. in the £ to meet the increased military budget. This time the papers used the Euston to Rugby line once more for the first stage of the journey north. Then the express turned north-north-east to Leicester and up via Derby and Normanton to York; so to Newcastle, then along the east coast route to Berwick and Edinburgh, and so to Glasgow where the merchant community was anxiously waiting for news of the Budget. (Wood did raise income tax but by 28 February caved in to widespread hostile criticism: the tax stayed at 7d.) The whole journey from Euston to Glasgow – 472 miles – took 10 hours 22 minutes (running time 9 hours 37 minutes) at an average speed of 49 m.p.h. This was remarkably fast: the record time for the short stretch from Derby to Normanton was only 7 m.p.h. faster.

Thus and thus did Smith's in the early railway age maintain the reputation William Henry I had boasted in coaching days of being 'first with the news'. The railway train, ordinary and special, was now harnessed firmly to W. H. Smith as a prime adjunct to much more speedy delivery by a kind of partnership between William Henry II and Mark Huish. Was it Huish or Smith who was the more anxious to make the pace? For all railway managers the 1840s and 1850s were a testing time in competitive speeds, and breaking records an almost daily phenomenon. The Grand Junction (from which Huish had recently graduated) was 'a line more famed for dividends than for speed'.[12]

The London & Birmingham (to which he moved) was likewise bottom but one of a comparative table of average train speeds read before the Statistical Society in 1843.[13] If, therefore, Huish was, as seems likely, anxious to acquire a reputation for better speeds on the LNW by 1847–8, William Henry II was no less anxious to be intimately associated with his initiative, to be known to the railway companies, and in turn to know them better. For railways offered not only the opportunity to carry newspapers at three or four times the speed and a fraction of the cost of a coach: they also offered him the opportunity to make a unique personal contribution to the expansion of a business still dominated by his father, whose whole philosophy of newspaper distribution had been moulded in the age of coaching.

What was to prove even more important was that every contact with the rapidly growing railway system, its managers and policies, convinced him that, quite apart from their improvements in speed, cost and punctuality, the railways must also offer a positive opportunity to expand the W. H. Smith business in entirely new directions through sales, not only of newspapers but a variety of other goods and services to railway passengers. William Henry was a *mechanophilus*, but he was not only a lover of what Tennyson in his *Ode* was to call 'wheel and enginery'.[14] His imagination stretched much further than that; and it fastened on the railway station as well as on trains. He was well aware that the figures for 1850 showed that more than 60 million passengers travelled over 40 million miles over 6,635 miles of track. All had to pass through two or more stations for each journey made.

The railway stations that spread over England from the 1830s were not just places where trains stopped or started. They swiftly became centres of amenity and social intercourse. The railway companies acquired hotels and refreshment rooms, built hospitals, churches, schools and houses – almost entire towns – where they owned manufacturing and repair sheds, marshalling yards, etc., such as Derby, Crewe, Doncaster and Wolverton. In the end, they became, collectively, the largest property owner of all. It might be said they provided everything, except newspaper and bookstalls. These came to be provided, in stages, by W. H. Smith.[15]

Broadly speaking, railway stations interested Smith's in proportion to their size. The great termini of the great cities provided, obviously, the best markets and therefore cost Smith's the highest rents. Conversely, there were village stations – like Elsham, Appleby and Frodingham on the Trent, Ancholme and Grimsby Railway in the bare windswept plains of north

Lincolnshire – where the rail proprietors were anxious to see Smith's involved but where the volume of passenger traffic of a sparsely populated countryside could not possibly support the relatively heavy costs of maintaining a bookstall and the necessary staff. Against such considerations Smith's themselves had to weigh others: for as railway co-operation and amalgamation grew relentlessly, the railway world shrank and even a small railway might be able to bring diplomatic and economic pressure to bear through discriminatory action by their larger friends via other, larger and profitable contracts for station bookstalls on the main lines. Nor were Smith's without a conscience about their public duties and reputation. Thus against immediate profit or, more likely, loss in such cases had to be balanced other less immediate economic considerations and some non-economic considerations.

Later in the 1850s William Henry II made some notes on the rents payable to the different railway companies for bookstalls or advertising or both from 1851 onwards. They showed roughly the order of profitability of the different lines (see Table V.2).

TABLE V.2 RENTS PAYABLE TO THE RAILWAY COMPANIES[16]

Company	Rental £ p.a.	Dates
1 London & North Western	3,500–4,200	1852–8
2 Great Northern	1,100–1,300	1851–4
3 London & South Western	850–1,400	1851–6
4 Midland (advertising only)	800–1,000	1851–4
5 Eastern Counties	600–1,050	1851–4
6 South Eastern	600– 700	1852–9
7 Lancashire & Yorkshire	600– 650	1851–5
8 London, Brighton & South Coast	300	1852–7
9 Manchester, Sheffield & Lincolnshire	200	1852–9
10 Chester Station	100	1852–6
11 North Staffs	80– 100	1851–4
12 North British	60	1851–6
13 Southampton Docks	10	1851–6

Even in 1848, Smith's had bought the exclusive right to sell to passengers along over 1,000 miles of track and the distance was increasing rapidly month by month. By the 1860s they would have bookstalls on all the main and many secondary lines. A journalist writing on 'Our Modern Mercury' in the magazine *Once A Week* for 1861, claimed that every railway except the Great Western was 'in literary possession of Mr. W. H. Smith.'[17] And there were major warehouses at Birmingham (1857), Manchester (1859), Liverpool (1868), and branches at Dublin (1850) and later Belfast (1870).

None of the expansion and proliferation of the railway network of Britain and, with it, the spread and growth of W. H. Smith's business, affected the general order of priorities established in 1851: the bookstall business (and, as we shall see, advertising business too) with the Great Northern, the London & South Western, the Midland, the South Eastern, the London, Brighton & South Coast, the Lancashire & Yorkshire, the Manchester, Sheffield & Lincolnshire, the North Staffs – all these showed increases in Smith's business gratifying to Smith's and (in spite of some grouses and protests) to the railways concerned.

To the early 1850s' list of agencies was to be added a greater number of new contracts in the 1850s and 1860s. The largest was the Great Western (gross rental £5,500) but some sixteen smaller contracts swelled the total volume by some £1,100–£1,200 a year.[18] All in all the years 1852 to 1867, the period of most rapid expansion of the railway network, saw the cost of Smith's outlay in bookstall and advertising rents increase more than threefold – from about £10,000 a year to about £34,000.[19]

Besides the cost of renting the right to bookstalls, William Henry II faced a proportionately much steeper rise in the cost of renting advertising space for re-sale to traders and manufacturers. Before 1861, 'advertising' had meant advertising within railway carriages (remembering that many carriages as yet were open to the weather). The Great Exhibition had given a brisk fillip to station advertising to which William Henry II, with his usual sense of business opportunity, lent his best efforts: but potential advertisers were sluggish and conservative. It was some time before profits caught up with the necessary and considerable investment laid out on 'frames', design work, printing and labour. Together, bookstalls and advertisement nevertheless provided a prophetic glimpse of the future, and permanent, character of the W. H. Smith business – essentially the provision of services rather than the manufacture of goods.

To this extent the business, increasingly under the direction of young William Henry II, followed on the lines meticulously defined by William Henry I: the ever-wider and swifter distribution of daily newspapers, journals, periodicals, magazines, reviews and so on (see pages 67–74). The growth of the business and the technological changes that underpinned it, far from changing the ethos and methods of the old business, only served to reinforce the need for minute attention to detail, punctuality and fair dealing. The problems of management in such a business became not only technically but humanly more complex. And it could be argued that the business, now with turnover rising into hundreds of thousands of pounds, was still built on farthings.

The precise origins of the railway bookstall are not entirely clear. William Vincent, an employee of Smith's who spent his working life on bookstalls and much later wrote his reminiscences in retirement,[20] thought the first railway bookstall was opened at Fenchurch Street Station, not by Smith's but by Horace Marshall & Son in 1841.[21] Marshall's were newsagency contractors to the Great Western: Walkley & Son serviced the Bristol & Exeter: Sampson (of York), Morrison (of Leeds) did the same for one or more northern lines. Collings of Brighton contracted for the Great Western: so for a time did the firm of Fraser & Co. Walker & Co contracted for the old North Eastern between Stockton-on-Tees and Saltburn. Menzies in Scotland and Eason in Ireland were the principal newsagencies for these countries and continue to be so in our own day. William Henry II, for all his successes, never became a monopolist. News distribution was highly competitive. Only the highest efficiency could protect the newsagent against its fundamentally precarious nature.

The rivals were mostly reputable agents. Some were to give way to the competitive efficiency of Smith's: others were to survive. But William Henry's astonishing progress in the 1850s was at the expense of more vulnerable rivals, especially in the metropolitan termini. '... within a week', wrote Samuel Phillips witheringly in *The Times* of 9 August 1851, '[we] visited every railway terminus in this metropolis. It was a painful and a humiliating inspection ... unmitigated rubbish encumbered the bookshelves of almost every bookstall we visited, and indicated only too clearly that the hand of ignorance had been indiscriminately busy in piling up the worthless mass [of literature].' On sale was a miscellaneous collection of publications 'of the lowest possible character, and vendors equally miscellaneous and irresponsible ... without credit, without means, without education ... They bought cheaply to sell at a large profit, and the more despicable their commodities the greater their gains.'[22]

Many of the vendors were former railway employees or their widows. Sometimes they were crippled or otherwise handicapped. The privilege of vending on the stations was treated as a kind of working pension: it hardly produced a satisfactory service. Soiled newspapers were the most respectable among the heterogeneous collection of oddities they offered for sale

– gingerbeer bottles, buns and tarts, and, as a later *Times* contributor put it, 'improper literature', including 'novels which no bookseller would dare to expose for sale'.²³

This was the near-pornography of the day which was about to be replaced by popular, 'radical' newspapers such as *Lloyds Weekly* and *Reynolds News*. Their presence was brought to the attention of the Select Committee on Newspaper Stamps of 1851 where abolitionists were moved by many motives; among them the desirable end of providing cheap newspapers to compete with the fiction which upset respectable observers like Samuel Phillips (see page 62).

The Smiths, father and son, though not 'abolitionists', shared the sentiments of those who deplored 'the literary condition' of the metropolitan railway stations. It was William Henry II who took the initiative to change things. His correspondence with the London & Birmingham and London & North Western Coaching and Police Committee for the mid-1840s underwent an important change. Before 1847 it had turned largely on such questions as the costs of carrying newspapers by rail, on the old bugbear of delays to mail trains occasioned by the late arrival of parcels of *The Times*, and so on. From August 1848, it turned increasingly on the offer by Smith's to tender for the exclusive rights to sell books and periodicals on stations. Due regard was to be paid to sitting tenants. '. . . we have for some time past supplied the parties (two only excepted) who now occupy the Stands . . .'²⁴ They would endeavour to employ them if the Smith offer was accepted. The following month the tender was accepted by the railway at a yearly rent of £1,500. W. H. Smith were to have 'the privilege of selling Newspapers etc. at all the Railway Stations now under the sole control' of the LNWR.²⁵ They were to provide a scale of their maximum charges for newspapers and any failure to provide the promised service on any station would give the railway the right to re-let their privileges on that station to another agent.

By 1849 the relationship had taken definite and detailed shape. When William Henry II wrote a 'Mem: of Privileges conceded by the L & NW Railway Company', it included the free carriage of library books (for WHS's station libraries), free 'Returns' of unsold books and papers from the outlying stations to London, special half rates for carriage of books, and a free pass for the use of 'Self and Servants whenever necessary for Station business.'²⁶ The stations to be served from Euston were Watford, Wolverton, Bedford, Northampton, Rugby, Tamworth, Stafford, Coventry, Birmingham, Crewe, Warrington, Liverpool and Manchester.²⁷ Thus the transport pattern of the old coaching days showed plainly through this first formal rail contract by which William Henry II ceased to be simply a wholesale distributor and became also his own retailer.

The remote and humble cause of what was to prove a momentous event in the Smith history is clearly indicated in the railway records. On 19 August 1846, it was ordered that one Samuel Mayhew, a newsvendor, 'be severely reprimanded for his misconduct, and his sale of books on the Euston plat-form confined to Railway Maps & Guides.'[28] Later that year the super-intendent was 'instructed to authorise the sale of *proper* books . . . as heretofore'.[29] Samuel had evidently been purveying something more questionable than *Bradshaw*. Earlier in the same year an LNWR under-messenger, by name Gibbs, had been given permission to sell newspapers at Euston 'in the room of Locock deceased'.[30] The appointment was only 'during pleasure' and Gibbs was to contribute from his profits to the Railway Friendly Society.[31]

Were Mayhew and Gibbs the two exceptional newsvendors who were *not* supplied by William Henry? We do not know: all we know is that Mayhew was among those members of his trade who hardly improved its reputation. To judge from the events of 1849, Gibbs was also another of the fraternity upon whose veracity and honesty it was not difficult to improve. For on 18 December 1849, Mr Justice Erle heard the case of Gibbs v. LNWR at Guildhall.

Gibbs, as plaintiff, claimed the stall and access to it, alleging that the defendants had denied him such access and taken his books. Counsel agreed that Gibbs had been given an order to quit in September 1848 (to make way for W. H. Smith) but had refused to go. '. . . on the 1st of November the plaintiff was removed from the platform, and the men of Messrs Smith, the eminent newspaper vendors in the Strand, were put in his place.'

Father Gibbs filled in with much detail the story of the expulsion from what was clearly a veritable little paradise: his son's net profits, the father revealed incautiously, totalled the very large sum of £1,021. 18s. 8½d. for 10 months. His annual rent was £60.

Gibbs, naturally anxious to recover the valuable privileges so rudely snatched from his grasp, searched desperately for some evidence to dis-credit the LNWR. The scapegoat he ingeniously chose was none other than the redoubtable, but hardly popular, Captain Huish. Upon becoming general manager of the LNWR, the plaintiff's counsel declared, Huish had discovered, unhappily for the innocent and diligent Gibbs, that his news-paper sales had become 'very profitable in consequence of the great industry of the plaintiff'; so much was true. But then Gibbs committed a major blunder. Huish, because of Gibbs's success, put out to tender the whole newspaper business at Euston and gave the contract to Smith's. 'Between Mr Smith . . . and Captain Huish there was some family connexion, and the plaintiff [Gibbs] was removed from the station.' Gibbs therefore claimed damages for the loss of the business created by his industry.[32]

The allegation of a family connection was a fabrication and easily shown to be such. Gibbs lost his suit on the simple ground that he possessed no evidence to support it. But given that there was an existing business relationship his story was just plausible enough to have left a nasty taste behind it. Two days later therefore, on 20 December 1849, W. H. Smith & Son, in a letter to *The Times*, firmly denied Gibbs's story. 'This statement of the plaintiff [of a family connection] is utterly without foundation.' When public notice of a tender was issued 'we made, we believe, the highest offer, and it was accordingly accepted by the Board [of the LNWR].'[33]

Gibbs disposed of, the new partnership became active and the cleaning up proceeded briskly. 'As we progressed north [through the metropolis]', *The Times* correspondent continued, 'a wholesome change, we rejoice to say, became visible in railway bookstalls . . . At the North-Western terminus [Euston] we diligently searched for that which required but little looking after in other places, but we poked in vain for the trash. If it had ever been there [it had] the broom had been before us and swept it clean away.' But not, it has to be admitted, at one fell swoop. Those 'young men . . . educated as booksellers', who returned such polite, intelligent and well-informed answers to the correspondent's queries, had an uphill and discouraging task at first. Deplorable as it might seem, it was revealed that 'persons who apparently would be ashamed to be found reading certain works at home, have asked for publications of the worst character at the railway book-stall, and, being unable to obtain them, in evident annoyance have suddenly disappeared.' It was to be feared the market for underground literature persisted (much as it does in the 1980s, allowing for the differences in what are regarded as moral standards).

Yet the campaign of the 'North Western Missionary' – as William Henry II came to be called – was highly effective. Persuaded by the great Macaulay himself, Longman's introduced a cheap and popular series called the 'Travellers' Library'. The traveller aspiring to culture could buy at Smith's Prescott's *Mexico*, Coleridge's *Table Talk*, George Borrow's *Gypsies*, the poems of Tennyson and Moore, the *Lays of Ancient Rome*. The Bishop of Exeter on *Baptismal Regeneration* and Baptist Noel on the Church sold like hot cakes 'while excitement on these questions lasted'.

Different people, different places, different tastes. Ladies (the regrettable truth dawned) were not usually partial to great literature. They preferred un-serious fiction like *The Female Jesuit*. At Bangor, Dissenting and Radical books in Welsh sold well (English books were well advised to be High Church and Conservative). Schoolboys bought Harrison Ainsworth 'and anything terrible'. Yorkshire didn't buy poetry and Liverpool didn't care for religion. The bookstalls between Derby, Leeds and Manchester found it 'very difficult to sell a valuable book'. Weales's drove a useful trade in their practical scientific works (at 1s. and 2s. each) to 'the mechanics, engine-drivers, and others employed upon the line'. *Warren Hastings* sold a thousand copies on publication, beating *Lord Clive* by 33 per cent. Washington Irving's works always sold well.

This early essay in market research concluded with words that would have been equally pleasing to Lord Macaulay and William Henry II:

> The Universities are exclusive, but the 'rail' knows no distinction of rank, religion, or caste. We cannot promise to instruct by steam, or to convey knowledge by express speed, but we may at least provide cheap and good books for willing purchasers, and make the most of that anxious and welcome desire for knowledge which locomotion has mainly introduced, and which cannot be gratified without adding to the happiness of the individual, and conducing to the permanent good of society.[34]

Such was the ideal of the new culture sketched, a trifle breathlessly, by *The Times* correspondent. When, in the twentieth century, the W. H. Smith 'house magazine', the *Newsbasket*, issued some potted biographies of the great personalities of the business in the past, it began with William Henry I – 'essentially a "newspaper man".'[35] The next portrait, of William Henry II, described him as a ' "bookstall" man'.[36] Had he shared the conservative character of his father, the history of the business might have been very different. But William Henry II seized upon the social, economic and technical developments which made a change of direction in the Smith business policy necessary: it was, specifically, the 'increasing length, and number, of journeys taken on the railways that gave its impetus to the sales of books'. To which might be added the growth of cities, of incomes and of publishing and printing developments. But to fulfil his plan William Henry II had to overcome 'by degrees, the resistance of the senior partner to the sale of "books".'[37]

The problem of organising the selection, buying and selling of books was entrusted in the late 1840s to Jabez Sandifer, a formidable disciplinarian but a skilful organiser with a gift for encouraging his small staff (of about 20) in the new Book Department to give their utmost efforts to the new venture – even to enjoy doing so.[38] Sandifer was to run Smith's Book Department for nearly forty years and his system survived into the twentieth century. By 1851 the 'rolling stock' of his Department was valued at £10,000 and the early resistance of a section of the customers to the idea of better books was overcome – or perhaps they went elsewhere to satisfy their less serious tastes. 'The North-Western Missionary', a contemporary journalist wrote, 'never undersells and he gives no credit. His business is a ready-money one, and he finds it his interest to maintain the dignity of literature by resolutely refusing to admit pernicious publications among his stock.'[39]

The 'moral improvement' of Smith's bookstalls gained momentum from another initiative of William Henry II: the development of cheap, so-called 'yellowback', fiction and non-fiction, books – mostly reprints specially for the bookstalls. He did not, as was sometimes thought, invent the 'yellowback', neither did he publish them himself over his firm's name: in the prickly world of authors, publishers, printers, distributors, this might have brought more problems than profits. William Henry II accordingly acquired the copyright of various popular authors – the perpetually hard-up Charles Lever, Harrison Ainsworth and others who 'partially' assigned their rights not to Smith's but to the well-known publishing house, Chapman and Hall. The series, called *The Select Library of Fiction*, appeared under their imprint. For many readers they were more associated with the name of W. H. Smith and Son, who did, in all probability, possess some legal rights over the 'yellowbacks', perhaps contained in an exchange of letters later lost.

Observers of the early railway age made much more of William Henry's purge of the railway literature; critics of the *fin-de-siècle* turned their eulogies upside down; for extremists, W. H. Smith became a synonym for stuffy puritanism, dreary, bourgeois respectability and hypocrisy (see page 367).

In truth, both praise and blame were exaggerated. Certainly William Henry II did lead the campaign to clean up the paper stands and their contents. He replaced scruffy touts and dirty papers by reputable papers, magazines and books displayed on well-designed permanent bookstalls run by trained staff. But he did not represent only himself, his own interests or his own 'moral' principles (or prejudices). His presence in the railway stations rested on the sanction of contracts with the railway companies, and their directors and managers were every bit as anxious about the reputation and respectability of their stations as William Henry. The ill-starred Mayhew and Gibbs had their counterparts on scores of the new stations that proliferated in the 1840s and 1850s. They were invariably unreliable and often dishonest; newsvending was not, by its nature and in the social conditions of the time, calculated to be 'particularly respectable'. Yet the provision of papers and books was not only a valuable amenity in the battle for passenger traffic: the carriage of newspapers was itself profitable freight business and their speedy delivery a matter of prestige to any railway company involved. Captain Mark Huish, laying before the General Road and Traffic (London) Committee (LNWR) in January 1852, proposals for 'accelerating the transmission of Newspapers to Birmingham, Liverpool and Manchester', put the point thus:

> It was important in every respect & more especially considering the coming competition of rival lines of Railway, to have the Newspapers delivered at those places at the earliest possible time and an acceleration of two hours, to two hours and a half might be effected by a change in time and the addition of a new fast train for part of the distance . . . [he] had ascertained that the delivery of papers at Euston might be accelerated a quarter of an hour: and that the proposed measure would be highly popular generally.

The Committee made haste to approve the changes 'required to effect this desirable result'.[40]

All this was a far cry from the attitudes of 1844 when Mr Smith was, for Huish's predecessors, 'only a News Agent'. Mr Smith the Newsagent was now an integral part of the LNWR business; significantly, Huish's proposals came only a month after he had presented his Committee with a new, extended contract with William Henry II (on 12 December 1851). A revised scale of bookstall rents rising to £4,200 over 7 years together with other increases (see page 113) would, reported Captain Huish with obvious satisfaction, raise 'the total receipts of the Company from these sources . . . [to] £6,100 per annum'.[41] And this, he added, was not the end of it if the Committee would allow him to negotiate further. Smith's business was a valuable asset to the LNWR.[42]

Given the growing size of the mutual commitment, these new arrangements came to be formulated in contracts which were to grow month by month, year by year, more detailed and explicit: but the clauses about the nature of the literature Smith's were licensed to sell and the advertisements they were allowed to exhibit varied very little from company to company. A standard LNWR clause provided that Smith's were not to sell indecent or immoral books, etc., or publish any book or advertisement 'of an indecent immoral or seditious character or relating to medicines for complaints or ailments of an indecent or indelicate nature'.[43] If they were to do so, the railway company was at liberty to remove the offending articles and prohibit their sale. Advertising 'dubious' medicines was a notorious problem. In these years more than half the patent medicines advertised in a popular, pseudo-radical Sunday paper like *Reynolds News* were of a type described by a Select Committee on the subject (1910–12) as 'disreputable': for example, for the 'removal of female obstructions', 'spermatorrhea', etc. The railways were also for a long time deadly opposed to the exhibition of any publicity in favour of the activities of trade unions, such as also appeared in *Lloyds Weekly* and *Reynolds News*. The Smith contract therefore prohibited advertisements 'of any Society or body of Workmen in combination against their Employers . . .'[44] Contracts with the Lancashire and Yorkshire Railway, the Midland, the Manchester, Sheffield and Lincolnshire railways and all the others were drawn with similar provisions, inserted at the insistence not of Smith's but of the railway companies.

The 'morality' of the 'North Western Missionary' (or 'Old Morality' as *Punch* was to dub him) was as much – or more – that of the London and North Western Railway as it was of William Henry II. He was, in fact, neither prude nor prig: he was personally kindly, open-minded and understanding by the standards of middle-class Victorian England. His religious aspirations, though frustrated, were still the springs of his spirit. Whenever he could he made time for social work; whether it was the management and finances of King's College Hospital, or the London School Board, or some other educational enterprise of his friend W. E. Forster, they inspired his sense of the need to serve his fellow-men. Just before the Franco–German War, in 1870, he visited Paris to inform himself of the state of the poor of Paris and how the French tackled the problems of poverty in a great city. Although a Low Church Protestant of Dissenting stock, with some traditional suspicion of the Roman Church, he was irresistibly impressed by the work of the Sisters of Charity. The care taken of the children by the Sisters touched his heart. The whole working of the system depended on them. 'I am afraid it could not be carried out at all without them.' At the Dépôt de Mendicité, he was deeply moved by the human misery he found there . . . 'enough to make one sad, especially as it was of the hopeless kind springing from past errors, infirmity or incompetence of some kind or other in most cases . . .'[45] His letters from Paris breathe compassion: they put to shame the unworthy gibes and sneers of later ages: for William Henry II was consistent in his ethical stance – as social reformer, employer, trader. His religious views, his social outlook, his moral ideas, his handling of his own material interests – were all of a piece. He was a middle-class man and he was not ashamed of his creed or status: he was neither 'progressive' politically or socially (he began as a Liberal and ended as a Conservative), nor prophetic. He did not reach forward to the permissive or the welfare state of society (in its modern form). Rightly or wrongly he believed, quite simply, that England would be a better place if more of its people were better educated, read more good books and less pornography, were employed usefully rather than un-employed and unskilled. He believed his business performed a valuable function in these respects and felt a deep sense of responsibility toward his workers and their service to society and themselves. His objection to Sunday work derived as much from his concern that his people should have one incontrovertible day of rest as it did from Sabbatarianism. Because few people, even among historians, take the trouble to contem-plate the fearful social evils which led reasonable, observant men to sub-scribe to their intolerance, such movements as teetotalism, Sabbatarianism, apparent shibboleths in matters of gambling, sex, extra-marital relation-ships or belief in the doctrine of work, have become the music hall jokes of history. William Henry II was broad-minded and compassionate: but he saw no reason to disregard ostentatiously the accepted moral codes of his day and class.

Hard Bargains, Happy Endings: Smith's and the Euston Confederacy

The railway connection – bookstalls, advertising on behalf of the railway companies, advertising goods and services in railway carriages and in and around railway stations, on hoardings, walls, bridges, and so on – was the spring from which flowed the unprecedented and continuous growth of the Smith business in the third and much of the fourth quarter of the Victorian age. It was channelled through a mass of contracts, usually in pretty general terms in the early years, but steadily becoming more detailed and precise as time passed and as both sides gained experience of this novel line of business.

With a few exceptions – when irritation at some seeming injustice burst the bounds of self-control – the negotiations followed a suitably gentle-manly course. William Henry II never wore his heart on his sleeve and was usually master of his emotions even when ruffled. As he grew to manhood and his experience of business and his fellow-men deepened he became more and more the imperturbable monument of Victorian self-control which was to become famous throughout the world of business and, later, politics. He made (a contemporary close observer said) 'the most of oppor-tunities and the least of difficulties and never took a false step'.[46] The last was exaggerated: he made the occasional blunder, either, in the 1850s, under pressure from overwork or lack of help, or perhaps because (as the same observer noted) he was very sensitive to other people's feelings. 'This sometimes caused him to show indecision, or rather hesitation, and deprived him of the art of repartee.'[47]

His detachment, though it took the edge off the natural liveliness he had shown as a boy, probably helped him as a judge of men: his appointments were good and he was popular with those who worked for him and with him, both in his business and later in Whitehall and Westminster. He was extraordinarily successful as a minister in the various ministries where he held office. He was accessible and reasonable: his civil servants respected and admired him.

All these useful virtues he cultivated as he met one committee after another representing the many railway companies whose business he sought. The basic area of agreement between them and him was that the distribution and carriage of newspapers, the presence of stalls and advertis-ing posters, meant more business, more profits and more amenities for everybody. Yet there were limits. William Henry II wanted to place his stalls and advertisements where there were most customers, readers and passers-by: the railway companies wanted the same things but they often wanted them in places where passengers were too few to make it worth-while for Smith's to maintain, at the considerable costs in outlay, manage-ment and labour involved, a bookstall or a hoarding. From the beginning arguments turned on how Smith's rent should be calculated. How long should a contract last? How should the rent be calculated – three, five or seven years ahead? As traffic grew, more railway managers began to ask themselves whether the time would come – was it perhaps already here? – when the company would do better to take the news business and advertis-ing into their own hands? William Henry (and later, his partners) were well aware that their business might become precarious if any slackening of punctuality or efficiency on their part were to deliver them into the company's hands – or those of one of the rival newsagents who were always waiting in the wings. Such risks were the essential spur to effort. The railway men invariably made the mistake of supposing the distribution and sale of newspapers, magazines, books (to say nothing of footwarmers, reading lamps, mufflers and other evidences of the trials of mid-Victorian travel) was a simple matter which any fool could master. The wiser ones recognised the immense expertise which such a complex business demanded: the less wise had to learn by trial and error. But usually – down to the end of the century at least – William Henry II and his partners won the day with astonishing regularity: though not without some staggering exercises in brinkmanship.

The men who faced William Henry II across the table and carried on prolonged, obstinate and complex arguments to improve their own terms and spoil his were formidable opponents. They included some of the toughest negotiators in the Victorian business world – the far from popular Captain Huish, of the Grand Junction and LNWR; James (later Sir James) Allport, reputed 'the Bismarck of Railway Politics', general manager and chairman of the Midland Railway; (Sir) Edward Watkin, chairman of the Manchester, Sheffield and Lincolnshire; Lord Chandos and Admiral Moorsom, chairmen of the LNWR; Seymour Clarke and Henry Oakley, successively managers of the Great Northern, as well as some ebullient figures from the smaller lines, like John Lewis Ricardo of the South Staffordshire who, threatened with absorption by Huish on behalf of the giant LNWR, immediately replied with an offer to buy up the LNWR.

The personalities of the railway managers varied as much as what the public came to think of as the images of the companies of which they were both the creators and the reflection. One thing they all shared in common. They were trained and tested in the tactics of the tribal warfare which broke out intermittently between the remaining survivors from the early euphoria of rail construction: this reached new peaks of ferocity in the 1850s with contests such as that between the LNWR, the Midland, the Great Northern and the Manchester, Sheffield and Lincolnshire. In this, Huish, Allport, Watkin, and Seymour Clarke were the chief protagonists. Huish, deserted finally by his ally, Allport, and by his pupil, Watkin, lost the battle to the Great Northern (Seymour Clarke). This was only one of the constant battles and skirmishes which took place in the areas of transport where the interests of the different companies overlapped. It was a tough school of diplomacy and the techniques it developed largely account for the length and obstinacy of the negotiations William Henry had to endure to reach agreements which would keep his business afloat and expanding.

Throughout these long-drawn-out contests certain patterns emerged which conditioned the investment outlay, running costs, turnover and profits of the Smith business. The bookstalls gradually gave Smith's many hundreds of retail outlets throughout most of England and much of Wales (the story in Scotland was different, see page 145).

The customers they served included many who had earlier been postal subscribers. (Postal subscribers did not disappear but their numbers diminished. Some still insisted on survival: the LNWR Road & Traffic (London) Committee in September 1854 showed a proper respect for the remains of feudal privilege when they deferred to the application from Lord Rokeby that the guard of the down morning train from Watford should be allowed to hurl out of its windows his copy of *The Times* when the train passed by his estate.[48] They only reserved the right not to be in any way responsible for its fate.) The travelling public at large asked for no more than to be able to rely on W. H. Smith's bookstall to provide a reliable supply of newspapers, journals and books: and the output of all three categories was growing fast by the late 1850s as the economy grew and the fiscal cramps on output were removed.

The bookstalls also acted as wholesalers of such literature to other newsagents in the areas within reach of the railway stations. Wholesaling had always been a function of William Henry I back in the coaching days. The increasing volume of newspapers – especially provincial papers – gave new emphasis to this facet of the distributive trade. It also added another – sometimes thorny – item to the agenda when bookstall contracts were discussed. For the wholesale part of William Henry II's bookstall trade fell outside the railway bookstall contract. The vitally important element of the cost of the carriage of newspapers was only normally covered for those papers sold on the stall. Obviously it was in Smith's interest to get all carriage rates included at the most favourable rates. The railways did not always agree. The strictness of the railway bureaucracy in dealing with what a century or more later seem trivial points is very striking. The cost of despatching a single newspaper, a privilege for William Henry II or his agent to have a free railway pass in order to oversee his railway business, the responsibility of William Henry II for the behaviour of his newspaper delivery boys on Euston Station, the prohibition of any illicit enclosures in newspaper parcels (even though invisible) – all such matters were the subject of grave, ponderous and prolonged consideration and argument by the rail directors.

The crux of the argument was, nevertheless, money: how much was a railway stall or an advertising contract worth? In the first Euston contracts of 1848 and 1851, the value and length of contract was simply determined

"The Times" Office.

The Manager of the Times begs to inform   that the Proprietors have determined that on and after the 3rd July 1854 all papers required by Mess.rs Smith & Son for distribution in the Country, shall be delivered to them by the Publisher before any other Agent is supplied.

"The Country" is understood to include all Railway Stations & to exclude London & the Metropolitan Districts as defined by the Post Office.

Mess.rs Smith & Son will distribute for the London Agents at a fair price, the Papers required by them for the service above defined.

Printing House Square,
Blackfriars.
21st June, 1854.

6 *The Times*: priority for Smith's, 1854

MODERN ADVERTISING: A RAILWAY STATION IN 1874.

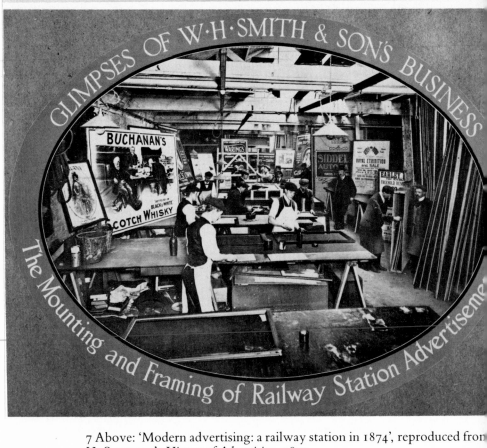

7 Above: 'Modern advertising: a railway station in 1874', reproduced from
H. Sampson's *History of Advertising*, 1874

8 Below: From the earliest days of railway advertising, the frames were
made in W.H. Smith's own Frames Department (seen here in a 1910
photograph)

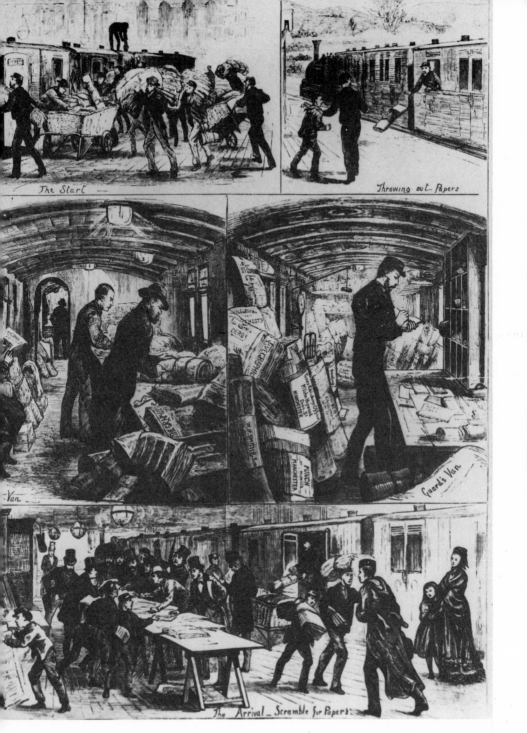

'Notes in an early newspaper train', reproduced from the *Graphic*, 15 May 1875

10 Left: W.H. Smith II, 1825-91,
grandson of the founder (portrait
by George Richmond, 1878)

11 Below: Lord Salisbury's
Conservative Cabinet, 1885.
W.H. Smith II, as Secretary for
War, is standing, third from the
right

by putting the matter out to tender. On 12 December 1851 Captain Huish reported that he had negotiated a contract for seven years with Messrs Smith. They would pay rent 'for the sale of Books and Papers & for purposes of Advertising' as shown in Table V.3.

TABLE V.3   THE 1851 7-YEAR BOOKSTALL AND ADVERTISING CONTRACT

Year	Rent £ p.a.
1st	3,500
Next 4	4,000
6th	4,100
7th	4,200

This represented 'an average annual increase . . . of £1,150 per annum . . . Mr Smith', Huish noted, 'was prepared to increase his payment if the Company would discontinue the practise [*sic*] of advertising in Carriages' (i.e. disallow rival advertising).[49] When the contract was renewed in 1859 it again covered rents for stalls and for advertising 'in proper frames' (to be previously approved by the company) on platform walls, fences and in waiting rooms and booking halls.[50] There were the usual admonitory clauses prohibiting offensive or indecent advertising (or what the directors of the LNW might think indecent), fines and penalties for any breach of covenant, however trifling. Railway discipline was as iron as the track on which its traffic moved.

In 1866, the rents were up again (see Table V.4). The extension of ten years demonstrates both the stability of the Victorian economy and a confidence in steady growth. Ten years later, 1876, there were significant changes. The term was only for five years and the rent paid a percentage of receipts subject to minimum guarantees of £10,500 to £12,000 per annum.[51] In 1886, the rent was again for ten years but at the very high fixed figure of £26,000 per annum.[52] The continuing increase in the rent William Henry II was willing to pay indicated that he, for his part, was confident of the future expansion of his business – and, in that age of industrial and commercial diversification, it was true expansion and not just inflation or monetary devaluation. Alongside the 'basics' – coal, iron, machinery, cotton, wool, silk, etc. – new products multiplied. They were mostly consumer goods, soap, chocolate, cocoa, tobacco, ready-made clothing, patent medicines, sweets – a strong mixture of hygiene, convenience and rubbish: but they all created employment, wages and profit.

So wages grew throughout industry, trade, agriculture, retail shops and offices. 'White collar' occupations multiplied while prices dropped. From the 1820s to the 1850s, the price of a 4lb. loaf in London was 8½d: then it

TABLE V.4 RENTS OVER 10 YEARS FROM 1866[53]

Year	Rent £ p.a.
1866	6,500
1867	6,700
1868	6,900
1869	7,100
1870	7,300
1871	7,500
1872	7,700
1873	7,900
1874	8,100
1875	8,300

dropped steadily until by 1887 it stood at 5½d. A 'basket of commodities of ordinary consumption' that cost 17s. 8½d. in the 1850s cost only 14s. 7d. by 1886 and was still falling in the mid-1890s.

Perhaps it was the buoyancy of a diversified economy that gave back to the directors of LNW enough courage to contemplate a future as long as ten years by 1886: lower coal prices may have cheered them up too. The 'Great Depression', as some historians have called it, had a silver lining, for some people at least. The more sophisticated 1876 method of percentage payments hedged the risk of being caught out either by uncovenanted prosperity or unexpected adversity – for both parties. The new 'covenant' initiative came, for advertising contracts, from Smith's; for bookstall contracts, from the rail companies and in some cases from Smith's. It was difficult, especially on smaller lines, to calculate fixed rents for advertising. Why not base the rent on a percentage of takings, so that the rail company would share in any benefit or loss? From the mid 1860s a 50/50 per cent sharing system was introduced. Smith's paid to the railway company half 'of the gross sums received . . . for the Exhibition of Placards at the stations', Smith's paying 'all the expenses of Canvassing, Printing, Frames, Collecting etc . . .'

In the early 1870s a similar idea was applied to the large bookstall contracts. By 1872, a formula was devised between Smith's and the Lancashire and Yorkshire Railway which combined in a single contract percentage arrangements for both bookstalls and advertising: after much haggling the percentages were fixed at 5 per cent of gross receipts for bookstalls and 50 per cent for advertising: but to safeguard the railways, Smith's agreed to guarantee a minimum payment in case business should fall so low that the percentages became unrewarding.

By 1875 these systems were in operation with the Lancashire and Yorkshire, London, Brighton and South Coast, and South Eastern companies; for advertising alone with the London and South Western, Great Eastern, Midland and LNW & Great Western joint lines. The percentage payment of rent for bookstalls at the great London termini was 10 per cent. (William Henry II resisted a claim for 10 per cent on large provincial stations, arguing – successfully and truthfully – that they cost much more to maintain in supervision, and, of course, in carriage charges.) The question whether Smith's should be liable to variations in rent according to variations in bookstall receipts or in the volume of passenger traffic remained an open one. What the percentage system did was to safeguard both parties against the worst hazards of fate. Prosperity beyond expectation would not leave the railway company that signed a long-term contract hopelessly behind. But if business sagged, Smith's liabilities were limited: provided they could meet the guaranteed minimum they could wait for a turn in events in their favour.

To organise an advertising system was less exacting than to organise the bookstalls: but for this very reason the advertising side of the business had its own hazards. Railway directors and managers suffered recurrent bouts of optimism that they could manage both types of activity without paying Smith's for their help. They did not usually take much persuasion that they were wrong over bookstalls, newspapers, books. They saw enough, at close quarters, of the trials of a bookstall clerk to realise that his responsibilities were heavy and exacting. As to advertising they were less easy to convince. Repeatedly, during stressful moments in negotiation they would fall back on the threat 'to take the advertising business into our own hands'. To this William Henry II and his partners could bring the (usually) effective rejoinder that their proposals were based on an unequalled nationwide network of information about markets, manufacturers, products and consumers which they had steadily constructed since they had pioneered national advertising after 1850. The strength and weakness of the railway companies was that they were quintessentially regional and local; and they knew it.

For a long time William Henry's confidence in the professional organisation of his advertising business held good – not quite universally or perfectly, but generally. All the railway company managers could do was to riposte through using their own collective intelligence organisation – joint committees and conferences between the individual rail companies, necessary personal relations over technical problems that demanded joint policy and action against Smith's. For in spite of the gang warfare that often seemed a front put up to the public, the railways were slowly but surely being compelled to concentrate, take over, amalgamate – the words change, the facts are the same – and behind the noise, fire and smoke of competitive warfare the pipes of peace were passed round at the St Pancras Hotel, the Great Northern or the Midland Hotel, Manchester. The collectivism was still fragile but railway directors such as James Allport, Mark Huish and Edward Watkin were always ready, in person or through an underling, to suppress old hatreds in an effort to find out what terms William Henry Smith II was offering their rivals. Joint committees were a necessary evil. Why not put them now and then to a mutually useful purpose?

On occasions they turned in need to what today would be called environmentalism or conservationism. To the directors of the Midland who claimed to be under strong pressure from the more sensitive and cultivated residents of Leicester and other towns about ugly advertisements on the local station (though they continued to accept the rent paid by William Henry II under his contract) William Henry wrote on 25 August 1859:

> I am as anxious as anyone can be to avoid disfiguring the Company's ornamental buildings, but in order to realize the Rent we have paid, and the larger amount we shall have to pay, we must contract with Advertisers to display their announcements in large numbers at the Stations and we do not feel we keep faith with our Customers so far as the Leicester and Hitchin [Railway] is concerned, or that we can get fresh orders for such an amount of publicity as is afforded on that line.[54]

The environmentalists (mainly members of the Leicester Town Council living near the station) continued to complain of the loss of amenity, and no doubt the depreciation of the value of their residences, for many years. The directors of the Midland were more easily mollified by the steady increase of Smith's rents as old contracts expired and new and more profitable ones took their place. William Henry's imagination, on the other hand, was more easily moved by moral and social than by aesthetic problems. Scrupulously conscientious as to the former, it must be confessed that it is doubtful if he was deeply stirred by the wounds inflicted by his hoardings on the members of the Leicester Council resident in London Road (the Council of which they were members was simultaneously busy erecting even larger and uglier ones in Rutland Street). As a contemporary noted: 'He was not imaginative; and had not, I think, much knowledge of, or a natural taste for, Art.'[55] The first part of the dictum was inaccurate; the second part was, on the whole, true. His response, nevertheless, was characteristic. The order was given. The offending hoardings were removed. William Henry did not repine. He could console himself that he usually won the important battles; he could afford to lose a trivial one.

For the most part, in the intervals between the renewal of contracts, business went along reasonably amicably. The LNW company's ally, the North London, came into the Smith empire on 1 March 1855. By 1866 a rent of £215 a year for the shared Broad Street Station and Hampstead Junction Railway gave William Henry II the right to the usual privileges for newspapers and other literature, but added specifically 'prints, stationery, railway reading lamps, travelling caps, wrappers, and straps for same (but not any other articles . . . without the permission of the said Company . . .)'[56] These trimmings were symbolic of what an observer called the 'gentility' of the North London suburban traffic – the stockbrokers of Highbury and Gospel Oak travelling first class, their clerks second: it was another decade before the North London bowed to pressure and introduced a third class.

From the early days William Henry II consulted the railways about the design, placing and layout of the bookstalls – at Euston, Liverpool, Crewe, etc. All the details were carefully discussed with the architect and bookseller on the station. 'The only motive I have had in troubling the Company about these little matters', he wrote to Liverpool in July 1849, 'has been to have them in each case suitable to the Station, and to secure the best accommodation for our people, with the least inconvenience to the Company's business.'[57] All his care could not wholly prevent minor frictions such as the 'objectionable mode of advertising the County Fire Office by putting up the small Insurance plates'[58] which drew a mild reproof from the line's secretary.

A much sharper disagreement over a contract for a joint station, Wolverhampton, in 1858, revealed how swiftly a normal relationship could overnight give way to bitter mutual recriminations. A contract giving Smith's the usual privileges as agent for seven years had originally included all stations belonging to the LNWR 'for the time being'. Wolverhampton Station had been included in an agreement of 1848 when it had belonged to the LNWR. Later it went out of use and a new one was built by associated companies which was therefore excluded from the next contract. Now the LNWR had it again for themselves.[59] In a letter to one of the signatories for the LNW, Edward Tootal, William Henry II claimed, courteously but firmly, that he had arranged with Lord Chandos (the chairman) and 'the Company's officers' that Wolverhampton was covered by the rent agreed for the whole LNW system. He wrote to Tootal:

> I think I have a claim upon you to see the agreement carried out as I view it . . . to include all L & NW Stations for the time being. When it was made there was a Wolverhampton Station at which I had a Bookstall & Advertisements, which I lost without a murmur when the business was removed to the Joint Station; but now that you are to have a separate Station again, you have not, I think, acquired a right to shut me out.

His letter provoked squeals of uncontrollable rage from Tootal. He scrawled on William Henry's letter:

> *If so* you acted most *uncandidly* and *unfairly* to us – I told you *distinctly* we wanted £100 per an. more PROFIT for what we THEN had [the note dissolves into total illegibility at this point] – you distinctly *understood* you were to pay us *£100* p. an. *more.* I dislike this special pleading – it is *unmanly* & UNFAIR. I DISLIKE IT *for* or against me . . . You have NOT exceeded it [viz. the rent] . . . if you *had* you'd [?] pay the *£100 as agreed* I shall *never* be satisfied until you do. The money is not much but I do not *like* to be *deceived.*[60] (All the emphases are Tootal's.)

The dispute dragged on into the following year and the LNWR's legal adviser pointed out the company was losing the rent on Wolverhampton. By February the explosive Mr Tootal had sufficiently regained control of himself to receive William Henry II, who proposed that the dispute should be left (as Tootal wrote obscurely to Chandos) 'to yr Lordship's decision as on [?] a matter of equity what was fair between the parties.'[61] The Marquis of Chandos gave – as he well might for he it was who had made the original agreement with William Henry – an exceedingly judicious and lengthy opinion. On the one hand the agreement appeared to him to include Wolverhampton: on the other he felt sure that Smith's 'would make a fair and liberal settlement of the question on which there was clearly a difference of understanding between the parties signing thereon' by agreeing to pay an annual sum equal to the rent formerly paid to the joint owners of

Wolverhampton Station.[62] Chandos plainly deserved his reputation as a skilful arbitrator which had caused the LNWR Board to employ him as trouble-shooter on other occasions. Tootal was entirely in the wrong. But William Henry was, as ever, conciliatory.

So the matter rested there and relations returned to normal. Nevertheless the incident had revealed how, without warning, the storms could blow up. This one concerned a trivial sum of money but two men's pride. It had shaken even the imperturbable William Henry II out of his normal serenity. It had caused hysteria in Mr Tootal wholly disproportionate to the importance of the dispute. The business connection of Smith's and the LNWR was to last for the best part of another half century before being finally upset: but the Wolverhampton dispute was remembered as an ominous warning that the Euston–Smith relationship was a delicate plant.

The Great Western

The railway network which gradually covered England in the mid-century seemed to many – and so it seemed on the map – to radiate outwards from London; to confirm and strengthen the grip of the metropolis on the rest of the country. In some respects it did, but not in all. A great deal of the capital and enterprise came from the provinces; from traders, manufacturers and bankers who saw how important the London market was to them. Thus the Midland Railway sprang from Derby; the Great Western was a Bristol invention. The capitalists in both cases, as in Manchester, Birmingham and Liverpool were the same men who made up Smith's 'country' customers for *The Times*; capitalists whose business depended on knowing what was going on in Westminster and the City and knew there were thousands like them. There was a two-way flow in this final stage of moulding the regions of Britain into an integrated state.

The original Great Western Committee of 1833 was purely a Bristol affair; only later was a second Committee formed in London. The coat-of-arms adopted by the new railway diplomatically blended the Arms of the Cities of London and Bristol, for these were the limits contemplated by the GWR Act of 1835. Only later did it extend into the farthest wilds of Devon and Cornwall and throw out tentacles north and south of the original line by acquiring other lines such as the Bristol & Exeter (see pages 121–2).

The engineering problems of the GWR in its early days were formidable and notorious. A major one was caused by uncertainties about the siting of their London terminus. Were they to run into Euston (by agreement with the LNWR)? There seemed to be much to be said for a solution which would save them the cost of a separate metropolitan terminus by sharing the most westerly of the north-midland termini. It was not to be. In those turbulent days the negotiations for common use, like so many others, broke down. They were fortunate to acquire a site at Paddington. Thus was created the need for the longest and most awkward London run by the bright red, horse-drawn vans which carried Smith's cargoes of newspapers, journals and books daily to the London termini for despatch to the provinces.

This, for Smith's, was a problem still in the future. By 1867, William Henry II would be paying tribute to the GWR at a rate of £5,500 a year; this made them second only to the LNWR, who were paid £6,700. And evidently this was a relatively novel situation. For the GWR had taken to William Henry only after a protracted process of trial and error with rivals – this time ones of substance, or so it was thought. Only seventeen years after the foundation of the GWR did he acquire the contract (in December 1863) for advertising and selling newspapers and books on their stations. His predecessors were the firms of Henry Collings & Co. and Fraser & Co., apparently acting together.[63] Whatever their expertise, they were, by 1859 when the first surviving reports of their affairs become available, in deep trouble. Their rent (£2,500 a year for advertising and £1,500 a year for bookstalls in 1863) was badly in arrears. Repeatedly assurances of repayment were made; repeatedly they were accepted by an extraordinarily compliant Board of directors. But no arrears of rent were paid and new arrears grew. Lord Shelburne, the GWR chairman, bravely took it upon himself to deal with the matter in 1861: but his Lordship had no better luck than his junior colleagues.[64] By 1863 the arrears had risen to about £2,000. This was the point at which William Henry II put in an appearance.

For at least two years he had had a contract with the South Wales Railway for advertising and bookstalls. Its special wording suggests they too had been having the usual trouble of finding a reliable news agent: it therefore provided a strictly worded paragraph which enjoined upon Smith's that '. . . each Bookstall shall be attended by competent persons at all convenient times & particularly on the arrival & departure of each train & that each train shall also be . . . provided with an adequate supply of newspapers . . .'[65] And if the job was not properly done, the company could appoint somebody else to do it, Smith's paying the bill. In 1863 the South Wales Railway was amalgamated with the GWR and no doubt the satisfactory services of Smith's speeded the GWR directors in their resolution to hand over to them the cure of the sins of omission committed by their predecessors. They also handed them, as a condition of getting the contract, the responsibility for paying the arrears. This was promptly done.

Equally promptly Smith's entered upon their task of rescuing and reviving the sick and sorry business they had acquired. The effects of the change of management were quick to show. In four years, they were able to pay over a third more rent than that paid by the predecessors.[66] By 1873, the new agreement was settled for £7,000 a year or more. By 1879 it rose again to £10,000 and now included other lines acquired by the GWR – the Bristol & Exeter, South Devon, Cornwall, West Cornwall, Portishead and Monmouthshire. They now controlled virtually the whole of the western lines except some small advertising contracts for lines west of Plymouth held by a local firm, Cross & Co. Two years later this also passed to Smith's.

William Henry's Great Western business was a late starter, but once launched its progress was rapid, even though much of the line passed through sparsely populated countryside, a good many stations were small and unprofitable and even its largest cities could not compete in size with those of the midlands and north. They were nevertheless cities of distinction serving a society crowned by a still prosperous and cultivated gentry who demanded the best and appreciated it when they got it. All this William Henry (and his new assistant, Lethbridge) understood; not for nothing had they both been at school together at Tavistock. It was no accident that one of their first moves on taking over the business from the departing contractors was to obtain permission from the GWR management to set up a circulating library on any GWR station where they saw a future for it. After that it was to be smooth, uneventful and profitable sailing for many years, during which the Great Western business kept up close behind the leader, in the shape of the LNWR.

The Smaller Lines of the West

After the launching of the Great Western in 1835 there was a pause of only a few months before the next west country line was opened, again on Bristol initiative. This was the Bristol & Exeter. Of its sixteen directors twelve were Bristolians.[67] Like the Great Western it fulfilled its ambition of having its own station in Bristol. 'Station' is a euphemism. Local contemporaries called it 'the cow-shed' but it stood, defiantly and as if to underline its independence, at right angles to Brunel's magnificent Temple

Meads Station of the GWR. Not without difficulty, the Bristol & Exeter maintained itself as an independent line until 1876 when it was finally amalgamated into the GWR.

The promoters of the B. & E. were town merchants. The promoters of another minor line with whom William Henry did business, the Devon & Somerset, were local gentry. A very short and unprosperous line, it nevertheless remained independent into the twentieth century (1901). Another, the Somerset & Dorset Railway was an amalgamation (1852) of two hitherto independent lines serving the two counties separately. The S. & D. was also unprosperous but an object of affection both to those who maintained that its initials stood for 'Swift and Delightful', and the dissenters who alleged they signified 'Slow and Dirty'. The line nevertheless survived, though bankrupt, until in 1875 it was finally filched from under the nose of the GWR (who regarded themselves as its natural parent) by a combination of the London and South Western (based on Waterloo) and the Midland (in the person of Sir James Allport).

The contractor for newspapers and advertising to both the Bristol & Exeter and the Somerset & Dorset in the early 1860s was Alfred Walkley, who also had railway news agencies in London. Walkley was doing reasonably well for himself but he was not popular with the railway management who regarded him as disingenuous and slippery. When William Henry II enquired of Moore, the B. & E. secretary, about Walkley's business (having had an offer by Walkley to sell it to him) Moore's reply was uncomplimentary. Walkley (he wrote, on 11 December 1863) had an arrangement dating back some twelve years and therefore long before he, Moore, had joined the B. & E. Walkley was liable for only a very small rent: Moore didn't know how much profit he made but he thought he had probably done well – the stations were 'well covered with advertisements, and his bookstands appear well stocked', but a considerable number of stations which could support a stall – Clevedon Junction, Wellington, Tiverton Junction for example – had none. Walkley seems to have been reluctant to pay his rent in cash. For a long time the company had done a kind of barter deal by which Walkley supplied them with paper and stationery etc. 'to square the account without his paying rent in cash'. All this rested on letters or verbal agreements. Similar improvisations existed on the Somerset & Dorset and the railways wanted a change. But Walkley was hinting darkly that he was actually *extending his business* in which a gentleman (could it be William Henry?) was *about to join him* – as a partner'.[68] Walkley suggested he might leave his Bristol-based business to the partner and himself go to greener pastures in London (the Charing Cross line).

William Henry's letter to Moore was in all probability prompted by similar kites flown for him by Walkley, who had long bought his papers wholesale from Smith's anyway. But William Henry would have none of it. William Henry knew Walkley and promptly interviewed him. His offer was to take over Walkley's business in Bristol and on the B. & E. and S. & D.: in return for this and the disclosure of all the necessary trading information he would pay for the bookstalls, stock, advertisement 'frames', etc., at Bristol, Ilfracombe, Glastonbury and Poole, and pay off the arrears of rent due from Walkley to the railway companies. There was to be an end to the sleasy confusion revealed when the Walkley stone was turned over. Two of Smith's reliable bookstall clerks received clear and sharp instructions from William Henry II on 31 March 1864. They would have enough assistance to enable them 'to do the work with perfect regularity'. They would first observe the work closely for a week or two before taking over responsibility. Bonham, the senior man, would 'order the Papers from us *here* for the supply of the entire business' just as Walkley had done in the past, and from various publishers as necessary . . . you will (the letter concluded) 'be made entirely responsible for its management, receiving credit if successful – and blame if you are not'.[69] When necessary William Henry II could speak in the stern voice of Victorian business.

Contracts were made. Some progress too. But the usual problem raised its head by the early 1870s. The railway management wanted Smith's to extend their business to small stations where Smith's could see little profit – Portishead was a case in point. Smith's were more concerned to develop in the stations where there were people, money and literacy. When they totted up the gross takings for the Bristol & Exeter line bookstalls in 1871 – Bristol, Bridgwater, Exeter, Highbridge, Taunton, Weston, Yatton, Yeovil – they came to just under £7,000. Bristol contributed one-third of the bookstall rent of £200 per annum and one-sixth of the advertising rent of £400 per annum.[70] When Smith's approached the Bristol & Exeter manager, J. C. Wall, in February 1874, asking for a concession on the Devon & Somerset line, which Wall helped to manage, they received – hardly surprisingly – a seasonably cold answer. Wall's energetic manner and a belief in the commercial value of aggressive tactics were not matched by his judgment (as the affairs of the B. & E. were to prove):[71] he was determined to squeeze Smith's out of business.

Having had some little experience in the Advertising business at our Stations and in our Carriages, we have found it so lucrative compared with the amount we have received from you that we intend taking all the business viz. Bookstalls, Advertising and Newspapers into our own hands at the expiration of your Lease.[72]

Smith's returned a soft answer: might they have an interview to explain why they felt bound to query Mr Wall's hopes? Wall saw them at Bristol. Afterwards he wrote to William Henry. 'We [Wall often used the royal 'we'] are rightly or wrongly impressed with the notion' . . . of making 'a very profitable business . . . [we] feel inclined to try our hands at it.' Nevertheless, he might consider putting 'an offer of £2000 per annum for Five or Seven Years' before the directors.[73] Smith's, expounding the merits of their nation-wide system, offered £1,500 over a 7-year period.[74] Wall could not agree: they would take the business into their own hands.[75] No rehearsal of the hard arithmetic of W. H. Smith's accounts showing that the contract was not worth even £1,500 as things stood moved him. 'Please therefore consider the negotiations at an end.'[76] Smith's thanked him, regretted his decision but accepted it.[77] This was 30 March 1874. Yet on 20 June 1874, Smith's could write to Wall to make an offer of £1,750 for all privileges of bookstalls and advertising on the Bristol & Exeter: it was now to be for ten years and Smith's were to enjoy a 25 per cent reduction in their rates of newspaper carriage.[78] This was accepted by Wall and the directors a week later.[79] A month later Smith's registered another advance in a new contract for the Bristol Joint Station.[80]

The Midland Contracts: or Allport versus Smith (Markham intervening)

The Midland connection was never Smith's largest source of business or profit during the great railway expansion of the 1850s and 1860s. Gross rents paid to the Midland by 1867 (when we can compare them with rents to other companies) were just over half those paid to the LNW. The Midland came somewhere between third and fourth in the 'League Table' of the great companies, after the LNW and the Great Western. The explanation lies partly in the comparatively late arrival of the Midland headquarters in the metropolis. In the 1840s and 1850s the Midland's home ground was not London but Derby. Even in 1868, when the St Pancras terminus was open to passenger traffic, Smith's were still arguing that the station was only half finished and that it was unfair to expect them to pay the full amount of rent recently agreed under a new contract.

There was perhaps another reason for the slower growth of Smith's profit on the Midland as compared with other railways: in James (later Sir James) Allport, its general manager for four decades and finally chairman of its Board of directors, William Henry II was confronted by a railway entrepreneur who was at least his match in business vision and negotiating ability and (sometimes) more than his match in the patient handling of detail. James Allport shared with William Henry I a simple belief in the importance of the farthings.

It was not least his combination of 'dogged perseverance' with his more spectacular innovatory genius that turned the Midland into one of the largest and most influential railway companies in Britain. Both his detailed mastery of business and the cunning for which he was renowned and feared by his rivals in other railway companies recur time and again in his dealings with William Henry II. Like him, he spent useful time in the 1840s experiencing in person record breaking runs like his return trip from Sunderland to London in 1846: 600 miles in 15 hours. He championed the right of his drivers to exercise the maximum independent responsibility on their own judgment. He introduced to England the Pullman car which he had seen operating in North America (and must thereby have reduced Smith's sale of footwarmers, tins filled with hot water or acetate of soda, for Pullman cars were heated from the engine). If he was the 'railway Bismarck' of legend, he was also respected as an honourable dealer, if an ambitious one, who never underrated his own importance. Amidst the clamorous confusion of parochial loyalties that enliven but muddy railway history, Allport stands above most of his rivals. Acworth, a shrewd judge, allowed that in his championship of the third-class passenger Allport conferred a boon upon his country comparable to that of Rowland Hill: he was 'a benefactor of his species'.[81] He died, at the ripe age of 81 and probably as he would have wished, in the Midland Grand Hotel at St Pancras, still within earshot of the familiar hiss of escaping steam, the clank of the carriage buffers and the noise of train whistles.

W. H. Smith's Midland business began in a modest way on 18 October 1848, between William Henry II and the secretary of the railway at Derby. Smith's agreed to pay £350 per annum for the privilege of selling papers etc., on the line.[82] Three years later they agreed to pay £800 to £1,000 per annum for a three year contract 'of placing placards' on the Midland stations.[83] In May 1854, William Henry II wrote to ask for a different system. His letter is an interesting *exposé* of the factors, psychological and technical, that were obstructing the growth of his business on the Midland Railway in particular. Smith's (he argued) had suffered very considerable loss . . .

We attribute this partly to the unexpected difficulty . . . in inducing the
Traders in the Midland District to adopt a new channel for their Advertisements – partly to the very great difficulty we have found in getting
the Advertisements placed attractively at the Stations – and partly to
the abolition of the duty on Advertisements in Newspapers, which has
reduced their cost so greatly as to induce Advertisers to make use of them
in preference to any other system . . .[84]

A note appended suggested a loss over two and three-quarter years of
£1,265 on orders for advertising of approximately twice as much.[85] Smith's
suggested therefore a comprehensive contract for selling papers and books
and exhibiting advertisements: an early example of what was to be usual
practice, based presumably on the traditional argument of swings and
roundabouts.

At this point James Allport took over. The idea of a comprehensive
contract he accepted. The price offered was too low. An accommodation
was reached, but henceforth every detail of Smith's business was subjected
to the personal scrutiny of Allport himself. What were the rates for carrying papers? Single or parcels? Who was responsible for loss or damage?
What payment, if any, should be made for 'returns' of unsold papers? To
which station should they go? Which papers should benefit by Allport's
innovation of prepaid labels ('to Midland stations from Euston . . . *Pink*;
from King's Cross, *Blue*') for newspaper parcels, a time- and labour-saving
device?[86] What precisely were Smith's special privileges with the Midland
to be? From whom were parcel labels to be obtained? (From Allport
personally – of course!)

Allport's farthings were much in evidence: but so were William Henry's.
Each of Allport's strokes was fielded neatly. Over the disposal of 'unsold
Provincial papers' he made a point which was a sign of the times which
would recur with increasing emphasis. 'When the original Contract was
made they were scarcely in existence for our purposes, but they have now
[1861] to a considerable extent superseded the demand for the London
papers . . .'[87] This expanding newspaper production not only demanded
prompt attention: it was ultimately to help to re-shape the whole structure
of W. H. Smith's business (see page 167).

There was the tussle over St Pancras. It had been open since the beginning
of the month, Allport wrote to W. H. Smith & Son in October 1868: if
Smith's continued to refuse to pay the increased rent agreed, 'we must of
course call upon you to remove the Bookstall and advertisements, if any,
from the Station and . . . let the privileges to some one else . . .'[88] W.

Lethbridge was moved to protest '. . . the building is not sufficiently complete to enable us to exhibit these boards.'[89] He suggested the new rental of £4,500 – over ten times the figure of twenty years earlier – should he begin in January 1869. Allport continued to insist: a *portion* of the business *had* been carried on and should be paid for. They compromised: half now, full pay from 1 January.[90]

Two years later Smith's got their own back. In 1871 Allport wanted a bookstall at his new station at Ilkley. Lethbridge regretted having to doubt whether it would be commercially successful: '. . . it certainly could pay only during the Season [Ilkley was a well-known inland holiday resort] and were we willing to make the experiment, it would certainly be a convenience to your Passengers and if we found from experience that the privilege has a commercial value we shall be quite ready to pay that value.'[91]

So the bargaining and counter-bargaining went on, a hard, keen battle of wits but conducted with a proper regard for good manners – a letter of 1865 from the Midland secretary goes out of its way to refer to 'the businesslike and courteous manner in which your business here has ever been conducted'.[92] Alas! less than two years later the atmosphere of businesslike courtesy was threatened by an abrupt and upsetting end. 'As you will be aware', wrote Allport to William Henry, 'your Contract for advertising &c in connection with our Stations, which expired some time ago, has not been renewed, and the Directors have now decided to take the business into their own hands.'[93] The bookstalls, he added, could go on – on suitable terms.

A severely shaken William Henry II wrote post-haste to explain that it was all an unfortunate misunderstanding. He had read Allport's last letter to propose that they should meet when 'the line was opened through' (presumably to St Pancras): in the meantime they would go on as yearly tenants.[94] He would be glad to go to Derby to go into matters. But Allport stood firm (or pretended to). Matters had gone too far to be reversed. William Henry could have four months to make his arrangements to depart. Seriously worried, William Henry turned for advice to a Derbyshire notable of influence. Charles Markham came of a Northampton family of standing with strong links with the law and commerce. Charles himself had taken a somewhat odd decision to become an engineer and in 1851 became assistant to Matthew Kirtley, the Midland superintendent of locomotives, a formidable character who had risen to, and then from, the foot-plate. It was Markham who gave Kirtley vital help in launching a method (which had eluded other inventors) for running engines on coal instead of coke. He crowned his success by marrying Rosa Paxton, daughter of the designer of the Crystal Palace and himself a director of the Midland; later he lived, after George Stephenson's death, in Stephenson's former home at Tapton House, Chesterfield. By the time William Henry sought him out he was an important figure in the railway world and managing director of the Staveley Coal and Iron Company.

From Staveley he sent William Henry his views. He had talked to E. M. Needham, one of Allport's managers, a devious and pompous bureaucrat who actively disliked Smith's and evidently had ambitions to run the Midland newspaper and advertising business himself. 'I found out as I expected that he was at the bottom of the movement ...' Markham wrote.[95] Needham had been gossiping with an informant in the Chatham & Dover Railway for whose business Smith's had made an offer. From thence he had retailed to Allport stories of the glittering profits made by that railway by doing their own advertising.

William Henry replied to Markham by return of post: 'I have no hesitation in saying that if I had access with you and Needham to the Chatham & Dover books I could prove that they have not received in hard cash a single farthing of *net* profit above the money I offered them, but that on the contrary they are worse off for the arrangement.' Neither the Midland (he continued), nor the North Eastern and West Midland (who had tried it) realised the enormous working expenses to be faced. Other competitors – Collings on the Great Western, Walkley on the Charing Cross – outbid Smith's 'and in neither case did the [Railway] Companies get their rents' (see pages 120 and 122). Those who stand to lose nothing can risk making offers they cannot fulfil. (This was almost identical with the argument used repeatedly half a century later by C. H. St John Hornby to contest the policies of the GWR & LNW against W. H. Smith. See pages 240–1).

> We are at a disadvantage ... as we must pay what we undertake to do ... it is a little hard to be turned off our farm ... in order that others may try an experiment at the risk of the Landlord. Do I understand you that I ought *now* to follow Allport up in order to get the Contract? I don't like to do that kind of thing unless it is expected and it is necessary.[96]

Markham was impressed but by now pessimistic. Another firm, Partington's, had made an offer of £4,000 to Needham. He could only advise William Henry to write to Allport openly and frankly, as he had written to Markham, telling him the true facts about the Chatham &

Dover line and pressing the point that it was he – William Henry II – who started the whole business of railway advertising.

Markham himself ended with some extremely frank comments to William Henry:

> I must say from what I have seen of the correspondence that you are very much to blame for allowing the question to remain open so long without a strong effort to close the transaction earlier. You will find Allport a very honourable man and the points you have raised will have much weight with him.

He added: 'Needham is at the bottom of the scheme and you may rely I will do all I can to assist you in that direction.'[97]

William Henry knew good advice when he saw it. On receiving Markham's letter, he did as he was told. He wrote tactfully but firmly and with dignity to Allport. He explained why he had not approached him earlier. Allport had 'expressed in writing' his intention to call on Smith's to arrange a new contract. He went on:

> I have personally a strong dislike to hunting up a Man after he has expressed his intention to do a thing; and in this case I really thought you waited intentionally for the completion of the line ... You will understand I do not call in question your perfect right to do as you have done – but I explain why we have appeared to be indifferent.

He had, he added, 'perfect confidence' in Allport's sense of justice.

There were also the arguments designed to convince Allport the man of business. Smith's, wrote William Henry, had '12 Travellers employed all over England ... to collect Advertisements for the Stations'. It was for Allport to decide whether an agency working for 'one or two Companies' could be as successful as Smith's system covering the whole country:

> I think it will turn out that one or two Railway Companies working the Advertising by itself will not obtain ... a *net* profit equal to the rental which a Contractor in our position could pay them; – while the Company will be encumbered with working expenses in the shape of boards &c and with trouble and loss in Advertisers' accounts – as they are a slippery class.[98]

What it was that moved Allport is not sure. Did he talk further to

Markham? To Needham? To the Chatham & Dover? Was it the sting in
the tail that worked – the doubts sown about the hope of profits or fears of
loss and of trouble? Or had Allport throughout been playing his own
game? Was the threat of 'taking the Advertising into our own hands' an
elaborate piece of shadow-boxing designed to strengthen his case for
increasing the rent to be squeezed out of Smith's? All these are possible.
We only know that both parties to the controversy emerged without loss
of face. Markham's intervention was sensible and crucial, his frankness
timely. But William Henry II, while recognising Markham's tactical wisdom, never budged from his position: Allport had promised to negotiate.
Allport, to his credit, seems to have admitted as much by agreeing to
resume diplomatic relations. His action was sound business as well as an
honourable retreat. Thus an ominous threat to Smith's was removed.
Relations between Smith's and the Midland resumed their normal course:
proper, civil, businesslike – no trimmings, no gush. But William Henry's
imperturbability had had a jolt which he did not quickly forget.

The London, Brighton and South Coast Railway

In the spring of 1851, William Henry II made an offer to the London,
Brighton Railway to contract 'for the privilege of advertising in the Company's Carriages, and at their Stations'.[99] He received a polite but firm
refusal to have anything to do with such a development. Then there were
second thoughts. Just before Christmas, it was the Railway directors who
revived the idea of advertising and asked their secretary to find what other
railways were doing.[100] He replied, after exhaustive enquiries, that all those
with London termini (save the GWR and the SER) 'had let the right of
placarding at their Stations, to Messrs. W. H. Smith & Son'.[101] Hearing
this the directors ordered him to find out without delay what Smith's
would offer for exclusive privileges for three years. By January 1852, it
had been agreed to let the advertising to Smith's for £300 a year for five
years.[102] Thus began a long and apparently generally easy relationship
which was to flourish and outlive some others.

The first bookstall contract began on 1 January 1861 at £1,800 a year,
by which time the advertising rent was £500 a year. A joint contract
covering stalls and advertising started in 1863 at £2,600 a year. Smith's
were to pay an initial rent of £3,250 a year in 1868 which it was hoped
would increase over the seven years of the contract in proportion to the
looked for increase in passenger traffic.[103] And so it did. When the renewal

negotiations took place in 1874, Smith's settled for a minimum guarantee for 1875 of £6,500.[104] The Railway Company's two large London stations – London Bridge and Victoria – were deemed to be worth a rent based on 10 per cent of receipts, country station bookstalls 5 per cent; advertising paid 50 per cent of receipts.[105] The relationship with Smith's (and the contract on which it was based) were both, reasonably enough, described by the Railway directors to each other as 'very satisfactory'.[106] And so it was to continue.

The growth of London, of the suburban traffic, of Brighton itself and its neighbouring south coast resorts – all combined to favour the sustained growth of the south of England business. By the turn of the century the London and Brighton was treading on the heels of the old leaders of Smith's business in terms of its turnover and rents. Proportionately this branch of the trade was to grow at not far short of twice the rate of that on the LNWR and the GWR. Relations, accordingly, continued appropriately cordial.

Northwards from King's Cross

The Great Northern dated from 1845: it was operational by the following year but it took a few years before King's Cross, under its famous roof, was working to full capacity. It was 1850 before its Board of directors listened while their secretary read two letters from newsagents applying for permission to sell newspapers on their stations. These were George Howes & Co. of 7 Thavies Inn, and W. H. Smith. Thomas Kennedy of 31 Royal Exchange 'who at present supplies newspapers to the Offices' was to be admitted to the *London* station – 'pro. tem'.: but plainly the Board was not entirely satisfied that he was the right answer to their problem and they added, therefore, 'such privilege not to give him any claim whatever upon the Company; and that Tenders for . . . selling newspapers on all the Stations on the line be advertised . . .'[107] By September 1850 twenty tenders were in their hands: W. H. Smith of 136 Strand for £500 per annum was accepted.[108]

In 1851 the Great Northern traffic had grown sufficiently to encourage Smith's to make a comprehensive offer[109] for a three-year contract, starting at £1,100 a year, then £1,200 and finally £1,300.[110] Ten years later the Railway Company was only offering a five-year contract at a rent of £2,000 a year and William Henry II was parrying their offer with £1,800 for three years and £2,000 for another four years (advertising included).[111]

William Henry explained why he wanted not less than seven years:

> . . . my business is a very costly one to conduct . . . the addition of the
> Library which I have recently made to the Book Stalls will for some
> time to come involve a larger outlay than any return I can possibly
> obtain will compensate me for. I believe it will ultimately be profitable,
> but my great motive in establishing it was to increase the general
> advantages of the system of business connected with the Book Stalls, on
> the principle that the more the wants of the Public are met by this
> business the broader will be its basis in public estimation.[112]

But Northern heads were hard. The directors were less impressed by
their travellers' amenities than their Western or Midland rivals. Even less
were they moved by William Henry's concern for the place his business
held in the public estimation. Five years and no concessions was all they
would agree: after that they were hoping for more traffic and bigger rents.
As on the Midland, Smith's first problem was the internal one: management. Seymour Clarke, the general manager, was not himself as tough a
bargainer as Allport. A graduate from the slower, gentler world of the
Great Western, he was a man of modest talents and less fierce ambition. He
once wrote to William Henry II turning down an offer for a contract with
obvious regret . . . 'for my own part, I like working with old friends', he
wrote, but he had to go via his Board.[113] Plainly Clarke, who enjoyed only
delicate health – his aspect was pale, melancholy, moustachioed, and
archetypally Victorian – was no match for his masters. '. . . the best of
traffic managers but the worst of negotiators' as one of them said.[114]
Dealing with this kind of Board through Clarke was a problem. While
Clarke survived – from 1850 to 1870 – relations were consistently amiable
but not conspicuously profitable.

For this there were other, non-personal reasons: principally the nature
of the territory through which the Great Northern lines ran. A W. H.
Smith advertising manager, surveying the territory with a trained eye
many years later, remarked that it consisted chiefly of 'rural districts' which
possessed not many 'stations of commanding importance' for advertising
except (of course) 'King's Cross, Peterborough, Grantham, Nottingham,
Derby, Leeds and Lincoln'.[115] Its potential as an advertising area was
obviously limited. Thus – relatively long stretches of track unembellished
with stations, a fitfully populated area with large patches where population density was low, and, perhaps, a people slower than their more
southern neighbours to respond to the wiles of advertising – all these

factors combined with less aggressive and less sophisticated management to keep the Great Northern at number 7 in Smith's League Table.

With Seymour Clarke's retirement in 1870, the general manager's post was filled by Henry Oakley (later to be Sir Henry). Oakley was strictly a northerner whose training had been almost exclusively in the office of the secretary of the Great Northern. This somewhat limited background had done nothing to damp Oakley's spirits. He was a man of inextinguishable wit, imagination and administrative precision. He flung himself into the battle to extend the Great Northern's profitability and contributed greatly (not least as a brilliant witness in Court) to its later progress against its rivals. Oakley was a man of stature comparable to Allport, Moon, Huish and Watkin: with his appointment in 1870 a new era began in Great Northern history.

Oakley's first confrontation with Smith's was in fact the fruit of some quiet work by Seymour Clarke who in 1866 had obtained from Smith's a list of railway stations where they sold papers but confessed he could not find out the amount of the business done. The Accountant's Department had privily extracted from the LNWR, the Great Western, the Great Eastern and others how much rent Smith's paid them and for what length of track. The LNWR, for example, were paid £6,500 rising to £8,300 under a ten-year contract covering 1,306 miles of track. The Great Western's rent stood at £5,500 for 1,150 miles of track. And so on. '... this', said the report, 'conclusively disposes of Messrs. Smith & Son's proposition' (that they could not afford more than £2,350 and deserved cheaper rates of carriage for their papers).[116] In 1872 Oakley elicited the terms of the Lancashire & Yorkshire Railway's contract with Smith's which gave them 50 per cent of gross advertising receipts (Smith's to bear all expenses) and 5 per cent of bookstalls' sales.[117] And so on, with larger companies like the London & Brighton and South Western. He even winkled out of the London General Omnibus Company that they received £3,762 for advertising in and on omnibuses. Indeed in a letter to Oakley their omnibus contractor, Thomas Smith (no relation) 'proffers his services in the event of your determining to conduct the advertising yourselves': £6,000 a year could be obtained from advertising and 'he [Mr Smith] would do all the work and receive 1/3rd of the net receipts, as his commission ...'

Before discussing any further the merits of the ebullient Mr Smith's proposals, Oakley cautiously added that he hadn't himself yet seen William Henry II. Before he did so he wanted to know what sort of a contract his directors had in mind – a fixed rent for a term without reference to increases or decreases in railway traffic? Or a first year of rent which would then vary with the future volume of traffic? Or 50 per cent of advertising and 5 per cent of bookstalls? He added that *pace* the other Mr Smith, the Lancashire & Yorkshire had told him they had tried to find competitors to W. H. Smith & Son but had 'found none who were apparently so able or so competent as Messrs. Smith . . .' who had accordingly been given their contract.[118]

After considerable haggling during which offers and demands swung backwards and forwards from £2,630 to £5,000, the difference was finally split at £3,250 a year, on 6 June 1872.[119] This figure was calculated on a base line of passenger receipts by the railway for 1871: the contract was to be for seven years and the rent was to vary according to variations in passenger receipts during its life.

As things were to turn out, Oakley's first encounter with Smith's was not a successful one. For at the Midland, Allport was busy cutting his fares. Unlike those shrewder calculators, the Midland and the Lancashire & Yorkshire, the Great Northern had not insisted on a guaranteed minimum rent: so, as traffic was checked by sharper competition, so too was their rent from W. H. Smith's. It was to take another five or six years to put this error right by (in the end) tying the rent to Smith's receipts and not to the railway's receipts. By 1878 Oakley got this done, with the advice and help of the Lancashire & Yorkshire (who had won a 45 per cent increase from Smith's out of it since 1872: the Lancashire & Yorkshire would have earned an increase of 43 per cent if they had implemented the Great Northern's system).[120] But by that time William Henry II had largely withdrawn from regular participation in the management.

The negotiations had brought two points forcibly to the attention of the Great Northern directors. First, their general manager had inaugurated or at least pursued a policy of exchanging information with rival companies on a scale probably more thorough and elaborate than ever before. Second, for all their stance as tough businessmen and no nonsense, they had failed to grasp that the form of contract they (not Oakley) had deliberately chosen for Smith's was not the better. Third, W. H. Smith's had won. They would leave more decisions to Oakley for the future.

The Eastern Counties

From the beginning – even when they were still associated with horses, not steam – railways were generally an adjunct of industry: not so in the eastern counties. East Anglia was a land of farming and fishing. In the eighteenth century its farming had been technically very advanced and often prosperous: its ports, Yarmouth especially, famous if not wealthy. By the railway age things had changed, generally for the worse. Farming ran into bad times after 1815, worse after 1846, worst of all after the 1870s as free trade and foreign competition bit hard into the profitability of arable farming. Herring and mackerel fishing was less prosperous than the deep sea fisheries of Grimsby and Hull. But, slowly, as the eastern seas ceased to feed England they began to offer something else – recreation: Hunstanton, Cromer, Clacton, Frinton, Southend became more important than Wells or Blakeney (once busy ports) as the holiday trade grew: Harwich became the terminal for traffic between England and Northern Europe.

Into this changing world came the Eastern Counties Railway; but it was no triumphal entry or progress. Population was still relatively sparse, towns still relatively small, industry relatively rare. The ECR (1836) enjoyed, if that is the right word, a decade and a half of unedifying domestic but widely publicised rows and faced dozens of apparently insoluble problems of organisation. Its services were poor, its unpunctuality a household word, its reputation deservedly low. Only in the mid-1860s, after its incorporation as the Great Eastern Railway in 1862, did its prospects have a chance of improving: even then its inherited burdens brought it into court and temporarily into the hands of a Receiver.[121]

The current repute of the Eastern Counties in its early decades was faithfully reflected in its arrangements for newspapers and advertising. Down to 1855 W. H. Smith's had had advertising contracts with them. In that year they had been invited to tender for bookstalls but had been rejected in favour of another firm (somewhat confusingly also called Smith) who had overbid them. The confusion was confounded by their also having their offices at an address in the Strand a few doors away from W. H. Smith's. The victorious Smiths (hereinafter called Smith Holmes to avoid more confusion) proved as unsatisfactory as many other of W. H. Smith's rivals. Their paper delivery to the railway was late: they illegally packed other articles into parcels labelled as newspapers: they underlet their bookstalls to their employees and did all manner of things '. . . calculated', in the words of the secretary of the ECR, 'to facilitate the continuance of the frauds . . . so extensively practised . . .'[122] Not least among their shortcomings was that having obtained the contract by offering to pay an annual rent of £2,100 they found themselves unable to pay more than £1,500.

At this point, in March 1857, William Henry II weighed in. He had felt (he wrote to the Board of the ECR) that what had gone on was scarcely fair to W. H. Smith but he had had no right to interfere: but now that it seemed both the railway *and* the newsagent contractors were alike dissatisfied he thought it 'not improper' to state he would still be ready to pay the £1,800 he had originally offered: he could do this at twelve hours notice and 'conduct the business in a manner ... satisfactory to the Company'.[123]

Horatio Love, the managing director of the day, was sympathetic. But the Eastern Counties, like their trains, moved in those days at a stately speed. Three years passed in legal arguments before the contract was put up for tender. William Henry's bid was not the highest – Sullivan of Slough and Thomas Kennedy of Royal Exchange (a familiar rival) offered more: but the ECR directors had learnt their lesson. William Henry's offer was finally accepted as 'the most eligible'.[124] 'Young Reliability' had conquered again. His victory survived for eight years. Then relations cooled – not so much because times were bad but because, for the GER, they showed signs of getting better. Since 1863 management had been reorganised, technically and financially, traffic between London, Norwich and the east coast ports had grown and the suburban traffic in and out of eastern London was increasing steadily. For some years, dreams were dreamed of a new passenger terminus to replace overcrowded Bishopsgate. It finally became reality – a very expensive one – in 1874–5. It was called Liverpool Street. By 1864 Smith's were paying a rental of £2,000 a year: discussions were already in progress for its replacement to include new suburban lines – Epping, Wormwood Street, and the Blackwall lines.[125]

But other thoughts were now stirring in the minds of the Great Eastern directors. The South Eastern (whispers reached them) enjoyed better terms with Smith's than they did. They would enquire from the Great Northern, Midland, London & North Western and Great Western how matters stood between them and Smith's. Did not the Metropolitan Railway advertise along the walls at the side of the line? Why should not the Great Eastern do the same? But in spite of earnest enquiry and desultory negotiations with other newsagent contractors, nothing came of these ideas. The main proposal petered out while both sides wrangled over whether the station managements were infringing Smith's contract by placing 'Copies of a Publication, Entitled [Thomas] *Cook's Excursionist* ... in Cloth reading cases on the Tables of the Waiting Rooms ...'[126]

Three years later, the advertising problem came up again in a more serious form. The metropolitan companies, it was said, were taking the advertising 'into the hands of the several Companies'.[127] The North London undertaking its own advertising and the London, Chatham & Dover employing an agent who managed all their advertising business on commission made, it was claimed, very large profits.[128] These highly-flavoured rumours sent them off in search of confirmatory evidence. But the evidence was not forthcoming. On the contrary, on 11 February 1874, the GER superintendent reported that the North London had now informed him 'that since writing to the large Companies to combine for Advertisement letting purposes – those Railways have made fresh Agreements on their respective lines and so ignored the North London suggestion'.[129]

Flummoxed by this vexatious turn of events, the Great Eastern had no alternative but to reconcile itself rapidly to the need to repair its relations with W. H. Smith's; for, after all, Smith's were already paying a sizable rental and could doubtless be induced to pay more. The new deal was closed by 15 March: a minimum guaranteed payment for all their services of £3,700.[130] In fact by 1878 they were to be paying over £5,450 a year.[131] It was enough to keep the Great Eastern quiet for a few years. As for William Henry II, he could hardly complain. Some unsigned notes, though difficult to interpret, suggest that gross receipts from his GER bookstalls had risen between 1871 and 1873 from £16,321 to £19,885 – though so too had expenses.[132] Income was becoming harder to earn; a sign perhaps of the onset of the phase in history from 1873–96 which became known as the 'Great Depression'. It hit the arable farming of East Anglia with special force in the shape of cheap grain imports from North America. But William Henry, like all businessmen who provided consumer goods or services, knew that the British economy was still not uniform in its movement: it remained a congeries of regional economies. What was poison to the eastern farmer was meat to the graziers of the west and north-west; just as cheap materials and food were to the cities and industrial areas of the north and midlands. *Pari passu*, his bookstalls and advertising business in the different regions experienced different, not identical, destinies. In any case, the Great Eastern ranked – roughly – only eighth on his list of railway clients.

The Lesser Lines

Outside the eight major lines to whom William Henry was paying rentals of over £2,000 a year in 1867, there was another score of lesser lines all over Britain with rental values that fell as low as the £5 paid to the Sirhowy Railway or the £7 to the Stamford and Essendine.[133] Of these lines, the largest was the Lancashire & Yorkshire Company, formed by amalgamation in 1847 and an independent line until its merger with the LNWR as late as 1922. W. H. Smith's rental in 1867 for its services was £1,850 a year.

The beginnings of the connection were humble – but significant. In 1848, Smith's were beaten by Mrs Robb in the competitive tendering for the Victoria Station, Manchester. Mrs Robb, the resident incumbent, offered 20s. a week, which just topped William Henry's offer of £50 a year.[134] There were other tenders: £15 per annum 'from the person at the Salford Station'; £10 per annum 'from the person at the Bolton Station'.[135] But a month later Mrs Robb (probably a railwayman's widow) had passed the way of so many of her kind – she 'had not paid according to the terms stipulated'. The company decided that 'Tenders be procured from some respectable Newsvendors for the privilege of selling Newspapers and periodicals at the Victoria Station and such other stations as may appear desirable'.[136]

The L & Y was of great importance – potentially at least. It covered, cross-wise, a vast area of the north of England, particularly the industrialised areas, from Liverpool, Manchester and Preston to Leeds and Halifax, and it linked up with the Manchester, Sheffield and Lincolnshire Railway and later the Trent, Ancholme and Grimsby line (opened in 1866), and thus with the growing Lincolnshire fishing port and the burgeoning neighbouring seaside resort of Cleethorpes. There were, therefore, two distinctly interesting prospects opened up by the L & Y for Smith's: a wider market for their London newspapers, to which was added the rapidly expanding trade in local provincial newspapers such as the *Halifax Guardian*, the *Manchester Courier* and the *Examiner*. The big stations at Liverpool and Manchester were respectable rivals to the London termini as centres for advertising placard business. Blackpool (and later Cleethorpes and Skegness) apparently attracted visitors from the south of England as well as from the north and midlands.

The system of 'Pre-paid Parcel Labels' for local newspapers (strictly not for London papers ... 'the circumstances attending the conveying of which are entirely different from that of the Local Press'), was introduced in 1855 by the L & Y.[137] It provoked an immediate protest from Captain Huish on behalf of the LNWR: the scheme (he complained) was not 'sufficiently well digested', by which he meant it was too cheap.[138] It threatened, thereby, the trade of the London papers in provincial England. But the L & Y traffic manager, Cawkwell, spoke loudly and clearly for the provincial press as well as the Midland, North Eastern, Manchester, Sheffield and Lincolnshire, and the L & Y:

It may be suitable to the London Press to have a minimum charge of 6d per parcel, but many of the Provincial Publishers could not afford it . . . the system to which the London and North Western Company object will work well, and . . . only very slightly affect the points where we divide the traffic . . .[139]

The scheme went ahead. The momentum behind the provincial press following the repeal of the newspaper stamp was too strong to be resisted and the labelling scheme added further to the momentum.

Smith's were by this time firmly established in the bookselling, news-vending and advertising sides of the L & Y stations' business: but they also early encountered Cawkwell's tough negotiating methods. Late in April 1856, their failure to reply to a peremptory notice that their contract was at an end brought an even more peremptory note of warning.[140] Any further delay in negotiating an agreement would mean an arbitrary charge of £1,500 a year rental. Another minute of the L & Y Board recorded their decision to take advertising into their own hands.[141]

All this was at least half bluff. The L & Y had no alternative arrangements to fall back on, a fact equally well known to William Henry II and Cawkwell. So, after some by now familiar rituals had been enacted, a comprehensive contract was signed. It was for five years.[142] It excluded, however, the station at Liverpool (which was jointly owned with the East Lancashire Company).[143]

The renewal in 1861/62 brought another clash, rather sharper than the formal, normal rituals of offers and refusals. William Henry wanted the Liverpool station included this time – obviously too valuable a franchise to be omitted. He could not, however, go higher than £1,500 overall 'advertising at the Stations not having been so satisfactory of late'.[144] The L & Y, in reply, demanded £1,600. This was (in William Henry's words) 'the last feather [that] broke the camel's back'. He had (he protested) given in time and again. He could not possibly face such a figure, even '. . . if I am solvent enough to pay it – of which I shall have great fear if our business is as dull during the next five years as it has been during the past five months. I really cannot do more than pay the old rent [now] and the new [from next January] . . .'[145]

The directors had to agree with great reluctance. They worked off a little of their chagrin by noting with sour relish a report that the W. H. Smith bookstall at Blackburn 'is in a disgraceful state, and requires painting'.[146] The owners were advised to have it done immediately.

The atmosphere was still fairly hostile when the renewal forms were considered again five years later. The directors grumbled about the cost of Smith's advertising. Thorley (the secretary) was ordered to consult with other rail companies and find out how, and at what cost, they got on with Smith's. Like all good railway company secretaries, he faithfully reported that the L & Y seemed to do 'a great deal of work for very little pay': but the figures he produced were not black enough to convince anybody that a change could bring much good.[147] The L & Y continued, all the same, to demand very much better terms (five years beginning at £1,850 and rising to £2,250 . . .). After a good deal of shuffling and muttering from the railway company and a letter from W. H. Smith's 'expressing their willingness to retire from the Line . . .' a compromise was reached.[148] But by 1871, the trouble broke out again with the expiry of another contract. The haggling had to begin all over again. But this time there were rivals — a local firm, Emmott & Savage, and 'Messrs Grant & Company, a large publishing Firm in London'.[149] Both the new rivals entered the lists with large offers and confidence to match. Both dwindled as the protracted bargaining went on and on.[150] In the end, in December 1871, Smith's were back in the field, alone, with their standard offers of 5 per cent on the sales at bookstalls, 50 per cent of receipts for advertising and a guaranteed minimum rent of £2,500 a year. It was accepted.[151] Smith's had won again: but the going was getting harder.

Oddly (but in fact understandably) Smith had an easier row to hoe with the L & Y's northern neighbours, the Manchester, Sheffield and Lincolnshire. The MSL was still a homely affair when William Henry fixed his first contract with them from 1 January 1852 at £200 a year. An 1860 contract arranged for the 'Station Clerks to sell the Manchester papers' at Guide Bridge, Dinting and Glossop: another herald of the rising northern press and its growing importance in W. H. Smith's affairs, long dominated by the London press.[152] The immediate result was a minor explosion over a minor matter: but it showed that in the MSL territory, minor, homely and human matters still counted. The MSL general manager wrote to William Henry II in September 1860:

> . . . I have to complain that in opposition to the understanding, your Mr Carter gave *direct instructions* to our Agent at Guide Bridge to remove an old man, who had previously been allowed to sell Newspapers inside that Station, to passengers in the train, and on the platform. His so selling them was a convenience to the Public, who complain loudly of his exclusion, and did not interfere in any way with the arrangement made with you, and I have ordered him to be reinstated.

William Henry drafted an urgent reply, having failed to catch the manager in person. Of course he consented to the old man remaining there and his man (Carter) understands this. But the MSL will surely understand that . . . 'The whole scheme has for its object the accommodation of the Public in these districts by an orderly and systematic arrangement, under proper control. It is scarcely likely to be profitable to us.'[153] For once, the railways were on the side of humanity. William Henry's excuse was, of course, sound enough: but he has the faintly uneasy air of a man apologising to his own conscience. Alas! In a Benthamite world the greatest happiness of mankind was not to lie with bearded and ancient newsvendors.

The MSL rapidly became the largest of the small railways – its potential, though much less than that of the L & Y, was much greater than its western and southern counterparts such as the Bristol & Exeter, Somerset & Dorset, Shrewsbury & Hereford, Bristol & Portishead or the Isle of Wight. And it was enmeshed with the other neighbouring lines which covered the north and east midland area, some more profitably than others. In the centre was a group of busy stations serving industrialised or industrialising areas which paid lucrative returns on their rental by 1868. Sheffield Victoria Station, London Road Station, Manchester and Retford were returning gross receipts totalling nearly £7,000. New Holland, the Lincolnshire terminal of the Humber paddlewheel ferry serving Hull, Grimsby and Barnsley together, yielded almost £800.[154]

With progress, the MSL grew more ambitious over rent; demanding now a guaranteed minimum of £1,000 a year. In 1869 Sir Edward Watkin, chairman of both the MSL and South Eastern Railways, advised William Henry not 'to boggle at the difference.' William Henry split it at £875: he was influenced largely by Watkin's advice that the MSL was 'now more important than it was'.[155] This may have derived less from actual growth of its profits than from the fact that it was part of the growing network of interests of this railway tycoon who was known as 'the Railway King' of the Manchester group of railway promoters. Sir Edward Watkin was a man of erratic talents and more erratic judgment – a 'Northern Philistine' with his origins in trade, as Hamilton Ellis has called him.[156]

Watkin certainly possessed a kind of impetuous vigour reminiscent of George Hudson. It took him into railway directorates and shareholdings all over Britain, not to speak of the presidency of the Grand Trunk of Canada. He was among the early enthusiasts for a Channel Tunnel. Later he changed the MSL into the Great Central, for, 'ambitious and wrong-headed' as Jack Simmons thinks him, he wanted, above all, to emulate James Allport and run his own line from the north into London:

thus Marylebone Station was created as the Great Central terminal.[157] But Watkin finally was a failure. The Great Central never paid a dividend.

By 1870, the MSL's ambitions were beginning to look exaggerated. And against the profitable stations of the MSL had to be set the much less profitable MSL and LNWR joint ones. Smith's adviser at Manchester wrote gloomily of their prospects. 'We are doing nothing on [this] line and I don't think there is anything to be done at these stations [of the Oldham, Ashton-under-Lyne & Guide Bridge Junction Railway].' The basic reason was the British system of competitive railway construction. Ashton had three stations, Oldham had five: '. . . you see the thing is so cut up that no station business can be worth much . . .' Ashton might support one bookstall – not more – either on the MSL *or* the L & Y station: the traffic was pretty evenly divided for London, Leeds and Manchester. '. . . then some day', he continued, 'something might even be done for Oldham. I have heard a *Manchester Guardian* man say that even in his time it used to be quite dangerous for a stranger to go to Oldham – the natives would be almost sure to trip him up while walking in the streets and then nearly kick him to death for tumbling over their clogs.'[158]

The Macclesfield, Bollington & Marple line (another MSL joint venture) was equally unpromising. The line was short (9½ miles), traffic limited 'and of a country sort'. The newspaper trade from Macclesfield to Bollington consisted of one copy of *The Times* and four penny papers. There was not enough business 'at either station to pay a lad's wages'.[159] Smith's wrote to the MSL: they put it mildly: 'the demand for Newspapers is . . . not great'.[160] They offered £5 per annum for all privileges. The MSL accepted without argument.[161]

The situation and problems of the MSL were summarised some years later by W. H. Smith's advertising expert.

> The large towns in which . . . the MSL company have exclusive property are limited to Sheffield and Manchester: the line for the most part runs through colliery and rural districts in which if there is any advertising at all, beyond what has been [already] developed . . . must be done at comparatively low prices. The chief stations are now fairly well filled with the [WHS] Firm's and the company's [own] advertisements and I see little or no room for any appreciable expansion of the 'inside' advertisements.

This could be achieved, if at all, only by the active canvassing 'peculiar to the system of the [WHS] Firm'.[162] The MSL proved that even by the

1870s and 1880s, Britain's industrialisation and its social effects were still very patchy.

Nowhere was it more patchy than in north Lincolnshire where the Trent, Ancholme & Grimsby line had been opened to public traffic in 1866: a stark corner of the Watkin empire, flat, muddy and unkind. Would Smith's (enquired Edward Ross for the MSL) like to make an offer for the advertising? The line, he explained hopefully, joined the South Yorkshire line at Keadby (where it crossed the Trent) and the MSL near Barnetby. There were four stations on the line – Gunhouse, Elsham, Appleby, and Frodingham.[163] A day would come when they would be at the heart of the great Scunthorpe complex of iron and steel works: but that day was still far off. In December 1866 a shivering inspector sent by Smith's from their Brown Street office at Manchester could only report that the line was about 15 miles long, with four small stations – 'mere sheds', the traffic small – only two trains had passed each way daily in November.[164] Smith's cool reply reflected their unpromising experience of Oldham: they would 'place the Stations on our list, . . . do our best to obtain Advertisements . . . pay to you 50% of the amounts so realised after deducting the cost'.[165] Ross accepted quickly – by return of post:[166] but three years later he was still lamenting that he had been paid nothing. The reason? There was nothing to pay.[167]

The MSL (*pace* Edward Watkin's optimism) was a patchy enterprise outside Leeds, Sheffield and Manchester. The notion grew in Smith's that by itself it was not worth the candle. But the MSL did not stand alone: it was part of the Watkin empire. And, as William Henry's deputy was to write in 1888: '. . . I do not quite like the idea of having a severance between W. H. Smith & Son and Sir Edward Watkin'.[168] Such was the nature of railway diplomacy.

The Bookstall Empire: Conclusions

The bookstall network spread at an extraordinary rate. In 1850 there were about thirty stalls with a prerogative to sell to passengers over somewhere between a thousand and two thousand miles of track. During the 1860s William Henry II had thirty to forty separate contracts for bookstalls and advertising with railway companies, great and small, controlling nearly 10,500 miles of track, and the process of growth was still continuing; so that in another twenty years the number of main bookstalls was up to between five and six hundred, and there were warehouses to handle the wholesale trade when this was too heavy for the local bookstalls – Birmingham (1857), Manchester (1859), Liverpool (1868).

In Ireland, too, in May 1850, William Henry II bought a bankrupt newsagency in Dublin. Six years of painful reconstruction followed. He wrote to his sister Gussie on 3 March 1853:

> I am going to Dublin as we are rather anxious about the state of the accounts there. Father wishes me to stay a fortnight but I don't think I ought to be away from him more than three days at the outside . . . I am almost afraid to go away, not knowing what violent changes may take place in my absence, in his desire 'to get rid' of the business.[169]

Dublin continued to test his patience severely. He was there again in 1856. Again, to Gussie:

> I am well and very cross, for the Irish are fast exciting all the dormant decision and anger in my character. I verily believe if I stay here much longer I shall be thought a fiend at the least for I do insist upon their doing that which is right in my own eyes this instant; and they always want to do something else tomorrow.[170]

The Irish problems were partially solved by appointing Charles Eason, former manager of the bookstall at the Victoria Station, Manchester, to take charge. He was chosen, as was explained in the letter inviting him to take the post, because of William Henry's conviction 'that you were under the influence of real and true religion'.[171] Be that as it may, Eason was also a good business manager and technician. By 1857 he had succeeded in concluding contracts with a number of Irish railways – the Great Southern, the Dublin, Wicklow & Wexford and the Dublin & Drogheda. Later came arrangements in Belfast to work the northern railways. Circulating libraries blossomed in a number of towns from Limerick to Athlone. Business looked up rapidly. William Henry wrote from Dublin to his wife on December, 1858: 'I am very much pleased with Eason, the head here. He is an odd little fellow . . . but he is thoroughly true, honest and good.'[172] Once again, William Henry had proved his capacity to choose men. It did not, however, totally relieve his conscience of the responsibility for the Irish business. 'I often wish', he wrote on a visit in 1859, '. . . to have done with this work, but . . . I feel it is a duty to do it thoroughly.'[173] And he was right. In 1861, there was 'evidence that I have been wanted. Nothing wrong but laxity and indolence which would grow into wrong in such a soil and such a climate if not checked.'¹⁷⁴

Some knotty problems of negotiation with the Irish railways could not be left entirely to Eason. In 1863 William Henry was becoming ever 'more tired of this sort of thing . . . I do feel very lazy indeed, as if I should like a long holiday absolutely to do nothing'.¹⁷⁵ Things were to get worse before they got better; there were losses on the libraries, an economic slump which hit the tourist trade, all gratuitously crowned by the generous permission to an employee to depart for the United States to attend at the bedside of his dying mother: but the occasion proved a sad one for his employers too, for with the departing traveller went a very large sum of the firm's money. After that better days dawned and Dublin was reasonably prosperous until 1886 when, for reasons quite extraneous to the business proper, it was decided to sell it to Easons. They still own it.

The problems encountered at Dublin may help to explain Smith's otherwise puzzling decision – if decision it was – to withdraw from Scotland. Early on, in 1851, they moved into the Edinburgh station with a bookstall for five years. Their business seems to have been the usual one in *The Times* and other London papers, later in the *Scotsman*, the *Glasgow Herald* and local papers from Inverness, Aberdeen, Dumfries, etc. There was a wide variety of choice in the Scottish reviews – *Blackwood's*, the *Edinburgh Review* and many others, together with fiction and biography, often with a Scottish flavour of some kind, including Boswell's *Life of Johnson*.

Then, in 1857, Thomas Murray, founder of *Murray's Diary*, outbid them; in turn Murray was to be displaced by John Menzies, the founder of the great firm which was to look forward to a long and distinguished future as booksellers, not only in Scotland but England too.¹⁷⁶ Oddly, William Henry's handling of the Edinburgh affair resembles, superficially, his apparent indecision over the Midland contract with Allport (see page 127).

Was it overwork or some kind of passing indolence or indecision about the future of Smith's that caused a delay of ten weeks before the North British Railway were compelled to write to him:

Not having heard anything further from you in regard to the Book Stalls at this Station, and several offers, largely in advance of the sum paid by you, having been made to us, we have, in concurrence with the Edinburgh & Glasgow Company, concluded a five years lease with another party . . .¹⁷⁷

That was the end of W. H. Smith's Scottish interests. William Henry never tried to return. Why? It is true that the episode came at a time of peculiar stress, when William Henry I had been feverishly engaged in hatching schemes to sell the Smith business to John Walter and *The Times*; when William Henry II was overworked and single-handedly doing his best to cope with the problems of an expanding business – including Dublin. But perhaps the Irish experience played a part in persuading him of the almost insuperable difficulties of operating news distribution successfully over such enormously long lines of communication. At all events, with the exception of very special cases in Paris and Brussels, Smith's had settled for a future predominantly English.

The negotiations by which they established their trading position in English news and book distribution, though tedious in themselves, fall into a pattern which helps to explain the contemporary character of the business and the path it was to follow. The first move was invariably the same, and it confirmed the opinion voiced by many a contemporary journalist and moralist that the state of popular literature and its purveyance was very far from being what it might have been. The business on line or terminus X was in the doubtful hands of a Robb or a Gibbs or one of the anonymous eccentrics who straggle through the records, all to a lesser or mostly greater degree unreliable, incompetent, insolvent. Their shortcomings, and the shortcomings of the literature they purveyed, constituted the first condition of William Henry's arrival, voluntary or invited, on the railway scene. Thereafter, progress depended on the already established reputation of Smith's as distributors to the country, wholesale to other retailers, retail mostly to individual subscribers, for the leading London newspapers and journals. Most of the old newsvendors, like so many of their kin, picturesque but imperfect utterers of the cries of London, faded away – with the exception of one category: the Sunday newsvendors on the larger stations.

They survived, often by agreement with Smith's, who would themselves have nothing to do with trade on Sundays. This was not Sabbatarianism in any doctrinal sense but common sense on the part of an employer often strict but always realistic. The work at Smith's, headquarters or bookstalls, was long and hard. One clear rest day was essential. This rule was relaxed only once, in the Crimean War, when Sunday work was allowed to enable soldiers' relatives to obtain the names of casualties at the Battle of Alma. As late as 1896 echoes could still sound occasionally, recalling the old arrangements by which the Sunday gap had been filled – for the highly popular and successful Sunday papers like *Lloyds Weekly* and

Reynolds News could not be ignored. On 20 April 1896, several years after William Henry II's death, his partners gave an interview:

> Saw Mrs Brown [their diary recorded] and her son, who exercise the privilege of selling papers at Charing Cross, Cannon Street and London Bridge, Brighton & South Eastern on Sundays. Told them they must not sell any papers which we refuse to sell. They produced a letter from Mr. W. H. Smith dated December 27, 1867, saying *inter alia* 'We have no intention of making any change ... you are the only person we recognise as having the right to sell papers'. This letter was addressed to Mr. Brown, who had several Bookstalls on the S.E.R before W.H.S & S. took it.[178]

Thus the ancient oaths and fealties passed down the years.

Such minor exceptions apart, Smith's rapidly established their new regime based on new standards of punctuality, reliability, organisation and service. But this did not, in itself, always produce plain sailing and perfect answers. Smith's stood in an uncomfortably exposed position between the newspaper publishers, the railway companies and the public.[179]

The railway managements, many of them initially gratified by the revolutionary changes and improvements introduced by Smith's (and some of them remained so), apparently often suffered an early form of amnesia where gratitude gave place to a desire to share the rewards. This became more common as the early euphoria of railway management gave way to cheese-paring when railway revenues levelled off and running costs increased. There were another two decades of buoyancy before the railways ran into really serious financial difficulties in the 1890s; nevertheless, the pace-setters – the Midland especially – were pulling in their belts in the 1860s and 1870s.

The growing consciousness of the need to increase revenue was manifested in two different but related ways. First, the old informal arrangements by which bookstalls, carriage advertising, inside station advertising, and outside station advertising were each settled separately and informally, year by year, gradually gave way to package deals in which all were included on terms which varied round a rental norm: for bookstalls 5 per cent of receipts, for London terminus bookstalls 10 per cent; for advertising, 50 per cent of receipts. All these were to be tightened up as the century went on its way: and the comprehensive contracts later came to include a guaranteed minimum rent, which was essential from the railway companies' viewpoint if percentages of takings were to be the mathematical principle of rent-fixing. Five per cent of what? was their question.

The negotiations themselves took strange forms, or at least forms which seem strange in cold print over a century old. WHS offer: the Railway Company says perhaps: WHS modify: the Railway refuses: WHS raise their offer: the Railway still refuses: WHS decline to bargain any further; they will withdraw; the Railway returns with a better offer; finally they agree. The impression of these strange ritual dances is that William Henry II (and later his assistant and partner) usually won, or at least succeeded in retaining the contract. But all the time the terms of rents were getting stiffer. True, this was mainly because the volume of business in popular literature and advertising of popular teas, soaps and watering places, was increasing steadily. The belief was common among the railway managements that while their profits were becoming harder to earn, Smith's were becoming easier.

On the face of it, Smith's bargaining position did not appear strong. Their business was conducted on premises built on railway property and removable at that. They had no security beyond what they could extract from the railways in their contracts. The railways could make the term longer or shorter according to the view they might take of future prospects. The longer the term Smith's asked, the higher the rent. Yet in reality the matching was less uneven than it seemed. The railways needed, for their travelling customers, the services Smith's could supply. The firm had established under William Henry I a reputation for punctuality and reliability: it had been confirmed and underlined by his son. Smith's managers knew the intricacies of their trade; railway managers who underestimated the problems of news distribution usually lived to regret their ignorance. On bookstalls and their business, Smith's could therefore usually put up a good argument.

Where advertising was concerned, matters were less easy. This involved Smith's being allocated space in and around the railway station to erect hoardings or place frames on station walls; these were let by Smith's to manufacturers to advertise the merits of the growing number of foods, drinks, tobaccos, soaps, patent medicines, etc., which represented a prominent trend in the British economy in the era which opened in the mid-century and grew throughout the third quarter of the century. This had appeared to some railway managements an easy and useful source of revenue; many continued to believe they could manage it for themselves. Yet at least one (the West Midland) had tried the experiment with results so meagre that they had abandoned it. Smith's argued, cogently for many years, that only a large advertising network – such as the one they had pioneered since 1851 – would work. Only by investing heavily in an expert staff of 'canvassers' on a national scale and thus bringing together producers and consumers over wide areas could the system be made to pay: the net profit was much exaggerated in the railway mind. This did not prevent the railways regularly using the threat, during negotiations, 'to take the advertising into our own hands'. The repeated use of exactly the same phrase suggested – and suggested correctly – that the railway companies' often bitter business rivalry over traffic did not prevent pretty regular consultations over their negotiations with Smith's.

In general, in an expanding economy, Smith's held their own well. A reputation for integrity usually persuaded the railways in the end to renew their privileges. A central point in the invariably tough bargaining was Smith's insistence that their ability to pay higher rents was inevitably limited by the heavy working expenses unavoidable in their operations. Labour costs were high (especially on the bookstalls and at the Strand headquarters): so were railway costs for carrying the newspapers. The final terms therefore involved considering rents in relation to carrying costs: the railways could not, Smith's argued, expect to have both always in their favour or William Henry I's traditional farthings would cease to flow.

There was one last problem which had constantly to be explained to the railways. The contracts which conferred the 'privilege' of opening bookstalls on the stations of the LNW, GW, GN, Midland or other, smaller and less prestigious lines, carried also a liability: it could be only potential, it could be real and immediate. Quite simply, the larger termini might generate business worth between two and three times that of a normal, average-size provincial station. This, in due course, created a demand from the railways that the rentals for such exceptionally profitable centres of concourse should be fixed at double, or more, the 'normal' 5 per cent of takings. This left out of account an important fact: that there were many bookstalls – on remote rural, village stations, in poor industrial districts, in places which enjoyed a short season as holiday resorts by hills, lakes or sea but which endured much longer periods of almost total desertion out of season – all these were positively non-profitable or of doubtful profit. The railway companies expected Smith's to supply them continuously with news, book and library services: but they did not *reduce* the 5 per-cent-on-takings rents to offset the rise to 10 per cent which they expected on the profitable London termini. In the 1880s an estimate of the net profit on the station bookstalls suggested that somewhere between a quarter and a third of all bookstalls did not 'suffice to pay Carriage & the Wages of a Boy . . .';

10–20 per cent of 121 London daily and weekly papers and periodicals on sale at railway stations were returned unsold.[180] Half of the 150 provincial dailies and weeklies left behind a residue of 20–40 per cent unsold. And this was certainly no new situation.

The newsagents' lot was, in reality, not the honey pot which the railway companies liked to pretend. But the ritual dances continued: their complexity was in direct proportion to the financial problems of the individual railway company concerned: those most seriously affected were the LNW and the GWR.

The early railway age was one of continuous expansion for Smith's: but it was very far from being one of internal peace. On the contrary, the business suffered a series of crises and eruptions which at times threatened its existence. Smith's was a family business: the crises were family crises, and their basic cause was the behaviour of William Henry I. From the early 1840s he was increasingly irascible, inconsistent, excitable (see page 78).

An undated letter from sister Emma to William Henry II put the problem delicately: 'I am sorry dear Father is so extremely diligent in business, but the time *will come* when in some way our God will answer our earnest and united prayers . . .'[181] But the ways of Providence in dealing with Father were more than usually inscrutable and the mills ground very slowly indeed. William replied more explicitly to his other sister Augusta (his favourite, 'Gussie') in November 1846, that:

> [Father was] testy but generally manageable. He came down on Monday for half an hour, walked into the Counting House, bowed to the people, then walked upstairs, had his leg dressed and then got into the carriage . . . vowing 'the place stunk' – 'couldn't breathe', and he 'would not come down again for some time'; it was 'wretched' – 'such a noise too'. So he has not been here since, and won't be, at all events till next Monday.[182]

So things continued for nearly a decade during which the practical day to day responsibility for the business fell on the shoulders of William Henry II.

As his majority came near there were inconclusive mentions of a partnership: but it took the death of William Henry I's brother and erstwhile partner – 'poor Uncle Smith' – in 1846 to bring matters to a head. The Rev. William Beal, William Henry II's brother-in-law and former tutor at Tavistock, pronounced suitably pious sentiments on the true happiness of an event which had sent 'poor Uncle Smith' to a destination where his 'eccentricities' would be no more. His nephew was more down-to-earth:

for the truth was that the 'eccentricities' – a form of alcoholism – had been a growing burden on the nerves of the whole family for many years. William Henry II, a dutiful nephew, had visited him at Putney, on 15 July. He was very excitable and disturbed, and two days later 'violently attacked by *delirium tremens*'. He was put under special care: then, on the 20th, in the early morning he died. Ten days later William Henry II became a partner.

A few days later he wrote:

> Poor Uncle Smith's . . . premature death is indeed an awful warning to all of the dreadful consequences of giving way to animal propensities – the appetites. If he had had the strength of mind to devote his time and powers to some useful purpose . . . he would have been alive and well . . .

Father seems to have taken his loss with a mixture of brotherly grief modified by intense relief. 'At first my Father . . . reproached himself . . . but feeling upon a longer consideration' that nothing could have helped his brother and that 'the eccentricities so frequently deplored' were the result of some malformation of the brain . . . 'he now appears more cheerful and resigned – almost himself again.'[183] There is no doubting where that cool streak which some observers remarked in William Henry II came from.

'Almost himself' was ambiguous. Faced with and exasperated by his son's continuing belief that his future lay in holy orders, Father, even ten years later, was turning his still remarkable energies into perverse concentration on plans for getting rid of the business altogether (see page 83). These extraordinary plans went into considerable detail of which only one or two salient features are relevant. A note of 1856 made as its first point: 'The Messrs Smith wholly to retire in 3 years. Mr. S. Junior to remain if desirable for a term of years – as Manager or as may [be] agreed upon on a Salary.'[184] The buildings at the Strand were all to be leased and the rest of the assets to be sold – to whom? None other than John Walter, proprietor of *The Times*! Later the plan was modified to become a sale of the premises but Smith's were to remain, in 'partnership [with] a gentleman nominated by Mr. Walter, with the view of carrying on business as Publishers of *The Times* exclusively . . . at a price to be now agreed upon' (endorsed in pencil '4d').[185]

The plans, like so many other figments of Father's fevered imagination came to nought: nor is it clear whether Walter and the managers of *The*

Times even knew of them. They remain simply a source of speculation for those who enjoy counterfactual history. Immediately, it may have helped to concentrate William Henry II's thoughts on the need to make up his mind about his own future. What he needed, above all, was help: someone he could trust to run the business on its traditional lines, take decisions when necessary and yet maintain the essence of W. H. Smith's success – a family business.

His thoughts went back to Tavistock: to two brothers of a Devon family who had laboured with him under the eye of William Beal. William Henry II, with his keen eye for human quality, remembered best William, Lethbridge *primus*. They were in the same class in 1839. Since then he had been at Cambridge (St John's), reading mathematics: at Rossall, St Paul's, and Highgate as a schoolmaster, at Lincoln's Inn for the Bar to which he was called in 1861. These apparently erratic changes of course did not bother William Henry II: William Lethbridge was the man he wanted. So, from 1862 to 1864, Lethbridge became his assistant. Stocky, bearded, portly, *bon viveur*, his appearance formidable but at heart warm and genial, Lethbridge rapidly made himself indispensable to Smith's at the Strand, sharing William Henry's burdens: so that after a couple of years he was already being considered as a potential partner. A close friend, the Rev. T. R. Maynard, a chaplain to the Forces, wrote to William Henry in Paris in 1861:

> . . . considering the *nature* of your business, & your *social* position as a married man . . . & the uncertainties which attend every man's life . . . you ought to have someone associated with you in your business (be he a partner or otherwise . . .) who could take your place whenever it was necessary . . . & in case of your death, carry on your business . . . Now there are two men, Lethbridge & Gatchell. Gatchell knows most about the details of business, but I consider Lethbridge to have the most decision & aptness for taking circumstances as they arise, & adapting things to them accordingly . . .[186]

The description was apt and seems to have carried weight with William Henry II. It was on Lethbridge that (in 1864) the first partnership outside the family circle was conferred. William Henry retained – it was mindful of his own junior partnership some years earlier – 'exclusive and absolute power and authority' over the business. Lethbridge was to obey William Henry's orders and directions but William Henry was to 'give only such time and attention to and engage in the said business so far as he may in his uncontrolled discretion think fit and necessary'.[187] Lethbridge received £1,000 a year: a manager at most, but the basic relationship was revealed by the terms of their correspondence. Later partners were to address the head of the firm as 'Dear Mr Smith': only Lethbridge wrote 'Dear Smith'. His authority inside and outside the firm was correspondingly weighty.

From this time on, much of the diplomatic business and a great deal besides, including William Henry's private financial business, investments and the like, were handled firmly and decisively by Lethbridge, without fuss or hesitation.

In 1860, William Henry had felt able to consider nomination as Member of Parliament for Boston. But this provoked a shower of outraged letters of protest from his father. How could he contemplate such desertion of the business? And just in case his son should remind him of his own plans of a year or two earlier to sell out to *The Times* he added cunningly:

Anything that takes you so much from Emily would be a severe trouble to her.

It will be little worse than Insanity for you to adopt a course that would occupy time to such an extent that the business must be neglected. You have a business & a name that should be carefully cultivated & by the time you are 44 you may think of what you judge highly – but what I am sure is a mere bauble & that would most probably destroy your health. You are now married & it cannot be told yet what a family may require.

If you value your Domestic happiness do not enter the House it will destroy all the hope I have of doing any real good to your Family – they have claims not to be neglected.

The plague of being an M.P. are [sic] great & very expensive.[188]

The next day another breathless and unpunctuated bombardment followed:

. . . the most detrimental thing that could be thought of for your future welfare . . . what real good will it confer on you, except the pleasing vanity of having after your name the letters M.P. – which would be very heavily paid for by being away from Emily & the Children [so much and injure the business] destroy your health & also all domestic happiness in which is more real comfort than anything else (except true heartfelt Religion) can afford in this Life . . . I am anxious that the *Character* & *extent* of your Concern should continue, not one tradesman in a hundred thousand in all England have so fine a prospect or so large a property do not I pray you endanger, nay I may say destroy it by choosing a trifle not better than a prettily coloured glass bead is to a child – it cannot lead you into any real good – & avoid mixing yourself up with either of the parties in *Political matters* have nothing to do with them.[189]

For the moment, the barrage was effective and silence closed down upon William Henry's political ambitions – but only temporarily. In 1862, however, Father's fears were aroused again. What lay behind the rumours reaching him that his son was contemplating taking in a partner? Was this another prelude to his departure into public life?

If you have any wish for peace of mind do not on any account have any Copartner in your business you will have much cause & time for repentance should you have a partner it will be very easy to get one but quite a different thing in getting rid of one who must have so much power in his hands. Your greatest error is being too fond of Public honor & pursuits. I observe by the Newspapers you are Chairman of Kings College Hospital. It thus appears your business in the Strand &c is not enough to occupy your time & attention but that it was needful that you had the details of that large establishment to look after.[190]

For one reason and another it was to be another six years before William Henry II entered Parliament. That he was able to contemplate a political career at all was largely because since his entering upon partnership in 1864, Lethbridge had shown himself well able to handle a large part of the responsibility for the conduct both of policy and detail. Even before that he had swiftly carved out for himself a notable place in the respect and affection of the Strand and Fleet Street. The Rev. T. R. Maynard wrote to William Henry in 1862 that he was sorry to hear Lethbridge had been ill – his bulk and *joie de vivre* belied a delicate constitution – but Lethbridge had *spirit*: 'The natural elasticity . . . of the Great Mogul has triumphed I hope . . . & his place at Simpsons knows him again as usual.'[191] Smith's was still – and was long to be – a family business, but with the appointment of Lethbridge it had taken the first of the successive steps which were to place it among the few professionally managed private enterprises. William Henry was at last free to enter public life – a surrogate and compensation for the devotional life of religion for which he had longed throughout his adolescence.

VI

Managing the Bookstall Empire

THE SPREAD OF Smith's business typified the general economic expansion of the 1850s and 1860s. It also created large problems. Not only the volume of new business but its far greater variety — books, libraries, magazines, a flood of cheap new papers, provincial as well as London, more wholesale and retail outlets — all this called for larger headquarters, more staff and above all more specialised staff.

From 1820 to 1849, the business had been centred at No. 192 the Strand. Then, for a short period it moved to No. 136.[1] Later, premises were rebuilt at No. 186 on the corner of Arundel Street and the Strand, originally the site of the old Arundel Palace.[2] Other outposts were to develop in Milford Lane and Water Street. But the new buildings kept to the old principle. They were near Fleet Street, Somerset House, the Post Office: there was room near by for stabling the horses and keeping the carts which sped the papers and books to the rail termini to the north, south and west — at this stage through streets clear of traffic in the early hours of the morning when Smith's most essential business was done. The new buildings were much praised for their modernity and novelty though this was perhaps due less to the architects than to the government. The window tax, which had long imposed a regime of darkness on the interior and imitation windows for real fenestration, had just been abolished. Smith's was apparently the first private building in the Strand to be equipped with windows that really did light.

It was what went on inside the building, however, that caught the imagination of journalists, visitors and even those who worked there. An historian writing recently on the history of the press at this time (and not particularly favourable to it or to Smith's) remarks a trifle irascibly that

Victorian journalists seem to have spent a considerable amount of their time showing their readers this 'hive of poorly paid industry' in the Strand.[3] There is no evidence that the conditions of work at the Strand were any worse, or the pay lower, than in scores of contemporary trades and industries. In regard to security of employment and opportunities for promotion it certainly compared favourably (see page 172).

It was indeed one of the sights of London, described vividly in a number of journals from the rebuilding in 1852–5. One article (in *Once a Week* for February, 1861, by Andrew Wynter, who combined practice as a physician with extra remuneration from journalism) was entitled 'Our Modern Mercury'.[4] *Chambers' Journal* followed in 1865 with 'How we get our Newspapers'.[5] Then in 1875 there was another account (certainly the best) though cribbing the *Chambers'* title, printed in *All the Year Round*.[6]

Wynter was most impressed by the growth of the Smith's business – in volume and variety. In the last days of coaching one man ('who is still in the establishment') could carry all the papers to the coaches under his arm. By 1861 the early trains despatched six tons of *The Times* alone, and the preparation, packing and folding in the great basement rooms in the Strand was 'one of the most remarkable sights in London'. Between 4 and 6 a.m., in a large square hall open to the roof, surrounded by two galleries and lit by a cluster of gas lights, the ritual was enacted. Much of the work was manual, an extraordinary sleight-of-hand, with some elementary and rather unsatisfactory mechanical technology for slitting, folding the papers and addressing the parcels to destinations all over Britain. Much of the labour was done by young boys, but not all. The supervision was strict, standards of accuracy and punctuality incredible. A great problem was posed by *The Times*, always reluctant to go to press without the latest news; always the last arrival at the stations, demanding hairsbreadth decisions by the managers. In all this William Henry I, William Henry II and later the partners all took part. Smith's was, in its own paternalistic way, a democracy.

More important than his descriptions of the process of the modern Mercury were Wynter's comments on the revolution taking place in the market for popular literature and its production. Partly by reason of the abolition of the stamp duty and other fiscal obstacles, but partly because the entire economy and society in industrial Britain was changing rapidly, the press had changed too, and with it W. H. Smith's business. The penny morning papers were 'beginning to monopolise the public market; and the thousands which daily leave Messrs Smiths' for the country is a proof that hundreds of thousands in the provinces now see a daily paper who never enjoyed that luxury before. As the *Telegraph, Star* and *Standard* have thus spread themselves over the country, all the high-priced daily papers, with the exception of *The Times* only, have lost a considerable part of their circulation, and must eventually come down to the standard penny, if they would avoid destruction.'

The old, slovenly papers and moribund weeklies were giving place to a higher class of journals – the *Saturday Review*, the *London Review*. The old high-priced provincial papers were rapidly giving way to livelier, cheaper papers. 'We cannot but pause', this mid-Victorian optimist declared, 'to pay our tribute of admiration to the spirit and ability with which the cheap press throughout the country is conducted. The sneer heretofore urged against the "cheap and nasty press" now falls harmless, and there can be no reasonable doubt that they will assume and exercise a very considerable influence, as an educational power, among the middle and lower orders of the population.' The same consideration applied to books. Railway bookstalls found few buyers for first class, costly books: but these could now be borrowed through the Smith lending libraries or bought cheaply *ex libris* provided the buyer was willing to exercise a little patience.

The 1875 account has all the vivid pseudo-Dickensian colour the others lack:

Towards St Clement Danes (at 2 a.m.) are tending carts, cabs, and men, bearing weekly newspapers of all sorts and sizes, of every shade of political and religious opinion, appealing to the serious, to the artistic, to the sporting fraternity. The centre of attraction is the huge building at the corner of Arundel Street – the establishment of Messrs. W. H. Smith & Son, just waking into life.

The ground-floor of this great focus of newspapers is furnished with a battalion of tables with passages between, like the alternate squares of a chess-board . . . a long strip of white paper pasted on . . . with the names of the weekly papers . . . so many *Sporting Gazettes*, so many *Broad Arrows, Bell's Lifes* (or should it be '*Lives*'?), *Examiners, Economists, Saturday Reviews, Dispatches, Lloyds, Licensed Victuallers' Guardians, Fields, Land and Waters, Volunteers' Gazettes* etc.

Sorting out, distributing and packing all these off to the stations is followed by similar treatment of the dailies. Wet from the press come five tons of 'The Thunderer' (*Times*), *Daily News, Telegraph*, etc. Not all depends on the Strand headquarters. Supplementing H.Q., at King's Cross, Paddington, and so on, is another trained team of W. H. Smith distributing staff ready to accept papers direct from the Fleet Street presses.

The early-morning mixture of order and chaos surveyed, the author went off to see the rest of the building. Bookselling and circulating library reminded him of 'a pyramidal system of book-keeping'. Under the central dome sat 'four-and-twenty book-keepers, not exactly "all of a row", but divided into eight sections of three in each'. As the books arrived from the publishers by hundreds or thousands, they were hoisted upwards by a lift to be checked:

> A mighty store, indeed! In packages, in bales and boxes, and in book-binders' boards – on floors, tables, and walls – are regiments, nay, armies of books, cyclopaedic and historical, didactic and controversial; books of prayer and books of praise: books of poetry and travel; novels and romances; tales and sketches; brand-new works not yet reviewed; and reprints of authors whose names are known wherever the English tongue is spoken; quaint volumes of maxims, and useful hints on finance and farming, dress and deportment; the art of spelling, and the art of cooking. It is a land of books, carefully divided into counties and wapentakes, cities and towns, hundreds and hamlets.

Books for sale were distinguished from books for the circulating libraries by different coloured labels. The affairs of the railway stall clerks were regulated with minute care from the Strand. 'As the stock of Mr. Cator, of Screwby Junction, is sold down, he writes to head-quarters for further supplies . . .' They are sent to him, accounted for, placed in a special crate with his name. Further up 'in the snug rooms, at the top of the house' were other special stores. 'There is a cap department . . . a card-room, for supplying the packs of playing-cards' sold at stations to while away the boredom of travellers; a rug room for railway rugs and straps . . . and 'a sweet-smelling collection of old tea-chests, used for packing books . . .' There were departments where books were printed and bound ('many of the best and pleasantest books in our language') and carpenters' shops where the bookstalls and advertising frames were manufactured.

The writer's dramatic imagination was most roused, though, by what was called 'the realm of King Runnyrede': in fact the Advertising Department. This monarch presided, not dictatorially but benevolently, persuasively, over the entire British railway system.

> In gold and in silver, in all the colours of the rainbow, he tells you that 'Crackstone's Cornflour is the Best', and adds the warning, 'Take no

other'. He does not mince the matter. He does not say it is merely good; he prefers the superlative . . . We are happy until we are told, in glaring black and yellow, that 'Crown and Bolster's Cornflour is what it purports to be' – a dig in the ribs for Crackstone evidently. An error on the part of King Runnyrede and he is going down in our opinion when he brings us up all standing with 'Why pay more?' Yes. Why? That is the question . . .

And so on. Facetious? To later generations certainly. The merits of Boreman's Baking Powder, Silvertop's Soup Squares, Hallamshire Relish, Stede's Patent Columbian Eye Sparkler, the juxtaposition of 'Accidents will Happen' and 'Dye at Home' are heavy comedy. The dramatic is never far away from the melodramatic, the satirical from the facetious. But as a period piece on the early phases of advertising in the almost-modern manner, it is worth recording. So too the final observation on leaving the Strand building. 'A placard hanging against the wall catches my eye, with the heading "Provident Fund", under which Messrs. Smith offer to take care of their workpeople's savings, and allow them six per cent on all sums of ten shillings and upwards – an excellent example to great employers of labour.'

To the end of his days William Henry I was at odds with his son. He had thwarted his wish to enter the Church. He had poured scorn on his proposal to stand for Parliament in 1860. He had rebuked him for considering making Lethbridge a partner in 1862. The son had on each occasion deferred to his father's wishes. But he had not been wholly deflected from his conviction that the life of business, successful, in some ways satisfying as it was, was not enough. Outwardly cool and reserved, there was an inward restlessness of spirit that sought deeper satisfactions from life.

As the older man grew physically weaker, mentally less alert and more erratic, the son was in a stronger position to sublimate some at least of his needs for outlets for his deeper emotional fulfilment. These were mostly philanthropic services or social reforms. From 1848 (to his father's disgust) he served on the Committee of Management of King's College Hospital (still today closely connected with Smith's). From 1855 he was elected to the Metropolitan Board of Works, part of the long overdue reform of London's local government, which was to culminate in the London County Council. Friend of W. E. Forster, father of the later Act for free popular education, he specialised not only in education but in Poor Law and housing.

In 1870 he visited Paris specially to find out how Paris tackled the problems of massive poverty and social deprivation (see page 108). Finally, overcoming his father's opposition, he stood as a candidate for Parliament (Westminster) in 1865. He was defeated. In 1868 he stood again and was returned as a Whig, soundly beating a formidable opponent in the shape of John Stuart Mill, standing as a Radical. The story of his political career has been told recently and fully: it is not necessary here to make more than a few basic points.[7]

William Henry II began as a Liberal and ended as a Tory (unlike Gladstone who did the opposite): his position was nearer to that of Disraeli and Tory reform. He quickly made himself well known in the House by a few good speeches on social reform and a capacity for getting on well with political opponents as well as political allies. His practical sense of organisation likewise stood him in good stead. In 1874 Disraeli made him Financial Secretary to the Treasury (usually a reasonable promise of future Cabinet office): Smith evidently did not disappoint him. 'After forty years experience of parliamentary life, I can sincerely say, that I never knew the affairs of the Treasury conducted with more thorough sense & efficiency, than while they have been under your management & control.'[8] Later, in 1877, Smith was chosen First Lord of the Admiralty, on the warm commendation of Disraeli. The Queen was at first less enthusiastic. '. . . she *fears* it may *not please* the Navy in which Service so many of the *highest rank* serve . . . if a man of the Middle Class is placed above them in that very high post . . .'[9] Eventually she gave in, but with a *caveat* that Mr Smith must not 'lord it over the Navy (which almost every First Lord does) & be a little modest & not *act* the Lord High Admiral which is offensive to the Service. . . .'[10]

She need not have worried. W. S. Gilbert tried to guy William Henry in *H.M.S. Pinafore*. (He later denied that Sir Joseph Porter could possibly have been intended as a caricature of Smith; but few were convinced.) In any event, William Henry's reputation gained rather than lost. He got on increasingly well with the Queen. His senior officers and civil servants liked him and respected him. His reorganisation of the dockyards was a task for which his business experience fitted him particularly well. Under his leadership the Navy brought into operation its first steam torpedo boats and breech-loading guns. Occasional minor storms he survived, as when Ponsonby, the Royal Secretary, observed that the First Lord was 'furious, outwardly calm' over the tactlessness of Prince Alfred (Captain R.N.) which Smith insisted on bringing to the Cabinet.[11]

The middle-class man was still rare in high politics. William Henry survived well. His family were justifiably pleased. Augusta ('Gussie') was particularly delighted with his political advance. On 6 August 1877 she wrote: 'Our dear Father never hoped for your being a Cabinet Minister but he used often to say "your Brother will be in Parliament. I may never live to see it, but you will".'[12] Distance had perhaps lent a little enchantment to her view of family history.

In Opposition he concentrated on naval affairs where his private intelligence network often left him strategically better placed than the reigning First Lord. But meanwhile Lord Randolph Churchill entered the lists as leader of the rebels of old Toryism against what he referred to sniffily as the antics of 'Marshall & Snelgrove' (being William Henry and Richard Assheton Cross) against the Byzantine hierarchy of the Party. But Randolph's ferocities did not prevent William Henry becoming Secretary of State for War in Salisbury's minority government in 1885. He handled his new post with his usual cool efficiency and this in turn led to his appointment as Chief Secretary for Ireland. Within six months he was back at the War Office, the battle with Lord Randolph resumed – and won. The Prime Minister, Salisbury, got rid of Randolph: William Henry became Leader of the House. By 1887 the Salisbury government reconstruction was virtually complete. William Henry was in the post which suited him best of all. 'The combination between Salisbury and Smith was a happy mixture of the most worthy influences of Toryism', wrote Lord George Hamilton. Each supplemented the qualities the other lacked. 'His [Smith's] common sense and perception (amounting to genius) rarely, if ever, failed him in his diagnosis of the agitation of the moment.'[13]

For five years, Smith was the pivot of the Administration: his strength was not in his oratory, effective though his homely style often was, but in his shrewd and sensitive handling of political business. In the House, as at the Strand, his judgment of men was basic to his success. But even his mastery of Parliamentary business faltered and failed when faced by the crisis over Parnell, the Piggott forgeries and the whole imbroglio over Irish affairs. His health was failing; his spirit depressed and distracted by what he saw as the declining standards of Parliamentary affairs. His re-election to Westminster, where he was acclaimed even by the Radical *Pall Mall Gazette* as 'the most popular man that has led the House of Commons for the last twenty years', failed to rally him.[14] He died on 6 October 1891, aged 66, on the same day as Parnell. The *New York Herald* wrote: 'The House of Commons killed Mr. Smith as it has killed many another man of smaller importance . . . The newspapers and the public do not realise how much heavier the strain has become than it was in former times.'[15] Queen Victoria wrote to his widow: 'He was so good, so honest, so amiable & of such a modest & unselfish character that everyone respected him & must regret him. He died from devotion to his work.'[16] His widow was soon afterwards created Viscountess Hambleden.

Any valedictory comment on William Henry must be more complex than such statements on great business men usually are. He had none of what are usually described as the dynamic qualities of the Victorian and Edwardian tycoons – the mobile, restless, roving energy of William Lever, the effervescent exhibitionism of Tommy Lipton, the temperament and emotionalism of a Northcliffe. As a tycoon he was atypical. The qualities that won him popularity in the House and respect in Whitehall were his imperturbable good nature and rationality; his almost inhuman patience and self-control. These were at once a facet of his deep religious feelings and probably a reaction against the hyperactivity and violently explosive temperament of his father.

They happened also – since the character of the entrepreneur and of enterprise itself are both derived in part from their context and circumstances – to be the qualities that were peculiarly appropriate to the growth of his business in the third quarter of the nineteenth century. For the two other business forces upon which his own depended were the railway companies and the publishers – especially the newspaper publishers and managers of *The Times*. The quality they looked for above all (and usually in vain) in the news distributor and bookseller was reliability. In the rumty-tumty world of road and rail transport in the 1840s and 1850s and later still, reliability was far to seek. It was the quality which above all enabled William Henry to rise above his numerous competitors for rail contracts and secure a favoured niche in the arcanum of Printing House Square: to construct (as green-eyed rivals asserted, not entirely without justification) something like a monopoly of certain areas of the distribution of popular literature. By the time of his death, his very success, and that of the professional subordinates who managed his business after his entry into politics, was exposing him and his business to criticism.

His armour was not without its chinks. He might well be called 'the reluctant entrepreneur'. His conscience and sense of duty kept him hard to his work once he had felt bound to yield to the intolerable pressure put on him by his father. But even his meticulous attention occasionally wandered away from duty to those interests in social and political work which were the ultimate compensation he sought for sacrificing his ideal of a religious vocation. Nor does it detract from his achievement to suggest that William Henry had, up to a point, the economic wind behind him from the 1850s to the 1880s: so did others who nevertheless failed as conspicuously as he succeeded. By the time of his death the economic climate was changing. The basic or older industries had for two decades felt the blast of foreign competition. By the 1890s even the new, secondary, light trades and industries – like Smith's itself – were having to adapt to more competition at home, more constraints and less favourable or less obvious openings for enterprise. Fresh ideas and new men were needed. Even if William Henry had not died when he did, one may doubt whether the methods he had applied round the mid-century would have brought the ship home to port in the early twentieth century. The enormous goodwill and inherent strength which he had created for his business nevertheless remained: it was a sound foundation on which his successors could build.

William Henry's political career has in itself little direct relationship to the continuing affairs of what still remained his own private business. Yet indirectly and in the longer term, it had very important consequences indeed: once he was involved in government, he had to renounce his connection with any government contracts. This he immediately did. In other respects he continued, for six or more years, to exercise a powerful influence on the general policy of management at W. H. Smith's. Yet even this slowly faded as the demands of Westminster grew. Smith's gradually became a 'managed' business: still privately owned – William Henry never allowed any doubts on that – but increasingly managed by a group of partners – Lethbridge from 1864 as senior, joined by others as time went by, together with a growing group of specialised expert managers responsible for the different sections of the business.

William Henry II's political involvement had one curious consequence: characteristically it concerned the Smith business in Ireland. From the start, the Dublin business had had problems. Even by the mid-1860s, when Charles Eason had brought it into remarkable order, William Henry was still cautioning him against being too ambitious. Ireland was too small a market to warrant grand schemes of expansion. The penny newspaper and general torpor of business were a warning against excessive optimism. This worked for a time but by 1867 Eason was becoming plaintive and fractious.[17] Not even his faith in the Almighty could reconcile him to the fact that he had now worked for seventeen years as a manager and never been offered the chance of a partnership, while in London men of no greater ability had achieved partnership status. It was not the least painful aspect of his situation that 'your [William Henry's] withdrawment from some of the oversight of your business causes the details to come less under your view . . .'[18] Lethbridge and White (head of the Counting House) had both expressed themselves satisfied with Dublin's progress. So the wrangle continued. 'The poor fellow', wrote William Henry to Lethbridge in January 1879, 'is evidently very much in earnest. He has come to the conclusion that he himself is a very remarkable man . . . Poor fellow I am sorry for him.'[19]

Eason continued to advertise his meritorious service to Smith's. William Henry, distracted by his daily political involvements, continued to put off a decision. It was probably politics, nevertheless, that created an upset in 1883, in the House of Commons. Eason had started publishing Catholic prayer books which were issued in his name. Tim Healy, one of the keenest Irish MPs in the House taunted William Henry ('friend of the Orangemen of Belfast') with selling Catholic prayer books. Shortly after (as Charles Eason's son later recorded) 'Mr. Smith made a present of the whole of the stock [of prayer books] to my Father . . . I have always felt that Mr. Smith dealt very generously with us.'[20]

The facts of the final act three years later were also put plainly by Charles Eason's son:

A crisis came in 1886 when Mr. Smith became Chief Secretary for Ireland. The excitement in the political world was intense, and my father at once suggested to Mr. Smith that the business might suffer. Mr. Smith responded most generously, and early in February the transfer of the business was settled in principle. My father suggested that a part ownership in the business might be retained but Mr. Smith preferred to withdraw altogether from Ireland and, accordingly, the whole business was sold to my father and myself, trading as Charles Eason & Son. Mr. Smith did not require any independent valuation of the business, he accepted the figures of the last Balance Sheet as the basis of payment without any addition for goodwill.[21]

Thus Ireland followed Scotland: with the exceptions of Brussels and Paris, W. H. Smith's became virtually an English business.

William Henry's departure into politics did not mean that he became an absentee landlord: very much the reverse. For at least six more years after he became Member for Westminster, his connection with what was still his own private business remained close and his influence still decisive. In this there was nothing either unusual or improper: the Parliamentary programme was itself organised on the principle that Members had their private business and professional interests and their private recreations: all were necessary: all were allowed for. Thus the grouse shooting season was one reason why autumn sittings of the House were rare. Nevertheless, it is doubtful whether he would have continued in the business to the extent he did if his constituency had not been Westminster. From the House to the Strand was only twenty minutes' walk. In Lethbridge he already had an able second in command: in 1864 Lethbridge became a partner, in much the same way as William Henry himself had become his father's partner in 1846.

Lethbridge settled down quickly and characteristically without fuss. '[He] seems to like his work', wrote William Henry from Dublin in November 1864, 'for he really gives time and attention to it with more interest and acuteness than I can show.'²² Nevertheless, the articles of partnership left no doubt that as the principal partner, W. H. Smith continued to have 'exclusive and absolute power and authority over the said business . . .' His decisions were to be binding on Lethbridge; Lethbridge was to obey William Henry's orders and directions; he was not to have any share in the capital or property of Smith's, or to bear any of their business risk. He was to give 'his whole time and best attention' to the business, so that William Henry was free to give 'only such time and attention . . . so far as he may in his uncontrolled discretion think fit and necessary'.²³ There spoke the voices of past and present – father, son and their friend and meticulous legal adviser, William Ford; but Parliamentary pressures, and the remote possibility of political office prompted a further move in 1868 which began the loosening of William Henry's ties with everyday conduct of his business.

Smith's were suppliers of newspapers to government offices. They acted as advertising agents for government. It was at least doubtful whether William Henry could 'with propriety' be continued in this function. In an agreement of that year he declared his wish to divest himself of any profit or interest in such dealings. Smith's would therefore henceforth have no dealings with any government department. *Lethbridge* might do so 'in his own name and on his own account': he might not involve Smith's name or capital.²⁴ So the partnership continued. Lethbridge, William Henry wrote to Ford on 12 September 1870, 'is manfully at work and seriously caring for everything . . .'²⁵ He had already proved himself well capable of negotiating with all those outside interests which together set the stage for the extraordinary growth of the Smith business down to William Henry's death. He was equally apt as strategist and tactician, yet palpably frank and honourable in his dealings. He was resolute but naturally friendly, patient and reasonable. Again and again, against all the apparent odds, he succeeded in reaching agreement with the railways; with patience and tact he fended off the attempts of *The Times* managers (egged on by their master, John Walter III) to browbeat Smith's over a variety of problems which were perennial sources of friction between the newspaper proprietors and the news distributors.

He dealt equally firmly with members of the public who tried to manage Smith's business in the light of their own ideas on public morality and responsibility: for example, the Headmaster of Sherborne, the Rev. E. M. Young, who pressed them to ban certain magazines from their bookstalls. Papers such as the *Sporting Times* and others had fallen into the hands of boys at the school. The very foundations of morality, declared Mr Young, were in danger. Lethbridge's comments to William Henry were a good example of his firm but relaxed, balanced and unflappable style of handling such situations, which were constantly plaguing the business. He wrote:

> My dear Smith . . . The question of offensive publications is very difficult . . . Honestly I confess I do not see my way to dealing with any but those which are undoubtedly indecent or obscene, and exclusion from the bookstalls stimulates the demand for publications so tabooed – coarse vulgarity – indelicacy – bad taste and an offensive style do not in my judgment justify our refusing publications a place on the Stalls . . . I daresay he [the Headmaster of Sherborne] thinks – as many of the public think – that if a publication is excluded from the Railway Bookstalls it is killed – The *Illustrated Police News* [long famous as a means of exploiting criminal proceedings for purposes more salacious than educational] has a circulation averaging some 100,000 copies a week of which not a single copy passes through our hands.[26]

As the rising tide of business showed, Lethbridge was worth the 20 per cent of net profits which his partnership was bringing him by the 1870s. He radiated the sort of quiet confidence which made political life, and even long absences from England, possible for William Henry. Everything was going on quietly, Lethbridge wrote to him in Canada, in August 1872. The Stations (bookstalls) were doing well, money coming in well. Chapman (of Chapman & Hall, Smith's dependent book publisher) was 'of course in his chronic state of tightness'. Cockett (of the Railway Advertising Department) had accepted a new contract. The printers were still asking for more. White (head of the Newspaper Department and 'Counting House') 'goes off for his holiday . . . on Friday . . . but everything goes smoothly. I have had a talk with Monger (head of Newspaper Dispatch) & he is of opinion that our hands are well satisfied . . . with their pay & position so I have satisfied myself at present by telling him to keep his eyes & ears well open . . .'[27]

Lethbridge was the embodiment of Victorian optimism and assurance. This was the stuff of his relationship with his senior partner, his business associates and the public. He was also (like William Henry) a realist where people were concerned. Ford – the solicitor and legal adviser – he wrote later 'is as gloomy as ever'.[28] Evans – Smith's medical expert – 'as mad as ever or rather more so'.[29] White was back from the north and midlands – not all well but it could be put right with a little thought. The manager of *The Times* was angry because he couldn't buy his *Times* at East Croydon the other day: he had been assuaged.[30] The strike of carpenters and printers was settled by a compromise: a new 54 hour week would begin in both departments.[31] There was too much money and little or no interest on the bank deposit. Should he re-invest? What about the Northern Canada Railway (in which both William Henry and he had substantial interests)? But generally Lethbridge had nothing special to worry his principal with. Business was going well, cash flowing in well. There was plenty of money available for normal business needs. If William Henry had any *special* expansion in mind would he let him know? Etc. It was all comfortable and reassuring. And so things went on through the 1870s. By this time Lethbridge was earning – and worth his hire – a quarter of the net profits of Smith's.

Yet, for all his comfortable stance, Lethbridge was himself now in need of help, as William Henry had been in the 1850s and 1860s. After the abolition of the stamp duty in 1855 and the paper duties in 1861, the national upsurge of trade and industrial output gave Smith's special opportunities: they also created more problems for management. New papers, magazines, books 'were started on every hand'. In 1821 there had been 267 in all – but almost no provincial dailies. By 1861 there were more than 1,100. The older, costly papers – *The Times* especially – had seen their London territory invaded by the new penny papers like the *Daily Telegraph* with a daily circulation of a quarter of a million (see page 175).

'It does not, of course, follow', wrote a contributor to the *Quarterly Review* in 1880, 'that this enormous increase in the circulation of the London daily papers is confined to the capital ... The provinces take a surprising quantity – so many, in fact, that the hour of "going to press" ... has ... been modified to meet the provincial demand.'[32] This, the *Review* continued, 'is due in a great measure, if not wholly, to the energy of one man'. And it recalled William Henry's defence in the House of Disraeli's appointment of the obscure Mr Pigott as the Controller of the Stationery Office. Accepting that Pigott knew nothing of printing or stationery, he had pointed out that:

practical knowledge was not always the best test of a good administrator ... He had ... appointed as his representative a gentleman who not merely had had no experience of news-agency, but who was one whose antecedents might be thought peculiarly unsuited to the manager of a vast business. Mr. Smith was then referring to the present head of the business part of his firm, Mr. Lethbridge, who was until 1862 one of the masters of a public school. Since Mr. Lethbridge assumed the management ... of 186 Strand, it has grown enormously ... the greatest extension ... since the institution of the 'newspaper trains' in 1876, which were entirely due to Mr. Lethbridge.

The London papers were folded and sorted *en route* for the great industrial cities of the midlands and north: yet this had not impeded the growth of the provincial press. London was not the power it once was: a simultaneous growth of local economic interest had accompanied the continuing need for Manchester, Birmingham and Liverpool to have access to *London* news. In 1855 the provincial press barely existed. By 1868, sixteen provincial towns had at least one daily paper. By 1900 over seventy cities had a daily, either morning or evening, selling at a penny or half penny. This had become possible 'thanks to the [electric] telegraph and to the various agencies for the transmission of information' that enabled the provinces to obtain almost simultaneous access to international intelligence with the metropolis itself.[33] (The writer might have added that William Henry had seen to it that he was in on the ground floor when the telegraphic agencies were initiated, invested heavily and confidently in them and later reaped a modest harvest of capital appreciation when he was bought out.)[34]

'The old-fashioned high-priced and somewhat ponderous organ' which was the provincial weekly paper still lingered on but its power and prestige had gone.[35] The only weeklies left were in London – the *Observer* and the *Sunday Times*: on a lower level *Lloyds*, *Reynolds* and the *News of the World*. But other flavours brought variety to the spreading foliage of the popular press – specialist periodicals to appeal to those moved by religious, temperance or sporting interests, cab-drivers, photographers, medicinal experts and non-experts, spiritualists, billiard players, licensed victuallers, architects, the deaf and dumb, the vegetarians, actors, race-horse owners, Freemasons, miners, musicians ... there was no end to the opportunities for enterprise opened up by the new, spreading literacy and relative affluence of England in the late Victorian Age: even the 'Great Depression' seems to have frightened historians more than it frightened most of those contemporaries who gazed out upon England between the 1870s and

1890s and saw it as a land where prices might be falling but real wages – at least for those with jobs – were rising.

The increase in real incomes helped to stimulate the publishers' and newsagents' search for wider markets and lower costs of production. New and cheaper methods of making paper, the introduction of high-speed presses for printing mass circulation papers, more accurate and rapid methods of reproducing paper and book illustrations, cheaper ways of publishing and binding novels and classics . . . all these increased the spreading circulation of popular literature and speeded the rise of new publishers – Macmillan, Routledge, Dent, etc., and the authors they popularised – Charles Dickens, Hall Caine, Kingsley, Rider Haggard, and so on. The growth of periodicals, magazines and more intellectual 'reviews' was even more important in cultivating the habits of those who have been called 'the common readers'. The grand culmination – for some – of this popular literary movement was to come with Pearson, Newnes and Alfred Harmsworth – *Answers* and *Titbits*. 'More and more', an American authority on the subject has commented disenchantedly, 'as the years passed, people would be buying reading matter whose chief function was to keep their eyes busy while their brains took a rest'.[36]

It is not necessary to admire, objectively, the popular press of late Victorian England to recognise that such judgments are subjective, detached from their historical environment. Material progress, relative affluence, relative freedom from traditional corstraints – all these brought losses as well as gains. It is not, however, self-evident that 'the reading habit among the masses was contributing nothing to their cultural improvement'. Had reading become merely 'a popular addiction . . . the soporific exercise that the earliest advocates of cheap religious reading matter had intended . . .'? Was it the betrayal of the ideals of the advocates of a free press who had stage-managed the abolition of the stamp? It was only so if the new readers are judged by standards different from those of an earlier age who had been able to afford the luxury of costly imported pornographic books[37] or who had known where to find their cheap equivalent in the back streets of towns and villages.

These are matters of opinion. The certain fact which faced William Henry and Lethbridge in the 1860s and 1870s was that the rising tide of popular literature, good, bad and indifferent, called for another instalment of managerial change in the Smith business. William Henry had his intellectual and emotional limitations: snobbery was not among them. Honours, titles, social symbols of status meant little if nothing to him: it was not 'Old Morality' but his widow who was ennobled as a tribute to his services. In February 1886, after he had laid down his seals of office as Chief Secretary for Ireland, he wrote to his sister Gussie. The letter was, characteristically, mostly about the death of Cyrus Elliman, a very senior member of the Smith staff at the Strand whose record dated back to the days of William Henry I . . . 'He died at 74 after having been in the Strand for 59 years. I was very sorry for him as indeed were the whole staff . . .' He added: '. . . The Queen was very gracious to me on Saturday when I gave up the Seals, but I am sure you will be glad to know I remain by my own strong wish, plain Mr Smith'.[38]

He did not hold it against other men that they had enjoyed easier social precedents or education superior to his own. If he was not a snob, neither was he an inverted snob. When he saw, in the late 1860s, that Lethbridge needed help, he looked round for another potential partner in the Lethbridge mould . . . 'some University man who might be trained to help in his business . . .'[39] He found the man he wanted in Charles Awdry, of a landed family in Wiltshire, son of the late Chief Justice of Bombay, brother of the Bishop of South Tokyo, a Wykehamist, sportsman, stroke of the New College, Oxford, Eight in 1868–9. Charles Awdry was to prove a very successful choice. He shared with Lethbridge a patrician yet liberal background. He entered immediately and without hesitation into the democratic ethos of the Strand, at the bottom of the ladder, sharing the heavy labours that attended the despatch of the London papers for the provinces. By accident or something less fortuitous, Awdry was to prove the first of the triumvirate of New College provenance which was to be charged with the responsibility for the W. H. Smith business after William Henry's death in 1891.

For some seven years, Awdry had acted as assistant manager to Lethbridge. In 1876 a deed of partnership was drafted: it recited Awdry's claims to have his services 'more beneficially exercised . . . [in] the status of a partner' . . . but strictly 'under the express direction' of William Henry or Lethbridge.[40] Awdry, returning the draft of the neat agreement to Ford in 1881 concurred: of course, he added, his two seniors could, if they chose, exercise their powers arbitrarily, but that 'appears to me inevitable, & practically of no consequence, as if we are to work together at all our relations must really rest on good faith, and you know well what entire confidence I have (& could not fail to have) in their good faith.'[41]

Awdry might not have the vision or originality of Lethbridge or (later) St John Hornby (see page 190), but his temperament was equable and reasonable, his sense of justice to employees strong. He was the top second-class man. A decade later, when a new deed of partnership set out the joint duties and powers of the proprietor, Lethbridge and Awdry, it reiterated the sole discretion of William Henry to give as much or as little time and attention to the business as he saw fit. Lethbridge was now to give such time and attention to the extent 'that may be necessary in reference to matters of general policy', but was no longer required 'to attend daily' or to 'details' except in case of emergency.[42] Awdry now took over virtually entire responsibility for the business to which he was to give his whole time and attention. His salary was £8,000 a year (the percentage arrangement earlier enjoyed by Lethbridge was not extended to Awdry) but on any unexplained termination of his partnership or the winding up or sale of the business, Awdry was to receive £10,000.

We shall see later the range of duties and problems that fell to the partners. They formed, however, only half of a double tier of management. Below them came a dozen or more – as time went on – specialised managers each charged with responsibility for his own professional expertise in the daily running of the business: newspaper distribution, periodicals, magazines, books, the circulating library, the superintendence of bookstalls district by district, advertising, framing, printing, transport, etc. The same technological advance in printing, photography and illustration that was transforming the whole industry of popular literature, combined with a decision in 1908 to launch what would later be called a 'house magazine' – the *Newsbasket* – has preserved the physiognomies of a number of these mid- and late-Victorian managers – some dating back to the days of William Henry I. Perfect reflections of the conventional image of middle-class Victorian England, they gaze into the camera; stiff, stern, strong-jawed personifications of the virtues of accuracy, discipline and punctuality for which the firm stood. Almost all are full-face portraits: perhaps the long drawn-out agony of the photographic sitting in those early days explains why few of them show much sign of the wit and humanity for which they were often known. (The portraits of the partners are significantly different, usually profile or semi-profile. Whether this represented a difference in the sophistication of the photographer or the wisdom of the sitter who can say? A sitter in the early days of photography had to remain perfectly still for at least fifteen minutes.)

The managers survived the rigours of a career with Smith's with remarkable resilience. Out of a group of eight top managers for whom evidence exists, the oldest survivor was 82 when he died: the youngest, 62. The average age at death was 68. The earliest was born in 1812; the last survivor died in 1915. Together they spanned the history of England from the Napoleonic Wars to the First World War. Their average length of service with Smith's was just under half a century: the one with the longest service could count sixty years – Elliman, to whose death William Henry referred in his letter (see page 170) – but in general the period of service was extraordinarily long. In September 1906 Charles Awdry wrote to Stanley Wilson, MP for Hull, who had been pursued by an aggrieved constituent, an employee of Smith's dismissed for irregularities and heavy drinking. Awdry explained that in addition to this, the constituent was in error in claiming uniquely long service: '... 25 years is in our employment almost to be regarded as short service: we have many who have been with us 40 years or more.'[43]

The main reason for this phenomenon was analysed later in a series of articles in *The Times* by a member of its editorial staff:

> W. H. Smith II established the system of scientific promotion from the ranks, which is essential to the peculiar efficiency of the organisation. The heads of departments and of provincial branches have in almost every case begun as paper boys at bookstalls, and have risen through the various grades of bookstall assistant, relief clerk, clerk-in-charge, and superintendent. By this system of education, the man at the head of the department knows his business absolutely from the bottom to the top. By this system, too, the feeling of loyalty to the firm is strengthened; every worker has the knowledge that he is not a mere tool to be used and cast aside, but an integral part of the great machine. How strongly this feeling exists is shown by the manner in which a son succeeds his father in many departments, so that in some cases there are as many as three generations on the firm's books.[44]

The records bear out the general truth of *The Times*'s remarks. The exceptions, when expertise had to be recruited from outside, occurred when some innovation was introduced into the traditional functions of the business. When the first Book Department was set up in 1849, Smith's were in some difficulty about finding someone to organise it and consulted Hamilton, Adams & Co, the booksellers. They recommended Jabez Sandifer who was in their employment at Cambridge. Somewhat reluctantly, Sandifer agreed; over the next 38 years he saw his department grow from about 20 to some 130 people. His successor, W. F. Kingdon, became equally well known in the bookselling trade. He was initiated on a modest reference from his former employer: he was 'perfectly honest and steady – Writes a good Hand and is tolerably apt at accounts' but suffered from a 'want of energy and activity ...' which would perhaps be removed by 'a brush of London business'.[45] It was: a quarter of a century later, when Sandifer died and a successor had to be found, Lethbridge wrote to Awdry: 'Of Kingdon I have formed a very good opinion, he has shown tact, firmness & good judgment in some cases of difficulty . . .'[46] There was no doubt about his promotion.

The training and organisation provided by Smith's steadily became famous in the Strand, Fleet Street and the whole publishing district of London. Edward Rossiter, a former employee, wrote in the *Journalist* in 1887: '. . . the training and insight into business the clerks [at Smith's] attained was very valuable to them. They were in demand in the commercial department of the press as publishers, managers, etc.' For example, Joseph Mansfield, manager of the *Graphic* and previously on the *Saturday Review*, had joined W. H. Smith's as a junior clerk in 1860.[47]

These upper echelons of management constituted an élite at the Strand. When William Henry went off to Cyprus on his first foreign trip as First Lord of the Admiralty in 1878, he was seen off like departing royalty at Charing Cross by Admiral Sir George Elliot, C-in-C Portsmouth, Lethbridge and 'to my surprise, White, Sandifer and Taylor, old Strand faces, came to shake hands and say, God bless you Sir'.[48] Their continued personal loyalty to William Henry – in White's case almost an obsession – (see pages 187–9) reminds one that at this period the relations inside English private businesses were sometimes more like those of nineteenth- and twentieth-century Japan than of modern Europe. More than once, in the 1860s and 1870s, William Henry seriously contemplated making the senior managers 'limited partners' in his business. Ford raised the even more revolutionary possibility of converting it into a limited liability company in 1876. Again, in 1886, Ford wrote to William Henry:

We have as you will remember from time to time taken the 'Limited Liability Bull' by the horns only to let it go again although I have always felt that it would have to be recaptured and put to the practical solution of the future of the business . . . What I want to evolve is the formation of a private company for a term, or until your death [Ford always took positive melancholy enjoyment in facing the worst] with an internal machinery for conversion into a public company on certain events . . . it would relieve you . . . from the greater part if not from all the contingencies . . . legal, moral, or sentimental; and it would have the great advantage of providing an almost automatic machinery for the disposal of the concern on your death. The private coy. could be so constructed as to give you practically the same powers as you have at present over the business & without impinging the *amour propre* of present partners and managers.[49]

Ford's advice was wise and far-sighted. Unfortunately it was not taken for more than another four decades. Meanwhile, the partners remained partners, the managers remained managers and William Henry remained sole proprietor. This form of organisation, commercially and socially ancient, was to give rise to serious difficulties as time went on. What were the respective duties and the qualifications of partners and managers? Did they consist in professional competence alone? Or in social status? Or both? If so in what degree? The problem was to arise in acute and embarrassing form in the case of John White, the manager of the Newspaper Department and the 'Counting House', described in an obituary on his premature death as 'the autocrat' of W. H. Smith's. 'He was practically Messrs W. H. Smith & Son. There was no appeal from his judgment in matters of "distribution", for the late Mr. W. H. Smith and the present partner [*sic*] had absolute confidence in him and seldom questioned his decisions, which were occasionally affected by his own very strong views on religious and political matters.'[50] But White never became a partner. Underlying these curious observations was a whole debate of principle about policy and the organisation of policy which becomes clearer in the light of later evidence (see page 393).

Among the transitional problems inherited by Lethbridge and the partners were those implicit in the six or so tons of *The Times* received every weekday morning at the Strand for distribution to the 'country'. The years between the reduction of the newspaper stamp by the Act of 1836 and its abolition in 1855 had been a Golden Age for *The Times*. All attempts to produce and sell a cheap rival to 'the Thunderer' – Dickens's *Daily News*, the *Chronicle*, the *London Telegraph* – failed equally dismally. Older rivals – the *Morning Herald* and *Post* – fell back. But its increasing monopoly carried within itself the seeds of change, and the gathering storm of criticism which culminated in the Parliamentary enquiry of 1851–5 united the criticisms and jealousies of provincial newspaper owners and journalists, middle class liberal prophets of laissez-faire and even government circles which resented the uninhibited opposition of 'the Thunderer'. This strange alliance achieved a short-lived but successful coup: even some of its individual members such as Henry Drummond, MP for West Surrey, were aghast at what was done. It was a 'dirty stab in the dark'. *The Times* had survived because it was produced and written with journalistic and business ability: if its profits were abolished 'it would dwindle down to the same twaddle as the *Morning Herald*'.[51]

This was the situation after abolition of stamp duty in 1855. During 1858 *The Times*'s circulation fell from 55,000 to 50,000. Its profits from advertising fell sharply. Competition both provincial and metropolitan grew. The *Manchester Guardian* (hitherto weekly), *Liverpool Post, Birmingham Mercury* and the *Scotsman* forged ahead. But the sharpest competition came from London where the *Daily Telegraph and Courier* of four pages, appeared on sale for 2d. (compared with *The Times* at 5d.). In less than two months, the *Telegraph* was in difficulties and sold out to its printer, Joseph Moses Levy. In September Levy gave London its first morning paper for 1d.

The Circulation of the *Daily Telegraph* [the *Courier* part of its title was dropped] EXCEEDS THAT OF ANY LONDON MORNING NEWSPAPER, with the exception of *The Times* . . . the Circulation . . . is greater than any FOUR MORNING Newspapers all put together. As an ADVERTISING MEDIUM, the *Daily Telegraph* stands second only to *The Times* . . . It is to be found at the chief Club Houses and Hotels, at every Railway Station and Commercial place of resort, at every Newsvendors and the corner of every street. The Banker, the Merchant, the Peer, the Member of Parliament, the Lords and the Commons, all now alike read the *Daily Telegraph*.[52]

Levy's advertising technique was modelled on the *New York Herald*: choose your target and claim you have already hit it. Yet the greater challenge came less from the *Telegraph* than from James Johnstone's *Standard* which he changed from an evening to a morning paper of eight full-sized pages looking very like *The Times*.

Recovering its wind after the abolition of the paper duties in 1861, *The Times* won back some of its lost circulation between 1862 and 1867 but then dropped again: its gains relatively fell behind those of its new rivals. The 'new journalism', which included afternoon papers such as the *Pall Mall Gazette* with contributions by Trollope, Charles Kingsley and Matthew Arnold, was conscious of the need to combat charges of 'vulgarity' if its challenge to *The Times* was to be more than a flash in the pan. John Walter III meanwhile grasped the need to reform 'the Thunderer's' techniques. New printing machinery incorporating new methods was combined with tougher advertising rates to cut down production time and costs and raise revenue. The battle grew sharper: Fleet Street bankruptcies more frequent. More than ever, success in newspaper publishing (and distribution) depended on business acumen.

Smith's inevitably felt the cross-currents flowing strongly in the news-paper world round about 1860. William Henry II had inherited a news distribution business built largely on the export of the London papers, above all *The Times*, from London to the provinces. Practically the whole of the country issue of *The Times* was bought by Smith's, and for many years they had paid some £4,000 p.a. for the privilege of having the earliest copies of the paper. A premium of a penny was charged to cover the extra cost of buying and carrying this unusually weighty paper. In 1860 *The Times* made up its mind to abolish the £4,000 charge in an effort to get itself sold uniformly and universally for the 4d. as printed on each copy.

This led to new collisions between the complex forces operating in the news market. *The Times* found itself obliged to allow discounts to agents (including Smith's) who sold large numbers of copies on station bookstalls and in the provinces. But regular London subscribers buying, for example, through the Strand, had to pay 5d. to cover the substantial costs of carriage. There were thus still two prices for *The Times* according to where it was sold. When the price was reduced to 3d., it was found impossible to per-suade many agents to charge less than 3½d. The dispute about price went on until 1871, when *The Times* was forced to tackle the basic problem: who was to bear the cost of papers sold to the agents by *The Times* but unsold by the agents to the public? In June 1871, John Walter finally instructed Mowbray Morris, his manager, to take back all copies 'unsold [by Smith] at the Railway Stations', such copies 'not [to] exceed a certain proportion [to be agreed upon] to the total railway sales.'[53] Combined with the spurt in sales created by the outbreak of the Franco-Prussian War, this sale-or-return system helped to prop up *The Times*'s falling sales. It also resolved a long conflict between *The Times* and their principal country agent: an analysis of this shows that the interests of publisher and distributor were far from identical. It was this fact which explained a long series of bitter conflicts between Smith's and *The Times*.

John Walter's manager, Mowbray Morris, though a man of thrust and vigour, did not include tact or patience among his qualities. Walter knew this very well when he urged Delane, his editor-in-chief in 1860 to 'set Morris at Smith'.[54] The aggressive tactics that suited Morris well had been much to the fore when he had given evidence before the Parliamentary Committee on Abolition of the Stamp Duty. Since the plan for *The Times* to buy out Smith's had fallen through (see page 151), Morris was to be let loose on William Henry. A trial shot was fired in January when Morris

wrote a sarcastic and irritable note to him agreeing to alter the arrangements by which Smith's had delivered him a daily parcel of *The Times* to
his house at Ascot.

> I cannot help observing that the service which you have been asked to
> perform for me does not seem to be a very unreasonable demand upon
> the powers of your establishment. However, since you cannot oblige
> me in this matter, & you have a monopoly of the railways, I must
> perforce submit.[55]

By the end of March, he was demanding that in return for the remission
of the £4,000 hitherto paid by Smith's for early copies of *The Times*,
Smith's should reduce the price of *The Times* to their customers. Any loss
they might sustain:

> [could] only result from your [Smith's] having demanded & received
> from the public, your customers, a higher price than that marked on
> the paper. It is true that we have acquiesced in this practice . . . we
> propose now . . . we should both forego this benefit. Your sacrifice may
> be greater, but so has been your gain.[56]

William Henry remained imperturbable as ever in the face of Morris's
repeated and officious attempts to instruct him in the rudimentary conduct
of his business, to say nothing of the continued habit of *The Times*, for
which it was notorious, of arriving late at the London railway termini and
holding up the trains. Against Morris's demands that a uniform high price
be charged for *The Times*, he argued in favour of a universal reduction of
the price to all purchasers and therefore of course to the distributing trade.
Morris, obviously alarmed, counter-attacked:

> . . . the Conductors of the *Times* are not prepared to make this sacrifice
> . . . your business must be very extravagantly conducted if you cannot
> afford to sell *The Times* at all places within the Bills of Mortality (includ-
> ing Railway Stations) at an increase of 27½% upon our wholesale price.[57]

When he received a report from Hitchin that Smith's bookstall had twice
sold out of *The Times* in a week, Morris's tone became more caustic than ever.

> . . . the practical monopoly which we have given you on the sale of our
> paper has produced the usual effect in deadening activity & stopping

enterprise . . .[58] I must not conceal from you my doubts whether the
rapid growth of your business has not exceeded your power to perform
it . . .[59]

William Henry kept his temper and refrained from comment on ponderous hints by Morris that *The Times* had other systems of distribution up its
sleeve if Smith's would not come to heel. He was sorry to note the tone of
a letter from Morris in December 1861 naming him 'the chief offender'
against the public interest in *The Times*.[60]

If arrangements were made in my favour in the Publishing Office they
were based upon an understanding making the interests of *The Times*
the first & chief object, and you have yourself admitted that although
bound only by my word I have acted throughout fairly and honourably.

But he could no longer keep quiet on Morris's offensive rhetoric and
concluded acidly that Morris was:

entirely in the dark as to the necessary charges which are incurred in the
distribution of the paper.
    The machinery of this office is available for promoting the interests of
The Times, to a larger extent than any other in existence. I believe it to
be now used for that purpose, and the evidence of the fact is in your
possession; where our Agencies do not exist the supply of the paper is
more scanty and the price higher than at our Stations and I believe there
are many parts of the Country which would be unsupplied, excepting
through the Post, if our men were withdrawn.

If no means could be found 'to place our mutual relations on a satisfactory footing', withdrawn they would be.[61]
    On that Olympian note the controversy was, for the moment, suspended.
William Henry was not often so blunt. Morris was quiet and when the
discussions were resumed ten years later, they ended with a letter from
Macdonald, Morris's successor, which conveyed a cordial message from
John Walter III offering to take back from Smith's 'unsold copies up to a
limit of 750 weekly'. *The Times* would leave it to Smith's to arrange with
their bookstall clerks the handling and pricing of any unsold copies. When
an extra demand 'of a speculative character is anticipated' and this was
intimated to *The Times*, 'we shall always be ready to halve the risk with
you . . .'[62]

This innovation certainly improved matters but it was not the end of the differences between Smith's and *The Times*. Faced by the competition of the penny papers, Macdonald himself would complain that Smith's did not 'push' *The Times* sufficiently.[63] In the 1890s, Macdonald's successor, Moberly Bell, though more courteous and patient than his predecessors, was still arguing hard with Awdry (see page 187). The differences were, in truth, exceedingly complex and obstinate. John Walter III, his editors and managers, were perfectionists. They were also dictatorial. Their reputation for carrying the latest possible news in the most perfect format demanded reporting and proof-reading at a standard higher than those of their cheaper competitors. This was difficult to operate in harmony with railway timetables and newsagents' arrangements for getting their papers to the readers. The price (at 3d.) remained much higher than that of its newer competitors and was able to remain so because (as Macdonald wrote to Smith's in October 1884) *The Times* '. . . is especially the Paper of the leisure class who are not as a rule early morning travellers . . .'[64] It was therefore always more difficult for the bookstalls to gauge satisfactorily the rate at which to sell their supply of these more expensive papers through the day. If they 'pushed' the sale too hard, by encouraging the paper boys to 'shout' *The Times* (as *The Times* managers constantly urged them to do) they might well find distinguished late-comers complaining bitterly that they were deprived and betrayed, and writing letters to *The Times* to denounce the incompetence of everybody concerned. If Smith's increased their order for copies, they would equally certainly be left on many days with more unsold copies than they were able to return to *The Times* – even after the 1871 agreement. Like the railway managers, the managers of *The Times* found it difficult – or pretended to – to grasp the unusual risks and running costs of newspaper distribution.

The perfect adjustment of supply and demand seemed to be a problem beyond human ingenuity to solve and the reason lay in the very nature of *The Times* and its readers. In both cases, the higher the quality the more intractable the problems. The only solution was to go on arguing: and that is precisely what they did.

VII

Change Partners: 1885–1905: A Crisis of Management

> Mr. W. H. Smith said . . . he had been at the head of a very large business . . . but what he had done was to exercise his judgement . . . in the selection of a manager, and he had always to rely upon the advice of faithful and able assistants.[1]

For some years before the premature death of William Henry II in 1891, there were signs and portents of more difficult times ahead. The uninterrupted expansion of newspaper business and especially the growth of the bookstall empire of which he was the architect seemed to be slackening. One of the first omens was the sour confrontation of Lethbridge and Awdry with the LNW Board in the early summer of 1885. Both sides were by now accustomed to ritual declarations of bad business, unsatisfactory levels of rents, threats to end the business relationship in part or in whole. But on this occasion the negotiations had a nasty air of real business. The railway company demanded larger percentages for rents of bookstalls, especially at large termini, special discounts for customers buying books and magazines on LNW stations, and they refused to discuss the future of advertising. Lethbridge, though now an ageing and tired man, conducted the negotiations with his usual blend of frankness and reasonableness. He refused, nevertheless, to agree to a shorter contract than 10 years, or to the proposed discount system, even though the LNW directors held over his head throughout the whole proceedings the threat to take advertising 'into their own hands' unless Smith's agreed to their terms. In mid-July a compromise was eventually reached for a bookstall contract for ten years on very stiff terms but there was no agreement until later about advertising.

In the course of the argument Lethbridge told the railway representatives: that WHS had '53 stalls and 45 sub-stalls at London and North Western Stations, but that it would pay the firm to shut up 20 of these altogether, because they were so unprofitable.'[2] In September he and Awdry in turn reported these facts to William Henry. Lethbridge told him:

> I quite expect that when we receive details we shall find that it will be wise to terminate some of them [i.e. the bookstall contracts] *if we are at liberty to do so*, in consequence of the low rates at which they have been accepted.[3]

William Henry replied from the War Office (where he was now Secretary of State) to Awdry.

> I am afraid you have got a serious task before you, but I am personally quite willing to see the profits lessened somewhat if the concern as a whole can be preserved for those who depend upon it in a vigorous and thriving condition: but you will no doubt require great energy in all concerned.[4]

William Henry's intuitions were prophetic: but not immediately. After a poorish year in 1886 total profits continued with ups and downs for the rest of the century. Turnover at the bookstalls and in general continued to grow as it had done steadily ever since figures for it began to be collected systematically in 1867 (see Table VII.1). Increased turnover was produced by more bookstalls (see Table VII.2). More stalls demanded more labour: so did headquarters staff and advertising staff. The total labour force had risen steeply in consequence (see Table VII.3). The wage bill rose with numbers employed (see Table VII.4). Wages still rose roughly in proportion to hands employed, or less. Rents, or guaranteed minimum payments, to the railway companies on the other hand were rising at rates which were threatening to reduce net profits in an economic situation where gross profits were becoming harder to earn. The total of minimum guarantees or fixed fees paid by Smith's to the ten largest railway companies rose accordingly (see Table·VII.5). Thus with capital employed that had increased nearly threefold, from 1866 to 1904/5, the net profit was becoming harder to obtain after 1899/1900: capital would clearly outrun the capacity of the business to yield an adequate net profit if the pressure from the railway companies continued to raise rents; and other costs continued to grow.

TABLE VII.1 BOOKSTALL TURNOVER, 1867–1904/5[5]

Year	Stalls Turnover (£)
1867	295,899
1885	953,183
1904/5	1,403,003

TABLE VII.2 GROWTH IN NUMBER OF BOOKSTALLS, 1851–1902[6]

Year	Stalls	Sub-stalls	Total
1851	35	—	—
1853	70	—	—
1870	290	—	—
1874	385	—	—
1880	450	—	—
1886	—	—	1166
1894	615	—	—
1902	779	463	1242

TABLE VII.3 GROWTH IN NUMBERS EMPLOYED, 1856–1905[7]

Year	Numbers employed
1856	350 (*approx.*)
1887	4,156
1905	8,285

TABLE VII.4 INCREASE IN THE COST OF WAGES, 1856–1904/5[8]

Year	Wages (total) £ (*approx.*)
1856	—
1870	64,000
1887	150,000
1904/5	275,000

TABLE VII.5 INCREASE IN RENTS PAYABLE TO RAILWAY COMPANIES, 1855–1904/5[9]

Year	*Total rental 10 companies* *(NW GW SW GE SC Mid SE L&Y GN NE)* ★ £
1855	10,110 (GW, GE and NE uncontracted)
1894/5	148,600
1904/5	192,000

★ *SC* = London, Brighton & South Coast.

From the late 1880s onwards, the management was conscious that its task was becoming more exacting. At the same time the proprietor was under heavy physical and nervous strain in the House, less and less able to spare time to advise his business colleagues. Since the 1860s Lethbridge had been the central figure on whom the progress of the business had depended. By 1885 he was only sixty years of age but he had come to regard himself as the elder statesman and wise man rather than the active manager. He was subject to recurrent bouts of poor health to which his increasing bulk doubtless contributed, for the shadow of the 'Great Mogul' certainly did not grow smaller with time. After 1880 his contract with William Henry II was renewed at intervals, but against increasing reluctance on the part of Lethbridge. In August 1886 he had written privately to William Henry that his 'own wish & feeling is . . . to vanish altogether' from the management: but in deference to his colleagues' wishes he was ready to stay on the understanding that he would be largely if not wholly free from regular attendance at the Strand. He would be prepared to act in case of emergency and prompt from the wings but, he added, 'I am fully sensible that I am not physically what I used to be'.[10]

William Henry II was himself conscious of this, as he had written to Sir Alexander Galt, former High Commissioner for Canada, in September 1884. (A number of the Smith partners were closely involved in investment in Canadian industry, coal and shipping especially, about this time. Lethbridge was the largest investor. The city of Coalbanks in Alberta was renamed Lethbridge after him in 1885 and still remains so.)[11] Galt had complained that Lethbridge was something less than courteous to him in correspondence. William Henry replied no less frankly:

> I am sure that his communications to you were not intended to be other-wise than cordial . . . He writes to me very rarely and then only in a

very few lines, so that if I did not know him well I should think him, as you do, cold or indifferent; but the fact is, he is simply lazy.[12]

On the face of it, Lethbridge's attempted semi-exit seemed well timed. In the same letter, he went on to discuss the accession of a new partner. This was A. D. (Alfred) Acland, who was married to William Henry's third daughter Beatrice and whose eldest brother, W. A. D. Acland, later married another daughter, Emily. Both brothers were sons of Sir Henry Acland, Regius Professor of Medicine at Oxford and an old friend and medical adviser of William Henry. Alfred was an engineer, who had served his apprenticeship with Maudslays of Lambeth, the pioneers of the machine tool industry. From there he had passed on to marine and civil engineering and to the railways: above ground the Great Western, below ground the Metropolitan and District. To his engineering expertise, which was doubtless thought to point him towards the printing side of Smith's (growing in the 1870s) Alfred added a passion which embraced both horses and motor cars: a handy if unusual combination of interests for a business which made use of traction in all conceivable forms. He was 27 years old. '. . . Acland', wrote Lethbridge tactfully, 'will have to be arranged for . . . [it] is somewhat difficult. He is of course at present of no great value but I see no reason why he should not become a decided success . . .'[13]

Having seen Alfred safely installed, Lethbridge, a devoted Devonian, withdrew to Wood, South Tawton, and a happy, bachelor semi-retirement of good works as JP, High Sheriff (in 1893) and Treasurer of the Church Congress at Exeter, emerging for some years afterwards to make the occasional intervention in Smith's affairs. Some tactful intercession between Alfred and his colleagues – Awdry especially – swiftly proved necessary. Alfred had his own ideas about the running of the Strand, which he did not hesitate to make public. There was friction with Awdry, who was always careful, correct and discreet. Lethbridge wrote to William Henry in April, 1888:

I fear you have not quite understood Awdry's view of Acland – personally he likes him much – Acland is in every sense a gentleman – but has he business capacity and tact & a disposition for hard work? . . . I should like to see Acland a success and [so] I am sure would Awdry and I am not prepared to say that he may not become one.[14]

To compensate for his lack of crystal clarity over Acland, Lethbridge made his views (they were those of Acland and Awdry too) clear about possible further elections to the partnership, presumably suggested, at least as possibilities, by William Henry. 'I am satisfied', he wrote, 'that it would not be wise to make White or Treadwell or any member of the staff as [*sic*] Partner.'[15] White (Treadwell and the rest did not really come in for serious consideration) was head of the Counting House and manager of the Newspaper Department which was itself the traditional heart of the business. It was around White, his place and func ions at the Strand that a muted but intense battle of wills was to take place over the next few years: in fact, until White's death in 1895. The match was Gentlemen v. Players with a vengeance: but the Gentlemen were not to have it all their own way.

The obituary in the *City Press* on White and notes in Smith's own house magazine were to make clear the partners' dilemma over White and the tragic ambiguity of White's own position in the 1880s and 1890s. By 1888 he had been with Smith's for forty-five years. He had originally been a bookstall clerk at Aldershot. As in so many other cases it was William Henry who had spotted White's ability. He was brought to the Strand where he became the unquestioned head of the office and in all respects, subject only to Lethbridge, William Henry's trusted (and very autocratic) deputy. Add to his zeal and ability that he was a powerful and active Christian, creator and leader of a Bible class at the Strand, a National Councillor of the YMCA and a bachelor with no domestic preoccupations to dilute his concentrated dedication to the Strand, and the picture of the dilemma becomes clear. He exercised (as a later writer in Smith's *Newsbasket* put it) 'a power and influence ... which would be hardly possible, or even desirable, today'.[16]

There was general, if reluctant agreement, even among the partners that in as much as the business owed its progress and prosperity to any one member of the staff, it owed it to John White. No one knew this better than William Henry who recognised his debt by constantly reciprocating White's loyalty to him and ultimately by a legacy twice as large as any other to either executors, friends or employees.

Other tributes were paid to White's charm and kindness. A less attractive, even faintly sinister aspect was recalled by one obituary:

> He had a habit of mentally summing up the man he had to deal with, by glancing at him with his eyelids half closed, and provided this inspection was satisfactory, an opinion would be passed in a low voice, and the business soon ended.[17]

St John Hornby, who was soon to supersede all the other partners in the contest for power, was more blunt. In a speech at the Jubilee Luncheon on

New Year's Day 1943, in celebration of the fiftieth anniversary of his own
entry into the business, he said of White:

> [He] liked to think that he was General Manager of the whole concern,
> and in order to preserve this fiction he had all the correspondence . . .
> brought into his room each morning and made a show of going through
> them, which was of course quite impossible . . . He was . . . austere and
> alarming . . . with a pontifical manner, [and] regarded himself as the
> real Head of the Business and . . . watch-dog on behalf of the Smith
> family to keep an eye on the doings of the Partners, of whom he had no
> great opinion.[18]

The pattern of the managerial kaleidoscope changed once more in 1890.
Frederick William Danvers Smith, William Henry's heir, 'Freddy',
entered the business on coming down from New College, Oxford. This
gave the liveliest satisfaction to Lethbridge and Awdry for more than one
reason. Lethbridge wrote to William Henry:

> If I judge rightly Freddy has a great deal more character & force than
> Acland and this idea has made me think much, perhaps too much, of one
> or two points on which it seems to me Acland is rather wanting . . . at
> no distant date Freddy would be the more important & influential
> partner . . . it does not appear to me that Acland's motto is business first
> & pleasure afterwards but almost the other way and though possibly
> much of this is due to feminine influence I do not think it is entirely so.
> Secondly, while he is ever a gentleman & in his personal relations with
> others everything that could be wished from the social point of view, he
> seems to me when the position of employer and employed arises to be
> somewhat deficient in that manner & tact which is necessary in order to
> ensure the hearty & loyal self-denying co-operation of the staff upon
> which the success of the business has so much depended & which is most
> important for its future well-doing . . . I may be mistaken and . . .
> attach too much importance to trifles . . .[19]

While Freddy was being installed, while Lethbridge and Awdry suspended judgment on Alfred, and while William Henry took short vacations
and cruises to try and break the grip of chronic ill-health, the partners
carried on what in retrospect seems a kind of caretaker government. It
had some important constructive jobs to do: the provision of more stabling,
the extension of head office down Arundel Street and plans for moving

the printing works from Water Lane to Fetter Lane. It also had to face a new flurry of bitter exchanges with *The Times*, this time in the person of the successor to Morris and Macdonald, Moberly Bell. Like the railways, *The Times* was feeling the edge of competition, especially from the *Daily Telegraph*, and vented its frustration on Smith's – and on Awdry in particular. He was accused of distributing *The Times* badly so that customers were left uncertain of their supply: of aiming at unreasonable margins of profit and of refusing Bell information he was entitled to expect.

By the autumn of 1892 relations between Smith's and *The Times* reached their lowest point since the days of Mowbray Morris thirty years before. Bell's allegations mounted to a crescendo in November when he referred to 'what is becoming a very serious matter of complaint with the public – the inefficient working of your monopoly'.[20] Even if Smith's need for higher profit was due to the larger rents being squeezed out of them by the railway companies, was that a reason why *The Times* should make the sacrifice and reduce *its* price and *its* profit? Bell exploded: he could see no end to it. 'The Railway Companies will have found an inexhaustible mine and will only have to make fresh exactions with each new contract.'[21]

There was some truth in what Bell said – and Lethbridge knew it. Lethbridge's influence was throughout thrown into the scales in favour of compromise. *The Times*, he argued, had moved a long way from its old arrogant position of Mowbray Morris's day. *The Times* 'is still to some extent a power . . . Whatever be the outcome, the more I think of it the more I am of opinion that we should do all we can to avoid a rupture, or give *The Times* any good ground for complaint.'[22] In the end his reasonableness won and this particular bout of trouble ended with both sides agreeing that it was all the fault of excessive competition in Fleet Street and excessive charges by the railway companies.

Yet over all this hung the unsolved and apparently insoluble problem of Acland versus White. A few months before William Henry's death, Awdry had written a fairly desperate letter to him to explain that he had been discussing future management at the Strand, the most delicate point being how best the necessary changes could be made 'without hurting a man intensely devoted to you' (viz. John White). Whether this was possible, Awdry couldn't say but though neither he nor Lethbridge wanted to impose extra burdens on William Henry, they felt that he was the only man who could handle the problem. Awdry was not shrinking from dealing with the matter simply to avoid an issue he ought to bear but 'because I believe that nobody else could possibly put back White's position to what it was some time before I ever came to the Strand except yourself

– even if you can – without creating intense soreness – possibly actual parting in bitterness – & this I am sure you desire to avoid'.[23]

But William Henry does not seem to have responded to Awdry's plea. And Awdry – if Alfred was telling the truth, which he probably was – was not on speaking terms with Alfred because, as Alfred said to Lethbridge, 'I know that my views [on White] are not acceptable to him'. In Alfred's view, the general move-all which was taking place in the offices after their geographical rearrangement provided the opportunity to grasp the nettle and put White in his place.

> . . . one of the principal objects of the arrangement of the new offices will be lost if the partners are to remain in the same position as regards White as at present, & except signing, are to do only such work as may seem good to him. What work there will be for three of us I don't know.

Alfred felt very strongly that it was quite wrong that White should open all letters (even those marked Private), and that he should be the sole channel through which outsiders could write to the firm. There should be a proper system of registering and distributing letters for the partners to deal with. The staff should come under proper control and not be allowed to go whenever they liked for so-called 'luncheon'. The question of introducing more telephones should be considered. To dodge all those issues was inexcusable weakness. Alfred concluded:

> I have talked over a good many of these matters with White, and I have yet to be persuaded that anything I have mentioned would be lowering to his position. I believe it entirely depends upon the way the changes are made & by whom, & I am sure that he knows we all have the highest appreciation of his business powers & [are aware] of the fact that the success of the business is largely due to him. I have also mentioned most of them to Mr Smith & my impression was that he thought the change of offices the right time for their introduction . . .[24]

Lethbridge, however, was not to be hurried. He agreed with Alfred. The changes were 'important and desirable'.[25] But they should be made with White's co-operation and all else would follow. It was all a matter of tact and patience. So Alfred battered on in vain: nor was White his only target. He questioned Kingdon's judgment (White assenting) in selling *Lloyd's Dictionary* at too low a price on the bookstalls. He questioned

Awdry as to why the 'mechanical & labouring hands' should not be members of the superannuation fund like the clerks?[26] And so on. Alfred wrote
bitterly to his brother-in-law (Freddy), now on a world tour designed to
broaden his outlook and help fit him for his future responsibilities:

> Things are going on much as usual at the Strand, & I am in my annual
> state of disgust at White being allowed to go away with all the business
> matters with which he has dealt (& many which we have to go on with,
> because they are not completed) locked up & the key in his pocket.[27]

Alfred's wife, Beatrice, took it all rather more light-heartedly and with
a sense of feminine mischievousness. She also wrote to her brother Freddy:
'The world wags on very much the same as usual here. Alfred & Mr.
Awdry have daily rows together, of which, let us hope, you will reap the
benefit.'[28]

White's position, it seemed, was impregnable. Neither Lethbridge nor
Awdry dared to grasp the nettle: the junior partners could not act over the
heads of their seniors. So all that could be done was to plan for the future
when Time, the great healer, would remove White by retirement. *Then* –
there was at least unanimity over this – it must never be allowed to happen
again. There would be a successor – but with strictly limited powers:
all supervision of the bookstall empire, its clerks, inspectors and the like,
all railway correspondence would be dealt with by the partners. Awdry's
idea of a 'private secretary to the partners', wrote Lethbridge to Awdry,
was good and worthy of consideration: 'he should be someone who can
write short-hand and hold his tongue.'[29] (Lethbridge had not been a
schoolmaster for nothing.) But when and how could White be retired
and by whom? *That* would be dealt with in due course.

It was among all these brave words in April 1895 that the apparently
indestructible White became ill and the partners at last had an adequate
excuse to put him on sick leave and relieve him of the duties which caused
Alfred (and everybody else, whatever they might say) so much chagrin. In
May he returned to work but not for long. He retired, mortally ill, to
Eastbourne where he died in September. Office gossip was that he was
never the same after William Henry's death. His will for work and life,
they said, withered. Perhaps they were right: but the evidence of those
four years suggests he was as energetic and autocratic as ever. Perhaps, after
all, he was not as invulnerable as he appeared to Alfred. Perhaps in the end
it was the criticism and the prodding and the daily tensions that destroyed
him.

Whatever the cause of his final illness and departure was, his resistance had shown up the weaknesses of the management. The only senior partner in residence was now Awdry. Lethbridge was an occasional visitor, increasingly out of touch with the changing economic and social conditions that ruled the press and the railways. William Henry was dead. Alfred was energetic and often fundamentally sound in his ideas and criticisms: but even when he was right he lacked the ability to get his ideas accepted by others. He possessed neither the habit of command nor the habit of persuasion. Freddy was still in his apprenticeship to the business and, in any event, his attention was already divided by his decision to go into politics and succeed his father as representative of the electors of the Strand Division in Parliament, by getting married and beginning a family. Faced with problems actual and potential of unprecedented difficulty, the management was hesitant, weak and divided against itself.

Salvation came, if indirectly, from an unexpected quarter. It was Freddy who was responsible for what was certainly the most important event in the history of the business since the mid-century. At Oxford, he had rowed in the New College Eight in 1888, 1889 and 1890 with his friend C. H. St John Hornby. Hornby had stroked the Oxford University boat which beat Cambridge in this last year. But for doctor's orders, Freddy might well have shared in that great victory with him. Together they had gone round the world in 1890 and 1891. In 1892, he was called to the Bar. On 28 November 1892, Freddy wrote from 186 Strand:[30]

> My dear Horn
> I have a proposition to make to you with regard to the business of W.H.S. & S. . . . it is not possible to go into details . . . Can you come and see me? . . .
> Your affec. friend
> W. F. D. Smith.

Hornby entered the business in 1893. The following year he was a salaried partner. In July 1896, Freddy wrote again: Awdry would let 'Horn' have the partnership deed which would give him the status of a profit-sharing partner 'with responsibility equal to that borne by Awdry & Alfred'.[31] Hornby had been a salaried partner for only two years, before which time he had begun training at the Strand and done eighteen months of early morning packing work in the Newspaper Department. The Partners' Diary for 2 January 1893, bore the historic entry: 'Hornby began work'.[32] From late 1894 his name was regularly among those of the partners attending meetings. It was not long before their minutes and decisions began to carry a sense of determination and direction that had long been lacking at 186 Strand. Freddy had inherited his father's capacity for judging men. In Hornby he had found a unifying force that was to reform and transform the W. H. Smith business. The age of indecision and the indecision of age were both at an end. But, first, things were to get worse before they could get better.

VIII

The Turn of the Screw, 1894-1906

Why should we pay for possibilities? We are quite ready to pay for them when they are realised.

The Partners: to the Great Western & Midland Railways Joint Committee, 1901[1]

Large advertising revenues are not created in a moment, even under the most favourable circumstances, especially in these days of very keen competition.

C. H. St J. Hornby: to C. J. Owens, London and South Western Railway, 1901[2]

Long credit is a fatal thing in the newsagency business.

C. H. St J. Hornby: to W. H. Manning, W. H. Smith's Newcastle Wholesale House, 1901[3]

. . . they [the railways] are like the old Yeomanry Cavalry, which moved at the speed of the slowest man . . . That is the only kind of logic — the logic of a strong position — that I have ever found the railway companies would listen to.

William Lever, 1888[4]

The Coming of the Seven Lean Years

After a little more than a year's training at the Strand, it was time for Hornby to take to the road — the iron road. A surviving letter to Charles Awdry written after dinner from the University Pitt Club at Cambridge on 6 May 1894, describes his impressions of the bookstall empire and its prospects in Suffolk. (Suffolk was in the Great Eastern bailiwick, lying fifth in order of importance for bookstall business.) It conveys the authentic flavour of the still young Hornby (he was twenty-six), his keen eye for people, things, and business prospects, his physical energy and his zest for life and action.

His first excursion from Cambridge (where he stayed at the *Bull*) was to Harwich – not, for once, by his favourite mode of transport, the bicycle, but by rail on a free pass from the Great Eastern. He was neither the first nor the last passenger to denounce Harwich, once a picturesque and attractive old port, as 'a thoroughly wretched place'. Railways and steamers loaded with fish and sanitary earthenware had not improved its ancient attractiveness: it was also, he noted, 'poor business'. Lowestoft, on the other hand, he visited with the stall manager, Pink, who 'struck me as a capital clerk, and he has a nice business there'. The stall at Yarmouth was 'not so good . . . as I should have expected from the size of the place – but the class of customer appears poor – the station is very badly situated, and the competition in the town sharp and rather bitter'. At Beccles 'I found Gibbard [the clerk-in-charge] rather disconsolate at the prospect of leaving as he had been having nice increases there for some years, and does not expect the same at Beverley'. Bungay 'should furnish a nice little business in time'. He had visited Framlingham where 'it is proposed shortly to open a sub-stall under Saxmundham'. He then proposed to go on to visit Newmarket, Bury, Haverhill, Ely and March and finally Oxford.

For an Harrovian only four years down from Oxford, with a First in Classical Mods and a Rowing Blue to his credit, Hornby had taken to 'trade' surprisingly quickly. 'I find it quite interesting work', he concluded, 'seeing the different Bookstalls, and getting an insight into the varying conditions of business . . . What a storm in the *Chronicle* over *Esther Waters*!' (see page 365). 'I thought Faux's explanation was well done, and the *Chronicle's* leader a sensible one.'[5]

East Anglia was a useful training ground; with its recent and current experience of deep agricultural depression, it no doubt impressed on Hornby's mind the weight of the burden which Smith's bookstall empire had to carry in the shape of small, unprofitable stations. The railway companies were apt to relegate these to convenient oversight when negotiating contracts: Hornby was to spend a considerable part of his working career reminding them that profitless places like Harwich and Yarmouth were very different from the London termini.

For the next few years Hornby gradually assumed his full duties as a partner. By the autumn of 1894 he was taking his turn in writing up the decisions recorded in the Partners' Diary: they normally comprised reproofs, punishments, and dismissals for backslidings, scrimshanking and embezzlement among the peccant members of bookstall (and other) staff: conversely, rewards, incentives and promotions for the virtuous. With something like a thousand stalls and sub-stalls spread all over England and Wales, staff management was a complicated but critical problem (see page 281).

Those who feared (and some who hoped) that they were libelled in newspapers or journals distributed by Smith's had to be soothed, compensated or dealt with firmly as the experts advised. Bishops, headmasters, clergy, parents who detected 'offensive', 'doubtful', even 'gross' matter in literature sold on Smith's stalls had to be reassured in one way or another. Publishers of indubitably doubtful material had to be warned off or refused service by Smith's. Those members of the staff who fell by the wayside for one reason or another (including the unhappy White, see pages 187–8) had to be succoured; widows and orphans pensioned; the convicted granted (or refused, according to circumstances) help to emigrate quietly overseas. Codd, head of the Stables, had to be warned of complaints of noise from his horses and told not to groom them in the street. Adams, of the Carpentry, was ordered to abate the noise of hammering in his works in the early morning: and so on.[6] All this was a necessary and not unimportant part of management's job. In the last analysis, though, it was less important than the negotiations of new rail contracts; into these Hornby came for the first time in August and September 1895. As the newcomer he was still third or fourth of the partners (after Freddy, Awdry, Acland) who discussed new terms with the top men of the LNW (Frederick Harrison especially, their general manager) and of the GWR (T. I. Allen). For these contracts were, after all, the main foundations of the Smith business.

The going was hard. Allen was still relatively amenable, friendly and ready to listen to the case against the steep rise in rentals put forward by the partners, still headed by Awdry as senior. For the LNW, Harrison (later Sir Frederick) was unusually difficult and aggressive; and the LNW were still Smith's largest client. The final terms agreed at Euston, appropriately on 5 November, were exceedingly stiff. For Smith's, Freddy Smith and Awdry had offered £26,000 p.a. as a minimum: they had to bring up their offer to £32,000 to secure a ten-year contract.[7] The gap between Smith's and the GWR negotiators was less wide. Smith's offered £23,000 p.a. for five years and £25,000 for the following five years; the GWR wanted (originally) £25,000 p.a. for the whole ten years.

After – doubtless – some of the by now usual exchanges of information between the two railway companies, the GWR directors agreed to put forward a new offer of £25,000 for five years, £26,000 for the following five.[8] Hornby was not, apparently, present when these terms were agreed. He was certainly far from happy with them: but his senior colleagues were at least able to congratulate themselves on having secured a long-term contract. In any case, they consoled themselves that turnover was still increasing; so was the number of stalls and members of staff employed on them. It was true that the rents charged by the railways for bookstall and advertising privileges were fractionally up, both as a proportion of turn-over and of total expenses, but with turnover so buoyant and net profits still moving up to what was to prove a record year in 1899/1900, there seemed, at least to the older generation of management, to be no reasons for worrying unduly. The rest of the railway business went on its way, with rents rising but relations pretty good.

The year 1898 began with nothing worse than a rather higher-than-average number of casualties among the staff. Clerks-in-charge of stalls seemed unusually prone to peculation, breaches of confidence, outright theft and drunkenness; juniors married without permission (against the rules). The wife of the clerk at Dalston 'called to say that her husband has gone off his head from worrying over the decreased receipts at his stall & the imagined displeasure on our part occasioned thereby . . .' She was duly comforted, reassured and promised that if her husband did not have to be put 'under control', he would be allowed at once 'a long holiday – say 2 or 3 months – to recover his health & spirits'.[9]

Such was the usual stuff of managerial life and problems: much more serious was the row which broke in the summer of 1898 between Smith's and the outstanding newcomer to the world of popular journalism, Alfred Harmsworth. With his three brothers, Harmsworth was already the personification of the new, cheap press. A strange, temperamental, lonely man, his obsessions in life were his mother, bicycles, motorcars, railways and journalism. His personality was electric, his understanding sharp but limited; but what he understood he commanded, and this meant not only the art of journalism but the whole organisation, science and economics of communication. By the time he came into head-on collision with the Smith partnership, *Answers* and the *Daily Mail* (the first newspaper to reach a circulation of a million) were facts of life. In Alfred Harmsworth, the future Lord Northcliffe, the partners were taking on the most formidable opponent the newspaper world could produce. His model in newspaper style was American (Horace Pulitzer in particular) and like Pulitzer (and later Beaverbrook), Harmsworth impressed his personal style on his editors and writers (Frank Harris in the *Saturday Review* called it '. . . brainless, formless, familiar, impudent'). It was certainly brief, brisk, pungent, sarcastic, aggressive.

All these qualities marked Alfred's conduct of hostilities which immediately broke out between him and Smith's. The apple of their discord was the price of the latest Harmsworth innovation, the *Harmsworth Magazine*. This was to be offered for sale at 3d. and not a farthing more. It was to beat out of existence the established reviews selling at 6d. like the *Strand*. Harmsworth claimed (in the *Daily Mail*) not only to have found agents in every district of Britain to stock his new magazine but to have sold out the first edition of half a million at his own price. The Smith partners immediately issued an advertisement regretting they were unable to execute orders for the *Harmsworth Magazine* because its proprietors refused to supply them 'except upon terms which make the sale of the magazine upon the railway bookstalls an impossibility, save at a considerable loss'. They had offered nevertheless to send copies to subscribers but Harmsworth had 'refused to supply them with a single copy, at any price whatever' and threatened to boycott any wholesaler who was found supplying Smith's.[10]

In July the battle was joined in earnest. The *Daily Mail* improved the shining hour by printing congratulatory letters from other newspaper proprietors including Frank Lloyd (who owned the *Chronicle* and *Lloyds Weekly*) applauding Harmsworth's defiance of Smith's and 'the first serious blow at a monopoly which has greatly injured the free distribution of popular literature.'[11] Next day it published a circular issued by Smith's to their trade agents which denounced Harmsworth's for their aim of getting 'the retail trade under their thumb by means of *skilfully veiled intimidation*. We are fighting the battle of the retail trade in this matter', declared Smith's. '*Do not leave us to fight it alone*. By backing us up at this critical time you are standing up for your own rights, and resisting an attempt on the part of a powerful publishing house to obtain entire control of the market, and impose what terms they will upon the retail agents, who, *unless they combine* for their common defence, are helpless single-handed.' This rather breathless onslaught (*Daily Mail*'s italics) drew the retort from Harmsworth that Smith's action was 'the most magnificent advertisement ever received by a publication . . . directing the attention of other capitalists to the enormous profits of the book-stall business'.[12] It was not the first time the point had been publicly made since William Henry II's Will was proved at over one-and-three-quarter million pounds.

Lloyd was joined by W. L. Thomas, editor of the *Graphic*, in his support for Harmsworth. The *Chronicle* printed a letter from Smith's explaining mildly that they had no wish to oppose cheaper magazines and that Harmsworth's profits were larger than theirs. Harmsworth joined in with a letter to the *Chronicle*: 'One of the extraordinary and amusing developments' was Smith's 'sudden affection' for the small retailer, hitherto treated by them 'with contempt'. Did the public at large know that Smith's were also *wholesalers*? That their aim was to absorb wholesalers throughout the country and thus 'tighten their grip on the throats of owners of newspapers and publishers of books?' If Smith's could not make do on more reasonable profits, they must expect 'to go the way of all monopolists, for to exist at all a monopoly must at least move with the times'.[13] It was not the first nor the last time Harmsworth was to raise the monopoly bogey: it was to feature a few years later in his greatest and most costly fiasco: the *Daily Mail* attack on the alleged Lever soap monopoly. All this reflected clearly the influence on Harmsworth of popular journalism in North America, where the muck-raking attack on trusts and monopolies was in full swing, with excellent results for circulation.[14]

The partners continued to reply in a low key. They repeated that neither they nor any other retailer could be expected to sell at a loss. They had no monopoly: on the contrary, competition in the retail newsagency business was very keen. Not they, but Harmsworth's, were out for a monopoly.

At this point, in mid-July, the trade association of the retailers, the Retail Newsagents and Booksellers' Union, entered the lists. The *Academy* published an article on their behalf which ingeniously pointed out that Smith's in particular bore the increasing burden of the bookstall rents being constantly squeezed upwards by the railways. They did not think Harmsworth would succeed in imposing their 'impossible' terms. 'They are very powerful, and they have worked this revolution – so far as it has gone – very cleverly. But . . . the Trade will quickly realise that they cannot allow the Messrs. Harmsworth to be dictators of their business.' England, it continued, is not America, which had 'an enormous, level, and homogeneous population to work upon' and any magazine (like *Munsey's* and *Cosmopolitan*) could sell for 10 cents. In England 'the public is many publics. Circulation is not everything . . . the advertiser needs to hit "*his* public" not the *general* public . . . hence we have myriads of papers with small circulations, but fat advertisement pages.'[15]

Other papers, London and provincial, now joined the dispute; some for Smith's, some for Harmsworth. The level of debate was revealing rather than elevating. Among its revelations was the fairly clear one that while the voices might multiply, the inspiration and momentum was still that of

Alfred Harmsworth versus W. H. Smith. 'We are not concerned to aid Messrs. W. H. Smith & Son' wrote the *Stationery Trades Journal* primly '... in fact, the necessity for a hard and fast system has at times given us a momentary annoyance, but their absolute impartiality is beyond question ...'[16] *Figaro*, the *Investors' Review*, the *Newsagents Chronicle*, the *Western Mail*, the *Newsagents & Booksellers Review* and many others added their *amen*. A supplement to this last provided what it described as 'a cloud of witnesses' – retailers all, naturally – 'all dead against Harmsworth and their dealings with the trade'.

Yet the cloud of witnesses did not go unchallenged. The *London Illustrated Standard* commented (and the comment may have borne fruit in unexpected quarters later) that Harmsworth 'have before now contemplated the establishment of news stands *outside the railway stations*'.[17] (Time was to prove that when the Smith bookstalls on their two largest lines had to close, it was Smith's, not Harmsworth, who acted on the prophetic hint of the *Standard*.) The most balanced comment came from an Irish newsagent of Glasgow. He regretted the brawl between Harmsworth and Smith's. He was opposed to the bookstall monopoly. The stalls should be thrown open to tender. But there was no point in small retailers 'out of resentment and desire to pay off Messrs Smith' putting Harmsworth in a position of 'pulling the cords to strangle' them 'more quickly'.[18]

That there was something in the contention that Smith's position *vis-à-vis* the railways was (rightly or wrongly) resented, was proved by complaints from other correspondents. One went further and deeper. 'For some years', he wrote, 'the central management of that concern [Smith's] seems to have greatly deteriorated.' The library had gone downhill. The stall clerks were still always civil and obliging: the fault lay with the central administration. 'It is always the way with monopolists, that they become inflated with prosperity, and end by supposing that they are necessary to the existence of society.'[19] Another correspondent who signed himself 'Ex-Bookstall Clerk' reminisced on the great days of W. H. Smith (now past) when 'the whole of their gigantic business was managed by five gentlemen who were superb organisers ... thorough men of business, and masters of tact and discrimination ... W. H. Smith, ... Lethbridge, ... White, ... Sandifer, ... Elliman ...'[20] The writer left the readers to draw their own conclusions. It is not likely they were intended to be favourable to the management of 1898. Yet, surprising as it may have seemed to the general public, Smith's quiet but knowledgeable exploitation of the fears of the small retailers proved more effective than Harmsworth's heavy artillery bombardment.

On 16 August the *Daily Mail* published a brief notice on the occasion of the second issue of the *Harmsworth Magazine*: 'In order that the heavy carriage on so bulky a publication should not fall on the newsvendor, he is entitled to charge 3½d a copy in future.'[21] The phrasing was an obvious attempt at a face-saver but however it was put, it was plain that Harmsworth knew he had lost the battle to a combination of the big distributors – including Smith's, Menzies and Graham (in Scotland), Eason and Olley (in Ireland) and Willing's (in London) – acting on behalf of the small retailers as well. Neither Conan Doyle nor Kipling (who both came to his rescue) could help.

As a diversionary effort Harmsworth switched his counter-offensive to a different front. Leading drapers, tobacconists and others – Boots, Swan & Edgar, Bon Marché of Liverpool and Manchester, Cranston & Elliott of Edinburgh – were entering (so claimed the *Daily Mail*) by 'the simple law of supply and demand', into competition with the avaricious but mis-guided followers of Smith's and their allies.[22] Another alarm followed: Smith's stalls were said to be 'boycotting' the *Daily Mail*, *Answers*, *Home Chat* and other Harmsworth publications. Frustrated readers of these journals were urged to write to the 'Boycott Department' specially created and entrenched for the occasion.[23] The general secretary of the Retail Newsagents and Booksellers' Union claimed at once to have seen through Harmsworth's tactics. Knowing that bookstall managers were largely masters of their own stalls, he wrote: 'Alfred conjured up the idea of start-ing the "boycott" cry so as to frighten the clerks and force the firm to order that all Harmsworth's goods should be kept to the front'.[24] *Und so weiter, und weiter, und weiter . . .*

By September, the public row died down. It had become humiliating to Harmsworth, embarrassing to Smith's and boring to everybody else. But in Fleet Street and the Strand it continued to rumble on into the autumn. The evidence is scanty but there are signs that Smith's partners did not see exactly eye to eye with each other about relations with Harms-worth. Hornby met Leicester Harmsworth (Alfred's brother) and had a long talk about the situation. Harmsworth's agreed to put their views in a letter. But Hornby's olive branch seems to have withered in the coolness generated by Awdry and Acland. On 2 November Alfred Harmsworth asked for a meeting: Awdry complied. When Awdry went in he said: 'It is you who have sought this interview not we'. A few days later one of Alfred's men, Young, came to the Strand. Harmsworth (he warned) was 'very much annoyed by our letter' which had followed his earlier talk with Awdry. Young said he 'supposed Mr. Acland would not come & see

A.H.?' Acland replied icily that he would be 'glad to see Mr. H. *here,* if he wished to see us'.²⁵ Young brought no reply to Awdry's letter and left after saying Alfred was going to write to the *Daily Mail.*

With that the dispute disappears from view. *Harmsworth's Magazine* never succeeded as a cheap rival to sixpennies like the *Strand.* Only when its price steadily went up – 3½d., 4d. and finally 6d. – did it find a foothold under a new name, the *London Magazine.* When evidence of renewed relations of Smith's with Harmsworth becomes available, in 1905, it suggests that the bitterness of 1898 had somehow been strangely transmuted into utmost cordiality and understanding. It is not too much to see the hand and brain of Hornby behind this – as they were behind so many of the fundamental changes of outlook and policy in those vital years.

No one supported more strongly than Hornby the policy of keeping profit margins at the bookstalls healthy and competitive: but he seems to have kept out of the particular dispute with Harmsworth. It is more than likely, in the light of his later, highly personal, policy of cultivating good-will among the new proprietors of Fleet Street, that the fracas of 1898 was a turning point in his ideas.

The criticisms of Smith's, the cries of 'monopoly', the divisions even in the newsagency trade, the proposals that the railways should put the stall contracts out to tender, that the newspaper proprietors should sell their papers from their own stalls or shops outside the railway stations – all these shafts may well have gone home. For the shades of the *fin-de-siècle* were beginning to close over the railway scene. In spite of a temporary alliance of newsagents in 1898, Smith's suddenly seemed very much on their own. One may guess that in Hornby's view neither side had won the battle of the Strand in 1898. Harmsworth had been blocked; but the prospect of his permanent enmity was alarming. It was time to look round for friends. This called for better lines of demarcation between the interests of the three major parties involved in the newsagency and bookselling trades: the railways, the publishers and the retailing and wholesaling sides of the trade itself. On its own, an empire founded solely on railway bookstalls and railway advertising began to seem perilously vulnerable.

Railways – predominantly established surface railways – still represented the basic source of Smith's profits on their business, shaped in the image of a bookstall empire created by William Henry II. To Hornby, the risks inherent in this situation were high, for two major reasons, both linked to the same source. First, the habit of inter-company consultation on policy, financial especially, had existed in embryo from the early days of the 'Railway Age', but it had been intermittent and punctuated by interludes

of bitter quarrels especially about the border territories where cowboy-
and-indian warfare continued for many years. But as the nineteenth century
approached its end, the level of warfare was gradually reduced to that of
friction (it never wholly disappeared) while occasional consultation turned,
in some important areas, into regular consultation which could sometimes
be justifiably regarded by parties whom it adversely affected as collusion.
The collusion became closer and more frequent as the opportunities for
profitable rail construction shrank away and the dire consequences of the
reckless manoeuvres of early constructors and speculators under the banner
of carefree *laissez-faire* doctrine were brought home to directors, managers,
and investors. At the roots of the depression which struck Britain in those
decades was the railway problem.

The economic problems of the railways were a fundamental reason for
their increasingly fractious relationship with Smith's. A perceptive railway
historian at the turn of the century explained the major problem, *tout court*,
in 1903.[26] 'The prevailing depression in the value of British railway property
dates from the second half of . . . 1899.' It had two main causes: 'the coal
"boom" . . . and the war' (in South Africa). Both had raised the price of
fuel, money and labour as compared with 1896–7. Yet trade at large was
booming and prices ruled high. Why were rails left out in the cold? 'Whilst
everybody else was putting up prices against them, they were unable to
raise their own prices against anyone. They were bound hand and foot by
the Railway and Canal Traffic Act of 1894': the prices of 1892 had been
frozen as maximum charges for rail transport. Companies tried to reduce
costs by building more efficient engines, larger freight trucks. Statistics
were called in to help. But, as Lord Allerton told his Great Northern shareholders in 1903, 'statistics will not help you. The real remedy is closer union
and more real disposition . . . to work together, and to try' (as the chairman
of the Great Central company had already remarked) 'to "put our horses
together," in order that we may pull a common load . . .' Since the 1870s
the dividend paid by the Great Northern had been halved – from 7 per cent
to 3½ per cent in 1903.

Grinling himself diagnosed the cause of the trouble as excessive competition which benefited nobody (by which he meant no railway company).
The only 'real remedy', to prevent every company from invading the
territories of the rest was 'monopoly' . . . a private or nationalised 'Railway
Trust'. With prophetic sense, he added gloomily that 'probably the remedy
would be worse than the disease'.[27] What he meant, of course, was that a
single monopoly should replace a series of regional monopolies. For the
Victorian economy, a self-proclaimed area of free trading, was here (as so

often) a loose federation of local monopolies or price rings: competition was, increasingly, restricted.[28]

Few of the supposedly perfect markets of Victorian England were in practice perfect: fewer still of Adam Smith's perfect Victorian disciples could stand in a white sheet and claim that their commercial practices followed the principles of perfect freedom from agreements to rig prices, share out markets and limit competition. After all, must there not be reason in everything, even in economic doctrine?

The evils stemmed, then, supposedly from 1894 and the Traffic Act. *Tout court*: perhaps *trop court*. Those statistics which Lord Allerton so distrusted told a longer, less simple story. From 1854 we can watch how the working expenses of running the railway system rose: in particular how they rose faster in relation to total working receipts. Down to 1872, expenses did not rise to above half total receipts. *Net* receipts stayed therefore above half: in 1873 the position was reversed (see Table VIII.1).

TABLE VIII.1   RAILWAY EXPENSES AND RECEIPTS, 1854–73[29]

	£ million Total working Receipts	£ million Total working Expenses	£ million Net working Receipts
1854	19.3	8.8	10.5
1873	55.2	29.3	25.8

Thereafter the relative burden of rail working expenses continued to rise and relative net receipts to fall in relation to total receipts. Down to the 1890s the deterioration was gradual. The price of decline then quickened (see Table VIII.2).

TABLE VIII.2   RAILWAY EXPENSES AND RECEIPTS, 1899–1905[30]

	£ million Receipts	£ million Expenses	£ million Net receipts
1899	98.0	58.0	40.0
1901	102.7	65.1	37.6
1903	106.8	66.1	40.7
1905	109.4	67.5	41.9

If Grinling's disaster year of 1899 was indeed bad, 1901 was worse. Thereafter the slide of relative net yields on the railways was continuous until 1911: only in one year (1908) did net *money* receipts actually fall: but as a proportion of total receipts, which rose until 1913, working expenses rose and *net* receipts fell. Table VIII.3 shows the proportions on the eve of the First World War and how the war only accelerated the deterioration.

TABLE VIII.3   RAILWAY EXPENSES AND RECEIPTS, 1913–20[31]

	£ million Receipts	£ million Expenses	£ million Net receipts
1913	119.8	75.7	44.1
1920	238.9	232.0	7.0

This is not the place to analyse in detail why the profitability of the British railway system declined: enough to say that it took place over a longer period and for more complex social (as well as economic) reasons than early analysts such as Grinling suggested.

Our concern is with its importance as a factor in the relations between the railway companies and Smith's. Behind the usual façade of gentlemanly exchanges these became steadily more tense in the early years of the new century until they broke, in October 1905. The traditional contracts of Smith's for railway stalls with the two larger companies, the London & North Western and the Great Western, terminated in what came to be called in Smith's the 'great upheaval'. This event was certainly a traumatic shock to Smith's staff as a whole but not to those at the top who were responsible for negotiating with the railway companies. Nor are the commonly accepted narratives of the breach a satisfactory explanation of what happened and why.

From the Smith defenders came stories of injustice, incompetence and bad faith on the part of the railways. From the railways came accusations of monopolistic practices and (to them) costly inefficiency on the part of Smith's. That the two railway companies behaved with less than the minimum of the practical consideration and even decent manners that might have been expected is true, but in the rapidly worsening situation they faced, their behaviour could be explained, though not excused, by a certain feeling of panic which led them to try and squeeze the drop after the last out of a victim who could be plausibly represented as profiting unreasonably at their expense (see page 237).

After all there was hardly any other victim who could be squeezed. For their part, Smith's could justly claim they held no monopoly either of the distribution of news and other literature or of advertising on the railways. Their books were constantly opened to the railway companies to prove their contention that *their* running costs were (like those of the railways) necessarily very high and rising, not least the very large rents they paid to the railways. Indeed *The Times* proprietors upbraided them on numerous occasions for allowing themselves to be blackmailed by the railways into paying even higher rents; for this, in turn, led to higher newspaper prices and therefore lower circulations. This, at least, was the contention of successive managers of *The Times* from Mowbray Morris to Moberly Bell.

The Smith partners defended themselves stoutly against the alternating and contradictory charges of being dictatorial and monopolistic or of being too weak before the railway onslaught and less efficient than in former days. But as Hornby watched the Harmsworth dispute and read and heard the accusations of monopoly and profiteering, he must have remembered the comments of a few years before when the press had similarly commented on the announcement of William Henry II's Will. The *Newcastle Daily Chronicle* wrote on 31 January 1893:

> The feeling of discontent among railway people and press men was accentuated by the announcement that the late Mr. Smith had died worth upwards of £2,000,000. This is thought to have been a large sum to have made out of a retail trade, and the railway managers are looking, as a consequence, for increased rentals ... But I should not be surprised if, in the end, the companies take the stalls into their own hands as they have taken the hotels, and make the distribution of literature another department of their huge business. Nor would I be surprised if English newspapers do as newspapers have done in America ... organise a system of sale and delivery of their own.[32]

The article has all the usual overtones dear to newspaper proprietors, publishers and railway managers alike: the references to retail trade were, as usual, patronising: that retailing required skill and experience or deserved appropriate reward was concealed by omission. The size of the Smith fortune was exaggerated (the actual valuation was £1,776,042. 0s. 10d.), but rounding it all up to two million helped to give the desired effect. It was not mentioned that William Henry II's private fortune represented the earning capacity of the family business he had inherited over the larger part of a century and included the accumulated earnings reserved over that period necessary for the financing of the growing business.

Nevertheless, the kind of criticism represented by the Newcastle paper (and others) had to be taken account of. It was the stuff which still came in handy to Alfred Harmsworth in 1898. A contributor to the *Daily Mail* correspondence columns in August 1905, Colonel W. F. Prideaux, complained about W. H. Smith's inefficiency in carrying out his order for newspapers. He concluded (rather confusingly): 'Of course one swallow does not make a summer, and at the other places, where they intend to start shops, the service of the firm may be conducted on a high level of efficiency, but like so many other British institutions, I fancy the old established firm of Messrs. W. H. Smith & Son might be none the worse for a little polishing up in the shape of competition.'[33]

Whatever the other partners might feel about such criticism, it is unlikely that it was resented by Hornby. For Hornby was already deep into the business of change, reform and renewal in the Smith organisation. Even disappointment was foreign to his nature: he was a realist who knew only too well from his daily work that human nature was fallible and the work of the stall clerks physically and mentally wearisome, especially when it included the supervision of a high-spirited and potentially disorderly army of adolescent delivery boys. The world could not be perfected entirely or at one fell swoop.

Hornby Takes Over

During the seven lean years between 1900 and 1907 problems of rising costs and stagnant trading faced Smith's just as they faced the railways. Up to a point they derived from the same sources. The British economy as a whole was disturbed, in large part, by the impact of the war in South Africa. The dislocation was patchy but certainly not disastrous. These were not years of deep depression. Some trades and industries felt little effect. Some even flourished. Unemployment fluctuated. Dislocation, such as it was, was not in itself enough to explain the anxieties of Smith's, though their trade may have suffered by the general upward trend of raw material costs – paper, for example.[34]

The basic trouble was that Smith's were bearing the railways' burden in the shape of the continually rising tribute which was levied by the railways on Smith's main sources of turnover and profit: railway bookstalls and railway advertising. Steadily, therefore, these years of poor trade saw the unrolling of Hornby's grand strategic plan.

Its essence was to liberate Smith's from what he saw as their perilous dependence on the judgment of the railways as to the size of tribute that could be screwed out of Smith's. By 1900 Hornby was no longer willing to accept the railway management's theory that rent fixing was the Art of the Possible. He opened the debate in the new century with – even for him – a more than usually tough statement to the London, Brighton and South Coast Railway about the liability of the railway and Smith's respectively for payment of local municipal rates on advertising sites, on the one hand inside the stations, and on the other on hoardings outside. He also signalled the bad times ahead for business in realistic language. '. . . the interests of the [railway] Company and ourselves are not mutual until the amount of the percentage earned exceeds the guaranteed minimum payment [rent], and we do not ourselves see any chance of exceeding this guarantee during this next ten years.'[35]

When the Crewe manager of the LNWR raised the question of Smith's charges for *The Times* and the *Field* (his own copies in particular) Hornby's reply adroitly combined equal parts of honey and vinegar. He would see that the complainant was given the normal terms for senior railway staff: but he emphasised that Smith's were bound to charge more where accounts were not paid in advance '. . . and so long as we have to pay such enormous rents as we pay the LNWR for the Bookstall privileges . . . we shall not be able to reduce our charges'.[36]

Impartially, to the Joint Committee of the Great Western and the Midland responsible for lines in the Bristol and western areas, he sent a firm refusal to consider higher rents. At Bristol, advertising receipts had been down for the last two years: at Worcester, they were stagnant, bookstall turnover down. So too on the Clifton Extension line:

> . . . when business is stagnant we do not think we can be justly asked to give such increases as are now suggested . . . We notice that you refer to some 'slight modification' of the terms of the Agreements. We presume from past experience that these slight modifications are not in our favour . . .[37]

Early in 1901 he told the North British Railway also that business was 'rather retrograde than otherwise'.[38] So, from Berwick to Bristol, from the Humber to the Isle of Wight, local railway companies were given due warning that Smith's could not pay increased rents out of stagnant or declining profits. Even at Waterloo, the directors of the L&SW were informed, politely but firmly, that their ideas of the advertising value of the Waterloo & City Railway were exaggerated even for the 'City Station which alone is of real value . . . advertisers do not seem at present to be particularly anxious for spaces . . .'[39] They also resented, he added, the higher rates of charges which the L&SW had imposed at the City Station.

The Midland and Great Northern joint lines were dosed with medicine from the same bottle. '. . . Bookstall business at small stations does not pay, and as we pay a rent for the privilege, we can hardly be expected to work stations which are not remunerative.' This disposed of the railways' idea of a great future for Fakenham ('hardly warrants keeping a second boy') and Sheringham (where a stall would be idle 'for half the year'). Hornby concluded: 'if we can meet your wishes . . . we will do so, though we rather doubt whether from our point of view it will prove a success.'[40]

The first tussle of the depression came in the spring of 1902: it was with the Lancashire & Yorkshire Railway, the important northern transverse line whose affairs were increasingly intermingled with those of the large companies linking the north of England with the metropolis, the LNWR in particular. By the summer of 1902 Hornby was locked in argument with James Aspinall, general manager of the L&Y. He had proposed that Smith's should pay an increased minimum rent for the L&Y and LNWR joint railways although it had been doubled less than five years before. Business had actually been declining in 1901 and the first half of 1902 was worse than the level of 1901. Smith's were willing to pay a bigger guaranteed rent but they could not raise the percentages of their receipts, nor would they pay rates on their bookstalls.[41] They were under pressure from the proprietors of newspapers and journals because higher rents portended higher publishing discounts for the goods they sold. Profits had not risen with gross takings, largely because rents had increased too steeply. The time had come to declare they could not carry any further burden and at the same time carry on their business creditably or profitably: thus Hornby.

By November the deadlock was still unbroken. Hornby wrote to Aspinall a characteristically blunt letter: he wanted a face-to-face talk: discussions between understrappers 'who had no power to negotiate definitely' could only waste time.[42] Aspinall agreed and the two protagonists met at Manchester on 8 December. The gap between them seemed unbridgeable. Aspinall at once declared that Hornby's offer 'could not be entertained'. Hornby replied that the Smith's partners' mind 'was *absolutely made up* . . .'[43] He asked for a final decision as soon as possible. This seems to have shaken the directors of the L&Y. By March 1903 they had decided to continue Smith's L&Y and LNWR joint contract for another five years. As regards the L&Y contract due to expire at the end of 1903, Hornby explained that he didn't 'wish to hurry' their decision 'unduly', but added helpfully that he needed their clear undertaking as soon as possible. '. . . if we have to move out . . . our possible successor . . .' would need several months to move in.[44]

Not only did Hornby stand firm: he saw to it that Smith's men working in Lancashire and Yorkshire territory did likewise. 'In general' ran an enquiring letter to their man in Manchester 'do you think we are favourably treated by the Company on the whole, or not?'.[45] The answer was no. This and other reports were passed to Aspinall by Hornby:[46] they fully bore out his criticisms, he declared. Not only were facilities enjoyed in the past being gradually curtailed but the interference of railway officials with advertising space was 'causing us great and continued loss . . . gradually alienating our Customers, who cannot understand such treatment'.[47]

As the wrangle over detail continued Hornby made no attempt to conceal his impatience. 'We offer you the best we can . . . If there are others who can afford to pay you more and do the work better . . . we cannot legitimately complain if they are preferred to ourselves.'[48] On 24 August he sent Aspinall a letter asking urgently for a final decision. It contained an historic sting in the tail: the matter could not longer be delayed. '. . . as we have certain property in the district, the letting of which depends upon the result of our negotiations with you.'[49] It needed no reading between the lines to unravel his meaning. Hornby had not concealed that he had been for some time carrying out surveys to find out whether, and if so how far and where, it might be possible to replace station bookstalls by shops in the towns through which the railways passed.

The knowledge of this seems to have had an immediate and pacifying effect on the directors of the L&Y. But they had to carry their allies in the LNWR with them and the LNW were less alarmed and less amenable. Hornby had to despatch a letter to their general manager (the formidable and domineering Sir Frederick Harrison). Curtly, without beating about the bush, it said that Smith's had come to the end of the road:

> Therefore, though the breaking of old ties is painful to us, we have come, after full and mature consideration, to the conclusion that rather than pay for privileges a sum which we consider to be largely in excess of their value, *we will turn our energies to the development of a business in which we shall enjoy a certain amount of independence* . . . We are sending a copy of this letter to Mr Aspinall . . .[50]

An anxious Aspinall seems to have remonstrated with the LNWR, for Harrison at once asked for an interview with Hornby. The business was thereupon satisfactorily settled – for the moment. On 17 November Hornby felt he could safely write to H. W. Lowther, Smith's superintendent of bookstalls in Lancashire, who had been exploring for suitable shop sites. Negotiations with the L&Y and LNWR had practically come to a successful end 'and the question of opening shops in the district is therefore not a pressing one . . .' There was no further need to pursue sites at Lytham or Blackpool 'at present'.[51] A shop at St Anne's (independently of the railway stall already there) was still possible.

That, for the moment, was the end of the battle: but the wording of Hornby's letter makes it clear that he was quite prepared for further trouble. His instinct was sound. The tussle with the L&Y was only a preliminary skirmish; the real battle was to come two years later but it was to centre not least on the personality and problems of one of Hornby's enemies in the L&Y dispute: Sir Frederick Harrison.

Meanwhile the business depression which underlay the attitude and actions of the railways continued to afflict Smith's too. That Hornby's continued reiteration of the gravity of Smith's problems was more than tactical window-dressing is shown by the internal finances of Smith's in this period. Turnover at the railway stalls, after reaching a peak in 1899/1900 (£1,470,317) fell away until it reached bottom during the crisis years 1905–7: after that the picture is complicated by the revolution in the fundamental structure of the whole business (see page 256): profits followed suit. They were at a record level (£189,243) in 1899/1900. Then they too declined, reaching bottom between 1905–7: after that there was gradual recovery. But it was 1914/15 before they topped the 1899/1900 figures.

Meanwhile, the rise in rents as a percentage of total expenses of running the business was gradual: the relentless consistency of the upward trend nevertheless showed that Hornby – indeed the partners as a group, for though Hornby came to manage almost single-handed Smith's external relations he certainly had the backing of his colleagues – was right to see the future darkly if the squeeze on bookstall rents was not checked. A few figures make the point (see Table VIII.4).

The same thing was happening to Smith's railway advertising income and expenses. So, too, the charges made by the railways for carrying newspapers and journals from London to the bookstalls increased.

The figures left no room for doubt: business was more or less stagnant, yet the expenses attributable to the railway connection showed no sign of deflation: on the contrary, as a percentage of turnover and total costs they were still rising. So were freight costs. So were labour and running costs internal to the business but in large measure an unavoidable consequence of the earlier expansion of the number of bookstalls and the diversification

TABLE VIII.4 COSTS AS PERCENTAGE OF TURNOVER AND TOTAL EXPENSES

1 *Bookstall rents*[52]

Year	(1) Rents £	(2) (1) as % of turnover	(3) (1) as % of all expenses
1870	15,550	4.07	25.47
1897/8	89,493	6.84	33.59
1904/5	103,444	7.37	33.91

2 *Advertising rents*[53]

Year	(1) Rents £	(2) (1) as % of turnover	(3) (1) as % of total expenses
1884	68,652	51.80	71.01
1895/6	134,692	69.18	80.46
1905/6	156,760	76.10	82.89

3 *Newspaper and journal carriage costs*[54]

Year	(1) Carriage £	(2) (1) as % of turnover	(3) (1) as % of total expenses
1892	30,231	2.65	13.40
1905/6	54,009	4.50	16.68

of the kinds of business they handled. In the mid-1880s the total number of stalls, major and minor, stood at between 1,100 and 1,200: by 1904/5, at between 1,200 and 1,300. Not a remarkable increase: yet the staff they required had almost doubled: from 3,324 to 6,129. The wage bill had risen correspondingly from c. £107,290 to c. £175,387, a rise of 63 per cent.

This was not, of course, the responsibility of the railways. Charles Awdry explained it and its consequences in a speech (to the Newsvendors' Benevolent Institution) on 16 November 1908. In 1840 only about 550 newspapers were published in the United Kingdom: by 1908, 2,353. The newcomers had to be delivered early ('Charles Dickens . . . said that the one absorbing passion of any member of the human race was to get his newspaper 10 minutes before his neighbour'), they were larger, heavier and they cost more to carry by rail, yet nobody wanted to pay more for his paper. Result: 'rates went up, carriage went up, rent went up, the cost of boy labour went up, expenses went up all round, and the small newsagent had increased work and increasing difficulty in making ends meet.'[55]

It was not the moment to add: 'so had Smith's', but it was true. The newsagency business had grown prodigiously; so had its costs. But its profitability had not kept pace. Some of the reasons for this were almost inevitable. Newsagents and booksellers were engaged in activities where profits were elusive – libraries, for example. Their unit margins of profit were (as W. H. Smith I had classically stated) minute, and the precarious price structure of the market left the risks high. Ironically they were highest of all for the firm which held what its detractors described as the railway monopoly. Smith's had repeatedly had to explain that large numbers of their small bookstalls ran at a loss. The 'monopoly' charge was one which the firm (and Hornby in particular) denied. Yet, as he pondered the current criticisms of the press and faced the mounting demands of the railways, he was increasingly aware that W. H. Smith's heritage, monopoly or not, was unlikely to be worth more than a mess of pottage unless it was radically reorganised.

First, he had no doubt that the rising tide of papers, books, journals, stationery, bill heads, ledgers, diaries and the dozens of articles provided by manufacturers, printers and publishers for a literate and commercial society demanding news, information, entertainment and equipment, provided vast opportunities for business. As matters stood, firms which conducted that business were more vulnerable than profitable. This was, above all, because they were being dragged in the wake of a monopolistic transport system which was itself steadily becoming less and less profitable and must, within the foreseeable future, face bankruptcy. What should be done?

The major issue was clear. Smith's had from the start been distributors of popular news and literature: some 'manufacturing' they had taken up – profits on the printing business in Water Street are recorded from 1867: they ranged from modest to very small, or less. Equally modest, if less erratic, were the profits from the Works Department where carpenters made the 'frames' which held in place the plates advertising the merits of Mazawattee Tea or Suttons Seeds on or outside the railway stations. Figures for these are preserved from 1868. Yet these were minor, necessary divergences – aberrations, some might have argued – from the central, classical activity of the firm: this was to buy papers, books, magazines, etc., from publishers and printers and sell them either to retailers (wholesaling) or to the final customers and readers (retailing). Wholesale or retail, Smith's distributed. They 'manufactured' only on the small scale demanded by their trading system and this was for a long time a 'country' trade: they helped the 'country' to find out what was going on, politically, economically, socially, culturally – in London – or at least what the London press *said* was going on.

One feature of their distributory activity stood out prominently. Their two major functions were wholesaling (selling to some person or business who re-sold – retailed – to the final customer) and retailing itself. On the relatively small scale on which business was conducted until the 1860s or 1870s, the division between these two branches of trade was by no means perfect. Even after the coming of railways, the growth of literacy, the increased urbanisation of Britain, a rise in incomes and living standards – the division remained blurred. Was a railway stall a retailer or wholesaler? It depended: on its size, location, and the economic and social nature of its environment. Many stalls were both.

From early days the south of England – south of London that is – was serviced from the Strand, which assumed a generally wholesale aspect. From the mid-nineteenth century the traditional reception areas for Smith's London 'exports' – in the industrial north-west, the midlands, Wales and Dublin – developed their own wholesale 'houses'. Thus the Dublin 'house' was a mixed business when it was bought from the Johnstons in 1850; Treadwell, the enterprising superintendent of the railway bookstalls at Birmingham, bought a combined newsround and wholesale business from Mrs W. Cooper, a diligent and business-like widow (and possibly relative of the Smith family) in Union Street – 'a small shop, with back parlour and three or four rooms over same' – as a later manager described it.[56] Such were the origins of the Birmingham House from 1857. Two years later, the Manchester House was bought from its owners, the Eldershaws. The Liverpool Wholesale House dated from 1867/8: Belfast from 1870. Cardiff (1896), Newcastle (1898), Leicester (1899) followed in rapid succession. Elsewhere, the local retailers were supplied by local wholesalers, or, in many places, through the W. H. Smith bookstall, combining wholesale and retail functions.

The inference may be drawn that this division of labour was a function of growing trade, growing markets, growing population, especially urban. Where large towns were outside the convenient catchment area of London, Smith's had set up separate wholesale houses. The average railway book-stall offered no adequate site from which to handle and despatch, with efficiency, speed and punctuality, a large quantity and variety of papers and magazines to local retailers while simultaneously providing morning papers for the traveller running for his train. Wherever the volume of trade justified it, it would be wise to find a separate site for a wholesale organisa-tion. The sheer volume, variety and complexity of the task – increasingly comparable to the traditional role of the Strand House itself – demanded it (see page 218).

This was an operation different in purpose and character from the pioneering experiments in retailing shops, which were also carried out between 1901 and 1905. The wholesale house ventures were practical and economic: so were the explorations in urban shops; but at this stage they were also political and tactical. In December 1905/January 1906, a series of articles on W. H. Smith's was to appear in *The Times*. They were modestly entitled 'The World's Greatest Newsagents' and they were inspired by Hornby. If he did not write them he almost certainly provided much of the material and the tone of moral vigour and enthusiasm which they exuded. Collectively they were a stout but carefully worded defence of Hornby's strategy. In anticipation of the facts (justified by the reflection that the facts were in his mind from the 1890s onwards) we may quote the paragraph on these 'new bookshops':

[They were] situated in the most agreeable and central parts of each town . . . either more convenient than the railway stations or equally so. It has been found by careful investigation of one line that 70% of the business at the railway stalls came, not from travellers, but from persons living in the neighbourhood of the stations . . . The shops will be larger than the stalls, better lighted, and better stocked . . .[57]

All of which was no doubt true: but whether these truths would have been revealed or accepted if certain of the railway companies – not all – had not, by their exigency, thrust them upon Smith's may still be doubted. In this instance, as so often, hard times and necessity certainly sharpened the spur to new enterprise in their victims. The private vices of the railways became the public benefit of Smith's and their customers. The railway companies which were ready to consider remaining with Smith's had to be confirmed in that inclination by rational, open argument and solid evidence of present stability and future potential.

The move into retail shops has often been regarded as a consequence of the breach with the LNWR and GWR in the autumn of 1905. This is too simple a view. It began, cautiously but quite deliberately, round the turn of the century, and may more accurately be thought of as the start of a rational reform of the structure of the news trade rather than merely a retrospective substitute for railway bookstalls. It was also a prophetic exercise hedging against railway pressure: but the railway relationship was never the entire story. The early retail shop movement and the (much larger and more positive) move into provincial wholesaling were both parts of a strategic whole (see pages 217–18).

In chronological order, the first shops (excepting Paris) were at Clacton (1901), Gosport (1902), Southport (1903), Reading (1904), and Torquay (1904). The Torquay shop was directly descended from premises on the Parade which dated back before 1863: Pembroke Dock was another ancient possession – it dated from at least 1874 and in 1901 was a possible victim for closure. The only feature this first group of shops had in common was that they were all by the sea – except Reading which was part-wholesale, part-retail and was at least on the Thames. What the basis for this choice was is not clear: possibly the simple music-hall moral that people do like to be beside the seaside? The principal scout who carried out Smith's search for new sites and businesses was E. D. Earle, a shadowy – not to say shady – figure, a freelance property broker. He worked on commission for Hornby until he was found out in 1905. His offence was to have proposed the terms of purchase of businesses for Smith's while taking commission from the vendor also. In March 1905, therefore, Earle received his marching orders from Hornby in his sternest style.[58] Yet by that time, Earle, Lowther (the Smith superintendent in Lancashire), and another agent, Horace Holmes, of Paternoster Row, had made good progress in expanding not only Smith's urban retail shops but (even more positively) their vital stake in provincial newsagency wholesaling (see pages 220–4).

In general, the policy was to go softly. When Lowther had agreed terms for the purchase of a shop at 31 Chapel Street, Southport, Awdry asked him to clinch the deal with the vendor . . . 'but as that will complete *the part of the transaction during which it was not desirable that our name should be known* . . .' (author's italics), the deeds of title etc. could now go to the Smith's solicitors (Bircham & Co) 'for dealing with in the usual way'.[59] This prudent strategy was no doubt partly designed to keep the railway companies operating in the area (the Lancs & Yorks and the LNW) guessing, partly to ensure that owners of desirable property and speculators were not encouraged to exploit Smith's predicament to their own advantage.

Lowther's projected purchase of shops in Lytham St Anne's and Black-pool was part of the same strategy to put counter-railway pressure on the L&Y (see page 209). The negotiations came to nothing in the end. Instead Horace Holmes found another business in Southport at 14–18 Neville Street, belonging to one Woodall. His business (Woodall assured Smith's) 'could not be sounder'.[60] Only his brother's death had persuaded him to give up. Hornby was interested. 'We had made up our minds to start a shop in Southport', he wrote to Manchester, 'and this might be a better way of doing it than opening in our own premises close to the station.'[61] So Woodall's were acquired in December 1903.

Holmes was less successful elsewhere. In the centre of Cambridge, at Rose Crescent, just off the Market Hill, was Jackson's, a newsagency. Holmes introduced them to Hornby. 'The business ... never belonged to us', Hornby wrote to Holmes, 'but was, we believe, founded by an entirely different W. H. Smith about the year 1830 ... We let you know this as you will no doubt want to inform him [Jackson] that you introduced the business to us.'[62]

It fell to Charles Awdry to try to complete the details of the Jackson purchase. In the course of it, Smith's put the usual clause into the agreement prohibiting Jackson from carrying on his business in Cambridge after its sale to Smith's. But 'what *kind* of business?' his solicitors – neighbours in Rose Crescent – asked. Awdry was a formalist but not without a sense of humour. The 'business', he replied, was that of 'Newsagent, Bookseller and Stationer': and he added, 'We have neither the right nor desire to hinder Mr. Jackson from being engaged in hairdressing or any other similar pursuit.'[63]

So assiduous was Holmes that Hornby had to shorten rein: in June 1904, he explained that another Maidstone business was not required in an area where Smith's was 'already well represented ... and [we] are not at present particularly anxious to open any more shops'.[64] The assiduous but suspect Earle, who returned to the scene in the autumn of 1904 was given a similar message: Hornby did not want a shop in Piccadilly at present and was doubtful about one in Felixstowe (though 'we already do a very good Business there at the Bookstall').[65]

The truth was that to absorb and digest the problems of shop manage-ment – a different matter from running station bookstalls – a little pause was necessary. Questions of organisation and control required thought. A man was needed to sort all this out; a reliable, resourceful, resilient man.

The same name occurred to both Hornby and Awdry. At Nottingham, commanding Smith's large midland area, was George Tyler. His empire included six different railway lines; it stretched from Marylebone north to Grimsby and Barnsley, from Luton to Manchester, from King's Cross to Retford and north-east to Lincoln and Louth. Here he had increased total retail income by 50 per cent by demanding prompt payment from customers and by refusing to countenance bad debts. In Nottingham he was a notable public figure, indefatigable in good causes though (as *Newsbasket* remarked) 'in business he knew neither creed nor party . . . [his] disposition is cheery . . . with a fund of generous repartee and lively anecdotes'.[66] It was, not surprisingly, to this versatile optimist that the partners turned. Hornby wrote to him on 12 July 1904:

> When . . . last in Town you may remember that we mentioned to you the possibility of appointing a Shop superintendent. His duties would be somewhat like those of a Bookstall superintendent but wider in their scope. He would have to control the managers of certain of our existing shops and of those which we may open in the future, to help and guide them in their selection of stock, to investigate and watch the condition of each business, and audit the accounts – to advise us where to open new branches, and to find and negotiate for suitable premises at such places, and generally in every way to see that this department was kept up, and progressive and profitable as a part of this concern.

The partners had concluded, Hornby wrote, that Tyler was their man for the job. They regarded it as most important. They proposed a salary of £700 a year with 5 per cent of net profits (a handsome income in 1904). 'In course of time with energetic and judicious management this should grow into a very important part of our business.'[67]

Just how important Tyler and shops were to be, even Hornby could, at this stage, only guess, but in the year that followed Tyler's appointment, and while an ominous lull seemed to settle over the railway scene, some eighteen shops were opened. About a third were located in or around London, another third in coastal resorts or spas – Bournemouth, Harrogate, Eastbourne, Scarborough, Penzance, Hove – the rest scattered over the west, midlands and east.

For the most part, at this stage of the operation, the shops were not primarily designed to replace bookstalls: they were to test the possibilities (in which Hornby firmly believed) which existed in the growing towns and cities of England for larger, more diversified and more profitable business than could be driven exclusively from railway bookstalls. All this notwithstanding, some of the new shops – Finchley Road, Clifton, Newbury, Penzance, Windsor, Reading, Torquay and Pembroke Dock – were later to figure effectively as replacements for former W. H. Smith bookstalls on the LNWR and Great Western. For the moment they represented trial grounds for a new kind of business and a new type of manager. For perhaps the most striking feature of the human side of the business in these years was the passing of a number of old names and faces – eminent Victorians of their kind like Faux (of the Library), Cockett (Advertising), French (White's successor at the Counting House), Treadwell (superintendent of the important Birmingham area), Monger (chief news dispatcher). Their places were taken by a new generation more open to new ideas and methods. Its members had often been trained under their predecessors – as Palmer had been inducted in the Library by Faux; C. W. Kimpton (later creator of a very successful Stationery Department) by Kingdon of the Book Department. Others, such as H. E. Morgan and Douglas Cockerell were brought in from the outside world, where they were already famous in their professions, through the personal influence of Hornby, himself a connoisseur of fine printing and book-binding (see page 226).

In all the postings, promotions and demotions of these years, the dominant influence was that of Hornby. Awdry was his senior in age by twenty years and as a partner by eighteen years. Awdry was not an old man – in 1900 he was 53 – but his health was not good. Though faithful and competent, he lacked the imagination and force which were Hornby's hallmark. Where Hornby relished the challenge of novelty, change and conflict, Awdry was increasingly tending to shrink from the new world of changes brought about by social, economic and technological innovation. By 1900 Awdry concentrated on what today would be called 'personnel matters', while the higher diplomacy of the business fell increasingly to Hornby: but in general they worked well together. Awdry appreciated the strength and judgment of a colleague still much his junior but gifted with the resilience needed to cope with a changing world. He does not seem to have resented the way Hornby directed and re-directed men and measures round the board with all the intuitive skill of a great chessmaster of business.

It was a sign of the different worlds they inhabited that Awdry's rather formal, squirarchical, hierarchical paternalism was merely upset by the irrepressible vigour and plain speaking of W. C. Smart, a rising star in the W. H. Smith management team, then head of the new Cardiff Wholesale House. Smart, no undue respecter of persons, was severely rebuked by

Awdry for asking the partners 'to come, if possible, to see you to-day' without adequately explaining why. 'You left us entirely in the dark', wrote an aggrieved Awdry, 'merely calling upon those under whom you work to come at your call.'[68]

To Hornby Smart was not a servant: he was one of Smith's most original entrepreneurs. It was Smart who had persuaded the partners to establish the Cardiff Wholesale House in 1896, the first of a dozen new wholesale houses which were to provide hope in the dark years of the new century, especially in the crisis of 1905–6. The man who to Awdry was simply a subordinate getting above himself was to Hornby a reformer and innovator, not only to be listened to but to be encouraged and promoted. It was a significant measure of the difference between the two men.

Yet their relations remained very friendly. On the occasion of his Jubilee, Hornby was to recall as the salient feature of his campaign of reform in the critical years 'the rebirth of our Provincial Wholesale Trade . . .' Characteristically, he gave the credit to Smart. But he recalled at the same time the earlier, more leisurely, golden years of the 1890s: how on a summer afternoon 'about 4 o'clock old Mr. Awdry, who was very fond of the game and no mean exponent' would say to him: ' "There doesn't seem very much to do today, what about watching a little cricket" and I, nothing loth, used to bowl off with him in a jingling hansom to Lords where we spent the rest of the afternoon.'[69]

The progress of the 'shop' policy was slow. In the early days, it showed no profit: it called only for more capital. As late as 1910/11 the 'A' shops, trading largely on their own initiative through buying and selling channels determined by themselves, and to a large extent independent of the Strand, showed nothing but losses. It was 1911/12 before they showed their first profit: £808. (For the post-1905 'B' shops, managed by the Head Office, see page 242.)

By comparison, Smith's penetration of the growing provincial wholesale market was positive, confident and highly profitable. In the decade between 1896 and 1906, twelve new provincial wholesale houses were added to the original five: by the end of the First World War, another six had joined them. The scale of turnover and profits was remarkable. In 1899/1900 (the first year for which they are available) turnover was £302,455: profits £12,585. By 1918/19 turnover had risen to over £2 million: net profits to just short of £148,000 – a handsome reward for enterprise.

These results were not achieved without considerable calls on capital investment – provided largely by the proprietor himself. During the second half of the nineteenth century the figures for capital employed had roughly doubled (1866–92). They began to climb steeply in 1905. The changes of the early years of the twentieth century – shops, wholesale houses, printing, etc. – made unprecedented calls on capital to cover the new fixed assets needed. By 1906/7 the capital employed stood at over £600,000. By the end of the war they were to be near to a £million and a half. The apportionment of this investment between the different branches of business and the relative returns they earned is not clear in detail: but there is no doubt that in the years before 1916, when the shops and bookstalls were pulling themselves up only painfully slowly, and other activities were at best unsteady, at worst loss-makers, the wholesale houses were the true *feste Burgen* of the Smith business: in the seven lean years from 1900–7 the wholesale houses in the provinces felt the draught of poor trade (like the retail stalls) but they survived to recover and grow. Nothing could shake them, nothing could stop them. They took competition, wartime restrictions, raw material and labour shortages, government controls and all else, from 1914–18, in their stride.

Nearly half a century later, in reminiscences of these critical years, Hornby generously gave all the credit for this providentially successful development to W. C. Smart. He was the 'begetter' of the policy of acquiring and developing the provincial wholesale houses: the skill and initiative of the remarkably able team of managers was developed under Smart's sharp eye and keen training. In the beginning it was Smart who 'persuaded us to open a wholesale branch at Cardiff in that year' (1896).[70] So much was true: but it was also undeniable that neither Hornby, nor Tyler, nor Smart could have done what they did without the confidence and backing of Freddy Smith, upon whose capital the new ventures drew heavily.

Smart, in the established W. H. Smith tradition, had come up the hard way, starting as an adolescent bookstall junior at the Cardiff Great Western Station in 1871. He was then 15 years old. He moved south to Bridgwater, east to Windsor, west to Gloucester, then back to his native Cardiff. Within twelve months he had persuaded the partners to give their blessing to a wholesale branch underneath the Cardiff GW arrival platform. The wholesale business quickly outgrew its subterranean nursery, surfacing to new and larger premises. Two wholesale branches were added, at Swansea and Newport, in 1901, with immediate success. When the final link in the wholesale chain was added in the shape of the Gloucester Provincial Wholesale House the western wholesale organisation was complete: turnover had expanded by '1,000 per cent' in a decade.[71] Nobody doubted that it was owed to Smart.

Like Tyler, Smart was an optimist, genial and extrovert, but at the same time a shrewd and, if necessary, exigent manager; always ready to reward good work but a martinet to those he suspected of carelessness or inaccuracy. He was an excellent leader of men with a gift for articulating and communicating his ideas to his team.

Smart's strategy at Cardiff and in the surrounding area was to be the model for a number of other wholesale businesses. His original enterprise was to hive off from the Cardiff bookstall a wholesale trade with a turnover of some £9,000 a year by the mid-1890s. By 1900/1 he had built this up to over £31,000, earning a net profit of over £2,500. He repeated the same division when he acquired the branch houses at Newport and Swansea in the spring of 1901. Newport took over the wholesale trade formerly done by the bookstalls at Newport itself, Chepstow, Abertillery, Merthyr and Brynmawr. Swansea did likewise at its own bookstall and those at Haverfordwest, Neath, Llanelly, Carmarthen, Llandilo, New Milford and Tenby. That left Pembroke Dock, where it was proposed to close the shop and carry on the whole trade from the station. The move worked brilliantly. By 1904/5 Smart's turnover at Cardiff had risen to over £50,000 and continued to rise through the two crisis years that followed (when Smart left South Wales). From 1907/8 to 1910/11 it went on rising – from £59,000 to over £68,000.

The specialisation of the newsagency business by Smart certainly increased efficiency and profitability. So did his conception of organising the wholesale trade on a regional basis. Both paths were followed by others. Sometimes the wholesale house originated in the Smith station bookstall as at Cardiff. Elsewhere a wholesale – sometimes a combined wholesale and retail – business would be acquired, then split up into its two specialised functions. The wholesale house would then acquire satellites. Thus the old Manchester Wholesale House, dating from its acquisition from Eldershaws in 1859, was later to acquire branches at Halifax (1904) and Chester (1911). At Bristol, Mapstone's business (a discovery by Hornby's scout, Earle) was acquired in 1903, later sprouting branches at Exeter and Plymouth. Tyler and Smart bought in Slater's wholesale business at Sheffield for Smith's in 1900; it was to acquire a satellite at Doncaster in 1903. Bromby, Gower's wholesale business at Hull, was spotted by J. C. Jones, Smith's Manchester bookstall superintendent, and bought in 1903. A few years later Hull acquired a satellite across the Humber at Grimsby to serve north Lincolnshire. Another branch at Lincoln followed much later.

Although Manchester was the oldest, largest and most noted provincial newspaper and wholesale centre, Birmingham was its senior as a Smith wholesale centre – Manchester 1859, Birmingham 1857 (see page 212). When turnover and profits can first be compared, in 1899/1900, Manchester was a long way ahead on turnover but Birmingham made better profits (see Table VIII.5).

TABLE VIII.5   MANCHESTER AND BIRMINGHAM HOUSES COMPARED, 1899/1900[72]

	Manchester £	Birmingham £
Turnover	111,662	35,057
Profits	1,640	3,437

For Manchester 1899/1900 was a bad year; but Manchester's trade and results tended to be more volatile than Birmingham's. They suffered worse in the lean years 1900–7 and reached the turnover figures of 1899/1900 again only in 1915/16. Birmingham, after a slow start, made steady, consistent progress. Eventually, the old high-flyers, Manchester and Liverpool, were toppled from their pre-eminence by Birmingham, Newcastle and Sheffield. Much depended on the quality of management and the state of the local economy. Cardiff owed everything to W. C. Smart in its first decade: it was to lose more than the others by the General Strike. At Newcastle, Smith's were fortunate to find in W. H. Manning a leader as spectacular as W. C. Smart himself. Between 1901 and 1925, Manning rescued Newcastle from its existing muddle and kept it among the top wholesale houses for more than two decades.

Birmingham developed three satellites; Wolverhampton (where Start's business was acquired in 1904), Walsall (1909) and Coventry (1920). In its early days Birmingham drove a modest trade with a handful of newsagents. Then, under J. B. Treadwell and his successor, H. A. Crook, business grew and flourished. As an old member of the staff wrote in 1910: 'The wholesale trade now began to take rapid strides upon the floodtide of the cheaper press, and has increased gradually until to-day it finds employment for some forty persons, with eight delivery vans . . .' Its business was mainly in newspapers and magazines. The writer concluded:

Time has worked many changes . . . The half-penny press . . . the great increase in periodical literature . . . the magazine list has trebled itself . . . Evening newspapers have arisen in nearly every town . . . rapid communication has placed the London publishing houses in very close touch with provincial distributing houses. The volume of matter handled has increased a hundredfold, while a perfect network of local newsagents' shops has arisen. To satisfy the demand of the trade and the public for early and regular supplies the machinery of distribution has been greatly developed.[73]

Hornby's instinct was sound: the wholesale trade was the area that cried out for most attention and repaid it best in these years. All the more reason (in Hornby's view) to keep euphoria within bounds. The vendors of ill-managed and unprofitable businesses were quick to offer them for sale at prices calculated to solve their financial problems. But Hornby drove such bargains hard. Before Mapstone's of Bristol was bought, he sent Jones from Manchester to give him 'your opinion of the general character of the business, stock, premises etc. and the value of the goodwill'.[74] The final terms were scrutinised long and hard in conjunction with Smith's solicitors, Birchams. When he bought Kitchingman's at Bradford, he subjected them to severe cross-examination on their figures, concluding: 'Though we have every desire to meet you fairly, we cannot pay an excessive price for the goodwill of any business, as *our own name is sufficiently good to make it cheaper for us to start independently than to pay too high a price.*'[75]

Hornby was only too well aware that provincial wholesale enterprises were very far from being instant gold mines. When the partners set up a new house at Leicester in 1899 they interviewed its manager-to-be, one Beckwith. They enquired of him as to its prospects. Beckwith cautiously answered: 'fair, but not brilliant.'[76] He was right. His turnover in that first year was c. £12,000: in 1903/4 it had risen to only c. £13,000. Leicester did not take off until the First World War.

In acquiring wholesale businesses, *caveat emptor* was Hornby's major weapon. In supervising them, he mingled two principles: maximum economy on costs and minimum interference with managerial enterprise. Occasionally, a discreet word of guidance was unavoidable:

Your stock of Stationery & Fancy goods appears to be somewhat large; very possibly this may have some connection with the coronation, when no doubt all kinds of fancy nick-nacks will be put on the market. Watch this sort of thing very carefully, for any overstock in this direction will be mere waste, & fancy stationery of all sorts depreciates very rapidly with the changes of fashion.[77]

Equally important was the principle of maximum freedom of management to manage – wholesale management above all, for its major need was utmost flexibility – flexibility to meet unforeseeable emergencies at no notice whatever, flexibility to decide what to sell, and when and how to sell it. The partners' task (as Hornby remarked forty or more years later) was to select the right men to manage and give them the support and freedom they needed to manage well. These principles were not invented by him: they were already strong in the oldest provincial wholesale houses when Hornby was still an undergraduate rowing in the Oxford boat. In 1906 Charles Awdry had to use stern words to induce old W. A. Barker, who had managed Liverpool House for forty years, to keep his promise to retire. Desperation sharpened Awdry's nib as he wrote on 15 February:

you have already enjoyed your superannuation allowance as well as your salary for several years & have reached a good old age – while your probable (& almost necessary) successor is hardly being treated considerately . . . This delayed hope must be most disheartening to him & consequently injurious to the future prospects of this firm.[78]

Already the managers of the provincial wholesale houses bore something of the aspect of fifteenth-century barons, given to conducting their far-flung and almost independent kingdoms as they saw fit, regardless of the central government. A correspondence between Charles Awdry's son, Charles Selwyn Awdry (who became a partner in 1904) and W. H. S. Barker, the manager of Bradford Wholesale House (and son of the reluctant, Liverpudlian Barker who hung on to office so tenaciously) illustrates the kind of problem sometimes created by managerial freedom. 'We have learnt with some surprise' began Awdry Junior's letter in 1906 'that you have sent to Mr. G. Vickers a list . . .': Vickers was another old-established London wholesaler; the list contained the number and the prices of the periodicals supplied to Barker by Smith's. It had come as a nasty shock to Vickers to realise that the publishers were supplying Smith's at cheaper rates than he himself was given. He had vented his indignation on the publishers. The publishers had vented theirs on the Strand. Barker's indiscretion (Awdry continued severely) was 'an extremely serious one . . .' It had broken the understanding that the W. H. Smith wholesalers might deal with Smith's, or with the publishers or with other wholesalers, whichever was the cheapest supplier. In this case Smith's had offered the cheapest price. '. . . we entirely object to your using our exceptionally good terms, when we are already the cheaper, as a lever for making another wholesaler cut still lower.'[79]

What limits ought then to be imposed on sharp trading? When did enterprise become an abuse of freedom? What limits, if any, should be placed on the independence of the wholesale houses? The case of Awdry v. Barker was only one of many. It was neither the first nor the last time questions were asked: when the proprietor of the then most famous ink on the market, Stephens, asked Hornby indignantly in 1905 why Smith's sold inks made by rivals while Smith's obtained revenue from Stephens's advertising, Hornby gently initiated him into the secrets of wholesale trading:

> ... we do not exercise any direct control over the goods which are sold by any of our Wholesale Branches in the Country. It would be possible for a dozen different Inks to be sold by them without our knowing anything about it, as each of these businesses is independently managed.[80]

That was a main spring from which their success flowed. It was also to be a source of some problems.

Compared with the wholesale side of the business, the so-called 'Stationery' Department was a modest affair. Yet its contribution was sufficiently large and consistent to be important in times when morale as well as profits were in desperate need of support: between its foundation in 1904 and 1948 it never made a loss. Turnover and profits were to rise steadily. It was Hornby's old opponent, Alfred Harmsworth, who (according to Hornby) gave him the idea of developing the sale of writing paper and things with which to write on writing paper.

Starting with the sale of 50,000 of the *Daily Mail* advertising fountain pens and a cautious stock of writing paper, the 'Sundries Department' was separated off from the Book Department and given an identity of its own. Its growth was satisfactory in the lean years when the main sources of turnover, railway stalls and advertising, were at stake and advertising especially under heavy fire from competitors. The figures of the turnover and profits of the new department brought a touch of loving comfort in a cold climate (see Table VIII.6).

The new branch of trade had grown out of the books and library connection. Book Department was therefore its original home. But when the new strategy suggested it as a serious diversification of business, it was separated off under a separate manager. This was C. W. Kimpton.

The new heads of the other special developments, Tyler (shops) and

Smart (wholesaling), were both ambitious, determined, genial, optimistic: Kimpton was ambitious and determined. He was still relatively junior in 1904/5 ('with less than twenty years' service' as Smith's house journal remarked, not entirely without *arrière pensée*, one suspects). He had come up, through books, library and bookstalls, with a speed that confirms the further observation that he 'has known all along that what he wants is well on top, and has been quite steadfast in letting no ordinary obstacle bar his

TABLE VIII.6 TURNOVER AND PROFITS OF THE SUNDRIES/STATIONERY DEPARTMENT, 1904/5–1918/19[81]

	Turnover £	Net profit £
1904/5	56,096	3,130
1910/11	125,816	7,442
1918/19	319,293	57,931

progress'. Kimpton was undoubtedly a great organiser and planner who worked indefatigably himself and expected his subordinates to do the same. Some might have said he was a slave driver: as the Smith house journal tactfully phrased it, his vigorous qualities enabled him 'to extract the last ounce from an appreciative staff'. However Kimpton may be rated as a person, his methods worked. It was not long before his new department had to be provided with new quarters, spilling over in the new Kingsway. Stationery never stopped growing. By 1909 it had a staff of 170 people, urgently propelled by Kimpton or as the journal blandly described it '. . . a constant living force, which [*sic* who] urges each man, by his own example, to do better work and more of it each and every day'.[82]

Kimpton's little empire diverged from the traditional distributory function of the firm. Its centre from 1908 (in Goldsmith Street) was a small factory, with machinery for cutting and folding paper, presses for box-labels and wrappers and die-stamping. These were expanded in the new purpose-built factory opened in 1911 in Kean Street, behind Kingsway (and were to continue after the move in 1935 to Bridge House). But after that the manufacturing element dwindled. Essentially the Stationery Department was a very successful exercise in finishing (checking, cutting, folding, boxing, labelling, die-stamping or printing) paper or card supplied from outside mills. At the same time, it still partook of the more familiar W. H. Smith general function of distributing, both wholesale and retail. It was a shrewdly timed intervention in a market where the fastest-growing occupations were offices, and their occupants more literate and numerate than either their predecessors – or their descendants after the Second World War.

It is almost a relief to turn from the tank-like energies of Kimpton to a very different scene: the new Printing and Binding Departments which were yet another diversification of these years. Neither activity was a novelty to Smith's in 1904/5: but in that year they were reorganised to assume a new and prestigious, though not conspicuously profitable, role in Smith's affairs. Their new role derived entirely from the personal interest of Hornby. There was a weekday Hornby and a Sunday Hornby: the weekday Hornby, who wrote lapidary and thunderous epistles denouncing the malpractices of railway directors, the Sunday Hornby, quietly busy at home with his private printing press. '. . . Hornby', a recent authority on the private printing presses has said, 'was a craftsman in his own right':[83] a craftsman who succeeded in producing some of the finest work ever to emerge from a private press, amateur in the original and best sense of the word, professional only in its supreme quality.

From an early meeting with William Morris at his Kelmscott Press in 1895, from the Daniel Press at Oxford, and from the University printer, Horace Hart, who had lent Daniel the seventeenth-century Clarendon Press Fell type, then from Emery Walker and Sydney Cockerell, Hornby learned his trade as amateur printer. He worked in the little garden-house of his father's home, Ashendene in Hertfordshire, on pamphlets, short stories, Christmas cards, orders of Church service. His printing studio was a small room some 10 feet by 5. His output was similarly miniature. In 1899, after his marriage in 1898 to Cecily Barclay (for which he printed the hymns and prayers himself) he moved to Shelley House on Chelsea Embankment. His press went with him. Hornby wrote that he worked mainly 'for my own pleasure and amusement': his taste was for 'a certain gaiety of treatment in the use of coloured initials and chapter-headings'. This was conveyed in the type developed for him by Walker & Cockerell. It was named *subiaco* after the fifteenth-century type produced at Subiaco in North Italy by two refugee German printers. It demanded 'good margins, close setting, a sound solid body of printed area and no nonsense'.[84]

How splendidly characteristic of Hornby. His choice of books to print was cultivated but in the convention that had grown up among the private printers of his time. Which was his finest book? His *Thucydides*? *Don Quixote*? *Faerie Queene*? *Utopia*? *Ecclesiasticus*? *Lycidas*? Dante's *Inferno*? Boccaccio's *Decameron*? Opinions vary, but none disputes Hornby's claim to be among the greatest artist-craftsmen of the renaissance of English printing. Hornby himself thought his best work was his larger, taller books (like his *Ecclesiasticus*, which was a response to a suggestion from Arnold Danvers Power, a Smith relative and publisher who became a partner in the firm in 1911). But the question did not worry Hornby as it might have worried Morris; Hornby 'printed for his pleasure – not for reform'.[85] Hornby could be grim when it was necessary to be grim: his pleasure kept breaking through in his books:

> Thus endyth the Boke of the Revelacion of Sanct Jhon the Devine the whych is ryght utile and profytable unto all Christian men, translated and drawen oute of Greke into oure Englysshe tonge by William Tyndale, and emprynted by me St John Hornby on my Presse at Shelley House, Chelsea, in the County of London, the same havynge bene begun in the moneth of October mdcccc, while oure gracious soverayn Ladye Queen Victoria yet raygned over us, and fynysshed in the moneth of July in the fyrste yere of the raygne of Kynge Edwarde the Seventhe, whom God preserve, the yere of our Lorde one thousande nine hundred and one.

Hornby regarded his printing press as primarily a pleasure, a hobby, a recreation and relaxation. This is not in conflict with its historical, social and business setting: indeed, it would be odd if there were no relationship between Hornby's hobby and his work. There was. As the history of book production, distribution and sale shows (see page 362) a revolution had disposed of the old three volume novel selling at 10s. 6d. These had been replaced by cheaply printed and flimsily bound reprints. The hobby of Hornby the printer was to revive art-and-craft printing of the greatest classics. His hobby brought him into contact with the other great private printers and typographers of his day – Emery Walker, Cobden-Sanderson, Sydney Cockerell (secretary of William Morris's Kelmscott Press and later director of the Fitzwilliam Museum at Cambridge), Eric Gill, Bernard Newdigate and many others. Charles Gere and Gwen Raverat were among his illustrators.

Books needed binding. Many of the Ashendene books were bound by the man whom many experts would regard as the Prince of English binders:

Douglas Cockerell, brother of Sydney, closely connected with the Arts-and-Crafts movement, and the 'Guild Socialist' movement. Cockerell, like Hornby, was elected a member of the Art-Workers Guild. Medieval romanticism, idealistic socialism, the ideas of Ruskin and William Morris, folk dancing and folk song, home weaving and English Catholic revival — such were some of the ideas and movements that formed the backdrop to the practical arts and crafts of printing and binding in the late years of Victorian and the early years of Edwardian Britain. Some of the private printers were men of means: those who had no private capital did not last long. For Hornby personally profit was of no account. 'Such books', he writes of his *Utopia* and *Thucydides*, 'present a more interesting problem to the printer, and as I have worked for my own pleasure and amusement without having to keep too strict an eye upon the cost, personal indulgence in this respect has been easy.'[86]

At the same time, Hornby could not help allowing his amusements and business interests to cross-fertilise. Ashendene formed the ideal to which W. H. Smith could aspire. The problem was to bring ideal and reality together. Smith's had been printing since 1861. The turnover and profit were never more than modest but the service was useful internally and to an extent externally: for bookstall notices, advertising and so on. In the first decade for which figures exist, printing turnover grew, then flattened out: profits fluctuated until the 1890s: then came bad times (see Table VIII.7).

TABLE VIII.7   PRINTING TURNOVER AND PROFIT, 1867–1907/8[87]

	Turnover £	Net profit £
1867	11,196	170
1877	33,552	6,639
1887	24,945	4,597
1897/8	23,958	(−578)
1907/8	81,142	(−5,078)

The vicissitudes of printing, its promise, its profits and its losses were a permanent feature of the business; they were especially erratic during the period of combined managerial weakness and poor trade from the 1890s to 1910. Somehow Smith's did not pick up the knack of printing. Perhaps the simple explanation was that their traditional expertise was in the arts of trade and distribution, not in manufacturing. Of all forms of manufacturing, moreover, printing was one of the trickiest: it demanded a considerable degree of literate intelligence among its principal operatives. Unions were strong, often politically minded and arrogant – or so employers and managers thought. For Smith's the management problem seems to have been chronically difficult and good managers hard to find. They came and went with depressing regularity and seem to have suffered more than the average attacks of sickness and sick leave. Wilson (the foreman) was a trial to the doctor and the partners in 1895. Wilson, the doctor reported, needed a prolonged rest. He was 'gouty & highly nervous & excitable, he sees no reason to regard him as intemperate but suspects him of "nipping".'[88]

An exasperated Awdry was still lecturing the harassed Wilson in the hard times that came seven years later. As Awdry had pointed out to Wilson in person, the past nine years since the printing office had been moved at great expense (from Water Street to Fetter Lane) had shown only four years of profits against five of losses. In the past five years only one profitable year could be claimed. The partners did not overlook Wilson's 'continual endeavours'. They were aware of the 'fluctuations common to all trades, but under the present working we do too little business independently of the work for this Firm – it is necessary that this item should be largely increased if the works are to become profitable once more, *as for so small a business as we now do the fixed charges are far too heavy.*' (Author's italics.)

Wilson was to have one more year's trial in the hope that he could put the business on a sound commercial footing. They did not (Awdry concluded) want 'to have to say "good-bye" to one of our old and respected Officers'.[89]

Awdry's hopes of Wilson were disappointed: so, too, those of his successor. All this Hornby, entrepreneur and printer, watched with growing concern. By 1905 he was satisfied that a new pattern of management was essential for the Printing Department. Two grades of manager were needed: a practical working printer to look after the technical business of printing, and, above him, a business manager to watch out for outside and inside markets and control costs, turnover and profits. For the first task, W. T. Welfare was recruited from Spottiswoode's where he had risen from compositor to departmental manager. Welfare was technically far ahead of Smith's earlier printers: he quickly relieved Alfred Acland of the responsibilities for supervising the machinery at Fetter Lane and left him more free to take part in properly managerial aspects of the business as a whole. Welfare was a dependable man, a Freemason, an inveterate smoker and (unlike some of his predecessors) 'almost a teetotaller'.[90] To Hornby it was nevertheless clear that the higher managerial aspects of printing called for a different kind of talent. The necessary qualities seemed to reside in H. (Herbert) E. Morgan.

Herbert (later Sir Herbert) Morgan was an 'ideas' man of a kind already (in 1905) more familiar in North America where he had received his education. It certainly had not dimmed the native eloquence he no doubt inherited from his father, a Welsh minister. He had already made his ideas on printing widely known. They were, in fact, the vehicle on which he had ridden to wider fame in the world of business. As the W. H. Smith house magazine remarked of him some years after he had held appointment in that business, Morgan 'not only saw the opportunity, but took hold of it with such purpose that within a few years his influence was felt in every printing shop in England'. His ingenuity lay 'in linking up the renaissance . . . in decorative art with the needs of commerce . . .': Morgan had brought about (it was claimed by his admirers) 'something akin to a revolution in advertising-printing'. His personality was stamped 'on the whole of constructive advertising. His was logical idealism . . .'[91] Morgan had already powerfully shaped an industry – advertising – still devoid of tradition, still in plastic condition.

The idea of harnessing the revived art of printing to the needs of business (and Smith's in particular) via advertising was one naturally attractive to Hornby: even more to Morgan. On 15 February 1905, Morgan was accordingly harnessed to Smith's. There were 'many difficulties' Hornby told him cautiously in 'creating for you such a position as you suggest' but he was ready to accept Morgan's services for developing the printing business 'on the lines' Morgan suggested. His salary was to be the generous figure of £1,000 a year plus 2½ per cent commission on all orders introduced after the first £10,000. As regards the rest of the business (where Morgan was anxious to spread his wings) Hornby was unwilling to assign him any definite duties but he would always be ready to consider 'any ideas for development' especially in advertising and to use his services 'in the creation of . . . business literature'.[92] Later in 1905, when Hornby mounted a carefully conceived campaign to burnish the Smith image with the press and public, a series of articles in The Times bore the clear imprint of Morgan's doctrines about the transforming power of printing and therefore of advertising on business: especially the piece on 30 December 1905, entitled 'Artistic Printing & Bookbinding by Messrs. W. H. Smith & Son'.

The central theme was straightforward: the art of printing had two principal uses. The first, familiar since the invention of printing, was to convey knowledge: the second, new and perfected only in very recent years, was to compel the reader, willing or unwilling, to learn certain facts or arguments. This must be 'of enormous value to the business man. If you can compel the public to read what you have to say about your business, you have won more than half your battle.' If you want to convey the merits of mineral water and can communicate them to fifteen people, it is likely that nine will buy. The new typography 'is a complicated and almost an exact science'.[93] Large or special type, curiously compelling titles, the use of colours – all can be employed for a well-defined purpose. Every letterhead, bill, catalogue and price can promote business:

> The reader may ask: 'But where can I obtain such printing?' The answer is, at W. H. Smith & Son whose Printing Department, recently removed to Fetter Lane and even more recently reorganised to supply effective and attractive business literature, posters, designs for advertising tea, soap, jam, railways, mineral water, insurance, tobacco, cigarettes, biscuits, confectionery, motor cars, whisky, beer &c. &c.

If the propaganda bore the mark of Herbert Morgan, Morgan still bore the mark of the USA. There was an evangelical ring about the 'philosophy', an ambition (as another great contemporary master of advertising put it) 'to put a halo round the article for sale' that was plainly transatlantic. To Hornby it began to seem all a trifle extravagant, but the times called for imaginative measures. No one could deny that Morgan had a lively imagination. A paper exists which seems to have been written by him after the loss of the LNWR and GWR contracts in October 1905. After judiciously (and correctly) prefacing his remarks with an apology for his defective knowledge of the business, he goes on to produce two suggestions: first, that 'the whole of the advertising literature and circulars used for the shops' should be produced by Smith's themselves: of course (he adds) he is aware that at present Smith's printing prices were too high to make such a move practicable. He ends, a trifle lamely, but 'I think this could be adjusted'. Second, he thought there were 'great possibilities in connection with the sale of articles through the post'.[94] Again, the influence of the American 'mail-order' business was evident.

After this, Morgan's influence seems to have waned inside Smith's, even as it waxed outside, with his publication of a characteristically transatlantic piece at once romantic, ethical and didactic. It was entitled *The Dignity of Business* (1914). Neither Hornby nor Awdry seems to have found Morgan's wide-ranging sermons on the universal truths of business specially useful. Unlike Morgan they were faced with hard facts, the need for specific knowledge, above all specific knowledge of how to raise profits. Morgan's patent medicines were ingenious but time was too pressing to teach the doctor how to apply them to the patient. They seem nevertheless to have recognised that Morgan might still be useful on the printing side: typography was his passion and his technical knowledge of it might be sufficient to combine fruitfully with his business management ideas. In December 1906, his contract was renewed, still as the 'Controller' of printing. But there was an ominous sting in the tail. If the printing business showed no profit from 1 April 1908, the partners would be free to terminate the arrangement in the following March.[95] It was fortunate for this 'artist in the business world and . . . business man in the world of artists' that as a result of his book 'his reputation soon began to grow beyond the particular enterprise in which he was engaged'.[96] For the partners were beginning to suspect that what they needed after all was a business man in the world of business. (Morgan was to seek a fuller life in wartime Whitehall, Smith's Potato Crisps – no connection with W. H. Smith & Son – the Licensed Victuallers' School and other areas of public affairs, including national festivals: he was 'one of the very first to further the idea which resulted in the Festival of Britain'.)[97]

Meanwhile, less visionary manifestations of Hornby's plan for printing and book production were going forward on other fronts. His own exercises in printing had brought him into close touch with many eminent figures connected with the renaissance of the arts and crafts and two in particular. Eric Gill, a polymath and prophet in the visual arts, designed the initial letters for Hornby's printed edition of More's *Utopia* (1906). He was to design the lettering for the W. H. Smith shops which sprang up after October 1905 in the towns dotted along the lines of the LNW and the GWR: and thus the name W. H. Smith & Son became associated in the popular mind with what it might have been surprised to know were letters derived from Imperial Rome – in Eric Gill's work from Trajan's column. Hornby probably came to admire this when he was at Oxford. Gill was closely associated with the private press movement and through it with Douglas Cockerell, who numbered Hornby among his first clients for bookbindings. Cockerell had first set up on his own as a master bookbinder at Hammersmith, then near the British Museum and later at Ewell, in Surrey. When the bookstalls were lost on the two great railways (see page 236), the programme of diversification already under way in distribution was joined to plans to expand and improve the printing works and develop as a 'house industry' the bookbinding which had for some time been farmed out to contractors, when necessary, for the bookstall libraries.

Hornby greatly admired Cockerell's work. In the direct line of descent from William Morris, Cockerell had developed an independent style which combined simple beauty with superb craftsmanship. Hornby sought his advice on his new project. In 1904 Cockerell was induced to give up one day a week to organising the new bindery in Goldsmith Street.[98] In spite of some mutterings from the morris-dancers and a few raised eyebrows among the anti-capitalist home weavers, Cockerell was sufficiently impressed by the potential value of the experiment after a few months to devote his whole time to Smith's.

Later the bindery went to Letchworth where it was alongside the Arden Press, then owned and managed by Bernard Newdigate at Letchworth, not far from Ashendene. At Letchworth was the 'First Garden City', only five years old in 1908. The idea of the garden city was to cultivate industrial growth of a suitable kind in village surroundings. Appropriately the Arden Press was one of its first settlers. Newdigate was himself impressed and influenced by Hornby's Ashendene printing: in 1907 he was in low water financially and seems to have turned to Hornby for help. In the end, though with some doubts, Hornby agreed that W. H. Smith could make use of the Arden business and it was bought: a rescue operation, executed by means of payment by instalments for the plant and machinery.

'We do not like to make too much of the point', Hornby wrote to New-digate in February, 1908, 'but there is no doubt that, to speak plainly, we are taking over a business which is not showing a profit . . . a far better bargain than you could possibly obtain . . . in the open market . . . we are not exactly what you would call willing purchasers.' He added that he regretted he could not increase Newdigate's guaranteed salary: it was 'only fair to both parties' that his salary should depend on the 'tangible results of your work'.[99] Hornby knew enough artists sufficiently well to know they were rarely endowed with much business sense.

In spite of these patchy origins the Arden enterprise went on to exercise a considerable influence, not least through the printing it did for other 'craft' presses (such as Chatto and Windus's Florence Press much of whose work was done by Newdigate at the Arden) and later, by lineal descent on its offspring the Shakespeare Head Press at Oxford under Newdigate. But from 1904 to 1915 (when the First World War broke up the experiment at Letchworth's new 'Garden City' and Cockerell and Newdigate went to the War) the remarkable experiment of a combined craft press and bindery formed part of the W. H. Smith expanding business. As an authority on the history of newspapers, printing and typography wrote of Hornby and Smith's, theirs was 'the first large commercial business successfully to incorporate the principles of the English private press movement into mechanical typographical production'.[100]

Neither printing nor binding ever made much profit: more often they showed losses (though these may mask beneficial prices charged by the two departments to other of Smith's departments who purchased their needs internally within the business). Perhaps profits were not the only object of the exercise: reputation was important too, not least in these years. It is easy today to lose sight of the old disrepute that had dogged the newsagent in early days. Certainly the reforms introduced by the two Smiths, by Lethbridge, Awdry and Hornby, made news distribution a very different story: what had often been a by-word for furtive publications and furtive people had become a national synonym for punctuality and morality. There remained the problem of explaining those complexities of the business which made it indispensable, and justified not only its existence but its profitability. It had become a business fit for gentlemen, true, but did they do anything that really justified their profits? Rightly or wrongly, this was the insinuation frequently dropped by the directors and managers of railways, the proprietors and managers of newspapers and publishers, and repeated and sometimes believed by the public.

This may have been in the minds of the partners when they launched into the printing and binding projects. They were useful internally to the business and if they did not make much money on the open market they undoubtedly brought interest and prestige and helped to get W. H. Smith & Son into the public eye. Cockerell, Newdigate, Gill . . . all names to evoke cultural revival and new attitudes to an industrial society inspired by William Morris and acceptable to middle (and upper) class, non-Marxist socialism. Hornby himself was by nature and endowment an artist and their equal on the level of creative achievement. He also presided magisterially over the process of bonding the Arts-and-Crafts movement into the Smith business. In a more deliberately publicist style, Morgan also found a place in this developing process. So did another young man of talent timely discovered by George Tyler of Shops Department and recruited in November 1905 when the crisis broke. This was F. C. Bayliss, a lively character who left his mark on the visual and practical aspects of the business.

It was Bayliss who was to put in hand the design and fitting out of some fifty shops in November 1905 and another hundred or so in December. By 1 January they were ready for business. Bayliss's functions were wide and steadily became wider; to fitting out individual shops and applying the standard designs, lettering, equipment, etc., he added the choice and development of new sites, the arrangements of leases, the building of new premises, maintenance and repair, decoration, lighting and heating; he prepared and circulated a series of *Guides* on shop management, including window-dressing, to shop managers. Much of what has since come to be common form in retail organisations was still quite new in 1905. Bayliss was the conduit through which the new ideas were diffused in orderly, standardised patterns. What remains unique about all this pioneer work was its quality, which derived directly from Hornby's intimate association with the new Arts-and-Crafts movement and its executants, and his own profound commitment to its ideals. All this combined to convey a very special image of a business which was to survive the trials of 1905 and continue to grow and develop both geographically and functionally.

'The Great Upheaval'

Wholesale houses, retail shops, printing, binding, stationery – these were the principal points of Hornby's strategy of diversification designed to meet the contingency of railway action against Smith's. All were well under way by 1905: and in the spring of that year, when Awdry and Hornby met the GWR general manager, Inglis, they felt strong enough to put to him a stiff programme of proposed rents and privileges for bookstalls and advertising 'to be understood to be final . . . we were to stand or fall by them', as Hornby recorded in the Partners' Diary. He added: 'Interview lasted 55 minutes, and was very friendly. Result to be communicated to us shortly.'[101]

It was the one and only Diary entry about relationships with the major railway lines for the year: but later developments were recorded in correspondence and they bore witness, by July, to a serious deterioration. On the 20th of that month Hornby wrote to Inglis of the partners' regret if the Smith bookstall connection with the GWR 'were to be terminated after so many years of friendly association': he added that the figures they were submitting by tender represented 'the fullest value' not only to Smith's but 'to any Firm in our own line of business which is prepared to conduct the Bookstalls in a creditable manner, and with strict impartiality' (i.e. no favouritism to particular newspapers or journals – a very important point).[102] The tender for bookstalls ran at 12½ per cent for Paddington on a slope down to 1 per cent for minor stalls: guaranteed minimum rent £12,000. For advertising, 65 per cent of receipts, guaranteed minimum

£19,000: total minimum £31,000 (which was what had been offered in April).[103]

A bitter wrangle with the GWR went on into August: Hornby complaining of the new and unreasonable demands of the railway. By early August the partners were aware that the railway was in negotiation with rivals, their identity as yet undisclosed. On 10 August he was 'completely staggered' to hear of an offer so out of all reason that it 'must have come from some party who knows nothing whatever of the business'. He enumerated the reasons why he felt this was 'a dangerous experiment' for the GWR. First, Smith's had built up a highly trained, reliable and expert staff whose equal would be hard if not impossible to find. Second, the company benefited by the continuity of tenure Smith's had enjoyed and their nationwide network of stalls, which reduced running costs to railway and customers alike. Only Smith's success, based on *their expertise and organisation*, could encourage an ignoramus to think a wildly increased rent could be squeezed out of the trade.

Hornby ended with an ominous warning. The railways should not overlook the trade which the Smith stalls brought into the station from the towns themselves:

At many Bookstalls half our business is done outside the Station, and could be done equally well ... from a shop, which would have the additional great advantage of being our own property, not subject to disturbance. We do not say this in any hostile spirit, or by way of threat, but simply as a frank statement of what our policy in the future must be, if we are driven from the Bookstalls.

It looked as if Hornby's policy, cautiously followed since 1900, of probing the potential alternative offered by urban shops to the railway bookstall empire, had been only too timely. His peroration suggested that Smith's were ready to face it as reality. It would be 'a bitter blow' to lose the stalls but they, as business men, must look to the future rather than accept conditions of business which offered only inevitable bankruptcy. In that case, he concluded:

we will carve out our future to the best of our ability upon new lines. We are not afraid of competition ... there is still a future before us even under changed conditions. Our immediate loss will be heavy, but it will be easier to bear than years of unprofitable trading with no hope for the future.[104]

Almost identical letters passed between Hornby and Sir Frederick Harrison, general manager of the LNWR. '. . . the blow of separation', Hornby wrote on 5 June, '. . . causes us great distress . . .' but they could not pursue 'an absolutely sure road to our own ruin. We are therefore determined that . . . we will, if necessary, content ourselves with a smaller business resting upon a sounder basis, rather than strive after a larger turnover which can only be done at a loss.'¹⁰⁵ Probably unconsciously, he was echoing William Henry II's words to Awdry in the difficult times just before his death (see page 181).

The same applied to their advertising. Could he have a reply by 30 June? There were thousands of clients to be dealt with. But no reply was forthcoming. Unknown to Hornby or his fellow-partners (though doubtless not unsuspected) the top management, if not the directors, of the two great railway companies concerned were deep in discussion – collusion might be a better word – to concert their strategy against Smith's. As Hornby guessed, the calculations on which the rival offers for the bookstall and advertising contracts were based did not come from the contractors concerned, experienced or otherwise. They came from the railway officials, or agents, motivated in equal parts by jealousy of Smith's, a desire to promote the interests of a rival already closely connected with the railways by an existing link of patronage, and perhaps the hope of ingratiating themselves further with the railway Board of directors at a time when the railways were feeling the draught of bad times and their jobs were none too secure. At some date unstated but probably between June and September 1905, the GWR Estate Agent put in a report on the bookstall, library and advertising business to his superiors. Its object was to place Smith's in the most unfavourable light possible: its calculations might be tendentious, its allegations inaccurate but its effect on influential opinion in the GWR was decisive. It concluded that the GWR were 'most inadequately paid for the facilities afforded to the Firm [Smith's]' who were represented as insulated against loss and overpaid for conducting a business which called for no expertise worth speaking of.¹⁰⁶ It was estimated that the rent for bookstalls ought to yield £24,892 to the GWR (an increase of nearly £14,000): advertising to yield £19,478 (an increase of over £4,000). If the GWR were to take over advertising themselves, the net income could reach even larger figures – £24,500 or even more.¹⁰⁷

In each case (for bookstalls and advertising) the report concluded, breathless with visions of limitless prosperity, with a list of possible alternatives if the negotiations with W. H. Smith (then in progress) should break down. In both cases the list was headed by Wyman's, already printing contractors to the GWR but lacking any experience of either bookstalls or advertising.

On 3 October, 'a call was made at Euston' by the GWR management to find out what the LNWR were doing in regard to their bookstalls and advertising (the Smith contracts for both railways coinciding in their terminal date, the last day of December 1905). There was no difficulty in reaching cordial agreement on one point: both railways wanted bigger rents. Some substantial increase – say, of the order of 25 to 50 per cent on advertising – would be appropriate. When the two sides began to nose more deeply into the offers made by the competing firms thus far, it was clear that Wyman's, their hopes doubtless encouraged by the Estate Agent of the GWR, had made by far the largest offer for the bookstall contracts. For the advertising there were several contractors on roughly the same level as Wyman's. The GWR, when interrogated about Wyman's 'stability', merely said they had no reason, so far as their enquiries had gone, to doubt it. The LNWR simply remarked that Wyman's were well placed to conduct both sides of the business.

Three days later, a meeting of GWR directors took place. It decided to consider the acceptance by the LNWR of Wyman's offer for bookstalls and an offer by a contractor called Kershaw for advertising. The question was put to the LNWR directors: why was Wyman's offer for *advertising* not accepted? The answer seems to have perturbed the GWR. Wyman's, it appeared, had based their original tender on guesswork and had reduced it substantially on second (and more cautious) thoughts. Mr Kershaw was restrained by no such prudential considerations; the minimum rent he had so generously offered was, in the opinion of the GWR Committee, 'considerably in excess of the sum which any contractor could reasonably afford to give, having regard to the existing business'. It was 'quite out of the question' to expect an increase to justify such a minimum. The GWR minute continued:

> The London & North Western Company admitted that the sum was more than they deserve, and it would appear that *they have accepted the tender simply to shew an increase on the present payment* [i.e. Smith's] *regardless of the consideration as to whether the contractor fails or not* [author's italics]. It certainly could not be recommended that the Great Western Company should adopt such a course.

Understandably, the LNWR made known to the Great Western their opinion that these strange, and it might be thought improper, proceedings should 'be kept secret for the present' so that their attitudes might be announced simultaneously. On the 9th a P.S. was received to say the LNW had no objection to the GWR using their figures; their only condition was that 'they should not be communicated to W. H. Smith & Son'.[108]

The final attempt to persuade or intimidate Smith's into making a larger offer came from Alfred Baldwin, chairman of the GWR and father of the future Prime Minister. It was aimed at what the GWR directors may have imagined was Smith's Achilles heel: the proprietor. They chose the wrong target. Freddy had pledged his total and convinced support to Hornby: 'It appeared to me', he wrote immediately to Baldwin, 'that I should be wasting your time and my own if . . . I had come up to see you.' He then went over the Smith case . . . 'merely a repetition of what you will have already seen in our letters and I have only written it once more to make it quite clear that I am convinced the sum . . . named is the largest . . . we can offer . . .'[109]

With that the gate was shut. On 17 October a railway press announcement appeared: the Smith contracts would expire, and not be renewed, on the last day of December 1905. That left just 10 weeks to rearrange a large part of Smith's entire business, get out of the stalls and into the shops. This put Hornby under very great pressure. The problem, vital to W. H. Smith's, had been under discussion since March. He had repeatedly reminded the railway companies of the growing urgency for them to give Smith's a decision. Nothing had been done. His exasperation, natural in the circumstances, at the irresponsibility of the railways, exploded when he learnt – only from his newspaper – that the decision had gone against Smith's. It was not only bad business but an offence against decent manners and confidence. '. . . this last courtesy', he wrote bitterly to Baldwin, 'at least was due to us.' The figures which Baldwin had been given by Harrison of the LNWR, and had been used by the GWR, had been given by Hornby to Harrison 'under the strictest pledge of secrecy, and under the distinct understanding that they were for his personal information . . . Such a gross breach of confidence has caused us almost more pain than losing the Bookstalls.'[110] But by this time Baldwin had sunk into that torpor which was the Baldwin flight from reality when life got difficult. Harrison, on the other hand, felt bound to try and exculpate himself from the charge of breaking confidence, explaining that the leak did not come from him personally. Hornby acknowledged his letter, only remarking that he would have expected reasonable notice: in a mere ten weeks Wyman's would probably 'find it as hard to get in as we shall do to get out . . .'[111]

The railway companies' behaviour was, viewed from any standpoint, extraordinary. Long after Wyman's had secured the new contract, the two companies were giving direct notice to Smith's bookstall clerks, while it was left to Wyman's, who as yet had no status *vis-à-vis* Smith's, to give notice to Smith's of their duty to vacate their railway stalls. Hornby quickly brought his feelings under control but even in November he wrote to an old friend (later 2nd Viscount Knutsford) whose brother was a director of the LNWR. He didn't want his brother or anybody else to think 'we feel any soreness' — he did, of course — at *losing* the LNW contract. But he and his fellow-partners had felt keenly the way they had been treated by the officials of that railway, Harrison in particular. He (Hornby) and Awdry (who was with him) were absolutely certain that Harrison *had* given a pledge that he would use the information and figures given him solely for the LNW.

Having shewn him the figures which were on a little piece of paper, I was putting them back in my waistcoat pocket when H. said, 'May I keep those?' I said 'Yes, if you will treat them as confidential, and return them to us' . . . we should not have been such idiots as to have left them with H., as we knew well that they would prejudice us in the eyes of other Railway Companies.

He was honestly of opinion that the LNWR had made a mistake in taking on Wyman's as bookstall contractors:

They are [price?] cutting printers, no more and no less . . . I do not wish them any harm . . . As to Kershaw . . . his chances are indeed poor, unless he receives very much better treatment from the Company than we have ever done. I gather, however, that he has nothing to lose, though I presume he has backers.[112]

But by this time the hostility of the railways had hardened into a phobia. Pride spoke louder than money. Rightly or wrongly they had voted for Wyman's. They were determined — apparently — to stick to them regardless. The GWR especially knew that they were taking a heavy risk: the LNW had acted partly out of spite against Smith's and for many years spite was to be the steam in their boiler. By 1908 retribution was on the way: the provisions for Wyman's carriage charges had to be amended to bring them into some kind of relationship to reality. By 1916 Wyman's were appealing desperately for financial help to both companies because their

12 Above, left: William Lethbridge, 1825–1901, 'The Great Mogul' (portrait by Frederick Sandys, 1882) 13 Above, right: Charles Awdry, 1847–1912 (portrait by William Strang, 1911)

14 Below: a day in the country: W.H. Smith staff, *c.* 1892. Presiding (centre), arms folded and wearing a top hat, is John White

15 Above: Finchley Railway Station bookstall, 1895
16 Below: Blackpool North Railway Station bookstall, 1896

17 No. 186 Strand, decorated for the Coronation, 1901

18 Above: the Newspaper Despatch Room in 1905

19 Below: the Kingsway shop in Central London, 1908. The descriptive commentary beneath the picture is from *The Shop Manager's Guide*, 1908

bookstall business was making heavy losses. Bending the rules in a manner extraordinary in companies which themselves held their monopoly privileges under law, the GWR and LNWR had to agree to abate Wyman's rent to enable them to balance their books. That was in 1916. In 1917 Wyman's asked for a larger amount to enable them 'to pay their cumulative preference dividend'.

Even this did not persuade the general manager of the GWR that it was time to apply the same rules to Wyman's as had always applied to Smith's: 'The firm's [Wyman's] financial position has throughout . . . been stringent . . . the firm have had to use revenue from the bookstall and advertising business for the purpose of their current liabilities by reason of the fact that they had not at any time a sufficient floating bank balance of their own to meet the current charges . . .' The chairman 'speaks confidently as to the future . . . a passing phase . . . aggravated by war . . .' but it 'may be *open to doubt whether the firm can ever become a sound financial undertaking* . . .' (author's italics).

All of which was a circumlocution to try and conceal the fact that the Wyman tender, with its contractual undertakings to pay the promised rents, was not and never had been worth the paper it was written on: a fact which had been plain to the GWR from the beginning; or should have been. Why then were Wyman's continued in office? Because (in the GWR's words) 'the two companies entered into contracts with Messrs. Wyman & Sons because they could not get what they regarded as satisfactory terms from Messrs. Smith & Son, and also because the latter were in the position and were prepared to exercise the powers of monopolists.' If Wyman's were not assisted – in fact, subsidised – Smith's 'would again enter the field as practically the only possible competitors, and would be very likely to insist upon their own terms'.[113] In 1918 Wyman's were still applying for help: the railway companies, themselves operating a legalised monopoly, appointing themselves public guardians against what they had decided was another monopoly, still propped up Wyman's at the public expense against Smith's, 'the monopolists'.

When George Tyler talked to a Midland Railway friend in 1920, the latter spoke of a discussion with an LNWR official dealing with their bookstall contracts who said, 'we are tired of & have no respect for the present Contractors . . .'; if only WHS would approach the railways he felt sure they would negotiate. 'I said,' wrote Tyler to Hornby, 'why do not the Company [LNW] approach the firm [WHS]? He replied, I fear that their pride will prevent this.'[114] So the extraordinary irony continued: a railway sytem which had emerged, historically, as a monumental tribute to *laissez-faire* economic doctrine, and itself detested by Victorian and Edwardian private enterprise as a tyrannical monopoly, had appointed itself arbiter in the competition ordained by law for its business, rusticating potential competitors by describing them (privately) as monopolists while creating protected monopolies for their own subsidised camp-followers.[115]

To return to the confusion of 1905. The moment was already overdue to put Hornby's strategic plan into full action. No time was lost once the news had been confirmed on 17 October that the two great rail contracts were indeed lost. The following day a notice went out to 'The Clerks in Charge of Railway Bookstalls, and all others whom it may concern'. It was signed by Hornby and announced that the bearer, Mr Horace Holmes, was 'travelling for us in a confidential capacity. Be so good as to assist him to the utmost of your ability, both with any information concerning our business in the town where you are resident' and any other information or help he needs.[116] Holmes, it will be recalled (see page 214), was one of those brought in (to replace the peccant Earle) in search of properties suitable for shops. It was the signal for the campaign to begin in earnest. Time was desperately short. There were only ten weeks to go.

Moving Out

The principal superintendents on the two lines affected were summoned for councils of war on 17 and 19 October. Between them the partners and the superintendents divided up their trading areas on the LNWR and GWR and decided which stalls were to be let go, which to be replaced by shops in the towns near by. Instructions were then prepared for the superintendents concerned to negotiate for premises. Where possible, existing businesses were bought and later taken over after valuation. Elsewhere shop premises were rented, or leased, or bought, in some cases and in due time, rebuilt. But even the temporarily fitted shops were redesigned and repainted to a standard pattern: cream lettering on a ground-colouring of green. It was not always easy to find suitable premises at short notice or even to find premises at all. For example at one Welsh town practically the whole business area was in the ownership of a landlord who was also a director of the GWR. In all, some 250 stalls, major and minor, were being lost. But between 18 October 1905 and 1 January 1906, 144 new shops were opened on LNWR and GWR 'territory'. The majority of these were what were called 'B' shops: some sixteen were 'A' shops. A 'B' shop was managed in a way similar to a bookstall, that is, it was responsible to the

Strand head office. An 'A' shop was closer to the model of the provincial wholesale house, with a larger degree of independence for its activity both in buying and selling. The whole of this enormous redeployment was directed, under the partners, by Tyler and Bayliss.

By 20 October instructions began to flow from the Strand to the bookstall staff. Most went either from Hornby or Awdry. Some contained good tidings, some less. The manager at Ruabon was no doubt relieved to hear that Smith's would be 'glad to retain your services'; pleased or frustrated when they added that he would have to move to 'a position no worse than you at present occupy'.[117] Mr Hull at Didcot must have been flattered to be told 'that with your energy, the many accounts which you have from the large district which you control ought to remain with us, and we are happy to say that we shall be able to leave you there in charge [of the shop]'.[118] Mr Hoskins at Monmouth was less fortunate: Monmouth would have to be abandoned. If he wished to start his own business Hornby would be pleased to write to all his customers encouraging them to transfer their business to him.[119] And so on, to some 200 or more clerks-in-charge.

The execution of a complex and – for the partners and top management – exhausting operation was meticulous. It was also done with meticulous consideration for fairness. Hornby wrote to a correspondent from Penrith later in October who had praised his local bookstall manager. 'We have reason to believe that all our Bookstall Clerks have acted in a most loyal manner during the past few weeks, and we have not yet, to our knowledge, lost a single good man.'[120] The record was not to remain quite as immaculate as that. Some newsboys deserted. 'Can not you get back the boys who have gone over [to Wyman's]?' Hornby asked the clerk at Tavistock. 'You may offer them higher wages than Wyman's have done, if you can retain their services. It is important not to lose boys at the last moment. We must not in any event abandon the rounds. You can pay *good* wages for *good* boys.'[121] Mr Hurford at Yeovil (whom Wyman's had attempted to lure away to Weymouth) was given both stick and carrot treatment. If he accepted Wyman's he would be 'strenuously opposed' by Smith's who had secured 'admirable premises, well situated' and by a very popular clerk. If he stayed with Smith's he would be ensured 'a position, at least as valuable as that you already have . . .'[122] Hurford stayed. Not everyone did and not everyone took the discomforts of the 'great upheaval' (as superintendent William Vincent entitled it) without at least grousing. Replying to a complaining clerk at Dorking, Awdry had to point out that his guaranteed salary on removal was £40–£50 a year higher than he had received before, that his opportunities to earn even more were bright. Everyone, Awdry

continued, had suffered a restless, anxious and busy six months but most
were thankful that dismissals had been so few and pecuniary loss small.[123]

On the whole the staff response to the discomforts and hardships created
by the upheaval reflected creditably on the partners' staff management
(see page 243). But it was not easy to meet Wyman's tactics towards either
staff or customers, especially as both the railway companies (but the LNW
especially) collaborated openly with their new satellite in a way they had
never done with their predecessor. Wyman's had no hesitation in demanding of Smith's bookstall clerks, as a condition of offering them the succession, that they should supply them with details of Smith's business —
salaries, commission, turnover. Their circular to railway ticket holders
which appealed for trade concluded thus:

> The trade at the Station and in connection therewith has not been
> created by the individual efforts of the Contractors, but has attained its
> present position *through the enterprise of the Railway Company*, the growth
> of travelling facilities, and the residential increase in the various neigh-
> bourhoods.[124]

To be fair to Wyman's, it is almost certain that in much of these manifestations of malice they were merely the instruments of the railways: in
particular of the LNW general manager, Harrison, whose fury at being
opposed by Hornby remained unplacated by second or even much later
thoughts. Time only served to keep green his memory of having his power
questioned and his proposals rejected. It was Harrison who personally
circulated an advertisement offering extra free amenities on behalf of
Wyman's — free delivery of papers and of books, through Mudie's Library
— to travellers.[125] All of which cost Wyman's not a little of their precarious
and as yet unrealised margin for profit. Finally Smith's were driven to
protest against these attempts 'by means not generally considered straightforward' to suborn or bribe staff directly without reference to their
employers.[126] Wyman's allegations of wholesale dismissals were flatly — and
with chapter and verse — contradicted. Another letter ended, nevertheless,
with an assurance that Smith's would be willing to carry on competition
'in the same fair spirit to which we have been accustomed in the past with
all our competitors' and discuss any matters of concern to both businesses
in that spirit. But that did *not* mean (Hornby assured an enquiring correspondent who may or may not have been inspired by Wyman's) that
Smith's 'were prepared to consider any negotiations for an amalgamation
with Messrs. Wyman & Co. Ltd.'.[127]

Hornby's rejoinder to the Harrison-Wyman axis in a *Spectator* advertisement (23 December 1905) was likewise soft: but barbed.

In a circular recently distributed it was somewhat humorously remarked that the success of the Bookstalls . . . was due, NOT to W. H. Smith & Son, but to the enterprise of the two Railway Companies. W. H. Smith & Son are now about to prove what their own enterprise can effect, now that the enterprise of these Railway Companies as applied to the Bookstall business is unfortunately no longer at their command.

There followed a list of the new shops with the assurance of 'less hurried and more pleasant conditions than was before possible': and a timely postscript that the new shops would, of course, be under the management of those same clerks 'who have so faithfully served their firm and the public at the Railway Stations'.[128] If Hornby had suffered any loss of spirit he had quickly recovered it.

Hornby, Harmsworth and Recovery

Hornby's recovery – and that of the W. H. Smith business as a whole – was speeded by a final aspect of his business strategy less palpable, more easily overlooked but no less crucial than those already discussed: public relations. As long as William Henry II had lived, the image of his firm had been linked in the public mind with the high politics of the Victorian railway age and the concept and achievement of prosperity which were its hallmark. With William Henry's death, with the retirement of Lethbridge from the City to rural obscurity, with the receding tide of economic growth and the vicissitudes of the *fin-de-siècle*, the firm had become more isolated from the sources of power in the news world.

Hornby had become acutely aware of this during the dispute with Alfred Harmsworth in 1898. He had also conceived a certain admiration for Harmsworth, differ though he might from many of his ideas and policies. He had accordingly set to work, quietly and deliberately, to repair the Smith fences, in and beyond Fleet Street. Conscious that some of the provincial press was hostile to Smith's (whom they saw as the instrument of *The Times* and the other London newspapers which still threatened their hopes of improved circulations) Hornby saw that the Harmsworth press could be an enormous source of strength, especially because *The Times* was

visibly wilting as the end of the long regime of the Walters came into sight
(see page 54).

Did he, perhaps, already foresee that 'The Thunderer' might itself end
up in Harmsworth's empire? Whatever his precise appreciation, there is no
doubt that from 1900 he built on the conviction that Harmsworth would
be a powerful ally. He went out of his way more than once to ease the
upward climb of Harmsworth and his papers. He cultivated his friendship
and Harmsworth reciprocated with the warm and emotional side of his
nature. When the rumours began to circulate of a coming railway *putsch*
against Smith's, he had warned Hornby of the threatening trend of Fleet
Street gossip: but in a letter referring to their conversations he added: 'I
cannot conceive it possible that anyone would be so foolish as to undertake
the venture' (of cutting out Smith's from the bookstalls).[129] That was on
22 September 1905. Then he offered Hornby a contract for display of the
'contents' bills' of the *Daily Mail*. Hornby accepted appreciatively on
5 October 'not only for the sake of the advertising revenue – which is very
welcome in these days – but because it sets a good example to others. I hope
you will find it as advantageous to you, as we find our advertisement in the
D.M.'.[130]

When Hornby confirmed his worst fears on 17 October, Harmsworth
sent an immediate and comforting reply. 'I cannot say how surprised &
sorry I am at the news . . . & I feel that my views will be shared by our
trade generally.' He could not think there was ground for a rumour they
had discussed at Harmsworth's home, Sutton Place.

> The people [Wyman's] have no money at all & I am much puzzled
> about the whole business . . . Meanwhile you have energy, & a great
> opportunity in which I trust you will allow us to assist to the best of our
> ability – the organisation of the much disorganised retail trade of the
> country.[131]

The revolution in attitudes since the quarrels of 1898 was indeed remarkable
(see page 195).

Hornby replied the following day. He was evidently touched and was
unusually forthcoming:

> [the] truly kind and sympathetic letter . . . brought a good deal of com-
> fort to me when I was naturally feeling a bit down in the mouth. For
> when you have held a business for over fifty years, and given your whole
> soul to it, it is a blow to lose it at one fell swoop. I am afraid we shall hear

that we have lost the G.W.R. tomorrow, and those two lines are a large part of our business. I can only feel some pride in the thought that we have carried on the Bookstalls in a clean fashion, and that we have not used our position to the detriment of the Trade in general. I don't intend to be disheartened. I think we can create a new business which in time will be better than the old, and I hope – without wishing to be revengeful – that I may live to see the downfall of our opponents. I can only see a heavy loss before them, unless the Railway Companies ... treat them much better than they have treated us.[132]

His prophecy was to prove accurate; so was his equally prophetic reservation. The following day he wrote again to confirm to Harmsworth Smith's loss of the GWR contract and assure him of his wish to reciprocate his offer of mutual help. 'Wyman's chief claim to be a Bookstall Contractor' he concluded 'appears to be that he can sell Bluebooks to Railway passengers!'[133] Two days later he wrote again to ask for one or two full pages of advertisement in the *Daily Mail*. 'Our campaign is going on splendidly. Our men are full of fight, and I think will give W. & Son a warm time.'[134]

Harmsworth's view of the crisis was not only encouraging: it was also critically constructive and perceptive, as Hornby was quick to see. Harmsworth wrote on *Daily Mail* writing paper on 19 October:

Everyone to whom I have spoken is entirely of your point of view with regard to the temporarily unfortunate check in your business. I cannot help thinking, however, that it will really prove a blessing to you in the future. Instead of the constant anxiety of the renewal of the contracts, you will be able – if you will get efficient managers – to entirely reorganise the News Trade in such a way that it benefits the public & the newspapers, and is a much less anxious form of business for yourselves. The progress of the electric tramway and motor omnibuses is only beginning, and the supply of newspapers to their passengers, quite apart from general trade, will be well worth securing.[135]

Harmsworth was one of the few newspaper men who did not underrate the complexity and value of efficient news distribution.

He was as good as his word in promising Hornby any help he might need. When a rumour began to circulate in the summer of 1906 that the *Daily Mail* was interested in acquiring Wyman's, Hornby asked Harmsworth if he would contradict it. Harmsworth responded immediately. The *Mail* not only flatly denied it had ever contemplated an offer for any newsagency:

it added that W. H. Smith had similarly declined ownership in newspapers and had given up book-publishing on the same principle of the division of labour and skills. It went on to say that the railways would be well advised to follow out the same logic and stop trying to supplant W. H. Smith. The latter's work was, on the whole, well done: the allegations of monopoly were ill-founded. Smith's share of news distribution was often exaggerated, e.g. the Horace Marshall newsagency took more of the *Daily Mirror* than Smith's . . . And so on. Harmsworth was a master of propaganda.

Hornby reciprocated. When the *English Review* published an article on Harmsworth, Hornby wrote to its manager on his own initiative regretting the publication 'in your issue of last week [of] a most scurrilous and objectionable article upon Sir Alfred Harmsworth': he gave notice (as in any case of possible libel he was fully entitled to do) that if any similar articles appeared in the paper about any individual, he would discontinue its sale at Smith's bookstalls and shops.[136]

But his concept of a 'public relations' strategy did not end with Harmsworth. He took note that in spite of a cold breeze that had sprung up with *The Times* over their proposal (in the middle of the railway bookstall crisis of 1905) to float a *Times* Book Club which would compete strongly with Smith's circulating library, Moberly Bell could still write him a genuinely sympathetic and friendly letter over the Wyman episode. Accordingly, when John Murray, the publisher, tried to involve him in a row with *The Times*, Hornby decided to tread cautiously: his predecessors had more often been at loggerheads with *The Times* than in friendly alliance with it. So, from time to time, had Hornby. But (as Lethbridge had remarked decades before, see page 187) 'The Thunderer' was still a force to be reckoned with. Hornby agreed, in spite of its currently moribund condition. When Murray called *The Times* Book Club 'unscrupulous & vindictive' and tried to persuade Hornby to join the publishers' alliance to defeat them, Hornby was unforthcoming.[137] His diplomacy contained a prudent element of *realpolitik*. The great newspapers, even when temporarily under heavy weather, were more vital to W. H. Smith's than a single book publisher, even than the entire book trade of the first decade of the twentieth century. Hornby was conscious that he needed the best and most powerful allies he could find.

But Hornby was building his bridges out beyond Fleet Street, Printing House Square and Sutton Place. They extended to the head offices of the great railway companies (other than the LNW and the GWR) – at King's Cross, St Pancras, Marylebone, Waterloo, Victoria and Liverpool Street: to the London Electric Railways, the Metropolitan and District too; even outside the metropolis, in the provinces, to Manchester, Sheffield and York; to Sir Guy Granet, general manager of the Midland Railway, an old friend to whom Hornby had sold – so he remembered, half a century later – his wig and gown when he had decided to give up the law and take to newspapers. Granet was a man after Hornby's own heart. A week before W. H. Smith's were due to yield place to Wyman's on the last day of 1905, Granet wrote to Hornby:

> Quite apart from business you may take it from me that so long as I have any influence on the Midland . . . we shall not leave you. I have already . . . infused my views into my chiefs . . . Whatever you like to say against Wymans I will endorse blind. I have the greatest prejudice agst. them. If Wymans sell tea or tobacco at any station where we have the refreshment contract I will raise Hades. All the above sentiments are based not upon friendship for you but upon prejudice. Prejudice agst. leaving a tried article. Prejudice – perhaps utterly unreasonable – agst. Wymans personally.[138]

In the north a good friend had emerged – after some stern tussles – in James Aspinall, the general manager of the Lancashire & Yorkshire Railway Company. Aspinall had negotiated as toughly and obstinately as the next, but he was fundamentally a square dealer who was not intimidated by his larger partners of the LNW at Euston Square. Unlike Granet, he had no personal ties with Hornby. Theirs was a purely business relationship but it stood the strains of the early 1900s. So, in the end, did the relationships with the other rail companies. No other major bookstall contract was lost after 1905 and relationships with the railway companies, though still marked by hard bargaining, became less critical.

To summarise the nature and consequence of Hornby's operations between 1900 and 1906 is not simple. Did he do right to stand out, as he did, against railway demands upon him and the firm he led? Or did he, by his opposition, drive the two largest railway customers into inevitable and ruthless hostility to Smith's? What were the gains and losses of his 'strategy'? To try to answer these questions means making up one's mind: is it worth asking – could history have taken a course different from that it did take? If it enlarges one's imaginative understanding of what actually happened yes: if it does not, no.

It is only too easy to see that Hornby could have given in. If he had done so, it seems most probable that the other railways (besides simply the LNW and GWR) would have followed the same course as Hornby's great opponents. If the statistics and arguments he put forward were accurate, he was probably correct in believing that Smith's would have collapsed, or at very least would have become a satellite of a railway system which was itself in steady and seemingly irreversible decline. The strategy he devised and followed, on the other hand, lost two of the largest railway contracts for bookstalls and advertising: this was due to opposition from the management of the two rail companies concerned which, however much one tries to see the conflict objectively, seems hopelessly prejudiced. Their calculations about Smith's actual operations and Wyman's potential operations were both equally fictitious. In the end their only excuse was their rhetorical denunciation of Smith's 'monopoly'. In modern terms,[139] there may have been an element of justification for this but, if it was a 'monopoly' it was a relatively efficient and profitable one that served the public and the publishing industry, and added to the railway's slender profits too: in any case, it was no more of a 'monopoly' than the railway companies' own business or Wyman's business to which the LNW and GWR granted not only monopoly right but long-term subsidy, even when the figures on the strength of which the monopoly was granted had been proved beyond question to be entirely fictitious.

Informed contemporaries believed that it would be necessary to call the railway companies' bluff if the Smith business were to be saved from extinction.[140] They seem to be borne out by the facts as they have emerged historically. Yet some further distinctions must be made. The newsagency business was one thing: it demanded a certain kind of professional knowledge combined with organisation designed to produce punctuality and reliability. The railway advertising business was different: the arguments in support of it less convincing, especially with the growth of efficient commercial communications. Already before 1900, the continued threats of the railways to take their advertising into their own hands were materialising. Hornby himself privately poured cold water on plans for an Advertising Contractors' Association in 1907: they were Canute-like in trying to hold back the inevitable; '. . . for to very few is Railway Advertising essential because of the various other excellent channels of publicity . . . newspapers, pamphlets, insets and the like.'[141] The railways were increasingly reserving the best spaces on stations for themselves so that the value of this kind of advertising was decreasing so far as Smith's were concerned.

The figures of net profit on railway advertising bore him out. Between 1870 (when the first figures are available) and 1891, profits rose (unevenly) from c. £26,000 to c. £44,000. Between 1892 and 1915/16 they fell from the record (1892) figure of c. £54,000 to c. £11,000. They only exceeded

the 1892 record once even in the prosperous first half of the 1920s – that
was in 1923/4 when they reached c. £56,000. In 1949/50, they were c.
£26,000. This telescoped history includes the loss, in 1905, of two large
rail advertising contracts, the gradual loss of others, the acquisition of some
new contracts. Moreover, losses on rail advertising were offset to some
extent by advertising on new forms of transport such as buses and Tubes
(as Northcliffe had forecast).

If the decline of Smith's railway advertising was 'natural' – it might be
argued 'inevitable' – the rise of news wholesaling and retailing via urban
shops was equally 'natural' or 'inevitable' – that does not mean 'easy'. The
developments of the first decade of the twentieth century grew out of
social, technological and economic changes in the world of which the
Smith business was a part: they also grew out of the skills and experience
comprised within Smith's, their management and staff. Seen in historical
perspective, the new urban shops which replaced the bookstalls on the
LNW and GWR lines were an improved adjustment in retailing, the outcome of conflict. Without that conflict they might not have come. They,
in turn, brought or encouraged growth elsewhere. One old hand (who
knew only too well what life was like on an exposed station bookstall on a
winter's day) pointed out that the large and prosperous stationery business
could hardly have developed in the conditions of a stall exposed to wind,
weather, water, dust and dirt. The stationery business (turnover and profits)
rose in concert with the shops, properly sheltered and equipped.

Again, if the railway companies and Wyman's had taken any account
of Hornby's 'shop' strategy, it was inadequate. For this they had no excuse.
Hornby had given them fair warning. The combination of long experience
and a bold new initiative was very nearly fatal to the new contractors.
Without the dubiously-legal help of the railway companies they would
have failed.

Hornby's policy of resistance had, temporarily, lost Smith's perhaps a
third of their railway business: about a third of their total bookstalls had
gone, and at least a third of their railway advertising profits. His policy of
replacing all this with shops and other enterprises created an immediate
demand for a great deal of capital, and profits were slow to materialise. The
capital in 1894 (it could be argued) was less than what was necessary in 1874.
By 1907 or 1908 it was three to four times as much – on account of the
demands made in the new century both for fixed and working capital to
meet the needs of Hornby's 'strategy'. This burden fell on Freddy as
proprietor and Freddy had no hesitation in carrying it. His faith in Hornby
was absolute.

When Hornby celebrated his Jubilee in 1943 he looked back on 1905 – a shock, a disaster, but in the end a blessing:

> Never shall I forget the enthusiasm that permeated the whole staff; the . . . scores of willing helpers scouring the country in search of shops . . . the Partners' Room at least for once a hive of industry; the fiery eloquence of George Tyler as he addressed squads of Bookstall men before they took up their new duties; Bayliss knee-deep in shop-fitting plans, working till any hour of the night or early morning . . . It was a great time . . .[142]

IX

'Pre-War': Reform, Recovery
and Diversification

AFTER 1918, WHEN boom turned to bubble, men were to look back
nostalgically to 'pre-war' as a Golden Age. In spite of a reputation as a time
of 'The Great Depression', the preceding period of late Victorian history
had witnessed massive economic advances, the benefits of which went in
some degree to all orders and kinds of men and women. The middle classes
did best but wage-earners also enjoyed remarkable advances in living
standards. '. . . it seems doubtful whether any generation tackled its
problems more successfully than the late Victorian'.[1]

It deserved its reputation for enterprise, judgment and humane social
instinct. In this respect, as in so many others, W. H. Smith & Son mirrored
their times: they had had their ups and downs but even their most serious
crises had been tackled with success. It was still like that as the Victorian age
passed into history. The new management, guided by Hornby, faced and
dealt with its own business crisis – a rail crisis – and their plans to cope with
it developed satisfactorily down to the outbreak of the First World War
in August 1914.

These were years of renewed if gentle expansion. They suffered only
one marked sag – in 1908/9. Like the steady downward movement of
prices from 1873 to 1906, the new upward movement was pretty steady.
There was little violence about it to disturb or dislocate. This benefited the
economy at large and Smith's in particular. If these were not conspicuously
fat years they were certainly not lean. Recovery was gradual but unmistakable. The worst was behind them; for the time being. The volume of
business done by the stalls and shops grew: the wholesale houses continued
their success story. New enterprises – stationery, printing, binding – all
expanded, though with degrees of good fortune that differed very widely.

First with the News

Even the library expanded. Only advertising seemed to be stuck at round about, or below, its levels of the turn of the century (see Table IX.1).

The profitability of Smith's different activities varied considerably. *Total* profits almost doubled – from £123,000 in 1907/8 to £231,000 in 1914/15. But within this circumference there were results good, bad and indifferent. The bulk of profits naturally came from the retail and whole-sale outlets. The 'A' shops (largely independent of the Strand headquarters)

TABLE IX.I TURNOVER, 1907–14[2*]

Years	(1) Stalls £	(2) 'B' Shops £	(3) 'A' Shops £	(4) PWHs £
1907/8	1,040,348	231,762	225,660	624,051
1914/15	1,317,034	503,738	185,410	1,024,097

Years	(5) News £	(6) Books £	(7) Ad. £	(8) Stationery £
1907/8	1,208,960	360,463	193,123	87,631
1914/15	1,727,389	610,982	185,564	183,580

Years	(9) Library £	(10) Printing £
1907/8	68,509	81,142
1914/15	101,354	125,157

* It is not easy to use these bookkeeping figures for statistical purposes. Very roughly 'turn-over' proper is contained in Cols 1–4. Cols 5, 6, 8 and 9 duplicate Cols 1–4 in so far as they represent stock sold through the retail outlets. This represents a high proportion but the figures should not be taken as more than an indication of orders of magnitude.

fell in numbers, from 58 to 26 (32 becoming 'B' shops) but slowly began to turn in a modest profit as the early teething troubles were overcome. 'B' shops and stalls (this in spite of the loss of the two great railway con-tracts) grew in numbers. After an initial drop in 1905, 1914 saw a recovery to 720 major stalls (compared with the 779 of 1902). Minor stalls (463 in 1902) nearly doubled (to 828) by 1912. Fifty new 'B' shops were added to the original 147 by 1914.

These were years when the partners hastened to take advantage of the combined talents of Herbert Morgan, F. C. Bayliss, Douglas Cockerell, Bernard Newdigate (and doubtless others) to effect the transition from a purely railway-stall regime to a mixed railway-stall-and-urban-shop regime. Their wisdom issued forth in several hand-books (often beautifully printed by the Arden Press) addressed to the shop manager on how best to discharge his manifold tasks. *The Shop Manager's Guide*[3] was designed to educate him on the economic, psychological (and moral) aspects of shop-keeping, its interior economy, bookselling, stationery, library manage-ment, bookbinding, window dressing, etc.

A central question was how to cope with new problems that arose in an urban street and had not arisen on a railway platform One illustration[4] is entitled: 'when your shop contains a *"bookstall"*, see that the dressing is typical of what it represents.' Like the early steamships which retained their sails, the early W. H. Smith shops were still hybrids. Some years later, F. C. Bayliss produced *The Master Salesman*[5] which went into these, and other matters (printing, paper especially), in absolutely precise detail. It was superbly produced and printed by W. H. Smith's Arden Press at their Stamford Street works. The presentation, style and content of these, and other, contemporary manuals accurately represented the partners' philo-sophy about their business. They aimed for high quality and reputation, in what they sold, in their staff and, for that matter, in their customers. And, so far as possible, they dealt individually with all three categories.

Stalls and shops must have provided worthwhile profits: the rest came mainly from the bustling, largely independent provincial wholesale houses. Their management was vigorous, brash, enterprising. They sold anything respectable they could lay hands on provided it made a profit. But retail or wholesale, profits still depended largely on the sale of newspapers, periodi-cals, and books.

Library business looked up in 1912 and an uncovenanted result of the outbreak of war in 1914 was a sudden demand for reading – in camps and tents, later in trenches and hospitals, and in homes. Turnover and profits on reading of all kinds soared unexpectedly. So did the demand for stationery as millions of letters went from families to fathers and sons serving in the Army and Navy and later the Royal Flying Corps. These windfalls were very welcome while they lasted. Elsewhere the results of the new strategy were less satisfactory.

The expansion into large scale printing, urged on enthusiastically by H. E. Morgan, brought large turnover but large losses too (except for the period 1910/11–1912/13 which showed small profits). There was a record loss of £17,604 in 1908/9: of £12,533 in 1914/15. The total profits of Hornby's brainchild, the Cockerell bindery at Letchworth, in these years were £349: the losses £6,966. Printing seemed necessary to Smith's. According to Morgan it promised great opportunities: but it also made new demands. It was a manufacturing activity. Apart from small-scale workshop exercises in making frames from wood for advertising, Smith's were unfamiliar with problems of manufacturing, with the complexities of the machinery, even less of the men who worked the machines. Was this Hornby's Achilles heel? We shall return to these problems again.

W. H. Smith & Son, from its earliest years, had been affected, to a greater or lesser extent, by the development of the national economy and society at large. Yet down to 1905 the sharpest impact on its fortunes came from a single source: transport. Roads, coaches, railways were the main determinant of Smith's fortunes and misfortunes. The crisis of 1905–6 was the last occasion when this particular set of conditions operated. After 1906, external and internal changes operated to make W. H. Smith & Son more sensitive to changes in British society and economy as a whole. The diversification in the activities of the firm, the diversification of the means of transport, the changing relations of capital and labour, of employer and employee, the growing need for capital, for technical expertise, the division of labour – all these, immediately or more remotely, began to alter the 'attitudes' of the firm towards its economic and social context. From the outside came additional positive, sometimes countervailing, influences – whichever they were they could not be ignored.

An important element, but in a new form, was the relative importance of the metropolitan and the provincial markets. Smith's original business was founded in London's West End; thence it had shifted to the distribution of London papers to the provinces. The growth of the provincial press had combined with the rise of the provincial wholesale houses to tip the balance of the business somewhat towards the economy of the provinces. But in the first decade of the twentieth century, as the growth of the national network of railways slowed down virtually to nothing, and contracts with some of the largest existing railway companies were lost, the only major opportunities offering new business came from London itself, especially in the form of the London Underground railways. These comprised both the older 'sub-surface' networks (the District, Metropolitan and City Lines) which dated back several decades, and the 'Tubes' (deep underground 'tubes' proper), which came into their own just after the turn of the century.

The London Underground

The 'Underground' rail system was neither the first nor the only passenger transport system called into being by the needs of travellers between outer and inner London. Surface railways had much earlier brought business-men, clients and customers in from Barnet and Chingford, Harrow and Ealing, Bromley and Chislehurst to the termini of north, east, west and south London, thence to find their way to Threadneedle Street, or West-minster, and back again: more occasionally their wives and families travelled too. Travel in and out of London – 'commuting', as it has come to be called, for business of one sort or another, or for expeditions for shopping or concert or theatre, increased with the growing density of Greater London. Its population grew between 1875 and 1895 from 4.2 to 6 millions – nearly 50 per cent in twenty years. The number of journeys rose by 300 per cent: per head of the population, from 65 to 165 a year. Unlike the provincial cities, London – at least the City and West End – remained tramless. With its old-fashioned horse-omnibuses, London was behind the times until 1905. In that year the first motor-omnibus appeared: the motor swiftly replaced the horse thereafter. This was followed in the same year by the opening of deep tubes, the Bakerloo and Piccadilly. Once again London was the hub of Britain; not only its government, business and finance but (with Shaw) its theatre, (with Beecham, Henry Wood and the Queen's Hall) its music, (with Wells, Bennett and Barrie) its popular literature. Only Manchester could offer a measure of local culture in any way comparable. For good and ill, Britain had become, culturally, politic-ally, financially, a single-city state.[6]

The 'Underground' was the principal means by which a sprawling metropolis was all tied together. It linked the West End and City to suburbia and the London termini with one another. Slowly the different Underground companies became linked together, until by 1918 they were to be concentrated into a single unit for management purposes, though they still retained their separate names. The acquisition of newspaper and bookstall agencies on the London Underground became a focal point of Hornby's strategy to offset the effects of the hostile policies of the LNWR and the GWR.

Reading on the train was not a new habit in Britain (neither was it restricted to Britain). It had been a main plank of W. H. Smith's business progress. The year before they lost a large slice of their traditional custom on the surface railways, Smith's seized the new opportunities offered by the London Underground and its daily thousands of strap-hangers. Since 1 June 1875, there had been W. H. Smith stalls on the sub-surface District Line — at Charing Cross, Hammersmith, Mansion House, Sloane Square and Victoria. By 1902 the original five had grown to thirteen. Now they secured their first 'tube' contract, a single event: Finsbury Park on the Great Northern and City Line, opened in 1904. Contracts with the Great Northern, Piccadilly and Brompton Lines followed in 1906; with the Charing Cross, Euston and Hampstead Lines in July 1907.

A sizeable plum remained in the shape of the Metropolitan Railway. It traversed London from east to west, linking up *en route* five major rail termini (Liverpool Street, King's Cross, Euston, Marylebone and Paddington): it also served the largest Underground junction station, Baker Street, which joined its own north-west extension with the Bakerloo and District Lines. Baker Street did more business in papers than any other Underground station. Its contract was in the hands of an old rival of Smith's, James Willing. In 1907 Willing's were in difficulties, short of capital, ideas and management. The Metropolitan were restive and Willing's were prepared to move.

Hornby had to pick his way carefully. R. H. Selbie, secretary of the Metropolitan since 1903 (he was to become general manager in 1908), was an old Lancashire & Yorkshire man. He and Hornby knew one another of old and got on well. Selbie was friendly and fair-minded but a firm and honest dealer.[7] There seems to have been no difficulty in securing in 1907 the bookstall contract to commence on 1 January 1909, but Hornby also wanted the contract for its joint line with the Great Central into Marylebone. Here, however, he met with an old enemy, Sam Fay, general manager of the Great Central. Fay had had a long dispute on his own line with Smith's, and with Hornby in particular, over the responsibility for rates and taxes on advertising hoardings. Selbie stood with Hornby. 'It appears [he wrote to the Metropolitan Board] that the Great Central Company have a long outstanding dispute with Messrs Smith & Son in regard to the question of rates on the advertisements at their stations.' Smith's 'absolutely decline to have anything to do with the payment of rates unless a very substantial concession is made to them in the matter of the rent . . .'[8] Fay dug in. So did Hornby (knowing that Selbie wanted him to replace the ailing Willing's). '. . . we really cannot understand' (wrote Hornby with that air of a man whose patience is stretched almost, but not quite, beyond endurance which so often proved an effective diplomatic weapon) 'how a Firm composed of business men could be expected to enter into an arrangement which might entail serious financial loss without the hope of making a profit which is, under the best circumstances, so very small . . .'[9]

On 17 June, Fay gave way. Hornby added the joint lines to his Metropolitan Lines contracts. Unlike most of the earlier Underground contracts these covered both bookstalls and advertising. There was no need to worry about Willing's: he had already dealt with that. 'I am very glad' (he had written to James Willing exactly one month earlier) 'that we were able to come to an amicable arrangement, and hope that we may work together in a friendly way for many years to come.'[10] After Frederick Harrison and Wyman's, Hornby was not leaving any part of Smith's flanks or rear at risk.

The Baker Street and Waterloo stalls (no advertising) followed in 1910, the Central Line in 1917, with the City and South London in the same year (no advertising). In 1911 Selbie had become dissatisfied with Willing's handling of the Western Joint Stations held by the Metropolitan and the District Railways (High Street, Kensington, Gloucester Road and South Kensington). '. . . in the hands of a more enterprising Firm like Messrs. W. H. Smith & Son the rental of the Companies should be materially augmented justifying the fixing of an increased minimum.'[11] By 1912 Smith's business with the Metropolitan Railway and its associated lines was worth over £43,000 a year; by 1913 it was over £45,000.[12]

By the time war broke out, the trade at the London termini and on the London Underground combined to make up a very profitable share of W. H. Smith's turnover. In 1913 the Bakerloo–Piccadilly–Hampstead trade of the London Electric Railway was worth over £50,000 a year: the Metropolitan and District joint lines over £30,000. Waterloo Station alone £30,000: if all the London and SW stations as far as Southampton were included (Tooting, Merton, Wimbledon, Epsom, etc.) the contract brought receipts worth nearly £200,000 a year. London business on this scale seemed to offer profits relatively easily gathered, compared with, say, the sparse rewards offered by the bare, swampy, windswept plains of north Lincolnshire where the gross receipts for one bookstall and advertising on the GN and GE joint lines for Gainsborough, Misterton, Haxey and a few other village stations brought gross receipts of less than £150 in 1911.

Not that London business was all profit. When invited by the Great Eastern in June 1914 to contemplate the wealth offered to an enterprising advertiser on the London & Blackwall Railway, Hornby gave an unenthusiastic answer. He would consider it: but at nothing like the estimated value placed on it by the Great Eastern.

> ... under £1,000 per annum ... with the exception of Fenchurch Street station, the line runs through so poor a district that there is practically no local business to be got, and the purchasing power of the surrounding inhabitants is so small that the stations will not be at all attractive to the large advertisers.[13]

Quite simply, Hornby divided contracts into profitable and unprofitable. The former had to carry the latter. The nature of the local economy decided which was which.

Yet Hornby rarely turned any offer down flat. The 'Sunday trade' had never been a traditional activity for W. H. Smith's, but in the pre-war years he came to the conclusion that it was foolish to refuse as a law of the Medes and Persians to take it on. He told the South Eastern Railway that he was willing to do it for principal stations 'but for various, and, we think, good reasons . . . not at all anxious to do it to any large extent'.[14] The faint malodour Tennyson detected in 'the Sabbath journal mixt with lust' still hung about the Sunday trade.[15] But to all the questions concerning his business, great or small, welcome or otherwise, Hornby applied the same minutely detailed attention: to Selbie about the Metropolitan carriage advertising, he offered a correction to the figures in a draft contract. They should read:

> ... not less in number than, or inferior in quality to, ...
> 4,500 spaces in compartment carriages.
> 10,000 side, end and corner spaces in corridor cars.
> 468 curved roof of corridor cars.
> 6,000 top lights of windows ...[16]

He added that the present numbers were:

> 4,580
> 10,150
> 468 and
> 6,454.

It is not difficult to understand why Hornby was sometimes more respected than loved in railway circles.

In 1914, the London Tube business was still growing. By 1919/20, in spite of wartime difficulties Smith's had 75 main stalls on the Underground: this compared with 103 on the London and South Western, and a grand total of 661. The total receipts were approaching a quarter of a million pounds. Thirty years later they were to be nearly £650,000. But London had another asset which in the mid-nineteenth century had been very valuable: the 'Town Trade' as it was called. This signified the supply of the London newsagents from the Strand House. It had been worth £60,000 to £70,000 in the 1860s and 1870s. Then it had wasted away until, in 1905/6, it was worth only c. £24,000. Hornby later blamed this on John White, the head of the Counting House. White '. . . impervious to new ideas . . . thought that the Firm . . . had only to sit still and all the business would fall into its lap . . .'[17] Whether this was the whole story or not, the revival of the 'Town Trade' certainly dates from Hornby's summons to W. C. Smart to leave his triumphs at Cardiff in 1906 (see page 218) and hasten to London to raise the town trade from the dead. This he did:

TABLE IX.2   THE TOWN TRADE[18]

Years	£
1907/8	51,467
1911/12	146,550
1914/15	186,937
(1930/31	534,545)

Thus Hornby helped to bring about the 'rational reorganisation' of the distributory trade on news which Harmsworth had urged on him ever since they had settled their differences over the *Harmsworth Magazine* after 1898.

Changes in Fleet Street and the Strand

Meanwhile great changes were overtaking the British press as a whole. In London Harmsworth had created the *Daily Mail*, taken over *The Times*, then the *Observer*. Three groups of proprietors controlled two-thirds of the London morning papers, Northcliffe being first with nearly 40 per cent. The same group controlled over four-fifths of the London evening papers, the first being the *Morning Leader* Group. A different group controlled four-fifths of the London Sunday papers, Northcliffe being fourth with 11.8 per cent.[19]

In the provinces, too, ownership of the press was becoming more concentrated. Yet concentration did not mean a reduction in the numbers of papers created, printed and published. On the contrary 9 million London daily and Sunday papers were printed every week in 1910: by 1930 the figure would be 25 million. Part of the increase was due to a Canadian financier and company promoter who had arrived in Britain in 1910: Max Aitken, later Lord Beaverbrook, was to purchase the *Daily Express*, launch the crusade for Empire Free Trade and become a Minister in Churchill's wartime Cabinet as Minister of Aircraft Production. There was, therefore, no shortage of papers (in peacetime, at least) or, correspondingly, of turnover. The problem was to make profits. The day of the farthing may have been past. Money had steadily fallen in value. Now a popular paper sold for two or four farthings: but profit had still to be calculated, when possible, at fractions of a farthing. Harmsworth, as Hornby recognised, was quite right. The distribution of papers had to be organised better than ever it had been if it were to yield any profit at all. There was therefore no let up in the eternal battle between newspapers and distributors on how prices should be set, how profits should be shared. London, with its ever increasing population and increasing control of the newspapers, was a necessary key to the market problem. So the Strand house was rapidly becoming too small for its increasing business as a wholesale supplier of London papers to the metropolitan retail trade. All this merely emphasised the top-heavy role which London had assumed in English life, politics and culture.

This, in turn, meant a strategy which – however justifiably – demanded capital, fixed and working, that seemed for a time likely to bring about a change in the basic financial structure of the firm. The capital was still as much the property of the owner of the firm as it had been in 1792. The figures down to 1904/5 suggest a stability which in turn helps to explain why no proposals by Ford or anybody else to move towards a public limited liability company were followed up (see page 173). Table IX.3 gives the figures of capital employed down to 1919/20.

The heavy demands of the latter years of change and expansion are easy to see: new property, new leases, new shops, the expansion of the Strand properties and adjacent sites for printing, binding, stationery etc., together with more working capital to bridge the gaps between spending and getting in a growing business – all these explain the capital expansion. It came

largely from the pocket of Freddy Hambleden. And this in turn explains a
significant change in the wording of the partnership deeds in 1908.

Ten partnership agreements exist for the period 1890 to 1907. All were
basically similar in purpose. They provided the legal foundation for a firm
owned by a single proprietor (in these years William Henry II or Freddy).
He was to provide the capital on which he received up to 10 per cent and
agreed to undertake whatever business responsibilities he chose. But the
net profit remaining was then to be divided between the partners (including the proprietor) in an agreed proportion: for 1896, for example, Freddy
and C. Awdry each took 33⅓ per cent, A. D. Acland 25 per cent, C. H. St
John Hornby 8⅓ per cent, and Lethbridge 'at his own desire' no share of
profits.[20] The 1907 agreement provided Freddy with only 5 per cent on his

TABLE IX.3   CAPITAL EMPLOYED[21]

Years	Capital employed £
1877	250,000
1901/2	272,000
1904/5	382,000
1905/6	602,000
1913/14	1,087,000
1919/20	1,464,000

capital. Profits were divided into 48 shares. Freddy received 8, Charles
Awdry 12, Acland 12, Hornby 12, Charles Selwyn Awdry 4. The reduction of interest reflected the drop in rates generally but also, like the
following innovation, anxiety at the rising volume of capital needed. The
supplemental agreement of 1908 therefore added: if further capital was
required and W. F. D. Smith was 'unwilling to find such additional
Capital', *any other partner* might find it, the amount so advanced to be
repaid out of the assets of the business *in priority to any other capital* at the
termination of the partnership.[22] Other clauses made it plain that anyone
supplying capital in this way would possess no additional rights as a result,
except the right to be paid interest (at 5 per cent) and the ultimate repayment of that capital. He would have no *right* to withdraw it during his
partnership.

Thus was created a possible alternative source of temporary additional capital if needed, constituting a prior charge (also temporary) on profits. As a source of aid it was entirely dependent on the ability and willingness of the partners, other than the owner himself, to lend money to the business. It therefore went only a small way to opening up the family firm to 'outside' investment – from a strictly economic standpoint, correctly, for it never proved necessary to bring it into operation on any sizeable scale. The necessary capital generally continued to be found by the proprietor. His percentage return on capital was reduced as his invested capital increased (dropping from 10 to 5 per cent). On the other hand his *profits* went up. Thus his holding was always a mixture of rights to fixed and movable returns – of preference and equity, as it were. Not the demands of the business but the demands of the Chancellor of the Exchequer were ultimately to change the capital structure of W. H. Smith & Son.

In the immediately pre-war years, London's traffic problems threatened to add another capital cost to the mounting bill for the redeployment of retail investment. Traffic congestion in the Strand was growing rapidly worse as London itself grew. The traffic jam preceded the arrival of the internal combustion engine. By 1910 both motor buses and taxis were clanking and snorting along the Strand, but as yet they were only flotsam on the older tide of dog-carts, broughams, victorias, flies, hansom cabs, growlers – and W. H. Smith's own red commercial carts. These, and their 130 horses, emerged from 2 a.m. onwards from their nearby stables where they were the pride and joy of L. E. Smith (formerly a Sergeant of the Royal Horse Artillery), a linchpin as unobtrusive as he was indispensable to the entire working of the firm. 'Suddenly annihilate the stables and a thousand managers throughout the country might whistle in vain for their supplies of newspapers, periodicals, books, and everything else they handle at their branches.'[23]

The Editor of *Newsbasket* was quite right in his high estimate of Sergeant Smith's functions; but the Town Clerk of Westminster was troubled. With military precision Sergeant Smith daily backed the W. H. Smith carts on to the pavement outside 186 Strand, loading them from hand trolleys. Since July 1906, rumbles of dissatisfaction over the Sergeant's tactics had been audible: Sergeant Smith, on behalf of W. H. Smith & Son, was causing serious obstruction of the public way (recently – 1902 – widened at the cost of over half a million pounds of public money) by 'unreasonable and excessive use' of the Strand.[24] Smith's returned a mild answer. They would do their best to lessen the obstruction; but they could do nothing about those vehicles (belonging to others) over which they had no control. In May 1909 the Westminster City Council, unsatisfied, were still alleging 'a public nuisance'. Smith's retorted that the interests of workers, as well as walkers, were at stake. There was no solution. In May 1910 the issue was joined in the High Court: a glittering legal grand opera – four distinguished KCs in full voice, two of them (one on each side) future Lord Chancellors.

The cases for prosecution and defence were equally simple. Smith's were frustrating the object of the costly widening of the Strand by excessive use: no, they were not; the authorities simply disregarded 'the claims of commerce'. Smith's were in business. As ratepayers they were conducting it in the only way possible. They were neither inconveniencing the public nor interfering with traffic. Witnesses supported them in this. Some deposed that the real culprit was Mr Gladstone (whose statue stood at the critical point of congestion in mid-Strand): others (including the polter-geist consulting engineer for the Strand-widening scheme of 1902) that one-third of the total Strand traffic had come to consist of business carts in general without which there would be neither business nor income for Westminster. There was also the matter of the lamp posts down the middle of the Strand which added to congestion. In the end, the presiding judge (Mr Justice Neville) was sufficiently impressed by the complexity of the issues involved to dismiss the case against all the Smiths with costs against the Westminster Council.

For W. H. Smith & Son this was good: so far as it went. But of course they – especially Hornby, trained as a lawyer and the man mainly respon-sible, via Birchams, the solicitors, for briefing counsel – knew that they could no more face the increasing traffic problems of the Strand than could the Westminster City Council and the Attorney General. Plans began to be made for a move. A site was offered in 1912. By 1914 the plans were taking real shape. In 1915/16 they would materialise. The Strand house (in the Strand) would be removed northwards to Portugal Street (behind the Aldwych) to become Strand House, Portugal Street, in 1916; just in time to be requisitioned for another five years by government for 'Government purposes'. This also cost a great deal of money.

Then there was stationery, printing and binding. Stationery looked after itself. From the start it created nothing but profit and satisfaction. Binding gave great satisfaction but little profit. Printing gave enormous turnover, no profit and a host of troubles. Why?

Ever since the original printing works was bought from Robert Waters of Bateman Row, Shoreditch, in 1860 by William Henry II, Smith's printing abode had been as unfixed as their printing policies. From Shoreditch it had gone to 82 Fetter Lane, then to 10 Water Street. It then rooted itself mainly in Fetter Lane until it removed to Stamford Street, across the Thames, in January 1916. But fine printing was centred at Letchworth, in the Garden City at the Arden Press (see page 233) next door to Douglas Cockerell and the bindery. This had also moved from an earlier site in Goldsmith Street and was to move back to London and around from site to site between 1918 and 1955. Another dozen or so small printing works were acquired in the course of time, thrown in as it were, with the purchase of shops and reluctantly kept on in a vague, and mostly unfulfilled, hope of future utility and profit. Charles Awdry wrote rather desperately to a correspondent in April 1909 that he was 'misinformed' as to Smith's 'starting many Printing Offices over the country – we have bought various businesses with printing attached, but we do not willingly do so; in many cases we try to get rid of existing ones, & in no cases when we are free to do as we like do we start printing works.'[25] There was obviously doubt and predicament here.

The purpose of buying Robert Waters's business was to provide the means of doing such printing as might prove a necessary or convenient appendage to Smith's other activities as booksellers or newsagents. In 1867 this was still the pattern: out of a turnover worth £11,664, Smith's own work accounted for nearly £9,500: third party orders for only £2,000. By the time Herbert Morgan arrived on his mission of reform and progress, this had already changed. Out of a total turnover of c. £22,000 in 1904/5 third party orders accounted for over £12,000, Smith's own work for c. £9,500. Morgan's efforts in the following year achieved a startling increase of turnover, to £48,000. He was more successful in extracting new orders from outsiders (£35,000) than from insiders (£13,000). But he was monotonously unsuccessful in making a profit: his first year recorded a resounding loss of £10,000.

Morgan set forth his ideas eloquently if not very precisely in a memorandum (of 1906) entitled 'Suggestions'. The suggestions, he wrote, might be open to objections 'which are outside my knowledge'. They certainly sound more like the bright ideas of a newcomer than the products of experience. 'Printing' is at the centre of his thinking. The main purpose seems to be to expand business in general by high-pressure salesmanship in order to boost orders for printing. Shops, stalls and advertising canvassers should be recruited to obtain printing orders from merchants, manufacturers and retailers (what happens to their own duties meanwhile is not explained). Maps should be printed showing these salesmen where to find the railway lines on which W. H. Smith operates. Departments – all departments – should advertise more. All printing for the proposed new Stationery Department, all order forms, advertisements, etc., should be printed by Smith's themselves. 'I believe that in the long run it would prove of advantage'.[26]

In some of this there was a degree of prophetic sense. But apart from Morgan's habit of thinking more of turnover than of profit, there were two other major difficulties. The problems created by the 1905 crisis were short-run as well as (perhaps more than) long-run, and competitiveness was essential. Smith's printing was, on Morgan's own confession, not competitive and he was not the man of meticulous attention to technical detail to make it so. Secondly, the partners were faced with two inhibiting prospects: the rising demand for capital combined with a delicate set of business relationships which cramped their style in the printing world.

The world of distributory services which was their principal activity was a relatively small one. It worked on personal knowledge and personal relations. Newspaper proprietors, book publishers, printers inhabited a village in and around Fleet Street and the Strand. Like all villages it was full of ferocious personal feuds and scandalous gossip. Business was fiercely competitive: but normally, especially in publishing and printing, the market was far from perfect. The legal requirements of the day in regard, for example, to tendering for contracts were scrupulously observed. But the protocol of gentlemanly conduct occasionally resulted in abstentions from competing. Feelings were also easily aroused in what (between craft unions for example) would have been called demarcation disputes. To publish or not to publish had long been a question (see page 106).

A few years later the partners codified their policy on publishing and printing. They would not act as publishers 'in the ordinary sense for general literature'.[27] They would stick to pamphlets, magazines, year books, annuals, catalogues, directories. Either 55 Fetter Lane (the general press) or the Arden Press could print such items, and such articles as diaries could bear the firm's name. The next year they enlarged on this. For 'the convenience of printing customers' they were ready to publish on commission or on their own via the St Catherine Press, which they had acquired in 1908. (It published such specialised items as *The Complete Peerage* and parts of the *Victoria County Histories*, almost as a public service rather than a commercial venture.) They would not 'publish ourselves any books in which we have a direct financial interest'. They would not canvass for publishing. They would not publish on commission novels or books of general interest 'likely to be sold at our Shops or Bookstalls in competition with those of other publishing Firms . . . The general principle of our decision is that we do not wish to enter into competition with publishers.'[28]

How far this was due to pressure from the publishers or how far Smith's were simply sensitive to the dangers of provoking their hostility it is impossible to know. In practice they certainly honoured the principles they had laid down, explaining, for example, to the proprietor of the *Car* that they were reluctant to tender for publishing and printing his journal against the existing publishers (Eyre & Spottiswoode).[29]

The policy of non-intervention was undoubtedly justified by the facts of Smith's situation *vis-à-vis* the publishing world: but it clipped Morgan's wings by putting a distance between W. H. Smith as printers and the book publishers. It did not eliminate them as printers: but it made their task more difficult. Their printing turnover continued to grow. Table IX.4 shows the figures for Morgan's last year (1917/18). Since 1907/8, Smith's own inside

TABLE IX.4   PRINTING TURNOVER, 1917/18[30]

Total	W. H. Smith's own work	Periodicals (outside)	General (outside)
£118,173	£6,932	£55,709	£55,532

orders had grown but little. Morgan's dreams of a vast expansion from this source had vanished. 'General' outside orders had slightly diminished (£55,607 to £55,532). Only the printing of (outside) 'periodicals' had grown (£21,821 to £55,709). The net result in 1917/18 was a loss of nearly £6,000. The rise in costs and labour shortage combined to frustrate Morgan's object of making Smith's competitive in printing. Printing, over a decade, had lost some £70,000 and made only some £10,000 profit. 'Vertical integration' in Smith's simply did not work.

Books were, traditionally, more central to Smith's affairs. 'Next in importance to the Newsagency business at our Shops and Bookstalls comes Bookselling' (said 'An Inquiry Concerning a Special Publicity Department', circulated in 1910). That was true. More circulars, it said, were distributed in connection with books than with any other business – except patent medicines. The 'Inquiry' came from the Shops Department and George Tyler: the style is more reminiscent of Morgan than Tyler. But it was not Morgan's work. It came from the hand of another recruit from outside. George Marshall, like Morgan, was an ex-Civil Servant who had emigrated to the Tabard Inn Library, acquired by Smith's. Here, like

Morgan, he had come under the influence of the Library's owner, an American with strong American ideas on advertising – especially the conviction that advertising was useless if it was not focussed specifically and accurately on a particular target. Marshall's drift was plain. Books are publicised and sold, by W. H. Smith's as by other booksellers, through the indiscriminate distribution of publishers' advertising material to their shops and stalls. This is not enough. Customers must be won by an appeal to their personal preferences and tastes . . . 'nothing is more gratifying than to find that an interest is being taken in catering for one's special tastes . . .' W. H. Smith deals with a ' "Reading" community' . . . why should we not recapture the 'lost art' of personal taste and the days of Johnson, Thackeray, Goldsmith and Richardson . . . when writers wrote for themselves and their critics?[31] Readers will be found! By the oldest method . . . introduction! A Register is the real *desideratum*. A register of customers, with their sex, tastes, addresses duly inscribed will restore the personal touch. A register would promote other things – stationery, the sale of remaindered books from the libraries, the collection of bad debts (for in 'the class of business conducted at our Shops and Bookstalls . . . one-third of the customers' lived upon credit).[32]

The reception of the Inquiry by managers was mixed. Some were vaguely friendly. The most detailed comments were sceptical: a bright idea but costly . . . and likely to require shops and stalls to carry a lot of dead stock. It was perhaps the ambiguity of theories about bookselling that partly explains why Freddy, on 1 July 1910, wrote the following letter to a cousin in the book trade, Arnold Danvers Power:

My dear Arnold,
Circumstances make it advisable for me to get another man of business experience & capacity as Partner in the business; briefly, I want to know if you will be that man . . . Awdry does not wish to go on after the end of this Partnership, Alfred [Acland] has command of our Yeomanry and will be on the Devon County Assocn which means a good deal of work out of town and two Partners with a third doubtful one would be tied to the office in London more than they ought to be if personal knowledge of the branches is to be maintained. Hence the need of a man whose previous experience would enable him to get a pretty rapid grasp of at any rate some important parts of the business. The fact that you are a member of the family would make you welcome amongst the Staff as they always look upon it as a family business . . .
your affec. cousin, W. F. D. Smith.[33]

Arnold Power's mother and Freddy's mother were sisters. Arnold himself had been in publishing for thirteen years in 1910, first with the all-round publishing firm of Hutchinson, more recently as London manager of Sir Isaac Pitman. He had travelled widely in Europe, America and the Empire and founded the Publishers' Circle in 1908, designed to foster good relations between publishers and booksellers. Hornby approved – indeed he may well have prompted – the new move. He was glad to hear Power was coming into the business (he wrote to him): 'I hope you will like it as much as I have done for the last 17 years.' Would he come and dine? 'I hope you won't mind my asking you without being formally introduced, as I don't think we have ever met.'[34]

The new partner's appointment was timely. He filled a gap in the partners' expertise not easily bridged. (Both turnover and profits on books were to improve by 1914.) He had business experience. He was cultivated, widely-read and a connoisseur in fine books and bindings. He therefore fitted with the firm and with Hornby and his tastes. He also fitted with the family. Freddy's sons were still small. It would be another decade and a half before the eldest was ready to enter the business. Awdry was not to enjoy his retirement long: he died in 1912. Above all, perhaps, Arnold was the nephew of Sir Juland Danvers, a faithful executor of William Henry II who maintained the family tradition of the Danvers as high public servants who knew everybody.

As the First World War came nearer, W. H. Smith & Son was still a family business, based still on an alliance of blood and marriage, a cousinhood strengthened by friendship, chance and prudence, timely admixed with meritocracy. Hornby and Awdry had also built up a strong team of professional managers. Between them the partners and managers had partitioned the business up into a series of specialised departments – news, shops, books, libraries, advertising, publicity. The provincial wholesale houses looked pretty much after themselves, not as a matter of doctrine so much as of practical common sense, and perhaps up to a point also in deference to the independent origins which many of them could claim. In 1914 W. H. Smith was broadly based: it needed to be.

X

War Without Precedent, 1914

As THE TWENTIETH century progressed, there was to be much argument (and more assertion) that Britain was in economic decline. The talk had begun at the end of the nineteenth century. It was both true and false. Some old industries – coal, iron, steel and textiles – were declining relatively to their counterparts in more recently industrialised countries, the USA and Germany especially. What is more difficult to establish is how far old, sick, tired industries were being replaced by new industries – engineering, chemicals, pharmaceuticals, ready made clothes . . . and newspapers, magazines and books too. The cloth cap was ceasing to be the sole symbol of a working class which included increasing numbers of 'white collar' workers.

All these economic and social changes resulting from international competition and technological change brought higher incomes to most: but they resulted in new tensions, at home and abroad. What was serious (and was to remain serious into our own day) was that few people yet realised, even after at least two centuries when Britain had become increasingly dependent on sea-borne trade with the rest of the world, how frighteningly vulnerable she would be if war should come. Nor were many people in the last years before 1914 fully conscious of the dangerous point to which domestic antagonisms were being pushed: semi-education, 'literacy', the ability to read without the ability to understand, had if anything sharpened the hostility of party against party, class against class, Irish against English, women against men. Confidence in Parliamentary democracy was running low. In industry there was an upsurge of those violent minorities (who are always present) ready to replace reasonable, peaceable negotiation of wages and working conditions by bitter strikes, lock-outs and demagogy in general.

The British people therefore lurched or slid into four years of appalling and unprecedented death and destruction in a mood of ignorant optimism. 'History taught' (that idiotic cant phrase responsible for so much political folly) that wars would be short and British victory assured. Mr Churchill's phrase 'Business as usual', intended as an injunction not to panic, was interpreted as encouragement to total complacency: a different matter.[1] On both sides, it was confidently believed in August 1914 that the soldiers would be home in time to see the autumn tints. It was assumed that taxes would pay for this war as they had (largely) paid for Napoleon's. The small professional army would be supplemented by volunteers. Munitions in war, like bicycles or fish knives in peace, would be produced by a free economy with as few controls as possible.

Only after nearly two years were such illusions dispelled. Conscription came only in March 1916, after a last desperate attempt to make voluntary recruitment suffice, under the direction of Lord Derby. Labour relations meanwhile were half sorted out by an improvised agreement between the government and 35 trade unions (excluding the miners) aimed against strikes, restrictive practices, etc.[2] This brought the unions' members greater security and confidence: but their leaders' word was often honoured in the breach by the membership, sensitive to excessive prices and profits and urged on by domestic militants who were ferociously pacifist only in international disputes.

Britain survived, but at fearful cost: nearly 10 per cent of the men of age to be fathers of families (as well as many younger and some older) were killed: in all three quarters of a million. Another 1,700,000 were wounded. This was the overriding horror brought by the military deadlock. But economic and social changes also vital to human life occurred. Britain's international trade was hopelessly dislocated, her apparatus of production distorted, relations of capital and labour soured by wartime profiteering on the capitalist side and by greed for affluence and power on the part of labour. Trade union membership doubled during the war (c. 4 million to c. 8 million).[3] As the war ended there was as much profiteering among workers as there had been among employers.

It is not easy to compare the state of industrial relations after 1918 with their state before 1914. For the most part it is probably true that the war only hastened social and economic changes already in motion. Trade union growth both strengthened the forces working towards socialism and the general moderation with which most of the labour leadership worked for its objectives.

Yet the closing stages of the war were unedifying. In spite of more

20 W.H. Smith's design–consciousness: the egg–shaped logo designed by
R.P. Gossop, and the Newsboy with Basket sign by Septimus Scott

21 Above: women at work in the Letchworth bindery, 1910

22 Below: King's Cross Station bookstall, modernised, 1910

23 Above: Counting House outing, 1911

24 Below: newsboys, with bicycles, at the West Drayton shop, 1913

25 Above, left: Alfred Dyke Acland, 1858–1937, in 1915   26 Above, right:
Charles Selwyn Awdry, 1877–1918, in 1915

27 Below: the Partners' Room at Arundel Street in 1920. Left to right:
C.H. St J. Hornby, W.H.D. Acland, the Second Viscount Hambleden and
A.D. Power

attempts at government control, or because of their weakness, a general scramble for scarce goods brought its usual benefits to the sharp-witted; the less fortunate went to the wall. Prices went on rising as the more strategically placed part of the labour force used their elbow power to screw higher wages out of employers. By 1920 the wholesale price index stood at just over three times its level when the war began.

Then, between February and July, markets in raw materials collapsed. They did not begin to recover until 1922. In 1921 two and a half million men and women were out of work. Just before the bubble burst, the unemployed figure was the lowest recorded in any boom year of the recent past. By 1922 it had risen to the highest level since records were kept. For the greater part of the next two decades it was to meander somewhere round an average between the two. 'It appeared', writes Professor Ashworth, 'that the rate of unemployment in boom years in the interwar period was such as in the late nineteenth and early twentieth centuries had been known only in the blackest years of depression.'[4] Such was the background to the W. H. Smith business in wartime and afterwards. How was its inside working affected?

In July 1914, Freddy (newly arrived at his delayed inheritance of the title as Second Viscount Hambleden – the first Viscountess, his mother, having died in 1913) entertained 400 guests, members of the staff and their families at his home at Greenlands, Henley-on-Thames. There were boaters and blazers, punts and parasols, cucumber sandwiches and strawberries, the hoarse bellowings of the coxes urging on their crews, the crowded banks cheering yet another victory for the Grand . . . Another two weeks and it seemed like a dream as the lights went out. For in Smith's, 1914 was not 'business as usual', and for this there was one basic reason. Whether for railway stalls or town shops, the railways were still the arteries of the newsagency business, W. H. Smith's lifeblood: and the railways were the first and largest business undertakings over which the State assumed wartime control.

This early stroke of emergency legislation took immediate effect. Hornby himself evidently assumed the worst the moment war was declared. He saw catastrophe looming for at least the railway part of the business. Stalls and railway advertising, he assumed, would be among the immediate sufferers. Fellow-sufferers had already sought his help: a letter from the humble but indispensable fraternity of billposters written to him on 17 August lamented that since the declaration of war 'our business has practically vanished, having regard to which we beg respectfully to ask your careful and sympathetic consideration of our position'.[5] Their rents would have to be suspended or reduced to nominal amounts or they were lost.

When Hornby approached Selbie, general manager of the Metropolitan Underground, *inter alios*, the following day, representing the gravity of the situation of the railway advertising business at large, Selbie replied that since all the railways were now taken over for the duration by government he could do nothing without government approval. What Selbie did, off his own bat, was to ask the newly constituted 'Railway Executive Committee' for their approval to agree reductions of rent for Smith's along reasonable lines (in fact payment of an agreed minimum rent for the time being). In the event the Executive decided that the whole problem of such contracts should be remitted back to the rail companies to be dealt with at their discretion.

Things turned out differently from expectations. Bookstalls (and 'B' shops too) were kept buoyant until 1916 by demand that often outran resources. Vast crowds waited around railway stations for the (often late) arrival of the London papers with news of the war. At Swanage the bookstall staff were compelled to lock themselves in an empty carriage for protection and sell papers through the window. Newsboys risked physical injury from crowds. When the supply of papers gave out, headlines telephoned from the Strand were posted up on notice boards. The insatiable thirst for news and the demand for books for the Front (and the rear) kept the dwindling staff frantically busy.

As the production of ordinary fiction fell away it was replaced by war books, embryonic science fiction such as H. G. Wells's *War in the Air* (published in 1908 and now enjoying a sudden topical revival), war magazines and anti-German propaganda. *The Times* published the French government's *Yellow Book*. Of the 600,000 copies printed Smith's sold nearly one third, an 'unprecedented figure' as *The Times* wrote.[6] Nearly as many copies of *King Albert's Book* were sold for the benefit of the Belgian Relief Fund on the initiative of the *Daily Telegraph*.[7] And so on. The threatened shortage of newsprint due to the closure of the Baltic and the elimination of Scandinavian supplies never took place. Scandinavian supplies were replaced by exports from Canada. Only the price of papers soared.

During the first two years of war the fortunes of W. H. Smith's rail business see-sawed. The statistical evidence for individual lines gives the impression that after the early uncertainty of 1914–15, the sales of stalls and shops gathered pace. The Great Northern stalls, for example, doubled their yield in rentals between 1913 and 1919. Advertising receipts, on the other hand, fell in the same period (from £9,841 to £7,131). The total sum paid by Smith's for both concessions rose from £15,832 to £19,377 – but these were in money terms.[8] Their true value was considerably reduced by the inflation which grew more strongly as the war dragged wearily on.

The Metropolitan Underground business told the same story. Hornby – never given to optimism in dealing with railway officials – admitted to Selbie in November 1916 that 1915 had been a good year for bookstalls, but added that in 1916 business was falling off 'partly by the absence on active service of thousands of our regular customers, and partly by the ever increasing difficulty, or rather impossibility of getting a competent staff to manage the Bookstalls in place of the men called up for active service'.[9] Hornby also remarked on the disturbing way rising costs were beginning to eat into trading margins: these were caused by the general rise in wages – and W. H. Smith, unlike some businesses, were unable to compensate by raising prices. The apparent increase in profits during the war was an illusion created by inflation. Demand certainly kept up better than had been anticipated. Even supplies of newspapers were reasonable in spite of sporadic problems. The most difficult problem was the supply of labour.

The staffing problem was central to the running of the business. It had worsened as the inexorable growth of military demands forced the government to move away from voluntary service to conscription. Even in the later transitional stages of the voluntary system under Lord Derby's direction, Hornby had to send him a sharp reminder that Smith's were doing their best to combine patriotism with the task, also set them by government, of maintaining a news service essential to the national morale.[10] Lord Derby was in error in saying Smith's had 'refused permission' to their managers to enlist. They *had* advised them to remain at their posts. His Lordship's statement that 'any women of ordinary intelligence could learn the work in a few months' was so ridiculous, Hornby said, that it hardly needed refutation ... and there followed much more in the manner to which Hornby had become trained by long dealings with ignorant newspaper proprietors and supercilious railway directors.[11]

This was in November 1915, after one year of war. Already some 1,200 men had left Smith's voluntarily to join up. They had been replaced by women but while women could, given time (which was as short as everything else), be trained to do much of a man's job on a stall or in a shop, the heavier physical work was beyond them. In any case, the process of replacement was only just beginning. Before the war Smith's had employed c. 700 women and c. 9,500 men. The number of men employed fell steadily through the war. It recovered to a figure of 8,268 only by 1921: by that date c. 3,500 women were employed. It was not to be exceeded again before 1940: in spite of fluctuations in numbers, one permanent legacy of the war was the employment of female staff.

Bookstall fortunes might fluctuate. The fortunes of railway advertising pointed consistently downwards. Most of the railway companies used the discretion given them by government in 1914 to ease the contractual terms in favour of W. H. Smith, at least temporarily. Hornby had argued convincingly that Smith's were under heavy pressure from their customers to release them from their obligations. What could Smith's do? Moreover, the future had to be considered. To the Lancashire & Yorkshire, who showed themselves more sluggish in coming into line than the others, he argued:

> In the future interests of the Railway Companies it is essential to maintain the popularity of railway advertising as compared with other forms ... Unless advertisers are treated generously ... it will be difficult ever to persuade them to agree to long contracts in future ... Advertisers who make use of the Press can cease ... at almost any time and we and yourselves ... do not wish the Press to be an even stronger competitor than it is at present ...[12]

Hornby was not exaggerating: there was a sharp drop in advertising receipts in the months following the outbreak of war. After a measure of recovery in 1916, the advertising business suffered another blow as economic controls by government began to bite early in 1917. A new Paper Restriction Order hit advertising especially hard. (Newspaper sales were less seriously affected.) 'Not only is the use of paper largely prohibited for advertising purposes', Hornby explained to Selbie, 'but enamelled iron plates [still much used for advertisements on railway station walls and hoardings] are almost impossible to obtain, and what is perhaps most important of all, advertisers are very loth to enter into new contracts ...'[13] All of which (as he said) was no doubt satisfactory to government and just what they wanted.

The First World War therefore saw an apparently irreversible decline in the already shaky fortunes of the railway advertising business. In this trend the shortages and problems of war only exacerbated the difficulties that had been setting in for several decades as the rail companies drew closer together for comfort and covered jointly a larger proportion of national advertising territory. Smith's original function as the co-ordinator of local or regional territories was growing correspondingly smaller. Shortages of paper, iron and labour only made their major existing problem more serious. It affords specific support from a particular branch of industry for the thesis that the war tended to push the economy not in new directions but in directions already set in peacetime.[14]

The same might be argued of the development of the printing side of Smith's. In 1915 a new printing works was completed in Stamford Street, on the south side of the Thames. To this new works was moved the old Fetter Lane press and the Arden Press from Letchworth. (The Letchworth bindery stayed a little longer, then its premises also were requisitioned by the government and it went back to Milford Lane, running down to the Thames from the Strand.) The Stamford Street establishment was built on a large scale. It had capacity for printing fifty weekly and monthly periodicals. It also printed for the St Catherine Press (see page 267).

This large affair, still under H. E. Morgan as 'Controller', continued to enlarge its turnover and regularly to return losses on its operations – this in spite of considerable engagements for the printing and distribution of enrolment cards for various national wartime campaigns and government committees, drives for economy in the use of coal, the salvage of waste rubber and other good causes.

Matters went from bad to worse in July 1918 when Hornby and Power became highly critical of Morgan's handling of the purchase of an advertising business (Powell Rees.) He had paid much more for it than it was worth and had kept the facts to himself afterwards. All this finally decided them to grasp the nettle. They would remove the printing business from Morgan's control. What was to happen to Morgan? He was already involved in several outside tasks for government. But perhaps there was a case for face-saving? There was, for example, the Railway & Tramway Advertising Department 'which requires a certain amount of new life infused into it'. Would this not (they enquired of Morgan) be a good time to make changes 'because your public work gives a good pretext for your giving up certain of your former duties without causing an undue amount of comment'.[15]

To this rather bald question, Morgan seems to have replied that he would prefer to be 'general adviser' on printing and advertising and continue with his outside appointments (which had already brought him a Lloyd George KBE). They grasped at the offer. 'We propose to say [they told Morgan unblushingly] that you have requested us in view of your exacting work for the Government and the fact that you are now obliged to be away from London, to relieve you of the responsibility which you now have for the

First with the News

Management of the three Departments, and that in future you will serve us in an advisory capacity in connection with them.'[16]

So, at last, Morgan went: a day or two later he was replaced in the Printing Department by a totally contrasting personality, the silent W. T. Welfare. Welfare was a printer by trade, 'a man of few words, preferring . . . action [to] speech . . .'[17] He took control of printing on 22 July 1918. It would not be fair to him to omit that in the next three years, the Printing Department made profits of more than £40,000. Even allowing for inflation, this made an agreeable change.

Morgan's departure surprised no one. What surprised some was that he had lasted so long. His appointment had been a mistake for which Hornby must bear some responsibility; not because he was a man of no ability, but because he possessed the wrong kinds of ability. His semi-philosophy, if it could be so described, was an eloquent but confused mixture of Herbert Spencerism, T. W. Taylor-ish theories of scientific management, current Whitehall neo-mercantilist beliefs in the government role in a mixed economy, all conveyed with an intensity reminiscent of Mrs Mary Baker Eddy. Not all his ideas were wind. His enthusiasm and powers of persuasion had their uses in the Whitehall world of wartime quangoes and elsewhere. But W. H. Smith's was not such a place. It was a compact and functional institution with no room for rhetoric. It demanded, as of old, precision and punctuality. Morgan did better on a wider stage with a more distant audience. He was not long in finding a more congenial milieu.

The partners themselves were the first to feel the impact of war in August 1914. Four partners held commissions in the Yeomanry and left at once on military service. Alfred Acland, William Henry II's son-in-law, commanded the 1st (Royal) Devon Yeomanry as Colonel. William Acland (always known as 'Robin' from his red hair) a nephew of Alfred, appointed a junior partner in May 1914, was a Lieutenant in the same regiment. (He was later transferred to the Royal Flying Corps, severely wounded and brought home for ground duties but not before he had won the Military Cross, the AFC, the Russian Order of St George and a mention in despatches.)

Charles Selwyn Awdry, son of 'old' Charles, was already a veteran of the Boer War. He was commissioned Major in the Wiltshire Imperial Yeomanry and went with them to France where he was later awarded the DSO. He died in action. The owner himself, Freddy, now Lord Hambleden, took over Alfred Acland's command with the Devon Yeomanry when Alfred was posted to France. Later he was landed with his regiment at Suvla Bay as part of the Gallipoli campaign. Suvla Bay was a disaster, militarily, climatically and in every other way. In December 1915, Freddy was invalided home.

Thus the partners went to war, along with many hundreds of their staff: in the end the total was to reach more than 4,000. The entire responsibility for carrying on the business fell back – where for many years much of it had always rested – on Hornby. He took over again with his usual imperturbable sense of command. But it was fortunate that (once again) he and Freddy had foreseen the need for reinforcement at the top some three years earlier. As a result Hornby had the very considerable help of Arnold Power, a cousin of Freddy on his mother's side, primarily, but not only, a book man. Power stood ready to tackle any problem that came along. Arnold Danvers Power was not an entrepreneurial genius but he was experienced in the publishing world, cultivated, shrewd, and reliable.

Two partners there were, then, still vigorous, to take the strain. Yet even Hornby would have been helpless without the support of a continuing body of highly trained managers, at the Strand and in shops and stalls throughout the provinces. Here he was helped by the W. H. Smith tradition of long service. Charles Awdry had once remarked to a grumbler that a quarter of a century's service was commonplace in Smith's: half a century might be worthy of remark. As the demands of conscription grew and the age for service fell, Smith's still had many seasoned managers over military age who were ready to hold on a year or two longer. They also embodied traditions of unquestioning service to the job which were, for the first time, to be called in question by some of the post-war generation before many years were out.

This was only a fraction of the whole story. The atmosphere and ethos of business at large were to change radically with the peace. Lloyd George might forget his own words: after all they were too numerous to be remembered. The returning soldiers did not. They might not be entirely clear what 'a land fit for heroes' meant: they had an idea that it meant more money and more say in the way things were run. And that was to alter the entire outlook and system of managing private business after 1918.

XI

Labour Relations

The Strand and the Stations

'LABOUR RELATIONS ARE the centre of everything.' Smith's 'labour adviser' put his finger on the problem which seemed to many increasingly to dominate the W. H. Smith business between the wars. Others might think that 'labour relations' of different kinds had always been at the centre of business.[1] Certainly the partners of the 1920s and 1930s devoted much anxious time and thought to problems of staff management, labour demands, salary and wage structure. Relations with the trade unions, the question of the 'closed shop', strikes and the threat of strikes took up a frustrating proportion of their time. More agreeably, they pondered matters of social welfare, pension arrangements, social and athletic clubs, and recreational activities. None of these was in reality new in the post-1918 world. Some were almost as old as the business itself: but the forms taken by the problems were different. As the business had grown, the handful of employees had swelled to thousands. After the First World War, they demanded all the privileges of formal representation to argue their demands concerning pay and conditions of service. In some degree this applied to all levels and managers, under-managers, foremen, skilled workers and unskilled, white collar and cloth cap.

A brief glance at earlier days points the contrast with the old informality of the Victorian relationship when one or more partners would deal, by letter or in person, with the individual superintendent, railway stall clerk or Strand Office foreman. This was not merely because the small scale of the business made direct personal relations between employers and employees possible: it was also because the employer believed that the business and its success rested positively on foundations of personal conduct which demanded his unremitting vigilance. But he too would have had no difficulty in agreeing that 'labour relations' were centrally important.

Before the coming of the railway stall, the proprietor in person – Messrs Smith, William Henry I or William Henry II – was directly in charge of a force of packers, drivers, clerks and office boys solely employed at the Strand. Some slept on the premises. Hours were long and hard; William Henry I was an exacting but just master. Somehow the business was carried along on a stream not only of farthings but of cockney resilience and humour. Remedies and penalties were alike blunt and immediate: a handshake, a pint of beer, the sack. But since cockneys were cockneys, and traditions of the common cause still strong in London working-class life, a strike was always possible: when printers began to be employed, more than likely. Lethbridge reported a strike of carpenters when writing to William Henry overseas in 1872: he wrote as if it were neither wholly unique nor particularly worrying.[2]

The arrival of railways and station bookstalls brought more staff problems for a management which itself was proliferating into a sizeable, organised bureaucracy headed by full-time partners such as Lethbridge and Awdry after William Henry II's departure into politics in the late 1860s. The diaries and letters of the partners thereafter devote much time to appointments of stall managers and lesser staff, their suitability for promotion to senior and more responsible posts (e.g. as district superintendents or later as managers of large provincial wholesale houses) or appropriate punishment for dishonesty, idleness, neglect of essential duties, drunkenness or outright theft. For the railway stall clerk lived a hard life, exposed to the wind and cold on stalls which were for the most part unheated. (This occasioned recurrent debate which always seemed to end, strange as it may seem, in a consensus against heating.) Work began early on Monday mornings; it went on through Christmas Day and Good Friday, starting at 6 a.m. A former stall clerk who wrote his memoirs recalled how an invalid lady who subscribed to his library was moved to knit mittens for him 'as . . . the stone platforms must be very cold'. She also brought with her in her bath chair a large hot-water bottle which 'lay quite unused'.

Oftentimes, however, I have sat at the table outside the stall (the stalls then were mostly shelves and cupboards and without offices) from 2.30, when the midday trains [from London] had gone, until 4.15, when another lot of trains began to arrive, feeling numbed from my feet, upon the stone platform, to my shoulders, bent over library subscribers' daily lists and orders.[3]

In spite of such hardships (or because of them), the health of the staff who survived was remarkably good. Occasionally, a weaker vessel would take comfort in excessive drinking and if heedless of cautions would have to go. Others occasionally suffered from nervous troubles, more the result of worrying about their considerable responsibilities than of the physical hardships they endured. Book-keeping was strict but inevitably there were plenty of loopholes to tempt the needy or hard-pressed clerk to whom the Strand seemed a comfortably long way away. These were the cause of such troubles as did crop up: but their relative infrequency suggests that Smith's chose their staff carefully and well. On 1 August 1862 there was an alarm at the Strand when William Henry II was compelled to instruct Mr Elliman, head of the Newspaper Despatch Department and therefore a sort of labour head, that whenever anyone in the House was 'detected in a theft of which the evidence is clear to your mind, it is to be your duty to give the Offender into Custody immediately; and *afterwards* to report the facts to me'.[4] This seems to have been an echo of a wholesale discharge two years earlier of some dozen members of staff who had 'each and all confessed to several acts of dishonesty'.[5]

It was possibly the same case which gave rise to tearful appeals by his family and friends on behalf of one Edward Collins, a W. H. Smith clerk at Lewisham Station, who had been taken into custody for embezzlement. William Henry was begged by 'highly respectable' friends of Collins not to prosecute 'as it would be the death of the Prisoner's aged Mother'. Ford, William Henry's lawyer and friend, who was present in court, 'stated the principle upon which you acted in such matters namely for the benefit of the numerous young men who were in your employment . . . but that you were always most willing to take a lenient view of a defaulter's conduct if the facts would possibly admit of your doing so'.[6] A day or two later Ford was instructed not to pursue the matter.

The pattern of Collins's case was from time to time repeated. The partners were Victorians but they were men of the world, and human. They took no pleasure in punishing for the sake of doing so, especially when it meant losing a valuable servant to the firm. They were very severe, however, if it were shown that the culprit had also influenced or involved others, especially juniors, in his peculation or theft. No second chances were given in such cases: and, generally, once a decision to dismiss had been taken it was rigorously kept. A trickle of correspondence over helping dismissed staff to emigrate runs through the records. But such cases were on the whole not numerous: one or two a year by the 1880s. In the 1890s the number rose to as many as four a year in two or three years: perhaps bad times and poor business? We cannot be sure. The general tenor of the diaries makes it clear that the partners were well aware that their bookstall clerks bore a heavy burden: too draconian policies of control and penalty might well do more harm than good.

Salaries and wages at the Strand headquarters, on the stalls and later in the shops varied widely at the partners' discretion. A straight wage with no commission on a small or medium stall might run at from 30s. to 40s. a week. A canvasser for railway advertising in Yorkshire might likewise be offered a basic wage of 30s. but would get in addition 10 per cent on all cash received from orders he could put on the books and '5% on all cash received on orders now current . . .'.[7] Until his business was properly launched he was to have an advance of £5 a week, which indicates what he might expect. He could live where he liked but W. H. Smith had the right to veto any place which seemed to them likely to damage his chances of doing his work efficiently.

In 1902 Awdry was looking for a clerk to fill a vacancy at Cambridge Station. He wrote to the superintendent at Shrewsbury:

He must be a strong man capable of dealing with the rough-and-tumble of Trade business and the sporting crowds which assemble for Newmarket etc: but he must also be a man of exceptional tact and some culture, or he will not properly represent us with the University population of that Town who no doubt (as is not unusually the case) are a little exacting both as to hours of delivery and terms, though very nice and real gentlemen.

Would, for example, Billinger, of Swansea Station, be capable of filling this exacting bill? If he would, it would be a relief to the superintendent, would it not, for his district 'to be no longer weighted with his abnormal salary'?[8] Billinger's 'standing' wage of 51s. a week (to which commission was added) was 'abnormal' because the wholesale trade at Swansea had recently been removed from the bookstall to a new house (see page 220). He was in the end offered the Cambridge vacancy at about £270 a year.[9]

By this time, the partners had put in much good work into improving the standards of recruitment of staff, systematising promotion chances, reorganising the grading of staff and grouping the stations into districts, each under the direction of a superintendent who *inter alia* kept an eye on the stall clerks, their staff and work on behalf of the partners. There was also the vexed question of the 'station boys' whose unruliness in the streets and excessive zeal in bellowing the names of the papers which it was their duty to sell brought complaints from such distinguished public figures as the Town Clerk of Aberystwyth.[10] Their level of pay and future careers also elicited anxious enquiries from the public spirited. Were they not very underpaid, enquired a well-wisher from Colwyn Bay? What (enquired the Rev. Spencer Gibb of Stockport) was to happen to them in later life? To which Awdry could only reply that since there were about 4,000 boys in Smith's and only 800 clerks in all 'it will be obvious that the prospects of advancement are not very great'. On the other hand, he added as an after-thought, all the bookstall clerks were created 'by promotion from those who have been in our service as boys. There is always a prospect for the best of uninterrupted employment.'[11]

This theory and practice of internal promotion was the central motor of labour relations in W. H. Smith. It met the needs of a business not too large to be comprehended personally by a small body of partners and senior managers. As long as that remained true – in some respects longer – it did admirable service, producing not only employees with extraordinary length of service but families which, like the owners themselves, could claim generation after generation of service. If the sociological implications of genealogy ever become a branch of social research, W. H. Smith's staff would make an excellent field for enquiry.

Curiously, William Henry II's departure into politics, far from diminishing these trends, actually increased them. For him, politics had always been closely bound up with his Christian faith, and with his sense of moral, social and philanthropic duty. Freed from the immediate chores of business he was able to devote more time and study to social problems, especially the problems of poverty, at a public and political level, local and national. In the 1880s he was so powerfully swayed by these preoccupations that at one time he seriously contemplated disposing of his business altogether. On 18 June 1885 he wrote to Cawkwell, deputy chairman of the LNWR (an ironical choice, in the light of later relations between Smith's and that company) about some ideas which had been discussed between Lethbridge and Cawkwell at his suggestion:

My great object in life now is to provide for the staff who have served the house faithfully and with great ability in the past, and it has occurred to me that it is just within the bounds of possibility that the Railway Company might form a Committee or a Syndicate to take over the whole concern, men and material together, and run it for their own interests . . . Do you think it is at all feasible to work out such an idea?[12]

In the end, nothing came of this astonishing scheme but perhaps William Henry put other ideas of social improvement into the partners' heads. One concerned the (then) 3,000 or more 'station boys' employed by Smith's and their chances of advancement. Lethbridge was briefed to draw up a memorandum proposing that all the boys should wear a special tunic. In their third year of service (normally, by regulation, their last) 'selected boys of good conduct and character . . . should . . . have a stripe on the arm . . .' This would be worth an extra 1s. a week in excess of their ordinary wage. Out of 'nearly 3500' boys (the memorandum went on) only '35 or 36 are promoted annually into the permanent Bookstall service. It is thought that the tunics might act somewhat as an incentive and cause a greater proportion of the boys to fit themselves for promotion.' At 'about, 9/–' a time, the total cost would be 'rather over £3000 a year'.[13]

Lethbridge became warmly attached to the idea of uniforms. He even thought of extending them to the van drivers. Awdry remained unenthusiastic. Awdry was by nature economical and cautious: the whole idea savoured of a 'stunt' and he could see no future in it save added expense. He seems to have worn down the enthusiasts for tunics. Yet in other respects Awdry was liberal. When an MP, Col. Welby, complained of the political behaviour of a member of Smith's bookstall staff at a political meeting in 1905 – a stormy year – Awdry replied stoutly: 'You will understand that however much we deprecate disturbances in connection with political or any other Meetings, we do not undertake to interfere with the views of our staff.'[14]

In most respects, the partners were abreast of the best contemporary practices *vis-à-vis* staff, and in some respects ahead. In the 1860s, for example, employees with five years service claimed 'a clear week's holiday once a year'.[15] Even older was the 'Provident Fund' for the benefit of Smith's clerks, of which William Henry II became Honorary Treasurer in 1857.[16] Later, in 1894 and 1895 the Superannuation and Pension Funds were set up. The Pension Fund was for the benefit of 'non-clerkly' staff—printers, joiners, frame-makers, drivers, porters, packers, etc., whose jobs had proliferated in number and variety by the turn of the century. Membership was made compulsory, partly to ensure fair treatment for all, partly to reduce the need for *ad hoc* eleemosynary gifts in hard cases. When the Shop Clubs Act of 1902 inadvertently risked making the partners guilty of a legal offence in insisting on compulsory membership of the Pension Fund,

Awdry sent a copy of the ambiguous Act to the lawyers. Although it was not aimed at *bona fide* social schemes, it seemed that it might threaten them:

> I hope you may be able to tell me that the legal mind sees it otherwise; for we attach great importance to the compulsory clause, without which we fear that many would not make the little effort necessary to secure some provision for their age or infirmity.[17]

That was in 1903 – five years ahead of Lloyd George's State pensions. Four years later it was Hornby's turn to explain to a retiring clerk who appealed for extra help in his distress that the firm could not both contribute to the Superannuation Fund and make substantial personal grants to individuals as well. But his letter ended by enclosing a cheque for £50.[18]

So much for a glimpse of social relations before 1914. On the employer's side they were marked by a kind of consistency that mingled humanitarian attitudes with the longer, larger interest of the business. There was no comparable consistency on the employees' side except perhaps the need to earn as good a living as they could according to their abilities. The Strand headquarters had its own corporate way of life, its cockney *esprit de corps* and the odd spasmodic demonstration of a collective spirit that suggested the continuance of ancient communal arrangements beneath a veneer of Victorian individualism. None of this overflowed or could overflow to the scores of widely separated stalls and later shops, each employing one or two, at most a handful of staff and spread over the face of England. Their ambitions were a mixture of ingrained ideas of service with a natural desire for more pay and promotion. Remuneration was arranged to stimulate these desires and increase efficiency and punctuality by bonuses and commissions. Except in London there was little to encourage association for common ends which barely existed. That was something delayed until the twentieth century: largely until after 1918, for in one way or another the conditions of the First World War encouraged the principle of association on both sides of industry. Until then the natural improvisations which were the predecessors of a conscious social policy did not work badly, as the staff response to the crisis of 1905 had shown.

Workers United and Divided

The necessary proximity of Smith's London headquarters to Fleet Street and the newspaper publishing area was the essential geographical prerequisite for trade union colonisation of the business after the First World War. In the formation of unions and the shaping of attitudes the size and location of the W. H. Smith staff was critical. Table XI.1 shows the total

TABLE XI.1   TOTAL NUMBER OF EMPLOYEES[19]

1911	1921	1932	1941
10,349	11,772	13,452	12,999

numbers employed. Of these, approximately four-fifths to five-sixths were engaged in the bookstalls, shops and wholesale houses spread over the whole country. The London staff engaged in news distribution, stationery, books, binding, printing (until the 1930s), etc., formed between a fifth and a sixth. In the struggle for union representation, it was the latter who were the main objective of the Paper Workers' Union. They were an integral part of the close but often turbulent news and printing world centred in and around Fleet Street. The bookstalls and shops were geographically scattered and diverse in character. What emerged in the end was to be a dual structure: the PPW, a very large union, secured up to perhaps 900–1,000 members in W. H. Smith's: not a very large number but all engaged in activities crucial to the firm. The union representing the shop and stall staff, the RBA (Retail Book, Stationery, and Allied Trades Employees Association), was a small union, but of its 3,000-odd members, most were W. H. Smith staff. Relations with both unions were of great importance. But the proximity of Fleet Street, the traditional militancy of the London craft unions and the complexity and immediacy of the distributory problem in the London news centre made relations with the PPW the more difficult.

The beginnings of the relationship went back earlier, to 1914, perhaps even to 1907.[20] At the end of 1914 Smith's were among the members of the Federation of Wholesale Newsagents to sign an agreement with the National Union of Paper Workers. It covered such matters as wages, hours to be worked, those workers to be included in the agreement and those allowed to remain outside it, re-employment of those on war service, terms of notice of dismissal, etc. It came into force on the first pay-day after the first Monday in January 1915 and was to continue – and did – until the last pay-day in 1920.

Two points should be made in passing. First, the union concerned had an (almost unique) mix of skilled and unskilled workers. Second, the branch with which the agreement was made was the London Branch of Printers, Warehousemen and Cutters: but its provenance was clearly that ancient nursery of radicalism, the printing trade. Within Smith's, however, support for the PPW came largely from the unskilled London workers – that at least was the case put by the managers, clerks and staff of the stalls and shops. Certainly a large majority of them were against any concessions to the PPW. The PPW itself became (like many unions) markedly more vociferous and aggressively militant as the grievances over rising prices and profits multiplied in the late stages of the war. There was a rash of strikes throughout industry and neither the news industry nor Smith's escaped the attention of the militants. It was in an effort to restore a degree of reason and consultation to a situation rapidly becoming chaotic that Hornby proposed a programme of 'round-table conferences' between the partners and managers and the union 'Chapel'.

The first took place on 10 April 1918: altogether twenty-eight meetings took place before the end of 1921, after which only a scattered few were held before the General Strike in 1926. Their purpose (as Hornby more than once had to remind the conference) was to enable both sides 'to air their grievances'.[21] But from start to finish, Haley, the PPW chief representative, an embittered malcontent, refused to listen to any grievances but his own. The conferences became bogged down in doctrinal arguments about principles of management. Why should appointments throughout Smith's Book Department not be made by seniority rather than ability? Why (on the contrary) should special ability not be recognised as a reason for special pay in the stables? (In the end Smith's agreed to pay 'ability money' provided it *was* for ability and *not* seniority.)[22] Why would the firm not alter the 1914 agreement and pay those ruled by it for a 44-hour week? Hornby pointed out that these men were now governed not by the 1914 terms but by a new agreement made by the Wholesale Newsagents Federation and Haley's own union. 'The principle of collective bargaining was one which should be maintained in the case of firms engaged in the same trade.'[23]

It might have seemed worthwhile to prolong these wrangles if they had visibly succeeded in avoiding strikes. They did not. On 20 February 1919 there was a sudden strike. Hornby reminded the conference that the strike was caused by mis-statements circulated to members of the union by one of its officials, who was not even employed by Smith's. This sort of thing was not calculated to promote mutual trust and good feeling. 'What was wanted was a just & fair settlement of disputes, not a desire on either side to snatch a victory from the other.'[24]

The causes of the strike were too deep and devious to be eliminated by Hornby's appeal for fair play. Even while the conferences were in session the PPW proselytisers (led by Haley) were busy trying to force the entire body of managers and assistants into their union. At a meeting held on 9 February 1919, their methods brought to his feet an outspoken member of the staff, Edward Bull, who wasted no time in living up to his name. He was a union man (he declared). Unions and collective bargaining were necessary in contemporary conditions to raise the status and conditions of the working class. There had been a ballot: 606 had voted for having a union, 140 for not having a union; 29 had voted for joining the PPW, 267 had not voted.[25] But the firm had never been allowed even to know of the ballot. No superintendent was told. The PPW had implied that the firm had approved. It had bullied the managers with threats of stopping their supplies if they didn't join the PPW. And so on.

Meanwhile (Bull continued) the PPW was dominated from top to bottom by unskilled men who knew nothing of the grades, conditions, promotions and other factors conditioning the rest of the business and its staff. The result was chaos. At a recent Chapel meeting at Strand House bookstall managers, carmen, packers, and skilled men from the Book, Stationery, and Library Departments were present, but there was no discussion of any problems relevant to the skilled workers. The meeting 'broke up in absolute disorder – three free fights, everyone flying at the other's throat . . .'[26] Skilled men in the Book Department would never attend another meeting. They wanted their own union.

Bull's supporters lost no time in having his speech printed and circulated to all the managers of Smith's stalls and shops. This provoked the PPW to send a deputation to call on the partners. They demanded the withdrawal of Bull's speech, the withdrawal of a letter from the firm agreeing to recognise a separate union proposed by Bull and his supporters, and the recognition of the PPW as the sole union for managers of stalls and shops.

This was the last straw for the partners. They were prepared to ask Bull to apologise for anything he may have said which the union took to be 'offensive and slanderous':[27] they were not prepared to consent to the other demands of the union 'against the express wishes of the large majority . . . sooner than allow their business to be controlled by . . . warehousemen and packers, they would close down the business'. A situation (they continued) had been created by the 'Chapel' of the Paper Workers' Union

which was 'intolerable to any self-respecting Firm, and they were determined to resist demands which they consider unwarrantable and humiliating'. Thereafter is a note in Hornby's handwriting: 'Upon this a Strike was
declared by the "Chapel" at 10 minutes notice.'[28]

That was, nevertheless, for all practical purposes the end of the PPW
attempt to create a 'closed shop' exclusively for their union. It was also
the end, effectively, of the round-table conferences in any significant sense.
Perhaps this was the moment when somebody (Hornby? A. D. Power?)
pasted the quotation from Carnot into the conference minute book: 'In a
free country there is much clamour with little suffering; in a despotic state,
there is little complaint, but much suffering.'[29]

A new union of moderates was formed in 1919. This became the Retail
Book, Stationery, and Allied Trades Employees Association, in 1920. The
Paper Workers' leaders continued to complain and strike: most of Smith's
distributive labour had been drawn into the PPW under pressure from
Fleet Street. One participant in events from the management side has left a
picturesque account of two of his PPW union opponents at this time:

> There were some very bad people in top Union positions . . . a very bad
> Father of Chapel in News Despatch Department, Butler . . . . although
> he was paid by us to work for us, [he] didn't work at all for us . . . he
> worked entirely for the Union, and he had built what he called his own
> office in our News Despatch Department, and he spent his whole time
> running Union business, and never did a hand's turn for the firm at all,
> although he was getting full wages.

After this rather old-fashioned view that a man ought to work for those
who paid him for working, he continued: 'The Secretary of the London
branch of the Paper Workers' Union . . . was a terrible sort of thorn in our
flesh . . .' After the end of the war he was a source of continual trouble and
lightning strikes in the News Department. At the Round Table Larcey (the
Branch Secretary) 'used to sit there absolutely stinking of beer, and he used
to pull out a great clasp knife and sort of pare his nails with this knife when
he was having talks with us'. Larcey was impossible to negotiate with
'. . . because he didn't listen to any reason at all. He said, "Well, I'm going
to do so-and-so and if you don't like it the business stops working in an
hour's time" . . . that sort of thing.'[30]

Butler and Larcey were not the most engaging of colleagues but they
exercised enough power to coerce their fellow workers to follow the union

line. The partners in turn seemed to have decided their best strategy was to accept the inevitable and favour the moderates in the RBA. On 29 November 1922, a letter went out from the firm to the bookstalls, shops and superintendents. Its sense was sweetly reasonable: collective bargaining had come to stay; not everybody liked it or agreed with it but while their point of view was appreciated 'we feel that the advantages gained by holding aloof are outweighed by the disadvantages . . .' The staff were therefore urged to join some 'recognised Trade Organisation' before the end of the year. Thereafter superintendents were instructed to see that no promotion was sanctioned for any member of the staff who did not hold the card 'of some recognised Trade Society'.[31] In most cases the 'recognised Society' was the RBA but the Paper Workers, misliking and mistrusting the RBA (a moderate and reasonable organisation) continued to proselytise for their own union among the retail staff down to 1926.

The militants were apt to sneer at the RBA as a 'tame Union': but in fact, through their meetings and discussions, Hornby and the partners from 1919 onwards were in regular and constructive contact with their chief representatives. Some staff had inaugurated the action for higher pay in September 1918, when inflation had really begun to bite. The RBA renewed an ancient and honourable controversy. Should bookstalls be heated or not? It was a question as old as bookstalls themselves.

Hornby put up a spirited defence for the traditional practice of not heating. The staff themselves had never in fifty years asked for it: only outside observers: and they were wrong. 'There was no healthier body of men in the country . . . once the heating . . . was allowed, colds (which now were very rare . . .) would become very prevalent . . . warm clothing and not heating apparatus was the solution . . . He promised to consult a medical authority . . .'[32]

From such relatively light-hearted (if cold-blooded) matters, the third meeting passed to sterner stuff: inflation and the rising cost of living, on which Hornby invited the union officials to prepare proposals: but warned them against 'the danger of making drastic alterations, either in regard to remuneration or conditions, in quick succession'. The nature of the business was 'that of Distributors, and not manufacturers, and therefore virtually of a fixed price to the public'.[33] Alterations in salaries, wages and organisation might end as complete reorganisation. It would be unwise, in his view, to force other big changes until the initial changes had been properly assimilated. If top salaries were increased too much, some stalls would undoubtedly have to be de-graded or shut down altogether and employment of lower grades would suffer. And so on.

The problem, like many economic problems, solved itself. The inflationary bubble suddenly burst. Turnover fell. Profits too. The burning question was no longer higher wages but reductions in wages when the current wages schedule expired. Smith's suggested reductions would be reasonable in view of the fall in the cost-of-living index over the previous eighteen months from 130 to 103 in November 1921. The current schedule (i.e. basic pay + cost of living bonuses) was based on 130: if wages were to stabilise permanently on that abnormal figure 'England would very soon lose all her trade, and industry would be brought to a standstill'.[34]

These were the opening salvoes in a stiff tussle between Hunt (the RBA president) and Hornby. Hunt felt that to agree to any reduction would be to give away the whole principle for which his union existed. Hornby replied that practically every trade in the country had already reduced wages. The proportion of management wages to a declining turnover had risen to 'breaking point'.[35] He begged the delegates to remember that if this disproportion worsened it would be impossible for the firm to continue in business.

Hornby had to pick his way very carefully: he was acutely aware that the Paper Workers were on the offensive and using some plausible arguments to seduce malcontents away from the RBA if its leaders showed any signs of weakness. In the deflation of 1922, for example, they tried hard to rally support by demanding the abolition or at least severe restriction of female labour. The wrangle over wage reductions versus the decrease in the number of stalls therefore went on into mid-1924. By then it was clear that the worst of the crisis was past: for the time being. It had in the end been surmounted without wage reductions and to this extent was a victory for the RBA, Smith's and the cause of moderate union policies.

Not all the retail staff agreed. The following year saw Larcey insisting that in the Paper Workers there were now 'numbers of your Bookstall Staff, members of our Society, and they undoubtedly joined in conformance with the wishes of the Firm that they should belong to a recognised Trade Union'.[36] This, as Arnold Power pointed out to Larcey, was casuistry. The Paper Workers had agreed to abide by the outcome of the ballot of 1919 which recognised the RBA as the union for retail staff and the Paper Workers for wholesale staff. Larcey and his union had earlier been blocked in the provinces too. There they produced a comprehensive schedule of wages and conditions for the wholesale provincial houses in co-operation with the other printers' union (the NSOPA). But here the militants did not get far. They came up against the provincial trade associations – the principle of association had spread widely and deeply among employers as well as employees since 1907 – but the atmosphere of discussions remained friendly. George Isaacs, of the NSOPA, its general secretary, a moderate and a good negotiator was 'a restraining influence . . . what he is prepared to do for his Members, no doubt the Paper Workers will also accept' (as E. C. Scott acting for Smith's wrote on 10 March 1925).[37]

At the close of the bargaining Hornby wrote his congratulations to Scott. They were laconic. 'Taking everything into consideration we do not think you can be considered to have done badly.'[38] Coming from one not given to lavish compliments, it was almost high praise.

The mid-1920s saw an unexpected boom for Smith's. Turnover and profits recovered, and with prices stable, it seemed as if the major problems of the post-war years – inflation, labour troubles, high costs – were being resolved. In the country at large the better days of 1922 and 1923 turned sour by 1924 but for Smith's the improvement was maintained until 1926. Then, suddenly, the General Strike broke on to the scene. It began in the coal industry, where lock-out notices went into effect on the last day of April. The TUC asked for a mandate to call a General Strike. They got it by a huge majority. The Labour movement was swept along on a wave of tumultuous enthusiasm. Ramsay MacDonald led the singing of the *Red Flag*. Ernest Bevin saluted the 'magnificent generation' that had placed its all upon the altar – as indeed events were to prove. It began on 3 May: it was called off on 12 May. It was a disastrous failure and did immense damage to the causes for which it was supposed to have been called. For the great 'vote' could not conceal the divisions, confusion and chaos with which Labour entered on the battle. The miners fought on until November. Then they too had to accept defeat. 'Nothing whatever' (wrote two committed sympathisers) 'had been secured by the greatest effort the British workers had ever made.'[39] They were right.

Brief, good-humoured and ineffective as the Strike was,[40] it was a critical time for W. H. Smith's. From the start, Fleet Street was the nerve centre of the Strike. It was an unofficial lightning strike by printers on the *Daily Mail* which resolved the government to hold to the sticking point. Winston Churchill's vigorous and controversial *British Gazette* was published from the *Morning Post* offices ('unscrupulous' propaganda 'in the coldly provocative tone of that paper . . .' as it was described by two ferocious critics of the left).[41]

As news distributors, Smith's were in an awkward predicament. Those members of the staff at Strand House who were members of the Paper Workers' Union mostly – but not all – went on strike. The members of the RBA, now affiliated to the TUC, should have done likewise: some did, some did not. Many bookstalls remained open. The partners themselves were generally against the Strike but there were different degrees of enthusiasm for the positive actions that were taken. The older partners, Hornby (senior) and Power lacked the physical strength required by a demanding role which they left to younger men. Sir William (Robin) Acland was invited by Churchill to run the *Gazette*: with the help of his cousin Arthur, and expert printers from the *Daily Express* and the *Morning Post*, and engineering assistance from Woolwich Arsenal, the presses began to roll. Special material was flown in from the north of England by the RAF. 'All I had to do' (Acland said), 'was ring up a secret number, and say what I wanted and there it would come.' There were pickets but they were fairly friendly – 'just in case of trouble Winston sent me round half a dozen men with machine guns of some sort mounted on various roofs all round in case there should be a renouncement, as there had been with some past agreements.'[42]

That archetype of energy, C. W. Kimpton, now the manager of the News Department and of the still traditionally-named Counting House, was put in charge of distributing the *Gazette*, with Michael Hornby (St John Hornby's son, now also a partner as his chief assistant. Since trains were either not running or running very erratically, distribution was done by means of a pool of private cars. Michael Hornby recalled:

> People would arrive with every kind of car . . . with Rolls, and Bentleys, and Morrises and they went off over the British Isles with these papers . . . The Prince of Wales sent his Rolls, . . . driven by one of his equerries. It used to turn up every night.[43]

As production became better organised, the *Morning Post* premises were too small, so Michael Hornby asked the senior partners for permission (granted) to use Strand House instead, since it was standing empty. Freddy Hambleden used to take round supplies of the *Gazette* to W. H. Smith shops and stalls in his own car. On the last morning before the Strike ended, some 2 million copies were distributed. Churchill came in for violent criticism for his editorially biased handling of the *Gazette*. He refused to give way. 'I decline utterly', he informed the House, 'to be impartial as between the Fire Brigade and the fire.'[44]

Smith's kept going: that, in its way, was important. But like the political parties, the unions, and Britain itself, this firm too was divided and unhappy about the Strike and relieved when it ended. Indeed, the really important aspect of the Strike came at the end, during a conversation in pyjamas and dressing gowns at Strand House between the managers and the partners. All had been on the night shift when some of the managers sought out the partners. They put it to them that they now had an opportunity to get rid of the Paper Workers' Union and establish 'open shop'. Freddy and Hornby agreed – but only on condition they could get the backing of the newspaper proprietors in the form of guaranteed supplies of newspapers from their own staff. Lord Burnham, chairman of the Newspaper Proprietors Association, was an old friend of the Smiths and of Hornby. The NPA gave the necessary assurances; they themselves would remain 'closed shops' but they would insist on Smith's being supplied, even though they went 'open'. Since Northcliffe's day the NPA had played along with the unions. It had been worth his while to pay wages his rivals could not afford. In Michael Hornby's words, Northcliffe was 'prepared to accede to any demand which the Unions made . . . because he knew that he could afford it, and that his competitors probably couldn't . . . he started the rot in Fleet Street . . .'[45]

The notice published on 14 May 1926 announced:

Acting in accordance with a Resolution unanimously passed by the Federation of Wholesale Newsagents and the Associated Wholesale Newsagents Ld., we have decided as from this date to conduct our business as a Free House. We have also decided to pay the same rates of wages, and maintain the same hours of work as before the Strike . . . We undertake to protect the interests of those who return to work within a reasonable time.

Such was the outcome of what became known in Smith's as 'the Pyjama Conference'.[46]

So too ended the Strike. The main body of workers lost no time in getting back to work. Only a tiny handful of known trouble-makers were refused employment. The Labour Member for Gateshead, John Beckett (later a leading Mosleyite), at once made allegations in Parliament that W. H. Smith's had dismissed all their active trade unionists and had brought in the police to throw them out. Smith's issued a counter-statement. All but four of their 43 trade union members had been re-engaged. At no time in the Strike had the police been called in. Beckett withdrew his statement and apologised.[47] That was the end of it.

'What followed for some ten years or more' (wrote Smith's first labour adviser) 'is the nearest we are ever likely to get to Utopia, where the smooth running of the business is concerned. Output increased with a much smaller labour force and costs were correspondingly reduced.'[48] Michael Hornby supported him. '. . . for twenty years we enjoyed absolute peace and quiet . . . Everybody was completely happy. A lot [of workers] did not have to pay their Union dues, and their conditions remained exactly the same, and we were freed from this appalling tyranny of the Union . . . It was a very crucial moment for the Firm.'[49]

This was the view that prevailed. Yet the lessons of the General Strike were not forgotten. From June until well into the autumn, the partners debated lengthily with the departmental managers whether or not to set up a system of representative committees to replace 'the old Union'. There were those ready to argue it was wise to 'take men into more confidence', to allow grievances to 'come to the surface & not simmer & grow below . . .' In the end the idea was dropped; largely because 'work was going on well & smoothly, far more so than ever before & the Staff were obviously happier . . .'[50] Men went straight to their foremen with their troubles: this direct contact had better results than the old collective system which multiplied imaginary grievances. That was the employers' view.

Not until the second half of the 1930s did Fleet Street, then very weak and nervous, try and force Smith's into joining them in the 'closed shop' again. But by means of a Conciliation Committee (1935–   ) relations were kept harmonious.[51] The years of Utopia were not to last for ever, however. During the Second World War, union membership and union pressure increased. The 'closed shop' was to come back in February 1949 after what were – from the employers' point of view at least – twenty-three years of blissful industrial tranquillity.

A bookstall empire was not favourable territory for the aggressive tactics of radical unionism. The areas adjoining Fleet Street might catch the enthusiasm or contract the ailments of its radicals. But Northcliffe's analysis (see page 388) went to the heart of the matter: Smith's were merchants. Their tradesmen were dispersed, in penny numbers, over the face of England and Wales. It was not a good recruiting situation for union organisers like Larcey or Butler. Their natural environment was the factory or the printing works. Smith's were no happier with factories or large workshops than the Paper Workers' Union was with the far-flung bookstall empire and its dispersed and individualistic inhabitants. From this ideological impasse emerged a not wholly unsatisfactory equilibrium.

XII

The Inter-War Years: Economic Contours

FOR W. H. SMITH & SON, the inter-war years were neither uninterrupted boom nor unrelieved slump. As late as 1926–7, there seemed to be a good deal to be thankful for. Between 1934 and 1939 business continued poor but not throughout the whole range of activities. Even in the depths of depression, rays of cheer penetrated the gloom here and there. Why then consider the years 1919–39 (as this chapter does) as a whole? What, if anything, gave these two decades their special character? The answer is, their uncertainty. The history of Smith's down to 1914 had had its ups and downs: from 1900 onwards and especially round 1905–6 there were times of apparently insoluble problems and bad trading. Yet no one had doubted that stability and prosperity would return. The mood of depression itself was transient. After 1918, for one reason or another, for producers and consumers, for employers and employees, and between 1929 and 1933 for all, the times were out of joint. Worse than that, no one was clear why, or how, or when they would be put back into joint.

The troubles manifested themselves in, broadly, two ways. Economic activity was marked by a series of violent spasms which convulsed economic and social life. Such were the strikes that characterised the 1920s, especially the General Strike itself and the business crises and crashes such as the Wall Street crash of 1929, the scandals, swindles and eventual suicide of Ivar Krueger, the Swedish 'match King', the lesser and less spectacular domestic frauds of Horatio Bottomley or Clarence Hatry. Yet the effects of these dramatic upheavals were less important in themselves than was their symbolic, symptomatic significance. In Britain the economic and political scene was dominated by the decline of the old basic industries and whole areas that were almost solely dependent on them. Here and there an

observer noticed that – as always – new infant industries were, simultaneously, emerging. But the conservatism of employers and investors on
the one hand and the even more deeply rooted conservatism of the unions
and labour on the other made the process of industrial transition more
difficult and more bitter than it was in more open societies like the United
States.

Behind these vicissitudes were the deep cultural and social changes that
had been accelerated by the First World War, with all its vast displacements
of men, products, industry and trade. After the war ended the economic
changes continued to be reflected in the fluctuations of prices, which broke
like waves over the economies of Europe and the world. These in turn were
felt in the fortunes of business, including those of W. H. Smith's. The
background was the long slow rise of prices, which had been in progress
continuously since 1906, had accelerated with war demand in 1915 and
reached its peak in 1920 (see Table XII.1).

TABLE XII.1 THE RISING TREND OF THE WHOLESALE PRICE INDICES[1]

Year	Index
(1900)	(100.0)
1905	97.6
1910	108.8
1915	143.9
1920	368.8

The bubble burst in 1921. After a sudden collapse of prices, the situation
had stabilised by 1922 but the tendency of prices was downward, fairly
gently until 1929, then breakneck until bottom was reached in 1933 (see
Table XII.2). After that, price levels recovered, though painfully, until
1937, relapsed and took off upwards once more only as war and the
rearmament programme took over.

The price upheavals briefly sketched here represented a revolution in
public finance unprecedented in history, the general substitution of un-
limited amounts of printed money for notes backed by gold, or gold or
silver itself. Swings of prices of the amplitude experienced between 1915
and 1934 were something new. Neither politicians, bankers nor businessmen

had any experience to guide them through the masses of problems which were created, and are still with us. How did Smith's survive?

Smith's (to repeat) were distributors, not manufacturers. They were nevertheless accustomed to find that in so far as prices might be one – not the sole – guide to the partnership's state of health, they did well when prices of the things they sold – newspapers, journals, books, stationery, etc.

TABLE XII.2 THE BUBBLE BURSTS: THE FALLING TREND OF THE WHOLESALE PRICE INDICES[2]

Year	Index
(1913)	(100.0)
1920	307.3
1921	197.2
1925	159.1
1929	136.5
1933	100.9
1934	104.1

– were up or rising: and less well when they were down or falling. Like everything else in a topsy-turvy economic world, this also ceased to be a rule to be relied on, as a brief analysis of the figures of W. H. Smith's trade shows. Let us take the general categories first: capital employed, wholesale and retail turnover, the wage bill, and net profit.

If capital employed were a true measure of prosperity, Smith's would have enjoyed a sense of contentment in the 1920s and 1930s. The expansion of capital went on. What did it finance and how? Mainly property purchases and development. For after 1905–6 W. H. Smith no longer represented simply a collection of movable wooden stalls erected on other people's property. Major stall numbers remained remarkably stable between 1920 and 1940 (652:636): but 'A' shops also grew in numbers, and 'B' shops much more so (see Table XII.3). Then there were the provincial wholesale houses, sometimes much larger properties than the shops. They increased from 35 to 45 in the same period. Again expansion continued even in the depression of the 1930s. 'B' shops rose from 266 to 337, wholesale houses from 45 to 64.

There were, in addition, massive outlays on the rearrangement of the London headquarters with its various subsidiary activities. The Strand House at 186 Strand was already too small by 1906 to supply the growing network of railway stalls and shops. Problems of distribution grew as London traffic increased (see pages 264–5). More staff, more accounting, more supplies demanded more head office space. So by 1912 plans were already being bruited to move away from the Strand, northwards to Portugal Street: to a large combined head office and distribution centre in the end nostalgically christened Strand House. It was not finished until 1915, just in time to be requisitioned by the government for war purposes in 1916. The Ministry of Works, as usual, hung on grimly to their capture. It was 1920 before continuous pressure restored it to its owners.

TABLE XII.3 'A' AND 'B' SHOPS

Year	'A'	'B'
1920	22	202
1930	39	266

Sheer pressure of business drove Smith's to find a site at Lambeth for the non-Strand House activities. The construction of Bridge House (as it came to be called) began in 1933. Before it was complete the Binding Department moved in. The Stationery Department followed in 1935: side by side, a new specialised business stationery enterprise called Business Forms Department (BFD). In a separate building near by, the Works Department was re-housed. In matters of transport the General Strike had brought to the public attention (including, especially, the W. H. Smith partners) the merits of motor transport. The old stables in Water Street and Tweezer's Alley, between the Strand and the Thames, holding 128 horses in 1912–13, were coming to the end of their century of usefulness. By the autumn of 1932 only three Yorkshire bays were left: and in that year Monarch, Lassie and Michael were also pensioned and put out to grass. Motor vans had been hired in increasing numbers since the First World War and in 1934 a special subsidiary company, W. H. S. Transport Ltd, was formed to run all the company's motor transport.

Such were some of the major factors which explain the growth of W. H. Smith's capital between 1920 and the Second World War: a growth, in real terms (i.e. adjusted for inflation) of some 300 per cent. The needs for capital have been briefly indicated. Its physical forms were brought for shelter and sustenance under the roof of special companies, Hambleden Properties in 1922–9 and Hambleden Estates Ltd from 1929. Frank Bayliss,

Estate Department manager of W. H. Smith & Son and surveyor of Hambleden Estates Ltd, acted in many capacities – guardian, architect and designer, valuer, maintenance manager, financier, estates manager. But on everything he touched he left a mark which was to become characteristic of W. H. Smith: a blend of the creative imaginations of Eric Gill, St John Hornby and Frank Bayliss brought forth the unmistakable style of the W. H. Smith shop. And this was as it should be, for the shops formed the collateral for the debentures of Hambleden Properties. Bayliss's organisation was to be an important element in the future financial structure of the firm (see page 349).

The comprehensive picture of business growth may be inferred from the figures for both retail and wholesale turnover. The wholesale turnover was the more impressively consistent: with only an odd, minor kink its graph was upward all the way, even in the depth of the 1930–3 depression (and, also, adjusted for price movements). Here was the steadiest winner in the race. Retail turnover also performed remarkably well, except for a drop in the late 1920s. These results were not, of course, strictly comparable. The injection of new capital described above had as its object not merely the alterations necessary to allow the existing business organisation to expand, but also to finance expansion through the purchase of new businesses. The Partners' Minute Book therefore contains evidence of their continuing plans to buy out existing businesses both wholesale and retail, as well as to create new shops – overseas as well as at home. (Paris had got its W. H. Smith in 1903; Brussels followed in 1920, the *Queen Mary* in 1936 her floating bookshop.) For some time before 1923 W. H. Smith & Son had been the principal shareholders in the old-established enterprise of Truslove & Hanson Ltd, the owners of three well-known bookshops in the West End of London. In September 1923 the entire business was acquired.

This particular church-marriage (as it might be called) was celebrated by a wedding breakfast and general rejoicings. It was not always so. The smaller news retail agents had formed their own organisation to protect their interests: the Retail Newsagents Federation. It was particularly nervous that Smith's, losing interest in bookstalls, might leave the railway stations and open up hundreds of shops in the nearby towns which would drive their members out of business. When Smith's told the Federation of their purchase of the business and premises of one Owen, at Oswestry, in the autumn of 1925, there was a heated meeting. The business, the Federation said, was not 'a newsagent's'. Smith's representative left the meeting proclaiming their right 'not only to transfer all the rounds [of Smith's existing railway bookstall] to the shop, but to carry on the business of a newsagent, without let or hindrance'. The Federation affirmed their determination to prevent this happening. 'They would see that 1905 was not repeated.' Thus, noted Smith's representative, 'the Oswestry case assumes a most important aspect'.[3] He was right. The dispute recurred almost regularly as proposals to buy a shop here or a shop there were put forward. Part of the difficulty lay in Smith's large stake in the wholesale trade. There were deep suspicions among their small retail competitors that they would obtain less favourable terms from Smith's (as wholesalers) than those given to Smith's own retail branches. This kind of mistrust was to persist for many years: until in fact the wartime arrangements proved that their suspicions were quite groundless (see page 399).

The retail trade was not the only area of expansion. In the summer of 1923 the old wholesale newsagency of Johnson's of Leeds, dating back to 1813, was acquired. This widened Smith's trade throughout Yorkshire. New premises were built at Liverpool in 1924–5. The Leicester House was burnt down and had to be rebuilt in 1927. From 1934 the partners had to spend much money and ingenuity over the part-purchase and reorganisation of the important business of John Heywood Ltd at Manchester.

By such policies the impetus of business growth was maintained through times at best indifferent, at worst disastrous. Wholesale turnover rose from c. £1 million in 1918 to over £3 million by the late 1930s. Retail turnover in the same period from c. £1 million to £2.5 millions. Where then was the crisis? Was it a myth? It was not. A glance at net profits reveals how vulnerable the business was – at least from the mid-1920s – in these inter-war years; how fragile the impression of prosperity and growth derived from the turnover and investment accounts. In real terms (adjusted for inflation and deflation) the record profits of 1918/19 (c. £250,000) slumped by 1920/1 to £150,000. They then rocketed again to £285,000 by 1924/5. Then they fell sharply until, by 1937, Smith's earnings stood below their level of the mid-1890s: this after all the massive investment of the 1920s, to say nothing of the first fifteen years of the century.

Vulnerable – fragile? Were then the investments and efforts all a waste of time and money? Certainly not. The story of human economic effort (especially of capitalism) is the story of calculated risks taken in the hope of economic improvement. A depression on the scale of the inter-war years exposed every weakness. It thereby showed the entrepreneurs how to reorganise their efforts. This has often been the function of crises in economic history: to act as the spur to reform and correction. It was the function of the 1930s. Before accompanying the partners on their own continuous

vigil of reformation, however, we should examine one further phenomenon: the rising cost of wages. The cost of Smith's total wage bill had
risen steadily from 1870, with only very slight pauses in the late 1890s and a
year or two immediately after the 1905–6 crisis. The first real drop came in
1932/3. But from 1917/18 to 1932/3 there was a steep rise and the uncertainties of 1933–41 were not unbroken. The year 1930/1 represented a peak of
high pay. This is the more extraordinary when it is realised that in 1931 a
labour force only marginally larger than it had been in 1918 was costing a
wage bill some twice its post-war size at a time when prices had actually
fallen by between twice and three times their 1918 level.

A smaller but by no means negligible cost was imposed in 1936 by a
decision which made Smith's liable at law for the payment of rates on railway bookstalls. The responsibility for rates on advertising hoardings on the
railways was a bone of contention between Smith's and the railways as old
as Victorian whiskers. Some degree of liability had nevertheless long been
conceded: not so for bookstalls. Here Hornby had taken up an immovable
stance. His contentions had been supported – in the first instance – by the
Railway & Canal Commission. It held that a bank, shops, *bookstalls and
bookcases* let out at Victoria Station should not be regarded as separately
assessable for local rates. But an appeal by the City of Westminster and
Kent Valuation Committee – the metropolis has always been hungry for
income and prodigal in spending it – was upheld in the House of Lords in
1936. This was a heavy blow for Smith's; for the decision not only affected
their 21-year contract negotiated relatively recently with the Southern
Railway. It applied to all their bookstall contracts with all the other
railways.

In the event, the improved atmosphere that resulted from the elimination of the railway advertising contest (except on the LMS where it had
finally been amicably settled) proved of great benefit to Smith's. The proportionate division of the rates bill differed widely from one railway company contract to another. But in general the sum was worked out fairly and
amicably by empirical enquiry. Even this did not alter the fact that Smith's
had to shoulder an added burden on their costs at a bad time.

These were the circumstances in which partners and managers alike took
a searching look at the source of those losses which were pulling down net
profits in the 1920s and 1930s. Turnover and profits alike came from the
commercial and distributive channels operated by W. H. Smith's: bookstalls, shops, wholesale houses (i.e. originally the Strand headquarters, then
joined by the provincial houses). The essence of the problem was that one
group of activities was still making enough profit to support those which

were not. Overall, profits had not disappeared; but they had shrunk dramatically; and they were becoming more difficult to make. The inquests of the 1930s were designed to identify the areas of real promise and to write off those of none. One decision could be delayed no longer, hard as it was. In 1937 the large enterprise, the Arden Press, taken over thirty years earlier by Hornby, publicised and enlarged by Morgan, but haunted through its life by persistent unprofitability, was closed down with the loss of 500 jobs. Smaller printing works continued to operate to supply Smith's own printing – Bridge House had one; so did several of Smith's provincial businesses. But the closure of the Arden removed a heavy burden: a decision that killed off Hornby's own brain-child symbolised the tougher, more realistic mood of Smith's policies vital to survival in the 1930s.

Paddington Revisited: 1924-30

A decade and a half after Smith's lost the contracts with the LNW and the GWR to Wyman's, rumours were circulating among W. H. Smith staff that all was not well between the GWR and their protégé. Ripples of curiosity, hope (and doubtless satisfaction) ran through Smith's, where old memories of the injuries of 1905 were still green – even at the top. Hornby might continue to believe (as he said) that he did not grudge either the railway or Wyman's their right to a change: he only objected to the way it was done: but in his eighties his son recalled that as children, he and his brothers and sisters were always expected not to buy papers at Wyman's unless it was absolutely unavoidable. Such was family tradition.

It is possible that the soundings which were taken by Smith's about the future of Wyman's contract for bookstalls and advertising with the GWR originated with Hornby; but it is not likely. When Mr Bluff, a former Smith man, called on Mr Pope (superintendent of the line's office) at Paddington on 9 June 1920, he explained that he was there on his own responsibility to ask whether the GWR would persuade the head of W. H. Smith's railway advertising to reopen negotiations.[4] This was not quite true. Bluff had, in fact, called at Paddington at the specific request of Grant Francis, head of the Railway Advertising Department.

Francis was a very remarkable man, a Scot, who had not only come up to the top of his department on ability and tenacity but had, in the manner of his compatriots, trained and educated himself in the same way: to such effect that he was elected Fellow of the Society of Antiquaries, and ultimately became President of the Royal Numismatic Society. He was not a man to let the grass grow under his feet: but that was what it was showing every sign of doing as, one after another, the railways had taken over their own advertising. With each cancellation, the turnover and profit of Smith's department fell. With them fell the commission due to Mr Francis: he was too good a numismatist (and Scot) to be ignorant of the fact.

As it turned out, Wyman's contract still had another five years to run. Another four years elapsed therefore before Hornby wrote to Sir Felix Pole, general manager of the GWR, to say he would be pleased to have a chance to negotiate. Pole invited him to talk, and talk they did; very frankly. Pole was at pains to scotch any rumours of a row between the GWR and Wyman's, though he admitted they had never 'attained the status of Messrs. W. H. Smith & Son . . . any difficulty [Wyman's] may have been in in the past certainly did not apply now' (see pages 247–9).

Hornby was equally outspoken. If W. H. Smith 'had been treated with the cordiality extended to Messrs. Wyman', they would have paid the GWR better than Wyman's. All Smith's had experienced in their day was obstruction and non-co-operation. If they came back he wanted to deal with the top; he did not 'look with favour on any reference to the higher officials . . .'[5] But, countered Pole, would Smith's divert business from the station bookstalls to their local shops? Hornby fenced this one with his usual skill: Smith's anxiety was the reverse – that customers who had left the bookstalls for the shops might, once again, leave the shops for the bookstalls . . . if they were properly run.

It was a friendly but barbed encounter. One major obstacle was clear. Hornby stuck to his conviction of twenty years' standing: he would not recommend his firm to join in a competitive tender for the contract. This Pole could not accept: in fairness to the present contractors, they must be allowed to tender and that meant so must the other contenders for the contract. There was the rub.

For a month in the summer of 1924 the discussions paused. Then on 6 August (possibly under persuasive pressure from Francis and others who felt that the future of Smith's railway advertising hung on the outcome of the GWR negotiations) Hornby articulated in great detail his objections to the practice of competitive tendering. Even to those who had sometimes been puzzled by his obstinacy on the point, it made impressive reading. Broadly, tendering was a wholly unreliable and potentially specious way of choosing the contractor most likely to do the best job for the railway. It was easy, for example, for a firm to offer to pay a higher proportion of receipts as 'rent' than it knew it could afford and save the necessary money

by giving inferior service. An inexperienced but ambitious firm could do
– what Wyman's had done in 1905 – namely, offer what their responsible
competitors '*knew* & said was an impossible tender, and so obtain the
contract . . .' A bookstall contract was 'not like a contract for building a
house or constructing a railway . . .' There the contractor could sack all his
staff when the job was finished. Or go on to a quite different contract. A
bookstall contractor was faced with heavy capital investment and he
depended 'on continuity with its resultant goodwill and with the feeling of
security which it gives to the staff employed . . .' who took many years to
train. He ended: if Smith's did not put in a tender, 'it is not from any feeling
of false pride or irritation about the past, but simply because they do not
consider that it is in their best interests to do so.'[6]

Hornby's arguments were compelling. They did not, apparently, persuade Pole and his directors, who politely but firmly insisted that Smith's
must tender. Even Smith's managers for once took issue with Hornby.
Grant Francis reported that the question had been discussed at some length
in the Managers' Room: everybody present except two were strongly in
favour of doing so – for both bookstalls and advertising. If Smith's didn't
compete, the idea would spread round the railways that they were losing
interest in bookstalls. Then again, he continued: 'The question of the
Union (PPW) is an important one, and doubtless weighs heavily with
you . . .' But it would surely be better to face the Paper Workers now
rather than later, on a line where few of Smith's own men are affected and
where a few of Wyman's people could have little effect 'in seducing the
employees on your own Stalls into the Paper Workers' Union'.[7]

With great reluctance, Hornby surrendered over advertising. Over
bookstalls he stuck to his guns. But all to no purpose. Whatever the reasons
(and they are now lost) the GWR continued their contracts with Wyman's
until 1930. But in 1929 the rumours were flying once again. Meeting him
in their Club (as Arnold Power noted down on 18 July 1929), Wyndham
Portal, who was a director of the GWR and a friend of Robin Acland from
Eton days, remarked to Power:

I suppose you'll be back on the G.W.R. in – what is it? – six months?'
(or words to that effect). I said, 'Is W's contract up then? and should we
be welcome?' He said: 'Judging from what I hear everyone would be
very glad to be rid of W's. But I've been a Director only a short time.
However I do really do some work & attend committees twice a week'.
I concluded it by saying: 'We shall be ready.' (Previous to this for two
or three years past F. J. C. P[ole] almost every time I have met him has

professed to be most dissatisfied with W's, & has said either 'When are you coming back?' or 'Why don't you buy up W's?') C. W. K[impton] says R. C[ope] told him the other day that the G.W.R. had great difficulty in extracting money from W's.[8]

Another snippet of Club gossip, different in detail but alike in the hopes it raised, was recorded by Robin Acland. He too had met Wyndham Portal, who asked how bookstall terms were arranged and why Smith's had left the GWR: 'He said, "*we* should start negotiations." ' Acland asked, 'who with?' Portal said he 'w[oul]d find out & use his influence & then come to lunch in September'. He 'was glad Felix P[ole] had left & said he was a friend of Wy's & unpopular at Padd[ingto]n.' Acland had said, 'we should like to be back but that there was not as much in the bookstall business as before, owing to costs & that we could not be expected to go in and outbid Wy's.' W. P. said, 'But your service is better & your men are of a higher stamp.' Acland replied, 'Yes. That costs us more.' W. P. said, 'You sh[oul]d get the contract on Service.'[9]

Portal lunched with Acland on 16 October 1929. All the Smith partners were present except Hornby and Seymour. Portal repeated what he had told Acland in the Club.

[He was] very friendly. Said he w[oul]d speak to Churchill [First Viscount Churchill, chairman of the GWR] this weekend & advised us strongly to ask for an early interview with J. Milne [the new general manager of the GWR] at Pad[dingto]n. He said J.M. was quite straight, & w[oul]d probably be influenced by "Service" & by our present heavy traffic to shops & Wh[olesale] Houses.[10]

(He was right about the last item at least. W. H. Smith were paying the GWR at this time £43,000 a year for carrying their freight.) It would, Portal added, be Milne who would virtually decide who was to have the contract.

Hornby met Milne at Paddington a week later[11] and they exchanged information. Wyman's, it seemed, had gross receipts (from all sources including bookstalls) from the GWR of £311,062.[12] It was a certainty, a plum. But not all Grant Francis's urgings and briefings could raise any real enthusiasm in Hornby. For Hornby remained as distant from the GWR management as they did from him. Their bureaucracy had a long memory:

so did Hornby. And, from what he heard of Milne via Acland and his friend Portal he suspected that the GWR officialdom had already persuaded Milne that the GWR should take over its own advertising anyway.

But Hornby was not one to sulk in his tent. He took part in the preparation (by Acland) of a draft tender to the GWR in June 1930. Even Acland's previous high hopes were dampened by now. '. . . I sh[oul]d let Portal see a draft of our letter' (he scribbled to Hornby 'In train to Portsmouth' on 6 June) 'to enable him to make certain that the Board does see it & not only hear a *précis* of our tender.'¹³

The draft letter to Milne was in Hornby's usual style, frank, forthright and making no attempt to conceal the problems. Its gist was that Smith's could certainly improve matters on the GWR stations: but at least 45 out of the 73 stalls owned by Wyman's had a turnover of less than £1,500 a year. Another twelve did less than £2,000 of business a year. There were thus only seventeen bookstalls 'on which any profit can be anticipated in their present state of turnover'. In all, bookstall receipts at stations other than Paddington were £33,500 *less* than in 1905 'the last year in which we were bookstall contractors [to the GWR]'.¹⁴ Allowing for the increase in prices since 1920, this meant that Wyman's business was not much more than half of what Smith's were doing fifteen years earlier. Comparisons with other lines suggested that Smith's would have been doing £362,000 worth of bookstall business in 1929 if they had been awarded the 1905 contract. Wyman's bookstalls turned over £179,541. This could only be remedied (a final paragraph helpfully explained) by reducing the excessive costs being incurred and applying all the talent and experience which Smith's, and only Smith's, had at their command.

If all this had been included in the letter that ultimately went to Milne, it would not be difficult to understand why Smith's did not get the GWR contract of 1930. Yet these home truths, which might well have upset the delicate feelings of the GWR, never reached Paddington. Acland explained why to Wyndham Portal. The memorandum 'as originally drafted', he wrote, contained:

> a paragraph which was not in the memorandum as finally sent to Paddington, because we thought that it might be considered as rather jeering at the mistakes the G.W.R. made in the past (although, of course, this was not the reason for its drafting) but I think you would be interested to see it . . . I think it was a mistake that this paragraph was not sent, *because I feel the Directors ought to have known these figures, and I*

gather that they did not, though if the Directors did not read our letter and memorandum perhaps it did not make much difference after all![15]

Evidently Hornby had been right: so had Portal. The directors of the GWR were, as they had been in 1905, men of straw. Power lay with those 'higher officials' whom Hornby had so rightly mistrusted. They neither forgave nor forgot. We cannot know for sure what happened at the Smith partners' meeting which considered the full uncut draft letter to the GWR. The most likely surmise is that Hornby persuaded his colleagues to leave out the references to Wyman's and to 1905. His brother, recalling their childhood and after, observed that his method in debate never varied: it was to use reasoned, logical argument. Speculation, denigration and innuendo were against his nature. The draft contained too much of all three: so the draft was scrapped. This time it lost him the game: elsewhere he was to win.

The Waiting Rooms at Euston 1930-3

The long and fruitless negotiations with the GWR had been conducted under the relatively stable and prosperous conditions of the 1920s – that at least is how they seemed in the retrospect of the 1930s. Economic conditions were already deteriorating when the GWR contract was lost in 1930 and at that seemingly unpropitious moment negotiations were opened with the LMS for their bookstall and advertising contracts. No one could feel sanguine about the outcome. The shadow of the 1929 crisis lay across the meetings: the arguments on both sides hinged on falling prices, declining business. Yet in the end Smith's were to emerge with a notable victory. In many respects the circumstances facing them and the two railways were similar. Why was the outcome of these two vitally important episodes different? The evidence is detailed enough to suggest some reasons, even if they are not definitive ones.

The whole structure of the British railway system had changed after 1922. Four major groups had emerged: the Great Western Railway, the London North Eastern Railway, the Southern Railway and the London, Midland & Scottish. The once great London & North Western (whose contract Smith's had lost in 1905 along with the Great Western's) disappeared as a separate entity: its properties were merged in the new LMS. The general trend in railway advertising was for the companies everywhere to take it into their own hands. This was nothing new: the threat was very nearly as old as the companies themselves.

310 First with the News

The root of Smith's problem with the advertising business had been the steady erosion of what had originally been their unique advantage: their coverage of England and Wales, originally very much wider than that of any single railway company, had given them a national network of customers to whom they could sell advertising space. This advantage had been whittled down by the steady substitution of inter-company collaboration in place of the original acute rivalries. The regrouping of the 1920s was the latest and most decisive phase (see also page 309). W. H. Smith's original network of agreements covering bookstall and advertising rights had numbered, at its height, 144: by 1930 the only great combined contract still surviving was the old Midland section of the LMS.

On the bookstall front, prospects were brighter. After the débâcle over the GWR contract just described, Robin Acland wrote to his friend Wyndham Portal that Smith's had just negotiated 'a long renewal of the whole L.N.E.R. bookstall contract, and the G[reat] C[entral] [Railway] is included in it'. This was a defeat for Wyman's, the sitting member. The figures showed, Acland recorded with satisfaction understandable in view of the GWR's opposition to Smith's, that at Marylebone Wyman's were doing little more than half the business Smith's had done there in 1919 and at the country bookstalls of the Great Central Railway only a fraction of their turnover of a decade ago. 'Such is life! I expect it will take some time to revive the suspended animation.'[16]

Meanwhile, the Southern Railway (with whom Smith's relationship had been consistently satisfactory) had gone the way of the rest. In 1929 the Southern took over its own advertising but Smith's retained the bookstalls for another twenty-one years: here, at least, Hornby achieved his perennial objective of long tenure.

That left open the combined privileges on the LMS – the only great railway not so far committed to managing its own advertising, but strongly inclined towards it, as preliminary conversations between Grant Francis and LMS officials clearly indicated. This was Francis's last chance to save his own department's claim to play a major role in the business and he brought to his task all his innate tenacity and negotiating skill. He had a few comfortingly high cards in his hand. As he wrote to the partners when the discussions were in mid-flight, 'the Chief Officers of the Company' were 'predisposed to W. H. Smith & Son'; the carping came from an ' "Executive Committee" . . . almost entirely composed of accountants'.[17]

In this judgment he was on fairly solid ground. Guy Granet (Hornby's old friend from his Oxford days; see page 249 for his remarks on the 1905 crisis) had risen to be deputy chairman and later chairman of the new

LMS group between 1923 and 1927. Then he resigned, but not before he had brought in Josiah Stamp to succeed him. Granet remained an influential adviser. He was an entrepreneur of great originality, spontaneous, unorthodox and very human. His influence would be exercised in the interests of the LMS but if Smith's deserved the contract he would not refrain from saying so simply because he was an old friend of Hornby. Stamp in turn would not ignore Granet's views and experience. The rest of the officials were likewise zealous for their company's interests but their zeal was generally combined with a sense of fairness and objectivity: only the accountants (as Francis observed) seemed to be attached to obstruction for its own sake.

Francis obviously induced Hornby to go into the negotiations with an aggressive programme designed to win. Hornby therefore made an offer of rent for advertising of 80 per cent of receipts; very high for Smith's.[18] It depended on Smith's gaining the whole LMS network (the old Midland section currently held by them plus the old LNW section currently held by F. Mason & Co).[19] It was conditional also upon Smith's being given the fullest co-operation of the LMS staff in an effort to maximise the income of both parties – a *desideratum* which could not be taken for granted in any railway organisation. Here the current 'appalling conditions of trade' as Francis described the prevailing depression, may have helped Smith's.[20] These were no times for gambling, as the LNW and GWR had gambled in 1905 and since. Smith's (and in particular Hornby's) reputation for reliability had never stood them in better stead.

For, strong though Smith's support might be at the top, the trouble came – as with the GWR – further down the line. The Smith team took a long series of almost unendurable cavillings from the LMS officials, especially from their chief accountant and his assistant (Taylor and Graham) over the whole gamut of secondary points. Thus, although the LMS vice-president (J. H. Follows) was said to have approved joint recommendations by both negotiating parties for a settlement on 10 June 1931, and final submission to be now merely a formality, another whole year of vinegary exchanges followed.[21] Finally Francis was stung into a solemn declaration doubtless calculated to bring the accountants to realise the risks they were running if they drove the bluff too far. 'We had made the last concession we were able to make in order to retain the contract and we were not prepared to go one iota further.' It worked: Davies (LMS chief commercial manager) asked if that was to be taken literally, and Francis replied, 'Yes'. Davies then said, 'Very well, I will concede the point . . .'[22]

Even this was not the end of the difficulties, however. The LMS accountants went back again to the problem of working out a guaranteed minimum rent for past years. This set off another long wrangle lasting into February 1933. Then at last Hornby himself (to whom the concept of guaranteed minima was always anathema) exploded in a blistering letter to Taylor, the LMS chief accountant. Their calculations (he concluded) were out of all relation to the current value of bookstalls. The accountants were working on 1932 figures. But receipts, for 'causes completely beyond our control have declined at a disastrous rate during the past five years'.[23]

Earlier, during the negotiation of the fresh contract for bookstalls, Follows, vice-president of the LMS, apparently decided that matters were being mis-handled. 'He seemed rather annoyed', Hornby wrote to Power, 'that things had been carried so far without his having had a say in the matter. I think now that he will take a hand personally in the affair . . .'[24] In the summer of 1933, it seems to have been decided that further meetings were the only hope.

Robin Acland, a sharp and amusing observer of men, kept some illuminating notes. On 1 June:

> The general tone was pig-headedness and suspicion on the part of Graham [the assistant accountant] coupled with a determination to tie us up in every conceivable way to forms of rigid accountancy, without any appreciable regard to justice or common-sense or the ultimate benefit of either party. The other L.M.S. people were more reasonable, but apparently were unable to agree to anything unless they were unanimous. The meeting was the longest and the most unproductive of results per hour that I can remember. Many things were discussed, but few of any importance were decided. There was so much talk that it was not quite clear what was settled.[25]

The detailed comment on Graham's interventions supports Acland's opinion: that it was shared by Smith's representatives generally is witnessed by the opening gambit of George Barker (Smith's Bookstalls Department manager) who minuted the next meeting a week later:

> Barker: In view of his attitude at the previous Meeting would he (Mr Graham) explain whether he was really anxious to complete this Contract, or whether he was out with wrecking tactics to break down the friendly relationship existing between the L.M.S. and W H Smith & Son Ltd?
> Graham: My main concern was to get the Contract through, but to have it worded in such a way as there can be no misunderstanding . . .

The minutes hardly suggest it but even Barker's final note was that 'Graham's attitude at this interview was much more friendly . . .'[26] The next, on 13 September 1933, began with a message from Sir Josiah Stamp conveying a small but friendly concession in the matter of the past rent.[27] Robin Acland noted that it 'was far more friendly and did more good' than the June meeting. 'Mr Graham obviously having been sat on but . . . still very tiresome and shewed a lamentable lack of knowledge of the subject. Mr Forster [LMS trade advertising department] was friendly and inclined to be helpful . . . obviously out to get the matter settled . . .' So far so good but . . . 'our arguments produced but little effect . . . and none on Graham.'[28] Nevertheless, Acland's feeling that things were moving and that time was running out for the sea-lawyers was justified by events. The agreements, which gave separate contracts for bookstalls and advertising rights, were finally completed with almost disconcerting speed in September 1933; but Smith's were unable to dislodge F. Mason (advertising) and Wyman's (bookstalls) from the old LNW section of the LMS. It had taken three years of hard bargaining.

Two subsidiary points about the meetings that led up to them deserve to be mentioned. First, among the problems encountered were the activities of the rival advertising contractor: almost the only one to have survived the rigours of competition and depression in this line of business. Frank Mason had replaced Kershaw's on that part of the LMS which had formerly, before the regrouping of 1922–3, been the LNW. They had been much accused by Grant Francis of 'undercutting' i.e. selling space on railway advertising spots to their customers at prices which were below cost and therefore calculated to ruin their competitors. Old Frank Mason had recently died and when Mason's were drawn into the discussions between the LMS and Smith's, they were represented by his son, Captain R. F. Mason, MC a retired wartime officer, newly elected chairman of the family business. Probably to the surprise of Francis, Mason spoke frankly and engagingly of W. H. Smith as advertisers. He had always admired their methods but, then, he was new to the business and 'had found it impossible to avoid giving way in the question of price when he was faced with the choice of either giving way or losing business . . . He congratulated Mr Francis' . . . but he (Mason) was 'fighting for his business life and that of his staff . . . one of his father's last actions was to tell him that he must not lose the L.M.S. Contract . . .' Could he not 'look upon Mr Douglas Francis as a "bridge" which he might use in approaching us for help . . .?'[29] Captain Mason was irresistible. This was the beginning of an association which was to end in the absorption of Mason's by Smith's.

The second point is the appearance at the meetings of the Third Viscount Hambleden ('Billy' Smith) who had inherited the business on the death of his father, Freddy, in 1928. In the 1932 meetings Billy is recorded as accompanying Hornby and Francis, perhaps to demonstrate the solidarity among the partners and management of the business and the continuity of the W. H. Smith family concern and proprietorship. And just as an important role was played by Michael Hornby – C.H.'s son – in the LMS negotiations, so too Billy's younger brother, David (and a future chairman) was present at the meeting on 8 June 1933; holding 'a watching brief'.[30] It was another confirmation of the persisting strength of tradition in a still firmly family business.

Fate and Paradox: the Decline and Fall of Railway Advertising

Euston was a notable victory; a source of great satisfaction to Hornby and to Francis, whose department it saved from virtual extinction. Yet behind the rejoicings there were also anxieties. More than a few of Smith's men felt doubt in their bones. They were right. Euston 1933 was to mark the end of an era in Smith's history. For the whole aspect of advertising was changing, and not only in regard to the rail reorganisation.

Much had been said in denigration of Smith's advertising policies and methods on the railways. Much had been said in their praise. But in the 1920s so many new factors entered into the calculations that what had been said either way in the past by Smith's friends or critics was no longer relevant. An understandable but unreliable mythology had grown up in the railway companies (and in Smith's) about their relationship and functioning. The railway view of Smith's, especially in regard to the advertising contracts, whether among directors, managers or officials, was invariably prejudiced, *ex parte* and, frequently, totally ignorant. This was less so among the London Underground management than among the great national networks. Especially at the 'Met' there was a more objective and understanding attitude to advertising and to Smith's advertising in particular. This did not, as will be shown, mean that it was uncritical. Selbie, the general manager, was an unusually just and equable north-country man. As the 1920s wore on, his relationship with Hornby was less close and he was occasionally rattled by Hornby's failure to improve his bookstall and advertising takings. The decrease, as Hornby explained, was part of a general falling-off in takings, largely because London newspaper prices had fallen in real as well as monetary terms, as a result of the great newspaper battle raging in Fleet Street (see page 322).

Selbie accepted the explanation about bookstall profits but remained not wholly convinced about advertising. In the summer of 1926 he complained again to Hornby of the falling advertising revenues of Smith's. This time Hornby blamed the state of the economy. '. . . the same causes which lead to a diminution of your traffic, are operating adversely to the advertising business, because advertisers are naturally very much alive to the number of possible readers of these advertisements.'[31] Trade for the past year had been none too good. The General Strike had made things worse: where trains had been out of the running, the full rent for advertisements in carriages could surely not be expected? Selbie admitted there was something in this but declined to concur in Hornby's somewhat '*non possumus* attitude' (as he described it).[32] If Smith's were in difficulties would they like to turn in the remaining (six) years which their advertising contract still had to run? No, they would not.

Nevertheless, Hornby was himself not satisfied with the situation. Francis and his department were asked for an explanation. One factor, it appeared, was the loss of a contract with Nestlé who had extracted a specially advantageous rate of rent from Smith's predecessors. The Met had objected, Smith's had demanded higher rent, Nestlé's had withdrawn. A large customer had thus been lost. But worse and more serious, other 'national' advertisers had recently transferred their rail publicity to road signs. '. . . *this policy must and will continue and extend*, because there is no question that advertisers are now being largely attracted to the roads by their increasing use for transport purposes.' 'Sensitive advertisers' (Francis went on to claim) watched the published figures showing the decline in rail traffic and rearranged their advertising budgets accordingly.[33] There were other problems: bad lighting on the Inner Circle stations, the common lack of space and overcrowding of platforms.

Simultaneously, Selbie was reading a report on advertising by his own staff.[34] It made interesting reading side by side with Francis's report. Its general theme was that the popularity of advertising was increasing and while fashion favoured newspaper advertising, railway advertising was 'holding its position and should share in a general increase'. The author (or authors) agreed that there was a current temporary decline which reflected 'the actual conditions of business . . .' They agreed too that roadside and road vehicle-advertising, electric signs and newspaper advertising all combined to threaten railway advertising receipts. How did the existing

arrangements, by which the Met contracted their stations and carriages out
to Smith's and Smith's contracted them out to advertising businesses or
their advertising agents, promise to deal with these threats?

The answer was: not well. '. . . only if radical changes are made in the
nature of the spaces offered to advertisers and the system of letting them,
can any large increase in revenue be expected.'[35] The trouble was (the
report explained) that many shapes and sizes of posters and iron plates were
displayed in an indiscriminate jumble. Smith's contracts were made on a
national system which was not tailored to the particular demands of Underground stations. It agreed that these were often old and ill-designed –
especially badly lit – for advertisers. Suburban stations were better but slow
to develop the advertising fashion.

Smith's, the writers also agreed, were poorly remunerated for their pains.
Any proposals they might make for improvements, however small, had
to run the gauntlet of a railway bureaucracy which had to pass and sanction
them. (They did best inside carriages where they sold spaces in 'wall panels
. . . window spaces [for] "transparencies" . . . and "roof cards" . . .
enamelled signs (on some seat backs) . . . and lately a small enamelled sign
incorporated in the hanger straps has proved popular.')

Smith's (they noted) employed about twenty-two canvassers, ten of them
in London and the Home Counties. But they worked on a commission
basis and their major concern was to obtain contracts covering the widest
areas. Their Met contracts were therefore best fitted into 'national' contracts. They had, in fact, '. . . little inducement to push the special claims
of the Metropolitan line except as a means of increasing the value of a
"National" contract.' Local orders, of a kind very desirable on the Met,
were less worth their while and were neglected accordingly. All this
reflected the fact that Smith's 'selling organisation was established when
competition was less intense than it now is. It was designed to handle
contracts for large numbers of advertisements . . . distributed over a
variety of railway property, and was for this purpose a most economical
means of selling from the companies' point of view. It has expanded to
meet present conditions, although it is open to question whether it has
entirely kept pace with the times.'[36]

This was the rub. The report emphasised that it did not reflect on the
individuals who operated the present system . . . 'their experience . . . is
undoubted.' But times had changed and Smith's had not. The experience
of, for example, the Hammersmith & City Line where advertising orders
were obtained by the Met '. . . suggests that Smith's organisation is not
indispensable to the Company . . .' And so to the damning peroration:

... it is an accepted business principle to-day that advertisement is an essential means of selling. This principle is so little in the minds of Messrs. Smith & Son, however, that they expend a negligible sum in *advertising railway advertising*, and adopt no other method than to exhibit cards and small posters in unsold advertising space. No articles are contributed to contemporary business publications, no circulars or booklets of up-to-date and striking tone are available for the information of potential customers. At the recent Advertising Exhibition at the White City, the stand shared by Smith's with other advertising agents was of entirely insignificant character. The representatives of the business are unprovided with statistics of the latest developments and traffic on the Railway.[37]

Conclusion? It would be best if the company handled its own advertising (but the Smith contract still had six years to run and to do anything in the interval would be exceedingly costly and difficult). This of course was only what many other railway companies had argued: and done. What was different was that the Met critics argued their case logically and with at least the appearance of fairness and genuine evidence. Ironically, the report was hardly complete, let alone examined or implemented when the Smith advertising results showed a marked improvement on the Met in 1929, though it was less brisk in 1930. Thereafter takings relapsed once more in 1931 and 1932 (see Table XII.4).[38] Changes both swift and slow

TABLE XII.4 ADVERTISING REVENUE ON THE METROPOLITAN LINE, 1926–32

Year	Revenue £
1926	36,644
1927	34,188
1928	35,446
1929	39,992
1930	40,363
1931	39,245
1932	35,068

followed in the Underground system and in W. H. Smith's. The Met was absorbed, in 1934, into the London Passenger Transport Board. Taking their cue – in this as in other matters – from Selbie's innovations, Lord Ashfield and Frank Pick, the architects of the new Board, took their advertising, in the time-honoured phrase, into their own hands.

At Strand House, too, the facts of a changing world had been recognised. In 1927, Railway Advertising (under Francis) was bracketed with Publicity (under P. R. Chappell) and an Advertising Agency (under Francis and Chappell) in a composite Advertising Department of which these two were joint managers. Chappell was another picturesque recruit who had come to Smith's from Messrs Spottiswoode & Co alongside Herbert Morgan and W. T. Welfare (see pages 229–30). The details are not immediately relevant: enough to say that the reorganisation and the individuals chosen to supervise it showed that Smith's had accepted the validity of at least some of the criticisms made in the Met report of 1927. It recognised that in the new world of competitive advertising, the simple renting out of railway hoardings was not by itself a worthwhile activity. Closely focused advertising, whether for others or for Smith's themselves, was also important, both on their own premises and outside, by a variety of media. In the end it was to be joined by the systematic dissemination of information about the business, its policies, activities and personnel called 'public relations'.

The changeover was gradual and accompanied by some painful transitional experiences. From its peak (in turnover and profits) railway advertising sank steadily back. It had in any case grown but little in the twentieth century before 1920. From 1927, after a brief septennium of prosperity, it sank to its bottom point with the outbreak of the Second World War, recovering slowly thereafter under the stimulus of new ideas and new activities.

G. R. Francis retired in 1934, much honoured as the last and not least valiant champion of railway advertising. At the farewell dinner in his honour, among the guests who applauded Francis's reply to the toast was the knight of advertising himself, Sir Herbert Morgan.[39] Morgan may have misunderstood the precise needs of Smith's in matters of advertising: but so had everybody else. His general instincts had been sound.

XIII

Hard Times and Heart Searchings: The 1920s & 1930s

EVEN IN THE 1920s the W. H. Smith partnership was not large enough to spend too much time on conscious 'policy-making', 'decision-taking' and other such exercises in the manner of the present day giant company. Its style was a family style, its accounting simple and relatively primitive; its partners shared responsibilities in one large room. There was a minimum of bureaucracy. Ultimately it was in personal ownership. Odd as it may seem to a generation educated in a mixture of ideas culled almost equally from Karl Marx and the USA business ethos, this worked against the maximisation of profits as much as in its favour. As distinct from the strict fulfilment of daily functions of the firm as newsagency, its 'policies' were flexible, sometimes to the point of casualness. If the owners and partners had a definable object, it was stability rather than growth *per se*.

In spite of the disasters of war – perhaps even because they had at terrible cost been overcome – the underlying mood of management and staff remained one of basic confidence. The boat might rock from time to time: it would be righted: it would not overturn and it would never sink. Charles Manning at Bradford would be warned of 'the seriousness of his excessive and increased stock' and he promised to 'amend his methods'.[1] Garner, manager of the new shop at Brussels would be 'severely spoken to for having spent so much money on stock without authority'.[2] So were others. But the only sign that Hornby was at all inclined to a 'policy' of capital economy were the instructions to Bayliss (Estate Department manager) and Bentall (Shops Department manager) 'not [to] embark upon any new enterprises in the way of either purchasing businesses or opening new businesses . . . before December 31st 1924. All propositions made to us of this nature must therefore be firmly declined until that date is passed.'

The ebullient Bayliss was rather a favourite with the partners. They therefore felt bound to explain why the rein was being tightened. Finance was short; the businesses in hand must be consolidated before new ones were added; good staff were scarce; the Estate and Shop-Fitting Department was fully employed for at least another twelve months. They realised that all this would probably mean missing good opportunities but they could 'afford to do, and, in any case, it is the lesser of two evils'.[3] This might have been merely the aftermath of the collapse of inflation: but it went on for years. In 1928, the partners went out of their way to interview Bayliss 'and told him frankly that [they] considered the decorations and in some cases the buildings of [the] shops . . . too elaborate . . .' They hoped 'in future he would make them much simpler'.[4] Bayliss, buoyant as ever, was undismayed. 'That' (he observed) 'was only a scrap of paper.'[5]

By 1930 the truth – that the difficulties long supposed temporary were chronic – had dawned. The problem of capital, cash flow and profits had taken on a different, and more pallid, complexion. In July 1931, Michael Hornby (who had taken on more and more of the policy responsibilities carried by his father) drew the partners' attention to the 'unduly great' increase in bookstall staff which seemed out of proportion to the relatively smaller growth in the number of bookstalls.[6] After an enquiry, there were further, more urgent, discussions of the need 'to arrest the fall in receipts or the progressive increase in expenses'. The decrease in turnover was 'startling' and the rates of gross profit were tending to fall on goods for which the selling price was fixed for Smith's.[7] There was clearly a great reluctance to join in the cuts in wages that were a general feature of industry at large by now; but in 1932, the retail side of W. H. Smith was prepared to settle for a 10 per cent cut.

It was not as drastic as it sounded. Less than a year later, when the union leaders asked for the cuts to be restored, Billy Hambleden told them – with obvious reluctance, for staff relations were always at the centre of his thinking – it was too early . . . 'business was only just beginning to increase, and . . . no change could be made yet'.[8] Hornby added that in any case any growth of turnover would be shared through the new 'bonus' schemes devised to protect the lower-paid members of the staff. In 1934 the cuts were abolished and a new and improved pay schedule was introduced. Billy Hambleden had never been happy about the wage cuts and had accepted them with the greatest reluctance. At least he now had the satisfaction of announcing their discontinuance.

Meanwhile, within a context of gradually sustained turnover and falling profits, some branches of Smith's activity were performing badly, some indifferently, some well. Printing and binding had never made much profit; now they were making less. Stationery continued pretty well; but after the mid-decade mini-boom, railway advertising profits fell away. So, even more, did library profits: but the libraries had always been defended on the grounds that their profits were partly indirect and invisible. The library, it was argued, brought customers to the stalls and shops who might otherwise never have come at all. Once there they bought. Perhaps. But it was disturbing when both the main props of the entire retail trade – news and books – drooped dismally after 1924/5.

The reason seemed to lie in both cases in the drop in prices. In 1929 additional rulings were added to the original Net Book Agreement of 1899; it was to survive (in modified form) even the 1956 Restrictive Trade Practices Act.

The Net Book Agreement of 1899, arranged by the Publishers' Association and the Associated Booksellers of Great Britain and Ireland, meant business. Its purpose was stated unambiguously in the preamble:

We, the undersigned several firms of Publishers being desirous as far as possible of ensuring that books published at *net* prices . . . shall not be sold to the public (including schools, libraries and institutions) at less than such net prices, hereby inform you that henceforth we shall only invoice and supply you *Net* books published by us or any of us, on our usual trade terms, provided you on your part agree to abide by the following conditions . . .

Retailers were forbidden to offer books for sale on any other terms than those thus set out. No second-hand copies were to be offered below the same net price within six months of publication. Wholesalers were to allow their usual trade terms only to retailers who agreed to abide by the same rules.

That the publishers' condition was desperate was shown by the edge they gave to the teeth provided for the successful working of the Agreement. Any infringement was to be visited by severe penalties including the withdrawal of all trade privileges on the price and supply of books by members of the Publishers' Association. Any bookseller rash enough to try to avoid its terms would be out of business. W. H. Smith's had no alternative: they accepted. Copies of the additional rulings of 1929 were sent out by Hornby to all the provincial wholesale houses, and 'A' shops.⁹ What the effects were on book sales it is difficult to calculate. It is impossible to separate them from the disastrous general conditions of trade which lasted in many respects through the 1930s: but it was more than a decade before book profits climbed back to their 1929 level; and the libraries went through several years of serious losses.

The story of newspaper supplies was even more disastrous. The basic cause (as Hornby told Selbie of the Metropolitan Railway and other railway managements) was the collapse of newspaper prices. The remedy was in a general sense similar to that to which the book trade had resorted; co-operation to maintain prices. However, it took different forms. For these were the decades when the 'circulation wars' exploded in Fleet Street; the time-fuse had been laid in 1896 with Harmsworth's launch of the ½d. *Daily Mail*. For years it had burnt slowly with the arrival of competitors such as Pearson's *Daily Express* (later bought by Beaverbrook) and Northcliffe's own *Daily Mirror*. By 1918 there were 3.1 million dailies circulating; by 1926, 4.7 million; by 1939, 10.6 million.

With the entry of the *Daily Herald* into the fight in 1929, the circulation war was truly on. The *Herald* was a socialist paper kept going from 1912 by the efforts of its editor George Lansbury. By 1929 it had run out of steam. It was bought by Julius Elias (later Lord Southwood) the self-made man who had turned Odhams, printers, into the *enfant terrible* of Fleet Street. It cost him dear. By 1933 he was paying out over £3 million a year to buy his readers with prizes and gifts; 'free' pens, tea sets, insurance policies, giant prizes for cross-word puzzles, complete bound sets of Charles Dickens, and so on.

Elias did not begin the battle of Fleet Street: he only sharpened its ferocity and reduced to naught the semi-chivalrous code which had previously governed its conduct on the battlefield. Ever since 1918, Lord Rothermere and Lord Beaverbrook had been in touch about competition between their respective papers (from 'Harold' to 'Max'). By the late 1920s the fighting was less of a game between friends: more an all-in wrestling match between professional pugilists – the newspaper managers and canvassers. And now the battle was spreading from Fleet Street to the provinces, where the Berry brothers' papers ruled the north, and the Iliffe papers and journals were firmly entrenched at Birmingham and Coventry. The provincial reader was generally hostile to London papers. The Beaverbrook manager in Scotland noted the 'apathy and occasionally active hostility' of newsagents to national newspapers.[10] Only the *Daily Herald* seemed to make progress in the densely populated working class areas of Yorkshire. In Birmingham, conversely, not all their free gift schemes enabled the *Mail, Express, News Chronicle* – or even the *Herald* – to improve their circulation in face of the prevalent local patriotism. Beaverbrook's son,

Max Aitken, reporting on sales of the *Evening Standard* in Birmingham in 1929 wrote: 'The Birmingham people would be very difficult to win over from the *Evening Mail*. They would read a four page paper with little or no good news in it as long as it was printed and owned by a Birmingham man.'[11] 'If my forecast is accurate' (wrote Rothermere to Beaverbrook in 1930) 'our troubles in Fleet Street are only now beginning . . . and 1932 is going to be an exceptionally bad year.' Advertisement revenue was likely to drop until '. . . newspaper profits for next year will "go west".'[12]

Facing such grim prospects the newspaper proprietors followed the same path as the booksellers. In February 1930 the Newspaper Proprietors' Association informed Smith's and other newsagents that they would reduce the number of copies of their three evening papers (*News, Standard* and *Star*) in a quire from 27 to 26 without compensation.[13] Hornby's policy of maintaining good relations with Fleet Street went back to the settlement of the dispute with Harmsworth over the *Harmsworth Magazine* (see page 200). But the crisis of the 1930s was proof against all cure, whether applied in friendship, retaliation or the surgery of open war. Thus while Smith's turnover of newspapers rarely fell much below a value of some £3 million between 1919 and 1940, the profits on the newsagency business were a different story (see Table XIII.1). It was falls of this magnitude in the profits

TABLE XIII.1 NEWSAGENCY PROFITS, 1919–40[14]

Year	£
1919/20	191,039
1924/25	143,305
1933/34	45,440
1940/41	25,520

of the basic sectors of the business that provoked some of the Smith management to ponder carefully the fundamental structure of their activities and the assumptions on which it was based.

In conditions of deflation and depression, low and ever lower prices were a fact of business life that could only be accepted, not remedied. The only help lay in methods of enlarging turnover at the expense of competitors and reducing costs by getting more value for money laid out in, for example, salaries and wages. This was the core of ideas round which a number of reforms revolved in the second half of the 1920s and especially during the

1930s. And it is evident that both the younger partners and managers were looking outside the existing W. H. Smith organisation for new ideas. Some of the managers concerned were not 'Smith men' by origin. They came – like Chappell and Marshall – from outside. Others, such as Goad and C. R. Charles were trained in the bookstall and shop trade: but they were men who had kept their eyes open for ideas introduced by competitors. Thus did hard times act as a spur to more concentrated effort.

Goad, in charge of shops, obviously – and rightly – chose 'Bob' Charles as his informant on shops. Charles had had (and was still to have) a remarkable career.[15] Like many of Smith's staff, he was the son of another Smith employee who himself rose to be manager of the King's Cross bookstall. At the age of six, he is recorded (by his proud father) as delivering papers for him. Later he had joined Smith's himself. At the time of this correspondence he was managing an 'A' shop at Richmond. He was known as a devil for work, with a coherent philosophy of business (his original ambition was to be a teacher), a keen interest in music and a willingness to go on thinking and learning. Goad was right to choose C. R. Charles to expatiate upon what was happening in the shops.

When C. R. Charles wrote to the Shops Department in August 1933, his letter was one which breathed a general sigh of relief. The depression was over its worst but during its painful course many valuable lessons had been learned:

> We shall have learnt how much there is to be gained from extra application to detail, which we have found necessary to give. We shall have found valuable side lines to increase turnover, which we should never have thought about in good times. We shall have lasting benefits from the economies which we have had to make in working costs [etc., etc.].

Charles had, in his day, managed a bookstall, a 'B' shop and an 'A' shop. While 'searching round for avenues of escape from the Depression' certain differences in the working of the two types of shop had been borne in on him. On the whole, the 'A' shop system seemed to him the better system (as it well might to a shop manager). His reasoning was nevertheless perceptive.

The 'A' shops (he confessed – rightly) had suffered more than the 'B' shops in the bad times. Nevertheless Charles felt sure that the 'A' system, with its greater flexibility for managers to handle local situations on their own judgment, offered the better way ahead. 'The day has gone when we are the only "Pebbles on the Beach" . . . and if we are not prepared to offer the goods the public require, then there are plenty of competitors ready to supply our customers.' If the manager was only one of thousands dealt with at headquarters, he could not be satisfied as swiftly and satisfactorily as he could if he had the freedom to go straight to the producer or wholesaler and get direct service on terms he could negotiate.

As to running expenses, the 'A' system also came out better. 'In the "B" Shop the manager lives for "Turnover", which means "Salary" to him. In the "A" Shop the manager lives for Profit, which is his only means of Salary.' This distinction was correct and important. The growth of retail turnover and the low profile of profit suggests that Charles was probably right in guessing that many 'B' shop managers who *thought* they were running a successful business 'would be astounded at the small margin of *net* profit . . .' they were in reality earning. This in turn explained a widespread insouciance about salaries and wages. The shop managers should reflect (he continued) on, for example:

> Does this or that Round pay for itself? If not, what had I better do about it, or if it does how can it be made to show even a greater profit? There are probably hundreds of rounds bringing 'Turnover and *Wages*' to the manager, but 'Turnover and *Loss*' to the Firm . . . To put it shortly, does the 'B' Shop system encourage a Manager to take the line of least resistance in Staff matters?

Again, the consistent rise in the wage bill, higher proportionately than the rate of *shop* growth, gave force to his argument – and indeed had been recognised by the partners in relation to the bookstalls two years earlier (see page 320).

Of course (Charles agreed) there were also risks of 'leakage' in the 'A' system, but 'the mental aspect of the "A" Shop manager is different from that of the "B" . . . The "A" manager has to stand absolutely upright on his own legs, unsupported by anybody or anything, while the "B" manager cannot, since the system demands that he shall lean on Head Office and his Superintendent . . .' And this led to delays. But (Charles concluded) both 'A' and 'B' systems needed more precise staff training. Staff were too often assessed for promotion on criteria of their efficiency in clerical and routine work: they should properly be judged by the way they could 'handle customers and build the business by their personality'.[16]

Charles's comments carry a ring of experience and conviction. It is not clear that they had much influence on shop policy. For the tendency (as always in bad times) was for central control, belief in bureaucratic wisdom, its all-seeing eye, and good intentions in the partners' room to encourage growth in the number of 'B' shops and stagnation, even decline, in the 'A'. At the same time, it may be that the working of the 'B' system itself was streamlined and generally improved by the more systematic training of shop managers.

Other proposals had already been considered. One, which received very careful consideration, was put forward by P. R. Chappell of the Advertising Department. Its main purpose was to recommend a new system of 'Cheap Shops' selling, among other things, 'Cheap Books'. Chappell, as we have said, was not (like Charles) originally a Smith man, though by 1929 – the date of his Cheap Shops scheme – he had spent over twenty years with the firm. He had migrated, along with others, at the time of the Hornby–Morgan printing enterprise, from Spottiswoode's, publishers and printers, where he was 'a printer's devil'. But Chappell was an original and lively character. He escaped from printing into 'publicity' in 1919 after his return from naval service and thereafter specialised in various advertising functions, including the post of joint-manager of a reorganised Advertising Agency with G. R. Francis (see page 318).

In June 1929 Chappell addressed a paper to the partners on the importance of devising what he called 'new methods of bringing business'. The railways were 'marking time'; turnover in the shops was slow. The cost of new sites for multiple shops was 'prohibitive' – except for shops which handled a very large turnover in necessities or cheap goods. Woolworths was quoted as an example of the latter. Chappell declared:

> This is an age of cheapness, and all classes – even the Queen herself – have patronised Woolworths. There is a limit to the amount of business to be obtained from the cultured classes to whom our handsome shops mainly appeal, and we want more people to venture further than the bookstall – which they do not do in sufficient numbers other than at Christmas time.

While Charles was concerned largely with economies and reforms of the internal organisation and management of the retail outlets, Chappell took a wider view. He had turned himself into an advertising and market man. This gave a new and sharper edge to his thinking: not to choose among the existing, traditional types of shop devised by Hornby and Bayliss, but to introduce a new kind of shop serving a different market, and a different class of customer with a smaller pocket. '. . . we should move with the times, and without interfering in any way with the establishment of shops of our present type ... undertake – by means of a subsidiary company – the establishment of Cheap Book Shops.' They would be sited so as to cost no more than the normal shops and be staffed 'by employing a similar class of assistant to Woolworths, and at the same time enormously increase the turnover'.

These new shops would deal mainly in books, at prices limited to (say) 3/6d., together with cheap lines in stationery, fancy goods, hardware 'on the Woolworths model but avoiding perishable things and keeping only to those goods which are always in demand'. Books would be produced by editions for the Cheap Book Company itself (*not* WHS). Fittings would be simple. Assistants would be 'girls employed at comparatively low but fair wages'. The present expensive style of shop would have to be forgotten: it would be all on the 'Woolworth standard'. Supplies would come through head office supply departments.

The question of 'identity' was important. Chappell did his best to deal with it.

Our Firm, by its size, is comparable with the many large trading organisations which in most cases have subsidiary interests apart from their main business. This idea of the Cheap Book Company would be but a natural off-shoot of W. H. Smith & Son Ltd, but of course it is essential for it not to be run under the Firm's name.[17]

He had actually registered the name, which would be assigned to WHS if they wanted to take up the scheme.[18] Along with it would go a Children's Book Shop in the West End and (he had 'no doubt') 'parents will turn with relief to such a shop where they can have a big variety to choose from and easily satisfy their gift-giving desires'.

The partners took a long time to make up their minds about Chappell's proposal. In the end, in the spring of 1932, they wrote to E. C. Scott at Sheffield (Provincial Wholesale) House that they had decided to go no further with the Cheap Shop scheme.[19] From their private minutes it seems pretty clear that Chappell's wave of enthusiasm broke on a rock charted as St John Hornby. If one side of Hornby's business statesmanship was his regard for 'quality', his other was his awareness of the intricate context of business diplomacy within which W. H. Smith & Son had to operate. It would be impossible to conceal the true identity of the Cheap Book shops and unwise to try. The scheme, whatever its marketing merits, would upset that delicate balance of interests within which he had always operated – the interests of publishers (a problem more than usually delicate in these thin times), other retailers, and the wholesalers. So Chappell was rejected. Scott was told he could experiment at Sheffield, if he wished, with a lesser scheme for selling cutlery by mail order. The Strand House mill ground slowly but exceedingly small.

Meanwhile, as the partners pondered the Chappell scheme, there emerged out of the welter of self-criticism and reformation, yet another, more radical onslaught, which combined some of Charles's 'internal' and Chappell's 'external' approach. G. A. E. Marshall, writing from the Stationery Department to the partners, seemed to have inherited not only the precision with which its first head, Kimpton, had endowed it, but some of his blunt energy as well. He was aware (he informed the partners) that his department was 'not yet perfect' and indeed that he himself suffered from 'many imperfections'; he did not intend to comment on individuals. He only criticised the 'system'. He nevertheless wished to state:

> That the Partners in W. H. Smith & Son, by reason of their birth, education and social environment, are incapable of understanding and appreciating the psychology of the lower and the lower-middle classes, who form the vast bulk of their customers and, also, of their own numerous staff.

To this theme – the imperfections of the partners – Marshall warmed with all the chilly enthusiasm inherited from a frustrated career in the Civil Service, an equally frustrated and abbreviated career in a commercial library and a general feeling that his efforts in Smith's Stationery Department were not appreciated as they should be. Others, for example, might think the partners would acquire a broader knowledge of society through contact with their staff. Mr Marshall ventured 'to suggest this is not true':

> The predilections of the Partners are well known to all of the staff and, human nature being what it is, any information given by the ordinary members of the staff to a Partner is almost of necessity coloured by that knowledge: in other words, the Partners are generally told 'what they want to know'.

After getting this rather personal burden off his mind, Marshall made some sensible points: for he was a man of considerable acumen, if not sensibility. The W. H. Smith bookstall business (he argued) had been built upon an appeal to all classes. So are all multiple shops and the rule must apply to Smith's own shops:

It is impossible to establish successfully a multiple branch concern upon a Bond Street policy. If Bumpus or Hatchards were to establish branches, they would be forced to adapt those branches to meet local conditions ... What will appeal to the customers at Wigmore Street may be scorned by customers at Merthyr Tydvil [*sic*] and vice-versa.

The size and location of a shop must govern its holding of stock: return on capital depended on managerial judgment. Then he made straight for the defences of the Bayliss establishment.

'Fitness of purpose' should be ('but is not') the principal idea underlying the construction and fitment of our shops. This was a far more radical thrust than Chappell's. Chappell had only proposed the addition of 'cheap shops': he had said nothing against the existing ones. The name Bayliss could not have been more plainly his target if it had been inscribed in Bayliss's own Gill type. Marshall went on:

Too much thought is given to their artistic appearance and not enough to their business needs. They are too ornate and expensive in appearance. If beauty is an important factor in attracting customers, how is it that when many of Boots or Woolworth's shops are crowded to overflowing, our nearby establishment is practically empty? One very rarely sees one of our shops crowded except at Christmas or during the height of the seaside season.

Shop design which perpetuated the idea, no longer true, that 'Smith's are dear', combined with faulty layout, bad lighting, poor showcases and, above all, wrong priorities of command within Smith's to produce poor results. The headquarters supply departments, *not* Bayliss's Estate Department, should be the authority charged with shop planning and arrangements for selling their specialities, for example (he added pointedly), *stationery*. '... the policy pursued in the Stationery Department during the past seven years [since he had been responsible for it] has not been altogether unsuccessful, neither has it been detrimental to the "better" class of business.'[20] Die-stamping was at record levels: so were the sales of high-grade fountain pens. Marshall's note had started with a pseudo-ideological bang: it ended with what was palpably a departmental whimper. He lacked those qualities, whatever they are, that made friends and influenced people. If the records do not mislead, his remarks received no formal consideration by the partners.

While some of this intellectual seed corn may have fallen by the way-side, or took root only later, other important, if less spectacular essays in reorganisation of a more practical and less ambitious kind, were realised in practice. One was a staff bonus scheme approved in 1933. This, like the Chappell and Marshall ideas (which reflected the influence of Woolworths, Boots, and so on), reflected another outside influence: an experiment by Smith's earlier rivals in Scotland, John Menzies of Edinburgh. Menzies had evolved a method of paying an incentive in the form of a quarterly com-mission. There were many objections to commission payments as usually organised: they tended to be too small to be noticed if paid weekly and they encouraged the tiresome importuning of customers if paid solely on the direct efforts of the assistant concerned. By paying a quarterly com-mission based on the whole of a bookstall's takings, Menzies were satisfied they had achieved 'considerably increased sales at little extra cost' over a period of many years.

T. Whitwell, whose initials appear on the report, introduced accounting machines and Organisation and Method techniques to Smith's. The partners agreed that it would 'place assistants in a position to recover ground lost through the business depression' and put in extra effort for the general recovery of trade.[21] On that understanding 'this great experiment' (as it was described) was approved and launched by an announcement on 9 November 1933.[22] What part it played in later recovery is difficult to isolate from all the other factors making for more general recovery.

The same could be said of two other reformations of these years: the library and advertising. The immediate stimulus to library reform was two-fold: the first was undoubtedly the severity of the competition from the new, so-called 'twopenny' libraries. 'There seems every reason to believe that the "Twopenny Library" has come to stay', said a report of 20 November 1933: 'some are of considerable size and well organised . . .' Timothy Whites, for example, charged 2d. for a first class volume for three days, 1d. for each additional two days and no deposit. Boots similarly. Most charged simply 2d. a week. To join the competition was something of a gamble. It was calculated that in order to compete, Smith's must acquire a mass of *new* business: but not to try was fatal. Here, without doubt, Smith's had fallen behind.

So too in the country and small bookstall libraries: this was the other stimulus to reform. Of the branch libraries 77 had fewer than 10 subscribers; 121 had fewer than 10 day-by-day readers; 157 branches had fewer than 200 books on the shelves; 43 had fewer than 100. These were included in the 680 Smith branches (out of a total of 1,250) which offered a library service.²³ It had been proposed to shut down these small libraries altogether: but in the event the old traditional argument for the libraries – even the small ones – that they brought direct contact *at least once a week* with potential customers, prevailed. Emulating the methods of the rival who had caused Smith's so much chagrin – *The Times* Book Club – it was recommended that the small libraries should be preserved: but instead of carrying their own stock of books, they would be supplied, to order, through a 'Country and Small Branch Service'. This would give any subscriber two books on exchange every week. It would enable 'an immediate and direct blow to be dealt at *The Times* Book Club, which already is developing on branch lines and has worked up a large business by post'.²⁴

All this was to the credit of a distributing business in the midst of the worst depression anyone could detect in history. The same snag, nevertheless, seemed monotonously to accompany each attempted reorganisation. Turnover went up: net profit remained disappointingly low or nonexistent. Library turnover, for example, more than doubled from 1918/19 to 1939/40 (£107,043 to £240,848): but net profit fell from £19,437 to £8,817. The Press Advertising section of the reorganised Advertising Department enjoyed an increase in turnover from its inception in 1927/8 to 1940/1 from £37,473 to £101,448: net profit rose only from a loss of £3,221 to a profit of £5,333. The remaining parts of the Railway Advertising and Outdoor Publicity – in this sense – managed better: its profit in 1940/1 was almost exactly the same as in 1918/19 (£11,333–£11,344): but its turnover fell (£150,195 to £90,647).

No wonder the partners looked with satisfaction on those unique sections of their enterprise which regularly seemed able to record both growing turnover and growing profits – and largely minded their own business: the provincial wholesale houses. Further down the line, among the headquarters managers, the satisfaction was mingled with other less felicitous emotions. The independence, and ambitions to greater independence, of the wholesale houses aroused exasperation, anxiety and not a little jealousy.

XIV

⌒⌒⌒⌒⌒

The Provincial Wholesale
Houses: A State within a State

THE INVESTMENT IN wholesale houses in the provinces (PWHs) had got
under way around the turn of the century. By the time Hornby replied to
the toast at his Jubilee dinner in 1943 he could describe them as 'the brightest
jewel in all our diadem'.[1] He gave the credit to W. C. Smart and the band
of able managers who had built up by 1943 the chain of sixty wholesale
houses and sub-houses that ringed the whole of England except the area
round London. For the original business of the wholesale houses was very
largely to serve, not W. H. Smith's stalls or shops (except in emergency or
war), but the independent retail newsagencies, most of them small. Smith's
own branches were served from Strand House directly, as in the past.
Strand and the PWHs shared the remaining wholesale function roughly
30/70. The total share of both in the entire national market was probably
never more than about a third: but that was enough to make them a
powerful influence with publishers.

The most jealously guarded privilege of the wholesale houses and the
often remarkable men who managed them was their independence of head
office control. As time went on they had their own liaison office at the
Strand headquarters. But from 1919 their growing and more complex
network of trade brought into being a kind of informal confederate government: it met twice a year, once at a hotel in London and once in the
provinces. 'Conference' elected its own chairman and an 'Executive', a
kind of Inner Cabinet, to carry out policies agreed by the Conference. Its
affairs went unrecorded until 1937 but from 28 June in that year the
evidence is full and clear.

The *leitmotiv* of its proceedings was the conduct of the business relations
of the wholesale houses with those suppliers who could serve them best.

This was stated unequivocally and repeatedly by chairman and speakers in Conference. '. . . the success of our business' said Hardy, manager of the old-established Birmingham House, who occupied the chair in 1939, 'depends on our relationship with the suppliers and the supplied'.[2] To his listeners, what he was doing was staking the standard claim, now part of the houses' tradition, to enjoy the maximum independence of the Strand headquarters. Especially did they claim the right to buy their supplies – newspapers, magazines, books, toys, stationery and the dozens of other commodities (wallpaper, furniture, even bicycles) in which they had come to deal – wherever they chose; certainly not to be tied to Strand House for them, any more than they in turn were allowed to supply Smith's retail branches, stalls, or shops. And it was true that this superior status was what distinguished Smith's managerial regime from that of such rivals as Wyman's or Horace Marshall.

The almost obsessive determination not to come under metropolitan-imperial control emerged in every Conference meeting in one guise or another. At the first meeting of which records exist, members were busily alleging overcharging by the London Book Department headed by David Roy, a forceful Scot who seems to have cherished a resolute ambition to bring the wholesale houses to heel. 'Methods of accountancy at the Leeds house' (Conference agreed) 'should be dealt with through our own organisation and not referred to Head Office.'

This kind of thing formed the stuff of much of the Conference discussions. Members were urged to realise 'the absolute necessity' that their discussions 'should on no account be divulged' to outside persons.[3] One manager would express his dissatisfaction at 'the present terms for Parker Pens' offered by the relevant Smith department at Bridge House, London. Why not a direct account with Parker's for the whole PWH group? Why not, it naturally followed, a central buying department to look after *all* buying of supplies for all the houses? And why should not every chance be seized for PWH managers to buy any promising wholesale news business that came on to the market 'and thus strengthen the Firm's hand'? Why not extend the principle of 'combined buying' already employed on a limited scale and buy more extensively abroad, especially when currency arrangements made it specially profitable, for example in Germany?[4]

Yet as the battle went on, the ambiguity of the position adopted by some of the PWH managers became apparent. True, their business acumen and the profits it brought were a tremendous boon during the inter-war years, when profits were hard to come by. They bought ingeniously. The structure of buying and selling in the newsagency business gave them rare opportunities. Their demands for working capital were relatively small. The reader bought his paper or book at his retailer's and paid cash. The retailer paid his bill to the wholesaler weekly. The wholesalers settled their accounts with the publishers every four or five weeks. They worked, in fact, on the publishers' capital. They exercised great influence on the fortunes of the papers and periodicals they sold. Without them it was difficult to launch a new national 'title'. The wholesale market provided a context within which enterprise could blossom and flourish.

The managers of the largest and most successful houses were men of initiative – Hardy at Birmingham, E. C. Scott at Sheffield, W. H. Manning at Newcastle, F. C. Edmunds at Manchester were names known throughout the newspaper world, synonymous with enterprise and ingenuity. At Manning's farewell dinner in 1925 Hornby said of him that he had found the Newcastle House 'a mere ledgerful of bad debts'. He left it a 'splendid business'.[5] Edmunds (who began as a newsboy) rose through the rank of superintendent to be head of the Manchester House in 1919 – the traditional centre of the northern news trade. A hard bargainer and a high talker, he used to claim that Sir Arthur Sullivan composed some of his music in his manager's office at the Weybridge bookstall, writing out notes and staves on his long white starched cuffs. Thus *The Pirates of Penzance* came into the world (so Edmunds claimed) inspired by the rhythm of the passing trains and the wheels clicking over the gaps in the rails.[6]

The 'constitutional' situation was in reality confused. Nobody was more proud of the firm's name and repute than the PWH managers: but some of them genuinely believed the firm was best served by their freedom to operate by themselves and not as agents of headquarters. They were not fundamentally hostile to London. They simply believed they knew their business better.

The claim to total independence (made only by a small minority) was inconsistent if natural. The houses themselves represented the investment of the firm's (i.e. Billy Hambleden's) capital. When Bayliss was 'introduced' to the Conference in 1937 – for nobody, not even Lord Hambleden himself, was allowed to attend uninvited – he had to explain that Smith's had 'a definite obligation to Hambleden Estates to keep [PWH] premises in repair . . .'[7] Conference was sobered to find that neither Hambleden Estates Ltd nor W. H. Smith & Son Ltd was responsible for any of the costs of repairs inside or outside a wholesale house. Charles Manning (Bradford) pointed out that managers were not experts in building construction. Couldn't the Estates Company make regular inspections for the PWH? Bayliss agreed, thanked the meeting and left. But this was not merely an administrative incident. It was an indication that however much, and with however much justice, the houses and their managers valued their independence of what they regarded as the London bureaucracy, they could not, either legally or practically, disentangle themselves from it. There was an element of unreality in their posture.

There was also a certain incongruity about meetings which in the same agenda would discuss whether it was right for some houses to sell *Mein Kampf* at 4¾d. a copy while others offered it at 4½d., and the propriety of balance sheets running into figures of quarter or half million pounds. Moreover, as the Second World War developed, transport difficulties increased, wage problems became more complicated, call-up reduced the number of staff, and bombing destroyed the Birmingham, Coventry, Plymouth and Hull Houses and severely damaged those at Cardiff, Swansea, Liverpool, Birkenhead, Grimsby and Wolverhampton. With such problems doubts arose about the ability of the provincial houses to live on their own.

As the war went on, it became more obvious that, at all points, the fortunes of the PWH were entwined with those of the firm as a whole. As regards wartime conditions and regulations, they could not afford to be out of step and they sorely needed advice from the centre in order to know how to avoid trouble. War damage insurance was a case in point, to be vividly illustrated by the bomb and fire damage just mentioned at ten or a dozen PWHs. Already before war was declared, some managers were themselves questioning the propriety of the policy of combined buying in Germany. Air Raid Precautions arrangements had to be broadly co-ordinated throughout Smith's as a whole. As war had approached, some concerted policy towards staff call-up had had to be thrashed out. Dealing with transport emergencies was clearly going to be of crucial importance to keeping the business going at all if (as Stanley Baldwin had gloomily predicted) the bomber 'would always get through'. When E. C. Scott (who knew both sides of the question – he had been head of Sheffield House and was now in practice 'general manager' of London headquarters) was invited to the Conference in July 1939, he was asked whether London would continue to act as wholesale supplier to the Smith retail branches. Scott said that they 'had to assume that it was possible that Head Office would not exist . . . customers would be dependent on provincial houses for supplies . . .'[8]

Superficially, in this as in other respects, history did seem to repeat itself. In the early confusion of war, newspaper business was badly dislocated. Urgent appeals (as before) were made from headquarters to the provinces to hold on to staff, sell National Certificates, keep prices of existing stock down and generally preserve and burnish the Smith image for reliability and patriotism. Billy Hambleden, now left in sole charge of headquarters with the help only of Hornby and Power (recalled from virtual retirement) became the most frequent voice in policy announcements. For both A. W. and W. H. D. Acland, Michael Hornby, the chairman's two brothers, James and David, and Eddie Seymour, the company secretary, had joined up. And though Billy knew and valued the contribution of the PWHs, his natural anxiety was for staff welfare, better relations with the unions, strictest conformity with official government policy and the laws and regulations governing business practice, particularly as regards wages and prices. His visits therefore, though friendly, often had as their central purpose the presentation of those ideas on staff education and welfare and post-war planning for the business as a whole which were at the heart of his thinking.

On their side (and despite the growing evidence that the PWHs could not really survive or grow in isolation) many of the managers stuck to the doctrines which they believed had made the PWHs the most profitable and promising sector of the business. On the other hand, head office and its supply departments – David Roy in particular – continued to grumble that the PWHs were not buying enough of their supplies from headquarters. Headquarters, for their part, were still complaining of short-comings in the procedures – book-keeping especially – of some of the PWHs. Bad debts were allowed to run too long. Stock valuations were misleading or wrong. (For it was true that while PWH independence generally nurtured enterprise, it also encouraged – fortunately not frequently – a certain free and easy approach to financial matters on the part of a small minority.) The PWHs retained their own suspicions that London – Bridge House, for example, in matters of its supplies – might turn wartime habits of rationing supplies to their own advantage. So the wrangles continued, as in any institution slowly but ineradicably becoming sub-divided into departments and sub-departments managed by departmentalised and sub-departmentalised management.

Wartime nervous irascibility no doubt explained the less than rapturous reception of Billy Hambleden's admirable aspirations for more staff welfare and education. 'Staff welfare', said Hardy from the chair of Conference in 1943, 'is here to stay . . . Lord Hambleden has made up his mind . . . and although some of us may think that this is not the right time we must co-operate to the fullest extent and support him.' F. C. Smart endorsed this with obvious lack of enthsuiasm: yes . . . but 'while we support his

28 Above: the Toy Department at Sheffield Wholesale House, 1922

29 Below: the Library at the Leeds shop, 1926

30 Above: Strand House yard, 1932. Left (wearing a bowler hat)
L.E. Smith, master of the stables, and centre, the Third Viscount
Hambleden

31 Below: motor vans in Strand House yard, 1932, after closure of the
London stables in that year

32 Above: the Partners in their Room at Portugal Street, 1935. Seated, left to right: W.H.D. ('Robin') Acland, C.H. St J. Hornby, the Third Viscount Hambleden, A.D. ('Arnold') Power, and E.W. ('Eddie') Seymour. Standing left to right, M.C. St J. ('Michael') Hornby, J.F.A. ('Jimmy') Smith, D.J. ('David') Smith, and A.W. ('Arthur') Acland

33 Below: over seas: the W.H. Smith shop aboard the *Queen Mary*, then the world's biggest liner, 1936

34 C.H. St J. Hornby at his private press, *c.* 1935

Lordship in looking after Staff Welfare we ourselves should look after the business'. Hardy replied mildly: '. . . there was nothing *new* as regards Staff Welfare.' This had been practised among the wholesale houses for many years.[9]

Up to a point this was true. The real issue was its scale and organisation. For the PWH managers suspected – correctly – that Billy Hambleden had something more far-reaching in mind. He had. It came to fruition only a month later: from September 1943 Smith's were to have a new Staff and Staff Welfare Department: its purpose; 'to provide for the business, through education and welfare, a well-trained and happy staff, and by so doing to benefit the community and the business'.[10] And that, the PWH managers reflected, was Lord Hambleden's order of priorities: was it theirs? A more difficult question. The duties of the new department were set out with less precision. 'Staff advancement' was one: recruitment, training, placing, education, medical services, sport, recreation, general welfare all followed. The department would co-operate and co-ordinate with all others. The PWHs recognised it as a noble aspiration: but clearly they felt it was an aspect of post-war planning that could have awaited the end of the war. (See also page 348.)

The wholesale managers might be a trifle sceptical about education. They were not against it. What concerned them far more and alarmed them not a little, were Lord Hambleden's other ideas on post-war planning which seemed positively to impinge on their fundamental need for 'independence'. Even when E. C. Scott was proposed as a link-man between London and the PWHs in these matters – and he a former PWH chairman – doubts were not at once dispelled. '. . . there was a feeling that an ex-member of Head Office was being appointed to do a job we should do ourselves . . . that Mr Scott was coming to us *with* a plan instead of coming to us *for* a plan' as one member of Conference put it.[11] Nevertheless, after a long debate during which arguments swayed backwards and forwards for an entire day, Conference finally agreed to accept Scott as liaison on post-war planning. The passage to agreement was eased by diplomatic massage by London, who sent down David Roy, now Scott's successor as 'head of the Counting House' (in traditional language): in effect he was general manager. Roy had made his name nationally as a bookseller and manager of the first order. He was a strict disciplinarian but he knew when and how to say the right thing. 'The Firm had a very great regard for the Wholesale House Managers, realising the Wholesale Houses were an increasing source of power to the Firm.'[12] The move worked. The Conference ended on a friendly note.

So, for the moment, the cracks were papered over. But the major question remained. What were the functions and powers of the PWHs to be? Before the war, the PWHs had not supplied the Smith branches or stalls: their customers were independent, mostly small newsagents. Smith's own branches were all supplied from the Strand, and their location was in large measure dictated by the existence of communications capable of making these channels of supply possible: first, rail, more recently road and rail. After October 1940 the traditional system was abandoned. Central supply had made way in wartime for decentralised supply, with the PWHs supplying retail customers both inside and outside Smith's. Many people thought this was an improvement because it removed the delay in the distribution of papers to the non-Smith customers which was alleged to be a 'source of irritation' to the trade.

Some PWH managers had genuinely come to believe that Hambleden had already committed himself to continue this wartime system. It was (said the PWH Report on post-war planning) 'the unanimous opinion of the Wholesalers that it would be in the interests of the Firm as a whole that such an arrangement [the supply of Smith's bookstalls and shops by the PWHs] should be continued, if not extended . . .' They had 'been led to believe' that the principle of decentralisation had been accepted by the 'Executives of Strand House . . . We appear to be suffering from a mild form of censure.' They agreed that all goods supplied to the W. H. Smith branches could have been sold to the 'trade agents, but I have not heard it said' (this from Hardy as chairman) 'that the [London] Book Department could have supplied everything we have done'.

Apparently Hambleden's objection to this was that if the PWHs permanently captured the supply of goods to the W. H. Smith branches, many of the staff now serving in the war would lose their jobs. Hardy did not agree. '. . . the extra business which will come gradually after the War is over will completely absorb the Staff who will wish to return . . .'[13] Strand House would find itself embarrassed by its added tasks.

Hambleden and the partners pondered Hardy's memorandum for a month. The essence of their reply to the PWH management was of great importance. Should they continue the dialogue of diplomacy? Or should they put their corporate foot down? In the end they put their foot down. Couched – as their reply was – in civilised terms, it left no doubt where they stood. Though, as things proved, it still left the PWH managers with the feeling that their options were open. The partners began by explaining patiently that their decisions on the merits of decentralisation (against centralisation) had not been taken lightly. They had never given their blessing to 'a general policy of decentralisation'. What they had done contained no element of surprise. It was done with the welfare of the whole business, not just a single section, in view. Not even 'a mild form of censure' was in question: anything of that sort was far from the mind of the firm. As regards books and stationery it would always be open to the wholesale houses to supply the retail branches in cases where head-quarters were unable to do so. Hardy had spoken of 'the advantage of local supplies': thus Manchester would supply the Manchester bookstalls, Newcastle the Newcastle bookstalls, and so on. But this was only a fraction of the true picture. Already 'Liverpool supplies Southport, Manchester supplies Bolton, Newcastle supplies Stockton, Bristol supplies Weston-super-Mare. Etc.' Post-war, branches might continue to draw supplies from a local PWH but 'always provided that nothing interferes with the principle that *the branch must look to the Head Office as the main source of supply*'. (Author's italics.)

The letter from Strand House went on: it was not the case (as Hardy's memorandum seemed to imply) that the wholesale houses were wholly responsible for the increase in turnover at the shops and bookstalls. The true proportionate increase in book supply, for example, was only a small percentage of the total – say 7½ per cent? The partners believed the wholesale houses had a great future just as they had a great past. But they and their managers were a part, not the whole of the story They must regard themselves as 'members of a team which includes leaders in all sections of the business'.[14]

How the partners' letter was received by the PWHs is not on record. Probably the majority accepted it in good faith. They had, after all, no alternative. In the last analysis, the firm belonged to Billy Hambleden. As Hardy himself had remarked on an earlier occasion, the PWH managers could make suggestions, but 'in spite of what we decide the powers that be will have the last word'.[15] But a few obstinate old hankerings after total independence lingered. They evidently took the form, not of rational debate but of maverick exhibitionism of a kind deeply upsetting to Billy Hambleden. For Billy Hambleden represented, in almost exaggerated form, a corporate rebirth of the ideals which were supposed to be personified by his grandfather – 'Old Morality', the 'North Western Missionary'. A manager who worked with him at this time and even agreed (as did many others) that 'paternalism' was 'the source of our greatness', also believed that the Third Viscount Hambleden 'worried himself to death about staff, caring more about welfare than about profits'. He cared deeply too – perhaps even more than William Henry II – in a period when private capitalism was increasingly under siege, about the W. H. Smith 'public image'. It was this last which compelled him to call a meeting of all the managers of the wholesale houses on 16 January 1946. The manager of the Partners' Office simply announced that Lord Hambleden would address the meeting. There would be no other speakers and no questions. Supporting him on the platform were Michael Hornby, A. D. Power, Arthur Acland, and his brothers James Smith and David Smith.

His opening remarks were pitched in a diplomatic key. He was not there to imply any condemnation of the wholesale system. It had made magnificent progress in the past thirty years. He was only going to call attention to certain danger signals which had been showing recently in the hope they might be eliminated before it was too late.

After that came the plain speaking. Smith's policy had always been to give a large measure of freedom to the provincial wholesale houses. But recently there had been a change of attitude on the part of the houses. They were a part of the firm. Their policy – whether towards the Wholesalers' Federation or the unions in matters of labour – must follow that of the firm as a whole. They could not follow their own noses regardless of the interests of the firm as a whole. There had recently occurred some 'very unfortunate cases' which pointed to the lack of a real sense of responsibility in the PWH system. Two cases had been before the Courts involving house managers. True, in both cases, there was an element of bad luck, even unfairness on the part of the authorities. But the cases 'should not have happened and . . . if the individuals concerned had acted wisely and with a full sense of responsibility' would not have happened. Worse still, in another case, the conduct of a manager had done 'untold harm' to the reputation of the firm . . .

It was this which had obviously shaken him most.

In the towns where you work . . . and live, you are, first and foremost, the Firm's representatives . . . and ambassadors. Your conduct and your general behaviour are every whit as important as your success in business . . . [there must be] no ostentation . . . extravagance, excessive drinking . . . etc. We were not at all pleased, for instance, to hear of the party given to the B.B.C. at a well-known Golf Club when Church bells were rung for your benefit, and far too much show was made. Gaudy entertaining is not the way by which we have obtained business in the past . . . anything of the kind will tend to decrease the respect in which the Firm and the local Managers are held by the community . . . the manager must do his utmost to gain the respect of the town in which he lives, by showing a proper mixture of dignity, discretion and friendliness.

All this was high moral diet in the traditional manner sometimes ascribed to 'Old Morality' himself. Other passages reflected the less exalted ideals of the other partners who had to deal with Smith's negotiations with railway companies, Fleet Street newspapers and their circulation managers. For example, serious leakages of information had occurred about W. H. Smith's managers' earnings. The wholesale managers had to realise how much harm this did: how misleading such gossip might be to the representatives of other businesses (who were presumably either paid lower salaries or kept quiet about their pay):

> Can we possibly expect generous treatment or improvements of any kind if the heads of those firms with whom we are trading are full of this type of gossip? Again, how can anyone have respect for a firm if its representatives go about boasting in this way?[16]

So it ended. The audience departed, their tails between their legs. As one of them said, for some of the older managers it was 'one of the most humiliating days of their lives'.[17] Hambleden's harangue was a curious mixture of simple idealism, common sense and rather naïve didacticism. Its composition (something of an anti-climax beginning with ideals and ending with business tactics) suggests that he had, in the end, written it himself. The heart of the matter was the reputation of Smith's — the aspect of business management which, next to staff welfare, Billy Hambleden had always taken most seriously. He felt himself to be speaking for the whole firm. One striking feature of Smith's policy towards its staff had always been its willingness to treat anything short of seriously criminal offences with remarkable clemency. It must (as one observer remarked) have cost Billy Hambleden dear to make such a fuss about church bells.

Yet the speech has to be considered in context: and seen in context it had a certain psychological relevance. The war had barely finished. It had left Britain with a vast apparatus of bureaucracy shaped to deal with austerity. In some senses the British had become addicted to austerity as a way of life in wartime. Men who held extravagant parties, boasted of high pay and had church bells rung for them were offending against the inherent, egalitarian puritanism which is never far below the surface of British life and was at this time insufferably on top. But tactless ostentation and church bells were only the trigger.

The drift of the PWHs had for years been towards independence. This had brought great benefits. Pushed too far it was not consistent with the *actual* dependence of the provincial wholesale houses on the firm for support, assistance and advice in many important respects. The wiser provincial heads were well aware of this. A minority continued to demand the best of all possible worlds; and that in a world still reeling and staggering under the impact of the most destructive war in history. Hambleden's speech, simple, naïve though it might sound to a later generation, probably struck a chord of sympathy in many quarters where it was seen as the almost inevitable climax to a problem that had been a long time a-growing.

As for any effects on the morale or growth of the wholesale side of the business, they can only be interpreted in a very general way: for the period that followed was one of uninterrupted and unprecedented growth. Whereas the PWHs had previously grown while other sectors of the business had stagnated or declined, they now simply continued to grow – still faster than other sectors. If post-war 'policies' had the effect of inhibiting a process of growth previously dependent on a 'freedom of movement and action' as interpreted by the PWH managers themselves, it is difficult to detect it from the figures. The answer to this conundrum may well lie in a fairly complete change which came over the relationships between W. H. Smith's and the rest of their surrounding context of railways, newspaper production, bookselling, and wholesale and retail competition. For from this world many – not all – of the time-honoured shibboleths and suspicions were to be eliminated. In the end, it was to prove possible for the PWHs to supply both their own retailers and the independent retailers without serious controversy.

XV

The Structure of the Firm: Plus ça Change . . . ?

CHARLES HARRY ST JOHN HORNBY died on 26 April 1946. The directors'
minute on 6 May following conveys something of feelings too deep and
complex to be easily translated into words:

> . . . their deep regret at the loss of their colleague and elder brother, for
> whom they all had the greatest respect and affection, and to place on
> record the warm sense of gratitude which they owe him for the services
> he rendered to the Company since its formation in 1929, but above all
> they desire to acknowledge their still greater indebtedness to him for the
> way in which he devoted wholeheartedly his rare talents to the develop-
> ment of the business prior to its formation as a limited company. To him
> more than anyone else is due the expansion of the Firm of W. H. Smith
> & Son since he first entered it fifty-three years ago.[1]

Hornby was the last of the great Victorians who had given W. H. Smith
a national reputation and made its history read rather like a Victorian novel.
He had been the driving force in W. H. Smith's for over half a century.
Among the entrepreneurs of his time he had demonstrated a unique combination of qualities. He had combined enterprise and a sense of justice,
shrewdness and honesty, intelligence and integrity, craftsmanship and
culture. He had steered his ship with all the skill of a trained navigator. Yet
there were no handbooks from which he could learn. He had simply learnt
as he travelled along. He had asked no favours and given none. His manner
and methods were totally professional.

Press lords, journalists, family, colleagues, and workers joined to pay
tribute to a man who had been the same to all men and put his duty before

all else. It was characteristic of the English society of his day that he received no public honour or recognition of his business enterprise. Had he been a politician, railway director or civil servant he might well have been a knight, baronet or peer. But among his peers, in Fleet Street and scores of trading houses up and down Britain, his name was honoured.[2]

His methods and achievements have been recorded throughout this book and need not be repeated. One achievement that needs to be emphasised (since it was spread over a lifetime) was his success in building up a staff of professional managers in W. H. Smith. Hornby joined the company at a time when its fortunes were turning downward: William Henry Smith II was dead, Lethbridge was in semi-retirement, and no comparable executives were coming up to replace them. Not only did Hornby fill the gap and inject a new stream of ideas and energy into the business. He released the business from the stranglehold of the railways; he set about looking for suitable men to help him build a team of management – and he found them: Smart, Bayliss, Tyler, Kimpton and many others, who severally and jointly set Smith's back on the road to recovery and growth that lasted many years. Looking to the outside world where relations with press, railways, trade federations, publishers, etc., counted for so much, he had mended many a broken fence and cemented friendships with Northcliffe, Burnham, Beaverbrook, Guy Granet, Selbie and scores of outside men in the world of newspapers, publishing, printing, railways and elsewhere, whose goodwill was invaluable to his business. The threatened isolation that could have wrecked the business was avoided.

Out of the scores of tributes paid to his memory – by colleagues, business rivals, scholars, craftsmen, printers, antiquarians, philanthropists, etc., none is more striking than that of Cecil King. Recalling the *Daily Mail's* dependence on his uncle, Cecil King contrasted the state of its management when Northcliffe died and his business was left leaderless and lost in chaos accordingly. He compared its decomposition with that of W. H. Smith and the management nurtured by Hornby, 'an organisation which went on its way unperturbed by the death of St John Hornby, to whom so much of the present enterprise is due'.[3] The tribute was the more remarkable since Cecil King had more than once made it clear that no love was lost between himself and W. H. Smith's.

Characteristically, Hornby himself had been more modest. The credit for the shops venture of 1905–6 he had given to Tyler and Bayliss; for the stationery enterprise to Kimpton; for his financial support throughout, to his old Oxford rowing friend, the Second Viscount Hambleden. Those who only saw him at a distance sometimes thought him remote and formidable. Those who knew him better knew better. Those who knew him well knew his deep sense of humanity and justice. His personality, with all its pragmatism, quick intelligence but firm integrity, was stamped on every activity of the business as clearly as if it were in his own superb handwriting.

One after another, the problems of the business had been tackled by Hornby in person, as they occurred. The gaping holes in the management of the 1890s, the crises with the great railway companies in 1905 and 1906, the need for diversified activities to spread risk, cut costs and add to profits thereafter, the emergencies of two wars, the proliferating questions of staff and labour relations, costs, wages and terms of service in the inter-war years, the striking of equilibrium between decaying activities and promising innovations, the passing of one generation of owners and partners, the arrival of new and the choice of successors . . . all these Hornby had settled by consultation; the partners were a team, not a collection of soloists. But ultimately it was almost always he who had taken the final decisions: in person. Doubtless he made up his mind as he bicycled between his Chelsea home and his Strand office. Sir Ernest Barker, a Professor who knew Manchester, London, Oxford and Cambridge Universities equally well, wrote of him:

> . . . a man of grave and kindly courtesy with a serious poise of mind which was united to a most winning smile. His judgement was unerring: he seemed incapable of making a mistake: he had a *mitis sapientia* and it might be said of him, in the words of Horace, that the votes of all men were given to the man *qui miscuit utile dulci* – who combined in a happy alliance the claims of business and beauty . . . Happy the firm which worked under such leaders and such auguries.[4]

The Professor of Political Science at Cambridge overstated the case a little; not much. Hornby was not infallible. He sometimes tarried in the interests of charity and justice too long. He prolonged the printing and binding investment longer than he should: perhaps because he was a devotee of those crafts. He sometimes continued to defend a cause because he distrusted his opponents' motives rather than because of any profound belief in the cause itself. He was sometimes too charitable in honouring his opponents' motives when in his heart he knew they were false. His manner could be formidable but it concealed a great fund of humanity. He was human in his desire not only to be just but to be seen to be just. His occasional letters to *The Times* on economic and social problems reveal a deep and genuine liberalism. To compare his contribution to the growth and reputation of the business he guided with that of his predecessors and successors is to waste time and effort. His contribution was unique, and ranks him among the foremost entrepreneurs of his time.

Less than two years after Hornby's death the partners had to face another serious loss; the death of Billy Hambleden. Since Freddy's death in 1928, Hornby had been guide and counsellor to his son (who had by inheritance acceded to the ownership of the business at the age of 25). Billy had proved a responsive and responsible pupil. The great business decisions of state (such as the Great Western and London, Midland and Scottish railway contracts) he had tactfully left to Hornby and the departmental chiefs: his personal contribution and responsibility had centred round staff matters, education, training and welfare. These, and the almost hereditary family involvement in philanthropic activities, in charities (hospitals especially), Billy had made his own: though he had always watched the commercial, financial and industrial affairs of the business with a keen eye.

Billy's dedication to human relations within the business was to be important. But at his accession the most pressing problems concerned the financial structure of the firm. In March 1929, largely in order to meet death duties payable upon Freddy's estate, a public limited liability company (Hambleden Estates Ltd) was formed to buy and hold the properties from which the old partnership of W. H. Smith & Son had traded. Most of the shares in the new company were held, directly or indirectly, by the former partners but a million pounds were borrowed from public subscribers in the shape of a debenture. W. H. Smith & Son now became a private limited company, W. H. Smith & Son Ltd, the ordinary capital in which was held by Lord Hambleden, he and the three senior former partners (Hornby, Power and Robin Acland) holding most of the preference shares. This company acquired the business, stock-in-trade, etc., of the old partnership and rented back its former trading properties (now held by the new public company) on lease from that company. This provided greater financial flexibility. In other respects the organisation, management and day-to-day running of the business were little affected. The 'directors' of the new companies were still known, inside Smith's, as 'the partners'.

Between 1946 and 1949 – years when many companies, smaller as well as larger than Smith's, had become public limited liability companies – Smith's had remained a partnership or a chiefly private limited liability company. Within this legal and financial structure, as Cecil King had observed, there had nevertheless been gradual change and reorganisation. The division and sub-division of responsibilities already described in many places in this narrative had resulted in the growth of a number of different London buildings with different functions – Strand House, Portugal Street, still the head office proper, combining the ancient nightly ritual of newspaper distribution to the shops and stalls, with accounting, salaries, wages, staff matters, pensions, etc., grouped round what was the still undivided Partners' Room. Bridge House, Lambeth, looked after stationery and binding. Until its closure in 1937, the printing works in Stamford Street, across the river, housed printing. Until 1932 the stables were accommodated at Water Street. And so on. Over each of these widely varying departments, each increasingly demanding specialised knowledge and a network of personal relations with the railways, shops, stalls, press and publishers, presided a departmental head. It was upon them – the descendants of the early staff of 1900 (almost literally, for Smith's retained throughout all its grades of staff and all its activities strong family connections) – that the smooth daily working of this high-pressure machinery of procurement, distribution and sale depended. The departmental chiefs who managed those proliferating activities were in turn now responsible to the directors. In 1932 there were seven, eight in 1933, nine in 1935.[5]

In 1932 five directors, by 1936 seven, were still either members of the Smith family or closely related. The close Hornby friendship dated back the best part of half a century. Between the 'partners' there were no strict dividing lines of responsibility: Michael Hornby had come to be regarded as the authority on the wholesale side of the business. He was the natural choice as Smith's director of John Heywood (Manchester) when a share in that concern was acquired. Arthur Acland kept a close eye on the Smith transport subsidiary and had special responsibility for the planning and organisation of the various buildings which formed the London headquarters. But there was nothing sacrosanct about such divisions of labour. Partners or directors, they were expected to have a working knowledge of everything that was going on and an acquaintance with as many sides of the business and as many of the staff as possible. This was physically symbolised by their occupation of one undivided room. This tradition was deliberately carried over from the Strand to Portugal Street.

Inevitably, though, time, size and the division of labour had put a distance between the partners and staff, even between departmental chiefs and staff. The days of Lethbridge and Awdry, when the partners would call the clerk of some remote village bookstall before them to congratulate him, explain the error of his ways or listen to the troubles of a widow of a departed newspacker, were becoming a memory. The successor of David Roy, chief of the Book Department (Tom Hodges, later president of the

Booksellers' Association) recalled that in the 1930s when he joined the firm, Roy was rarely seen even by his own department. 'The Manager was a very remote figure.' So was promotion. 'Smith's were very paternal, a happy firm to work for.'[6] Staff stayed with them: but they also tended to stay put. It was not easy to treat promotion as a single problem in a business whose structure consisted of headquarters in London and over a thousand operating units spread over the face of England and Wales, most employing a staff that could be counted on the fingers of one hand. There was some disaffection in the Book Department among, for example, young men from grammar schools who felt they had fitted themselves for more responsible jobs. This lack of opportunity was, again, a common feature (and complaint) in many Victorian businesses. There were too many Bob Cratchits. It was without doubt this kind of inelasticity of the business structure which had caught Billy Hambleden's eye and stimulated his plan for a special Staff and Staff Welfare Department.

Billy's concern was therefore much more than a conventional top dressing: more than the paternal friendliness of the Victorian or Edwardian days. In the new society that business faced in the post-1918 world, active development of staff relations and their increasing involvement in the running of essential business activities were of critical importance. Billy's personality was important in a role which some men might have interpreted trivially, others patronisingly. His cousin Lord David Cecil, critic and writer and Oxford don, wrote when Billy died:

> I have never known anyone who made a stronger impression or had a more compelling influence on those who knew him . . . His gentleness masked a courageous determination to do only what he thought right, and a simple honesty which made it impossible for him to say what he did not think.[7]

This was not an overstatement, as the provincial wholesale house managers had discovered.

In the first half of the twentieth century, there had been a number of pointers to a problem which beset the W. H. Smith business, though not to a critical point until Billy's death. The problem was one common enough among individuals and institutions everywhere whose endowment was entirely or largely in land and property – as W. H. Smith's largely was. A thrifty owner might save enough to face the odd exceptional demand for capital if and when it arose. The unthrifty had often drifted into the hands of the usurer or the bankruptcy court. The records of the old English nobility and gentry are littered with such cases. Sometimes the more careful, faced by unavoidable necessity and guided by suitable legal advice, had recourse to mortgages or bank loans which were prudently redeemed over the years.

At least three times the proprietor of W. H. Smith found himself in a similar situation. For a high proportion of the W. H. Smith capital assets took the form of offices, shops, warehouses, etc., in London or the provinces. The first time was in the period of the loss of the great rail contracts when large sums of money had to be found to buy the alternative outlets of urban shops. This caused a sharp rise in the volume of capital employed between 1905 and 1913. To finance purchases on this extra-ordinary scale (previously most of Smith's properties outside the Strand were merely wooden, more or less removable, structures) Freddy Smith provided more capital. Later there was talk of bringing these scattered purchases together under an umbrella formed by a property company. It was set up in 1922. Its name was Hambleden Properties. Its existence and function were to be important in the more critical situations of 1929 and especially 1949.

It will be remembered that in 1908 the normal provision in the partner-ship deeds which made Freddy responsible for producing all the necessary capital for the business was varied for the first time: if it was desired and necessary, and if W.F.D.S. (Freddy) was 'unwilling to find such additional Capital', any other partner might find it.[8] This provision became a regular feature for the future, and had brought about those financial interests of additional partners which were to be an important feature of the new companies formed in 1929.

By the ingenious essay in borrowing in 1929, Smith's had escaped from the tight corner into which they had been pushed by the illiquid nature of their capital, their shortage of cash for business purposes, including an unusual number of business acquisitions, together with the urgent need to settle the estate duties payable on Freddy's death. This left control and continuity of policy safely in the hands of the existing partners while simultaneously opening up channels to the public through which cash for working the business and meeting emergencies might be found if necessary.

Or so it seemed. The two decades in which Billy Hambleden represented the Smith tradition were very far from easy. Economic depression, labour unrest, war and all its problems were the context within which he had to work. For him, as his advisers urged upon him, there were additional financial disadvantages arising out of the 1929 settlement. As the owner of

the ordinary shares in W. H. Smith & Son Ltd, his potential income from
them was continuously placed to reserve.⁹ The longer this went on the
more difficult it would be to find the money to pay the duties on *his* death.
Billy was in fact financing the business himself out of what should have
been his private income. It is fair to infer from the correspondence that
ensued that his major objective *was* what he said it was: to pass on the
business and its control 'in as nearly as may be the same condition as that in
which he inherited it' and at the same time assure the future of the present
managing directors (as the former partners were now called) 'in the event
of his dying before them'.¹⁰

All this resulted in a scheme to capitalise a part of the undivided profits of
the business and sums placed to reserve so that the ordinary shareholder
might be compensated by an issue of debentures which he could then sell
for cash. This was late in 1936. It was 1940 and the Second World War was
on before correspondence with Smith's solicitors, Birchams, shows that a
similar scheme to avoid or reduce the impact of death duties 'in the event
of your death' was turned down by counsel.¹¹ '. . . the whole matter is
now in abeyance until the War is over.'¹² They referred to the matter
having become more acute because of the greater risk to life in wartime
and higher rates of tax. That was undoubtedly true: whether it was also
pressed by Billy with some intimations of mortality that were not mentioned one can only guess.

When Billy Hambleden died, in 1948, the assets of W. H. Smith &
Son Ltd were valued at £10 million. (This was later, and reluctantly,
reduced by the Estate Duty Office to £9.75 million.) Lord Hambleden's
share in this came to £8,182,450. Duty was calculated (75 per cent) at
£6,136,837.10.0. Smith's solicitors were told to accept these figures 'with
the reservation that it might not be possible to raise the amount of duty
required . . .' They would therefore proceed with the formation of a
holding company to acquire all the issued share capital of W. H. Smith &
Son Ltd. A proportion of the shares would then be offered for sale to the
public in order to raise the amount of duty required.

The name of this new holding company was immaterial. Why not
W.H.S. (Holdings) Ltd? As sometimes in high tragedy, this evoked a
comic interlude: there was (it seemed) a small Yorkshire firm incorporated
with this title sixteen years before. So the holding company was turned
into P.J.D. (Holdings) Ltd – 'any name would suffice so long as it did not
indicate the connection . . . [with] W. H. Smith & Son Ltd' and thus give
rise to speculative dealings.¹³ So it went forward. The public would be
offered a large proportion of the preference shares in the new company so

that as much as possible of the equity of the holding company should be left in the hands of the Smith family and their friends, safe from outside raiders intent on altering the traditional business (and business ethos) of Smith's.

And so it was done: under, let it be said, some pressure. For times were not good. A crisis involving devaluation of the pound was impending, and there had been a long lull in capital issues to the public induced by an equally long decline in gilt-edged prices. The underwriters made it clear that if underwriting did not begin by 25 August, they were doubtful if it could be done at all. Matters were all the more urgent since the Midland Bank was owed £2 million advanced to Lord Hambleden's executors to enable the grant of probate to be obtained.

In the event, the authorisation came in time, the issue went forward, brilliantly successful. It attracted offers calculated at £33 millions and the ordinary shares were over-subscribed 5½ times. The death duties of £6,136,837.10.0 were paid. The proportion of ordinary shares (which carried the votes and therefore the ultimate control of the business) owned by Billy Hambleden had been 100 per cent: now the proportion owned by his successors in title and members of the family was reduced to 34 per cent. This proportion was boosted by allotments to current or retired staff and 'friends' to about 52 per cent, and reduced allotments to (presumably) less 'committed' shareholders from outside fragmented their voting power.

The 1949 operation was primarily due to the pressing need to find money for death duties; not for the business. In the end it left the same people in charge of W. H. Smith as were there before. Billy's brother, David, succeeded him as 'Governing Director'. He, Michael Hornby, A. W. Acland, and a newcomer back from a German prisoner of war camp, Charles Troughton, continued their contracts as managing directors for another ten years. Thus the original Smith family which created the original business, with their friends who had helped them to sustain and quicken its growth, were still in possession of sufficient shares to control the destiny of the business. 'Going public' – in a purely financial sense – was important but it was less of a managerial watershed than might have been expected, less the passing of an old order than its rescue from the fiscal storm. In many respects and for several years, W. H. Smith & Son Ltd went about its business much as it had done before.

As things were to turn out, the business was on the brink of a new period of expansion. The new financial structure was there to back this if need be: the more urgent task was once again – as in the 1860s, the 1890s and the 1930s – to find the right management team to meet the needs of a new age.

Except for the death duty problem which had brought a company structure with limited liability into being, the business was to continue, as it had in the past, to generate its own capital. The only recourse to outside help (from the City) was to bridge temporary gaps in capital supply caused by large building projects.[14]

PART II

Enterprise and Popular Culture

XVI

The Circulating Library

ON 16 JUNE 1860, the *Athenaeum* published a notice:

> Messrs. W. H. Smith & Son, taking advantage of the convenience
> afforded by their railway bookstalls, are about to open a Subscription
> Library on a large scale, something like that of Mr Mudie's. The book-
> stalls will, in fact, become local libraries, small but select, with the
> immense advantage of hourly communication by train, with a vast
> central library in London.[1]

This new venture into which W. H. Smith II launched himself was
destined to become, side by side with the bookstalls, the emblem by which
the firm was to become best known to the travelling, literate, professional
and business middle class of Victorian England. Its immediate inspiration
was, as the *Athenaeum* rightly diagnosed, the library founded in the 1840s
by Charles Edward Mudie. Originally in Southampton Row, it had moved
in 1852 to New Oxford Street and Museum Street, later spawning offspring
in the City and branching out to Birmingham and Manchester. Mudie's
was not only an inspiration: it was a provocation to Smith's. For in 1859
Smith's seem to have put a proposal to Mudie's that it should set up libraries
at Smith's railway bookstalls.[2] Mudie refused. Either Smith's offer was too
low (rumoured to be £1,000 a year), or possibly Mudie's felt that its resources would be stretched too tightly: circulating libraries were a sponge
which absorbed capital and managerial resources like water, and Mudie
knew it. It seems a fair inference that it was Mudie's rejection which
impelled Smith into what would be exactly a century of activity as a
competing circulating library (the Smith library was to last until 1961).

Mudie's was almost certainly the immediate model for the new Smith enterprise: but there were many older and remoter precedents. So far in the history of popular literature, high costs of production and relatively primitive technology on the one hand, low incomes and a limited degree of literacy on the other, had combined to foster the collective purchase and use of newspapers and magazines: of books also (see pages 33–6). Many potential readers who could not afford to buy for themselves even a cheap reprint, let alone the standard, massive, three-volume novel, were happy to pay an annual subscription to a book club or society or to a bookseller. (Direct descendants of these ancient collective aids to reading still exist, for example in the Cambridge and Oxford colleges.)

The first recorded circulating library in Britain – characteristically – was founded in Scotland: education had long been high in the Scotsman's order of priorities. To hire a book instead of having to buy it could mean the difference between one or two meals a day. Hence the founding about 1725 of a library at Luckenbooths in Edinburgh by the poet, Allan Ramsay, at his bookshop. Ramsay's library survived until 1832. Meanwhile the idea had taken root in many English towns – many an Athenaeum and Lyceum embellished even small provincial market towns. Birmingham, Liverpool, Leeds and Bristol similarly provided for the needs of a well-to-do merchant middle class between 1757 and 1772. London already had its private libraries, to which in 1841 (largely by the efforts of Thomas Carlyle) the London Library was added, steadily fulfilling its ambition '... to contain books in all departments of literature and philosophy and in all languages ....'.

None of this passed without criticism. The need to protect the public morals of Scotland against London vice called up thunder from the ecclesiastical historian, the Rev. Robert Wodrow, against '... all the villanous profane and obscene books and playes printed at London by Curle and others ... gote down from London by Allan Ramsay, and lent out for an easy price, to young boyes, servant women of the better sort, and gentlemen, and vice and obscenity dreadfully propagated'.[3]

The heterogeneity by social class of those exposed to the moral threat is interesting. The propensity of servants to imitate their masters and mistresses was a commonplace of social observers of the time. In *The Rivals*, Sheridan later, tongue in cheek, developed the *motif* of the infectious quality of immorality:

Madam, a circulating library in a town is an evergreen tree of diabolical knowledge. It blossoms through the year. And depend upon it, Mrs

Malaprop, that they who are so fond of handling the leaves will long for the fruit at last.⁴

Suspicion of novels and plays persisted among respectable people and even grew until late Victorian days (and after). It was offset by the novels of Walter Scott, Bulwer Lytton, Harrison Ainsworth and the whole school of romantic, respectable and, preferably, historical novelists who simultaneously shaped and ministered to the taste of Victorian Britain. 'Trashy novels' still continued but to a considerable extent were to be eliminated by a process of silent censorship from the contents of the circulating libraries. When Ruskin objected to circulating libraries it was not on moral but on hygienic and economic grounds: in his lecture *Of Kings' Treasuries* Ruskin wrote: 'We call ourselves a rich nation, and we are filthy and foolish enough to thumb each other's books out of circulating libraries!'⁵

The fact was that attitudes had changed since the first half of the century, with its social violence, its deep political divisions over reform and its agonising transition from an agrarian to an industrial society. Prose fiction had become respectable – 'a rational amusement', an accepted way for a professional man or woman of letters to make a living. 'We have become a novel-reading people', said Anthony Trollope in one of his *Four Lectures* in 1870, 'from the Prime Minister down to the last-appointed scullery-maid ... Poetry we also read, and history, biography and the social and political news of the day. But all our other reading put together hardly amounts to what we read in novels.'⁶

As an interested party, Trollope may have been guilty of a little understandable exaggeration: his picture of English culture is nevertheless true to life. Compared with the Germans, the English might inhabit a *Land ohne Musik*; compared with the Italians or the Dutch, they might have to count their geniuses in the visual arts in (relatively) penny numbers. Their culture was, and remains, above all a literary and, in its way, democratic culture, and the reading public which had inhabited its railway trains from earliest days down to the rush-hour London Tubes of the present day bears witness to it. This was the public whose tastes or preferences were W. H. Smith II's opportunity: tastes and preferences which he, in turn, encouraged and for a time helped to shape, in directions in which they seemed to want to go.

The problem of the book market – high costs and low incomes – was a commonplace. W. H. Smith saw further. The W. H. Smith library was primarily launched in response to the strong demand, especially from customers in rural areas, for books – to be borrowed. Smith's had already been selling books on their railway bookstalls since the later 1840s: hard on the heels of their first contract with the LNWR. in 1848, they had put a plan before that company for a 'Travelling (or Circulating) library' specifically for their bookstalls serving the LNWR.[7] The large enterprise of 1860 must be viewed against this smaller pilot enterprise of over a decade earlier.

In selling and lending books, they had been brought up sharply against the problem of the price and availability of suitable books. But this was only one aspect of the matter. The root of the trouble had been discerned by that acute observer of economic affairs in the late eighteenth century, Dr Johnson. Johnson himself was the son of a Lichfield bookseller and stationer. He remembered how old Michael Johnson had gone far and wide as a travelling bookseller to fill the gap in the book trade left by the scarcity of provincial booksellers. When Samuel carried out his famous investigation of the inadequacies of the Clarendon Press, he pointed above all to the disastrous squeeze imposed upon country booksellers by publishers. Denied a fair profit, they had inevitably been driven out of existence. This faulty structure persisted. In his station bookstalls W. H. Smith II saw a means of repairing it and adding another valuable facet to his enterprise. Books, to be borrowed – and sold – were added to newspapers as an increasingly important article of trade.

In the 1850s, Jabez Sandifer, manager of the Book Department since the 1840s and later responsible also for the library, entered into an arrangement with Chapman & Hall, the publishers. Sandifer was a man of diligence and perception who knew the book trade intimately. He had long experienced the difficulty of laying hands on an adequate supply of light fiction, cheap enough and readable enough to give travellers a means of passing long and tedious rail journeys. One answer might have been for Smith's to publish themselves. Sandifer was shrewd enough to see that this would almost certainly arouse opposition among their publishing clients and open the way to retaliatory policies by the publishing industry against Smith's. Better therefore to use the service of a reliable and friendly publisher: a discreet arrangement with Chapman & Hall would serve them and Smith's equally well. Smith's apparently acquired the copyright of a number of authors of successful novels: Chapman & Hall did the printing and publishing (under the title of the Select Library of Fiction). Thus was launched a partnership which lasted for some twenty years and put into Chapman & Hall's lists such popular writers as the Irish novelist Charles Lever, Ouida, Charles Reade, Hawley Smart, Edmund Yates, R. D. Blackmore and many others, now mostly forgotten. The arrangement ameliorated the problems of the bookstalls and library: it did not by any means solve them completely.

Nevertheless, the library grew. A circular of 1862 advertised the resources it offered. A small selection of books could be found at each of the company's principal bookstalls. Subscribers could change books daily at the library where they were registered but they could transfer their registration from one bookstall to another by giving notice. Table XVI.1 shows the subscription rates for London. Clubs and reading societies paid special rates for 24 volumes or more.[8]

TABLE XVI.1 W. H. SMITH LIBRARY SUBSCRIPTION RATES, 1862

No. of volumes borrowed at a time	6 months			12 months		
	£	s.	d.	£	s.	d.
1		12	0	1	1	0
2		17	6	1	11	6
4	1	3	0	2	2	0
8	1	15	0	3	3	0
15	3	0	0	5	5	0

In one sense Smith's were old hands at the library game. An early innovation when W. H. Smith I had moved from Mayfair to 192 Strand was the 'New Reading Room'. A notice in *John Bull* for 9 December 1821 called the attention of friends and public to the offer of an agreeable Christmas present: for a modest subscription of 5s. a month, or larger sums for longer periods, up to £1. 11s. 6d. a year, subscribers could read newspapers, reviews, magazines any weekday, 'from Nine o'Clock in the Morning till Nine in the Evening'.[9] Yet a reading room was essentially single and simple in its organisation and function. Circulating libraries were multiple and complex. Of their very different problems Smith's had no experience. And in some ways their experience as booksellers and newsagents was unhelpful to running a library: for it became evident that traditionally the circulating libraries that had developed since the eighteenth century had influenced publishers towards maintaining higher, not lower, prices for books: expensive books were an insurance against the risk that readers would borrow rather than buy. Moreover in any competition Smith's had the edge over the retail bookseller by reason of the extra

discount on book prices which they were able to extract from publishers.
Few market structures are more complex than that of the book trade. In
their predicament as new entrants to the library business on a scale involving
large numbers of bookstall-libraries, W. H. Smith took one obvious model
for guidance (and improvement): Mudie's.

In his old age, in 1884, Charles Edward Mudie left on record the motives
for founding his library in 1842:

> Seldom could I get a book that I wished for, and I was fain to buy what
> I wanted. The idea suddenly struck me that many other young men
> were in similar case with myself. I had by this time accumulated a
> number of books, so I determined to launch out a library on my own
> lines.[10]

For nearly another century Mudie's lent books of all kinds to its subscribers,
fiction and non-fiction; it sold tickets for the opera and the theatres, and
absorbed other Victorian London booksellers and libraries such as Hook-
hams and Booths. In 1864 Mudie's became a limited company in which
half the capital was provided by Mudie, the other half by such publishers
as John Murray and Richard Bentley; naturally enough – Mudie was their
best customer. But Charles Edward retained control and management
until about 1884. His last five years were overshadowed by the death of his
eldest son: a younger son, Arthur, took over a rather ramshackle and old-
fashioned business. But from the 1860s to the 1890s, Mudie's was the
most powerful of the lending libraries. W. H. Smith's library was its only
real competitor and duly flattered it by imitating – but simultaneously
improving on – its methods.

To Wilkie Collins, W. H. Smith II and Charles Edward Mudie were
'the twin tyrants of literature'. When Mudie, in 1873, asked Bentley (the
publishers) to change the title of Collins's *The New Magdalen*, the author's
fury was loosed on Bentley. The letter reveals the helpless indignation of
an author powerless before the might of Mudie's:

> Nothing will induce me to modify the title. His proposal would be an
> impertinence if he was not an old fool . . . But the serious side of this
> affair is that this ignorant fanatic holds my circulation in his pious hands.
> Suppose he determines to check my circulation – what remedy have
> *we*? What remedy have his subscribers?[11]

The trouble was that in general publishers did pretty well out of the prime business of the libraries – so long as the style and form of the novel remained what it had been since the success of Walter Scott's *Kenilworth* established it: a solid two- or three-volume affair. On this ponderous, formidable base Mudie's rule was built. It crumbled for two kinds of reasons. Internally, it was conservative, shunning innovation, declining orders proposed on the new-fangled telephone, maintaining hand-written correspondence by the proprietors as the medium of business and keeping provincial branches under strict surveillance from the London headquarters.

Any sharp edge which the competition with the new rival might have had was blunted by the extraordinary similarity and sympathetic relationship between the 'twin tyrants' themselves. Their lives and careers spanned much the same period. Both were deeply religious – W. H. Smith II was a thwarted ordinand, Mudie a devout nonconformist preacher and hymn-writer. Both were dedicated social reformers. They served together on the first London School Board. Both were resident in Westminster. Each viewed the business he organised and developed as a vital part of his moral responsibility to the public. Neither was shaken by occasional criticism from a minority avant-garde in his belief that he had a mandate to protect public and private morality against any corrupting influence in the literature he distributed. Moral sword in hand – in three volumes or one – they advanced on the enemy of illiteracy or 'trashy' literature; conquest of the growing army of satisfied subscribers confirmed their confidence in their judgment. 'All considerations of their practices, all praise of their usefulness, all protests against their monopoly must be placed against this background of steadily increasing numbers of pleased Victorians.'[12]

The differences between the two firms were often impalpable. All the same they were important, perhaps in the end decisive. Smith's subscription charges and terms were almost a replica of Mudie's, but their growing railway network gave them an important advantage in the number of their outlets (though it may have increased their running costs). It was also an automatic reminder of the indispensable need for punctuality and efficiency. Among the many problems of running a railway bookstall was shortage of space. This in turn led Smith's to look less favourably than their older competitor on the ponderous weight and size of the three-volume novel. They therefore inclined towards the cheap single-volume reprint: what came to be known as 'yellowbacks'. Not only did these take up less room on the stall: they were more convenient for the travelling reader to carry, hold or read in the confined space of a railway carriage. '. . . a Railway' (*Punch* had commented with good reason) 'is decidedly the best vehicle going for circulating a Library.'[13] While therefore Mudie's deliberately fostered the three-volume novel in spite of – one could say because of – its high cost, Smith's developed the cheaper single-volume through a number of publishers – not only Chapman (whose specially produced volumes were cancelled in the early 1880s) but also Blackwood, Bentley, Routledge and a number of other publishers. The long predominance of the three-volume novel, far too costly at more than 30s. a set for any but a small minority of buyers, and even for library subscribers at least three times as heavy on their borrowing subscription as the single volume, was already being undermined by W. H. Smith's innovatory library methods in the 1870s. Not only were publishers encouraged to produce cheaper and smaller books for circulating and for sale – a yellowback sold on the railway bookstalls for 2s. – but other ways of reducing book costs were explored. Sandifer and his successors, Faux and Palmer, would negotiate with publishers for unbound sheets. Michael Sadleir found a copy of George Eliot's *Felix Holt* – normally bound by its publisher, Blackwood, in brown – bound in bright blue by Smith's.[14] The discovery of the economics – and possible profits – of binding were to lead to an important diversification of Smith's in the twentieth century (see page 233).

So Smith's library was established and grew. Table XVI.2 shows its turnover in the half century after its foundation. This picture of growth is

TABLE XVI.2 TURNOVER OF THE LIBRARY, 1860–1913[15]

Year	£
1860	2,410*
1870	33,963
1880	44,281
1890	52,661
1900/1	69,120
1910/11	88,635
1913/14	114,835

* Half a year only.

misleading without a framework of reference and comparison. Neither the turnover nor the profits of the library ever represented more than a very modest fraction of Smith's main sources of business in the years before the First World War: there were other reasons for the importance which was attached to it by public opinion as well as by the firm itself (see page 321). The growth was less even than Table XVI.2 suggests. It slowed down in the 1880s, stopped and reversed about 1893–4, picked up in the 1890s, suffered along with the rest of the business between 1904–6 and rose to unprecedented heights in the better pre-war years. These vicissitudes call for comment, concealing as they do important – even revolutionary – changes in the book trade.

First among these was the steady decline and finally dramatic disappearance of the old three-volume novel. Smith's had always liked it less than Mudie's. Authors mostly disliked it because they had little or no benefit from books designed for the use of library subscribers and proprietors. Publishers were divided about it. By the 1880s Mudie's had been forced into line with Smith's by economic circumstances. Traditionally Mudie's profits had come to an appreciable extent from the sale of second-hand (*ex libris*) books. Now, as the popularity of the novel brought forward ever-growing numbers of novelists, cheap reprints became a profitable activity for publishers. They often appeared a few months after the original issue. Together with the increase in free libraries in London and provincial England, these developments hit Mudie's hard. When Arthur Mudie took over from his father about 1884 one of his first actions was to propose a meeting with the publisher (also his partner in Mudie's) George Bentley. There was, he wrote to Bentley, serious over-production of books and this was pressing hard on the libraries: for several years 'not one in twelve' of the three-volume novels had paid its way.[16]

Difficult as things were, another decade passed before anything positive was done. Then, in 1894, on 27 June, the bomb was dropped. Smith's and Mudie's sent out letters to the publishers, making the same basic points. They had noted with concern (wrote Smith's) the growing demand by library subscribers for two- and three-volume novels. This was creating a serious problem. The multi-volume novel was as expensive as it was ephemeral. The original issue was rapidly overtaken by cheap reprints: the result – mountains of unsaleable stock. They therefore submitted that from the following January, the price of novels in sets should not exceed 4s. a volume, less discount. No cheap reprints should appear until twelve months after the date of first publication.[17]

A week or two later, the Society of Authors came into line with the libraries. Novelists had long been unhappy with their lot. The publishers and booksellers, on the other hand, were thrown into hopeless disarray. The *Publishers' Circular* was torn between an immediate instinct to denounce this 'revolution in literature', to lament chivalrously its consequences (unemployment and poverty for the novelists) and express the conviction that writers generally should 'urge publishers to withstand the demands of the libraries' (7 July 1894). They were also convinced that the libraries would be hoist with their own petard. If cheap novels were to become standard practice, the public would forsake the libraries and flock to the booksellers. They ended with a call to close ranks. 'Since such ancient rivals as Messrs. W. H. Smith & Son and Messrs. Mudie can combine to protect their own interests is it not time for publishers to follow their example and that of their friends the authors and book-sellers?'[18]

The call fell on deaf ears. The authors, though not in love with the libraries, objected to the publishers of three-volume novels no less. The more astute publishers hastened to make their peace with the libraries. Among them were Chatto & Windus, A. D. Innes and William Heinemann who, two days before the foregoing militant issue of the *Publishers' Circular*, announced a new novel, *The Manxman*, by Hall Caine. A special note, with three asterisks, made all clear: 'There will be no edition in three vols.'[19] As the din of battle was swiftly stilled, it was plain beyond doubt that the time for valour was gone: the new motto was *sauve qui peut*. There took place the belated formation of the Publishers' Association to try to match the collective action of the libraries, the booksellers and the authors.

A letter to the *Publishers' Circular* from Andrew Tuer, of the Leadenhall Press, struck a new note of realism. The situation that had prompted the libraries' letter had to be faced: briefly 'trade is bad, library subscriptions are falling off, and *there are too many books*.' It used to be believed that one in every three books paid for the losses on the other two: Tuer questioned whether one in twenty now paid. The masses '. . . from whom was expected so much, buy their literature in weekly penn'orths . . . Not so very long ago I wrote a paper (copied by Messrs. Smith & Son) the keynote of which was *there are too many books*. Things were bad then, but they are worse now, and will be worse still. *There are too many books*, and yea, verily, they are mostly bad.'[20]

That was the end of the argument: there was nothing left to do but agree to blame the free public libraries and urge the offending circulating libraries – Smith's especially – to reduce their subscriptions and improve trade. And, in due time, that is what happened. The Smith Library Department turnover, after dropping to a level only four-fifths of that of 1890, rose until, in the year before the outbreak of the First World War, it reached a record figure of nearly £115,000. Net returns, similarly, having fallen to a loss of a few hundreds in 1893–4, rose to a profit of over £20,000 in 1914/15 or some three times the annual profits previously shown in good years.

So far the difficulties faced by the Victorian libraries were economic in character: it was the general opinion that these were bad times for trade in general. But for the libraries there were quite different problems as the century drew to a close: they arose from changes in the structure of society, in social habits and moral opinions – and these created awkward problems for those responsible for providing literature to be borrowed by, or sold to, the public. Broadly, the circulating library was vulnerable to two risks: it could be criticised – even taken to law – for circulating any literature that a plaintiff could allege was libellous or obscene: or it could be attacked, by authors, readers, members of the avant-garde, for failing or refusing to circulate reading matter – 'censoring' it as critics alleged – because it might be offensive to majority opinion among library subscribers or even potentially libellous or obscene. In short, the management of the circulating library found itself perpetually walking the tight-rope; its equilibrium depended on a constant vigilance for the law, opinion and, of course, the goodwill of its business.

An instance of the kind of problem the library faced emerges from an incident in the life of Bishop Walsham How. The W. H. Smith library had made up the number of volumes required with a 'realistic' novel which one of the Bishop's sons began to read. Finding himself unable to continue reading it, he piously took the book to his father and told him that though no prude, he was unable to wade through this 'unclean matter'. Whereupon the Bishop wrote to W. F. D. Smith ('Freddy', son of W. H. Smith II), already a Member of Parliament. The book was withdrawn and the Bishop was assured that any other books by the same author would be carefully examined before being allowed to circulate.[21]

The exact date of the incident is unknown, and we do not know if the author was the same whose novels created the major furore in connection with the refusal by W. H. Smith's library to circulate in 1894. This was the Irish novelist, George (Augustus) Moore (1852–1933). An early novel, *A Modern Lover*, had been the subject of a brush between the author and Smith's in 1883. Two lady subscribers wrote in to complain of a passage in the novel describing how a girl sat as a nude model to the artist. The book was at once placed on 'limited circulation', i.e. it was supplied only to readers who asked for it.[22] In 1894, *Esther Waters*, Moore's new, probably his best, novel and certainly the one by which he was to be best remembered, was published. Smith's declined to circulate it: so, at first, did Mudie's. They were promptly attacked by Hall Caine, himself a highly successful writer whose works had been attacked by critics for exploring situations thought best left alone by much Victorian opinion.

Moore himself was not slow to attack. Of a land-owning gentry family of Ballyglass, County Mayo, Moore was a characteristic figure in the *fin-de-siècle* 'decadent' movement; his Irish pride and his artist's sensibilities were both outraged by Smith's decision that they would neither circulate nor sell *Esther Waters*. Moore – not for the last time – illustrated the link which Dublin was to forge with Paris and the dent which was to be made in conventions of literary respectability which had been accepted for over half a century. Moore himself had left Ireland for France when he was 18 years of age to be a painter. He became the friend of Manet (who did three sketches of him) and a number of painters and writers who frequented the Café *Nouvelle Athène*. His *Autobiography* and *Reminiscences of the Impressionists* were to record his memories of Paris which he finally left for London in 1882, as a result of a decision to forsake painting for writing. His novels immediately revealed the influence of Flaubert, Balzac and Zola – a combination of realism and naturalism which was to have a profound influence on contemporaries.

Esther Waters was a story of a servant girl. Her trials and hardships were told simply and compassionately. Illegitimacy, drink, horse-racing and gambling mingle on its pages. To a modern reader its leading characteristics are its naïveté and harmless realism. If Moore's sojourn on the Left Bank had corrupted him there is little evidence of the fact in *Esther Waters*. Yet to a Victorian library manager the thought of her reception in hundreds of middle-class family homes was alarming. And it can hardly be doubted that Faux, Smith's library manager, knew his subscribers, their tastes and phobias. Smith's policy towards Moore represented a clash of concepts of what was acceptable morality and a precedent in the rebellion against a consensus of Victorian opinion which had so far dominated the publishing world and middle-class reading habits.

Moore left an account of his meeting with William Faux, whom he significantly describes as 'Mr Mudie's co-adjutor'. It was written in 1933, forty years after the event, is highly coloured and not wholly accurate. Moore was then living again in Ebury Street, to which he had returned disappointed by Dublin and Ireland's reception of his work. The bitterness and disillusionment of old age and neglect by the new literary world is reflected in his account. The memory of affront had nevertheless been kept green:

I mounted a long concrete staircase to arrive on the third storey at lack-lustre rooms in which I discovered a long, lean man, one of those men who have grown old without knowledge of life or literature in the dim shadows of their book-shelves. Mr Faux was particularly attractive as a specimen. A tangle of dyed hair covered a bald skull, and as he smiled, or rather giggled, his false teeth threatened to jump out at me. His withered face betrayed amusement when he heard that I had called upon him to ask his reasons for excluding *Esther Waters* from his library.

'You see,' he answered 'we are a circulating library and our sub-scribers are not used to detailed descriptions of a lying-in hospital.'

'So you do not aim at distributing good literature, but exclude certain aspects of life which you have decided dogmatically are not suitable to your subscribers in Belgravia and Mayfair.'

'There is much in good literature that we are bound to exclude.'

'But can you explain how it is, Mr Faux, that everybody in England has praised the book, except you and Mr Mudie, and I heard yesterday that Mr Mudie had decided to admit the book into his library. Is it wisdom, Mr Smith – but I changed the words on my lips to Mr Faux – when all the newspapers in England have published articles in favour of the book – the *Athenaeum*, the *Spectator* and the *Guardian* – the religious papers are specially enthusiastic?'

'No. I have read some of the articles in praise of the book, Mr Moore, but they have said nothing that has shaken my opinion that the book is not suitable to our library.'

I spoke of classical literature, of Shakespeare and the Bible, but Mr Faux shook his long lean head and smiled dolefully. Classical literature was another matter . . .[23]

Moore concludes by recalling with satisfaction that after consulting an accountant he had calculated that Smith's had probably lost £1,500 by their refusal to circulate *Esther Waters*.[24] No less his pleasure at hearing that the partners had instructed Mr Faux to avoid such heavy losses for the future by not excluding books that Mr Gladstone was likely to read and approve in the *Westminster Gazette*.

A contemporary account ('Mr George Moore's new Novel') in the *Publishers' Circular* on 5 May 1894, gives a less subjective view of Mr Faux's argument.

Our subscribers [Faux told the *Pall Mall Gazette*] rely upon us to give them such books as they can carry into their homes . . . We are merely caterers, and we have to spread our table with fare which will please, and not . . . displease, our customers . . . If we refused it in the library,

368 First with the News

where our profit is small, and placed it on the stalls [i.e. for sale], where our profit is large, people would naturally impute motives, and say what prigs we were. If anybody likes to order the book from us we gladly supply it . . .

The book's publishers had assured him, Mr Faux continued, that they would not be a party to any action contemplated against Smith's whom they had always regarded as their best friends 'for our fairness'.

. . . there are only about twenty lines of what I may call Mr Moore's pre-Raphaelitic nastiness. The removal of those would make the book acceptable to us . . . I should think Mr Moore is so anxious to secure our market that I believe he will make the suggested alterations . . .

Personally I can enjoy *Tom Jones* as much as another, but I never forget that I am not aiming to suit my own palate. I have to taste for the 15,000 subscribers . . . who include a large number of women . . . Between Berwick-on-Tweed in the north and Penzance in the south [Faux told the *Daily Chronicle*] we have 15,000 subscribers, and we have only received one complaint in the matter of not circulating *Esther Waters*.[25]

The clash over *Esther Waters* (like later, similar clashes) has often been treated simplistically as one between right and wrong, between the self-evidently admirably progressive and the equally self-evidently deplorably repressive. It was much more complex. It was a clash of personalities, economic interests, and genuinely held principles. Moore was an artist, headstrong, emotional, dedicated – but with a keen eye to his royalties. Faux (*pace* Moore) was gentle, courteous, dutiful, limited, self-educated in the Smith business where he had by 1894 spent forty years. The background, apart from the disagreement ten years earlier about *A Modern Lover*, was one of steadily changing markets for both authors, booksellers and libraries.

Further clashes were inevitable: and they duly occurred. Four years later, Smith's decided to exclude a highly moral novel about a peasant girl who was rescued from a Brussels brothel into which she had been sold by a satanic mother. The difficulty lay not in the story or narrative but in the title which the author, an obscure writer, a Mr T. Mullet Ellis, chose to give it: *God is Love* (1898). This was considered 'irreverent' in the context by Kingdon, the department manager who promptly removed it from

35 Above: a near miss. Portugal Street: broken windows at Strand House
after an air raid, 1940

36 Below: the Paris shop under Nazi occupation in the 1940s

37 Above: the Partners' Room, Portugal Street, 1948. Seated, the Hon. David Smith. Standing, left to right: C.H.W. Troughton, M.C. St J. Hornby, A.D. Power and A.W. Acland

38 Below: Bridge House, Lambeth, dressed for the Bookstall Centenary, 1948

39 Above: W.H. Smith rolls into Toronto, 1950

40 Below: the warehouse at Swindon. W.H. Smith's proud boast was that 'in no circumstances would they allow an ugly building to be put up'

41 Above: Beverley Nichols autographing copies of his new book at the Birmingham shop, 1958

42 Below: the Gatwick Airport shop, 1958, when the airport was inaugurated

the bookstalls.[26] Another public wrangle ensued, which added nothing to the substance of the issue between Smith's and George Moore.

More important was the clash with a much more important author, Compton Mackenzie, in 1913: the trouble – a new, later very famous novel, published in two volumes by Martin Secker, *Sinister Street*. This raised two suspicions in the library mind: first, it reverted to the ancient custom of multi-volume publication and thereby raised financial anxieties rooted in the troubles, avoided since 1894, connected with this uneconomic type of publication. Second, like *Esther Waters*, it raised problems of suitability for the circulating library subscribers.

Sinister Street is a perceptive, now very dated, exploration of the feverish emotions and imagination of boyhood and adolescence and of youthful passions. Its *aperçus* of the complexity and ambiguity of sexual relations might well have caused some perplexity to a circulating library manager of 1913. In Compton Mackenzie's accusing phrase to the *Daily Mail*, Smith's were projecting their anxiety about money into anxiety about morals. True or untrue, fair or unfair, this was his argument: it was pseudo-moral censorship.

The root of this censorship exists in the head office of W. H. Smith and Son. Here is their method: On September 1 my new book *Sinister Street* was published. On August 20 four copies were sent round to the four libraries. Mudie's and *The Times* Book Club subscribed generously. Smith's and Boot's declined to order; the book was still under consideration. On eight successive days my publisher's traveller called round in person at Smith's. 'Still under consideration' was the reply. The eighth day was the day of publication, and when this was pointed out to the manager of the library department he said, 'I can't help that, I've been away'. On Tuesday (September 2) there was still no order from Boot's or Smith's, notwithstanding many long and important reviews, including a column on the leader page of the *Daily Mail*.

On Wednesday my publisher wrote and demanded an explanation ... The manager of Smith's said my publisher's letter was his first intimation of the book's existence! Then on Thursday, four days after publication, Smith's ordered 200 copies to supply over 1,500 bookstalls and shops. This was finally increased to 750 in order to take advantage of subscription terms.[27]

The turn of the century saw the forces of conservative opinion closing ranks against the avant-garde. At the end of the nineteenth century only two organisations for the defence of what they called 'social purity' existed. By 1910, the National Social Purity Crusade, founded by the National Vigilance Association in 1901, was able to organise a Conference of Representatives of London Societies Interested in Public Morality. They included the Church Army, the YMCA, the Society for the Rescue of Young Women and Children, the Social Purity Alliance, the Alliance of Honour, and many others: they were led mainly by the clergy and lay social reformers, with MPs and members of the Upper House in support. As an American liberal observer has said, they had 'no support at all from the serious intelligentsia'.[28]

The self-appointed leaders of 'liberal' opinion, contemporary and later, had nothing but contempt for these conservative, allegedly repressive bodies of fuddy-duddy opinion – the C. of E. Mothers' Union, for example, was designed, so they said, to impose repressive censorship on literature. Fair or unfair, accurate or false, this view of the 'reactionary' movement seems, at first sight, to be borne out by the response of the circulation libraries in 1909. In that year the libraries formed an Association. They explained their purpose in a letter to the publishers. They were concerned with the problem of circulating books regarded as 'transgressing the dictates of good taste . . .' Much undeserved adverse criticism (they continued) had fallen on the libraries who 'in their endeavours to avoid giving offence, have repeatedly called in such books from circulation, and in consequence have suffered considerable loss'. They had therefore decided, in order to protect themselves and satisfy the wishes of their clients, not to 'place in circulation any book which by reason of the personally scandalous, libellous, immoral, or otherwise disagreeable nature of its contents is, in our opinion, likely to prove offensive to any considerable section of our subscribers'.

They accordingly asked the publishers to give them a week's notice at least of any book likely to cause such difficulties and hoped that they would not thereby be accused of any attempts 'to become censors'.[29] *The Times*, the *Spectator*, even the Publishers' Association, were sympathetic. There was ferocious opposition from Edmund Gosse, writer and critic and, at this time, Librarian at the House of Lords. Maurice Hewlett, another well-known figure of the literary establishment, agreed with Gosse. Both objected to the action of the libraries, less perhaps on any high moral views that censorship *per se* was objectionable. What was objectionable was censorship by 'commercial gentlemen' (Gosse) and 'tradesmen' (Hewlett).[30]

The 'alliance', never more than uneasy, between the Circulating Libraries' Association and the crusaders for social purity, lasted for several years. It culminated in deputations to the Home Secretary in 1911–12, organised by the National Council of Public Morals and including publishers, booksellers, librarians and journalists. Their object was to obtain legal support for the campaign to control the publication and distribution of doubtful literature liable to attract legal action for libel or obscenity. It was a squib. The following year saw the total failure of attempts to suppress three novels: *The Woman Thou Gavest Me* by Hall Caine; *The Devil's Garden* by W. B. Maxwell; and *Sinister Street* by Compton Mackenzie. All three were numbered among best-sellers of the year.

That, in the opinion of one American historian of this episode in Victorian-Edwardian social history, was the end of the affair. The 'crusaders' were countered, in part, by the resistance of authors and readers, but 'the true cause of the defeat of Organised Morality was not . . . primarily the resistance of individuals; at bottom the cause was economic'. The 'power of the libraries' was on the wane; their audience was diminishing; the old ladies whose threats had frightened Mr Faux and his like had disappeared; public libraries had begun 'to render circulating libraries unnecessary . . . they became unimportant in the economics of publishing. The War of the Circulating Libraries was not a war that anybody won: the battlefield simply disappeared'.[31]

In further retrospect, this picture of the forward march of progress, the defeat of conservative, puritanical attempts at repression, the heroism of authors, the dangerous and disreputable behaviour of tradesmen, and the final victory of an alliance of the avant-garde, the popular reader and library democracy, calls for some reconsideration. That there was a change in the intellectual climate from the 1890s (even from the 1880s) to 1914 and after is undeniable: equally undeniable (though oddly unpalatable to current self-proclaimed radical opinion) there was an economic basis for this: wealth – the real value of salaries and wages – was increasing. This was an age of new consumers demanding new commodities; they included literary commodities. The 'democratic' parallel to *Esther Waters* was provided by *Reynolds News* and *Lloyds Weekly*. Moore, Hall Caine and Mackenzie were not moral prophets. They were artists in popular entertainment earning a living out of novelty, keeping a wary eye on their royalties, providing higher amusement in the teeth of the doubts and fears of those older orders to whom the new style of journalism, fiction and the social morality it represented was anathema. The organisation of 'crusades' to defend the older order was not a symbol of strength but of the diminution of strength – and of fear: fear of the unknown social risks which the new order carried with it. All these sectors of opinion had perfectly legitimate and understandable objectives. So did the libraries. They were in trade to provide services to the public which only they could provide: they could provide them only if they were profitable. They could only remain profitable by attending to the desires, beliefs, prejudices, superstitions (if you like) which ruled the market they served. Among the penalties for this was the hostility of authors on the make, and of a literary establishment which preserved a high-minded dislike for trade. This internecine war of opinion and interest did not end in an unquestionable moral or philosophical victory of 'progress': it resulted not in progress but in change: in fact, the war did not end at all: it merely shifted from one phase into another. It would have been surprising if Edmund Gosse or Maurice Hewlett had supported the publication of *Lady Chatterley's Lover*.

Amidst all the shifting uncertainties, one thing, nevertheless, can be stated with confidence. The circulating libraries did not disappear. This may have been plausibly deduced from selected economic and social facts: thus, the circulating library had its origin in the scarcity and dearness of books. When books ceased to be scarce and dear, libraries were unnecessary. They therefore disappeared. Q.E.D. But the deduction is in reality false: higher incomes and more and cheaper books did not in themselves destroy the libraries. Some of the older ones might shrivel away because they were ill-managed. The Smith library (together with Boots, *The Times* and others) could look forward, even in 1914, to nearly another half century of life during which its turnover more than trebled.

This survival and growth of the library is not to be explained by considering its situation in isolation from the rest of the W. H. Smith business. In spite of a general growth of incomes, book prices in real terms remained high for many readers. There was therefore still a large body of readers who preferred to borrow rather than buy. From the business point of view, the library investment was not an easy one. It locked up a considerable volume of capital. It yielded profits that were only modest and fluctuating. The running costs were heavy, especially book distribution and transport between London and the stalls and shops.

On the credit side it could be argued that a large part of the library management was simply added to the general duties of local staff in stall or shop. Their greatest merit as an investment was probably that the libraries represented a natural extension of the book trade, especially in conditions where competition was limited: and — sovereign merit — libraries generated other business. They drew to the stalls and shops thousands of subscribers who visited their library regularly and were likely buyers to satisfy their other needs — newspapers, magazines, stationery and so on. They were at once automatic multipliers and stabilisers of business. As the *causes célèbres* of *Esther Waters*, *Sinister Street* and others demonstrated, the task of managing the libraries, of balancing the often conflicting demands of subscribers, authors, publishers, progressive reformers and preservers of the *status quo*, was delicate and sometimes vexatious. Yet even publicity of a kind at first blush unwelcome probably helped to keep the name of the firm itself in the news. Thus the function of W. H. Smith & Son as librarians played a role in the public eye quite disproportionate to its modest place in the whole gamut of their business activities measured in terms of direct profit. This image was to survive until in 1961 it finally faded away (along with that of the other popular circulating libraries) in face of a new cycle of affluence, the cheap paperback – and the 'free' public library. Boots were the last survivors. They finally went in 1966.

XVII

Taste, Morality and the Law: The Distributor's Lot . . .

LETHBRIDGE AND HORNBY, the principal partners chosen by William Henry II and by his son to guide their business, both had legal training: so too did Charles Awdry and several other later partners and directors. This could have been fortuitous, a relic of ancient tradition that took young landed gentlemen to the Inns of Court to acquire a smattering of culture and enough law to help them maintain their estates and be sure their stewards were not swindling them. It may, on the other hand, have been connected with the peculiarly exposed position which the distribution of news and literature occupied in the eye of society and of the law courts. This repeatedly raised questions, legal or semi-legal, where a mind trained in the law was essential to the taking of management decisions.

William Henry II was praised (or gently teased) in his day as 'Old Morality' or 'the North Western Missionary'. He was indeed a man with a strong sense of the public interest; but in fact the remedial mission with which his name was associated was not a particularly personal creation: it was the joint contrivance of Victorian railway companies, Victorian Parliaments, Victorian judges and Victorian society at large. William Henry II had found himself leaning heavily on William Ford, his solicitor, for constant advice. Birchams, who succeeded Ford's firm, were to be equally indispensable to his successors on all manner of legal problems. The distribution of literature was beset by legal issues, involving a complex of interests.

Three distinct but related problems repeatedly occupied the attention of the partners: they were moral, contractual and legal. They were not solely the responsibility of the distributors: indeed it was always Hornby's conviction that they were primarily the concern of the author and his publisher, and that distributors were required to bear an unjustifiable burden under English law as it had developed. This view was also put to the London publishers by the Circulating Libraries' Association and subscribed to by Mudie's Select Library, W. H. Smith & Son's Library, Boots' 'Booklovers' Library, *The Times* Book Club, Day's Library, and Cawthorn & Hutt in December 1909; this was when (in the view of some authorities) the campaign for censoriousness was reaching its high (or should it be low?) watermark in the immediately pre-war period (see pages 369–70). The letter ran:

> In order to protect our interests and also, as far as possible, to satisfy the wishes of our clients, we have determined in future that we will not place in circulation any book which by reason of the personally scandalous, libellous, immoral, or otherwise disagreeable nature of its contents is, in our opinion, likely to prove offensive to any considerable section of our subscribers.[1]

This was not mere academic moralising. Smith's, in particular, were acutely aware that it was the first climax in a half-century when social opinion at large, the common law and (1857) statute law had combined to give a keen edge to questions of defamation, especially in written or printed form, and to heighten the possibility of action by the government (the Home Office) and the police, in matters of 'obscenity'. In the case of Smith's, their situation contained a definite, contractual element: in every contract for maintaining a W. H. Smith railway bookstall, the railway company inserted a specific clause that forbade the distributor thus enfranchised to sell or advertise any literature of an obscene, indecent or offensive character. Wording varied slightly from company to company. This did not deprive the distributor of the right, or relieve him of the duty, to exercise his discretion in defining what was meant by these descriptions. The surviving evidence simply shows that the distributor was under heavy pressure to regulate carefully what he sold on his bookstalls or risk serious consequences. The contracts drawn up by the railway companies merely embodied current ideas of what constituted, publicly, decent or indecent literature, acceptable or unacceptable.

In 1862, W. H. Smith refused to sell a still novel journal, the *National Reformer*, edited by the young atheistical, republican, free-thinking editor, Charles Bradlaugh (later unseated as MP for Northampton for refusing to take the customary MP's oath). Customers complained. Bradlaugh complained. Smith's refused to budge – as, legally, they were entitled to do.

In 1869 another satirical author and journalist, Mortimer Collins,[2] complained that Smith's had refused to stock a pamphlet of his which described William Henry's victory over John Stuart Mill in the recent Westminster election:

> . . . The old, old story still –
> Wide-incomed Smith beats narrow-minded Mill.[3]

He omitted to mention that most other booksellers did the same. In the House of Commons in 1887, T. P. O'Connor accused William Henry II, then First Lord of the Treasury, of boycotting Liberal newspapers while encouraging the Tory variety.[4]

All this was political tittle-tattle. A different kind of tittle-tattle – oddly enough, with more serious historical consequences – was involved in the case of the attractive Mrs Weldon. She sued Smith's for distributing a libel on herself which she alleged was contained in an innocent book called *Great Composers* (1887). Writing of Gounod, the author described him as 'strangely unsettled' by a spell cast over him by 'a beautiful adventuress' with social and musical ambitions.[5] This reference, Mrs Weldon claimed, was clearly to herself. She sued for libel and substantial damages. Smith's gave in. They did all they could to recall all copies of the book and agreed – as distributors of the book – to pay her £200. The publishers agreed to pay £300.[6]

Yet even as they tacked to avoid the Scylla of Mrs Weldon, the Charybdis of *Science Siftings*, the *Hawk*, the *Bat* and other dangerous hazards came into view (1892). When *Science Siftings* attacked a prominent London business man, he shrewdly threatened to recover any consequent damages not from the journal itself (which he judged to be incapable of paying) but from two newsagents (W. H. Smith's and Willing's) if they sold any copies of the offending journal. The paper was at once ordered off. Both agents were thereupon sharply attacked by the *Star* newspaper, refounded in 1888 by T. P. O'Connor.[7] What kind of freedom of speech would exist if Smith's (who had meanwhile had an offer of indemnity from *Siftings*) declined to circulate papers directly anyone put pressure on them?

Smith's replied with the same argument they had advanced on earlier occasions. They regretted having to take a paper off the bookstalls: but they would not knowingly distribute any publication alleged to contain libellous matter. Nor would they accept any consideration from a publisher to cover them for handling what they had been advised was libellous. To this the *Star* retorted that it appeared that in addition to the growing power of the libel laws, newspapers and publishers were to have to face private censorship by W. H. Smith. Smith's reply – often reiterated later – was that the proper remedy of the predicament lay in a reform of the libel laws: only the writer, or the publisher – not the innocent vendor – should be held responsible.

This defence – 'innocent dissemination' – had in fact been used in a case heard a few years earlier (Emmens v. Pottle 1885). A newsvendor, it was held, though *prima facie* liable for a libel published in a newspaper he sells, may plead (if he can prove it to the satisfaction of the court) that he did not know it contained a libel; that his ignorance was not due to any negligence on his part; that he neither knew, nor had ground for supposing, that it was likely to contain libellous matter.

Smith's QC deployed this argument persuasively in a case brought by a manufacturer of a sewing machine ('*So-All*') who sued Smith's – having failed to extract any damages from the new paper owner involved who was himself in gaol. On this occasion, the judge took the rather sensible view that it was quite impracticable, indeed impossible for Smith's to peruse all the papers at their distributing office before sending them out for sale. The point was to come up again in a crop of cases round about 1919 – the peak of vigilantes' activity for stricter censorship – and again in the 1930s.

Meanwhile, a different problem was facing Awdry. He had to confront an indignant Rev. E. M. Young, Headmaster of Sherborne School, who had discovered some of his pupils importing undesirable literature – *Town Talk*, the *Bat*, *Modern Society*, the *Sporting Times* and *Bird of Freedom* – into his school. All had apparently been purchased at the local W. H. Smith stall. This was in 1888. William Henry II, at a particularly difficult and delicate stage of his Commons career,[8] was kept in close touch with the Headmaster's complaint by Charles Awdry – a custom followed by his son and grandson when such delicate matters (which would today be called public relations) were concerned. *Town Talk*, Awdry assured William Henry, had been banished by Smith's. The *Bat* was '. . . dead some little time & before that we had stopped it because of its libellous tendencies'. It was not 'suggestive of indecency', nor was *Modern Society*, its weakness being only 'an offensive tendency to disloyalty . . .' As for the *Sporting Times*, '. . . to say the least of it, its taste is as bad as can be, but its proprietor is now clever enough to avoid passing the border land' (presumably into obscene libel).[9] All of which shows that Smith's did exercise a considerable measure of what those who approved it called moral supervision and those who opposed it called private censorship.

Another offender in a class similar to the old *Sporting Times* was the
Winning Post. To its proprietors, in 1905, Hornby addressed a lapidary note
regarding 'several indecent paragraphs' and 'a number of very objectionable advertisements': he continued '. . . we shall be unable to continue the
sale of the paper at our Bookstalls, as we do not care to be responsible for
the sale of this class of literature'.[10] They were invited to let him know of
any comments they might wish to make.

If they did, these have not survived. But it is evident that the charge of
indecency made the case of the *Winning Post* serious for Awdry. Quite
apart from the railway company contracts, it had long been an offence
under common law to publish – or distribute – obscene matter. The
Obscene Publications Act of 1857 had given magistrates added powers of
seizing and destroying offending publications. Thus Charybdis grew more
menacing. Awdry was kept busy from 1906 onwards, corresponding with
the Home Office, the editor of *The Times* and others (including administer-
ing a severe wigging to a too lenient bookstall clerk who disobeyed instructions and sold the *Winning Post* by private treaty to Smith's customers) on
the offending journal.[11] Hornby wrote to the Home Office in February
1909 that 'Sievier' (proprietor and editor) had given him 'an undertaking
in writing (for what it is worth) that in future the "fun would be harmless".'[12] The W. H. Smith-Hornby policy was, in general, that it was
preferable not to ban this kind of journal to the dark corners of the back
streets: better keep it on the stalls and within the bounds of reasonable
decency.

To return to the problem of responsibility for libel; Hornby took a
prominent role in a press debate which kept the newspapers and weeklies
busy in 1909. In a letter proposing a 'guarantee fund' to help libelled persons
to prosecute those who had libelled them, the Rev. Herbert Bull, an earnest
reformer of public morals, had grouped together the culprits as 'author,
publisher and distributor', as though all were equally culpable. Hornby
wrote a comment to the *Spectator* under the signature 'A London Bookseller' explaining to St Loe Strachey, the editor, why he did so. There was,
in his view, a fundamental difference between the author and publisher, on
one side, and the distributor on the other:

> The author and publisher, and they alone, are jointly responsible for the
> production of a book, and produce it with a full and intimate knowledge
> of its contents. The individual distributor has no control over publica-
> tion . . . Therefore, while admitting fully the responsibility of distribu-
> tors *as a body* . . . it would be more in accordance with justice if it were

forbidden to take action against any individual distributor until the question of the immorality of the book had been decided in an action brought against the really responsible parties, either the author, or the publisher, or both . . .'[13]

It is important to place these expressions of opinion in their historical, chronological order. Four years after Hornby wrote the foregoing letter – the voice of Hornby the lawyer and distributor as it might be dubbed – he wrote the following letter to the manager of the *English Review*:

. . . we regret that we cannot place upon our Bookstalls in Pamphlet Form the Article entitled 'The Doctors and Venereal Disease' . . . Admirable as the Article is in many ways, we hardly think it is suitable for display in so public a place as a Railway Bookstall, and besides this, most of our Railway Contracts specially debar us from selling books &c. dealing with this subject. Properly and judiciously distributed, the Pamphlet should, in the opinion of the writer, do a great deal of good.[14]

It would be difficult to find a better example of Hornby speaking as the voice of good sense, balancing reason against the contemporary forces of interest and prejudice in a problem of great social importance but submerged still, in the pre-war world, beneath layers of fear and ignorance.

The cases quoted run the entire gamut of law, contract and taste. For reasons which defy precise analysis the 1930s saw the distributors' dilemma over the law of libel become much more costly and serious. Whether this was a by-product of the depression, or accompanying social malaise, or of the dawning realisation by those who regarded their chances (as plaintiffs) as favourable and increasingly profitable, the 1930s, especially from 1933, were to be an age of litigation over the distribution of libellous, or allegedly libellous, material. Glimpses multiplied of new versions of the old unexpurgated, imperishable underside of popular reading. The directors had to spend much anxious discussion (and doubtless private reading) of 'dubious' publications with hypnotic titles like *Ballyhoo, Hooey, Razzle.*[15]

Other cases were of a quite different character. Early in 1933 an article appeared in *John Bull* referring in a banner headline to the apparent failure of a firm called Machine Made Sales Limited as the 'Combine Crash Sensation'. Smith's lawyers promptly advised the recall of the magazines from all shops and bookstalls, advice which the firm acted on equally promptly. Curiously enough, in this instance Smith's, saved from a certain libel action, fell foul of the Periodical Proprietors' Association, who took the firm to task in a pompous letter which described the withdrawal of the magazine as 'precipitate and unprecedented', and asked for an undertaking of 'no such interference with, or interruption of, the circulation of any newspaper or periodical in the future without consulting the views of the proprietors of the publication concerned'.[16]

In the next affray Smith's were not so fortunate. The difficult position in which the firm was so often placed was never better demonstrated than in June 1933 when an action claiming damages for alleged libel was brought by the Sun Life Assurance Company of Canada which had been suddenly denounced in an ephemeral and sensational periodical called the *City Mid-Week* as a 'gigantic ramp'. Smith's sold 287 copies of the offending issue and exhibited a poster reading 'More Grave Sun Life of Canada Disclosures'. This was a very odd blunder; for the Sun Life of Canada had assets of £125,000,000 and an income of £33,000,000, and the company's accounts were by law inspected and passed by the Canadian government auditors. As the plaintiff's counsel pointed out, although there was not a scintilla of truth in the charges made by the *City Mid-Week* the plaintiffs had suffered incalculable damage from the fact that W. H. Smith's had spread a 'foul libel' about them throughout London.[17]

On behalf of Smith's Sir William Jowitt, KC took the familiar and still formidable line that Smith's could not possibly have a system of scrutiny at every one of their branches. Smith's had 48 wholesale branches, 311 bookshops, 1,400 bookstalls and a host of agents and sub-agents to whom they had to supply publications. They employed about 13,500 persons and handled in the year about one thousand million copies of daily newspapers, 350 million weeklies, and a myriad of books and magazines. A Smith's director supplemented these figures in evidence by again showing that if every item had to be examined, hardly anything at all could be distributed in reasonable time after publication.

Nevertheless, the poster proved an insuperable obstacle to acquittal and Smith's were found liable, though only on the charge of negligence, and ordered to pay damages of £3,000. But on the point of principle – that innocent dissemination should be a valid defence – Smith's were supported by press comment in general. One of the main cases cited by Sir William Jowitt was that of Mallon v. W. H. Smith and Son (1893) in which judgment had been given for this principal premise and the defendants. But the Court of Appeal, to which Smith's had recourse, was unable to disregard the offending poster and upheld the lower Court's decision.

Before the year was out Smith's had to face yet another threatened action. This time it was as the printers of a paper called the *Independent* that a writ was issued against them and the paper's proprietors for an alleged libel against the Nottingham Corporation. The *Independent* was owned by Benn Brothers Limited, and Sir Ernest Benn's promise to indemnify Smith's against costs from any action that might be brought against the paper saved the firm in this instance.

Four years after losing their Sun Life appeal Smith's were involved in a less austere libel suit brought by a 22-year-old lady whose professional name was Miki Hood. At the age of 13 Miss Hood had appeared as a film actress in two films devoutly entitled *Rock of Ages* and *Ave Maria*. She had also in her teenage years been a photographer's model. In November 1937, when Miss Hood brought her libel action against Smith's in the High Court of Justice, she claimed damages on two main counts. Firstly, Smith's had published a libel on her by distributing the *Paris Magazine* for March 1936. The cover photograph of this issue, she claimed, clearly implied that she was a 'loose and abandoned woman who would allow her photograph to appear either gratuitously or for reward in a filthy and degrading magazine'. Secondly, she demanded damages for infringement of what she considered was her own copyright in the photographs.

The train of events which led to this action was unusual. Under the photograph there was a reference to an article in the magazine which read: 'Dans le Numéro. Confidences d'une Amoureuse'. This article Miss Hood's leading counsel, Mr G. D. Roberts, KC, described forthrightly as a pornographic tale about a woman who met a man on a beach near Cannes and told him about her experiences with a man on board ship. Some readers might have connected the photograph outside the magazine with the article inside; but Sir Stafford Cripps, KC, who led for Smith's, won Miss Hood's agreement that the portraits of a number of film stars and actresses had appeared on the cover of various issues of the *Paris Magazine*. 'When that is done,' he asked Miss Hood, 'there is nothing in any way to connect the picture with the contents of the magazine?' 'I think that that depends,' she replied. 'There might be. I object to having my photograph on the magazine with these words written underneath.'[18]

At the outset Miss Hood's counsel had said that Smith's had sold 959 copies of the March *Paris Magazine*, a transaction which he admitted was 'a small one in view of the size of Messrs. W. H. Smith's business'. He admitted also that in July of the previous year the company had realised that this was not a publication which they would like to see on their bookstalls and had given instructions that it should only be supplied to customers who had ordered it in advance. Nevertheless it had appeared on certain bookstalls, and this was the gravamen of the offence.

On the following day Sir Stafford Cripps, after regretting that Miss Hood should have been injured or pained in any way by having her picture on the cover of the magazine, stressed the very difficult position in which Smith's found themselves when it came to censoring the papers which had to be distributed. He pointed out that the firm's directors put a great deal of thought into framing their policy and reviewing it from time to time, in the face of demands for publications like *Paris Magazine*. They did not regard themselves as entitled to censor what the public read; for they believed this under the law to be the function of the government, acting through the Home Office and the police, or, with regard to foreign literature, the Customs authorities. On the other hand they were anxious generally not to encourage the sale of such magazines. In their experience sales were boosted either if these magazines were displayed publicly on bookstalls, or if they were banned by someone but were still allowed by the authorities to be sold in this country. In one recent instance a magazine had actually brought out a special poster describing itself as the magazine which was banned.

As a matter of policy Smith's therefore refused to display such publications, but they also refused to ban them. All they could do was to try to diminish their circulation in order to minimise the harm which might be done. That was why they had given instructions that *Paris Magazine* should be supplied only when specially ordered; and since the Customs authorities had taken action in the spring with regard to a number of imported magazines, with the result that imports of *Paris Magazine* were stopped, Smith's had thought themselves justified in refusing to deal with a number of others.

Miss Hood, it appeared, had transferred her interest in the copyright of her photographs to the photographer himself, so on that count at least her action against Smith's was not in order. But as regards the allegation of libel, Sir Stafford Cripps pointed out that there was nothing in the magazine to suggest that the portrait was of Miki Hood, and no one had suggested that he had thought there was any association between the photograph on the cover and any of the contents.

On the question of innocent dissemination, Smith's had no knowledge that a libel, if indeed there was one at all, was being circulated in *Paris Magazine*. They had to deal with hundreds of millions of copies of publications at an extremely high speed. They had of course instructed their staff to keep an eye open and to draw attention to anything which appeared to them to be libellous, but that was the maximum possible precaution that could be taken. As the company's secretary explained when questioned by Sir Stafford Cripps – and as he had explained once before in the Sun Life of Canada case – it would be quite impossible to scrutinise the very large number of books, periodicals and newspapers which they distributed. It would not be a commercial proposition to do so and the time factor alone would make it utterly impossible.[19]

Summing up on the third and last day of the hearing the Lord Chief Justice condemned Smith's for selling the *Paris Magazine* at all, since it was 'an abominable disgrace to the printing press'. He also suggested that Miss Hood could suffer professionally from having her picture unknowingly on the cover of such a periodical. Finally he put a number of questions to the jury, of which the salient ones with their answers were as follows:

Did the *Paris Magazine* of March, 1936, contain a libel on Miss Hood? – Yes.
Did Messrs. W. H. Smith know that the magazine contained a libel? – No.
Did they know that it was likely to contain a libel? – No.
Ought Messrs. W. H. Smith, if they had carried on their business properly, to have known that the magazine contained, or was likely to contain, a libel? – Yes.[20]

The jury fixed the damages at £355, which suggests that they did not take too grave a view of Smith's culpability.

Some of their customers, however, took a different view. The head office in-trays brought the partners a riot of outraged letters. One of the most dignified of these said simply: 'I am instructed by the Dowager Lady . . . to say that in view of the recent case in which W. H. Smith & Son appeared, she does not wish to continue to obtain her papers from the firm . . .' Others were more outspoken: 'I was amazed to read this morning . . . of an actress's libel suit against you. Counsel for the plaintiff said "the *Paris Magazine* contained indecent photographs on nearly every page and sometimes indecent sketches" . . .'[21] With perhaps less relish and more outrage there was also a letter in which the writer piled disgrace upon disappointment and invoked 'Old Morality's' shade. He said he was 'shocked beyond measure at the disclosures . . . As one who remembers the Rt Hon. W. H. Smith, the embodiment of personal, political and commercial integrity, I have always traded when possible with the firm he founded . . .'[22] But not (he added) in the future.

These outcries illustrate the bookseller's perpetual dilemma, which is to serve and satisfy a wide variety of customers in situations where the most stable factor perhaps is his right – like that of any trader – to deal in the goods he has faith in, and not, if he can avoid it, in those in which he has none.

The clamour in these cases was not nearly as serious as the charge laid against Smith's in 1957 when they were called to answer the only accusation of contempt of court they have ever had to face. When a case is pending or in progress in the courts, the law is concerned to see that nothing shall be published which might prejudice a fair trial. This is particularly important in criminal cases, of which the Adams case was an outstanding example. Dr John Bodkin Adams of Eastbourne was alleged to have persuaded some of his wealthy patients to alter their Wills in his favour shortly before their demise; and when further accusations brought him to trial for murder at the Old Bailey, the respectable and responsible American magazine *Newsweek* published what in retrospect could hardly more clearly be seen as a breach of this rule. Directly the police called their attention to the matter, Smith's knew they were in danger. They called in every copy of *Newsweek* by telephone and confirmed by a special posting to all the firm's shops and wholesale houses not only that the offending number, which unfortunately had been on sale for three days, should be withdrawn, but also that the next one should not be put on sale at all. Everything was done to get the detonator out of the bomb.

Not that Smith's alone were concerned, though by 1957 they were selling 3,200 copies a week of the magazine whose importer, the Rolls House Publishing Company, was a firm of the highest status and throughout its 42 years had been absolutely unsmirched by any similar cases. This company in fact sent about 4,300 copies to other agents in the trade. Smith's therefore neither published, nor imported, nor even were the sole agency for the magazine.

From Smith's the police went first to the importers, and then to the *Newsweek* London office in Jermyn Street. There they questioned the magazine's chief European correspondent, a British subject domiciled in New York. He, as it happened, aroused some prejudice against himself by asking why Smith's and the Rolls House Publishing Company had resolved to stop circulating *Newsweek* without notifying the magazine, asking whether they had done it because the police had told them to or of their own volition, and by insisting that he must confer with his New York office before taking any further action himself. The court, incidentally, was to be much influenced by the fact that *Newsweek* had no responsible editor or manager in this country who could be brought to book.

After the acquittal of Dr Bodkin Adams, writs of attachment were served on this representative of *Newsweek*, on the Rolls House Publishing Company and its circulation director, and on W. H. Smith & Son Limited. Realising that the matter must soon come to trial, Smith's took the unprecedented step of withdrawing all the foreign newspapers and periodicals which went direct to their bookstalls and shops from the importers. Clearly the firm could not scrutinise each one for any suggestion of contempt of court, and in any event they were printed in 31 different languages. In tandem with this, efforts were made to examine as carefully as possible the 50–60 foreign periodicals and newspapers handled through Strand House. 'But in spite of all our care,' declared one of the directors, 'at least one paper got out and was promptly recalled, because counsel, who had had a copy, said it contained a dangerous contempt which would probably not be apparent even to a well-informed layman'; which shows how insuperable was the problem of always vetting everything in every publication.[23]

At the trial before the Lord Chief Justice and two other judges, the Attorney-General himself led for the prosecution. In his opening speech he said that the case raised an important question of principle – whether or not those who brought into this country and distributed matter published abroad, which if published here would certainly constitute contempt of court, were by the same token guilty of contempt. He cited two precedents for showing that they were. The first was the case of Rex v. Hutchison (1936), often referred to as the Gaumont Film case. The head note to the official report on this tells the story clearly:

> During a procession in London, in which the King was riding, a revolver fell close to His Majesty's horse. It appeared that it was either thrown by or knocked out of the hand of a man who was subsequently charged with being in unlawful possession of firearms. A news film of the man's arrest was shown with the caption 'Attempt on the King's life': – HELD: the caption was liable to prejudice the accused's fair trial and was a contempt of court.[24]

The second case was Regina v. Bryan (1954), which concerned a man awaiting trial in Canada. American publications commenting on the case were brought into Canada and sold there, and contempt proceedings naturally followed. Among those charged was a Mr Bryan who had distributed the magazines in question in the part of Canada where the case was to be tried. His defence was that he had not seen the offending material. But the judge, after sympathising with the difficult position imposed on the unfortunate distributor by those who publish magazines for gain – not that he himself seemed to gain much from it all – went on to say:

> Had he examined the magazines he would surely have seen that there were offensive articles in them . . . I think the only effectual way to control the matter is to control the distributor who actually puts them in circulation in the locality in which they are likely to do most harm.

Rather sadly no doubt, since he had earlier said he was 'very sorry' for him, the judge decided to control Bryan by sending him to prison for 10 days.[25] This was hardly likely to be an exact precedent for the fate of Smith's chairman.

Of the defendants, *Newsweek*'s representative claimed he had sent cables to his New York office advising it to steer clear of the Adams trial, and disclaimed all responsibility by transferring the onus to his American employers who could not be charged in an English court. Both the Rolls House Publishing Company and Smith's pleaded 'innocent dissemination'. There had been every reason to trust *Newsweek*'s discretion; if they were found guilty, that would impose an impossible burden for the future on all distributors. Many of the larger of these, such as John Menzies and Wyman's, had not been charged, and took no such precautions as Smith's had done, at no small cost in profitability, let it be said, against indiscretion in imported publications.

Despite the cogency of counsel's arguments, the court held that the defence of 'innocent dissemination' was not available in cases of contempt. But the Lord Chief Justice did recognise that both the importers and Smith's had taken every step in their power to stop the circulation of *Newsweek* as soon as their attention had been directed to the 'scandalous paragraphs'. He concluded:

> It is regrettable that in holding them guilty of a contempt we cannot also deal with those who are far more responsible but are out of the jurisdiction. We shall impose a fine (albeit of a nominal amount) and we do so to emphasize the risk which is run by dealing in foreign publications imported here but which have no responsible editor or manager in this country . . . Now that the risk and responsibility have been exposed in this case, should offences occur in the future similar leniency may not be extended. It was argued that if these two respondents are liable so every small newsagent or street seller who sells the paper would equally be liable. Logically this may be so, but the court would not regard with

favour applications against such persons to whom no real blame would attach.[26]

He then fined Smith's and the Rolls Publishing Company £50 each, and each had to meet half the costs.

Though the fine itself was nugatory, a member of the firm was to point out soon after that: 'During the last 20 years we have suffered three actions for libel and one for contempt of court; and although the damages never exceeded £3,000 the total costs of these actions amounted to over £35,000.'[27]

As Smith's directors saw it the really wounding and dangerous aspect of the judgment was its implication that Smith's, because and only because, they were the largest firm in the trade, would be liable to be singled out for prosecution even though they were completely innocent disseminators.

In recent years the 'censorship' controversy, in so far as it affects Smith's, has been almost entirely centred on their decisions not to handle certain books. In this they have been guided by legal advice that they might lay themselves open to prosecution, either for libel or for obscene libel if they did.

In one respect the bookseller's difficulties here have been lightened by the Obscene Publications Act of 1959, which now provides a defence analogous to the defence of 'innocent dissemination'. But in other ways the Act may be said to have increased his responsibilities and problems. No longer is it enough, where the bookseller has notice of the contents of a book, to consider whether it tends to deprave and corrupt. He must further consider whether the publication is likely to promote the general interests of science, literature and the arts. This is especially difficult when, as at present, standards seem to be changing in the direction of greater licence, not uniformly and evenly throughout society, but by fitful leaps and occasional bounds in different classes and generations. As we have seen, it is virtually impossible to cater for all shades of taste and opinion all the time.

Nor is the bookseller's task made easier by the seeming reluctance of the authorities, ever since the *Lady Chatterley's Lover* case in 1960, to prosecute for alleged obscenity under section 2 of the Act, where the issues would be determined by a jury. Usually section 3 seems to be invoked, which means that proceedings are instituted in the magistrates' courts in the hopes of obtaining a forfeiture order. The best and fairest way of dealing with this situation seemed to be to supply certain books, which they themselves do not consider suitable for general sale, only to special order.

It would have been strange if, in an age of economic reform, the expensive lawsuits mentioned above had had no effect on management policy. They did. When the failure of the appeal against the Sun Life verdict was reported to the Board, Smith's took steps to tighten the scrutiny by W. H. Smith management of 'contents bills' for newspapers and journals displayed at their branches. This duty they tried to concentrate at the Head Office so that the scrutiny could be as thorough and expert as possible. But even this measure could have only a limited effect: it could not prevent the publication of libel but it could make it possible 'to detect anything of the sort within 24 hours of the publication'.[28]

They went further; out to the bookstalls and shops for added safety. From 1934, the standing instructions referred to the dangers of libel,[29] and from 1938 they urged, in specially large print in a SPECIAL NOTICE, every manager and all responsible members of the staff to be constantly on the watch for it.[30] It was the manager's duty to train and indoctrinate his subordinate staff to think on the same lines. The Sun Life action cost £3,000 in damages and £35,000 in costs: it was bad finance and bad publicity.

The history of this business – 'great merchants of literature' as Northcliffe had once described them – was a history of strategic equilibrium maintained in face of perpetual risk of upset with one or more of the several elements upon whose confidence and goodwill its prosperity depended.[31] They included the railway companies, the publishers and newspaper proprietors, the authors, the trade unions, the readers and customers – of many different tastes – the trade associations, the sometimes conflicting interests within the firm itself (headquarters management and staff, branch managers, the provincial houses) and that strange amorphous and fickle force called public opinion. This last swayed according to still powerful religious and political beliefs, economic interest and detached conviction, between contradictory demands for utmost freedom and firm censorship of the offensive and corrupting. Smith's policy was at all times a residuum after all these (and other) considerations had been put through a sieve as close-meshed as it could be made. But the odd exception slipped (and would continue to slip) through. The special appeal to managers continued to appear prominently each year in the annual edition of instructions. Eternal vigilance was the price not only of freedom but – in times of unprecedented difficulty – of solvency too.

PART III

1949-1972

XVIII

The Contours of Change

Going Public

THE FLOTATION OF W. H. Smith & Son (Holdings) Ltd, in August 1949, was, like the changes of 1929, rooted not in any need for 'business capital' but (again) in the urgent need for resources to meet death duties. The issue of 1 September 1949 was a spectacular success, a tribute to the legendary reputation the old partnership still held in the public estimation. Henceforth this new company was the source of the greatest proportion of capital required for business activities. In practice, like the old partnership, W. H. Smith & Son (Holdings) Ltd continued to meet its capital needs from profits. In this, as in many other respects, this further exercise in 'public' ownership continued the long-established practice of the previous generation of partners. W. H. Smith was to be developed and expanded between 1949 and 1972 from retained profits. But the more open form of organisation now made necessary was to play an indispensable role in business development: when emergencies, sudden demands for capital or temporary shortages occurred (as was inevitable with revolutionary changes in the physical size and structure of the business) the outside contacts in the City, and the relationship with banks and financial institutions, gave the new company more ready access to new sources of capital.

Family influence was by no means extinguished. Together with the holdings of friends and staff, the 'inside' investments in W. H. Smith & Son (Holdings) Ltd still counted for just over a half of the ordinary shareholding. Moreover the governing directorship of the Third Viscount Hambleden's brother, David, continued until 1968; in 1967 he was to renounce the right (which was legally his under the Articles of Association) to nominate his successor. It was characteristic that in spite of a deep sense of family tradition he told the Board of directors in November 1967 that he felt this was a right which should be sacrificed, that the title of governing director should be discontinued and his successor as chairman be appointed by the Board.[1]

Other continuities arose from the division of the ordinary shares into 'A' and 'B' categories, the 'A' shares being five times the nominal value of the 'B' shares. Each class of share had the same voting rights per share, but by the purchase of more 'B' shares the family holdings were to gain a significant voting advantage as time went on: and the controlling interest by the traditional complex of family, friends and staff continued. Internally, the ten-year agreements held by the governing director and three 'managing directors' gave them a strong grip on company policy.[2]

In the history of any business, the relationship of ownership to management policy makes the conversion from individual, family or partner ownership to potentially fragmented public shareholding a critical phase. Many variants have been tried as solutions of this central problem.[3] The W. H. Smith arrangements of 1949 offered a flexible mechanism for future development which combined tradition with wide possibilities of managerial innovation.

The new business was directed by two Boards: that of W. H. Smith & Son (Holdings) Ltd, and that of W. H. Smith & Son Ltd. The governing director (chairman) and three other directors (M. C. St J. Hornby, A. W. Acland, and C. H. W. Troughton)[4] were common to both Boards. J. F. A. Smith (Jimmy), the chairman's brother, and J. G. Morrison (Lord Margadale), his brother-in-law, were 'non-executive' (i.e. advisory) members of the Holdings Board.[5]

A. D. Power had joined Smith's nearly forty years earlier on the strength of his experience as a book publisher and specialist, but had broadened into a general manager who had done splendid work in keeping the business going during the war. Now over 70 years of age, he was a member only of the W. H. Smith & Son Ltd Board. These directors constituted the core of the two-tier Board system. Later appointments underlined the respective basic functions of the two organisations. 'Holdings' represented the proprietorial, financial, and therefore policy-making (or policy-approving) aspect of Board functions. This was emphasised by later appointments of City finance experts to its number as non-executive members.[6] Other non-executive members were men of experience in other important business roles.[7]

From 1956, a different series of appointments to the Limited Board pointed to its increasingly 'operational' role. In all, between that year and 1972, ten appointments of existing, or newly recruited, members of the managerial staff were made to that Board.[8] They were most numerous in the 1960s. From this time onwards, they held office under specific titles defining their managerial functions – Wholesale, Staff & Training, Merchandise, Retail director and so on. Their appointments derived from experience, ability, proven merit, often but not invariably demonstrated by their careers within the company. They signified not only the growing need for specialised knowledge of the different managerial aspects of the business but the dawning realisation that such knowledge must be recognised by promotion to the highest posts available. The days of undifferentiated responsibilities by the 'partners' came to an end. The changes were witness also that in a world undergoing radical social transformation, the 'Gentlemen and Players' conventions that had marked, for example, the controversy over the powers of John White in the 1890s, were a thing of the past.[9]

Two staff members elected, first, to the Limited Board, later became members of the Holdings Board.[10] One outside recruit to the business from Canada became a member of both Boards in 1951.[11] These appointments brought expertise from within and without to the developing directorate.

A third category bore witness to the continuing sense of tradition and need for continuity derived from the family business. Since the appointment of William Lethbridge to a partnership in 1864 the management of the family business had been the responsibility of the head of the firm, and of partners related by marriage to the Smiths, or partners appointed by reason of their personal merit recognised through personal knowledge. From H. W. Smith onwards the proprietor was a Smith. In the second category (related) were A. D. Acland, Arnold Power, W. H. D. Acland, A. W. Acland and E. W. Seymour; in the third category (unrelated) were W. Lethbridge, the Awdrys, father and son, C. H. St John Hornby, Michael St John Hornby and (most recently) C. H. W. Troughton and P. W. Bennett.[12]

It was these three groups that seemed to offer a source of younger recruits who might provide new blood and continuity to the management or Board at one and the same time. Between 1950 and 1958, three appointments were made, one each from family, relatives and close associates; J. D. Smith (1950), D. A. Acland (1952) and S. M. Hornby (1958). All became directors but only after some years of training and performance in management which entitled them to be measured by the same professional standards as other members of the Board.

Thus fortified from a variety of sources and of suitably mixed provenance, the top management in the 1960s set about the task of modernising, controlling and streamlining a business which was of national repute yet was still traditional, and had grown by responding instinctively to immediate needs rather than to any discernible plan. Loose ends and dead wood were among its major targets. Nevertheless, even after a decade or more of 'public' ownership, the pace of change remained deliberate.

Until 1960 the functions of the two Boards ('Holdings' and 'Limited') were, in practice, only vaguely defined. In 1960, a 'Holdings Executive' was formed to assume a more deliberative role, to specialise in setting objectives, making longer-term plans, policies and standards: thus the Limited Board could concentrate on its essentially operational business responsibilities. As long as the governing director (The Hon. David Smith) was chairman of both Boards, their functions necessarily overlapped: the Holdings Executive acted as a link between the making of policy and its execution. When, in 1969, the two Boards had different chairmen, their functions were more clearly differentiated. The Limited Board controlled all operations of the entire group, subject only to the final approval of the Holdings Board in matters of high finance and basic policy. But, especially in a public company whose affairs were now open to scrutiny, this latter was of fundamental importance. As a public company, W. H. Smith & Son (Holdings) Ltd was responsible to its shareholders: the Holdings Board had the supreme responsibility for seeing that this duty was not only discharged but was 'seen and believed' to be discharged.

The business for which the new Boards were finally responsible was complex; it comprised the purchase and sale of millions of newspapers, magazines, periodicals, journals, books, tons of stationery and writing materials, games, toys, 'fancy goods' and so on. Its operations had, from the start, been complicated by delicate relations with suppliers and manufacturers over price and methods of sale, by the basic fact that much of the literature sold carried a date and was virtually worthless if it was not sold within a matter of hours, or at most days, after its publication. Nor did trade flow smoothly from day to day or week to week: it was highly seasonal. Christmas was the central focus of gifts in the shape of books, toys, games, greetings cards and the like. What in holiday seasons were dead months inland might be boom times by the seaside. This variable, seasonal factor called for foresight and experience in buying stocks of the right kind and judging their size accurately.

Within the normal scope of their business in popular literature there had been important adjustments over time. The W. H. Smith railway book-stall had turned into a national symbol in Victorian England. But it had been badly shaken by the dispute with the LNWR and GWR from 1905 onwards. Smith's response – the urban shop – had changed the nature of their business and provided new, more convenient, more spacious and less vulnerable outlets for their retail trade. This, however, had enlarged the already intricate problem of managing a business composed of many hundreds of individual units, as these were now spread even more widely over the whole of England and Wales. Top managers such as Bayliss were kept busy laying out the art and craft of shop management for staff instruction after 1906.

Beneath these changes, the basic, dual structure of the business was simple: it was a combination of a direct retail trade to customers for litera-ture of all kinds (including the provision of lending libraries) via Smith's own shops and bookstalls: and, simultaneously, the wholesale supply of similar types of literature to other, independent newsagents – 'trade agents' as they were called. Some of this trade went through special wholesale houses – in effect, warehouses; and these had grown – providentially – most rapidly and profitably at a time when the retail stalls were experienc-ing their classic problems with the railway companies.[13]

It did not take the post-1949 management long to discover that winds of change were blowing through their traditional trading areas. Retailing outlets and methods were meeting heavy competition. Wholesaling was no longer the almost automatically expansive business it had once seemed to be. Libraries were encountering new rivalry from the post-war free public libraries. Railways were in decline and had been nationalised: Smith's whole position was at risk. The structure of both the retail and wholesale trades and their methods of distribution needed to be looked to.

First, what was the pattern of the W. H. Smith retail outlets? Out of a total of just over 600 major railway stalls in 1929–30, roughly one-third were within 15 miles of London. The retail shops were more widely scat-tered. Out of a total of some 260 shops only 50 were in a 30-mile ring round London.

The retail branches, stalls or shops, received their supplies of 'news' from Strand House (as well as from the newspaper offices or other sources). For supplying the wholesalers with news the old 'Trade' and 'Town Trade' departments at Strand House had been amalgamated in 1931. Newspapers went by rail to 'country' agents: 'Town' agents were supplied from Strand House by road – 'Town' meant not more than 30 miles from Charing Cross. There had been a steady increase in the 'Town' trade from 1907/8:

in that year receipts were £51,000. By 1930/31 they were well over half a million pounds.

The distributive organisation of Smith's was to be under continual scrutiny from the 1950s. With the growth of newspaper printing in Manchester and Glasgow, most news supplies came from London or those provincial centres: and three-quarters of the wholesale houses' business was 'news' by 1955. Books and other 'non-news' were distributed from Bridge House, Lambeth, after 1956 or directly from the suppliers. By then, both Strand House (old-fashioned and far from ideally designed as a despatch centre) and Bridge House were likewise congested. Few subjects occupied more of the directors' time than the future of the London centres of the distributive organisation.

Not the least problematical aspect was the rapid development of road transport. From 1932 to 1947 Smith's needs were supplied by contractors. Then the build-up of a W. H. Smith fleet began. By 1961 they were to have 383 of their own vehicles: another 226 were hired from contractors. The needs of the 'Town' trade made the old Fetter Lane building and London Garages (Caledonian Road) the largest transport centres. There were also some thirty district garages serving provincial wholesale houses. Here was a new and dynamic factor which promised, or threatened, an impact on distributive arrangements comparable with that of the early railways.

Such, in brief outline, was the structure of the W. H. Smith national business. The major debates of the quarter century after 1949 centred on the organisation and location of the retail and wholesale trades; these raised the immensely complex problems of the location and functions of the London office – Strand House (the name remained the same, whatever the address) had traditionally been the dynamo of the whole W. H. Smith machine. But already in the 1950s, the role of the large London centres of news and non-news distribution (Strand House and Bridge House, Lambeth) was beginning to be questioned as traffic congestion grew and London costs of all kinds continued to rise steeply.

Reorganising the Retail Trade: 'The Dawn of Understanding'

Smith's retail trade continued in this period to be conducted through the two types of outlet which had become its major feature since Hornby had taken the decision in 1905/6 to break away from the exclusive grip of the railways. Railway stalls, great and small, were still the most numerous outlets. In 1951 the total was still 944. Ten years later it had been reduced to 755. Ten years later still, it stood at 383. The largest reductions had been effected among the smaller stalls and sub-stalls.

The total number of urban shops was smaller than the number of stalls: the adjustment of numbers proportionately less – in 1951, 376, in 1961, 393, and by 1971, 319. Within this total, the emphasis was on bringing the shops more directly under the guidance of headquarters and (as we shall see) concentrating new effort on larger, more profitable retail units.

The reduction in the importance of the railway stall emerged clearly from the renegotiation of W. H. Smith's contract with British Railways. Railways in Britain were nationalised on 1 January 1948. The negotiations were strung out (largely through procrastination by the new railway organisation) until 1953. When the arguments began in 1949 there were still 571 main and 404 sub-stalls. When they ended, these figures had gone down to 537 and 392. They were to fall to a total of 287 in 1972 when this history comes to an end.

Characteristically, the railway representatives were drawn from the Estate and Rating Department of British Railways. Their approach was that of the steward of a needy landlord combined with the suspicions of a tax inspector. Their object (as they freely confessed) was 'to make the hardest possible bargain ... because of the serious position in which the Railway Executive find themselves.' (In short, what the railways wanted, following ancient tradition, was the maximum rent regardless of the effect on the business which had to sustain it.) The assumption was that they were dealing with the proprietors of a bottomless gold mine.

Exasperated finally by a wrangle which was as absurd as it was fruitless, Smith's decided to disclose their situation in total detail. Their money rent had risen; their net profit had fallen by nearly one half. In spite of a small increase in turnover the increased costs of running the railway stalls had simply not been absorbed. Smith's freely conceded that the Railway Executive might well find it difficult to understand this basic fact as they failed to understand many others. Why were net profits so small?

The answer was that four-fifths of the railway stall turnover came from the sale of daily or weekly newspapers. The profit on newspapers was notoriously low. Costs on railway stations were very heavy. Many stalls were, in postwar conditions, an increasingly unremunerative facility provided for the sole benefit of the railways and their passengers. The prospects of improvement were poor. It was more likely that business would deteriorate given the outmoded position of the stations, the infrequent and unreliable train services and the considerable number of quite profitless branches. Smith's explained nevertheless that they continued to value this traditional branch of their business. In addition they had done their best to maximise their own commercial use of rail transport.

These detailed representations did little or nothing to imbue the Railway Executive with any sense of urgency. They continued to sit on the proposals for another 18 months. In the end they agreed to renew the contract for another 21 years though they rejected all Smith's ideas for substituting a rational form of profit-sharing to divide the burden or advantage between the two sides. Smith's, therefore, continued to be charged according to the size of the station and stall and the volume of produce sold. In the same year the contract with the London Transport Executive was renewed. The best that could be said for the settlement reached was that the conditions under which the railway stalls had to operate financially were a modest improvement on the exactions of the past. But the prospects for the railway trade remained sombre and shrinking.

The urban shops also faced some of the problems of the railway stall but they were freer to develop according to the commercial criteria which were gradually taking shape in the minds of Smith's own management. There had been rumblings of criticism of the style and management of the shops for over a quarter of a century.[14] Some intelligent and knowledgeable observers had remarked that this was outmoded by social changes and old-fashioned shop design.[15]

By 1949, these criticisms had not produced any radical reforms. The wartime boom in popular literature of all kinds had helped to postpone it. So had wartime controls, paper shortages, staff shortages, etc. There was also a growing problem with an old and honourable feature of the shops, as of the stalls; the Smith libraries had never been particularly profitable. They had nevertheless survived on the strength of a widespread belief that though their profits might be small they helped to attract into the shops customers who not only borrowed a book but made other purchases as well.

By 1950 these suppositions were being questioned. The price of books was unprecedentedly high. The availability of large, free public libraries finally brought things to crisis point. Rival booksellers and private libraries facing similar problems thought that a remedy might be found by limiting competition and dividing up the market on the basis of a 'this one for you, that one for me' principle. Smith's rejected this. The smallest and most unremunerative libraries were shut. More gradually the libraries as a whole came under the scrutiny of the management as it tackled the problems of retail reorganisation in its entirety.

At the root of the retail shop problem lay the same difficulty of high running costs that bedevilled the fortunes of the railway stalls. But whereas stall development was hampered by the conditions on the stations themselves – bad physical location, overcrowding, poor working conditions for staff – the cramps on shop development were imposed by the nature of Smith's own business structure. From 1949 there was an increasing determination to get out of shops with small turnover, high costs and low profits into something large enough to be profitable and more in keeping with the new patterns of trade and changing social conditions.

An early start was made in and around the so-called 'new towns'. The first was at Crawley in 1949. Others followed between 1952 and 1962 at Hemel Hempstead, Harlow, Stevenage and Basildon. The 'new towns' were the result of a deliberate government policy of reducing overcrowding in the ancient cities, London especially, and of providing manufacturing activities and industrial employment in what had previously been sleepy, semi-rural areas. Smith's was conscious of opportunities for retail expansion in these areas; but its 'new town' expansion had another aspect which reflects an important obstacle to retail expansion in older established trading areas.

The modest rate of expansion of modern shops in the 1950s may be partly explained by the fear that existed throughout the wholesale division that the independent retailers whom they supplied would be upset by the appearance in their trading area of a Smith retail branch. How far this fear was real or imagined is difficult to establish, but the influence of the small trader was certainly a factor to be reckoned with, and the establishment of new retail branches was hampered by this anxiety of the wholesalers.

In the 'new towns' there were fewer traditional restrictive influences and vested interests to be considered. Here there was more room to experiment, less risk of repercussions and bruised feelings. But the age of spectacular expansion of the retail unit was to come later in the 1960s with new shops of unprecedented size and scope at Bradford (1960), Brighton and Stockport (1968) and Nottingham (1969). It awaited not only real recovery from the war and the ending of the post-war restrictions which acted as a brake on business development. It also awaited the arrival of a fully articulated programme of retail reform by management. This had to answer two questions: what were the criteria by which uneconomic outlets should be pruned and those by which new and economic outlets should be created? These answers could be discovered only by a comprehensive analysis of the retail marketing system itself; in brief, of customers' needs, what articles they would buy and how, in turn, Smith's could obtain those goods on the most advantageous terms in order to supply them to their shops and stalls.

It was 1957 before the Board confirmed its approval of a 'Plan for Improved Retail Profits' and the establishment of a 'Retail Management Group' to achieve its objectives. The titles were self-explanatory. Other accompanying moves were less so. A flurry of appointments and disappointments suggested that the managing director responsible, P. W. Bennett, was ready to inject more 'hire and fire' into the retail reformation. The formation of a Market Research Organisation and enquiries through specialist consultants into the establishment of 'a co-ordinated theme and standard of taste in the visual presentation of W. H. Smith & Son in all its aspects to the public', bore witness that these rough recognitions of the need for human changes were accompanied by a more reflective philosophy of retail methods, also based on North American models. Other aspects of change were complicated by the fact that they encompassed other activities besides retail trading, for example wholesaling and Head Office activities; staff and especially managerial recruitment, training, and mobility impinged on all aspects of the business. It had to be made clear to staff throughout the business that 'it was one business, and not three separate and sometimes opposed organisations'. This discussion[16] was to have far-reaching consequences.

Meanwhile the new Retail Management Group asked the Board for permission to look for premises for new shops in some 29 towns and cities, all outside Smith's London area. The list was not therefore complete. It simply made a start in the search for 'first-rate shops in main shopping centres' (not in residential areas and subsidiary areas already served by newsagents). Almost simultaneously, the Group submitted a list of 38 retail branches where the library should be closed and the space so released used as selling space for other articles of sale. One line in the forefront of their thinking was gramophone records; technology had revolutionised the quality of sound reproduction and new types of popular music had combined with changes in popular taste and with social change to create an extremely buoyant new market, especially among the young. Records and tapes were soon to become a major feature of shop turnover.

From 1962 onwards the Retail Group vigorously attacked its problems, urged on by the Boards and the Holding Executive. The main objective was 'to inspire more positive selling, as distinct from simply handing customers what they ask for; to concentrate on salesmanship, especially in the January–August period of the year'. In regard to these 'dead months' especially, but also in a much more general sense, the consensus of opinion throughout the Board was that the future of the company lay with the retail side: in P. W. Bennett's phrase, there had already been a 'dawn of understanding' among branch managers of the basic economic principles of retail trading: and it was aided by the new training programme. There seemed to be a 'promising and exciting future' especially from the refitting and modernisation of existing shops and the acquisition of other business. Things were less hopeful for railway and airport bookstalls. Much depended on keeping up pressure on the rail and airport authorities concerned to persuade them of the importance of allowing the firm to put well-designed structures in the right places. Given that, this kind of business could also be reasonably profitable.

In 1950, most of Smith's bookstalls and shops had changed little in style or appearance since Hornby and Bayliss had stamped their own clear image upon them in the second and later decades of the twentieth century. By 1962 it was clear that the best results in retail trading had been achieved at the new or redesigned branches; all of these were 'virtually up to budget'. Times were not good for business in general: without these innovatory successes, the general W. H. Smith picture would have been considerably worse. To the Holdings Board 'the moral seemed to be that continuous attention to the presentation of goods and the premises in which they were offered for sale, was a first essential'.

The inference was plain: shop design and development paid dividends. The Retail Group's early plans began to look modest after 1960 when a large store was built at Bradford with 12,000 square feet of sales area and a staff of fifty. Another at the Elephant & Castle (1965), sited in a £2 million pedestrian precinct, was less successful.

These very large retail shops were necessarily the product of co-operation between market research enquiry, architects, property developers, builders, public and private land owners and local planning authorities. They brought the advantages of proximity to other large shops of quality. Smith's shared with them the attractions to shoppers of a complete market place and the commercial rewards that went with it. But not all the new shops were on this scale or of this type. New towns such as Crawley or Harlow where the idealism and utility standards of the post-war years mingled uneasily, called for something smaller, less expansive. Historic cities often presented acute puzzles in the art of the appropriate. (The Chester shop of 1925 was designed on lines which were later described as 'fake'.) At Exeter an old shop was successfully reconstructed in five weeks. Not all the larger shops and bookstalls were equally successful: but at least one ancient leak in the W. H. Smith boat – the ones that were too small ever to make a profit – was being stopped up.

The problems of what to sell and how to sell it were inextricably bound up with the problems of what to buy, how to buy it and especially at what price. A paper put to the Holdings Executive in August 1961 argued forcefully the advantages to be gained by setting up a Central Purchasing Agency. It declared:

> Multiple organisations have prospered because the system allows . . . for centralised buying to take place. This produces better [profit] margins and through the placing of large orders, the setting of standards on price, quality, etc. Being a big buyer also makes available a larger number of sources of supply, both national and international.

Such methods were becoming standard practice in the manufacturing as well as the retailing world. In Smith's, such an agency should be concerned with all merchandise other than news, periodicals and magazines, and it should buy for the wholesale side as well as for the retail. As branches grew, the number of 'lines' carried would be reduced. To reach the competitive standards of other business connections where retailers were supplied direct from the manufacturer, and the wholesaler eliminated, the system was essential and would greatly facilitate the conduct of the business.

The proposal was accepted. A specialist Merchandise director, W. K. Oliver, from Boots, was appointed a year later and the other critical appointments were made. The Central Buying Group – its final title – was set up by Oliver and came into operation on 31 December 1962. It was to be 'of first-line importance in the Retail and Wholesale sides' but its first task was to act for the Retail (Wholesale was planned to follow); before any new lines of merchandise were introduced, its urgent business was to 'raise the level of stock, at the shops, of traditional W.H.S. lines (books, stationery, and fancy goods) so that each one was able to offer the best possible selection, at competitive prices, for its neighbourhood' and ensure 'the yield of the best possible gross profit on these goods'.

The reorganisation of retail selling and central buying formed the basis of a revival of this side of the business, stopping up many of the sources of waste. But no system is perfect. No system satisfied everybody. Two years after its induction, Michael Hornby could still enter a mild but firm protest that the W. H. Smith shops still sold too many unsuitable lines – 'china, glass, toast-racks, carving knives, coffee pots, electric light bulbs . . . alien to our basic business and . . . not, from the point of view of total revenue,

very profitable ... and almost certainly tended to drive out customers.'
His view did not go unsupported.

Nor did the new ideologies of buying and selling stand alone as remedies
for the problems of the retail side. Among the ideas (of North American
provenance) thrown off by the fertile imagination of Herbert Morgan,[17]
mail order was not the least plausible. In the 1960s it returned. A new and
improved system 'would actively seek mail-order business' – mainly in
books. The literary journals would carry advertisements informing readers
that W. H. Smith could supply any books reviewed or advertised in those
journals. Lists would then be sent to customers direct. The whole scheme
would be subject to publishers being willing to give Smith's the special
discount on books ordered by mail order: this was basic. By July 1964,
eight publishers had been interviewed and agreed to these conditions in
principle. The scheme was therefore to go ahead: its headquarters would
be Bridge House. But this was not to be the whole of the idea of direct
relations between Smith's and their customers for books (see page 422).

Wholesale Reform

To modernise retail trading was difficult enough: but ample experience of
its problems was available, treatment was systematic, most of the factors
calculable. The problems of the wholesale side were more complex, the
variables unusually variable. They were not merely economic or statistical.
They were diplomatic, social, human too.

The provincial wholesale house management had made an enormous
contribution to the development of W. H. Smith & Son. This was not lost
on the new directors at the top. They too were sensitive to the situation of
the wholesale side of the business and its cautious attitude to retail expansion. Relations between wholesalers and independent retailers were necessarily delicate. The retailer's relations with his customers are relatively
straightforward: but a wholesaler was a supplier dealing with retailers who
were in turn suppliers to their customers. In their function as suppliers,
retailers could be disadvantaged by their wholesaler if he was also a retailer,
especially in times of general expansion. Every move by Smith's was carefully watched not only by local retailers but by the Associations representing the Newspaper Proprietors and Periodical Proprietors. If there was a
case for doubting the wisdom of granting total *laissez-faire* to the provincial
wholesale managers, this was the core of it. A false move could unite
Smith's great suppliers and their smallest retail customer against them.

Not surprisingly, therefore, the first move towards greater freedom of trade was negative. In November 1954, the Limited Board pondered the wisdom of decentralising the sale of periodicals and magazines from Strand House (the usual vendor and distributor) to the provincial wholesale houses. This (as they observed) had been considered 'over a period of years'. The decision went against change: the main reason was the certainty that 'the Trade Union members of the Company's staff would oppose Decentralisation, and so would make the system impracticable for the Company to operate'.

Almost a decade passed before the conventions governing relations between the provincial wholesale houses and retail branches were reconsidered – and relaxed. In September 1963, there was a discussion on the pros and cons of allowing retail branches to draw supplies (other than news and magazines) from the Smith provincial houses. 'Hitherto it has not been the practice to allow this except under specific control. It would be inadvisable to depart from this practice, though the principle should not be too rigidly applied.'

This judicious concession to the provincial houses in regard to supplies other than news is explained by the intervention, two years earlier, by the Holdings Executive into headquarters-provincial houses relations. On 5 October 1961, C. H. W. Troughton made a brief intervention in the Executive's proceedings; 'it was now accepted', he declared, 'throughout the [wholesale] Houses that the departments, other than News, which between them had an annual turnover of £4–£5,000,000, made no profit, and that reorganisation was necessary'.[18] Action followed swiftly. A fortnight later, he reported that a meeting with twelve provincial wholesale house managers had been 'a very good one'. He felt sure that 'everyone left the meeting fully accepting the need for rationalisation, and with enthusiasm for the work that would be entailed'.

The 1961 meeting was seminal. Thereafter the full implications of its economic analysis were explored. Had the time come for a complete re-think of wholesaling? Would not more profit be made if provincial wholesaling were to be confined to news only (including periodicals and paper-back books) accompanied by resiting of the houses in smaller buildings on less expensive sites? These were the ideas which were ultimately to lead to a judicious centralisation of this traditionally independent provincial wholesaling organisation under headquarters supervision. The old wholesaler 'baronage' was to be organised in regional groups: but under 'Exchequer guidance'.

By 1967 the plan was fully matured. In all, twelve new provincial houses were built of which nine were in the north-west. Another eighteen existing houses had been extended or refitted especially in the midlands or north. The Provincial Wholesale House Conferences, once a bi-annual occasion of rejoicing and free speech where wholesale managers aired their ambitions and criticisms of headquarters, were discontinued. Henceforth the subjects for an annual meeting would be decided by headquarters. The houses would be grouped into three or four regions, each under a 'Regional Manager of Head Office Manager rank responsible directly to the Wholesale Director'. If there had ever been any serious tension between London and the provinces it was at an end. The wholesale organisation was now prepared to concentrate its efforts on relating expanding capital investment to those activities known to be profitable.

In London the wholesaling system was in special need of rationalisation. Smith's were only one out of a number of competing wholesalers and there was strong pressure from the Fleet Street newspaper proprietors for a concentration of effort. In particular they had indicated they would favour Smith's entry into the Sunday wholesaling trade (which traditionally Smith's had left alone). Thus alongside the decentralisation of newspaper distribution to the Smith retail branches from Strand House to some 27 of Smith's provincial wholesale houses, began to emerge a plan to remove news distribution to independent newsagents from Strand House also. This would move to special London wholesale houses to be acquired or designed for the purpose. Two wholesale houses had already been added to help with the problem: Dalston House and Peckham House, to which Croydon House was added in 1964. This fitted in not only with the Board's own plans to expand the increasingly profitable, revitalised wholesale trade but even with those of Mr Cecil King (head of the *Daily Mirror* group) who thought that the concentration process should move even faster.

This was all very well, but, as the chairman remarked, Mr King 'was concerned more with the streamlining of the distribution system than with the profits of those concerned in its operation'. For Smith's, expansion was a welcome development 'but expansion must be governed by profitability, and it was not practicable to buy a business simply because it was running at a loss, and which offered no prospect of being made profitable'.[19]

In C. H. W. Troughton's opinion, it was best to confine expansion to the acquisition of Sunday news wholesalers wherever possible, adding daily or periodical wholesalers in towns where Smith's already had a wholesale house. Otherwise, they should concentrate on reorganising existing businesses to higher standards of efficiency. He cited as a prime example of potential expansion the case of the John Heywood business in Manchester, which had been wholly acquired in January 1964; it was now the linch-pin of the 'North West Area Plan' designed to redistribute and rationalise existing arrangements for trading.[20]

The London schemes moved slowly, not least because of the difficulty of finding suitable premises to accommodate the very large business of distributing news to thousands of trade agencies. (Newington Butts, acquired in 1963 was unsatisfactory but it served 786 trade agents: if it were to be closed, it would leave 400 agents unprovided for.) In the end, there were to be two very large London wholesale houses, one for the north (King's Cross) and one for the south (Hammersmith). These changes were not accomplished until 1975. They were inextricably bound up with the decision to sell Strand House (Portugal Street) and this in turn was a step in the long process of moving Smith's operational centre out of its original metropolitan location.

The Major Sources of Expansion 1960-7

A decade of reform and reorganisation in retailing and wholesaling elapsed before Smith's began to reap the harvest of some hard thinking and painful decisions of these years. But by 1960-1 the new order began to register in sustained growth of turnover and a steady rise in real net profits (interrupted only once by the move to Swindon and the incidence of Selective Employment Tax); this was to continue until the end of our period in 1972.

In the critical period of early growth between 1960 and 1967, expansion in the wholesale trade, in 'actual' (money) terms, slightly exceeded comparable expansion in the retail trade. By 1967, however, retail growth was proportionately greater than wholesale growth, measured against sales volume in 1960. In precise terms, 60 per cent compared with 48 per cent. Moreover, this proportionately larger expansion was spread over a diversified group of commodities and was not limited to newspapers or 'dated' literature.

This divergence between retail and wholesale development emerged as the result of the conscious analysis by management of the characteristics and potential inherent in the two types of trading. This analysis had suggested strongly contrasting priorities of commercial opportunity and profitability. The new direction of retail trading earned a gold medal, for example, for the gramophone record, a relative novelty to Smith's business. Starting from scratch in 1958 gramophone record sales rose to over £2,000,000 by 1966/7. Next in the stakes came stationery, an old and proven line but one which showed its remarkably resilient nature by an increase of more than 100 per cent over the 1960/1 sales figure. Books too were up by nearly 90 per cent. There had been days when all these might have been considered secondary to the newsagent's main business. Now they represented alternative sources of profit, indeed antidotes for the classic weakness inherent in 'dated' literature, here today and worthless tomorrow. In another sense, they represented the exploration of the growing market for leisure activities in an age which seemed to have caught up with the problem of producing and distributing the basic necessities of life and could now afford to explore the pleasures and potentialities of spare time.

Nevertheless, enterprise assumed, as always, different forms. What was appropriate and profitable for retail enterprise might well prove less appropriate and less profitable in wholesale enterprise. Lengthy enquiry revealed that the most profitable activity of the wholesale side of the Smith business was the distribution of 'news' in a broad sense. The supposed profitability of a wide range of other commodities which had once been a highly prized part of the commercial role of the provincial houses, proved on closer enquiries to be an illusion. Accordingly, the switch in wholesaling policy that ensued brought a renewed concentration on 'news'. This made far the largest contribution to the upward surge in wholesale trading between 1960/1 and 1966/7. By contrast the sale of books, stationery, etc., by the wholesale trade remained inert or even declining. The stars of the retail trade were the *etcetera* of the wholesaler.

All in all, the new business had generated enough profits by the 1960s to provide its working cash, together with the capital required for new warehouses, shops, plant and major building needs as far ahead as 1972. The only recourse to the outside world was an 8 per cent debenture issue for £2,000,000 in 1966/7 and short term overdraft facilities from Lloyds Bank (see page 413).

The programmes formulated in the later 1950s and executed in the 1960s were essentially exercises to reduce costs while increasing turnover and, more basically, profit. This meant turning the company's back on the past. The impressive but diminishingly effective coverage of the face of the country by well over a thousand railway stalls and shops was abandoned. Between 1951 and 1971, the number of stalls was reduced by 561: they were mainly in the smaller, or sub-stall categories. The number of shops was reduced by 57. In all, in 1971, retail outlets numbered 702, but they were on average larger, some unprecedentedly large, their business more valuable and diversified than in the past: and more profitable.

The statistics of turnover and profit indicate the operational consequences of the new concept and structure (see Tables XVIII. 1–4). The
increased momentum was achieved without increases in staff – indeed,
ultimately, with fewer staff. In 1957 (when the plans for retail reform
matured) W. H. Smith & Son employed 19,213, full and part-time. In
1967 it was 18,838, and in 1972, 17,514.

Most striking was the increase in net profit: a steady upward trend until
1968/9; in that year there was a spectacular take-off, culminating in record
profits in 1971/2. By the end of our period, Smith's still commanded cash
resources of £9.7 million.[21]

TABLE XVIII.1 TURNOVER, 1949–72

| | Turnover (unadjusted) | |
| | Retail | Wholesale |
Year	£	£
1949/50	11,443,000	14,855,000
1959/60	17,259,560	22,648,849
1969/70	42,039,463	54,504,332
1971/72	53,059,809	66,294,482

TABLE XVIII.2 NET PROFIT, 1949–72

| | Net Profit |
Year	£
1949/50	1,319,597
1959/60	1,795,763
1969/70	4,068,000
1971/72	6,518,000

TABLE XVIII.3 COMPARATIVE RETAIL TURNOVER, 1960/1–1966/7

			(£000)* (Actual)				
Year	News	Books	Stationery	Records	'A' Shops†	Other	Total
1960/1	8,335	4,581	4,593	178	1,892	2,129	21,708
1961/2	9,130	5,070	5,193	344	1,684	1,994	23,415
1962/3	9,418	5,783	6,165	614	—	1,808	23,788
1963/4	9,777	6,291	6,932	862	—	1,772	25,634
1964/5	10,271	6,993	7,795	1,170	—	1,802	28,031
1965/6	11,256	7,767	8,912	1,669	—	2,002	31,606
1966/7	11,937	8,675	10,173	2,067	—	1,928	34,780

* See also Appendices.   † No separate analysis available.

TABLE XVIII.4 COMPARATIVE WHOLESALE TURNOVER, 1960/1–1966/7

		(£000)* (Actual)			
Year	PWH	News (Strand House)	Books (Bridge House)	Stationery (Bridge House)	Total
1960/1	23,621	4,004	1,191	241	29,057
1961/2	25,730	4,185	1,128	245	31,288
1962/3	26,612	4,123	1,122	152	32,009
1963/4	28,543	4,084	1,080	166	33,873
1964/5	30,732	3,893	613	168	35,406
1965/6	34,898	4,120	504	137	39,659
1966/7	38,416	4,271	523	—	43,210

	(£000) (Actual)			
	(PWH split into News Books Other)			
Year	News	Books	Other	Total
1960/1	22,718	2,512	3,827	29,057
1961/2	24,967	2,412	3,909	31,288
1962/3	26,059	2,334	3,616	32,009
1963/4	27,940	2,326	3,607	33,873
1964/5	29,606	2,057	3,743	35,406
1965/6	33,516	2,195	3,948	39,659
1966/7	36,893	2,385	3,932	43,210

* See also Appendices.

XIX

Planning for the Future

Decentralisation and Automation: The Move to Swindon

UNTIL 1956 BOOK turnover had been increasing annually. Some of the most experienced members of the Board certainly saw the brightest future for the firm in books. Like most developments this one stemmed partly from market conditions, partly from internal management. A long tradition of managerial expertise in Smith's Book Department had culminated in its direction in the 1920s and 1930s by David Roy. Roy was one of the best managers in W. H. Smith's history. Out of bad times he had created a hard school of training which bore fruit in the 1950s and 1960s.

So heavy did the load of distribution become then that the Book Department had to be relieved of responsibility for the distribution of magazines and it was moved from Strand House to Bridge House. Even an enlarged Bridge House was still hard pressed: but a committee which pondered its future in 1959 finally reported that it 'should be left as it is'. This decision did not stand for long. In December 1963 another Distribution Committee was set up, under the chairmanship of C. H. W. Troughton, 'to consider the whole question of the supply of goods to our retail branches, including the suitability of Bridge House as a distribution centre and the part that the Wholesale Houses should play'.

Finance was a major issue. By 1965 the estimate for replacing Bridge House was £3 million, some of which would come from Lloyds Bank as overdraft: but prudential notice was given to the Stock Exchange of the company's intention to issue a large debenture. In any case, capital expenditure would have to be very tightly controlled until the final bill was settled. The project was to be kept secret. One comment by the Holdings Executive deserves to be recorded: it was 'an overriding decision that in no circumstances would they allow an ugly building to be put up'.

The detailed story of the results has been told elsewhere[1] and no more than the salient points will be elucidated here. The hard core of the Committee's problem was the supplies of books, stationery, games, toys, fancy goods, etc., to Smith's 310 retail shops and 420 railway station and airport bookstalls. The greatest problem and the greatest opportunity in the new age of relative affluence was the retail trade.[2]

The hardest core within the core was at Bridge House, through which passed two-fifths of the goods (other than news) retailed by the company; the rest went straight from manufacturers or wholesalers to the shops or stalls. Bridge House (the Committee agreed) was almost at the limit of its capacity and could not be extended. Moreover, its working costs were inordinately high – hence the rising costs and falling profits of the books and stationery trade. Bridge House, it was reckoned, had accumulated a total loss of half a million pounds in the three years 1961–4. As in the pre-war depression, the beginnings of reform can be traced to the growing consciousness of the urgent need to reduce costs.

In retrospect the replacement of Bridge House seems predestined. As a distribution centre in modern conditions it had become impossible. It had been built (1933–5) when the volume of Smith's trade and transport was relatively small. Its original purpose was to be a stationery warehouse. By the 1950s, it was difficult to get transport in and out. There was no room for horizontal expansion of any kind. Another serious drawback was that when 'books' moved to Bridge House from Strand House, restrictive labour practices moved with them.

By the mid-1960s one entirely new positive factor could be taken into account. When the first committee reported on the future of Bridge House in 1959, Smith's did not possess a computer: by 1962 they did. By 1963 they had a head office manager detailed to supervise experiments in the operational use of computers at Bridge House.[3]

The experiments and calculations made it clear that, given the necessary conditions of space and access, the entire methods of working could be revolutionised, and very large economies secured, by computerisation. Given computer control, orders could be co-ordinated, recorded, executed. Stocks could be arranged to correspond to the calculated expectation of orders. Despatch could be timed and simplified so that transport could not only match requirements but be at the right place at the right

time. The labour force could be assigned according to the supply calculated, so that restrictive practices could be circumvented to the maximum
extent. In a score of ways the new computer-based efficiency was to be
reflected most dramatically in the retail branches, where books and
stationery (the goods which would principally be handled at the new
warehouse) represented nearly 50 per cent of total turnover.

So the search began for a new site: it was to be of some 10–12 acres,
suitable for a single-storey warehouse, if possible with direct rail access,
unencumbered with the massive internal pillars and multiple storeys of
the Lambeth building. It should be outside Central London, but somewhere within a 50-mile arc between due west and due north of London.
It was to cost in the region of £1 million; but Bridge House would probably sell for two, three or more times as much. (This, like so many similar
estimates, was to prove too optimistic.) Where was the ideal site? Basing-
stoke? Letchworth? High Wycombe? Reading? All were considered and
none chosen. The search widened – to Bristol, Bracknell, Peterborough,
Northampton, Wellingborough and, finally, Swindon. In an exhaustive
competition, Swindon proved to be the site that divided the searchers
least. The dimensions as originally planned were now thought to be too
cramping. Swindon could offer 12–15 acres – freehold moreover – and
this was held to be a *sine qua non*. Housing for staff who would need to
move, with their families, seemed easier to find than at other locations.
The Swindon Corporation was interested and co-operative. So Swindon
it was.

In as much as it enabled the major part of Smith's retail distribution
system to be completely reorganised and modernised, the move was highly
successful. The labour force was reduced by some 250 workers. Two
hundred volunteers were moved from London – enough to provide the
experience necessary to set the new warehousing system in motion. A few
weaknesses there were: in concentrating on maximising the clear ground
floor space available, the architects were compelled to use a triple-arched
roof which limited the use – soon to be desirable – of a mezzanine floor.
Second, Swindon's importance as a rail junction was exaggerated, but this
error was compensated for by the decline of rail in favour of road traffic.

'No-one', writes Professor Loasby, 'has any doubt that Swindon was the
best available [location], for no other town could match its pattern of
advantages.' By 1967 the Smith warehouse emerged as a model of modern
distribution methods. Most important, what could have proved, if clumsily
handled, a dangerous source of labour-company friction, went through
with remarkable speed, rationality and smoothness. The union concerned

had a reputation in Fleet Street as tough negotiators, but they, and especially the Father of their Chapel, stuck to their main and proper duty of looking after the interests of their members. With the assistance of Smith's specialist Labour Adviser, terms of transfer for those willing to move and of compensation for those who did not, were negotiated justly and humanely. From Smith's point of view a major gain was the reduction in the excessive and costly overtime working which had, over the years, become a familiar but increasingly unacceptable element in the inefficiencies of Bridge House. Smith's were concerned in this, as in many other respects, with the interests of the business. But, as Professor Loasby has written, their attitude and actions were not wholly self-interested. 'The formulation and execution of a policy which owed something to the recognition of the firm's moral responsibilities was an essential element in the success of the company's plans.' And that, in turn, went back a long way in the history of the family business. One of the Chapel officials summed it all up with a telling understatement: 'They would never knowingly do you a bad turn.'[4] It was not a bad explanation of the success of the Swindon experiment.[5]

Not all the targets were hit at once. Early computers were fallible: their human operators even more fallible. But after one or two years of teething troubles Swindon was working to plan. Historically, it had been an extraordinary feature of W. H. Smith's that it had made little use of 'fixed' technology of its own: of others – railways especially – yes: but in the computer drive Smith's, for the first time, was in the van with the exploitation of a revolutionary technology and well ahead of all its retail neighbours and rivals. Swindon was built round the computer and would have been impossible without it.

An immediate consequence of the cost of the move to Swindon was intense pressure on the firm's resources of capital and cash. Before the warehouse was completed in 1967, plans were in the making for the removal of the traditionally central operation of news despatch from Strand House. By 1966 other related changes were under way. The result was an urgent need for more capital. The Holdings Executive was agreed that it would be necessary to raise more capital: there was less agreement about how and when it should be done. By July it was clear that there would have to be tighter control over capital expenditure and the use of working capital. It had to be accepted that this would necessarily slow down the expansion of the Smith group, at least for a time.

At the end of August there was a formal decision to issue £2 million 8 per cent debentures (redeemable 1987–92). The temper of the times and government was cautious: it was reflected in a talk the chairman had with Lloyds Bank in mid-September. They reminded him that the overdraft they had agreed to provide (and had provided) was simply to bridge the gap between the payment for Swindon and the prospective sale of Bridge House.

For over a year the financial stringency was acute. All manner of ways of easing the demand for capital (e.g. leasing – instead of buying – computers, motor vehicles, property, increasing bank overdrafts, issuing debentures) were explored. Then, as suddenly as it had arrived, the crisis eased. A tender of £1.9 million was accepted for Bridge House: by 1970 the sale of Strand House for £3.78 million was under negotiation. It became possible to resume plans for further expansion. But it had been a baptism of fire: uncomfortable but salutary. It was the sharpest experience of that stop-go which operates in the private as well as the public sector of finance. The result was to tighten the screws on the mechanisms for reducing all unnecessary waste and rising costs. To the extent that this meant closer budgetary control, it gave added justification for more detailed, centralised management of cash flow and capital investment. For if the company was to remain competitive it had both to save and invest. There was, for example, the problem of the headquarters offices and operating organisations at Strand House.

Operation 'Streamline' and the Decentralisation of London News Despatch

By the latter part of 1964, the reorganisation of the retail trade, the rearrangement of news despatch and the birth of ideas about Swindon had their repercussions on thinking about the future of Strand House in Portugal Street. The proposed decentralisation of news from London and the move of book distribution to Swindon meant that Strand House, originally built as a warehouse, was now being used largely as an office block. This was unsatisfactory and uneconomical. It was old-fashioned in design, it lacked light and was generally unsuitable for offices. A committee was set up to consider its future in relation to the other current changes in total organisation.[6]

It became known that the London School of Economics, adjacent to Strand House and themselves very short of space, were interested in its future. In 1967, they renewed their enquiry in more positive terms: they were promised an answer in six months' time (which they did not get).

Finally the 'Streamline Committee' (as it was called after the name given to the whole operational reorganisation) recommended that News Despatch and Transport for the London area should be dispersed from Strand House to King's Cross, Wembley, Fulham, Dalston and Peckham. It was no longer possible to combine operational services and management offices in one Strand House. But until the terms on which the Newspaper Proprietors' Association were willing to supply news to these depots were known, it was not sure whether the result would be a large gain or an equally large loss.

The conundrum now became: who should move and where to? This in turn was further complicated by current trends in the newspaper publishing industry towards regional newspaper printing, which could have important consequences on W. H. Smith's organisation. The Holdings Executive therefore entered upon a complicated series of calculations which compared current total operating costs with those which would prevail if the whole of headquarters departments and news handling were moved out of London (for example, to Swindon or some location nearer to London). Was the total move out of London too expensive, too complicated? How about using the lower floors of (old) Strand House for news handling and leasing the upper floors to the LSE?

The solution finally came by adding together several adjacent sites in Smith's ownership, buying others and exchanging yet others to form a site worth developing for a building 'of the type and size desired' – a 10-storey tower block, designed by Casson, Conder & Partners as offices for the Boards, top executives and head office service and other departments. All distributory or selling operations were to be moved elsewhere. The new building would, *D.V.*, be occupied by March 1975. Meanwhile, in October 1970, terms were agreed to sell old Strand House, Portugal Street, to the London School of Economics for £3.78 million plus legal costs and surveyors' fees, etc.[7]

A Philosophy of Development

David Smith was the seventh successive member of the family to lead the firm; the fifth to lead the firm which bore the name W. H. Smith & Son and was recognisably the progenitor of the company as it exists today. Yet his retirement as chairman on 25 May 1972 was more than a break in a dynasty that had lasted 180 years. His colleagues on the Holdings Board recorded his period of office as:

an example of integrity, of consideration for others and of devotion to the interests of this business which can never be forgotten by any who worked with him ... under his leadership this Company has met with success the several challenges it has faced and is now in an exceedingly strong financial and competitive position.

They did not exaggerate. The changes and growing strength of the business were owed to many persons and circumstances; but without the meticulous care he had brought to the guidance of the business, the choice of colleagues and understanding of human relationships, the successes they described might have been delayed or been totally missed. For his twenty-three years of office[8] he represented not merely the end of one tradition but the beginning of another – the transformation of the business itself into a highly organised modern public company, as highly organised techno-logically, financially, and administratively as it had always been com-mercially. This in turn was made possible by his acceptance of the need to cultivate new talent in the top management, especially C. H. W. Troughton and P. W. Bennett, who were successively to follow David Smith as chairman of the Limited Board, then of the Holdings Board, and by the addition of directors recruited both from inside and outside the company whose knowledge and experience made possible the steady evolution of business policy in the early decades of the reorganised public company. In 1949 it faced massive problems, severe constraints; by 1972 it had achieved notable successes, suffered a few failures and was still engaged in the never-ending pursuit of its goals.

Many of the post-war problems were temporary: some were unavoid-able, some were due to the unnecessary bureaucratic paralysis caused by a government to whom interference with the economy had become a per-manent anodyne, a habit of mind that persisted in Britain long after it had disappeared from most of Western Europe. Unavoidable were those con-straints which arose from the very nature of a distributory business, especially the distribution of literature, above all 'dated' literature, such as newspapers and magazines, on a vast scale. They were almost immediately commercially 'perishable'; their purchase, distribution and sale therefore called for judgment, vigilance and experience. Supplies did not flow freely and unimpeded in an open market (as they could in, say, the food or cloth-ing trades). They were subject to such collective associations as the News-paper Proprietors' Association, the Publishers' Association, the several Associations representing the independent newsagents, the trade unions, especially in the printing trade where militancy and restrictive practices went back more than a century; to say nothing of price maintenance and the Net Book Agreement. The major retail outlets down to 1906 (and still very important thereafter) were the railway bookstalls, and their business hung on agreements, reached – if they were reached – with increasing difficulty as the scores of rail companies had gradually consolidated into the nationalsed British Railways of 1948. A peculiar irritant among the (happily) transitory constraints was the so-called 'Selective Employment Tax'. This was a device of the Labour Party for resuscitating perhaps the most antediluvian of all those economic monstrosities which placed a special burden on the employment of so-called 'non-productive' labour, comparable only to Adam Smith's relegation of merchants, alongside comedians, as a 'non-productive' form of economic activity. It caused a distributory trade, like Smith's, great anxiety and a temporary reduction in profits.

W. H. Smith's had to learn to live, if possible harmoniously, with all these forces: but they were not without punch. This consisted in the experience they had acquired over more than a century of their trade and the reputation that went with it.

With the floating of the public company in 1949 came the need for a reorganisation of top management to deal not only with the transitional problems of the immediate post-war years but to identify the fundamental problems, arrange them in order of priority, and evolve consciously ways and means of recovering the old decisiveness of the era of the Hornby benevolent autocracy. The methods of those days were no longer possible in the conditions of the 1940s and after. W. H. Smith & Son (Holdings) Ltd came into being for reasons irrelevant to the business it undertook; but once created it had (in the phrase used more than once by its directors) to be 'seen and believed' to represent the interests of the shareholders and somehow balance the interests of all those, inside and outside the business, to whom the company owed a duty – staff, working force, customers. The responsibilities of top management were now very broad and they were long-term. They could not be left to improvisation, though the readiness and ability to improvise when improvisation was unavoidable (as it sometimes was) remained a vital *desideratum* of management. Planning therefore had to become a normal part of management's task. It may be seen in physical form in many of the structural changes of these years; the creation of departments to study special problems and increase the effectiveness with which they were tackled (such as Organisation and Methods and Marketing Research), new – 'more drastic' – procedures to control capital expenditure and identify the amounts of capital and its source; more specialised attention to staff and training activities and to what had come to be called 'public relations' problems, and so on.

These had led to the identification of the traditional major activities of Smith's – retail and wholesaling of news, periodicals, books, etc. – as the central areas to be given first priority for reorganisation. In the process that followed, the idea had emerged and solidified that planning, like peace, was indivisible; in short, that what was needed was 'Corporate Planning' covering the entire business, not just bits of it. A department had come into being to initiate, develop and execute such plans. But it was soon apparent that (here as everywhere) it was easier to recognise the limitless merits of planning as a way of life than to define and organise it in practice. Shortly before C. H. W. Troughton became chairman of the Limited Board in September 1969, he examined some of these aspects of corporate planning; his comments were frank. 'There must be', he wrote, 'some fundamental principles . . . But I find it difficult to find anything which all have in common – apart from the appalling jargon to which most writers seem to conform.'

Accordingly, he set down what he saw to be the assumptions on which the firm's objectives should be based and the outlines of means 'to get the planning procedures off the ground'. The 'assumptions' were a broad prediction of 22 conditions and probabilities likely to hold good over the next decade. They included the existence of a mixed private/public economy, a shift towards indirect taxation, a majority age of 18, expensive money, rising living standards for 'all but the highest groups', more literacy but probably not a higher degree of education . . . etc.: a broad and on the whole pretty accurate set of predictions.

The 'objectives' were to make a profit sufficient to pay a reasonable dividend and allow enough to be ploughed back and itself earn 20 per cent in the second and subsequent years. Factors affecting the size of the profit included the right attitude to those working in the company, i.e. 'ruthlessness in decision but generosity as a result to those who suffer by the ruthlessness . . .' This he saw as a traditional W. H. Smith 'attitude'.

There are things more important than the shareholders' share of the loot . . . there has been awareness that we ought to be in the van of those who saw the need for social change and innovation. Though we lost some of the latter as the rest of the world have followed us it is likely, I hope, that we will continue to advance on this front.

He listed the constraints of the past and present. The family 'stake' in the company could have been one in the past: but no longer. The main constraint was 'an inability to break out from the cyclical nature of the trade we are in . . . which deals with the written word in dated form. This still dominates us.' Lack of management capacity had sometimes been believed to be a constraining factor (on mergers and acquisitions for example). With the widened 'base of the Board' this was no longer true. Finance had been a constraint because 'we tended to have a more conserving attitude than an expansive one'.

From these reflections emerged the basis for the next five years' planning. It should aim at expanding existing operations, accelerating them by acquisitions or merger, entering upon new types of business operation, and cutting out 'deadwood operations'. But how should it be done? *Not* by expanding a costly, special department labelled 'Corporate Planning'. It should be for the directors and managing directors to do the planning themselves. The size of the Corporate Planning Department must be kept 'extremely small . . . I would recruit no one to it at all until the Chief Executive feels the need or until the Managing Directors see the requirement.'

These were to be the lines on which the company was to go ahead, and they were a fair indication of the extent to which the new management had recovered the capacity for articulate decision-making based on broad, bold but not rash, thinking.

Pruning and Planting

The Board naturally traced the paths they knew with surer tread than others they knew less well. Decisions to shed existing ventures were not easy to take, involving as they did getting rid of staff. In 1961, nevertheless, they managed to abandon long-held hopes for the enterprise once known as BFD (Business Forms Department) and more recently christened Alacra. Its performance under the new name showed no improvement on the old. In its 27 years it had never consistently been profitable: it was decided to sell. The following year it was bought by Spicers, the paper and stationery manufacturers.

Another doubtful investment was Versatile Fittings, whose profits (1961) were not felt to 'justify the attention required . . .'. The company had been launched because Smith's needed its products – ready-made shop fittings. Since no one else would take it on Smith's had done it itself. It survived the doubts of 1961 for another eleven years, in the hope that better management might improve the prospects of selling to a buyer with a larger and more direct interest in its product. These hopes were not realised. In 1972 it went.

The fate of the library had been virtually sealed in the 1950s. Another ancient and honourable monument, the Binding Department, had been closed (with some regret) in 1963. The printing works at Stafford sealed its own fate by being burnt down in November 1962. Its goodwill was transferred to the firm's Hambleden Press at Huntingdon, where it was already planned to concentrate the modest remains of Herbert Morgan's printing ambitions.[9]

Even more reluctantly, but in the end decisively, the decision was taken in 1972 to reduce the scale of operations of WHS Transport Ltd. Here, it had been hoped, was the skeleton of a transport network which could be expanded for parcel distribution nationally: and its operations were actually increasing. But heavy investment would have been required to buy sites and erect the depots necessary for expansion. That would raise costs instead of reducing them by comparison with those of established competitors. Transport was therefore left to concentrate on covering Smith's own needs, at least for the time being. Here was a real victim of the new round of inflation.

Of a quite different order were the cutbacks of the smaller bookstalls and shops in the mid-1960s. These arose first and foremost out of the priority given to the reform of the retail side of the business in the battle for greater profitability. An early request of the Retail Group had been permission to close down unremunerative branches. A thorough enquiry into the turnover, rents and profits of 209 main bookstalls on British Railways in 1965 showed that the group of the 33 smallest stalls (with a turnover of up to £10,000 each) was making a loss. Another 100 or so stalls in the £10,000–£25,000 category made an inadequate profit. When C. H. W. Troughton took over the problem early in 1969, he pointed out[10] that while British Railways were, by the terms of their existing contract signed in 1953 and valid until the end of 1973, 'interested in turnover', 'We are interested in profitability'. Probably the railways thought the contract was 'very much more valuable to us than it is in money terms'. If 'central expenses' were charged, it provided between 3 and 5½ per cent of Smith's net profit. While it would be better than nothing to renegotiate the contract, it would be better still to go for an entirely new joint company between British Railways and Smith's: to be managed by Smith's. At present all Smith's reward for enterprise went to the railway, which contributed nothing.

The firm line Smith's felt able to take is the best indication of the declining importance of the railway bookstalls in general. Only the largest would finally survive with any profit. Meanwhile a similar trend was showing in the shop sector. In both sectors, costs were high and profit margins small: an unpromising combination which could be countered only by aiming for size, large turnover and relatively small overheads. As long ago as the days of W. H. Smith II, Lethbridge and then Hornby had argued long and hard with the railway companies about the inordinate costs of maintaining stall service on small stations with few travellers. Now it was more true then ever. The aged newsvendor at Guide Bridge, for whose disappearance W. H. Smith II had to apologise over a century earlier, was as prophetic as his appearance (see page 140).

That the profit figures at last followed the example of turnover and capital and turned decisively upwards in 1961 was largely due to the positive contribution of the reform of the retail and wholesale trade. But the elimination of uneconomic operations (including those just described), certainly contributed. The fact that a number of them were manufacturing enterprises throws some doubt on the arguments (sometimes used in Board discussions of potential areas of expansion) favouring 'vertical integration'. The exploration to date of this type of diversification – printing, binding, shop fittings, business forms – had not been by any means consistently profitable. They were all of the type sometimes described in the infelicitous jargon of economists as 'backward integration', i.e. back into manufacture. And that demanded an expertise not traditional to Smith's.

Horizontal expansion (i.e. mergers, acquisitions in the retail or wholesale field) had been brisk, but this did little to lessen Smith's dependence on the suppliers of news, books and stationery which was causing some anxiety. Further 'forward integration' seemed – at this stage – hardly possible except in terms of continuing efforts in the retail shop trade. The sale of gramophone records was booming: they had more than filled the gap left by the libraries, physically and financially. On the wholesale side, further acquisitions, especially in the Sunday trade, were possible. Were there other fields left to be explored? Smith's believed so.

In the late 1960s the phrase 'leisure activities' became a popular way of describing the general field of commercial activities suited to the W. H. Smith tradition and ethos. Apart from books and magazines about leisure activities was there not merchandise used in such activities which might provide a natural extension of Smith's retail expertise? For example, sports equipment, fishing tackle, sports clothing, etc.? If Lillywhites or Liberty's could specialise, why not Smith's? What about travel? Should there be a new look at outdoor advertising? Should the record business be extended further into the more recent market for cassettes and films? And was the mail-order and book-club market being developed as rapidly and thoroughly as it might be?

A number of these suggestions were to bear fruit. Three fall within the period of this book. In November 1970, W. H. Smith Cassettes Ltd came into being in response to the rapidly growing interest in cassettes and enquiries from numerous sources. But it looked further ahead to the development and distribution of video cassettes and cassette players. C. H. W. Troughton felt that 'to maintain our position and reputation for being first in the distribution field' Smith's could not afford to neglect opportunities to join in investment projects for production too. W. H. Smith Cassettes Ltd was therefore authorised to invest up to £50,000 in such projects subject to reporting fully to the Holdings Board.

So far, so good. But it was a third and novel exploration of what had, after all, always been Smith's major interest in leisure – viz. reading – that was to prove the most immediately and strikingly successful among the new ventures. 'Book Clubs' were not new in the 1960s. In the United States they were already well established. They were, in one respect, a form of customer service by post rather than over the shop counter. The phrase 'mail-order' formed part of the business vocabulary which Herbert Morgan had acquired during his education in America: he was probably the first in W. H. Smith's to initiate discussion of its merits. But it had never made more than limited progress in W. H. Smith's before the Second World War. Other publishers ran book clubs – Foyles and Odhams notably – and one, the Reprint Society, already had a large membership. By 1963 the 'incidental supplying of books by post' by Smith's, as it was described, catered only for customers out of reach of any W. H. Smith branch. Its total turnover was about £40,000 a year. When the proposal to broaden this marginal activity into a major line of business on the North American model was considered, the chairman was hesitant: more thought would have to be given to the English application of the American systems outlined before any major decision could be taken.[11]

Nevertheless, the idea had taken hold. By July it was decided to enter the mail-order field in modest force: £24,000 was allocated for a start in 1963/4. A year later, an experimental scheme was initiated. A special company, Heron Books, would advertise in the *Sunday Times*, offering to supply any books advertised or reviewed in that issue. Smith's would supply, pack and despatch books to customers who asked for them. Heron Books would be charged for titles ordered at a suitable discount, would collect payment, and conduct any necessary correspondence. By the summer, an American book marketing and publishing consultant had advised on the full-scale development of the scheme. Eight leading publishers were ready to join in a scheme of special discounts for mail-order promotion. It was to operate from Bridge House.

The 'Direct Book Service' made rapid progress: so rapid that by 1966 the full conversion to a 'book club' was under active consideration with the American publishers, Doubleday & Co. Inc., who were experienced and successful operators in the American book club field. In October Milton Runyon, their vice-president, joined Smith's in the discussion of a proposed merger of the Reprint Society and other book clubs with the Smith Direct Book Service, under the umbrella of a Smith-Doubleday partnership to be known as Book Club Associates. It was to be a 50/50 partnership: that meant it either went with a swing or not at all. It went with a swing.

One obstacle which had seriously hobbled book club development in Britain was the Publishers' Association's rule which prohibited the issue of a cheap edition of any new book until twelve months after the publication of the library edition. The essence of a book club was that subscribing members received the books of their choice at a special reduced price. When the Holdings Executive discussed P. W. Bennett's proposal to tackle this basic problem with the publishers, they agreed with his initiative, but were careful to warn him against doing anything to rock the boat so far as relations with the publishing industry were concerned. They need not have worried. As book distributors Smith's carried considerable counterpunch. Even before the publishers formally agreed to remove the obstructive rule in 1968, Book Club Associates had already forged ahead. The Cookery Book Club, launched in September 1966 with a target of 25,000 members within two years, already had 28,000 members by January 1967. The Reprint Society, with 40,000 members when it was acquired in November 1966, expected a membership of 100,000 by the end of 1967. On the form they were showing in early 1967 a turnover of nearly £1 million seemed likely by the end of the year, on which the new partnership could expect a return of about 10 per cent net. That this return did not materialise was due to the mixed blessing that Book Club Associates' business expansion temporarily outran their capacity to contain and control it.

The accommodation problem was ultimately and satisfactorily solved by BCA's removal to Swindon. Here, like Smith's own normal distributive system to their own branches, it became a technology-based scheme steadily expanding until it was to have in 1983 a membership of 1,700,000. Its own initial impetus received an additional push from an agreement with the British Printing Corporation in 1970 for the exchange of franchises and services.

The success of the book club venture was extraordinary: at first sight surprising. If the competition of free public libraries had put the private commercial libraries out of business so completely, how was it that a scheme to sell more books could achieve such spectacular success, presumably in a market more or less similar to that for book borrowing? The answers are not beyond doubt; they are certainly multiple. First, there had always been a market for the supply of books (by post) to areas remote from a good public (or private) library or bookshop. Mail-order or some alternative type of supply had always found a market in such areas. But so far as sales were concerned, the Publishers' Association's ban on simultaneous publication in a book club series had been a serious drawback. Their decision of 1968 blew the whistle for a new game to begin.

There were other attractions. Membership of a book club was an easy Christmas or birthday present to give and a gratifying one to receive. For those who paid for their own membership, the discount involved represented a bargain: a thing of beauty and interest was a joy forever; even more so when it was a bargain. Finally, the book club system had devised a psychologically ingenious appeal to a wide spread of human desires, interests and weaknesses. It was a convenience to those who knew where their reading interests lay and therefore what they wanted, with expert advice available to help in the process of selection. But it also appealed to those who rarely entered a bookshop; who had neither the leisure nor inclination nor perhaps the necessary educational background to select the books they wanted and who felt relieved of a burden they were unable to shoulder: perhaps in some cases too mentally lazy to face. There was also still an agreeable element of surprise and pleasure in receiving a book by post: though what was a benefit to the members could be a curse to the organisers. A prolonged postal strike was the weakest spot in the armour of any book club. This apart, BCA was a spectacular success, an harmonious partnership which showed that, like charity, business success was often to be found nearer home than had been suspected. For book selling was Smith's second oldest major activity. Like some of the directors of the Holdings Board, William Henry I had distrusted his son's enthusiasm for books and seen nothing but trouble ahead in such new-fangled ideas. In the 1960s an adroit twist in the application of marketing skills to the techniques and technology of book selling and distribution proved a more than adequate compensation for the ending of Smith's libraries. And it left the membership, the partners and the publishers all as satisfied as could, in the imperfect world of popular literature and its distribution, be expected.

The 'Pedigree Book Shops'

Some of the factors that helped to explain the growth of book clubs and the general increase in book sales also help to explain the successful entry into a different field of bookselling in the shape of what came to be called the 'pedigree book shops'. The idea of creating a group of specialised book shops of 'quality' sprang mainly from the important changes that were taking place in government policy on higher education in the 1950s.

The Robbins Report[12] of 1963 was only one of the channels through which came the message that Britain needed more universities and institutes of higher education than were provided by Oxford, Cambridge, Durham, a handful of ancient Scottish, Irish and Welsh foundations and the modern, municipal 'red brick'. There were to be new foundations at York, Brighton, Lancaster, Stirling, Norwich, Warwick, etc.

At a stroke, the new educational policy added a new dimension to the already growing market for books. (Robbins envisaged a doubling of the higher education student population from under a quarter of a million to more than half a million.) Since the 1920s W. H. Smith had owned a few specialised bookshops, under the name of Truslove & Hanson in London. In the 1950s a new venture was born in a different but more appropriate place: in Cambridge, and it was called Bowes & Bowes. The building, known to every Cambridge don and undergraduate, stood in the heart of the academic centre of the city, flanked on the south by Great St Mary's, the University Church; facing on the west side Gonville & Caius College, James Gibbs's elegant Senate House, and King's College Chapel. Bowes & Bowes was picturesque, well placed, but small.

The Bowes & Bowes building had a long and curious history. In the 1840s it had fallen into the hands of a northern adventurer from the Isle of Arran, Daniel Macmillan, as a centre of bookselling and publishing. The firm prospered. Its first resounding success was the publication of Charles Kingsley's *Two Years Ago*. It went on to publish other works by Kingsley, Huxley, Tennyson, Lightfoot, J. R. Green, Lewis Carroll, and many other rising authors . . . in short, Macmillans were to become 'one of the most important publishing houses in the world'.

Between 1882 and 1907 the firm was styled Macmillan and Bowes

(Robert Bowes was a nephew of the Macmillans). 'Old Bowes', as he was known, faithfully reflected the character of the business itself; scholarly, eccentric, surrounded by a small staff mostly as antique as the books they bought and sold.

This home of true if dusty learning had passed after the Second World War into more ambitious hands. The ambition centred on printing and publishing. But the times were not propitious. Paper was scarce and capital scarcer. By early 1953, Bowes & Bowes was again on the market and it was acquired by W. H. Smith at an appropriately reasonable price. The new acquisition was quickly on the move, but not always in the right direction. The building, as has been already remarked, was small, and planning restrictions made it impossible to build out or up. Frank Reeve, the old Bowes & Bowes anchor man, son of a printer at the Cambridge University Press, and an experienced academic bookseller with a shopman's wry sense of humour and an equally wry sense of business, plainly thought little of Smith's as booksellers.

Their early decision to abolish the second-hand book trade he condemned forthrightly as 'a gross mistake'. Still, he stayed on (at a much improved salary) as assistant manager. Bowes & Bowes expanded by opening two sub-shops, specialising in modern language and scientific books, farther down Trinity Street. But as the Robbins dream materialised over other parts of Britain, Bowes & Bowes became the first of a growing chain of 'pedigree' shops, designed to serve the new or expanded universities elsewhere.

The Cambridge shops formally assumed their function with style and title of head of the new group in 1961. But some of the 'pedigree' shops dated back much earlier. Truslove & Hanson dated from 1923. The Bath shop in Milsom Street was of even earlier provenance (1906). Southampton University College bookshop was already present as a subsidiary to a town branch in the early 1930s. At Manchester, the Sherratt & Hughes shop had been acquired in 1946. The main Bowes & Bowes shop at Trinity Street, Cambridge, had emerged as the potential leader of the 'pedigree' group in 1953. New university shops in East Anglia were opened at Norwich and at Colchester in 1963/4 and 1964/5. In London, W. J. Bryce was acquired in 1965 (and later resold). Two shops opened at Sheffield in 1967/8. Thus the Bowes & Bowes group spread its services over the British universities old and new. In the field of academic literature the 'pedigree' shops (thirteen in all by 1971) were beginning to represent for Smith's a new type of professional bookselling.

The new retail shops and stalls were the spearhead of the drive to reorganise an ageing business for a new era, a new economy and a new society with changing needs and changing tastes. Like any piece of complex machinery, the new retail system had to be purpose-built, functional and, above all, flexible enough to allow for a continuing rate of economic and social change.

The Bowes & Bowes group served a growing academic market. Yet it was not simply a 'market of academics'. There was general agreement with C. H. W. Troughton when he argued on 20 March 1967 in favour of developing the Bowes Group 'on broader lines than simply University bookselling'. He envisaged over the next three or four years the establishment of a chain of 25 or 30 'books-only bookshops'. There was room 'in many towns and cities for both W.H.S. and Bowes shops. For this kind of business a first-class High Street position was not essential.' Where no premises were available they must consider 'buying into established businesses . . .' And that, in the age of the Open University, was logical.

XX

～⌒⌒⌒⌒～

Progress and Profitability

Overseas Expansion

SMITH'S BUSINESS WAS essentially a home business. From the start, it had bought, sold and distributed (mainly) newspapers and books in English to English-speaking readers. This had been its main function in the British economy and its main contribution to a national 'culture'. The same circumstances that provided a firm base in Britain circumscribed its frontiers and inhibited growth abroad – certainly growth of the kind that was open, for example, to manufacturers, whose products were more or less equally attractive to French and Germans or Africans and Indians. Yet the nineteenth and twentieth centuries were above all centuries of development in transport and travel. The British were foremost in both. Hence Smith's also developed, but on a modest scale, export trade and overseas branches: probably most of their export trade and the business of their (two) overseas shops was due to British customers resident abroad: but not all.

When the partners published for private circulation in 1921 a little book describing the firm,[1] the author found the export departments the most exciting of all.

> . . . for it is there that the romance of the Firm's worldwide distribution can be most clearly realised. It is the proud boast of that Department that there is not one reasonably civilised portion of the globe where the firm of W. H. Smith & Son is not in some way represented, by agents or otherwise, and to which books, newspapers, and periodicals are not sent out . . . by steamer, train or aeroplane, on pack mules or the heads of native porters . . .

Much of this commerce was doubtless with British expatriates helping to govern, or educate throughout the Commonwealth, or to develop trade in Europe. But the writer also noted '... Many requests ... in all the languages of the globe, or couched in the quaintest so-called English ...' These asked for information and literature, and a 'little book' of prices and information was prepared. The export trade was described as 'already large', though after decades of removals, waste-paper drives and the like, when records were lost, it is impossible to know exactly what this meant. It can only be said that though hindered by strikes, wars, riots, tariffs, prohibitions and other manifestations of the progress of twentieth century national and international civility, the trade continued to grow. It reached a figure of over £1,200,000 in 1956/7.

For reasons already mentioned there was little national scope for Smith's foreign enterprise to transform itself from the 'export phase' to that of local manufacture; to follow, in short, the path towards the multinational model that seemed the natural development for so many large manufacturer/ exporter industries which found thereby a way to meet problems of tariffs and local preferences. Abroad, Smith's task was to provide for its customers the same distributory services it produced at home. It was over a hundred years before it had acquired its first overseas shop, in the Rue de Rivoli in Paris. In 1903 this was bought from two English brothers called Neal for the modest sum of £5,500, and its clientele was plainly English: the vendors undertook not to re-start a similar business in Paris or in 'towns on the Riviera, such as Nice, Cannes, Mentone, and *those most frequented by English visitors*'. It was one of a number of St John Hornby's acquisitions of the period – but a rather special one. Plainly he saw (or foresaw) the world that was already taking shape, to be brilliantly described later by P. G. Wode-house and Agatha Christie, a world to which upper- and upper-middle-class English were to be carried to the holiday of their dreams by the 'Golden Arrow', the 'Blue Train', in Napiers and later Rolls Royces ... that kicked up clouds of dust that enveloped and no doubt enraged hundreds of peasants in France as they enraged (see *The Wind In the Willows*) Kenneth Grahame and R. C. K. Ensor at home.[2]

For these classes, Smith's provided the usual services. Their homesickness was abated by prompt and regular supplies of *The Times* or the *Morning Post*, plenty of books to buy or borrow at the well-stocked library, familiar stationery on which to write home and, perhaps above all, a tea-room where real English tea and buns could be drunk and eaten. Result, a quite prosperous if modest business which paid profits that had risen by the 1920s to £10,000 a year. 'Big Bertha' failed to close it down in the First

World War. Its English pleasures continued to be dispensed behind its nostalgically green front and WHS sign. Even after the French government moved to Bordeaux, W. H. Smith's remained in Paris with a welcome to British servicemen on leave.

The Continent, it seemed in 1920, was perhaps worth another modest step forward. Feelings towards Belgium had been warm in wartime England. Brussels and Ostend had seemed close to England. A site for a shop was found in the Rue du Marché aux Herbes, suitably near the proposed Central Railway Station. The Brussels enterprise was modelled closely on Paris, with all the usual features of an English news-shop, plus, of course, a tea-room. Among those who were ready to encourage the partners were the family of the great Hachette publishing house of Paris. M. Fouret, head of Hachette, wrote to Hornby in the summer of 1921 with an admiring welcome for the skill he had shown in promoting '. . . la fortune de votre grande maison, presque unique dans le monde entier. Quel magnifique exemple, et quels encouragements à donner aux jeunes gens qui entrent dans les affaires . . .'[3] Among them, it appeared, was his nephew Louis. He would be in London next week on business '. . . would it be possible . . . etc.?'

This was all very well. But there were also signals which suggested that M. Fouret's vision of a special relationship might have a less acceptable side. From the great, but now ailing, Northcliffe himself in his villa at Roquebrune on the coastal fringe of the Alpes Maritimes, came a warning rumour. He had heard from Garner, Hornby's man in Brussels, that it was believed '. . . the Germans have bought up Hachettes. According to your man, Hachettes have bought up Dechennes . . .' What was going on?

Hornby was impressed. Garner was sound. Hornby's partner, Sir William Acland, had also come back from Paris and Brussels full of rumours:

> . . . Hachettes are backed by German money, and . . . making a strong bid for the control of the Belgian, and subsequently of the Dutch, newspaper distributing and bookstall business, with a view . . . to propaganda work, from which German influence will not be excluded.

The Kaiser still ruled. Hornby was all for the English newspaper proprietors standing behind Northcliffe, with a veto on supplies to Hachette if necessary, to stop this pernicious penetration of Belgium. 'An English Firm starting in Belgium should, I think, have all the support possible from English Newspaper Proprietors.'

How much truth there was in this feverish gossip is not easy to assess; probably not much. The basic fact was to emerge that – Germans or no Germans – Brussels, and its short-lived subsidiary at Ostend, were much less successful than had been hoped. Profits were small, losses frequent. Nevertheless, Smith's held on. Garner – still in office – could write in 1934:

> The great hopes we had in 1919 of creating very great business in Belgium were quickly dissipated when we got down to real work here. The situation . . . then most favourable changed very rapidly, and has never since been the same. As Brussels was the first House created abroad, we had to work very much in the dark, so it is not at all surprising that we 'barked our shins' very badly.

In spite of setbacks, Paris and Brussels survived the Second World War. Enthusiasm for Continental potential remained. And there were still vast English-speaking communities far away overseas. What, for example, of Canada? Even perhaps the USA?

The Canadian enterprise was launched in the post-war era when 'multinationals' were the latest thing: but this was a multinational with a difference. The majority of such ventures consisted of manufacturing subsidiaries of large American or European concerns anxious to explore the promise of less developed but often heavily protected markets in other countries. To clear the tariff walls which obstructed an established export trade, a local manufacturer would be set up. The successful launch of such an enterprise often brought with it the secondary but substantial merits of closing the gap of distance between the goods and the customer. Local manufacture (and management by locals) often reduced the problems involved in meeting the requirements of local laws, regulations, religious or customary taboos, labour laws and the like. It also enabled manufacturers to assess more closely local tastes and preferences of consumers and take advantage of local supplies of labour and raw materials. True, there were disadvantages. They included growing nationalist sentiment, and legislation and discrimination against foreign capital and entrepreneurs. Nevertheless, multinational investment grew, to become a leading characteristic of the international economy in the second half of the twentieth century.

To a point, therefore, Smith's was following in the train of a growing body of commercial experience when it founded W. H. Smith & Son (Canada) Ltd, incorporated on 7 November 1949. In 1951 the chairman's Annual Report proclaimed that the company:

[had] opened its first shop in Toronto at the end of September, 1950 . . .
While it will be some time before this Company will be operating at a
profit, I am convinced that it will turn out to be a wise investment, and
that, as time goes on, further branches will be opened.

Both predictions proved well-founded. In 1953/4 a first measure of
'physical expansion' of the Canadian business was announced. It arose from
the purchase of the bookshops of the Canadian booksellers, Burtons Ltd.
Burtons had book stores in Ottawa and Montreal. They were timed for
takeover in 1954 and 1955. The belief on which the investment rested was
that Smith's had found a vacuum in Canadian commercial organisation
which they could best fill: it was not so much as newsagents but as booksellers that they went to Canada. Their judgment was not wrong: as one
of the largest booksellers in Europe, Smith's had a tradition of expertise in
books and bookselling which few if any North American rivals could
equal. Was their expertise a commodity which could itself be profitably
sold in Canada? This could only be answered by trying it out. Smith's
were unlucky with conditions of trade and money in the early years.
Their vision was of a chain of prime bookshops stretching from coast to
coast and making profits – very necessary for a British economy which
was still suffering from the economic drain of the war and the persisting
shortages of its aftermath, much longer than even the pessimists had
predicted. In the 1950s, as Peter Bennett, himself a Canadian, rightly said
'Britain was broke . . . and exporting *retailing* was a terribly difficult thing
to do.'

That was the point. W. H. Smith's, traditionally, were not – like most
firms which entered the field of multinational investment – manufacturers.
They had no manufactured article of their own for which they were
renowned. They were famous as skilled, well-informed and punctual distributors of literature. It was this skill in supplying the highly specialised
products of world publishers which they believed Canada could use: but
this was not a bright decade, even for booksellers in Canada.

In 1955/6 therefore 'progress' was 'slow': there was 'some way to go
before this subsidiary makes a profit'. In 1957/8 'Like many British businesses which have established themselves in Canada we have found that
progress has been slow' . . . This must be regarded as 'a long term development'. 1960/1 saw the first small profit but this happy augury was disappointed the following year. From 1962/3 business improved but even by
1965/6 the chairman could still make only the modest claim that: 'The
trend of profits is satisfactory but not their size'. The later 1960s saw

profitability and returns on capital improve. Turnover in 1967/8 rose to £1.3 million, profit before tax to £38,000. By 1971/2 turnover had risen to £2.1 million, profit before tax to £75,000. As the hoped-for 'long-term investment' of the 1950s, the Canadian venture was slowly beginning to take shape. But it remained small, representing only 1.6 per cent of the group turnover and 1.1 per cent of group pre-tax profits. Its fourteen retail shops (confined to Toronto, Montreal and Ottawa) and one wholesale house justified the claim of the originators that this was a worthwhile venture: and its slow improvement had been effected in the face of most difficult circumstances. The optimists were sufficiently satisfied to use Canada as a justification for further overseas ventures. The debate was to continue, as new factors – the computer in particular – were brought into play to change or rearrange the kaleidoscope that was the book trade. The thesis that the art and science of book retailing was generally for profitable export remained to be proved beyond doubt. Yet without risk, business enterprise would not exist. The cost of failure, certainly, was increasing; but as Peter Bennett put it: '. . . caution, by itself, leads nowhere'.

The first W. H. Smith shop had opened in Toronto in 1950. Fourteen years later, from the Special Holdings Board Meeting called at the Royal Albion Hotel, Brighton in December 1964, emerged a brief and rather wintry conclusion on the advisability of investing in businesses overseas. 'The Board felt that this was a matter which should be approached with a great deal of caution because of the difficulties of remote control management.' That did not mean overseas development was ruled out: four years later, in their discussions of possible areas into which Smith's could diversify and expand, the managing directors still included Australia and Canada. Any plans for Australian developments had to remain tentative until the future in Canada was clearer. The Canadian business was not yet self-supporting and this had to be achieved as soon as possible. The real hope for the future seemed to be in the east of Canada and from there possibly into the USA.

'Doubtful Titles', Censorship and Sales

The long saga of the battle for and against censorship runs right through the history of W. H. Smith's.[4] After the formation of the public company, the contrasting and contradictory arguments continued: should Smith's be reproved and if necessary prosecuted for selling, without censoring, books they should have censored themselves? Or should they be rebuked for censoring (e.g. by refusing to sell) books that should have been sold freely and without prudish interference? In 1963 a firm policy at last emerged. Books and periodicals were to be divided into three categories: (a) titles to be sold without restriction; (b) titles to be sold only to customers who ordered them individually; and (c) titles not to be handled at all. (Brussels and Paris shops were exempt from these rules; presumably on Laurence Sterne's conviction that 'They order this matter better in France' – or at least differently.)

A lingering concern for what an earlier observer had once called 'common decency', by now a generally less regarded aspect of the controversy, was still apparent: for example in the instructions to area managers that they should watch the display of paperbacks: lurid covers were not to be allowed to elbow out Penguins. But in a changing world, Smith's had to consider what they should sell in the light of current opinion. This was in fact what they had always done, even in days when Victorian moral opinion ruled most severely. What was new was that they no longer waited for trouble: they went out to meet it. When *The Times* and *The Times Literary Supplement* commented in 1966 that Smith's were still conducting a form of censorship in their marketing system, C. H. W. Troughton went and talked to their editors. He was able to report that they were:

> much more ready to see the Firm's point of view – that [WHS] had the right to decide what books they should sell, and that they ought not to be attacked for 'censorship' if they preferred not to sell the more unsavoury of today's outspoken books, or if they declined to handle books which they were advised carried a risk of prosecution for libel.

The matter arose again when Smith's agreed to join a panel on 'censorship' at a forum organised by the Publishers' Publicity Circle and the Society of Young Publishers. Their practice (it was agreed) remained as before:

> the vast majority of British books are available at or through all branches. A tiny minority are not stocked, but are available to order. And an even tinier minority are not handled at all (either on legal advice, or simply because we, in common with all other retailers, exercise the right to decide the kind of goods we handle).

The same point was reconfirmed in 1970, though with a small but significant change of emphasis. W. H. Smith's (the managing directors recorded) should be 'marginally ahead of public taste – in looking back on the rows of the past, i.e. *By Love Possessed⁵* which eventually won – we look ridiculous'. They might have added – what was doubtless in their minds – that there was no point in their continuing to fight battles that were already lost and by so doing make their own battle for business unnecessarily more difficult.

Unity in Diversity

The growth, development and diversification of the business in the 1960s carried with it important consequences not only for finance but also as regards management responsibilities. Some directors did not hesitate to speak out critically about the methods of control exercised over subsidiary companies and other sections of the business. C. H. W. Troughton enlarged on the methods adopted by other businesses whose systems of management were known to them. NAAFI exercised, in his opinion, too much direct control from the centre over the perimeter. At the other end of the spectrum was Unilever, who 'controlled' only through financial and management selection. In W. H. Smith's, managing directors and directors spent far too much time on the subsidiary businesses and became too much involved in detail. Subsidiary companies should be responsible directly to the Limited Board who should do no more than allot capital and choose management (in fact, on Unilever lines). One member of the main Board might sit on the Board of each subsidiary.

Out of this discussion emerged more detailed plans in 1969 and 1970. Their purpose was to provide in the Holdings Board 'the control, direction, and supervisory resources for an organisation . . . geared for expansion whether by acquisition, mergers, or diversification'. It should be the 'controlling vehicle' for all finance, appoint directors for approval by the shareholders, initiate future policy and be entirely responsible to the shareholders for the progress of the group and its annual results.

The group would continue to be run on a policy of 'centralised decision-making with decentralised execution'. It would incorporate 'the marketing function'. This had been defined as 'the whole concept of satisfying customers' needs profitably'. Integrated data processing, from which would flow a management information system, would be developed 'with speed and purpose'. The resulting system can be seen in Table XX.I.

Two features need a word of comment. First, W. H. Smith & Son (Canada) Ltd was shown as directly responsible to the Holdings Board

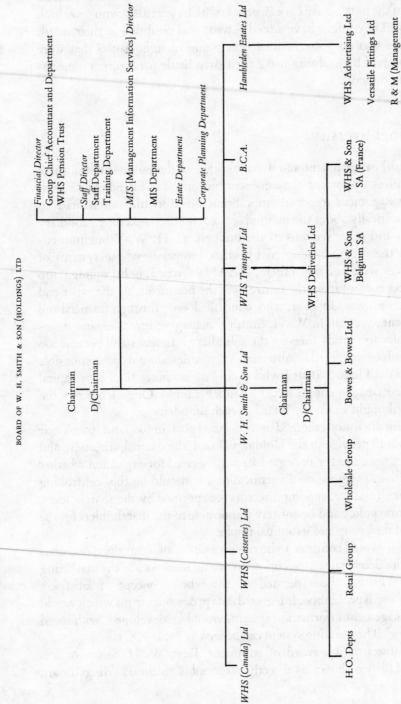

TABLE XX.I THE MANAGEMENT STRUCTURE, 1969/70

BOARD OF W. H. SMITH & SON (HOLDINGS) LTD

Financial Director
Group Chief Accountant and Department
WHS Pension Trust

Staff Director
Staff Department
Training Department

MIS [Management Information Services] Director
MIS Department

Estate Department
Corporate Planning Department

Chairman
D/Chairman

Hambleden Estates Ltd

B.C.A.

WHS Advertising Ltd
Versatile Fittings Ltd
R & M (Management Consultants) Ltd
WHS Bridge House Ltd

WHS Transport Ltd

WHS Deliveries Ltd

WHS & Son SA (France)
WHS & Son Belgium SA

W. H. Smith & Son Ltd

Chairman
D/Chairman

Bowes & Bowes Ltd

Wholesale Group

Retail Group

H.O. Depts

WHS (Canada) Ltd   WHS (Cassettes) Ltd

rather than, as the European subsidiaries were, to the 'operating' Board of W. H. Smith & Son Ltd. The Canadian company was now 'a Canadian Company with a Canadian Chairman and four of the five Board members Canadian nationals'. It would be invidious if it were made 'a subsidiary of a subsidiary'. The risks of 'remote control' were evidently less a source of anxiety than they had once been. Second, Book Club Associates were similarly treated. They were a partnership (actually an Anglo-American partnership) run by a management committee. They were not technically a subsidiary company and should not be treated as such.

The chart of responsibility projected visually the legal and administrative relationships inside the company. It symbolised the work of over two decades during which the old partnership had become a public company with binding Articles of Association under the law. It embodied the formal and practical consequences of public ownership. That was basic and important: it was not all. W. H. Smith's had also a public face. It was reflected in advertising, in goodwill, and in reputation. In 1969 all these public aspects were concentrated symbolically in the concept described as 'corporate identity':

> The way in which a company projects itself visually is known to affect public judgement of that company's standing . . . a clear visual identity used consistently on shop fronts and in the shops, stationery, packaging, vehicles and all printed matter certainly helps to project a good and modern image of a company.[6]

On this the new chairman of the Limited Board, C. H. W. Troughton, wrote the following comment on 11 December 1969:

> Once we were far ahead of anyone else – the Eric Gill lettering; the symbol; the Newsboy sign; the decoration of our shops was something which was absolutely unique. All this put a stamp on our public image which was strong and persistent. The origins of it were Mr C. H. St. J. Hornby backed up by a brilliant, resourceful and dominating designer in Mr Bayliss. One has only to see the decorative treatment of Shelley House[7] and the old ground floor of Leeds Shop to see exactly the same style and taste.
> I think we lost this and the strong discipline which is needed to insist on obedience to the required standard.[8]

He went on to say that it was strange that in matters of accountancy,

taxation, law and other disciplines, business invariably used expert advice:
but in aesthetics 'every man thinks he is his own expert . . .' He had therefore been having conversations with the Royal College of Art and its
principal, Sir Robin Darwin. 'They are not concerned with gimmicks. For
many years the late Lord Hambleden was Chairman of the Royal College
. . . I do not think their services will be expensive, though their recommendations may be.' History must be the judge of that.

A year later he introduced the plan for the development of W. H. Smith
& Son Ltd for the next five years (1970/1–1974/5) with the following
statement. It summarises better than the historian can do the practical
objectives of the company and the philosophy that lay behind them:

In origin, W. H. Smith & Son Limited is a corporate body made
up of a variety of human beings, governed by a number of legal rules
and guided by certain moral conventions. Its aim is to perform
certain desirable economic and social tasks which are related below.

The first economic task is to make a continuing and increasing profit,
the measure of which is more fully defined in the strategic concept which
follows, and the action programmes which support it. Secondly, this
continuing and increasing profit must give both a competitive return
and the prospect of growth on the money invested by the shareholders.
Finally and perhaps overriding all else, the continuing and increasing
profit must provide a secure base for the development of the lives of the
people who work in the Firm. This profit will be made by providing
our customers with worthwhile merchandise of good value sold in
attractive conditions; and the purposes we serve and the manner in
which we serve them must make a contribution to the civilised life of
our country.

I now turn to the strategic plans which go towards achieving the aim
which I have expressed in the previous paragraph. In dealing with people
it must be our strategy to create an atmosphere of excitement, interest
and enthusiasm which spreads to the activities of the people who work
here and enhances the attraction of the things they sell, and which,
properly organised and directed and supported by specialist and professional services, will achieve the profit target which we have set
ourselves.

A further consideration is that this strategic plan must include a proper
financial plan which will support the activities and ideas which will
flourish in the atmosphere we have created. Believing that we possess
both extraordinary skills and the ability to put these skills into practice,

we have conceived an expansion programme which will require all the energies and expertise we possess, which will recognize change and opportunity and which will be effective in a very short period of time . . .

Finally we believe that disciplines are needed in the business, not only as a management tool, but also to give people who work in it satisfaction and the feeling that they are working for the winning side. So we have conceived plans for the cost control of services, for the aggressive use of money and for the relentless divestment of time-absorbing hobby farming.

This deals with the philosophical and practical aims, objects, efforts and tactics which we should pursue in the next five years. Perhaps the most valuable part of this operation has been the knowledge to me that every word in this statement has been contributed to by every section of the business.

Turning Points

Time was when professional historians frowned on conjectural history. 'If' was a forbidden word. Today, what is called 'counter-factual' – imaginary – history is in vogue: imagined alternatives to the history that 'happened' are said to stimulate comparisons and deepen understanding of the all-too-solid flesh of conventional narration. So the argument goes. Certainly, those types of history in which individuals, and individual decisions, influenced the course of events often persuade the historian that it is worthwhile to ponder the possible consequences of different decisions.

Historians have scrutinised and analysed some of the crises that from time to time struck manufacturing industry, banking and finance. The operations of trade and distribution have had less attention. And these were the basic activities of W. H. Smith & Son – Northcliffe's 'great merchants of literature' as he described them.

Different activities produced somewhat different problems. Smith's problems did not spring directly from those decisions about technology or investment so dear to economists' thinking about industry and finance. For though they relied heavily, and successively, on the technology of transport, Smith's borrowed it from others (coach proprietors, railway companies, road haulage contractors). Their own investment in technology was for long minimal. Only when the twentieth century was well advanced did Smith's take the lead in computer-controlled distribution. Finance they provided, except in emergency, from their own resources.

Smith's crises arose rather from the problem of managing a delicate complex of relationships with suppliers, customers, transporters, publishers, readers, libraries, newspaper editors and proprietors, unions, trade associations and the like. Their success in solving their dilemmas lay in a system of top management (i.e. a choice of top managers) who could generate confidence in their word and their reliability. The history of W. H. Smith contains a number of such crises; we can identify at least three 'cross-roads' where history might well have taken a different route from the one it in fact took.

In the 1840s and 1850s[9] a battle of will and conscience raged between W. H. Smith I and his son about the son's future. In the end W. H. Smith II gave in and agreed to enter the business instead of the Church. But in the mind of this reluctant entrepreneur there always lingered a vision of higher ideals. These caused him to think from time to time of selling the business. In the end he found an alternative solution to his problems and entered public life and Parliament. This had two consequences. W. H. Smith II became the abiding emblem of the business to which he devoted his impressive talents, and the repute of which he actually enlarged by his ascent into high politics. This required him to hand over the day-to-day responsibility for his business to others – 'professional' managers (trained 'on the job' by trial and error). Smith's thus had the best of two worlds: the high talent of the proprietor and the dedicated abilities of the managers. This was, in consequence, an early, rare, and (in some respects) unique example of a 'managed enterprise'. What would have happened if W. H. Smith II had denied his father his wishes is anybody's guess: the only certainty is that this business history would have read very differently.

The second cross-roads was encountered in 1905/6. By this time the controlling influence in Smith's was Harry St John Hornby, himself one of the latest additions to the new managers.[10] It was Hornby, by an autocratic decision characteristic of his day (and person), who opted to fight the railway tycoons. His strategy was the strategy of urban shops. In the end, after a series of breath-taking crises, Hornby won. The future lay with shops, not with railways or railway stalls: that, in brief, was to be the future history of Smith's. Here again was an irrevocable decision. Assuming *ceteris paribus* as our guidelines (i.e. the ineluctable decline of railways) W. H. Smith were saved from parallel decline only by Hornby's personal decision: without it, they must have slid downhill alongside the railway system which was so precipitated partly by external events beyond its control, partly by a mechanical management whose commercial sense matched that of the grand old Duke of York. Hornby switched the points.

The third cross-roads was in 1949: 'going public'. This, as has been explained, was not a 'business decision'. It was an involuntary act, transacted under duress – from government – because no one had had the vision to foresee the full consequences of the demand for death duties which could threaten the very existence of the business in the event of the unexpected death of its proprietor. The unforeseen happened: the only way to raise the £6 million needed for death duties was to sell the partnership to the public.

This was clean contrary to all the instincts and inclinations of the proprietor's brother and successor, David Smith. David was a natural conservative. He would have liked to see everything continue as it had in the past. In some respects he and his advisers ensured that it did – in regard to the public reputation of the firm in the eyes of its customers, managers, employees, competitors, suppliers. But he also accepted the facts of a changing world. If the business was to survive and thrive it needed not only to keep up, neck and neck, with its competitors, but to outdistance them in matters of marketing, technology, planned finance, and managerial training. When David Smith and his team came to believe that this could be achieved without sacrificing fundamental principles, their attention came to be concentrated not on preserving but on modernising the new company. It was in 1968/9, the year after Swindon came on stream, that the new pattern of retail outlets and the continuing reorganisation of the wholesale trade led to a sharp but sustained rise in net profits, which reached a climax in 1971/2 dwarfing all precedent. This was essentially the product of the co-ordinated planning and reorganisation made possible by the new structure of the business after it became a public company. Operations on such a scale would not have been within the range of the resources available to the old partnership.

The bridging of the gap from private to public, from traditional to modern, was the third of the cross-roads, where the chosen signpost pointed to new techniques of expansion blended with the maintenance of a general business ethos as old as the partnership itself. The public company did not turn its back on its heritage. Like the old partnership, it was also something more than a machine for maximising profits, more than a house built on farthings; it was a house built also on family fealties.

Since its foundation (somewhere between 1787 and 1792) six members of the Smith family from the male side and one – Anna – from the distaff side had guided its fortunes. The marriages of William Henry II's three daughters, Emily, Helen and Beatrice, had brought (over three generations), four members of the Acland family, and Eddie Seymour, into the partnership. Arnold Power was nephew by marriage of William Henry II and a cousin of Freddy, the Second Viscount Hambleden.

Beyond the relatives by marriage and blood were the 'friends'. William Lethbridge was an old school friend of William Henry II, who remembered his qualities when he felt the need of support in the management of affairs in 1862. Harry St John Hornby and Freddy were undergraduate friends at Oxford who rowed together in the Oxford University trial Eight.[11] The habit of regarding close personal relationship as a reliable guide to quality – in contemporary society demoted if not deemed positively scandalous – was not exclusive to the 'élite' of the firm. When Freddy welcomed Arnold Power into the partnership in 1911, he was confident his member-ship of the family would ensure a warm reception for him among the staff because '. . . they always look upon it as a family business' (see page 269).

The sociological features of the business – the appointments by internal promotion, newsboy to boss; the traditions of long service, generation after generation; the 'W. H. Smith' family – have been analysed earlier.[12] W. S. Gilbert's sneer at the civilian 'Ruler of the Queen's Navee' may not have been aimed at William Henry II: but if it was, his employees certainly saw themselves as those sisters, aunts, cousins by the dozens, male and female, who constituted the lesser family dynasties incorporated in the staff of the business.

Far from resenting the wealth and status of the partners, the employees accepted it as a natural and well deserved consequence of the characteristic common to everyone, the proprietors and those co-partners they recruited to the service of the business – total devotion to the welfare of the business and those who worked in it, which was seen as overriding even the indivi-dual interests of the partners and their families: a concept of an Ark of the Covenant: the prime duty of the 'brotherhood' was its safe keeping.

Personal relations gave the partnership its peculiarly 'organic' quality. They helped to turn the original little news-walk into a national institution in Victorian England. Even after 1949, its traditional, private characteris-tics were still clearly discernible beneath its vastly expanded 'public' structure. And in a world where the ownership of business had become largely anonymous, management often hardly less so, it was not un-important that for investors, staff, suppliers and customers, W. H. Smith still possessed an identifiable image and ethos.

Appendix I

DIRECTORS OF W. H. SMITH & SON LTD AND
W. H. SMITH & SON (HOLDINGS) LTD 1949–72

Note: In order to simplify the following entries, the expression managing director has not been employed in connection with W. H. Smith. Generally speaking, those who were executive directors of W. H. Smith & Son (Holdings) Ltd in 1949–72 bore that title and those who were executive directors of W. H. Smith & Son Ltd alone did not. The title chief executive was not used formally in the period 1949–72. Had it been, it would have attached to the chairman of W. H. Smith & Son (Holdings) Ltd.

1 ACLAND, ARTHUR WILLIAM, 1897–
  Father of 2; cousin of 8, 16, 21, 22, 23
  OBE (1946) MC (1917) TD (1937)
  W. H. Smith & Son (1920) partner (1924)
  W. H. Smith & Son Ltd: director 1929–63
  W. H. Smith & Son (Holdings) Ltd: director 1949–68

2 ACLAND, DAVID ALFRED, 1929–
  Eldest son of 1; cousin of 8, 16, 21, 22, 23
  W. H. Smith & Son Ltd (1952) director (1958) financial 1960–8, distribution 1968–74, chairman 1974–7
  W. H. Smith & Son (Holdings) Ltd: director (1971) finance 1971–4, chief executive 1977–8
  Chairman of Barclays Unit Trusts and Insurance and director, Blue Circle Industries, English and New York Trust

3 BAGNALL, PETER HILL, 1931–
  W. H. Smith & Son Ltd (1961) director (1968) systems & computer/management information services 1968–74

W. H. Smith & Son (Holdings) Ltd: director (1974) merchandise/retail 1974–9, staff & services 1979–
Formerly a management consultant with Peat, Marwick, Mitchell & Co.

4 BENNETT, PETER WARD, 1917–
Brother-in-law of 25
OBE (1945)
W. H. Smith & Son (Canada) Ltd (1949)
W. H. Smith & Son Ltd: director (1951), deputy chairman 1969–72, chairman 1972–4
W. H. Smith & Son (Holdings) Ltd: director (1951), deputy chairman 1974–7, chairman 1977–82
Director: Lloyds & Scottish, Thorn-EMI

5 CORBETT, JOHN THALBERG, 1903–81
W. H. Smith & Son (Holdings) Ltd: director 1971–4
Senior partner in Peat, Marwick, Mitchell & Co.

6 ELMS, STANLEY REES, 1908–67
W. H. Smith & Son (1925) wholesale house assistant & manager, head office manager
W. H. Smith & Son Ltd: director (1960) supply 1960–4, wholesale 1964–7

7 FIELD, MALCOLM DAVID, 1937–
W. H. Smith & Son Ltd (1962) director (1970) wholesale 1970–4
W. H. Smith & Son (Holdings) Ltd: director (1974) wholesale 1974–8 retail 1978–80, retail & wholesale 1980–
Formerly with family wholesale newsagency taken over by W. H. Smith

8 HAMBLEDEN, LORD, *earlier* HON. WILLIAM HERBERT SMITH, 1930–
Nephew of 12, 21, 22; cousin of 1, 2, 16, 23
4th viscount (1948)
W. H. Smith & Son Ltd 1952–5
W. H. Smith & Son (Holdings) Ltd: director 1956–

9 HARCOURT, LORD, *earlier* HON. WILLIAM EDWARD HARCOURT, 1908–79
2nd viscount (1922) KCMG (1957) OBE (1945) MBE (1943)
Vice-Lieutenant of Oxfordshire 1963–79
W. H. Smith & Son (Holdings) Ltd: director 1951–4
Chairman of Morgan Grenfell & Co.

10 HORNBY, MICHAEL CHARLES ST JOHN, 1899–
Father of 11

Prime Warden of Goldsmiths' Company 1954–5, chairman of National Book League 1959
W. H. Smith & Son (1921) partner (1924)
W. H. Smith & Son Ltd: director (1929) vice-chairman 1944–65
W. H. Smith & Son (Holdings) Ltd: director 1949–69

11 HORNBY, SIMON MICHAEL, 1934–
Eldest son of 10
Chairman of National Book League 1978–80
W. H. Smith & Son Ltd (1958) director (1965) supply 1965–7, merchandise 1968–74
W. H. Smith & Son (Holdings) Ltd: director (1974) retail 1974–8, chief executive 1978–82, chairman 1982–
Director: S. Pearson & Son

12 MARGADALE OF ISLAY, LORD, *earlier* JOHN GRANVILLE MORRISON, 1906–
Brother-in-law of 21, 22; uncle of 8, 23
1st baron (1964) TD (1944) JP (1936)
MP (Conservative) 1942–64, Lord Lieutenant of Wiltshire 1969–81
W. H. Smith & Son (Holdings) Ltd: director 1949–77

13 MORRIS, KENNETH JAMES, 1920–
W. H. Smith & Son Ltd (1947) shop assistant & manager, area manager, head office manager; director (1968) retail 1968–74
W. H. Smith & Son (Holdings) Ltd: director (1974) retail 1974–8, wholesale 1978–80; deputy chief executive (1977)

14 OLIVER, WALTER KEITH, 1909–77
W. H. Smith & Son Ltd (1962) director (1962) merchandise 1962–8
Formerly general sales manager of Boots Pure Drug Co.

15 PHILLIMORE, JOHN GORE, 1908–
CMG (1946) DL (1979)
Prime Warden of Fishmongers' Company 1974–5
W. H. Smith & Son (Holdings) Ltd: director 1954–73
A managing director of Baring Bros & Co.

16 POWER, ARNOLD DANVERS, 1875–1959
Cousin of 1, 2, 8, 21, 22, 23
W. H. Smith & Son (1911) partner (1911)
W. H. Smith & Son Ltd: director 1929–51

17 PRIDEAUX, SIR HUMPHREY POVAH TREVERBIAN, 1915–

Knight (1971) OBE (1945)
W. H. Smith & Son (Holdings) Ltd: director (1969) vice-chairman 1977–81
Chairman of Brooke Bond Liebig

18 ROWE, GEORGE WILLIAM, 1914–
W. H. Smith & Son (1928) bookstall assistant, wholesale house manager, head office manager
W. H. Smith & Son Ltd: director (1960) wholesale 1960–4, retail 1964–8; deputy chairman 1971–4
W. H. Smith & Son (Holdings) Ltd: director (1968) wholesale/operations 1968–74, non-executive 1974–8

19 SAUNDERS, HUGH NORMAN, 1910–
OBE (1945) TD (1950) JP (1961)
W. H. Smith & Son (Holdings) Ltd: director 1956–78
Deputy-chairman of Lloyds Bank International & director of Rio-Tinto Zinc Corp.

20 SCOTT BAILEY, VICTOR EDWARD, 1902–
W. H. Smith & Son Ltd (1937) assistant & manager outdoor publicity department; director (1960) retail 1960–4
Formerly in advertising and publishing in England and America

21 SMITH, HON. DAVID JOHN, 1907–76
Father of 23, brother of 22, brother-in-law of 12, uncle of 8, cousin of 1, 2, 16
CBE (1964) JP (1946)
Lord Lieutenant of Berkshire 1959–75
W. H. Smith & Son Ltd (1930) director (1935) chairman 1948–69
W. H. Smith & Son (Holdings) Ltd: chairman 1949–72, director 1972–6
Director: Lloyds Bank, Union Discount Company of London

22 SMITH, HON. JAMES FREDERICK ARTHUR, 1906–80
Brother of 21, brother-in-law of 12, uncle of 8, 23, cousin of 1, 2, 16
OBE (1945)
Chairman of Sadler's Wells Foundation 1948–61
W. H. Smith & Son (1928)
W. H. Smith & Son Ltd: director 1933–46 and 1957–69
W. H. Smith & Son (Holdings) Ltd: director 1949–74

23 SMITH, JULIAN DAVID, 1932–
Eldest son of 21, nephew of 12, 22, cousin of 1, 2, 8, 16
W. H. Smith & Son Ltd (1950) director (1965) services 1965–8, staff 1968–74

W. H Smith & Son (Holdings) Ltd: director (1974) staff & training 1974–9, external affairs 1979–

24 SPICER, WALTER, 1909–81
W. H. Smith & Son (1925) wholesale house assistant & manager
W. H. Smith & Son Ltd: director (1967) supply 1967, wholesale 1967–70

25 TROUGHTON, SIR CHARLES HUGH WILLIS, 1916–
Brother-in-law of 4
Knight (1977) CBE (1966 MC (1940) TD (1959)
Chairman of The British Council 1977–84 (president 1984–   ), president of National Book League 1984–
W. H. Smith & Son Ltd (1946) director (1948) deputy-chairman 1965–9, chairman 1969–72
W. H. Smith & Son (Holdings) Ltd: director (1949) deputy chairman 1970–2, chairman 1972–7
Director: Barclays Bank, Wm. Collins & Sons, Times Newspapers

26 VAN STRAUBENZEE, HENRY HAMILTON, 1914–
DSO (1945) OBE (1947)
W. H. Smith & Son Ltd (1957) director (1960) staff 1960–4, staff & supply 1964–8
W. H. Smith & Son (Holdings) Ltd: director (1968) staff & property 1968–71 co-ordination 1971–4, non-executive 1974–7
Formerly a regular soldier

27 YATES, GEORGE CHARLES HENRY, 1898–1956
W. H. Smith & Son (1912) bookstall assistant, shop manager, superintendent, head office manager
W. H. Smith & Son Ltd: director (1956)

Appendix 2

W. H. SMITH STAFF NUMBERS, FULL & PART-TIME IN U.K.

Year	Numbers	Year	Numbers	Year	Numbers
1856	350*	1942	12,684	1958	18,842
1887	4,156	1943	12,415	1959	18,696
1905	8,285	1944	12,407	1960	18,780
1911	10,358	1945	12,270	1961	18,574
1917	11,000	1946	12,964	1962	17,859
1921	11,772	1947	14,141	1963	17,475
1932	13,452	1948	14,554	1964	18,154
1933	13,312	1949	15,312	1965	19,177
1934	13,790	1950	16,814	1966	19,547
1935	14,273	1951	17,012	1967	18,838
1936	14,506	1952	17,370	1968	18,867
1937	14,610	1953	17,629	1969	18,823
1938	14,547	1954	17,918	1970	18,523
1939	14,720	1955	18,104	1971	18,009
1940	14,554	1956	18,677	1972	17,514
1941	12,999	1957	19,213		

* Approximately.

Appendix 3

TURNOVER AND PROFIT, W. H. SMITH & SON (LTD)

Actual Figures, pre 1949

Year	Retail Turnover £000s	Wholesale Turnover £000s	WHS Net Profit £000s
1867	296		
1868	320		
1869	337		
1870	382		45
1871	406		38
1872	439		43
1873	491		57
1874	547		58
1875	589		55
1876	638		78
1877	705		69
1878	734		85
1879	749		95
1880	792		91
1881	810		86
1882	860		80
1883	875		100
1884	912		92
1885	953		99
1886	971		96
1887	990		102
1888	1,014		123
1889	1,051		136

Year	Retail Turnover £000s	Wholesale Turnover £000s	WHS Net Profit £000s
1890	1,110		131
1891	1,110		130
1892	1,111	213	162
1893*	1,113	222	151
1893/4	1,134	302	157
1894/5	1,193	312	164
1895/6	1,247	323	149
1896/7	1,320	338	177
1897/8	1,309	345	159
1898/9	1,318	354	159
1899/1900	1,470	702	189
1900/1	1,429	704	158
1901/2	1,405	738	140
1902/3	1,407	714	133
1903/4	1,407	837	140
1904/5	1,403	932	124
1905/6	1,321	1,021	58
1906/7	1,510	1,036	68
1907/8	1,498	1,194	123
1908/9	1,513	1,281	126
1909/10	1,563	1,380	162
1910/11	1,666	1,519	174
1911/12	1,682	1,565	181
1912/13	1,772	1,513	190
1913/14	1,834	1,594	191
1914/15	2,006	1,804	231
1915/16	1,977	1,895	222
1916/17	2,096	1,987	265
1917/18	2,583	2,589	458
1918/19	3,265	3,286	628
1919/20	3,625	3,591	523
1920/1	3,836	4,038	390
1921/2	3,629	4,105	397
1922/3	3,707	4,134	467
1923/4	3,927	4,242	528
1924/5	4,148	4,400	570
1925/6	4,054	4,409	539
1926/7	3,878	4,253	479

Year	Retail Turnover £ooos	Wholesale Turnover £ooos	WHS Net Profit £ooos
1927/8	4,063	4,331	467
1928/9	4,063	4,462	495
1929/30	4,138	4,485	436
1930/1	4,141	4,548	386
1931/2	3,986	4,510	322
1932/3	3,835	4,474	283
1933/4	3,884	4,649	294
1934/5	4,035	4,765	328
1935/6	4,180	4,970	256
1936/7	4,399	5,064	281
1937/8	4,483	5,436	312
1938/9	4,512	5,657	334
1939/40	4,478	5,840	373
1940/1	4,443	5,977	365
1941/2	5,341	6,934	728
1942/3	6,074	7,272	918
1943/4	6,875	7,992	1,252
1944/5	7,178	8,722	1,290
1945/6	7,875	9,785	1,535
1946/7	9,358	11,573	1,520
1947/8	10,438	12,607	1,521
1948/9	10,907	13,138	1,390

*9 month year adjusted to give 12 month comparison

Indexed Figures, pre 1949 (1900=100)

1867	228	
1868	246	
1869	259	
1870	294	35
1871	312	29
1872	314	31
1873	351	41
1874	421	45
1875	453	42
1876	532	65
1877	542	53

Year	Retail Turnover £000s	Wholesale Turnover £000s	WHS Net Profit £000s
1878	612		71
1879	624		79
1880	660		76
1881	675		72
1882	717		67
1883	729		83
1884	829		84
1885	866		90
1886	971		96
1887	990		102
1888	1,014		123
1889	1,051		136
1890	1,110		131
1891	1,110		130
1892	1 111	213	162
1893★	1,113	222	151
1893/4	1,134	302	157
1894/5	1,326	347	182
1895/6	1,386	359	166
1896/7	1,320	338	177
1897/8	1,309	345	159
1898/9	1,318	354	159
1899/1900	1,470	702	189
1900/1	1,429	704	158
1901/2	1,405	738	140
1902/3	1,407	714	133
1903/4	1,407	837	140
1904/5	1,403	932	124
1905/6	1,321	1,021	58
1906/7	1,510	1,036	68
1907/8	1,362	1,085	112
1908/9	1,375	1,165	115
1909/10	1,421	1,255	147
1910/11	1,515	1,381	158
1911/12	1,529	1,423	165
1912/13	1,611	1,375	173
1913/14	1,528	1,328	159
1914/15	1,433	1,289	165

Indexed Figures, pre 1949 *continued*

Year	Retail Turnover £000s	Wholesale Turnover £000s	WHS Net Profit £000s
1915/16	1,236	1,184	139
1916/17	1,048	993	133
1917/18	1,123	1,126	199
1918/19	1,306	1,314	251
1919/20	1 295	1,283	187
1920/1	1,475	1,553	150
1921/2	1,728	1,955	189
1922/3	1,854	2,067	234
1923/4	1,964	2,121	264
1924/5	2,074	2,200	285
1925/6	2,134	2,321	284
1926/7	2,041	2,238	252
1927/8	2,138	2,279	246
1928/9	2,138	2,348	261
1929/30	2,299	2,492	242
1930/1	2,436	2,675	227
1931/2	2,491	2,819	201
1932/3	2,397	2,796	177
1933/4	2,428	2,906	184
1934/5	2,522	2,978	205
1935/6	2,459	2,924	151
1936/7	2,588	2,979	165
1937/8	2,491	3,020	173
1938/9	2,507	3,143	186
1939/40	2,132	2,781	178
1940/1	1,932	2,599	159
1941/2	2,225	2,889	303
1942/3	2,430	2,909	367
1943/4	2,644	3,074	482
1944/5	2,659	3,230	478
1945/6	2,813	3,495	548
1946/7	3,227	3,991	524
1947/8	3,367	4,067	491
1948/9	3,408	4,106	434

★9 month year adjusted to give 12 month comparison

Appendix 4

TURNOVER AND PROFIT, W. H. SMITH & SON (HOLDINGS) LTD

Actual Figures, 1949/50–1971/2

Year	Retail Turnover £	Wholesale Turnover £	WHS Holdings Net Profit £
1949/50	11,443,000	14,855,000	1,319,597
1950/1	12,041,120	15,692,967	1,347,356
1951/2	13,612,546	19,124,900	1,756,459
1952/3	14,005,838	19,936,112	1,802,099
1953/4	14,538,298	20,904,064	1,811,629
1954/5	14,764,226	21,569,063	1,774,365
1955/6	15,409,813	22,363,397	1,475,911
1956/7	17,265,373	25,238,329	1,673,549
1957/8	17,720,469	26,316,066	1,825,861
1958/9	20,373,729	28,680,882	2,279,199
1959/60	17,259,560	22,648,849	1,795,763
1960/1	21,707,623	29,057,359	1,753,138
1961/2	23,415,103	31,288,337	2,101,167
1962/3	23,787,696	32,008,761	2,227,275
1963/4	25,633,516	33,873,939	2,577,080
1964/5	28,030,639	35,405,059	2,753,000
1965/6	31,605,881	39,659,416	3,049,000
1966/7	34,779,891	43,210,387	2,622,000
1967/8	37,665,486	47,910,508	2,488,000
1968/9	39,743 870	52,087,165	3,834,000
1969/70	42,039,463	54,504,332	4,068,000
1970/1	45,942,088	59,736,158	4,689,000
1971/2	53,059,809	66,294,482	6,518,000

Indexed Figures, 1949/50–1971/2 (1950 = 100)

Year	Retail Turnover £	Wholesale Turnover £	WHS Holdings Net Profit £
1949/50	11,443,000	14,855,000	1,319,597
1950/1	10,962,811	14,287,625	1,226,697
1951/2	11,374,866	15,981,082	1,467,727
1952/3	11,391,416	16,214,705	1,465,708
1953/4	11,668,895	16,778,262	1,454,073
1954/5	11,257,723	16,446,409	1,352,954
1955/6	11,190,460	16,240,085	1,071,792
1956/7	12,105,607	17,695,840	1,173,409
1957/8	12,010,540	17,836,445	1,237,529
1958/9	13,808,862	19,439,265	1,544,793
1959/60	11,569,594	15,182,197	1,203,755
1960/1	14,086,862	18,856,371	1,137,676
1961/2	14,574,708	19,475,393	1,307,872
1962/3	14,510,494	19,525,346	1,358,640
1963/4	15,181,015	20,061,266	1,526,233
1964/5	15,832,120	19,997,303	1,554,935
1965/6	17,213,917	21,600,219	1,660,616
1966/7	18,448,464	22,920,291	1,390,800
1967/8	18,988,385	24,153,233	1,254,282
1968/9	19,089,574	25,018,245	1,841,529
1969/70	18,995,612	24,627,883	1,838,132
1970/1	18,935,591	24,620,984	1,932,631
1971/2	20,356,278	25,433,732	2,500,618

Appendix 5

Retail and Wholesale Turnover, W. H. Smith & Son Ltd
1867–1950

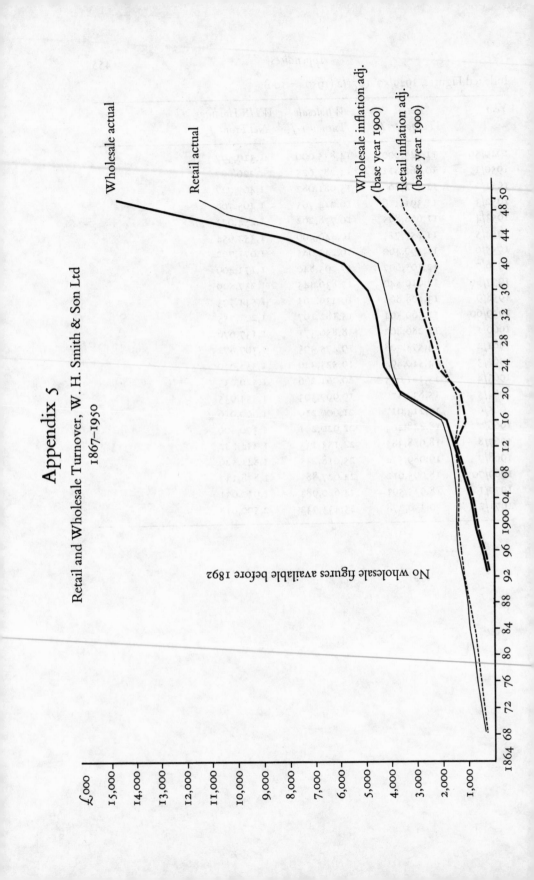

Wholesale actual

Retail actual

Wholesale inflation adj. (base year 1900)

Retail inflation adj. (base year 1900)

No wholesale figures available before 1892

£ooo

15,000
14,000
13,000
12,000
11,000
10,000
9,000
8,000
7,000
6,000
5,000
4,000
3,000
2,000
1,000

1864 68 72 76 80 84 88 92 96 1900 04 08 12 16 20 24 28 32 36 40 44 48 50

Appendix 6

Capital Employed, W. H. Smith & Son Ltd
1867–1950

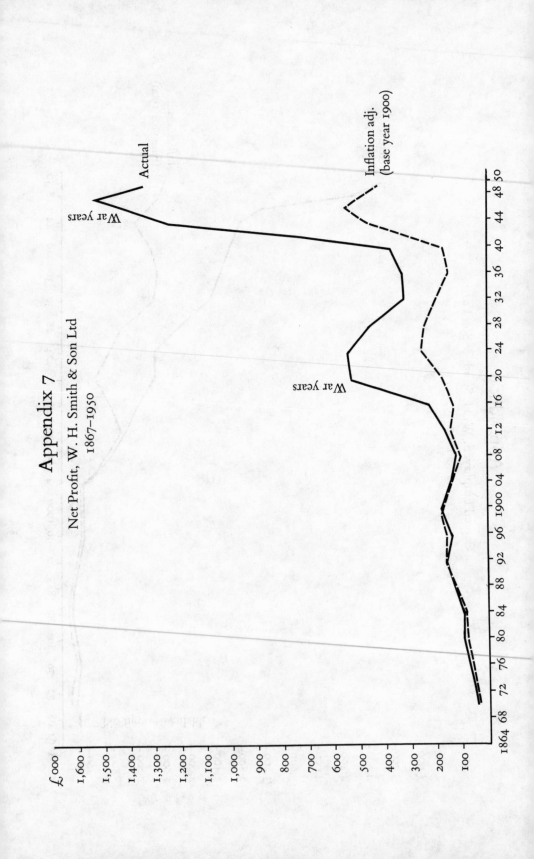

Appendix 7

Net Profit, W. H. Smith & Son Ltd
1867–1950

£'000

Actual

Inflation adj.
(base year 1900)

War years

War years

Appendix 8

Turnover, W.H.S. Holdings PLC
1950–1972

£M

75
70
65
60
55
50
45
40
35
30
25
20
15
10
5

1950 51 52 53 54 55 56 57 58 59 60 61 62 63 64 65 66 67 68 69 70 71 72

Actual turnover ⎰ Wholesale ———
                ⎱ Retail — — —

Inflation adj. turnover ⎰ Wholesale ———
(base year 1950)   ⎱ Retail ·····

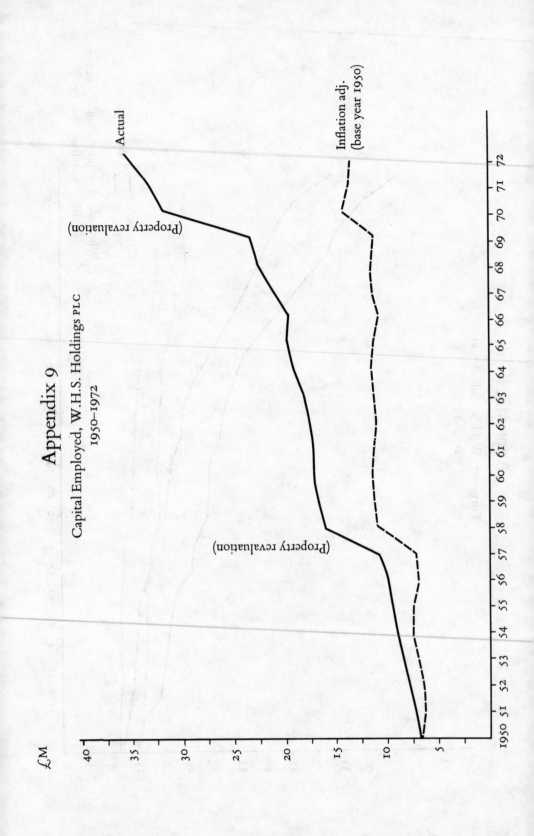

Appendix 9

Capital Employed, W.H.S. Holdings PLC
1950–1972

Actual

(Property revaluation)

(Property revaluation)

Inflation adj.
(base year 1950)

£M

40

35

30

25

20

15

10

5

1950 51 52 53 54 55 56 57 58 59 60 61 62 63 64 65 66 67 68 69 70 71 72

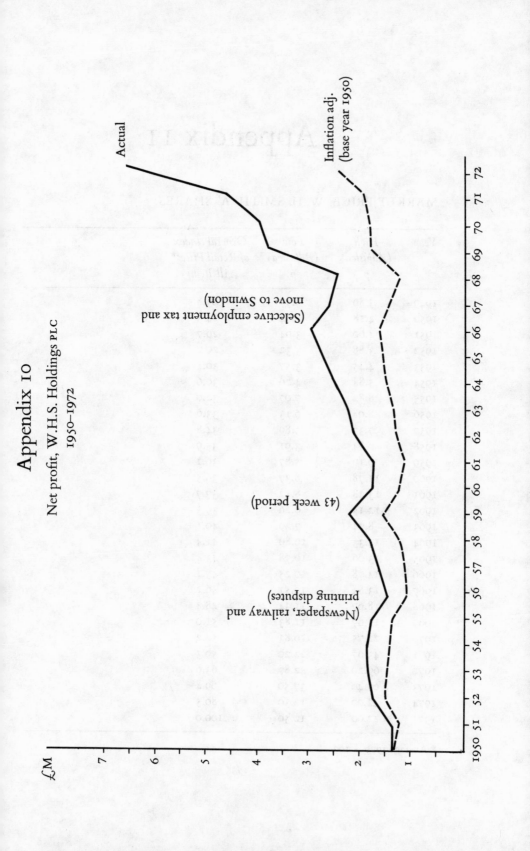

Appendix 10

Net profit, W.H.S. Holdings PLC
1950–1972

£M

Actual

Inflation adj.
(base year 1950)

(Selective employment tax and
move to Swindon)

(43 week period)

(Newspaper, railway and
printing disputes)

7

6

5

4

3

2

1

1950 51 52 53 54 55 56 57 58 59 60 61 62 63 64 65 66 67 68 69 70 71 72

Appendix 11

MARKET PRICE, W. H. SMITH 'A' SHARES

Year	High (Adjusted) p	Low (Adjusted) p	General Index of Retail Prices* All Items
1949	3.89	3.37	23.8
1950	4.18	3.64	24.5
1951	4.60	3.64	26.7
1952	3.88	3.32	29.2
1953	4.45	3.57	30.1
1954	5.84	4.26	30.6
1955	8.82	7.07	32.0
1956	8.08	6.13	33.6
1957	7.37	5.89	34.8
1958	6.84	3.91	35.9
1959	9.16	5.87	36.1
1960	11.78	8.37	36.5
1961	13.48	8.52	37.7
1962	12.15	9.26	39.3
1963	8.74	7.29	40.1
1964	14.33	10.89	41.4
1965	13.06	10.78	43.4
1966	14.78	10.25	45.1
1967	13.84	10.51	46.2
1968	18.67	11.34	48.4
1969	18.67	11.83	51.0
1970	22.75	16.83	54.2
1971	43.67	22.20	59.3
1972	69.20	42.87	63.6
1973	67.40	37.50	69.4
1974	42.00	12.30	80.5
1975	42.00	12.50	100.0

* Average 1975 = 100.

NOTES

Abbreviations:

HMs denotes the Hambleden Papers.
WHS denotes the Records of W. H. Smith & Son.

I A TALE OF TWO CITIES

1 Quoted, Charles Wilson, *Economic History and the Historian*, 1969, p. 181.
2 G. M. Young, *Victorian England: Portrait of an Age*, 1949, p. 159.
3 Wilson, op. cit., pp. 181, 187, passim.
4 WHS 87/1, 1 July 1910.
5 College of Arms Grants 66–72, 10 May 1842 (copied in WHS 217 f. 12).
6 I.R.56: *Introduction to the Index to Records of the Stamp Duty on Newspapers* (Public Record Office).
7 HMs HA/38/1, n.d.
8 Ibid.
9 Cottonian Collection, Plymouth, Envelope 256 No. 5, 1783.
10 HMs HA/38/1, n.d.
11 Christ Church, Spitalfields, Marriage Register P93/CTC1/15, 27 October 1784 (GLC Record Office) (photocopy in WHS 216/32).
12 Bank of England Consolidated 3% Annuities Ledgers, 1783–7 (copied in WHS 217 f. 29).
13 St George's, Hanover Square, Baptism Registers, 27 July 1787 and 10 March 1789 (copied in WHS 218/9).
14 Ibid., 6 August 1792 (certified copy in WHS 216/4).
15 Rate Book C.489 (1792) f. 43 (Westminster City Archives) (photocopy in WHS 1/20).
16 WHS 1/18, n.d.
17 Quoted, *History of The Times*, vol. 1, 1935, pp. 35–6.

18 Bank of England Consolidated 3 % Annuities Ledgers, 1793–1807 (copied in WHS 217 f. 30).

19 HMs HA/15/1, 7 October 1800.

20 WHS 1/18, n.d.

21 HMs HA/8/2, 28 September 1860.

22 HMs HA/8/4, n.d. (incomplete).

23 Ibid.

24 Ibid.

25 *During Six Reigns 1776–1926*, privately printed by H. & M. Massey Ltd (copy in WHS PA.38), 30 May 1815. Masseys continued in independent existence, until 1927, trading as H. & M. Massey of 27 North Audley Street. Their custom and name were acquired by W. H. Smith's in 1927 and the former transferred to W. H. Smith's subsidiary shop, Truslove & Hanson, Sloane Street, in 1941.

26 HMs HA/38/1, n.d.

27 PROB 10 Box 4260, April 1816 (Public Record Office) (photocopy in WHS 217 ff. 15–17).

28 Bank of England Navy 5 % Annuities Ledgers, 1809–16 (copied in WHS 217 f. 32).

29 HMs D/13, 11 January 1842.

30 WHS H.1, 22 July 1818.

31 St George's, Hanover Square, Marriage Register, 25 June 1817 (certified copy in WHS 216/7).

32 *Post Office London Directory*, 1819.

33 Rate Book B.243 (1820) f. 30 (Westminster City Archives).

34 Stanley Morison, *The English Newspaper 1622–1932*, 1932, p. 250.

35 *Gentleman's Magazine*, New Series, vol. 37, 1852, p. 306.

36 WHS A.14, Sep. 1825–Nov. 1827 and Cocks, Biddulph & Co Ledger, 1831.

37 *John Bull*, 9 December 1821 p. 1 (copy in WHS A.13/1/73).

38 *London Gazette*, 1828, p. 1560 (copied in WHS 1/19).

39 Sir John Summerson, *Georgian London*, 1970, p. 211.

II COMMUNICATIONS AND CULTURE

1 *Reminiscences of a Gentlewoman of the Last Century: Letters of Catherine Hutton*, ed. Mrs Catherine Hutton Beale, 1891, p. 176, August 1821.

2 *Miss Weeton's Journal of a Governess 1811–1825*, ed. Edward Hall, 1939, p. 343, April 1825.

3 Stella Margetson, *Journey by Stages*, 1967, p. 60.

4 Quoted, Margetson, op. cit., p. 62.

5 *The Torrington Diaries 1781–1794*, ed. C. B. Andrews, 1934, vol. 1, p. 6.

6 Ibid., vol. 1, pp. 72, 161, 315; vol. 2, pp. 84, 289.

7 *Maria Edgeworth: Letters from England 1813–1844*, ed. C. Colvin, 1971, p. 41, 1 May 1813.

8 Ibid., p. 303, 29 December 1821.

9 G. O. Trevelyan, *Life and Letters of Lord Macaulay*, 1877, p. 99n.

10 R. D. Altick, *The English Common Reader*, Chicago, 1957, pp. 289–92.

11 *The Monthly Magazine*, vol. 51, 1821, pp. 397–8.

12 R. D. Altick's very valuable book (op. cit.) seems to me to underrate the 'culture' of eighteenth- and nineteenth-century Britain; rural Britain especially, probably for want of printed records.

13 J. A. Langford, *A Century of Birmingham Life 1741–1841*, 1868, vol. 1, p. 238 and vol. 2, pp. 247–8, 496.

14 *Manchester Guide*, 1804, pp. 223–6.

15 *Manchester and Salford Advertiser*, 2 March 1833, p. 1.

16 Thomas Oliver, *A New Picture of Newcastle upon Tyne*, 1831, pp. 17, 52.

17 W. M. Childs, *The Town of Reading during the Early Part of the 19th Century*, 1910, pp. 73–4.

18 Sir Francis Hill, *History of Lincoln*, in 4 vols., 1948–74.

19 Sir Francis Hill, *Georgian Lincoln*, 1966, p. 16.

20 Ibid., p. 294.

III LONDON AND PROVINCIAL: THE FIRST W. H. SMITH

1 *Bell's Life in London and Sporting Chronicle*, advertisement, n.d. (copy in WHS PA. 133).

2 Ibid., 15 June 1828 (copied in *Newsbasket*, vol. 42, 1949, p. 335).

3 *Morning Post*, 3 December 1829, p. 1 (copy in WHS PA. 103).

4 WHS 4/1, 28 November 1822.

5 *Standard*, 3 January 1829, p. 1 (copy in WHS A.13/1/82A).

6 WHS 4/4, 5 May 1829.

7 WHS 4/6, 21 December 1834.

8 WHS 4/2, 29 May 1836.

9 WHS 15/90, 27 November 1839.

10 WHS 15/30, 16 May 1838.

11 WHS 4/7, 23 February 1835.

12 WHS 15 passim.

13 *Westminster Review*, vol. 10, April 1829, p. 474.

14 Ibid., pp. 475–9.

15 *Westminster Review*, vol. 12, January 1830, p. 69.

16 *Second Report of Select Committee on Postage*, 1838, pp. 197, 134–5.

17 H.O.42/213, 11 April 1798 (Public Record Office), quoted in Kenneth Ellis, *The Post Office in the Eighteenth Century*, 1969, pp. 160–1.

18 *Westminster Review*, vol. 10, January 1829, p. 228.

19 *The Times*, 4 July 1832, p. 5.

20 *London Gazette*, 1828, p. 1560 (copied in WHS 1/19).

21 WHS A.16, 1840–2.

22 *Newcastle Chronicle*, 5 June 1824, p. 1 (copied in WHS 1/21).

23 Quoted, *The Times*, 5 March 1928, p. 12 (copy in WHS A.13/1/82F). Author's italics.

24 *Once a Week*, vol. 4, 1861, p. 161 (copy in WHS 222/4).

25 *The Times*, 9 August 1939, p. 6 (copy in WHS A.13/1/112).

26 See G. R. Pocklington, *The Story of W. H. Smith & Son*, 1921. The precise date of the use of this expression is unknown.

27 HMs AA/1, 23 July 1830.

28 Charles Knight, *London*, 1843, vol. 5, pp. 337–52.

29 Ibid.

30 *The Times*, 28 December 1836, p. 3.

31 Ibid., 5 January 1837, p. 1.

32 HMs D/11, 21 December 1841.

33 HMs D/7, 27 October 1841.

34 HMs D/8, 10 November 1841.

35 HMs D/13, 11 January 1842.

36 HMs D/18, 15 February 1842.

37 HMs D/20, 18 April 1842.

38 HMs D/6, 20 October 1841.

39 HMs D/17, 8 February 1842.

40 HMs D/20, 18 April 1842.

41 HMs D/14, 22 January 1842.

42 Charles Knight, *Passages of a Working Life during Half a Century*, 1864, vol. 1, p. 129.

43 Quoted, *History of The Times*, vol. 1, 1935, p. 465.

44 Ibid., p. 201.

45 Ibid., p. 211.

46 Ibid., p. 368.

47 T. S. Eliot, *The Sacred Wood*, 1928, p. viii.

48 Baron A. de Stael-Holstein, *Letters on England*, 1825, pp. 139, 158–9.

49 Ibid., p. 162.

50 Ibid., p. 163.

51 *Westminster Review*, vol. 10, January 1829, p. 227.

52 *Edinburgh Review*, vol. 98, October 1853, p. 491.

53 Quoted, *History of The Times*, vol. 2, 1939, p. 207.

54 A. J. Lee, *The Origins of the Popular Press 1855–1914*, 1976, p. 45.

55 *The Times*, 9 February 1854, p. 7, quoted Lee, op. cit., p. 45.

56 *Select Committee on Newspaper Stamps*, 1851, p. xi, quoted Lee, op. cit., p. 46.

57 J. Curran, *Newspaper History from the 17th Century to the Present Day*, 1978, p. 60.

58 *Select Committee on Newspaper Stamps*, 1851, p. 215, q. 1322.
59 Ibid., p. 234, q. 1425–6.
60 Ibid., p. 228, q. 1389.
61 Ibid., p. 93, q. 600.
62 Ibid., p. 94, q. 604.
63 Ibid., p. 341, q. 2330.
64 Ibid., p. 397, q. 2676.
65 Ibid., p. 439, q. 2978.
66 Ibid., p. 307, q. 2025.
67 Ibid., p. 323, q. 2196.
68 Ibid., p. 324, q. 2200.
69 Ibid., p. 325, q. 2206.
70 Ibid., p. 326, q. 2213.
71 Ibid., p. 241, q. 1471.
72 Ibid., p. 242, q. 1479.
73 Ibid., p. 224, q. 1495.
74 Ibid., p. 247, q. 1523.
75 Ibid., p. 196, q. 1214.
76 Ibid., p. 198, q. 1217.
77 Ibid., p. 196, q. 1214.
78 Ibid., p. 197, q. 1215.
79 Ibid., p. 198, q. 1218.
80 Ibid., p. 205, q. 1263–4.
81 Ibid., p. 381, q. 2534.
82 Ibid., p. 381, q. 2536.
83 Ibid., p. 377, q. 2498.
84 Ibid., p. 377, q. 2502.
85 Ibid., p. 377, q. 2504.
86 Ibid., p. 374, q. 2490.
87 Ibid., p. 375, q. 2492.
88 Ibid., p. 376, q. 2493.
89 Ibid., p. 372, q. 2482.
90 Ibid., p. 374, q. 2490.
91 Ibid., p. 379, q. 2515.
92 Ibid., p. 379, q. 2517.
93 Ibid., p. 379, q. 2521.
94 Ibid., p. 383, q. 2556.
95 Ibid., p. 162, q. 995.
96 Ibid., pp. 168–9, q. 1032.
97 Ibid., p. 174, q. 1067.
98 Ibid., p. 172, q. 1056.
99 Ibid., p. 352, q. 2364.
100 Ibid., p. 362, q. 2414.

101 Ibid., p. 363, q. 2418.
102 Ibid., p. 468, q. 3196.
103 Ibid., p. 469, q. 3198.
104 Ibid., p. 476, q. 3240.
105 Ibid., p. 477, q. 3247.
106 Ibid., p. 478, q. 3247.
107 Ibid., p. 479, q. 3254.
108 Ibid., p. 296, q. 1936.
109 Ibid., p. 326, q. 2216.
110 Ibid., p. 326, q. 2218. Author's italics.
111 Ibid., p. 420, q. 2810.
112 Ibid., p. 420, q. 2812.
113 Ibid., p. 420, q. 2815.
114 Ibid., p. 420, q. 2817.
115 Ibid., p. 420, q. 2819–20.
116 Ibid., p. 421, q. 2822.
117 Ibid., p. 422, q. 2832–4.
118 Ibid., p. 424, q. 2848.
119 Ibid., p. 424, q. 2854.
120 Ibid., p. 424, q. 2856.
121 Ibid., p. 425, q. 2858.
122 Ibid., p. 431, q. 2920.
123 Ibid., p. 432, q. 2931.
124 Ibid., pp. 432–3, q. 2932.
125 HMs D/29, 16 March 1855.
126 *Select Committee on Newspaper Stamps*, 1851, p. 425, q. 2862.
127 Ibid., p. 428.
128 Ibid., pp. 524–43 (in part).

IV FATHER AND SON: A CRISIS RESOLVED

1 HMs D/3, 15 April 1839.
2 HMs D/2, 7 June 1839.
3 HMs B/1, 24 July 1834.
4 HMs D/3, 15 April 1839.
5 HMs D/36, 23 April 1842.
6 HMs D/12, 29 December 1841.
7 HMs D/14, 22 January 1842.
8 HMs D/15, 26 January 1842.
9 HMs H/24, 6 November 1845.
10 HMs H/22, 22 April 1845. Sir Herbert Maxwell, *Life and Times of the Rt. Hon. W. H. Smith, MP*, 1893, vol. I, pp. 14–48; Viscount Chilston, *W. H. Smith*, 1965, p. 8 et seq.
11 HMs H/20, n.d.

12 Ibid.
13 HMs H/23, 28 October 1845.
14 HMs H/22, 22 April 1845.
15 HMs H/23, 28 October 1845.
16 HMs H/24, 6 November 1845.
17 HMs Q ff. 6–8, 6 August 1846.
18 Ibid., f. 8, 6 August 1846.
19 WHS 701, 28 September 1846.
20 WHS 1/4, n.d.
21 WHS 1/16, 1 October 1859.
22 HMs H/22, 22 April 1845.
23 WHS 307/6, 24 April 1855.
24 WHS 307/7, 12 March 1856.
25 WHS 307/8, 25 November 1856.
26 WHS 307/9–15, April–May 1858.
27 HMs N/39, 24 October 1853.
28 WHS D.2, 7–8 June 1856.
29 HMs B/38, 4 May 1858.
30 HMs A/7, 9 March 1858.
31 WHS 307/15, 11 May 1858.
32 WHS 702, 1 July 1857.
33 HMs B/55, 31 March 1865.
34 Viscount Chilston, *W. H. Smith*, 1965.

V BUILDING THE BOOKSTALL EMPIRE, 1848–75

1 Henry James, 'Essay on London', *The Century Magazine*, vol. 37, December 1888, pp. 235–6 (copied in WHS 471).
2 WHS 244/2, n.d., *c.* 1851.
3 W. J. Reader, *Macadam*, 1980, p. 186.
4 Quoted, Charles Wilson, *Economic History and the Historian*, 1969, p. 196.
5 Charles Graves, *Mr Punch's History of Modern England*, 1921, vol. 1, p. 67, quoted C. R. Fay, *Great Britain from Adam Smith to the Present Day*, 1932, p. 200.
6 Tennyson, 'Mechanophilus', *c.* 1833.
7 For a survey of nineteenth-century railways see Jack Simmons, *Railways of Britain*, 1961, Sir William Acworth, *Railways of England*, 1899, revised 1900 and the multi-volume series by different authors, *A Regional History of the Railways of Great Britain*, published by David & Charles.
8 RAIL 1007/353, 18 September 1838 (photocopy in WHS 56).
9 RAIL 1008/100, 20 January 1844 (photocopy in WHS 415).
10 Ibid., 1 February 1844 (photocopy in WHS 457).

11 T. R. Gourvish, *Mark Huish and the London & North Western Railway*, 1972.

12 Acworth, op. cit., p. 30.

13 Ibid.

14 Tennyson, *Ode*, 1851.

15 For a short but highly readable account of rail development see Simmons, op. cit., esp. ch. 3.

16 WHS 20, n.d.

17 'Our Modern Mercury', *Once a Week*, 1861, p. 162 (copy in WHS 222/4).

18 WHS 22/2, n.d.

19 Ibid.

20 William Vincent, *Seen from the Railway Platform*, 1919, p. 13.

21 Ibid.

22 Samuel Phillips, *The Literature of the Rail*, 1851 (copy in WHS PA.42).

23 'The World's Greatest Newsagents', *The Times*, 21 December 1905, p. 7 (copy in WHS A.42 f. 46).

24 RAIL 410/873, 28 August 1848 (photocopy in WHS 56/4).

25 WHS 56/1, 9 September 1848.

26 WHS D.1, 1849.

27 RAIL 1008/100, 11 September 1848 (photocopy in WHS 56/4).

28 RAIL 410/141 f. 104, 19 August 1846.

29 Ibid., f. 118, 8 October 1846.

30 Ibid., f. 55, 18 March 1846.

31 Ibid., f. 60, 25 March 1846.

32 *The Times*, 19 December 1849, p. 7 (copied in WHS 57).

33 Ibid., 20 December 1849, p. 4 (copied in WHS 57).

34 Phillips, op. cit.

35 *Newsbasket*, vol. 1, January 1908, p. 3.

36 Ibid., February 1908, p. 3.

37 Ibid.

38 Ibid., November 1908, p. 3.

39 *Athenaeum*, 1851, p. 947 (copy in WHS PA.42).

40 RAIL 410/140 f. 51, 9 January 1852.

41 Ibid., f. 46, 12 December 1851.

42 For Huish's managerial abilities see Gourvish, op. cit.

43 RAIL 410/835, 14 June 1860.

44 Ibid.

45 HMs A/316, 20 January 1870.

46 HMs X/3, n.d.

47 Sir Herbert Maxwell, *Life and Times of the Rt. Hon. W. H. Smith, MP*, 2 vols, 1893. The notes were jotted down for his first biographer, Sir Herbert Maxwell, perhaps by a private secretary or a civil servant who worked for him. For Smith's occasional hesitancy see pages 127 and 145 below.

48 RAIL 410/146 mt. 7671, 13 September 1854.
49 RAIL 410/140 f. 46, 12 December 1851.
50 RAIL 410/835, 14 June 1860.
51 RAIL 410/981 No. 239, 1 January 1876.
52 Ibid., No. 289, 1 January 1886.
53 RAIL 410/866, 27 August 1866.
54 WHS 45/4, 25 August 1859.
55 HMs X/3, n.d.
56 RAIL 410/979 No. 75, 5 November 1866.
57 RAIL 1008/100, 19 July 1849.
58 RAIL 410/101 f. 30478, 13 March 1873.
59 RAIL 410/866, 2 December 1858.
60 Ibid., 20 December 1858.
61 Ibid., 11 February 1859.
62 Ibid., 7 April 1859.
63 RAIL 250/18 f. 106, 19 December 1861.
64 Ibid., f. 101, 12 December 1861.
65 RAIL 250/23 f. 383, 2 February 1861.
66 WHS 22/2, n.d.
67 For all the Western lines see the classic account by O. S. Nock, *The Great Western Railway in the Nineteenth Century*, 1962.
68 WHS 40/2, 11 December 1863.
69 WHS 40/27, 31 March 1864.
70 WHS 41/8, 1871.
71 D. St. J. Thomas, *The West Country*, 1960, pp. 15–17 (vol. I in the *Regional History of the Railways of Great Britain* series).
72 WHS 41/28, 28 February 1874.
73 WHS 41/16, 13 March 1874.
74 WHS 41/17, 16 March 1874.
75 WHS 41/18, 17 March 1874.
76 WHS 41/22, 25 March 1874.
77 WHS 41/24, 30 March 1874.
78 WHS 41/25, 20 June 1874.
79 WHS 41/26, 27 June 1874.
80 WHS 41/29, 31 July 1874.
81 See Acworth, op. cit., p. 206, Hamilton Ellis, *British Railway History 1830–1876*, 1954, pp. 351–2, and Simmons, op. cit., pp. 145, 163.
82 WHS 42/1, 18 October 1848.
83 WHS 43/14, 1851.
84 WHS 44/2, 12 May 1854.
85 WHS 44/3, n.d.
86 RAIL 491/828 f. 47, 28 November 1860.
87 WHS 46/1, 10 April 1861.

88 WHS 277/4, 19 October 1868.
89 WHS 277/5, 20 October 1868.
90 WHS 277/6, 26 October 1868.
91 WHS 277/9, 3 June 1871.
92 WHS 48/6, 1 July 1865.
93 WHS 50/1, 11 February 1867.
94 WHS 50/2, 13 February 1867.
95 WHS 50/8, 22 March 1867.
96 WHS 50/9, 23 March 1867.
97 WHS 50/12, 26 March (1867).
98 WHS 50/14, 27 March 1867.
99 RAIL 414/68 f. 158, 26 May 1851.
100 Ibid., f. 262, 8 December 1851.
101 Ibid., f. 270, 15 December 1851.
102 Ibid., f. 282, 5 January 1852.
103 RAIL 414/75 f. 129, 20 November 1867.
104 RAIL 414/76 f. 599, 9 December 1874.
105 Ibid., f. 605, 23 December 1874.
106 RAIL 414/81 f. 402, 4 April 1900.
107 RAIL 236/15 f. 352, 6 August 1850.
108 RAIL 236/71 f. 74, 24 September 1850.
109 RAIL 236/16 f. 187, 29 April 1851.
110 RAIL 236/72 f. 82, 23 May 1851.
111 WHS 66/6, 30 November 1861.
112 WHS 66/8, 20 December 1861.
113 WHS 66/13, 19 September 1866.
114 Charles Grinling, *History of the Great Northern Railway*, 1903, p. 153.
115 J. E. Cockett, see p. 166 below. WHS 66/23, 10 December 1885.
116 RAIL 236/313 No. 5 ff. 2–3, 10 October 1866.
117 Ibid., memo. of 6 April 1872, f. 1.
118 Ibid., ff. 3–5.
119 Ibid., 6 June 1872.
120 RAIL 236/332 No. 22, 29 November 1878.
121 Cecil J. Allen, *The Great Eastern Railway*, 3rd edition, *passim*, and D. I. Gordon, *The Eastern Counties*, 1968, ch. 1 and *passim* (vol. V in the *Regional History of the Railways of Great Britain* series).
122 RAIL 186/15 f. 194, 24 July 1857.
123 WHS 55/3b, 21 March 1857.
124 RAIL 186/46 f. 403, 21 November 1860.
125 RAIL 227/90 f. 61, 6 January 1864.
126 RAIL 227/173 f. 260, 22 June 1870.
127 RAIL 227/175 f. 204, 7 May 1873.
128 RAIL 227/177 ff. 11–2, 14 January 1874.

129　Ibid., f. 43, 11 February 1874.
130　Ibid., f. 52, 25 February 1874.
131　RAIL 227/94 f. 22, 25 February 1878.
132　WHS 37/10, n.d.
133　WHS 22/2, 1867.
134　RAIL 343/493 ff. 236–7, 28 October 1848.
135　Ibid., f. 248, 8 November 1848.
136　Ibid., f. 264, 25 November 1848.
137　RAIL 343/503 ff. 262–3, 27 June 1855.
138　Ibid., f. 297, 11 July 1855.
139　Ibid.
140　WHS 58/7, 30 April 1856.
141　RAIL 243/26 ff. 338–9, 30 April 1856.
142　WHS 58/8, 21 May 1856.
143　RAIL 343/26 ff. 456–7, 28 May 1856.
144　RAIL 343/70 f. 50, 16 December 1861.
145　Ibid., ff. 387–8, 27 January 1862.
146　RAIL 343/72 f. 10, 27 February 1862.
147　RAIL 343/124 f. 326, 13 November 1866.
148　RAIL 343/126 f. 346, 9 January 1867.
149　RAIL 343/174 f. 82, 30 August 1871.
150　Ibid., f. 460, 25 October 1871.
151　RAIL 343/176 ff. 195–6, 13 December 1871.
152　WHS 61/2, 8 September 1860.
153　Ibid.
154　WHS 62/3, 1868.
155　WHS 62/8, 25 May 1869.
156　Hamilton Ellis, op. cit., p. 309.
157　Simmons, op. cit., p. 29.
158　WHS 63/2, 7 March 1870.
159　WHS 63/6, 24 August 1870.
160　WHS 63/7, 25 August 1870.
161　WHS 63/8, 26 August 1870.
162　J. E. Cockett, WHS 64/9, 30 January 1880.
163　WHS 30/1, 20 November 1866.
164　WHS 30/2, 3 December 1866.
165　WHS 30/3, 4 December 1866.
166　WHS 30/4, 7 December 1866.
167　WHS 30/5, 5 October 1869.
168　WHS 64/15, 10 April 1888.
169　HMs B/22, 3 March 1853.
170　HMs B/27, n.d.
171　WHS 16/2, 20 March 1856.

172 HMs A/31, 9 December 1858.
173 HMs A/59, 19 June 1859.
174 HMs A/70, 15 May (1861).
175 HMs A/130, 16 July 1863.
176 BR/NBR/1/8, 11 September 1857 and BR/NBR/1/10, 14 November 1862 (Scottish Record Office).
177 WHS 26/4, 12 September 1857.
178 WHS D. 44, 20 April 1896.
179 See also Chapter VI for relations with *The Times* and other publishers.
180 HMs BB/75, 14 April 1886.
181 HMs N/6, n.d.
182 HMs B/9, 26 November 1846.
183 HMs Q ff. 12–3, 10 August 1846.
184 HMs BB/17, 1 January 1856.
185 HMs BB/19, n.d.
186 HMs N/81, 23 April 1861.
187 HMs HA/16/3, 3 June 1864.
188 HMs HA/8/1, 27 September 1860.
189 HMs HA/8/2, 28 September 1860.
190 HMs HA/8/3, 7 June 1862.
191 HMs N/83, 25 January 1862.

VI MANAGING THE BOOKSTALL EMPIRE

1 *Morning Post*, 16 March 1849, p. 1 (copy in WHS A.13/1/72).
2 *Illustrated London News*, 24 May 1856, pp. 549–50 (copy in WHS A.13/1/82D).
3 A. J. Lee, *The Origins of the Popular Press 1855–1914*, 1976, p. 64.
4 'Our Modern Mercury', *Once a Week*, 1861, pp. 160–3 (copy in WHS 222/4).
5 Quoted Lee, op. cit., p. 250 and note 101.
6 'How we get our Newspapers', *All the Year Round*, 1875, pp. 305–9 (copy in WHS 222/8).
7 Viscount Chilston, *W. H. Smith*, 1965.
8 HMs PS 5/34, 7 April 1877.
9 Royal Archives E.53/38, 4 August 1877 (copied in WHS 232/5).
10 Royal Archives E.53/43, 7 August 1877 (copied in WHS 232/5).
11 Arthur Ponsonby, *Henry Ponsonby: Queen Victoria's Private Secretary*, 1942, p. 105.
12 HMs C/9, 6 August 1877.
13 Lord George Hamilton, *Parliamentary Reminiscences and Reflections 1886–1906*, 1922, pp. 252–3.
14 *Pall Mall Gazette*, 13 May 1891, p. 3 (quoted Chilston, op. cit., p. 348).

15 *New York Herald*, 11 October 1891, p. 21 (copy in WHS A.47 f. 114).

16 HMs PS 16/88, 8 October 1891.

17 WHS 17/24, 17 June 1867.

18 WHS 17/26, 20 January 1873.

19 WHS 17/29, January 1879.

20 WHS 18/44, 29 September 1920.

21 WHS 18/47, 17 February 1936.

22 HMs A/152, November 1864.

23 HMs HA/16/3, 3 June 1864.

24 HMs HA/16/7, 3 June 1869.

25 HMs N/107, 12 September 1870.

26 HMs BB/81, 5 June 1888.

27 HMs DD/2, 21 August 1872. For the managers, their duties and personalities, see also Chapters VII and VIII.

28 HMs DD/3, 28 August 1872.

29 HMs DD/5, 26 September 1872.

30 HMs DD/6, 4 October 1872.

31 HMs DD/4, 4 September 1872.

32 *Quarterly Review*, vol. 150, 1880, p. 505.

33 Ibid., pp. 506, 509.

34 POST 81/16 and 19, 1853–70 (Post Office Record Office).

35 *Quarterly Review*, vol. 150, 1880, p. 519.

36 R. D. Altick, *The English Common Reader*, Chicago, 1957, p. 364.

37 James Pope Hennessy, *Monckton Milnes: The Flight of Youth 1851–1885*, 1951, pp. 115–22. Milnes's imports were transported for him, through the good offices of friends, by such convenient channels as the British Embassy diplomatic bag from Paris or a Queen's Messenger.

38 HMs B/95, 12 February 1886.

39 *Newsbasket*, vol. 1, April 1908, p. 3.

40 HMs HA/16/9, 30 March 1876.

41 HMs HA/16/10, 24 August 1881.

42 HMs HA/16/12, 1 January 1887.

43 WHS A.227 f. 591, 18 September 1906.

44 'The World's Greatest Newsagents', *The Times*, 21 December 1905, p. 7 (copy in WHS A.42 f. 46).

45 WHS 247/3, 10 May 1861.

46 WHS 247/5, 27 February 1887.

47 'A Big House in the Strand II', The *Journalist*, 1887, p. 269 (copy in WHS A.13/1/43).

48 HMs S/1, 21 October 1878.

49 HMs BB/72, 13 February 1886.

50 *Leader*, 11 September 1895 (copy in WHS A.46 f. 44).

51 *History of The Times*, vol. 2, 1939, pp. 209, 298.

52 Ibid., p. 295.
53 *Times* Managers Letter Book 1st Series, No. 16, f. 649, 9 June 1871 (*Times* Archives).
54 *History of The Times*, vol. 2, 1939, p. 355.
55 WHS 104/4, 4 January 1860.
56 WHS 104/11, 30 March 1860.
57 WHS 104/37, 19 December 1860.
58 WHS 106/1, 4 January 1861.
59 WHS 106/3, 11 January 1861.
60 WHS 106/15, 12 December 1861.
61 WHS 106/16, n.d.
62 *Times* Managers Letter Book 1st Series No. 17a f. 17, 4 November 1873.
63 Ibid., No. 19 f. 160, 17 July 1877.
64 Ibid., No. 20 f. 667, 25 October 1884.

VII CHANGE PARTNERS: 1885–1905: A CRISIS OF MANAGEMENT

1 *Hansard*, 1877, 3rd Series, vol. 235, cols. 1710–11.
2 RAIL 410/66, No. 134, 17 and 18 June 1885.
3 HMs DD/18, 7 September 1885.
4 WHS 112, 13 August (1885).
5 WHS X.108, 109 and 126, 1867, 1885 and 1905.
6 WHS PA.42, HMs BB/13, WHS X.108, WHS A.24 ff. 267–93, WHS X.109, HMs BB/75, WHS A.229 and WHS 277/6.
7 WHS A.290 f. 17.
8 WHS X.108, 109 and 126.
9 WHS A.23, 27 and 29.
10 HMs DD/20, 1 August 1886.
11 B.T.31/2974, 1882–92 (Public Record Office).
12 HMs HA/19/9, 25 September 1884.
13 HMs DD/20, 1 August 1886.
14 HMs DD/22, 1 April 1888.
15 Ibid.
16 *Newsbasket*, vol. 1, September 1908, p. 3.
17 Supp. to the *Newsagent & Booksellers' Review*, 14 September 1895 (copy in WHS A.46 f. 44).
18 *C. H. St J. Hornby Jubilee Celebration*, 1 January 1943, p. 12 (copy in WHS 165/2).
19 HMs DD/27, 5 October 1889.
20 *Times* Managers Letter Book 2nd Series, No. 6, f. 634, 8 November 1892.
21 Ibid., f. 808, 3 December 1892.
22 WHS 110/12–3, 25 and 27 October 1892.

23 HMs BB/88, 9 March 1891.
24 WHS 111/3, 23 May 1891.
25 WHS 111/4, 27 May 1891.
26 WHS 111/10–11, 11 January 1895 and 19 March (1894).
27 HMs HA/22/12, 7 September 1890.
28 HMs HA/22/50, 12 February 1891.
29 WHS 110/34, 6 April 1895.
30 WHS 127/1, 28 November 1892.
31 WHS 127/2, 30 July 1896.
32 WHS D.41, 2 January 1893.

VIII THE TURN OF THE SCREW, 1894–1906

1 WHS A.225 f. 213, 6 February 1901.
2 Ibid., f. 226, 23 February 1901.
3 Ibid., f. 366, 13 August 1901.
4 Quoted, Charles Wilson, *History of Unilever*, 1954, vol. 1, p. 35, 3 March 1888.
5 WHS 128/1, 6 May 1894.
6 WHS D.45, 8 October 1897.
7 WHS D.43, 15 October and 5 November 1895.
8 Ibid., 3 September and 13 November 1895.
9 WHS D.46, 10 June 1898.
10 Quoted, *Daily Mail*, 12 July 1898, p. 5 (copy in WHS A.49 f. 9).
11 *Daily Mail*, 14 July 1898, p. 3 (copy in WHS A.49 f. 11).
12 Quoted, *Daily Mail*, 15 July 1898, p. 5 (copy in WHS A.49 f. 12).
13 Ibid., 16 July 1898, p. 5 (copy in WHS A.49 f. 13).
14 Charles Wilson, op. cit., vol. 1, ch. 6 *passim*.
15 *Academy*, 16 July 1898, p. 68 (copy in WHS A.49 f. 17).
16 *Stationery Trades Journal*, 1898, p. 394 (copy in WHS A.49 f. 33).
17 *London Illustrated Standard*, 30 July 1898, p. 2 (copy in WHS A.49 f. 39). Author's italics.
18 *Book and News Trade Gazette*, 23 July 1898, p. 88 (copy in WHS A.49 f. 44).
19 Ibid., p. 89 (copy in WHS A.49 f. 45).
20 Ibid., 30 July 1898, p. 106 (copy in WHS A.49 f. 53).
21 *Daily Mail*, 16 August 1898, p. 6 (copy in WHS A.49 f. 56).
22 Ibid., 18 August 1898, p. 4 (copy in WHS A.49 f. 57).
23 Ibid., 23 August 1898, p. 6 (copy in WHS A.49 f. 60).
24 Supp. to the *Newsagent & Booksellers' Review*, 27 August 1898 (copy in WHS A.49 f. 64).
25 WHS D.46, 27 October, 2 November and 7 November 1898.

26 Charles Grinling, *History of the Great Northern Railway*. New introduction to 1903 edition, pp. vii–xv.

27 Ibid.

28 Charles Wilson, op. cit., vol. 1, ch. 5.

29 B. R. Mitchell and P. Deane, *Abstract of British Historical Statistics*, 1962, pp. 225–6.

30 Ibid.

31 Ibid.

32 *Newcastle Daily Chronicle*, 31 January 1893, p. 5 (copy in WHS A.13/1/96).

33 WHS 127/3/6, 9 August (1905).

34 For a general account see J. H. Clapham, *Economic History of Modern Britain*, vol. 3, 1938, ch. 1.

35 WHS A.225 f. 19, 12 June, 1900.

36 Ibid., f. 122, 11 October 1900.

37 Ibid., f. 195, 16 January 1901.

38 Ibid., f. 210, 4 February 1901.

39 Ibid., f. 225, 23 February 1901.

40 Ibid., f. 409, 15 October 1901.

41 Ibid., f. 625, 25 August 1902.

42 Ibid., f. 725, 24 November 1902.

43 WHS D.50, 8 December 1902.

44 WHS A.225 f. 830, 2 March 1903.

45 Ibid., f. 959, 21 May 1903.

46 Ibid., f. 973, 26 May 1903.

47 Ibid., f. 983, 5 June 1903.

48 WHS A.226 f. 11, 23 July 1903.

49 Ibid., f. 28, 24 August 1903.

50 Ibid., f. 78, 16 October 1903. Author's italics.

51 Ibid., f. 110, 17 November 1903.

52 WHS X.108, 119 and 126, 1870, 1897/8 and 1904/5.

53 WHS X.109, 117 and 127, 1884, 1895/6 and 1905/6.

54 WHS X.112–13 and 127, 1892 and 1905/6.

55 *Newsagent, Bookseller's Review & Stationers' Market*, 21 November 1908, p. 574 (copy in WHS A.46 f.34).

56 *Newsbasket*, vol. 3, 1910, p. 131.

57 *The Times*, 1 January 1906, p. 7 (copy in WHS A.42 f. 50).

58 WHS A.226 f. 856, 15 March 1905.

59 WHS A.225 f. 970, 25 May 1903.

60 WHS A.226 f. 126, 26 November 1903.

61 Ibid., f. 119, 24 November 1903.

62 Ibid., f. 141, 5 December 1903.

63 Ibid., f. 148, 9 December 1903.

64 Ibid., f. 410, 7 June 1904.

65 Ibid., f. 603, 10 October 1904.

66 *Newsbasket*, vol. 2, 1909, p. 121.

67 WHS A.226 f. 467, 12 July 1904.

68 WHS A.225 f. 437, 22 November 1901.

69 *C. H. St J. Hornby Jubilee Celebration*, 1 January 1943, p. 15 (copy in WHS 165/2).

70 Ibid., p. 16.

71 *Newsbasket*, vol. 2, 1909, p. 169.

72 WHS X.121, 1899/1900.

73 *Newsbasket*, vol. 3, 1910, p. 131.

74 WHS A.225 f. 837, 6 March 1903.

75 WHS A.226 f. 176, 17 December 1903. Author's italics.

76 WHS D.47, 4 May 1899.

77 Awdry to Lawrence at Sheffield House. WHS A.225 f. 567, 8 May 1902.

78 WHS A.227 f. 375, 15 February 1906.

79 Ibid., f. 626, 9 October 1906.

80 WHS A.5 f. 810, 10 June 1905.

81 WHS X.126, 132 and 140, 1904/5, 1910/11 and 1918/19.

82 *Newsbasket*, vol. 2, 1909, p. 145.

83 Colin Franklin, 'Ashendene and the Qualities of a Gentleman', *The Private Presses*, 1969, pp. 50–63.

84 Ibid., p. 56.

85 Ibid., p. 63.

86 Quoted, ibid., p. 52.

87 WHS X.108, 109, 119 and 129, 1867, 1877, 1887, 1897/8 and 1907/8.

88 WHS D.43, 29 January 1895.

89 WHS A.225 f. 746, 17 December 1902.

90 *Newsbasket*, vol. 5, 1912, p. 169.

91 Ibid., p. 25.

92 WHS A.226 f. 823, 15 February 1905.

93 *The Times*, 30 December 1905, p. 11 (copy in WHS A.42 f. 49).

94 WHS 89, n.d., pp. 18, 26.

95 WHS A.227 f. 730, 31 December 1906.

96 *The Times*, p. 8 and *Daily Telegraph*, p. 4, 5 July 1951 (copies in WHS A.92, f. 153).

97 Ibid.

98 *Newsbasket*, vol. 5, 1912, p. 75.

99 WHS A.228 f. 71, 14 February 1908.

100 Stanley Morison on Hornby, *Dictionary of National Biography 1941–1950* 1959, p. 411.

101 WHS D.53, 5 April 1905.

102 WHS A.227 f. 28, 20 July 1905.

103 Ibid., f. 32, 20 July 1905.

104 Ibid., f. 45, 10 August 1905.

105 WHS A.226 f. 962, 5 June 1905.

106 RAIL 258/238, 1905–30.

107 Ibid.

108 Ibid.

109 WHS 67/4, 12 October 1905.

110 WHS A.227 f. 136, 19 October 1905.

111 Ibid., f. 144, 21 October 1905.

112 WHS 128/16, 6 November 1905.

113 RAIL 258/238, 1905–30.

114 WHS 265/27, 30 March 1920.

115 Charles Wilson, op. cit., vol. 1, p. 35.

116 WHS A.227 f. 133, 18 October 1905.

117 Ibid., f. 141, 20 October 1905.

118 Ibid., f. 163, 27 October 1905.

119 Ibid., f. 143, 20 October 1905.

120 WHS A.8 f. 222, 31 October 1905.

121 WHS A.11 f. 326, 26 December 1905.

122 WHS A.8 f. 682, 9 November 1905.

123 WHS A.227 f. 460, 19 April 1906.

124 WHS A.42 f. 1a, 11 December 1905. Author's italics.

125 Ibid., f. 7, December 1905.

126 WHS A.227 f. 284, 27 December 1905.

127 Ibid., f. 300, 1 January 1906.

128 *Spectator*, 23 December 1905, p. 1070 (copy in WHS A.42 f. 45).

129 WHS 264/2, 22 September 1905.

130 Northcliffe Papers, vol. XX, f. 183, 5 October 1905 (British Library).

131 WHS 264/1, 17 October 1905.

132 Northcliffe Papers, vol. XX, ff. 185–6, 17 October 1905.

133 Ibid., f. 188, 18 October 1905.

134 WHS A.7 f. 564, 21 October 1905.

135 WHS 127/3/7, 19 October 1905.

136 WHS A.12 f. 382, 10 January 1906.

137 WHS 264/8, 10 January 1907.

138 WHS 265/2a, Christmas Day 1905.

139 The Oxford English Dictionary defines monopoly as 'exclusive possession': in the current jargon of most economists (and the Monopolies Commission) it has come to mean a share large enough to threaten 'the public interest.'

140 William Vincent, *Seen from the Railway Platform*, 1919, p. 154.

141 WHS A.227 f. 818, 5 April 1907.

142 *C. H. St J. Hornby Jubilee Celebration*, 1 January 1943, p. 17 (copy in WHS 165/2).

IX 'PRE-WAR': REFORM, RECOVERY AND DIVERSIFICATION

1 W. Ashworth, *An Economic History of England 1870 to 1939*, 1960, p. 260.
2 WHS X.129 and 136, 1907/8 and 1914/15.
3 Printed for private circulation by W. H. Smith & Son, 95 Fetter Lane, 1908.
4 Ibid., facing page 114.
5 F. C. Bayliss, *The Master Salesman*, 'Being a handbook of technical informa-tion and instruction compiled for the use and training of salesmen', n.d. but possibly 1916.
6 James Agate, *Ego*, 1935, ch. 4.
7 He was to administer the Metropolitan until 1930 'with marked and excep-tional ability and success', as his colleagues said in an obituary tribute.
8 MET 10/264, 29 January 1908 (GLC Record Office).
9 Ibid., 11 June 1908.
10 WHS A.228 f. 161, 18 May 1908.
11 MET 10/266, 24 May 1911.
12 MET 10/265, 4 March 1914.
13 WHS A.224 f. 313, 23 June 1914.
14 Ibid., f. 317, 25 June 1914.
15 Tennyson, *In Memoriam*: eds Susan Shatto and Marion Shaw, 1982, p. 153.
16 WHS A.224 f. 272, 5 March 1914.
17 *C. H. St J. Hornby Jubilee Celebration*, 1 January 1943, p. 13 (copy in WHS 165/2).
18 WHS A.290 f. 85, 1907/8–1930/1.
19 A. J. Lee, *The Origins of the Popular Press, 1855–1914*, 1976, p. 293.
20 WHS 711, 11 December 1896.
21 WHS X.108, 123, 126–7, 135 and 141, 1877, 1901/2, 1904/5–1905/6, 1913/14 and 1919/20.
22 WHS 675, 12 November 1908.
23 *Newsbasket*, vol. 5, 1912, p. 265.
24 WHS A.50 p. 2, 11 July 1906.
25 WHS A.228 f. 425, 5 April 1909.
26 WHS 89 (?1906), pp. 1, 18.
27 WHS A.215 f.2, 24 March 1911.
28 Ibid., f. 11, 15 April 1912.
29 WHS A.224 f. 109, 22 August 1912.
30 WHS X.277/25, 1917/18.
31 WHS 86, 1910, pp. 1, 5, 7.
32 Ibid., p. 20. For more on Marshall see page 328.
33 WHS 87/1, 1 July 1910.
34 WHS 87/3, 14 July 1910.

X WAR WITHOUT PRECEDENT, 1914

1 According to the *Newsbasket*, vol. 8, 1915, p. 143, the famous slogan was invented and disseminated by Herbert Morgan.
2 W. Ashworth, *An Economic History of England 1870 to 1939*, 1960, p. 279.
3 Ibid., p. 295.
4 Ibid., p. 411.
5 MET 10/264, 17 August 1914.
6 WHS 237/1–2, 21 December 1914.
7 WHS 237/3, 7 December 1914.
8 RAIL 236/420/12, 12 April 1921.
9 MET 10/264, 17 November 1916.
10 He did not use the word, which only came into common use in the Second World War.
11 WHS 130/3, 17 November 1915.
12 WHS A.224 f. 347, 27 August 1914.
13 MET 10/264, 31 March 1917.
14 Ashworth, op. cit., *passim*.
15 WHS A.215 f. 47, 11 July 1918.
16 Ibid., f. 49, 17 July 1918.
17 *Newsbasket*, vol. 5, 1912, p. 169.

XI LABOUR RELATIONS

1 A. A. Abbey, WHS memo., 'History of Trade Unions in the Firm over Fifty Years', 1964.
2 HMs DD/4, 4 September 1872.
3 William Vincent, *Seen from the Railway Platform*, 1919, p. 65.
4 WHS 3/10, 1 August 1862.
5 WHS 3/9, 18 August 1860.
6 WHS A.40 f. 118d, 18 March 1861.
7 WHS A.225 f. 668, 1 October 1902.
8 Ibid., f. 508, 10 February 1902.
9 Ibid., f. 509, 12 February 1902.
10 WHS A.6 f. 19, 30 June 1905.
11 WHS A.5 f. 184, 17 April 1905.
12 WHS 569, 18 June 1885.
13 WHS 110/6, 18 August 1890.
14 WHS A.226 f. 913, 9 May 1905.
15 WHS 3/4, 4 June 1867.
16 WHS 3/5, n.d.
17 WHS A.225 f. 986, 16 June 1903.

18 WHS A.227 f. 782, 4 March 1907.

19 WHS A.290 ff. 17–19, 1911–41.

20 C. J. Bundock, *The Story of the National Union of Printing Bookbinding and Paper Workers*, 1959, p. 147.

21 WHS A.261 f. 23, 10 March 1919.

22 Ibid., f. 25, 14 April 1919.

23 Ibid., f. 28, 12 May 1919.

24 Ibid., f. 23, 10 March 1919.

25 WHS PA.74, 9 February 1919, p. 15.

26 Ibid., p. 7.

27 WHS 549/1, 20 February 1919.

28 Ibid., n.d.

29 WHS A.261.

30 WHS 154/3, 23 November 1965.

31 WHS 153/6, 29 November 1922.

32 WHS A.39 f. 5, 25 September 1919, item 9.

33 Ibid., f. 7, 16 January 1920, item 4.

34 Ibid., f. 21, 7 December 1921, item 1.

35 Ibid., f. 22.

36 WHS 912/1, 20 August 1925.

37 WHS 912/2, 10 March 1925. George Isaacs was an amiable and popular M.P., later Parliamentary Private Secretary to A. V. Alexander as First Lord of the Admiralty; later still an (unsuccessful) Labour Minister.

38 Ibid., 12 May 1925.

39 G. D. H. Cole and R. Postgate, *The Common People 1746–1938*, 1938, p. 571. Their account is in all other respects tendentious and unreliable.

40 A. J. P. Taylor, *English History 1914–1945*, 1965.

41 Cole and Postgate, op. cit., p. 568.

42 WHS 154/2, n.d. (c. 1965). It is impossible to check the accuracy of this statement – only to note that it was made twenty years after the event when the author was in his late 70s.

43 WHS 154/3, 23 November 1965.

44 *Hansard*, Commons, vol. 197, col. 2216, 7 July 1926.

45 WHS 154/3, 23 November 1965.

46 WHS 154/10, 14 May 1926.

47 *The Times*, 13 July 1926, p. 9 (copy in WHS 154/11).

48 WHS 882, January 1972, p. 2. This could be misleading. Productivity per man increased. Total numbers employed continued to rise, though slowly, until 1939 and the outbreak of the Second World War.

49 WHS 154/3, 23 November 1965.

50 WHS A.215 f. 110, 12 October 1926.

51 WHS 1080 f. 6, 23 June 1952.

XII THE INTER-WAR YEARS

1 B. R. Mitchell and P. Deane, *Abstract of British Historical Statistics,* 1962, p. 476 *Board of Trade Wholesale Price Indices: 1871–1920.*
2 Ibid., p. 477 *Board of Trade Wholesale Price Indices: 1920–34.*
3 WHS A.215 f. 106, 2 November 1925.
4 WHS 67/8, 10 June 1920.
5 WHS 68/3, 7 April 1924.
6 WHS 68/7, 6 August 1924.
7 WHS 68/11, 23 December 1924.
8 WHS 69/1, 18 July 1929.
9 Ibid., 30 July 1929.
10 Ibid., 16 October 1929.
11 WHS A.215 f. 135, 23 October 1929.
12 WHS 69/8, n.d. (for 1929).
13 WHS 69/18, 6 June 1930.
14 WHS 69/19, 16 June 1930.
15 WHS 69/24, 14 July 1930. Author's italics.
16 WHS 69/26, 18 July 1930.
17 WHS 70 f. 26, 14 May 1931.
18 Ibid., f. 2, 20 October 1930.
19 Ibid., f. 32, 22 May 1931.
20 Ibid., f. 20, n.d.
21 Ibid., f. 46, 18 August 1931.
22 Ibid., f. 64, 21 July 1932.
23 WHS 71 f. 26, 27 February 1933.
24 Ibid., f. 10, 4 June 1931.
25 WHS 72 f. 10, 2 June 1933.
26 Ibid., f. 15, 8 June 1933.
27 Ibid., f. 19, 13 September 1933.
28 Ibid., f. 26, 13 September 1933.
29 WHS 70 f. 66, 25 July 1932.
30 WHS 72 f. 15, 8 June 1933.
31 MET 10/266, 20 July 1926.
32 Ibid., 21 July 1926.
33 Ibid., 3 June 1927.
34 Ibid., n.d. (probably July 1927 by N. Norman).
35 Ibid., pp. 11, 1, 1.
36 Ibid., pp. 3–4, 16–17.
37 Ibid., pp. 17–18. Author's italics.
38 Ibid., n.d. (for 1927–32).
39 *Newsbasket,* vol. 27, 1934, p. 94.

XIII HARD TIMES AND HEART SEARCHINGS: THE 1920s & 1930s

1 WHS A.215 f. 89, 3 July 1923.
2 Ibid., f. 75, 3 February 1921.
3 Ibid., f. 96, 26 November 1923.
4 Ibid., f. 129, 25 September 1928.
5 WHS 587/5/200, 17 September 1930, p. 8.
6 WHS Y.119 f. 13, 20 July 1931.
7 Ibid., f. 57, 5 October 1931.
8 WHS Y.120 f. 139, 28 November 1933.
9 WHS 330, 20 September 1929 (enc. copies of original 1899 agreement and 1929 additional rulings).
10 Beaverbrook Papers BBK H/17, 21 March 1928 (House of Lords Record Office).
11 Ibid., H/2, 14 January 1929.
12 Ibid., C/283A, 15 November 1930 and 2 December 1931.
13 WHS 225/7, 26 February 1930.
14 WHS X.141, 146, 155 and 162, 1919/20, 1924/5, 1933/4 and 1940/1.
15 Shortly after writing these letters, Charles was appointed manager at Brussels, escaping only just in time when Belgium was invaded by the German Army. He ended as manager of the Manchester Wholesale House and *doyen* of the PWH management.
16 WHS 157, 3 August 1933.
17 WHS 156/1, 28 June 1929.
18 WHS 156/2, 11 April 1929.
19 WHS 156/4, 3 May 1932.
20 WHS 452, 21 February 1930.
21 WHS 184, 10 October 1933.
22 WHS 185, 9 November 1933.
23 WHS 182, 20 November 1933, pp. 20, 4a.
24 Ibid., p. 18.

XIV THE PROVINCIAL WHOLESALE HOUSES: A STATE WITHIN A STATE

1 *C. H. St J. Hornby Jubilee Celebration*, 1 January 1943, p. 16 (copy in WHS 165/2).
2 WHS 493, 7 February 1939, p. 3.
3 Ibid., 28 June 1937, p. 1.
4 Ibid., 29 June 1937, p. 4.
5 *Newsbasket*, vol. 18, 1925, p. 94.
6 Ibid., vol. 47, February 1954, p. 29.

7 WHS 493, 30 June 1937, p. 9. See below for the Company structure after 1929.
8 Ibid., 5 July 1939, p. 8.
9 Ibid., 23 June 1943, p. 5.
10 WHS A.64 f. 66, 2 July 1943.
11 WHS 493, 6 October 1943, p. 8.
12 Ibid., p. 6.
13 Ibid., 16 February 1945, pp. 1–2.
14 Ibid., 23 March 1945, pp. 1–2.
15 Ibid., 23 June 1943, p. 6.
16 WHS A.215 f. 171, 16 January 1946.
17 W. Spicer verbally, 1980.

XV THE STRUCTURE OF THE FIRM: PLUS ÇA CHANGE...?

1 WHS Y.123 f. 285, 6 May 1946.
2 Even the *Dictionary of National Biography* describes him primarily as 'printer and connoisseur'. The account of him as entrepreneur is perfunctory.
3 Cecil King, *Strictly Personal*, 1969, p. 96.
4 *C. H. St J. Hornby: An Anthology of Appreciations*, 1946, pp. 35–6 (copy in WHS 167/6).
5 In order of seniority Lord Hambleden (Billy), St John Hornby, A. D. Power, W. H. D. Acland, A. W. Acland, E. W. Seymour, Michael Hornby, James Smith and David Smith.
6 T. W. Hodges verbally, 1981.
7 *Viscount Hambleden: An Anthology of Appreciations*, 1950, p. 5 (copy in WHS 162/6).
8 WHS 675, 12 November 1908.
9 Prospectus, 15 March 1929 (copy in WHS 197/1).
10 WHS 912/7, 8 October 1936.
11 WHS 587/4, Oct. 1939–Sept. 1940.
12 Ibid., 5 December 1940.
13 Bircham & Co, Memo., November 1949 (unclassified).
14 See page 410 for the Swindon project.

XVI THE CIRCULATING LIBRARY

1 *Athenaeum*, 16 June 1860, p. 825.
2 WHS 13/1, 10 November 1859.
3 D. Keir, 'First with the News', 1969, pp. 112–14 (typescript history of W. H. Smith & Son).

4 R. B. Sheridan, *The Rivals*, 1775, Act 1, Scene 2.

5 John Ruskin, *Sesame and Lilies*, 1865, Lect. 1, p. 32.

6 Anthony Trollope, *Four Lectures*, ed. M. L. Parrish, 1938, p. 108.

7 RAIL 410/142, ff. 141, 145, 18 April and 2 May 1849.

8 WHS 248/1/6, December 1862.

9 *John Bull*, 9 December 1821, p. 1 (copy in WHS A.13/1/73).

10 *Pall Mall Gazette*, 11 March 1884, p. 11.

11 G. L. Griest, *Mudie's Circulating Library and the Victorian Novel*, 1970, pp. 24, 32, 75.

12 Ibid., p. 5.

13 *Punch*, vol. 16, 10 February 1849, p. 61 (quoted Griest, op. cit., p. 31).

14 M. Sadleir, *The Evolution of Publishers' Binding Styles, 1770–1900*, 1930, p. 95.

15 WHS A.102, X.108–9, X.122, X.132 and X.135, 1860–1913/14.

16 Quoted Griest, op. cit., p. 168.

17 WHS 122/1, 27 June 1894.

18 *Publishers' Circular*, vol. 61, 7 July 1894, p. 5.

19 Griest, op. cit., pp. 182, 185.

20 *Publishers' Circular*, vol. 61, 21 July 1894, p. 57.

21 F. D. How, *Bishop Walsham How*, 1898, pp. 343–4.

22 Keir, op. cit., p. 383.

23 G. Moore, *A Communication to my Friends*, 1933, pp. 74–5.

24 Ibid., p. 77.

25 *Publishers' Circular*, vol. 60, 5 May 1894, pp. 464–5.

26 S. C. Nelson, *The Latest Literary Boycott*, n.d., p.4 (photocopy in WHS 289/4).

27 *Daily Mail*, 9 September 1913, p. 5.

28 Samuel Hynes, *The Edwardian Turn of Mind*, 1968, p. 280 et seq.

29 *Spectator*, 4 December 1909, p. 943 (copy in WHS 263/1).

30 Quoted Hynes, op. cit., p. 299.

31 Hynes, op. cit., pp. 304–5.

XVII TASTE, MORALITY AND THE LAW: THE DISTRIBUTOR'S LOT

1 *Spectator*, 4 December 1909, p. 943 (copy in WHS 263/1).

2 Immortalised in the *Oxford Dictionary of Quotations*, 1943, p. 102b, for two lines:

> A man is as old as he's feeling,
> A woman as old as she looks.

3 HMs HA/19/5–6, 25 and 28 June 1869.

4 *The Times*, 23 April 1887, p. 10 (copy in WHS A.13/1/44).

5 G. T. Ferris, *Great Composers*, 1887, p. 304.

6 WHS 123/6, 19 May 1888.

7 *Star*, 22 October 1892, p. 4, and 26 October 1892, p. 2 (copies in WHS A.13/1/67–8).
8 Viscount Chilston, *W. H. Smith*, 1965, ch. 12 *passim*.
9 HMs BB/82, 6 June 1888.
10 WHS A.7 f. 375, 14 October 1905.
11 WHS A.228 ff. 155, 181, 13 May and 3 June 1908.
12 Ibid., f. 366, 2 February 1909.
13 *Spectator*, 4 December 1909, p. 943 (copy in WHS 263/1).
14 WHS A.224 f. 225, 27 October 1913.
15 WHS Y.120 f. 60, 26 June 1933.
16 WHS 416/4, 17 February 1933.
17 WHS A.56/1, pp. 3, 6, 14, 29.
18 *The Times*, 3 November 1937, p. 4 (copy in WHS A.81 f. 19).
19 Ibid., 4 November, p. 4 (copy in WHS A.81 f. 19).
20 Ibid., 5 November, p. 4 (copy in WHS A.81 f. 19).
21 D. Keir, 'First with the News', 1969, p. 397 (typescript history of W. H. Smith & Son).
22 Ibid.
23 Ibid., p. 400.
24 *All England Law Reports*, 1936, vol. 2, p. 1514.
25 *Dominion Law Reports*, 1954, vol. 3, pp. 637–40.
26 *Law Reports*, 1957, Q.B., vol. 2, pp. 204–5.
27 Keir, op. cit., p. 403.
28 WHS Y.120 f. 136, 27 November 1933.
29 WHS List of Branches and Rules, 1 September 1934, p. 45.
30 Ibid., 1938, p. 44.
31 WHS A.53, 27 October 1920.

XVIII THE CONTOURS OF CHANGE

1 He retired as chairman of W. H. Smith & Son (Holdings) Ltd on 25 May 1972, after a tenure of twenty-three years.
2 From 1949 to May 1972 the Hambleden Trustee holding of B (high-voting) shares stood at c. 40 per cent of the total B issue.
3 E.g. William Lever never parted with any ordinary shares in Lever Brothers after it became a public company in 1894. He held this to be an essential condition for achieving clear, unquestioned policy control. The preference shareholders were entitled to their 5 per cent interest; they faced little or no risk. That, and the rewards for carrying it, were the prerogative of the sole ordinary shareholder. See my *History of Unilever*, 1954, vol. 1, pp. 46, 48. Similar, if less draconian, arrangements were frequent in family businesses 'going public'.

4 See Appendix 1 for all curricula vitae of directors.

5 The Fourth Viscount Hambleden was still a minor when his father died in 1948. On coming of age he spent 1952 to r955 in the company. He became a director of the Holdings Company in 1956. For the family interest see page 392.

6 In 1951, Viscount Harcourt of Morgan Grenfell; in 1954, J. G. Phillimore of Baring; and in 1971, J. T. Corbett of Peat, Marwick.

7 In 1956, H. N. Saunders of Unilever and Rio Tinto Zinc; in 1969, Sir H. P. T. Prideaux of NAAFI and Brook Bond Liebig.

8 In 1956, G. C. H. Yates; in 1960, S. R. Elms, V. E. Scott Bailey, G. W. Rowe and H. H. van Straubenzee; in 1962, W. K. Oliver; in 1967, W. Spicer; in 1968, P. H. Bagnall and K. J. Morris; and in 1970, M. D. Field.

9 See Chapter VII.

10 G. W. Rowe and H. H. van Straubenzee.

11 P. W. Bennett.

12 See the Family Tree, page xv.

13 See Chapter VIII.

14 See Chapter XIII *passim.*

15 See Chapter XIII.

16 Inaugurated by Charles Troughton, 20 November 1962.

17 See Chapter IX.

18 See Tables of Wholesale Turnover, page 409.

19 At a special Holdings Board held in Brighton, 2 December 1964.

20 There were two separate Heywood firms in Manchester: Abel Heywood and John Heywood. (For Abel Heywood's evidence on the Newspaper Stamp question in 1851 see Chapter III, pages 62–4 The John Heywood business had fallen on bad times. Smith's and Abel Heywood had co-operated to attempt its rescue. In the end Smith's became the sole proprietors.

21 For fuller details see Appendices 3 and 4 and graphs.

XIX PLANNING FOR THE FUTURE

1 B. J. Loasby, *The Swindon Project*, 1973, *passim.*

2 See pages 401–2 on site development.

3 P. H. Bagnall. The appointment, and the purchase of the computer, like many of the innovations of these years in connection with retail reorganisation can be traced to P. W. Bennett.

4 Loasby, op. cit., p. 70.

5 The whole project was planned and executed by a committee successively under the chairmanship of C. H. W. Troughton and Peter Bennett. Two recently appointed directors were closely involved in its work: David Acland and S. M. Hornby (the youngest member of the Limited Board). It

was just over seventy years since his grandfather, C. H. St John Hornby, entered on his long partnership in W. H. Smith.

6 Its membership, like that of the Distribution Committee, included one of the young directors, Julian Smith, representing the sixth generation of the Smith family since the commencement of the business.

7 It is now known as the Lionel Robbins Building. The new building was, like its predecessor, to be called Strand House; neither was in the Strand.

8 He served another four years (until his death in 1976) as a member of the Holdings Board.

9 See Chapter IX.

10 Cf. the chairman's comments on Cecil King and the London wholesale trade, page 405.

11 D. J. Smith, 19 February 1963.

12 *Higher Education*, HMSO, Cmnd 2154.

XX PROGRESS AND PROFITABILITY

1 G. R. Pocklington, *The Story of W. H. Smith & Son*, 1921.

2 R. C. K. Ensor, *England 1870–1914*, Oxford, 1936, p. 510.

3 '... the success of your great House, almost unique in the whole world. What a magnificent example and what encouragement for the young who are starting out in business ...'

4 See Chapter XVII.

5 A 1958 book by J. G. Cozzens which Smith's nearly refused to sell.

6 From a paper by S. M. Hornby, later to be chairman.

7 The former Hornby home on Chelsea Embankment.

8 For the Smith connections with aesthetic movements see Chapter VIII.

9 See Chapter IV.

10 See Chapter VIII.

11 See the Family Tree, page xv.

12 See Chapter XI *passim*.

Select Bibliography

MANUSCRIPT SOURCES CITED IN THE NOTES
Bank of England Ledgers, Bank of England
Beaverbrook Papers, House of Lords Record Office
Board of Trade, Public Record Office
Christ Church, Spitalfields, Registers, GLC Record Office
Cocks, Biddulph & Co. Ledgers, Barclays Bank (Cocks, Biddulph Branch)
College of Arms Grants, College of Arms
Cottonian Collection, Plymouth City Museum & Art Gallery
Hambleden Papers, W. H. Smith & Son Ltd
Home Office, Public Record Office
Inland Revenue, Public Record Office
London Transport Records, GLC Record Office
North British Railway Records, Scottish Record Office
Northcliffe Papers, British Library
Post Office Records, Post Office Record Office
Probate Records, Public Record Office
Railway Records, Public Record Office
Royal Archives, Windsor Castle
St George's, Hanover Square, Registers, St George's Church
Times Archives, *The Times*
Westminster Rate Books, Westminster City Archives
W. H. Smith & Son Records, W. H. Smith & Son Ltd

PARLIAMENTARY PAPERS AND LAW REPORTS CITED IN THE NOTES
All England Law Reports (1936)
Dominion Law Reports (1954)
Hansard (1877 & 1926)
Law Reports (1957)

Second Report of Select Committee on Postage (1838)
Select Committee on Newspaper Stamps (1851)

NEWSPAPERS, PERIODICALS AND DIRECTORIES CITED IN THE NOTES
Academy (1898)
All the Year Round (1875)
Athenaeum
Bell's Life in London and Sporting Chronicle
Book and News Trade Gazette (1898)
Century Magazine (1888)
Daily Mail
Daily Telegraph (1951)
Edinburgh Review (1853)
Gentleman's Magazine 1852)
Illustrated London News (1856)
John Bull (1821)
Journalist (1887)
Leader (1895)
London Gazette (1828)
London Illustrated Standard (1898)
Manchester and Salford Advertiser (1833)
Manchester Guide (1804)
Monthly Magazine (1821)
Morning Post
Newcastle Chronicle (1824)
Newcastle Daily Chronicle (1893)
Newsagent & Booksellers' Review
Newsagent, Booksellers' Review & Stationers' Market (1908)
Newsbasket (W. H. Smith & Son house magazine)
New York Herald (1891)
Once a Week (1861)
Pall Mall Gazette
Post Office London Directory (1819)
Publishers' Circular (1894)
Punch (1849)
Quarterly Review (1880)
Spectator
Standard (1829)
Star (1892)
Stationery Trades Journal (1898)
The Times
Westminster Review

WORKS CITED IN THE NOTES

Acworth, Sir William, *Railways of England*, 1899, revised 1900

Agate, J., *Ego*, 1935

Allen, C. J., *The Great Eastern Railway*, 1961

Altick, R. D., *The English Common Reader*, 1957

Andrews, C. B. (ed.), *The Torrington Diaries 1781–1794*, 1934

Ashworth, W., *An Economic History of England 1870 to 1939*, 1960

Beale, Mrs C. H. (ed.), *Reminiscences of a Gentlewoman of the Last Century*, 1891

Boyce, G., Curran, J., & Wingate, P. (eds), *Newspaper History from the 17th Century to the Present Day*, 1978

Bundock, C. J., *The Story of the National Union of Printing Bookbinding and Paper Workers*, 1959

C. H. St J. Hornby: An Anthology of Appreciations, privately printed, 1946

C. H. St J. Hornby Jubilee Celebration, privately printed, 1943

Childs, W. M., *The Town of Reading during the Early Part of the 19th Century*, 1910

Chilston, Viscount, *W. H. Smith*, 1965

Clapham, J. H., *Economic History of Modern Britain*, vol. 3, 1938

Cole, G. D. H., & Postgate, R., *The Common People 1746–1938*, 1938

Colvin, C. (ed.), *Maria Edgeworth Letters from England 1813–1844*, 1971

Dictionary of National Biography 1941–1950, 1959

During Six Reigns 1776–1926, privately printed, *c.* 1926

Eliot, T. S., *The Sacred Wood*, 1928

Ellis, H., *British Railway History 1830–1876*, 1954

Ellis, K., *The Post Office in the Eighteenth Century*, 1969

Ensor, R. C. K., *England 1870–1914*, 1936

Fay, C. R., *Great Britain from Adam Smith to the Present Day*, 1932

Ferris, G. T., *Great Composers*, 1887

Franklin, C., *The Private Presses*, 1969

Gordon, D. I., *The Eastern Counties*, 1968

Gourvish, T. R., *Mark Huish and the London & North Western Railway*, 1972

Graves, C., *Mr Punch's History of Modern England*, vol. 1, 1921

Griest, G. L., *Mudie's Circulating Library and the Victorian Novel*, 1970

Grinling, C., *History of the Great Northern Railway*, 1903

Hall, E. (ed.), *Miss Weeton's Journal of a Governess 1811–1825*, 1939

Hamilton, Lord George, *Parliamentary Reminiscences and Reflections 1886–1906*, 1922

Hennessy, J. P., *Monkton Milnes: The Flight of Youth 1851–1885*, 1951

Hill, Sir Francis, *History of Lincoln*, in 4 vols, 1948–74

Georgian Lincoln, 1966

History of The Times, vol. 1, 1935, and vol. 2, 1939

How, F. D., *Bishop Walsham How*, 1898

Hynes. S., *The Edwardian Turn of Mind*, 1968

Keir, D., 'First with the News', typescript, 1969

King, C., *Strictly Personal*, 1969

Knight, C., *London*, vol. 5, 1843

—— *Passages of a Working Life during Half a Century*, vol. 1, 1864

Langford, J. A., *A Century of Birmingham Life 1741–1841*, 1868

Lee, A. J., *The Origins of the Popular Press 1855–1914*, 1976

Loasby, B. J., *The Swindon Project*, 1973

Margetson, S., *Journey by Stages*, 1967

Maxwell, Sir Herbert, *Life and Times of the Rt. Hon. W. H. Smith MP*, 1893

Mitchell, B. R., & Deane, P., *Abstract of British Historical Statistics*, 1962

Moore, G., *A Communication to my Friends*, 1933

Morison, S., *The English Newspaper 1622–1932*, 1932

Nelson, S. C., *The Latest Literary Boycott*, c. 1898

Nock, O. S., *The Great Western Railway in the Nineteenth Century*, 1962

Oliver, T., *A New Picture of Newcastle upon Tyne*, 1831

Oxford Dictionary of Quotations, 1943

Parrish, M. L. (ed.), *A Trollope: Four Lectures*, 1938

Phillips, S., *The Literature of the Rail*, 1851

Pocklington, G. R., *The Story of W. H. Smith & Son*, privately printed, 1921

Ponsonby, A., *Henry Ponsonby: Queen Victoria's Private Secretary*, 1942

Reader, W. J., *Macadam*, 1980

A Regional History of the Railways of Great Britain (various authors and dates, published by David & Charles)

Ruskin, J., *Sesame and Lilies*, 1865

Sadleir, M., *The Evolution of Publishers' Binding Styles 1770–1900*, 1930

Shatto, S., & Shaw, M. (eds), *Tennyson, In Memoriam*, 1982

Sheridan, R. B., *The Rivals*, 1775

Simmons, J., *Railways of Britain*, 1961

Stael-Holstein, Baron A. de, *Letters on England*, 1825

Summerson, Sir John, *Georgian London*, 1970

Taylor, A. J. P., *English History 1914–1945*, 1965

Tennyson, Lord, *Mechanophilus*, c. 1833

Thomas, D. St J., *The West Country*, 1960

Trevelyan, G. O., *Life and Letters of Lord Macaulay*, 1877

Vincent, W., *Seen from the Railway Platform*, 1919

Viscount Hambleden: An Anthology of Appreciations, privately printed, 1950

Wilson, C. H., *Economic History and the Historian*, 1969

—— *History of Unilever*, 1954

Young, G. M., *Victorian England: Portrait of an Age*, 1949

Index